PHYSICAL ACTIVITY, EXERCISE, AND MENTAL HEALTH

This edited collection delivers contemporary international perspectives on the critical relationship between physical activity, exercise, and mental health, providing essential insights for researchers, practitioners, and stakeholders committed to promoting psychological well-being through movement.

Bringing together leading researchers and practitioners in exercise and physical activity psychology, this book covers a wide range of topics, including the effects of physical activity on mood, anxiety, and cognitive function, as well as personal experiences of body image and weight in physical activity contexts. It also explores the promotion of physical activity and exercise around the world, as well as the role of psychology professionals in promoting physical activity. Each chapter features contributions from international experts who examine research implications through diverse cultural and social lenses, offering nuanced insights into how physical activity influences mental well-being across different populations and contexts.

Offering a comprehensive and accessible resource on the links between physical activity, exercise, and mental health, this is an important volume for students, researchers, and practitioners of exercise and physical activity psychology across the globe.

Yu-Kai Chang is Chair Professor, Department of Physical Education and Sports Sciences, National Taiwan Normal University, Taiwan.

Alessandro Quartiroli is Professor, University of Wisconsin – La Crosse, USA and Visiting Professor, University of Portsmouth, UK.

International Perspectives on Key Issues in Sport and Exercise Psychology

Series Editor

Robert J. Schinke

International Perspectives on Key Issues in Sport and Exercise Psychology is a series of edited books published in partnership with the International Society of Sport Psychology. Each title reflects cutting edge research in the psychological study of high-level sport, written by key researchers and leading figures in the field of sports psychology.

Mental Health in Elite Sport
Applied Perspectives from Across the Globe
Edited by Carsten Hvid Larsen, Karin Moesch, Natalie Durand-Bush, Kristoffer Henriksen

Mental Health in Sport and Physical Activity
Selected Writings from the ISSP Academy of Science
Edited by Robert J. Schinke

Culture and Inclusion in Sport and Physical Activity
Selected Writings from the ISSP Academy of Science
Edited by Robert J. Schinke, Alessandro Quartiroli and Tatiana V. Ryba

Physical Activity, Exercise, and Mental Health
An International Approach to Research and Practice
Edited by Yu-Kai Chang and Alessandro Quartiroli

For more information about this series, please visit: www.routledge.com/ISSP-Key-Issues-in-Sport-and-Exercise-Psychology/book-series/KISEP

PHYSICAL ACTIVITY, EXERCISE, AND MENTAL HEALTH

An International Approach to Research and Practice

Edited by
Yu-Kai Chang and Alessandro Quartiroli

Routledge
Taylor & Francis Group
LONDON AND NEW YORK

Designed cover image: Getty Images @ Justin Paget

First published 2026
by Routledge
4 Park Square, Milton Park, Abingdon, Oxon OX14 4RN

and by Routledge
605 Third Avenue, New York, NY 10158

Routledge is an imprint of the Taylor & Francis Group, an informa business

British Library Cataloguing-in-Publication Data
A catalogue record for this book is available from the British Library

ISBN: 9781032852799 (hbk)
ISBN: 9781032852812 (pbk)
ISBN: 9781003517474 (ebk)

DOI: 10.4324/9781003517474

Typeset in Times New Roman
by codeMantra

CONTENTS

CONTRIBUTORS

Jing-Yi Ai, School of Sports Science and Physical Education, Nanjing Normal University, China.

Brandon L. Alderman, Department of Kinesiology and Health, Rutgers University–New Brunswick, USA.

Garcia Ashdown-Franks, Institute for Health and Care Improvement, York St John University, York, UK.

Nikoletta Barka, Doctoral School of Education, ELTE Eötvös Loránd University, Budapest, Hungary and Sport Office, Budapest University of Economics and Business, Hungary.

Kimberlee B. Bonura, School of Psychology, College of Psychology and Community Services, Walden University, Minneapolis MN, USA.

Szilvia Boros, Department of Psychology and Health Management, Faculty of Health and Marta Borrueco, Institut de Recerca de l'Esport, Universitat Autònoma de Barcelona, Barcelona, Spain.

Marius Brazaitis, Sports Science and Innovation Institute, Lithuanian Sports University, Kaunas, Lithuania.

Attilio Carraro, Faculty of Education, Free University of Bozen-Bolzano, Italy.

Cristina Carvalho de Melo, Postgraduate Program in Sports Sciences, Federal University of Minas Gerais, Brazil.

Yu-Kai Chang, Department of Physical Education and Sports Sciences, National Taiwan Normal University, Taiwan, and Institute of Sport Science and Innovations, Lithuanian Sports University, Lithuania.

Chien-Heng Chu, Department of Physical Education and Sports Sciences, National Taiwan Normal University, Taiwan.

I-Hua Chu, Department of Sports Medicine, College of Medicine, Kaohsiung Medical University, Kaohsiung, Taiwan.

Simon B. Cooper, Department of Sports Science, School of Science & Technology, Nottingham Trent University, UK.

Marta Duina, Faculty of Education, Free University of Bozen-Bolzano, Italy, and Department of Neurosciences, Biomedicine and Movement Sciences, University of Verona, Italy.

Francisco Enrique Garcia Ucha, Vice President of Sociedad De Latinoamérica Y Del Caribe De Psicología De La Actividad Fisica Y Del Deporte SOLCPAD, Cuba.

Scott G. Goddard, Physical Activity, Sport, and Exercise Research Theme, Faculty of Health, Southern Cross University, Coffs Harbour, Australia.

Renato Gomes Sá de Moraes, Postgraduate Program in Sports Sciences, Federal University of Minas Gerais, Brazil.

Christy Greenleaf, Kinesiology, Zilber College of Public Health, University of Wisconsin-Milwaukee, Milwaukee, WI, USA.

John Elvis Hagan Jnr, Department of Health, Physical Education and Recreation, University of Cape Coast, PMB-Cape Coast, Ghana, and Neurocognition and Action-Biomechanics-Research Group, Faculty of Psychology and Sports Science, Bielefeld University, Postfach 10 01 31, 33501, Bielefeld, Germany.

Caitlyn Hauff, Department of Health, Kinesiology and Sport, College of Education and Professional Studies, University of South Alabama, Mobile, AL, USA.

Rebecca M. Hawkins, School of Psychology, Sport Science and Wellbeing, University of Lincoln, Brayford Pool, Lincoln, UK.

Chen-Sin Hung, Institute of Sport Science and Innovations, Lithuanian Sports University, Lithuania and Department of Physical Education and Sports Sciences, National Taiwan Normal University, Taiwan.

Patricia C. Jackman, School of Psychology, Sport Science and Wellbeing, University of Lincoln, Brayford Pool, Lincoln, UK.

Leighton Jones, Sheffield Hallam University, UK.

Costas I. Karageorghis, Department of Sport, Health and Exercise Sciences, Brunel University of London, Middlesex, UK.

Dimitrios Kokaridas, Department of Physical Education and Sport Science, University of Thessaly, Greece.

Garry Kuan, School of Health Sciences, Universiti Sains Malaysia, Malaysia.

Matthew A. Ladwig, Purdue University Northwest, Indiana, USA.

Maria Fernanda Laus, Department of Health Sciences, Ribeirão Preto Medical School, University of São Paulo, Ribeirão Preto, Brazil; Department of Psychology, Faculty of Philosophy, Science, and Letters of Ribeirão Preto, University of São Paulo, Ribeirão Preto, Brazil.

Ruei-Hong Li, Department of Physical Education and Sports Sciences, National Taiwan Normal University, Taiwan.

Caitlin Liddelow, School of Human Sciences, University of Western Australia, Perth WA, Australia.

José Marcelo Roffé, President of Sociedad De Latinoamérica Y Del Caribe De Psicología De La Actividad Fisica Y Del Deporte SOLCPAD, Argentina.

Angela Meadows, Department of Psychology, University of Essex, Colchester, UK.

Miranda Miller, California State University, Bakersfield, California, USA.

Franco Noce, Sports Department, Federal University of Minas Gerais, Brazil.

Nikos Ntoumanis, Department of Sports Science and Clinical Biomechanics, University of Southern Denmark, Denmark, and School of Sport, Exercise, and Rehabilitation Sciences, University of Birmingham, UK.

Kurtis Pankow, Department of Sport and Exercise Science, Swansea University, Swansea, Wales, UK.

Athanasios Papaioannou, Department of Physical Education and Sport Science, University of Thessaly, Greece.

Eva Pila, School of Kinesiology, Western University, London, ON, Canada.

Joan Pons, Department of Psychology, University of Balearic Islands, Spain.

Alessandro Quartiroli, University of Wisconsin - La Crosse, La Crosse, WI, USA, and University of Portsmouth, Portsmouth, UK.

Giampaolo Santi, Faculty of Education, Free University of Bozen-Bolzano, Italy.

Jacob Owusu Sarfo, Department of Health, Physical Education and Recreation, University of Cape Coast, PMB-Cape Coast, Ghana.

Matthew J. Schweickle, Global Alliance for Mental Health and Sport, School of Psychology, University of Wollongong, Wollongong NSW, Australia.

Yan Shi, Department of Health and Physical Education, The Education University of Hong Kong, Hong Kong SAR, China.

Medina Srem-Sai, Department of Health, Physical Education, Recreation and Sports, University of Education, Winneba, Ghana.

Fenghua Sun, Department of Health and Physical Education, The Education University of Hong Kong, Hong Kong, China.

Jordan T. Sutcliffe, Military Psychology and Leadership, Royal Military College of Canada, Kingston, Ontario, Canada.

Christian Swann, Physical Activity, Sport, and Exercise Research Theme, Faculty of Health, Southern Cross University, Coffs Harbour, Australia, and Manna Institute, Southern Cross University, Coffs Harbour, Australia.

Peter C. Terry, School of Psychology and Wellbeing, University of Southern Queensland, Australia, and Centre for Health Research, University of Southern Queensland, Australia.

Stewart A. Vella, Global Alliance for Mental Health and Sport, School of Psychology, University of Wollongong, Wollongong NSW, Australia.

Christopher R. D. Wagstaff, University of Portsmouth, Portsmouth, UK.

Feifei Wang, School of Public Health, Fudan University, Shanghai, China and College of Medicine, Jiaxing University, Jiaxing City, China.

Amanda Warner, University of Portsmouth, Portsmouth, UK.

Claudia Ming Yu Wong, Department of Health and Physical Education, The Education University of Hong Kong, Hong Kong, China.

Zachary Zenko, California State University, Bakersfield, California, USA.

ACKNOWLEDGMENT

The advancement and deepening of academic work rely on the support of devoted individuals. I am truly grateful and honored to have worked with Prof. Quartiroli and all the contributors in fulfilling this shared aspiration. I would also like to express my appreciation to my mentors, colleagues, students, and assistants for their invaluable guidance, collaboration, and dedication throughout this journey. Heartfelt thanks to my beloved family, Eileen, Joanna, Matthew, and Sydney for their unwavering understanding and companionship, which have made it possible for me to pursue this path and contribute meaningfully to the academic community.

Yu-Kai Chang

I am deeply grateful to Prof. Chang for the opportunity to co-edit this volume and for the chance to learn from him throughout the process. My sincere thanks go to all the contributing authors whose expertise and collaboration made this book possible. I also thank the International Society of Sport Psychology for its continued support and for promoting globally relevant scholarship in our field. I am especially appreciative of the colleagues, mentors, students, and friends who supported me along the way. Most of all, heartfelt gratitude to Team ShAleMaAr! I love you all dearly and am endlessly thankful to always have you in my corner.

Ale Quartiroli

PREFACE

Founded in 1965, the International Society of Sport Psychology (ISSP) is the first and leading global organization dedicated to the advancement of sport and exercise psychology. As a multidisciplinary society, its core mission is to promote research, professional practice, and development in the field worldwide.

In line with the ISSP's commitment to disseminating up-to-date and high-quality knowledge, we are pleased to present the forthcoming edited volume, *Physical Activity, Exercise, and Mental Health: International Perspectives on Current Status and Implications*, as part of the ISSP Book Series. In addition to providing contemporary scientific insights into the relationship between physical activity, exercise, and mental health from a global perspective, with this book, we also aim to highlight practical and research-based implications. This book aims to offer valuable guidance for a wide range of stakeholders seeking to promote psychological well-being through physical activity and exercise.

This book is structured into five parts, each addressing a critical dimension of this evolving field. It opens with a bibliometric analysis tracing the development of exercise psychology from 1988 to 2025, offering a foundational overview of the field's intellectual landscape and thematic trajectories. Subsequent sections examine core mental health constructs, including, but not limited to, affect, mood, anxiety, and cognitive function, as well as personal experiences shaped by body image and weight-related stigma in physical activity contexts. Emerging topics are addressed in dedicated chapters on the effects of exercise on sleep, the psychology of flow, and the role of music in exercise settings.

A global perspective is further emphasized through region-specific case studies from sub-Saharan Africa, Oceania, Asia, Southern Europe, and Latin America, showcasing culturally grounded approaches to enhance mental health through physical activity. This book then closes with a final section focused on professional development of psychology practitioners interested in delivery exercise and physical activity psychology services, detailing key competencies, training pathways, and the essential role of integrating scientific knowledge with applied practice.

Each chapter is co-authored by leading researchers and practitioners from at least two countries, ensuring content that is evidence-based, current, and internationally relevant. This cross-national collaboration fosters a diversity of cultural and social perspectives, enriching the discussion of how physical activity supports mental health across varied contexts.

Physical Activity, Exercise, and Mental Health: International Perspectives on Current Status and Implications is a timely and comprehensive resource for students, scholars, and practitioners. With its focus on global contributions and translational knowledge, this volume advances both academic inquiry and practical application in the pursuit of psychological well-being through physical activity.

Yu-Kai Chang and Alessandro Quartiroli

ABOUT THE EDITORS

Yu-Kai Chang, PhD, FNAK, ISSP-R

Dr. Yu-Kai Chang is Chair Professor in the Department of Physical Education and Sports Sciences at National Taiwan Normal University, Taiwan, and serves as the Director of the Physical Activity and Cognitive Neuroscience Laboratory. He is the Vice President (2026-2029), Treasurer (2022–2025), and Member-at-Large (2018–2021) of the International Society of Sport Psychology (ISSP), Vice President of the Asian-South Pacific Association of Sport Psychology (ASPASP), and former President of the Society for Sport and Exercise Psychology of Taiwan (SSPET).

Dr. Chang's research primarily focuses on sport and exercise psychology, with particular emphasis on exercise and mental health, sport/performance psychology, and mindfulness, approached from a cognitive neuroscience perspective. To date, he has published over 270 articles in leading domestic and international journals, authored more than 10 chapters in international textbooks, and translated six academic books. Dr. Chang has been recognized as an International Fellow of the USA National Academy of Kinesiology (NAK), listed among the World's Top 2% Scientists in the field of Sport Science since 2021, and received the Distinguished Alumni Award from the School of Health and Human Sciences at the University of North Carolina at Greensboro, USA. He was also the recipient of the Outstanding Research Award from Taiwan's Ministry of Science and Technology in both 2019 and 2025, and the Early Career Distinguished Scholar Award from both the North American Society for Psychology of Sport and Physical Activity (NASPSPA) in 2014 and ISSP in 2013. In addition to his academic accomplishments, Dr. Chang is a skilled practitioner of Chinese martial arts, including Bagua, Xingyi, Taiji, and Shaolin, and has represented Taiwan in numerous national and international martial arts competitions.

Alessandro Quartiroli, PhD, CMPC, FAASP, NCC, AFBPsS, CPsychol, HCPC, RAPPS, ISSP-R/S, EuroPSY

Dr. Alessandro Quartiroli is Professor of Psychology at the University of Wisconsin–La Crosse (USA) and Visiting Professor at the University of Portsmouth (UK). Originally from Italy, he received academic and applied training in Italy, Spain, and the United States. In the United States, Dr. Quartiroli is a Certified Mental Performance Consultant (CMPC), an approved mentor, a Fellow of the Association for Applied Sport Psychology (AASP), and a National Certified Counselor with the National Board for Certified Counselors. In the United Kingdom, he is a Health and Care Professions Council (HCPC) Registered Practitioner Psychologist in Sport and Exercise Psychology and Counselling Psychology, a Chartered Psychologist with the British Psychological Society (BPS), and an approved supervisor. Internationally, he is a member of both the ISSP Registry (as practitioner and supervisor) and EuroPsy.

He is actively engaged in several professional organizations, including AASP, ISSP, and FEPSAC, where he has held various leadership roles. He currently serves as President of the International Society of Sport Psychology (2026–2029) and previously served as a Member-at-Large on the ISSP Managing Council (2022–2025). Dr. Quartiroli's professional and scholarly work focuses on supporting the development and sustainability of future and current practitioners. He has published over 70 peer-reviewed journal articles and 30 book chapters and has delivered more than 150 presentations at national and international conferences. His research and applied interests center on enhancing the professional journey of practitioners – supporting their identity development, competence, and well-being – to ensure the ethical, effective, and culturally grounded delivery of services across exercise, sport, and performance contexts. In addition to his academic work, he maintains an active applied practice and supervises professionals pursuing CMPC (US), HCPC (UK), and ISSP-R (international) credentials.

SERIES FOREWORD

The International Society of Sport Psychology and its members have increasingly engaged in the subject area of athlete mental health. Within this new contribution to the International Perspectives series, we are pleased to support the expansion of mental health knowledge to exercise and physical activity. This edited contribution is unique in its contribution to the field. The co-editors and contributing authors skillfully provided an expansive list of ideas that augment and impact the human condition via movement. The perspectives are international and global, with each subject area considered from the vantage of several countries, with their accompanying challenges and local solutions. I highly recommend this book for any reader who wishes to understand the human condition and mental health via physical activity from the vantage(s) of the world around us.

Robert J. Schinke
Series Editor

PART 1

Exercise Psychology from a Bibliometric Approach

1

GLOBAL TRENDS AND HOTSPOTS OF EXERCISE PSYCHOLOGY

A Bibliometric Analysis from 1988 to 2025

Yu-Kai Chang, Chien-Heng Chu, Ruei-Hong Li, Chen-Sin Hung, Alessandro Quartiroli, and Nikos Ntoumanis

1.1 Introduction

1.1.1 Conceptualizing Exercise Psychology and Its Scholarly Significance

Exercise psychology is a multidisciplinary field positioned at the intersection of "psychology," the study of human thought, emotion, and behavior, as well as "exercise science," which investigates the physiological, biomechanical, and behavioral aspects of kinesiology, exercise, or physical activity (Gill et al., 2017; Lox et al., 2019). The scientific field aims to explore two primary domains as the application of psychological principles to promote the initiation and maintenance of regular exercise and physical activity, and the examination of how exercise and physical activity influence psychological processes and mental health outcomes (Lox et al., 2019).

The relevance of exercise psychology has grown exponentially due to global health trends. According to the World Health Organization (WHO), approximately one in four adults worldwide fails to meet recommended physical-activity guidelines (Cardon & Salmon, 2020; Strain et al., 2024), contributing significantly to the global burden of noncommunicable diseases such as cardiovascular disease, type 2 diabetes, and obesity. Psychological determinants, including motivation, self-efficacy, cognitive appraisals, enjoyment, and social support, are critical in shaping individuals' engagement in and adherence to exercise and physical activity (Hagger, 2025; Smith et al., 2017). Hence, leveraging psychological frameworks is essential for the development of public health interventions targeting sedentary behaviors and promoting lifelong exercise habits.

A growing body of evidence also highlights the mental health benefits of exercise, showing that regular exercise or physical activity reduces symptoms of

DOI: 10.4324/9781003517474-2

depression, anxiety, and stress, while enhancing mood, self-esteem, vitality, and resilience. These effects are especially important, given the global rise in mental health issues. According to the WHO, over 300 million people worldwide suffered from depression in 2017 (Nagy et al., 2020). Additionally, it ranked third in global disease burden in 2018 and is projected to become the leading cause by 2030 (Malhi & Mann, 2018). These trends underscore the urgent need for preventive, accessible interventions such as exercise to support mental well-being. Given this context, exercise psychology provides scalable, non-pharmacological approaches to addressing mental health challenges.

1.1.2 Disciplinary Origins: The Transition from Sport Psychology to Exercise Psychology

The conceptual foundation of exercise psychology can be traced to its origins within sport psychology. Historically, research on psychological processes in physical contexts primarily focused on athletic performance, competition, and elite training. Over time, however, scholars recognized the need to explore how similar psychological principles could be applied to non-competitive exercise and physical activity, thereby initiating the evolution of exercise psychology as a distinct domain.

One indicator of this disciplinary shift was the revision of foundational textbooks in the field. An example is the textbook originally titled Psychological Dynamics of Sport (Gill, 1986), which was reissued in 2000 as Psychological Dynamics of Sport and Exercise (Gill, 2000). Gill emphasized that this change signified a deliberate recognition of the growing interest in the psychological dimensions of exercise and physical activity. The revised title also reflected a broader theoretical expansion, acknowledging that exercise contexts entail distinct motivations, challenges, and psychological outcomes that differ from those associated with competitive sport settings. This integrative trend was also reflected in several widely adopted textbooks. *Advances in Sport and Exercise Psychology* (Horn & Smith, 2018), *Foundations of Sport and Exercise Psychology* (Weinberg & Gould, 2024), and *The Routledge International Encyclopedia of Sport and Exercise Psychology* (Hackfort & Schinke, 2020), all emphasize a dual-domain approach that bridges the knowledge bases of both sport and exercise contexts.

Changes in journal nomenclature further reveal this disciplinary transformation. *The International Journal of Sport Psychology*, established in 1970, was reissued as the *International Journal of Sport and Exercise Psychology* in 2003, marking an explicit shift in thematic scope for the International Society of Sport Psychology (ISSP). Similarly, the *Journal of Sport Psychology* was renamed the *Journal of Sport and Exercise Psychology* (JSEP) in 1998, reflecting the North American Society for the Psychology of Sport and Physical Activity's (NASPSPA) expanding interests. In response to this broader focus, several new journals have emerged, including *Psychology of Sport and Exercise* (2000), *Sport, Exercise, and Performance Psychology*

(2011), and the *International Review of Sport and Exercise Psychology* (2015). These developments have laid a strong foundation for the independent growth of exercise psychology as a legitimate and impactful discipline.

1.1.3 The Emergence and Growth of Exercise Psychology as an Independent Field

While exercise psychology initially developed as an offshoot of sport psychology, it has gradually asserted itself as an autonomous field with its own research agenda, conceptual frameworks, and applied implications. This independent growth is evident in the literature of the 1990s and 2000s, which marked a turning point in recognizing exercise psychology as a stand-alone discipline.

One of the earliest textbooks to explicitly address this focus was *Exercise Psychology: The Influence of Physical Exercise on Psychological Processes* (Seraganian, 1993). The volume explores how stress and psychological factors influence health and illness, offering theoretical insights, empirical research, and clinical approaches for understanding and improving mental and physical well-being. Shortly thereafter, *Physical Activity and Mental Health* (Morgan, 1997) provided empirical grounding for the clinical applications of exercise. Morgan's work demonstrated the efficacy of exercise as a non-invasive, low-cost intervention for depression, anxiety, and psychological distress, based on both human and animal studies, expanding the field's relevance to mental health professionals and public health practitioners alike.

By the early 2000s, a surge of dedicated exercise psychology textbooks reflected growing academic interest. Among these were *Foundations of Exercise Psychology* (Berger et al., 2002), *Exercise Psychology* (Buckworth & Dishman, 2002), and *The Psychology of Exercise: Integrating Theory and Practice* (Lox et al., 2003). One of the notable signs of the field's maturation is its continuous development and updating of diverse and interdisciplinary research themes. Contemporary editions have begun to incorporate new and emerging topics, including cognitive function (Berger et al., 2015; Buckworth et al., 2013; Lox et al., 2019), fatigue, sleep, and pain (Buckworth et al., 2013). Another example is *The Psychological Benefits of Exercise and Physical Activity* (Etnier, 2025), which integrates research findings and focuses on psychological outcomes such as the effects on depression and anxiety, as well as the impact on cognitive performance, memory, pain, and sleep. These developments indicate that exercise psychology has evolved beyond its foundational focus to explore the complex biopsychosocial mechanisms underlying behavior and well-being.

1.1.4 Scientific Contributions and Societal Relevance of Exercise Psychology

Exercise psychology has far-reaching implications for both science and society. Its contributions extend beyond theoretical knowledge to inform health policy, clinical practice, and public health programming. Health authorities worldwide, including the American College of Sports Medicine (ACSM), the U.S. Department of Health and Human Services, and the WHO, have recognized the psychological benefits of exercise in their official recommendations.

The ACSM's *Guidelines for Exercise Testing and Prescription* highlight that regular physical activity improves mood, reduces symptoms of anxiety and depression, enhances cognitive functioning, and contributes to better sleep quality (American College of Sports Medicine, 2022). *The Physical Activity Guidelines for Americans* (2nd ed.) further emphasizes the cognitive and emotional benefits of exercise, including reductions in depressive symptoms and improvements in executive function (U.S. Department of Health and Human Services, 2018). Importantly, these benefits are not limited to high-intensity exercise; even moderate physical activity, such as brisk walking, has been associated with significant psychological improvements. The WHO's Guidelines on Physical Activity and Sedentary Behavior extend this message globally, affirming that regular exercise reduces the risk of depression and anxiety while enhancing well-being across the lifespan (World Health Organization, 2020). For children, physical activity is linked to better academic performance and emotional development. For adults, it reduces stress and burnout, while in older adults, it serves as a protective factor against dementia and loneliness.

The cumulative evidence presents a compelling case for integrating exercise psychology into healthcare delivery systems and community health initiatives. By identifying psychological factors that facilitate or hinder physical activity, exercise psychology offers a foundation for targeted interventions and policies capable of positively influencing population health at scale.

1.1.5 Rationale for Employing Bibliometric Analysis and Objectives of the Chapter

As exercise psychology continues to grow, synthesizing its expanding and dynamic body of literature presents significant challenges. Traditional review methods, including narrative reviews, systematic reviews, and meta-analyses, provide valuable insights and have become the predominant approaches to evidence synthesis. However, while narrative reviews may introduce subjective bias, systematic reviews and meta-analyses often address narrowly defined research questions within limited time frames, making it difficult to capture the field's broader and longitudinal development.

Bibliometric analysis offers a data-driven alternative by mapping the intellectual structure of the discipline through publication trends, citation patterns, co-authorship networks, and keyword co-occurrences (Donthu et al., 2021; Kumar et al., 2023). This method captures both the productivity (e.g., publication and citation counts) and structure (e.g., thematic clusters, co-authorship patterns) of the scholarly landscape, providing useful information for identifying emerging research fronts, influential authors, and underexplored topics (Donthu et al., 2021). For instance, Lindahl et al. (2015) analyzed 1,140 articles from 5 core journals, identifying 73 thematic clusters and 14 major research areas. Their findings highlighted recurring themes and theoretical overlaps between sport and exercise psychology. For instance, Lindahl et al. (2015) analyzed 1,140 articles from 5 core journals, identifying 73 thematic clusters and 14 major research areas, highlighting recurring themes and theoretical overlaps between sport and exercise psychology. More recently, Smolinski et al. (2024) offered a complementary, author-focused approach to portraying the field by identifying highly cited researchers based on h-index criteria. While insightful in highlighting individual contributions, their study does not extend to thematic trends. Given the substantial growth and increasing differentiation of exercise psychology in recent years, an updated, field-specific bibliometric analysis is warranted to capture its thematic evolution and inform future research directions.

This chapter aims to present an updated bibliometric analysis of global research trends and hotspots in exercise psychology from inception to 2025, focusing on the highest-impact factor journals that include both 'exercise' and 'psychology' in their titles. The objective is to systematically map the intellectual structure and thematic evolution of the field over nearly four decades. Specifically, the chapter seeks to provide a synthesis of both historical and contemporary research patterns in exercise psychology, as well as to identify thematic hotspots and emerging domains that warrant further investigation. Together, these efforts aim to inform the strategic development and future direction of the discipline.

1.2 Method

1.2.1 Data Source and Search Strategy

To map the knowledge structure and thematic evolution of the field of exercise psychology, this study conducted a bibliometric analysis using the Web of Science (WoS) Core Collection database. The analysis focused on the five highest-impact factor journals that include both "exercise" and "psychology" in their titles, including *International Review of Sport and Exercise Psychology (IRSEP)*, *Psychology of Sport and Exercise (PSE)*, *International Journal of Sport and Exercise Psychology (IJSEP)*, *Journal of Sport & Exercise Psychology (JSEP)*, and *Sport, Exercise, and Performance Psychology (SEPP)*.

Articles were selected based on the keywords "exercise" or "physical activity" in their titles. The search strategy employed the following formula: (SO=(INTERNATIONAL REVIEW OF SPORT "AND" EXERCISE PSYCHOLOGY) OR SO=(PSYCHOLOGY OF SPORT "AND" EXERCISE) OR SO=(INTERNATIONAL JOURNAL OF SPORT "AND" EXERCISE PSYCHOLOGY) OR SO=(JOURNAL OF SPORT EXERCISE PSYCHOLOGY) OR SO=(SPORT EXERCISE "AND" PERFORMANCE PSYCHOLOGY)) AND

TS=("exercise" OR "physical activity"). All data were retrieved from inception to June 10, 2025. The document types were limited to empirical articles and review articles, with no other restrictions.

1.2.2 Bibliometric Analysis Techniques

This study employed bibliometric analysis techniques to examine a) publication trends, b) productivity and collaboration networks, c) most cited references, and d) keyword analyses.

a) Publication trends: Publication trends represent the temporal distribution of the number of publications in each year in the exercise psychology field and were retrieved from the WoS Core Collection database. b) Productivity and collaboration networks: Productivity was identified by the top 25 highest publications of countries and the top 20 highest publications of authors. We also calculated the average citations per item (ACI) for countries and authors, representing the mean number of citations per publication, obtained by dividing total citations by the number of publications. We used this metric to gauge the impact and influence of research output. Collaboration networks were analyzed using the total link strength (TLS) of countries and authors. TLS represents the strength of collaborative relationships by measuring the frequency of co-occurrence between two countries or authors within publications. Both ACI and TLS were calculated through VOSviewer (1.6.20) (van Eck & Waltman, 2010). c) Most cited reference: Most cited references represent the top 25 references with the highest number of citations, extracted from the WoS Core Collection database. d) Keywords analysis: Keywords analysis included most prevalent, clusters, and burst phenomena of keywords. Most prevalent keywords represent the top 25 keywords with the highest number of counts, extracted from the VOSviewer. Clusters of keywords represent the top 20 clusters of keywords, conducted through clustering analysis of keyword co-occurrence, where the log-likelihood ratio method was used in CiteSpace (6.4.R2). Keyword burst phenomena represent the hot topics and developmental trends within the field of exercise psychology, with CiteSpace identifying the top 25 keywords and sorting them based on their occurrence time points. (Chen, 2006).

1.3 Result

1.3.1 Publication Trends

The description of five journals was presented in Table 1.1. A total of 2,071 publications were retrieved from the Web of Science Core Collection database spanning 1988–2025, comprising 1,885 empirical articles and 186 review articles. The publications exceeded 20 articles annually beginning in 2003. From 2009 onward, annual publications surpassed 50, and from 2017, the number exceeded 100 publications per year. The publications reached its peak in 2021 with 180 articles (Figure 1.1).

TABLE 1.1 Description of the Five Selected Journals

Est. Year	*Journal*	*Association*	*Publisher*	*IF*	*No. of Pub.*
1979	JSP JSEP (~1988)	NASPSPA	Human Kinetics	2.0	501
2000	PSE	FEPSAC	Elsevier	3.1	1,052
2003	IJSEP	ISSP	Taylor & Francis	2.3	286
2011	SEPP	APA division 47	APA	2.6	120
2015	IRSEP	-	Taylor & Francis	6.4	112

Note: JSP = *Journal of Sport Psychology*, renamed to JSEP (*Journal of Sport and Exercise Psychology*) in 1988, PSE = *Psychology of Sport and Exercise*, IJSEP (*International Journal of Sport and Exercise Psychology*), SEPP = Sport, Exercise, and Performance Psychology, IRSEP = International Review of Sport and Exercise Psychology, NASPSA = North American Society for the Psychology of Sport and Physical Activity, FEPSAC = European Federation of Sport Psychology, ISSP = International Society of Sport Psychology, APA = American Psychological Association, Est. Year = Established Year, IF = Impact factor (based on 2023 data), N of Pub. = Number of Publications.

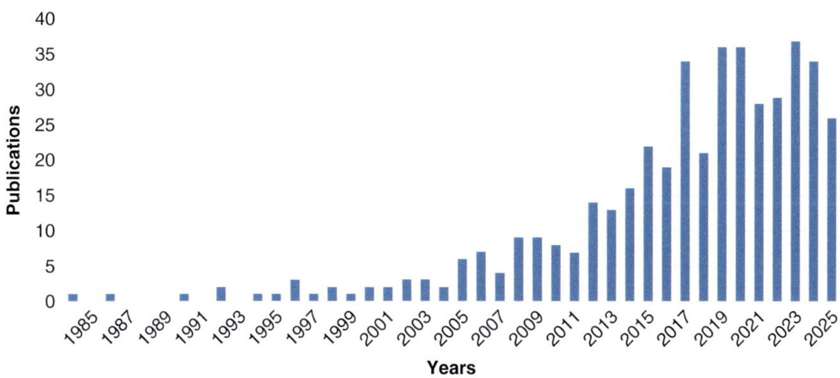

FIGURE 1.1 Years and Publication Trends in the Field of Exercise Psychology (1988–2025).

Note: Number above the bar represent the number of publications. The publication data for 2025 is incomplete due to the search period ending on June 10, 2015.

1.3.2 Productivity and Collaboration Networks

1.3.2.1 Country of Researcher Affiliation

A summary of country-level productivity ranked by the number of publications is provided in Table 1.2. The United States dominates with 658 publications (31.77%), followed by Canada (484, 23.37%), the United Kingdom (416, 20.09%), and Australia (300, 14.49%). These four countries represent 89.72% of total publications. Citation counts range from 530 to 27,018. The United States leads with 27,018 citations, followed by the United Kingdom (19,917), Canada (16,850), and Australia (11,434). ACI values span from 12.20 to 57.90. Wales achieves the highest ACI (57.90) despite producing only 39 publications. Singapore (44.32), New Zealand (43.50), and the United States (41.06) follow. Among the countries exceeding 100 publications, the United Kingdom records 47.88, Australia 38.11, Canada 34.81, and Germany 26.69.

In terms of geographic distribution, Europe dominates the research landscape, accounting for 17 of the top 25 contributing countries (68%) and top 4 contributors are the United Kingdom (3rd), Germany (5th), France (7th), and Switzerland (8th), reflecting the region's leading role in shaping the field. Asia contributes four countries (16%): China (6th), Taiwan (17th), Singapore (22nd), and Japan (24th). North America is represented by the United States (1st) and Canada (2nd), while Oceania includes Australia (4th) and New Zealand (11th); each region accounts for 8% of the total.

The collaboration network among the top 23 countries is illustrated, where larger nodes indicate higher citation counts and thicker connections represent stronger collaborative relationships (Figure 1.2a). The countries are organized into

TABLE 1.2 Top 25 Countries Ranked by Publications

Rank	*Country*	*Publications*	*Citations*	*ACI*	*%*
1	United State	658	27,018	41.06	31.77
2	Canada	484	16,850	34.81	23.37
3	United Kingdom	416	19,917	47.88	20.09
4	Australia	300	11,434	38.11	14.49
5	Germany	172	4,591	26.69	8.31
6	China	90	1,098	12.20	4.35
7	France	80	2,170	27.13	3.86
8	Switzerland	65	1,700	26.15	3.14
9	Spain	56	874	15.61	2.70
10	Scotland	45	1,193	26.51	2.17
11	New Zealand	44	1,914	43.50	2.12
12	Sweden	41	1,289	31.44	1.98
13	The Netherlands	40	995	24.88	1.93
14	Wales	39	2,258	57.90	1.88
15	Finland	38	1,310	34.47	1.83
16	Italy	38	1,226	32.26	1.83
17	Taiwan	38	1,097	28.87	1.83
18	Greece	35	1,030	29.43	1.69
19	Belgium	33	1,283	38.88	1.59
20	Portugal	29	708	24.41	1.40
21	Norway	25	944	37.76	1.21
22	Singapore	22	975	44.32	1.06
23	Ireland	19	560	29.47	0.92
24	Japan	18	558	31.00	0.87
25	Denmark	18	530	29.44	0.87

Note: ACI = average citations per item (citations/publications); % = the percentage of the total 2,071 publications.

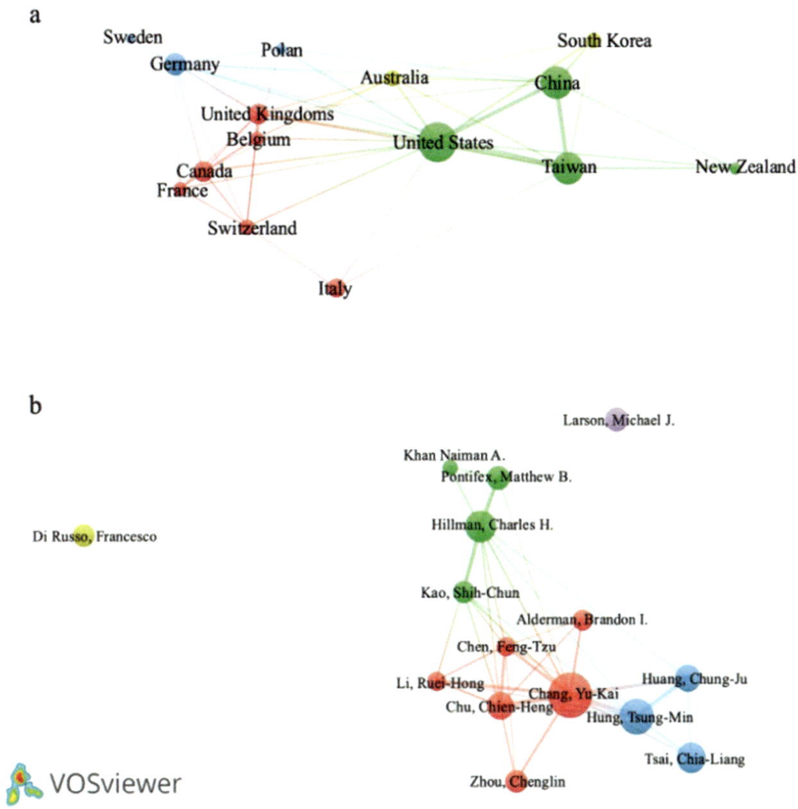

FIGURE 1.2 Collaboration Network of Countries and Authors Based on Citation.

four clusters. Cluster #1 (red) led by the United States, cluster #2 (green) led by Canada and the United Kingdom, cluster #3 (blue) led by Australia, and cluster #4 (yellow) led by New Zealand and Portugal.

1.3.2.2 Authors

A summary of the top 20 most productive authors (with 20% being female) is provided in Table 1.3. Catherine M. Sabiston leads with 41 publications, followed by Martin S. Hagger (32), Nikos Ntoumanis (26), and Yu-Kai Chang (24). The authors' citation counts range from 918 to 3,073, with Brett Smith recording the highest citations (3,073), followed by Stuart J. H. Biddle (3,007) and Martin S. Hagger (2,685).

The ACI values range from 40.61 to 1,004.00. Vanessa Tobin achieved the highest ACI (1,004.00) with one publication, followed by Susan A. Jackson (628.50) with two publications and Charles J. Hardy (386.33) with three publications. The

TABLE 1.3 Top 20 Authors Ranked by Publications

Rank	*Authors*	*Country*	*Pub.*	*Citations*	*ACI*
1	Catherine M. Sabiston	Canada	41	1,665	40.61
2	Martin S. Hagger	United States	32	2,685	83.91
3	Nikos Ntoumanis	Denmark	26	1,286	49.46
4	Yu-Kai Chang	Taiwan	24	1,199	49.96
5	Panteleimon Ekkekakis	United States	21	948	45.14
6	Costas I. Karageorghis	United Kingdom	18	970	53.89
7	Stuart J. H. Biddle	Australia	17	3,007	176.88
8	Kerry R. McGannon	Canada	16	2,245	140.31
9	Martyn Standage	United Kingdom	16	1,382	86.38
10	Brett Smith	United Kingdom	14	3,073	219.50
11	Jennifer I. Etnier	United States	14	994	71.00
12	David M. Williams	United States	10	918	91.80
13	W. Jack Rejeski	United States	8	1,711	213.88
14	Heather A. Hausenblas	United States	8	1,340	167.50
15	Albert V. Carron	Canada	8	1,163	145.38
16	Steven J. Petruzzello	United States	8	1,073	134.13
17	Herbert W. Marsh	United Kingdom	7	1,203	171.86
18	Andrew C. Sparkes	United Kingdom	7	1,149	164.14
19	Daniel M. Landers	United States	7	1,146	163.71
20	Nikos L. D. Chatzisarantis	Australia	4	1,433	358.25

Note: Pub. = publications. ACI = average citations per item (citations/publications).

next three highest-ranking authors are Brett Smith (219.50), W. Jack Rejeski (213.88), and Stuart J. H. Biddle (176.88).

The geographic distribution of the 20 authors spans six countries. The United States contributes eight authors (40%), followed by the United Kingdom with five authors (25%), Canada with three authors (15%), and Australia with two authors (10%). Denmark and Taiwan each contribute one author (5%).

The collaboration network of the top 18 authors is illustrated, where larger nodes indicate higher citation counts and thicker connections represent stronger collaborative relationships between authors (Figure 1.2b). The authors are organized into four clusters: cluster #1 (red) is centered around Yu-Kai Chang and Panteleimon Ekkekakis; cluster #2 (blue) around Sabiston Catherine; cluster #3 (green) around Nikos Ntoumanis and Martin Hagger; and cluster #4 (yellow) around Brett Smith and Kerry McGannon.

1.3.3 Most Cited References

The most frequently cited references with citation counts ranging from 287 to 1,471 are listed in Table 1.4. Four publications have exceeded 1,000 citations. Smith and McGannon (2018) received 1,471 citations for their review on developing rigor in qualitative research. Hardy and Rejeski (1989) follows with 1,112 citations for their

TABLE 1.4 Top 25 Reference Ranked by Citations

Rank	*Authors (Years)*	*Citations*	*Title*	*Journal*	*Type*
1	Smith and McGannon (2018)	1,471	Developing rigor in qualitative research: Problems and opportunities within sport and exercise psychology	IRSEP	Review
2	Hardy and Rejeski (1989)	1,112	Not what, but how one feels - the measurement of affect during exercise	JSEP	Empirical
3	Hagger et al. (2002)	1,078	A meta-analytic review of the theories of reasoned action and planned behavior in physical activity: Predictive validity and the contribution of additional variables	JSEP	Review
4	Markland and Tobin (2004)	1,006	A modification to the behavioural regulation in exercise questionnaire to include an assessment of amotivation	JSEP	Empirical
5	Kendzierski and Decarlo (1991)	911	Physical-activity enjoyment scale -2 validation studies	JSEP	Empirical
6	Jackson and Marsh (1996)	828	Development and validation of a scale to measure optimal experience: The Flow State Scale	JSEP	Empirical
7	Biddle et al. (2019)	702	Physical activity and mental health in children and adolescents: An updated review of reviews and an analysis of causality	PSE	Review
8	Castelli et al. (2007)	525	Physical fitness and academic achievement in third- and fifth-grade students	JSEP	Empirical
9	Etnier et al. (1997)	501	The influence of physical fitness and exercise upon cognitive functioning: A meta-analysis	JSEP	Review
10	Hausenblas et al. (1997)	477	Application of the theories of reasoned action and planned behavior to exercise behavior: A meta-analysis	JSEP	Review
11	Spence and Lee (2003)	474	Toward a comprehensive model of physical activity	PSE	Review
12	Sparkes and Smith (2009)	463	Judging the quality of qualitative inquiry: Criteriology and relativism in action	PSE	Review

(*Continued*)

TABLE 1.4 (Continued)

Rank	*Authors (Years)*	*Citations*	*Title*	*Journal*	*Type*
13	Williams et al. (2008)	456	Acute affective response to a moderate-intensity exercise stimulus predicts physical-activity participation 6 and 12 months later	PSE	Empirical
14	Terry et al. (2003)	446	Construct validity of the Profile of Mood States - adolescents for use with adults	PSE	Empirical
15	Jackson and Eklund (2002)	431	Assessing flow in physical activity: The Flow State Scale-2 and Dispositional Flow Scale-2	JSEP	Empirical
16	Reed and Ones (2006)	369	The effect of acute aerobic exercise on positive activated affect: A meta-analysis	PSE	Review
17	Reinboth and Duda (2006)	334	Perceived motivational climate, need satisfaction and indices of well-being in team sports: A longitudinal perspective	PSE	Empirical
18	Wipfli et al. (2008)	327	The anxiolytic effects of exercise: A meta-analysis of randomized trials and dose-response analysis	JSEP	Review
19	Edwardson and Gorely (2010)	310	Parental influences on different types and intensities of physical activity in youth: A systematic review	PSE	Review
20	Lonsdale et al. (2008)	306	The Behavioral Regulation in Sport Questionnaire (BRSQ): Instrument development and initial validity evidence	JSEP	Empirical
21	Wilson et al. (2006)	306	The psychological need satisfaction in exercise scale	JSEP	Empirical
22	Hausenblas and Downs (2002)	304	Exercise dependence: A systematic review	PSE	Review

(Continued)

TABLE 1.4 (Continued)

Rank	*Authors (Years)*	*Citations*	*Title*	*Journal*	*Type*
23	Chalabaev et al. (2013)	302	The influence of sex stereotypes and gender roles on participation and performance in sport and exercise: Review and future directions	PSE	Review
24	Jackson et al. (2008)	288	Long and short measures of flow: The construct validity of the FSS-2, DFS-2, and new brief counterparts	JSEP	Empirical
25	Craft and Landers (1998)	287	The effect of exercise on clinical depression and depression resulting from mental illness: A meta-analysis	JSEP	Review

Note: IRSEP = *International Review of Sport and Exercise Psychology*; PSE = *Psychology of Sport and Exercise*; IJSEP = *International Journal of Sport and Exercise Psychology*; JSEP = *Journal of Sport & Exercise Psychology*; SEPP = *Sport, Exercise, and Performance Psychology*.

work on affect measurement during exercise. Hagger et al. (2002) achieved 1,078 citations for their meta-analytic review of reasoned action and planned behavior theories in physical activity. Markland and Tobin (2004) garnered 1,006 citations for their modification of the behavioral regulation in exercise questionnaire.

The distribution between empirical articles (12 publications, 48%) and review articles (13 publications, 52%) demonstrates the field's balanced emphasis on both empirical research and systematic knowledge synthesis. The JSEP dominates the list with 15 publications (60%), followed by PSE with 9 publications (36%), and the IRSEP with 1 publication (4%).

1.3.4 Keywords Analyses

1.3.4.1 Most Prevalent Keywords

The most prevalent keywords, with frequencies ranging from 94 to 1,049, are presented in Table 1.5. Two keywords exceeded 500 occurrences: "physical activity/physical-activity" (1,049), and "exercise" (789). The keyword distribution reveals four distinct domains, including physical activity-related (e.g., physical activity, exercise), psychological (e.g., motivation, self-determination theory), methodological (e.g., validation, model, meta-analysis), and population-specific keywords (e.g., children, adolescents).

TABLE 1.5 Top 25 Keywords Ranked by Counts

Rank	*Keywords*	*Count*	*Rank*	*Keywords*	*Count*
1	physical activity/physical-activity	1,049	14	meta-analysis	129
2	exercise	789	15	participation	123
3	motivation	327	16	intervention	121
4	sport	303	17	fitness	115
5	validation/ validity	288	18	perceptions	110
6	performance	278	19	intrinsic motivation	109
7	health	274	20	adults	108
8	behavior	186	21	anxiety	105
9	self-determination theory	184	22	planned behavior	100
10	children	164	23	depression	96
11	self-efficacy	162	24	women	95
12	model	156	25	cognition	94
13	adolescents	130	—		

1.3.4.2 Burst Phenomena of Keywords

The burst phenomena of keywords in the field of exercise psychology are illustrated (Figure 1.3). "Planned behavior" shows the strongest citation burst overall, while "mental health," "childhood," and "executive function" demonstrate notable recent bursts over the past five years, with "executive function" leading among recent topics.

1.3.4.3 Clusters of Keywords

The cluster analysis indicated a highly significant clustering structure ($Q = 0.8788$) with highly convincing and well-defined clusters (silhouette value = 0.9441). All keywords were divided into 20 clusters, including the largest cluster "self-determination theory" (#0), followed by "physical inactivity" (#1), "inhibitory control" (#2), "optimal experience" (#3), "executive function" (#4), "social relationships" (#5), with "action planning" (#19) representing the last cluster (Figure 1.4).

1.4 Discussion

Based on the 2,071 included publications, comprising 1,885 empirical and 186 review articles, authored by 5,313 researchers from 68 countries, this bibliometric analysis explores the intellectual landscape and thematic evolution in the field of exercise psychology from 1988 to 2025.

1.4.1 Publication Trends

The publication trends in exercise psychology are categorized into three distinct stages based on the top five exercise psychology journals from 1988 to 2025.

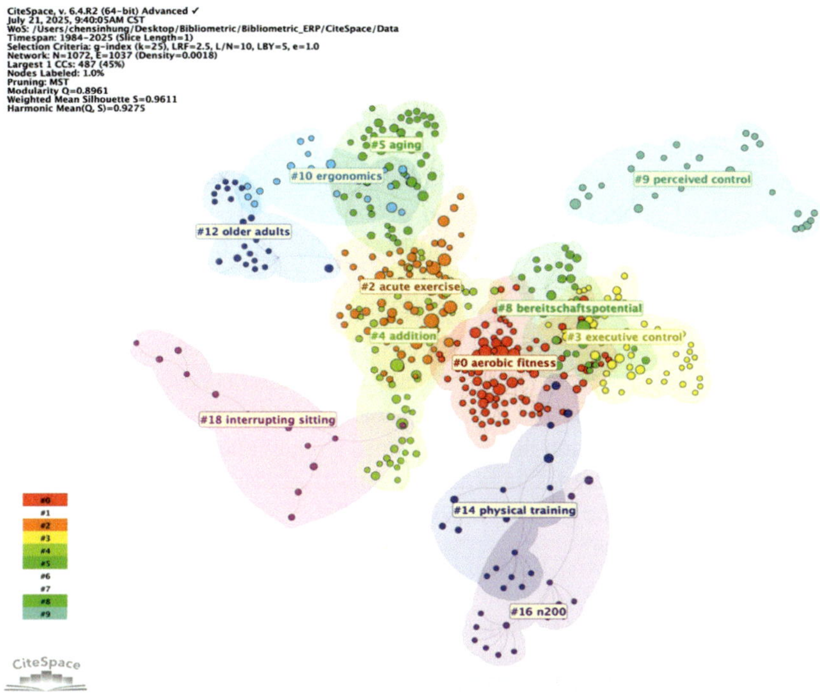

FIGURE 1.3 Top 25 Keywords with the Strongest Citation Bursts.

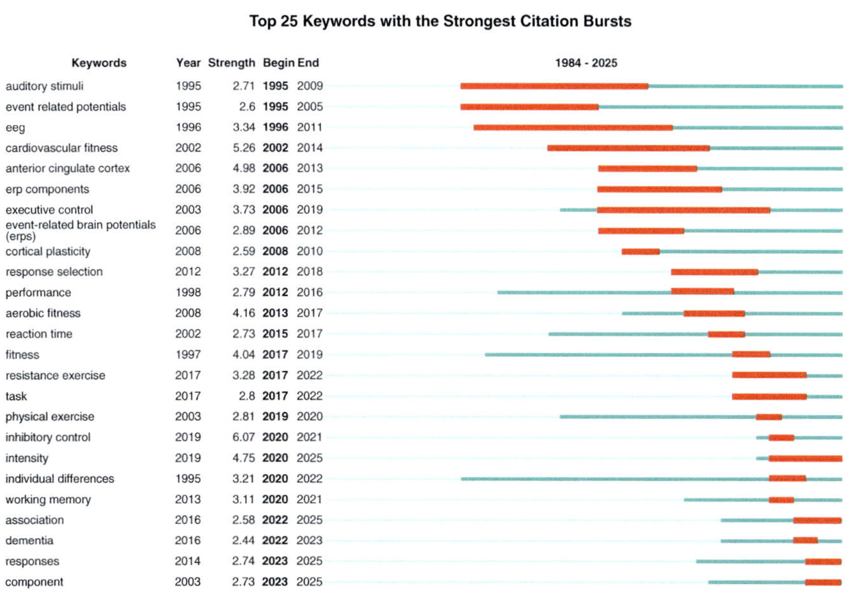

FIGURE 1.4 The Cluster Map of Keywords.

The first stage (1988–2002) was characterized by relatively low and stable output, with fewer than 15 publications per year, reflecting the early developmental phase of the field. This limited output may also reflect the print-only format of many journals at the time, which constrained research visibility and dissemination. The second stage (2003–2014) showed a gradual and steady increase in productivity, rising from 15 to 90 publications annually. The third stage (2015–2022) marked a period of rapid growth, peaking in 2021 with 180 publications. This sharp rise, particularly during 2020–2021, was likely influenced by the COVID-19 pandemic, during which researchers faced fewer competing demands and had more time to write, leading to an overall increase in scientific output (Aviv-Reuven & Rosenfeld, 2021). Additionally, the heightened focus on mental health and physical activity during lockdown conditions may have further contributed to the surge in exercise psychology publications (Papaioannou et al., 2020; Stockwell et al., 2021). Although publication numbers declined slightly after 2022, they remained higher than in earlier decades, indicating sustained scholarly engagement. Overall, the trend underscores the growing importance of exercise psychology in addressing modern health concerns.

1.4.2 Productivity and Collaboration Networks

The country-level analysis reveals a pronounced imbalance in global research productivity, with the United States serving as the central node in publication volume, citation impact, and collaborative connectivity. This dominance reflects the United States's robust funding infrastructure, global academic visibility, and role in hosting leading journals and conferences. The U.S.-led cluster underscores its integrative influence, while adjacent clusters, led by Canada and the United Kingdom, highlight the sustained impact of historically aligned, English-speaking nations. These countries benefit from shared academic norms and institutional support, especially within Commonwealth networks.

While European countries account for 68% of the top 25 contributors, the collaboration network reveals a more complex global structure. The centrality of the United States reflects ongoing geopolitical and linguistic advantages in shaping research flows. Additional clusters led by Australia and by New Zealand–Portugal indicate the emergence of regional research nexuses. Despite increasing output from Asia, particularly China and Taiwan, the region remains underrepresented in centrality and impact. Structural barriers such as language and limited integration into dominant citation networks (Goyanes et al., 2025) may contribute to this gap. Addressing these disparities through inclusive, cross-regional collaborations could enrich global scholarship and diversify the field's intellectual foundations.

The author-level analysis reveals a nuanced interplay between productivity, impact, and collaborative dynamics in exercise psychology research. As shown in Table 1.2, leadership in the field appears geographically diverse but unevenly distributed, primarily concentrated in North America and Europe, with more limited representation from Australia (n = 3) and Asia (n = 1). Catherine M. Sabiston, Martin S. Hagger, Nikos Ntoumanis, Yu-Kai Chang, and Panteleimon Ekkekakis emerge as the five most prolific contributors. Notably, country classification is based on current affiliation and may not account for scholars' international mobility. For instance, some leading scholars, such as Hagger and Ntoumanis, have held positions across multiple countries, including the United Kingdom, Australia, and the United States. Lastly, Martin S. Hagger and Stuart J.H. Biddle display higher ACI, suggesting that the relevance and focus of one's work may contribute more to academic visibility than sheer output alone (Donthu et al., 2021).

Viewed through a thematic lens, author clusters help illuminate the main areas of inquiry within the field. Mental health remains a central strand, with Yu-Kai Chang and Jennifer L. Etnier investigating the effects of exercise on cognitive function (Chang et al., 2014; Kao et al., 2025; Ren et al., 2024), while Panteleimon Ekkekakis, Steven J. Petruzzello, Ralf Brand, and Zachary Zenko elucidate how exercise influences affect, emotion, mood, and psychological well-being (Brand et al., 2025; Ekkekakis et al., 1999, 2021, 2024). Additionally, Costas I. Karageorghis examines the specific contribution of music to the exercise experience (Karageorghis et al., 2025; Karageorghis & Priest, 2012). Research on motivation and behavioral interventions is spearheaded by Nikos Ntoumanis, Martin S. Hagger, and Martyn Standage (Hagger, 2025; Megakli et al., 2017; Sivaramakrishnan et al., 2024; Standage et al., 2012), with mental health issues addressed by Ryan E. Rhodes also aligning with this thematic cluster (Grant et al., 2022; Haider et al., 2024). A complementary cluster led by Catherine M. Sabiston and Eva Pila explores the psychosocial dimensions of physical activity, including body image, motivation, and self-conscious emotions (Pila et al., 2022; Sabiston et al., 2014; Sick et al., 2022). Finally, Brett Smith and Kerry McGannon advance qualitative and sociocultural perspectives, with a focus on disability, identity, media representation, and equity in sport and physical-activity contexts (McGannon et al., 2021; Smith & McGannon, 2018).

1.4.3 Most Cited References

The most cited references, published between 2002 and 2018 and cited between 287 and 1,471 times as of 2025, can be categorized into four core topics: mental health, methodological approaches, measurement, and theoretical frameworks. Studies in the mental health category examined the effects of exercise on affect, anxiety, depression, and cognition (Biddle et al., 2019; Etnier et al., 1997; Reed & Ones, 2006; Williams et al., 2008; Wipfli et al., 2008). These works reflect the increasing societal focus on mental health and the growing recognition of exercise as a viable intervention strategy. The methodological approaches category includes synthesized research such as systematic reviews and meta-analyses (Edwardson & Gorely, 2010; Etnier et al., 1997; Reed & Ones, 2006), as well as methodological critiques (Smith & McGannon, 2018). Systematic reviews and meta-analyses are highly cited for their capacity to aggregate findings and draw robust conclusions across multiple studies. Their critique of traditional rigor in qualitative research quickly gained high citations.

The measurement tools category consists of nine out of twelve empirical research articles among the most cited references, focusing on constructs such as affect, enjoyment, and flow (Hardy & Rejeski, 1989; Jackson & Eklund, 2002; Kendzierski & Decarlo, 1991). These validated instruments serve as foundational tools for empirical research in exercise psychology. Their frequent citation underscores the field's reliance on standardized assessment tools to ensure methodological consistency and scientific rigor. Finally, the theoretical frameworks category encompasses studies grounded in established motivational theories, such as the theory of reasoned action, theory of planned behavior, and self-determination theory (Hagger et al., 2002; Markland & Tobin, 2004). These models offer critical insights into the mechanisms underlying exercise motivation and behavior. The high citation rates of these works highlight their enduring relevance and foundational role in shaping theoretical discourse within the field.

1.4.4 Keywords Analyses

1.4.4.1 Prevalent Keywords and Burst Phenomena of Keywords

Keywords represent core conceptual elements in scientific discourse, with frequency analysis revealing major research emphases in exercise psychology (Cui et al., 2024). Four distinct domains emerge across three temporal periods. Physical activity-related terms dominate the top 25 keywords, with "physical activity" and "exercise" collectively exceeding 1,800 occurrences, complemented by "sport" and "fitness." This prevalence demonstrates movement constructs as central to the field's identity (Rhodes et al., 2019; Ruissen, 2025). Psychological keywords bifurcate into motivational processes (e.g., 'motivation,' 'self-determination,' 'self-efficacy') and health outcomes (e.g., anxiety, depression, cognition), with meta-analyses suggesting the potential efficacy of exercise across these domains (Chang et al., 2025; Horcajo et al., 2022; Manninen et al., 2022; Panza et al., 2020; Wipfli et al., 2008). Methodological keywords including "validation," "meta-analysis," and "intervention" signal empirical rigor, while population-specific terms ("children, adolescents, women") indicate demographic research priorities (Anthony et al., 2023; Matheson et al., 2025; Zhu et al., 2022).

Citation bursts occur when keywords experience sudden acceleration in citation frequency, signaling rapid recognition and dissemination within the research community (Chen, 2006). Burst strength indexes the magnitude of that acceleration, whereas burst lag measures the waiting time between a concept's first appearance and its surge. Across the 25 keywords, burst strength values range from 6.03 to 13.62. "Planned behavior" demonstrates the highest burst strength, reflecting the decisive influence of the Theory of Planned Behavior in forecasting exercise intention and behavior (Hannan et al., 2015). "Sedentary behavior" demonstrated the second-highest strength, marking a fundamental shift from exclusively promoting activity to recognizing inactivity as an independent risk factor (Sui et al., 2021). Supporting evidence shows that sedentary time predicts adverse psychological outcomes regardless of physical-activity dose (Maher et al., 2014; Rong et al., 2024). Burst lags vary even more widely (0–28 years). Zero-lag adoptions (e.g., methodological staples such as "validation") indicate that requisite tools and theory were already in place. In contrast, concepts with prolonged lags signal either methodological barriers or disciplinary inertia; for example, "mental health" required 28 years to burst, reflecting the time needed to accumulate compelling evidence and overcome field boundaries. Thus, the joint inspection of strength and lag reveals not only what topics matter but how and when they become influential.

1.4.4.2 Temporal Evolution: Three Periods of Field Development

The burst phenomena analysis revealed striking variation in both burst strength (6.03–13.62) and lag times (0–28 years), necessitating temporal contextualization to understand adoption patterns. Our analyses identified three distinct periods: Early (1993–2004), Mid-Period (2005–2014), and Contemporary (2015–2025).

Early Period (1993–2004). Early burst phenomena concentrated on measurement validity and affective responses, reflecting exercise psychology's emergence as distinct discipline. "Attitudes" demonstrated both immediate adoption (0-year lag) and extended duration (17 years, 1993–2010), indicating sustained need for understanding exercise-related beliefs using established social psychology methods. "Validation" (burst strength: 7.58, 1996–2004) similarly achieved immediate recognition, as developing psychometrically sound exercise-specific instruments represented foundational necessity. "Feeling states" (7.27, 1997–2010) expanded beyond attitudes to encompass acute affective responses, recognizing that exercise experiences, not just beliefs, influence adherence (Hagger et al., 2002; Hazzard et al., 2020; Treasure & Newbery, 1998). Extended burst durations suggest systematic field building rather than paradigmatic shifts, with researchers establishing empirical foundations before theoretical advancement.

Mid-Period (2005–2014). This period witnessed unprecedented theoretical activity with nine keywords achieving burst status—the highest concentration across all periods. This surge reflects transition from measurement development to theory testing. "Planned behavior" dominated with the highest recorded burst strength (13.62), providing behavioral prediction through intention-mediated pathways (Schüz et al., 2017). Related constructs emerged sequentially: "intentions" (8.11, 2005–2014) preceded "implementation intentions" (8.01, 2011–2016), demonstrating theoretical refinement addressing the intention-behavior gap (Hagger et al., 2002). Theoretical pluralism defined this period, with complementary frameworks addressing different behavioral aspects. "Self-determination theory" (7.95, 2010–2014) shifted focus from prediction to motivational quality, its ten-year lag reflecting adaptation time for exercise-specific contexts (Teixeira et al., 2012). "Self-efficacy" (8.30, 2006–2012) bridged cognitive and motivational approaches, requiring 15 years to translate Bandura's theory to exercise settings. Overlapping burst periods and moderate durations (averaging six years) indicate rapid theoretical testing rather than prolonged exploration.

Contemporary Period (2015–2025). Contemporary keywords bursts reveal expansion beyond behavioral frameworks toward health outcomes and novel populations. Four ongoing bursts characterize current priorities: "sedentary behavior" (9.18, 2019–2025), "mental health" (7.33, 2021–2025), "executive functions" (7.63, 2022–2025), and "childhood" (7.21, 2021–2023). These signal integration with clinical psychology, cognitive neuroscience, and developmental science. "Sedentary behavior" represents a paradigmatic shift from promoting activity to reducing inactivity, recognizing distinct behavioral determinants (Melvin et al., 2020). Its rapid adoption (four-year lag) indicates aligned measurement technology and conceptual frameworks. Conversely, "mental health" exhibited the longest lag (28 years), reflecting institutional barriers between exercise science and psychiatry (Biddle et al., 2019; Klemmer et al., 2023). "Executive functions" represent the current frontier, its 19-year lag reflecting requirements for neuroimaging advances and standardized cognitive assessments (Chueh et al., 2022; Kao et al., 2025).

1.4.4.3 Keyword Clusters: Mapping the Intellectual Landscape

The cluster analysis revealed 20 distinct research communities within exercise psychology, demonstrating exceptional clustering quality (Q = 0.8788, Silhouette = 0.9441). These metrics indicate well-defined research boundaries with minimal conceptual overlap. Critically, the visualization maps both temporal evolution (left to right) and research impact (cluster size reflecting citation volume), revealing how different research streams emerged and gained influence over time.

Early Clusters (Left Region). The leftmost clusters represent exercise psychology's foundational concepts. "Narrative" (#10), "optimal experience" (#3), and "inhibitory control" (#2) emerged early, establishing qualitative, phenomenological, and self-regulatory research traditions. Despite their temporal precedence, these clusters show moderate citation accumulation, suggesting foundational but specialized influence. "Physical inactivity" (#1) appears as an early orange cluster, presaging the field's later embrace of sedentary behavior research. Mid-Period Clusters (Central Region). "Self-determination theory" (#0) dominates the central position both temporally and in citation volume, confirming its emergence during the Integration Period as the field's theoretical anchor. Its massive size reflects sustained citation accumulation since the mid-2000s. Surrounding clusters including "executive function" (#4), "affect" (#7), and "children" (#17) emerged contemporaneously.

Contemporary Clusters (Right Region). Recent clusters reveal current research frontiers. "Exercise adherence" (#13) has rapidly accumulated citations despite recent emergence, indicating urgent applied focus. "Missingness" (#9) and "structural equation modeling" (#16) in the right region confirm methodological sophistication as a contemporary priority. The rightmost position of "Australian-health-and-fitness-survey" (#18) demonstrates how recent landmark studies can quickly establish focused research programs. Together, these clusters illustrate the field's development from foundational theories to applied priorities, while highlighting the evolving interplay between conceptual innovation, methodological advancement, and real-world relevance in exercise psychology.

1.4.5 *Strengths and Limitations*

This study is the first to conduct a bibliometric analysis specifically targeting global trends and thematic hotspots in exercise psychology from 1988 to 2025. By systematically mapping the intellectual structure and development of the field, the study provides a foundational reference for scholars, practitioners, and interdisciplinary researchers engaged in exercise-related psychological inquiry. However, several limitations warrant consideration. First, the analysis was limited to the Web of Science Core Collection and employed two bibliometric tools (i.e., VOSviewer and CiteSpace). Although these tools are widely recognized, additional platforms such as Bibliometrix may offer complementary functions and deeper analytical granularity. Second, the article selection followed an exclusion strategy, retaining publications from leading exercise psychology journals that included the terms "exercise" and "physical activity" but excluded those containing "athlete" or "athletic." While this approach sought to avoid traditional sport psychology content, some studies rooted in sport contexts may still have been included. Third, although the analysis focused on journals with "exercise psychology" (e.g., IJSEP, IRSEP, JSEP), the inherently interdisciplinary nature of the field means that relevant research published in areas such as health psychology, public health, or medicine have been overlooked. For example, only 7.7%–25.3% of 10 most prolific authors listed in Table 1.2 published their research in outlets beyond these five selected journals, potentially leading to an underestimation of the broader impact of exercise psychology.

1.5 Conclusion

This bibliometric analysis provides an overview of the conceptual development, temporal progression, and emerging themes in exercise psychology based on selected journals. Keyword analyses identify three key phases, beginning with an initial focus on measurement and affective responses, followed by a period of theoretical expansion, and more recently, a growing emphasis on mental health, sedentary behavior, and executive functions. The observed patterns in keyword bursts and cluster structures reflect how theoretical developments, methodological advances, and demographic considerations have shaped the field over time. These findings suggest that exercise psychology has gradually evolved into a multidisciplinary area of research, influenced by both foundational inquiry and applied concerns. To ensure its continued relevance and contribution to global health, the field will benefit from sustained efforts to broaden research scope, enhance inclusivity, and uphold scientific rigor.

References

American College of Sports Medicine. (2022). *ACSM's guidelines for exercise testing and prescription* (11th ed.). Wolters Kluwer.

Anthony, J., Kinnafick, F. E., Papathomas, A., & Breen, K. (2023). Physical activity for adolescents with severe mental illness: A systematic scoping review. *International Review of Sport and Exercise Psychology*, *16*(1), 176–209. https://doi.org/10.1080/1750984x.2020.1833360

Aviv-Reuven, S., & Rosenfeld, A. (2021). Publication patterns' changes due to the COVID-19 pandemic: A longitudinal and short-term scientometric analysis. *Scientometrics*, *126*(8), 6761–6784. https://doi.org/10.1007/s11192-021-04059-x

Berger, B. G., Pargman, D., & Weinberg, R. S. (2002). *Foundations of exercise psychology* (1st ed.). Fitness Information Technology.

Berger, B. G., Pargman, D., & Weinberg, R. S. (2015). *Foundations of exercise psychology* (3rd ed.). Fitness Information Technology.

Biddle, S. J. H., Ciaccioni, S., Thomas, G., & Vergeer, I. (2019). Physical activity and mental health in children and adolescents: An updated review of reviews and an analysis of causality. *Psychology of Sport and Exercise*, *42*, 146–155. https://doi.org/10.1016/j.psychsport.2018.08.011

Brand, R., Sudeck, G., & Ekkekakis, P. (2025). Affective experiences from exercise. Youth-adult differences and prediction of exercise behavior. *Psychology of Sport and Exercise*, *76*, Article 102755. https://doi.org/10.1016/j.psychsport.2024.102755

Buckworth, J., & Dishman, R. K. (2002). *Exercise psychology* (2nd ed.). Human Kinetics.

Buckworth, J., Dishman, R. K., O'Connor, P. J., & Tomporowski, P. D. (2013). *Exercise psychology* (2nd ed.). Human Kinetics.

Cardon, G., & Salmon, J. (2020). Why have youth physical activity trends flatlined in the last decade? Opinion piece on "Global trends in insufficient physical activity among adolescents: A pooled analysis of 298 population-based surveys with 1.6 million participants" by Guthold et al. *Journal of Sport and Health Science*, *9*(4), 335–338. https://doi.org/10.1016/j.jshs.2020.04.009

Castelli, D. M., Hillman, C. H., Buck, S. M., & Erwin, H. E. (2007). Physical fitness and academic achievement in third- and fifth-grade students. *Journal of Sport & Exercise Psychology*, *29*(2), 239–252. https://doi.org/10.1123/jsep.29.2.239

Chalabaev, A., Sarrazin, P., Fontayne, P., Boiché, J., & Clément-Guillotin, C. (2013). The influence of sex stereotypes and gender roles on participation and performance in sport and exercise: Review and future directions. *Psychology of Sport and Exercise*, *14*(2), 136–144. https://doi.org/10.1016/j.psychsport.2012.10.005

Chang, Y. K., Ren, F. F., Li, R. H., Ai, J. Y., Kao, S. C., & Etnier, J. L. (2025). Effects of acute exercise on cognitive function: A meta-review of 30 systematic reviews with meta-analyses. *Psychological Bulletin*, *151*(2), 240–259. https://doi.org/10.1037/bul0000460

Chang, Y. K., Chi, L., Etnier, J. L., Wang, C. C., Chu, C. H., & Zhou, C. L. (2014). Effect of acute aerobic exercise on cognitive performance: Role of cardiovascular fitness. *Psychology of Sport and Exercise*, *15*(5), 464–470. https://doi.org/10.1016/j.psychsport.2014.04.007

Chen, C. (2006). CiteSpace II: Detecting and visualizing emerging trends and transient patterns in scientific literature. *Journal of the American Society for Information Science and Technology*, *57*(3), 359–377. https://doi.org/10.1002/asi.20317

Chueh, T. Y., Hsieh, S. S., Tsai, Y. J., Yu, C. L., Hung, C. L., Benzing, V., Schmidt, M., Chang, Y. K., Hillman, C. H., & Hung, T. M. (2022). Effects of a single bout of moderate-to-vigorous physical activity on executive functions in children with attention-deficit/hyperactivity disorder: A systematic review and meta-analysis. *Psychology of Sport and Exercise*, *58*, Article 102097. https://doi.org/10.1016/j.psychsport.2021.102097

Craft, L. L., & Landers, D. M. (1998). The effect of exercise on clinical depression and depression resulting from mental illness: A meta-analysis. *Journal of Sport & Exercise Psychology*, *20*(4), 339–357. https://doi.org/10.1123/jsep.20.4.339

Cui, X., Xue, T., Zhang, Z., Yang, H., & Ren, Y. (2024). A bibliometric and visual analysis of cognitive function in bipolar disorder from 2012 to 2022. *Annals of General Psychiatry*, *23*(1), 13. https://doi.org/10.1186/s12991-024-00498-x

Donthu, N., Kumar, S., Mukherjee, D., Pandey, N., & Lim, W. M. (2021). How to conduct a bibliometric analysis: An overview and guidelines. *Journal of Business Research*, *133*, 285–296. https://doi.org/10.1016/j.jbusres.2021.04.070

Edwardson, C. L., & Gorely, T. (2010). Parental influences on different types and intensities of physical activity in youth: A systematic review. *Psychology of Sport and Exercise*, *11*(6), 522–535. https://doi.org/10.1016/j.psychsport.2010.05.001

Ekkekakis, P., Hall, E. E., & Petruzzello, S. J. (1999). Measuring state anxiety in the context of acute exercise using the state anxiety inventory: An attempt to resolve the brouhaha. *Journal of Sport & Exercise Psychology*, *21*(3), 205–229. https://doi.org/10.1123/jsep.21.3.205

Ekkekakis, P., Hartman, M. E., & Ladwig, M. A. (2024). When studying affective responses to exercise, the definition of "intensity" must reference homeostatic perturbations: A retort to Vollaard et al. *Journal of Sport & Exercise Psychology*, *46*(2), 66–72. https://doi.org/10.1123/jsep.2024-0064

Ekkekakis, P., Zenko, Z., & Vazou, S. (2021). Do you find exercise pleasant or unpleasant? The Affective Exercise Experiences (AFFEXX) questionnaire. *Psychology of Sport and Exercise*, *55*, Article 101930. https://doi.org/10.1016/j.psychsport.2021.101930

Etnier, J. L. (2025). *Psychological benefits of exercise and physical activity* (1st ed.). Human Kinetics.

Etnier, J. L., Salazar, W., Landers, D. M., Petruzzello, S. J., Han, M., & Nowell, P. (1997). The influence of physical fitness and exercise upon cognitive functioning: A meta-analysis. *Journal of Sport & Exercise Psychology*, *19*(3), 249–277. https://doi.org/10.1123/jsep.19.3.249

Gill, D. L. (1986). *Psychological dynamics of sport* (4th ed.). Human Kinetics.

Gill, D. L. (2000). *Psychological dynamics of sport and exercise* (4th ed.). Human Kinetics.

Gill, D. L., Williams, L., & Reifsteck, E. J. (2017). *Psychological dynamics of sport and exercise* (4th ed.). Human Kinetics.

Goyanes, M., de-Marcos, L., Durotoye, T., Kurniasari, T., & Gil de Zúñiga, H. (2025). Editors-in-chief in social sciences: Mapping the institutional, geographical, and gender representation between academic fields. *PloS One*, *20*(2), e0317931. https://doi.org/10.1371/journal.pone.0317931

Grant, S. J., Lithopoulos, A., & Rhodes, R. E. (2022). Understanding action control of physical activity among mothers with young children. *International Journal of Sport and Exercise Psychology*, *20*(2), 569–585. https://doi.org/10.1080/1612197x.2020.1869805

Hackfort, D., & Schinke, R. J. (2020). *The Routledge international encyclopedia of sport and exercise psychology* (Vol. Applied and Practical Measures). Routledge London.

Hagger, M. S. (2025). Psychological determinants of health behavior. *Annual Review of Psychology*, *76*, 821–850. https://doi.org/10.1146/annurev-psych-020124-114222

Hagger, M. S., Chatzisarantis, N. L. D., & Biddle, S. J. H. (2002). A meta-analytic review of the theories of reasoned action and planned behavior in physical activity: Predictive validity and the contribution of additional variables. *Journal of Sport & Exercise Psychology*, *24*(1), 3–32. https://doi.org/10.1123/jsep.24.1.3

Haider, I., Brown, D. M. Y., Bray, S. R., Dutta, P., Rhodes, R. E., & Kwan, M. Y. W. (2024). Understanding the intention-to-behaviour relationship for adolescents: An application of the multi-process action control model. *International Journal of Sport and Exercise Psychology*, *22*(1), 52–69. https://doi.org/10.1080/1612197x.2022.2138496

Hannan, T. E., Moffitt, R. L., Neumann, D. L., & Thomas, P. R. (2015). Applying the theory of planned behavior to physical activity: The moderating role of mental toughness. *Journal of Sport & Exercise Psychology*, *37*(5), 514–522. https://doi.org/10.1123/jsep.2015-0074

Hardy, C. J., & Rejeski, W. J. (1989). Not what, but how one feels: The measurement of affect during exercise. *Journal of Sport & Exercise Psychology*, *11*(3), 304–317. https://doi.org/10.1123/jsep.11.3.304

Hausenblas, H. A., Carron, A. V., & Mack, D. E. (1997). Application of the theories of reasoned action and planned behavior to exercise behavior: A meta-analysis. *Journal of Sport & Exercise Psychology*, *19*(1), 36–51. https://doi.org/10.1123/jsep.19.1.36

Hausenblas, H. A., & Downs, D. S. (2002). Exercise dependence: A systematic review. *Psychology of Sport and Exercise*, *3*(2), 89–123, Article Pii s1469-0292(00)00015-7. https://doi.org/10.1016/s1469-0292(00)00015-7

Hazzard, V. M., Schaefer, L. M., Mankowski, A., Carson, T. L., Lipson, S. M., Fendrick, C., Crosby, R. D., & Sonneville, K. R. (2020). Development and validation of the Eating Disorders Screen for Athletes (EDSA): A brief screening tool for male and female athletes. *Psychology of Sport and Exercise*, *50*, Article 101745. https://doi.org/10.1016/j.psychsport.2020.101745

Horcajo, J., Santos, D., & Higuero, G. (2022). The effects of self-efficacy on physical and cognitive performance: An analysis of meta-certainty. *Psychology of Sport and Exercise*, *58*, 102063. https://doi.org/10.1016/j.psychsport.2021.102063

Horn, T. S., & Smith, A. L. (2018). *Advances in sport and exercise psychology* (4th ed.). Human Kinetics.

Jackson, S. A., & Eklund, R. C. (2002). Assessing flow in physical activity: The Flow State Scale-2 and Dispositional Flow Scale-2. *Journal of Sport & Exercise Psychology*, *24*(2), 133–150. https://doi.org/10.1123/jsep.24.2.133

Jackson, S. A., & Marsh, H. W. (1996). Development and validation of a scale to measure optimal experience: The Flow State Scale. *Journal of Sport & Exercise Psychology*, *18*(1), 17–35. https://doi.org/10.1123/jsep.18.1.17

Jackson, S. A., Martin, A. J., & Eklund, R. C. (2008). Long and short measures of flow: The construct validity of the FSS-2, DFS-2, and new brief counterparts. *Journal of Sport & Exercise Psychology*, *30*(5), 561–587. https://doi.org/10.1123/jsep.30.5.561

Kao, S. C., Chen, F. T., Moreau, D., Drollette, E. S., Amireault, S., Chu, C. H., & Chang, Y. K. (2025). Acute effects of exercise engagement on neurocognitive function: A systematic review and meta-analysis on P3 amplitude and latency. *International Review of Sport and Exercise Psychology*, *18*(1), 111–153. https://doi.org/10.1080/1750984x.2022.2155488

Karageorghis, C. I., Guérin, S. M. R., Fessler, L., Howard, L. W., Pinto, C., Ojuri, O., Kuan, J. Y., & Samwell-Nash, K. G. (2025). One-HIIT wonder: Can music make high-intensity interval training more pleasant? *Psychology of Sport and Exercise*, *76*, Article 102717. https://doi.org/10.1016/j.psychsport.2024.102717

Karageorghis, C. I., & Priest, D. L. (2012). Music in the exercise domain: A review and synthesis (Part II). *International Review of Sport and Exercise Psychology*, *5*(1), 67–84. https://doi.org/10.1080/1750984x.2011.631027

Kendzierski, D., & Decarlo, K. J. (1991). Physical activity enjoyment scale: Two validation studies. *Journal of Sport & Exercise Psychology*, *13*(1), 50–64. https://doi.org/10.1123/jsep.13.1.50

Klemmer, B., Kinnafick, F. E., Spray, C., & Chater, A. M. (2023). The effectiveness of structured sport and exercise interventions in enhancing the mental health of adolescents with mild to moderate mental health problems: A systematic review. *International Review of Sport and Exercise Psychology*, 1–24. https://doi.org/10.1080/1750984x.2023.2266823

Kumar, M., George, R. J., & Anisha, P.S. (2023). Bibliometric analysis for medical research. *Indian Journal of Psychological Medicine*, *45*(3), 277–282. https://doi.org/10.1177/02537176221103617

Lindahl, J., Stenling, A., Lindwall, M., & Colliander, C. (2015). Trends and knowledge base in sport and exercise psychology research: A bibliometric review study. *International Review of Sport and Exercise Psychology*, *8*(1), 71–94. https://doi.org/10.1080/1750984X.2015.1019540

Lonsdale, C., Hodge, K., & Rose, E. A. (2008). The Behavioral Regulation in Sport Questionnaire (BRSQ): Instrument development and initial validity evidence. *Journal of Sport & Exercise Psychology*, *30*(3), 323–355. https://doi.org/10.1123/jsep.30.3.323

Lox, C. L., Ginis, K. A. M., Gainforth, H. L., & Petruzzello, S. J. (2019). *The psychology of exercise: Integrating theory and practice* (5th ed.). Routledge.

Lox, C. L., Ginis, K. A. M., & Petruzzello, S. J. (2003). *The psychology of exercise: Integrating theory and practice* (1st ed.). Routledge.

Maher, J. P., Doerksen, S. E., Elavsky, S., & Conroy, D. E. (2014). Daily satisfaction with life is regulated by both physical activity and sedentary behavior. *Journal of Sport & Exercise Psychology*, *36*(2), 166–178. https://doi.org/10.1123/jsep.2013-0185

Malhi, G. S., & Mann, J. J. (2018). Depression. *Lancet*, *392*, 2299–2312. https://doi.org/10.1016/S0140-6736(18)31948-2

Manninen, M., Dishman, R., Hwang, Y., Magrum, E., Deng, Y. Y., & Yli-Piipari, S. (2022). Self-determination theory based instructional interventions and motivational regulations in organized physical activity: A systematic review and multivariate meta-analysis. *Psychology of Sport and Exercise*, *62*, Article 102248. https://doi.org/10.1016/j.psychsport.2022.102248

Markland, D., & Tobin, V. (2004). A modification to the behavioural regulation in exercise questionnaire to include an assessment of amotivation. *Journal of Sport & Exercise Psychology*, *26*(2), 191–196. https://doi.org/10.1123/jsep.26.2.191

Matheson, E. L., Schneider, J., Gentili, C., Tinoco, A., Silva-Breen, H., White, P., LaVoi, N. M., & Diedrichs, P. C. (2025). A systematic review and meta-analysis of interventions that target the intersection of body image and movement among girls and women. *International Review of Sport and Exercise Psychology*, *18*(1), 467–502. https://doi.org/10.1080/1750984x.2023.2258379

McGannon, K. R., Smith, B., Kendellen, K., & Gonsalves, C. A. (2021). Qualitative research in six sport and exercise psychology journals between 2010 and 2017: An updated and expanded review of trends and interpretations. *International Journal of Sport and Exercise Psychology*, *19*(3), 359–379. https://doi.org/10.1080/1612197x.2019.1655779

Megakli, T., Vlachopoulos, S. P., Thogersen-Ntoumani, C., & Theodorakis, Y. (2017). Impact of aerobic and resistance exercise combination on physical self-perceptions and self-esteem in women with obesity with one-year follow-up. *International Journal of Sport and Exercise Psychology*, *15*(3), 236–257. https://doi.org/10.1080/1612197x.2015.1094115

Melvin, A., Elliott, C. G., Bang, F., Roberts, K. C., Thompson, W., & Prince, S. A. (2020). Population health measurement of social norms for sedentary behaviour: A systematic review. *Psychology of Sport and Exercise*, *47*, Article 101631. https://doi.org/10.1016/j.psychsport.2019.101631

Morgan, W. P. (1997). *Physical activity and mental health*. Taylor & Francis.

Nagy, C., Maitra, M., Tanti, A., Suderman, M., Théroux, J.-F., Davoli, M. A., Perlman, K., Yerko, V., Wang, Y. C., & Tripathy, S. J. (2020). Single-nucleus transcriptomics of the prefrontal cortex in major depressive disorder implicates oligodendrocyte precursor cells and excitatory neurons. *Nature Neuroscience*, *23*(6), 771–781. https://doi.org/10.1038/s41593-020-0621-y

Panza, M. J., Graupensperger, S., Agans, J. P., Doré, I., Vella, S. A., & Evans, M. B. (2020). Adolescent sport participation and symptoms of anxiety and depression: A systematic review and meta-analysis. *Journal of Sport & Exercise Psychology*, *42*(3), 201–218. https://doi.org/10.1123/jsep.2019-0235

Papaioannou, A., Schinke, R., Chang, Y., Kim, Y., & Duda, J. (2020). Physical activity, health and well-being in an imposed social distanced world. *International Journal of Sport and Exercise Psychology*, *18*(4), 414–419. https://doi.org/10.1080/1612197X.2020.1773195

Pila, E., Gilchrist, J. D., Kowalski, K. C., & Sabiston, C. M. (2022). Self-compassion and body-related self-conscious emotions: Examining within- and between-person variation among adolescent girls in sport*. *Psychology of Sport and Exercise*, *58*, Article 102083. https://doi.org/10.1016/j.psychsport.2021.102083

Reed, J., & Ones, D. S. (2006). The effect of acute aerobic exercise on positive activated affect: A meta-analysis. *Psychology of Sport and Exercise*, *7*(5), 477–514. https://doi.org/10.1016/j.psychsport.2005.11.003

Reinboth, M., & Duda, J. L. (2006). Perceived motivational climate, need satisfaction and indices of well-being in team sports: A longitudinal perspective. *Psychology of Sport and Exercise*, *7*(3), 269–286. https://doi.org/10.1016/j.psychsport.2005.06.002

Ren, F. F., Feng, S. H., Li, R. H., Chu, C. H., Chang, Y. K., & Chen, F. T. (2024). The effects of acute aerobic and resistance exercise on the planning aspect of executive functions in children with preterm birth. *International Journal of Sport and Exercise Psychology*, *22*(9), 2137–2150. https://doi.org/10.1080/1612197x.2023.2268852

Rhodes, R. E., McEwan, D., & Rebar, A. L. (2019). Theories of physical activity behaviour change: A history and synthesis of approaches. *Psychology of Sport and Exercise*, *42*, 100–109. https://doi.org/10.1016/j.psychsport.2018.11.010

Rong, F., Li, X., Jia, L. Y., Liu, J., Li, S. Q., Zhang, Z. X., Wang, R., Wang, D. N., & Wan, Y. H. (2024). Substitutions of physical activity and sedentary behavior with negative emotions and sex difference among college students. *Psychology of Sport and Exercise*, *72*, Article 102605. https://doi.org/10.1016/j.psychsport.2024.102605

Ruissen, G. R. (2025). Establishing causal inferences from experimental and observational data: A critical review and primer for sport and exercise psychology. *Sport Exercise and Performance Psychology*, *14*(1), 7–23. https://doi.org/10.1037/spy0000357

Sabiston, C. M., Pila, E., Pinsonnault-Bilodeau, G., & Cox, A. E. (2014). Social physique anxiety experiences in physical activity: A comprehensive synthesis of research studies focused on measurement, theory, and predictors and outcomes. *International Review of Sport and Exercise Psychology*, *7*(1), 158–183. https://doi.org/10.1080/1750984x.2014.904392

Schüz, B., Li, A. S. W., Hardinge, A., McEachan, R. R. C., & Conner, M. (2017). Socioeconomic status as a moderator between social cognitions and physical activity: Systematic review and meta-analysis based on the Theory of Planned Behavior. *Psychology of Sport and Exercise*, *30*, 186–195. https://doi.org/10.1016/j.psychsport.2017.03.004

Seraganian, P. (1993). *Exercise psychology: The influence of physical exercise on psychological processes*. John Wiley & Sons.

Sick, K., Sabiston, C. M., Maharaj, A., & Pila, E. (2022). Body image and disordered eating prevention in girls' sport: A partner-driven and stakeholder-informed scoping review of interventions. *Psychology of Sport and Exercise*, *61*, Article 102215. https://doi.org/10.1016/j.psychsport.2022.102215

Sivaramakrishnan, H., Gucciardi, D. F., McDonald, M. D., Quested, E., Thogersen-Ntoumani, C., Cheval, B., & Ntoumanis, N. (2024). Psychosocial outcomes of sport participation for middle-aged and older adults: A systematic review and meta-analysis. *International Review of Sport and Exercise Psychology*, *17*(1), 398–419. https://doi.org/10.1080/1750984x.2021.2004611

Smith, B., & McGannon, K. R. (2018). Developing rigor in qualitative research: Problems and opportunities within sport and exercise psychology. *International Review of Sport and Exercise Psychology*, *11*(1), 101–121. https://doi.org/10.1080/1750984x.2017.1317357

Smith, G., Williams, L., O'Donnell, C., & McKechnie, J. (2017). The influence of social-cognitive constructs and personality traits on physical activity in healthy adults. *International Journal of Sport and Exercise Psychology*, *15*(5), 540–555. https://doi.org/10.1080/1612197x.2016.1142459

Smolinski, A., McIntyre, O., Martin, D., & Martin, J. J. (2024). An imperfect list of eminent sport and exercise psychology researchers. *Kinesiology Review*, *13*(4), 521–535. https://doi.org/10.1123/kr.2024-0024

Sparkes, A. C., & Smith, B. (2009). Judging the quality of qualitative inquiry: Criteriology and relativism in action. *Psychology of Sport and Exercise*, *10*(5), 491–497. https://doi.org/10.1016/j.psychsport.2009.02.006

Spence, J. C., & Lee, R. E. (2003). Toward a comprehensive model of physical activity. *Psychology of Sport and Exercise*, *4*(1), 7–24. https://doi.org/10.1016/s1469-0292(02)00014-6

Standage, M., Gillison, F. B., Ntoumanis, N., & Treasure, D. C. (2012). Predicting students' physical activity and health-related well-being: A prospective cross-domain investigation of motivation across school physical education and exercise settings. *Journal of Sport & Exercise Psychology*, *34*(1), 37–60. https://doi.org/10.1123/jsep.34.1.37

Stockwell, S., Trott, M., Tully, M., Shin, J., Barnett, Y., Butler, L., McDermott, D., Schuch, F., & Smith, L. (2021). Changes in physical activity and sedentary behaviours from before to during the COVID-19 pandemic lockdown: A systematic review. *BMJ Open Sport & Exercise Medicine*, *7*(1), e000960. https://doi.org/10.1136/bmjsem-2020-000960

Strain, T., Flaxman, S., Guthold, R., Semenova, E., Cowan, M., Riley, L. M., Bull, F. C., & Stevens, G. A. (2024). National, regional, and global trends in insufficient physical activity among adults from 2000 to 2022: A pooled analysis of 507 population-based surveys with 5.7 million participants. *The Lancet Global Health*, *12*(8), e1232–e1243. https://doi.org/10.1016/S2214-109X(24)00150-5

Sui, W. Y., Sui, A., & Prapavessis, H. (2021). Relationships between indices of sedentary behavior and hedonic well-being: A scoping review. *Psychology of Sport and Exercise*, *54*, Article 101920. https://doi.org/10.1016/j.psychsport.2021.101920

Teixeira, P. J., Carraça, E. V., Markland, D., Silva, M. N., & Ryan, R. M. (2012). Exercise, physical activity, and self-determination theory: A systematic review. *International Journal of Behavioral Nutrition and Physical Activity*, *9*, 78. https://doi.org/10.1186/1479-5868-9-78

Terry, P. C., Lane, A. M., & Fogarty, G. J. (2003). Construct validity of the Profile of Mood States - Adolescents for use with adults. *Psychology of Sport and Exercise*, *4*(2), 125–139. https://doi.org/10.1016/s1469-0292(01)00035-8

Treasure, D. C., & Newbery, D. M. (1998). Relationship between self-efficacy, exercise intensity, and feeling states in a sedentary population during and following an acute bout of exercise. *Journal of Sport & Exercise Psychology*, *20*(1), 1–11. https://doi.org/10.1123/jsep.20.1.1

U.S. Department of Health and Human Services. (2018). *2018 Physical activity guidelines for Americans* (2nd ed.). U.S. Department of Health and Human Services

van Eck, N. J., & Waltman, L. (2010). Software survey: VOSviewer, a computer program for bibliometric mapping. *Scientometrics*, *84*(2), 523–538. https://doi.org/10.1007/s11192-009-0146-3

Weinberg, R., & Gould, D. (2024). *Foundations of sport and exercise psychology* (8th ed.). Human Kinetics.

Williams, D. M., Dunsiger, S., Ciccolo, J. T., Lewis, B. A., Albrecht, A. E., & Marcus, B. H. (2008). Acute affective response to a moderate-intensity exercise stimulus predicts physical activity participation 6 and 12 months later. *Psychology of Sport and Exercise*, *9*(3), 231–245. https://doi.org/10.1016/j.psychsport.2007.04.002

Wilson, P. M., Rogers, W. T., Rodgers, W. M., & Wild, T. C. (2006). The psychological need satisfaction in exercise scale. *Journal of Sport & Exercise Psychology*, *28*(3), 231–251. https://doi.org/10.1123/jsep.28.3.231

Wipfli, B. M., Rethorst, C. D., & Landers, D. M. (2008). The anxiolytic effects of exercise: A meta-analysis of randomized trials and dose-response analysis. *Journal of Sport & Exercise Psychology*, *30*(4), 392–410. https://doi.org/10.1123/jsep.30.4.392

World Health Organization. (2020). *WHO guidelines on physical activity and sedentary behaviour*. World Health Organization.

Zhu, Y. X., Li, J. B., Zhang, M. G., Li, C. X., Lau, E. Y. H., & Tao, S. S. (2022). Physical activity participation and physical aggression in children and adolescents: A systematic review and meta-analysis. *Psychology of Sport and Exercise*, *63*, Article 102288. https://doi.org/10.1016/j.psychsport.2022.102288

PART 2
Exercise and Mental Health

2

PHYSICAL ACTIVITY MOVES ME

Affect, Emotion, and Mood in the Context of Physical Activity

Zachary Zenko, Leighton Jones, Miranda Miller, and Matthew A. Ladwig

2.1 Preface

Over two decades ago, Ekkekakis (2003) introduced the Dual-Mode Theory (DMT) to explain the complexity of affective responses to physical activity and shed a light on both physical and cognitive influences; the field was forever altered as a result. In the years since, research on affective responses has blossomed. This chapter provides a broad overview and brief sampling of this literature.

We first provide a brief introduction to dual-process models like the Affective-Reflective Theory of physical inactivity and exercise (ART; Brand & Ekkekakis, 2018, 2021) and the Theory of Effort Minimization in Physical Activity (TEMPA; Cheval & Boisgontier, 2021) that suggest physical activity and exercise behavior are determined by complex reflective processes based on cognitive appraisal, and automatic affective responses and valuations that are not dependent upon cognitive appraisals and evaluations. These dual-process models highlight the role of automatic affective responses in shaping physical activity as well as the role of self-control as a moderating variable.

Given the theoretical importance of affective responses to exercise as a predictor of future exercise engagement, and support from empirical evidence (for example, see a systematic review by Rhodes & Kates [2015]), we discuss the complex dynamics of affective responses to exercise and affective exercise experiences. We note that careful consideration must be given to both the choice and timing of measurements of affective responses (Andrade et al., 2022; Ekkekakis, 2013; Henriques et al., 2023). Using evidence from the laboratory and real-world, free-living situations, this chapter provides a broad overview of how (a) physical activity can change our affective experience and (b) our affective experience can influence future physical activity. This chapter also addresses affectively charged motivations and the impact of physical activity on emotion regulation.

DOI: 10.4324/9781003517474-4

More than 25 years ago, Blumenthal et al. (1999) presented seminal research on the benefits of exercise on depressive symptoms. In the decades since, the field has evolved with many randomized-controlled trials and meta-analyses demonstrating, with clear consistency, that physical activity has beneficial effects on depression and depressive symptoms. This chapter provides a brief overview of this literature and describes implications for these complex interactions between physical activity, affect, emotion, and mood. We highlight some recommendations for future research directions and emphasize the importance of mixed methods and consideration of diverse populations and basic and applied research.

2.2 Affect

The DMT (Ekkekakis, 2003) was proposed in the literature with the aim of understanding patterns and mechanisms of affective responses to exercise (Ekkekakis, 2009). This conceptualization of affective responses changing as a function of exercise intensity has driven a gamut of research studies testing and supporting the accuracy of the theory (e.g., Ekkekakis et al., 2011; Sheppard & Parfitt, 2008; Welch et al., 2007). The DMT offered an alternative perspective on understanding exercise through in-the-moment affective responses, an approach that was not present in other theories and models commonly applied to understand exercise behavior (e.g., Theory of Planned Behavior [Ajzen, 1991]).

In this section, we primarily discuss affect under the definition of *core affect:* "the most elementary consciously accessible affective feeling" (Russell & Barrett, 1999, p. 806), with two dimensions of affective valence (pleasure–displeasure) and arousal/activation (activation–deactivation) in line with the circumplex model of affect (Posner et al., 2005; Russell, 1980). However, we will also see examples of research that have deviated from this model presented under the umbrella of affect. Similarly, although affect and emotion refer to distinct concepts (Ekkekakis, 2013), emotions "are affective states with objects" that require cognitive appraisals (Clore & Ortony, 2000, p. 28). They are thus related concepts, and we will see examples where the terms overlap and have sometimes been conflated.

2.2.1 Theoretical Perspectives

Understanding and effectively promoting physical activity behavior is crucial, especially as rates of aerobic and muscle-strengthening activity are critically low (Garcia-Hermoso et al., 2023). Contemporary theoretical approaches seeking to understand exercise behavior are now embracing dual-process models. Dual-process models propose that engaging in exercise is determined by two mental processes: automatic and reflective. Automatic processes are rapid, sometimes nonconscious, and not dependent on cognitive resources. Reflective processes are deliberate, effortful processes underpinning reasoned action (Rebar et al., 2021). The dual-process models typically follow a default-interventionist architecture whereby behavior is driven by automatic processes unless there is sufficient motivation and self-regulatory capacity to inhibit them. Two dual-process models proposed to understand the decisions behind exercise behavior are ART (Brand & Ekkekakis, 2018, 2021) and the TEMPA (Cheval & Boisgontier, 2021). These models reflect our growing understanding that automatic processes are important in determining exercise behavior. Over the past decade or so, there has been increasing awareness and acknowledgment that automatic processes are important in exercise (Conroy & Berry, 2017).

2.2.1.1 Affective-Reflective Theory

The Affective-Reflective Theory of physical inactivity and exercise (ART; Brand & Ekkekakis, 2018; 2021) predicts that both affective (automatic, Type 1 processes) and reflective (cognitively mediated, deliberate, Type 2 processes) influence physical activity and exercise behavior. The affective valuations of physical activity are automatic, connected with the concept of physical activity through prior experience, and result in a feeling of pleasure or displeasure. If there is pleasure, then one is likely to experience an approach impulse toward physical activity. However, if the automatic valuation of physical activity is negative, perhaps due to repeated unpleasant exercise experiences, then an avoidance impulse is expected (Brand & Ekkekakis, 2021). Although one can override avoidance impulses and carry on with action plans and intentions to complete exercise goals, this is less likely if self-control resources are low (Brand & Ekkekakis, 2018). Thus, according to ART, it is important to facilitate both positive automatic, affective valuations of physical activity through repeated pleasant associations and positive experiences, and positive, favorable reflective evaluations of physical activity (e.g., through enhanced self-efficacy, cognitive appraisals of benefits of an active lifestyle; see Brand & Ekkekakis, 2018, 2021).

2.2.1.2 Theory of Effort Minimization in Physical Activity

The Theory of Effort Minimization in Physical Activity (TEMPA; Cheval & Boisgontier, 2021) also incorporates automatic associations with physical activity and suggests these automatic associations can help explain the intention–behavior gap. Like the ART, the TEMPA posits that self-control may override negative automatic associations and that automatic associations are more likely to influence behavior if self-control resources are low (Brand & Cheval, 2019). Following these theories, it seems that increasing self-control resources and promoting positive reflective processes toward physical activity (e.g., attitudes, goals, intentions) is highly recommended. But, recognizing that self-control resources may not always be high (e.g., in times of high stress; Maier et al. [2015]), it also seems essential to create positive automatic associations with the concepts of physical activity and exercise through repeated pleasant exercise experiences.

2.2.2 Dual-Process Models

The incorporation of dual-process models into exercise psychology signals a shift away from or beyond theories that have dominated research in the field for decades (e.g. transtheoretical model [TTM; Prochaska & DiClemente (1983)], Theory of Planned Behavior [Ajzen, 1991]). In their article describing the history of behavior change theories within physical activity, Rhodes et al. (2019) presented dual-process models as advancing prior frameworks by adding the understanding of nonconscious and hedonic determinants of physical activity. Excitingly for our field, these newly proposed dual-process models are not "borrowed" from other fields (e.g., TTM and smoking cessation), but they are developed for a better understanding of the specific context of physical activity, based on exercise-related literature, and they acknowledge the role of bodily movement in changing our feelings.

2.2.3 Affective Exercise Experiences and Anticipated Affective Responses

Hedonic theory (i.e., the theory that people choose to repeat that which makes them feel pleasant and avoid that which makes them feel unpleasant, especially in self-determined leisure-time) has existed for millennia (Ekkekakis & Dafermos, 2012). With the emergence of affective responses and automatic affective valuations as predictors of exercise behavior comes an increased attention to understanding and measuring affective processes and constructs. Ekkekakis and colleagues (2021) developed the Affective Exercise Experiences (AFFEXX) questionnaire. This questionnaire accounts for six antecedent appraisals (liking–disliking group exercise, showing-off–shying away, empowerment–damage, pride/honor–shame/guilt, competence–incompetence, interest–boredom), which influence core affective exercise experiences (pleasure–displeasure, energy–tiredness, calmness–tension), which in turn influence attraction–antipathy toward exercise. Ekkekakis et al. (2021) provided evidence for internal consistency, test–retest reliability, construct validity, convergent validity, discriminant validity, and criterion validity. Attraction–antipathy toward physical activity shared a meaningful correlation with self-reported moderate-to-vigorous physical activity ($r = 0.48$) in a sample of over 1,000 individuals, with a stronger correlation with vigorous activity ($r = 0.55$). In another sample, Nieves and Zenko (2023) found that attraction–antipathy toward exercise shared approximately 32% of the variance with the frequency of aerobic exercise, 36% of the variance with the frequency of resistance exercise, and 15% of the variance with overall aerobic exercise. Recent evidence indicates that the AFFEXX predicts exercise behavior in a home-based cardiac rehabilitation program; Piva et al. (2025) found that antecedent appraisals influenced core affective exercise experiences, which predicted attraction–antipathy toward exercise, which in turn predicted physical activity behavior (also see Brand et al., 2025). These studies underscore the importance of understanding affective constructs related to physical activity and suggest that affective predictors of physical activity are based on prior affective and emotional experiences related to exercise.

There are several other affect-laden constructs to consider in addition to automatic affective associations and affective exercise experiences. These include affective judgments, affectively charged motivations (discussed later), remembered affect, and anticipated affective responses (Stevens et al., 2020; Williams & Rhodes, 2023). Theoretically, remembered affect is a global retrospective evaluation of an experience that is predictive of future behavior (Stevens et al., 2020; Williams & Rhodes, 2023; Jones & Zenko, 2021), with initial evidence indicating that active people have more positive remembered affect of physical activity than inactive people (Anderson et al., 2023). This has also been supported by empirical evidence demonstrating correlations between remembered pleasure and future exercise behavior (Kwan et al., 2017).

Remembered pleasure or recalled affect may influence anticipated or forecasted affect (e.g., predictions of how one will experience future exercise). Anticipated affect (e.g., anticipated regret, guilt) is associated with some health behavior (Magnan et al., 2017). However, a recent review suggests that existing evidence is insufficient to make claims about the ability of anticipated affect to predict physical activity directly (Feil et al., 2023).

Acknowledging that anticipated affect may influence physical activity behavior, Kurth et al. (2023) examined the factors associated with anticipated affect. The researchers found that both physical context and physical activity intensity were closely associated with anticipated affect. Kurth et al. (2023) recommended focusing on light-intensity physical activity and physical activity that is performed outdoors (alone, with family, or with friends) for physical activity promotion as these types of activities were associated with the most anticipated pleasure among the least physically active.

2.2.4 Measuring the Affective Responses: The Relevance of Timing

As we seek to further understand the role of affective responses in determining future exercise behavior, we need to carefully consider our choice of measurement approach (Ekkekakis, 2013). Moreover, we need to be aware that *when* we measure affective responses is important. An oft-cited study on the role of affect in predicting future exercise behavior is by Williams et al. (2012). In this study, 146 insufficiently active adults walked on a treadmill for 10 minutes and rated their pleasure during and after the activity. This happened on three occasions at six-month intervals as part of a physical activity lifestyle promotion trial. When the pleasure ratings from the treadmill tasks were analyzed with self-reported physical activity, results showed that pleasure during the treadmill walk was associated with physical activity, but pleasure reported afterward was not predictive. This notion of affective responses during exercise being particularly important for understanding future behavior was reinforced in a review by Rhodes and Kates (2015). From the 24 studies included in their review, they found that affective responses during moderate-intensity activity were associated with future activity, but that affective responses recorded after exercise were not.

The timing of when we capture affective responses is important if we are aiming to understand how people feel *during* exercise. While this may sound obvious, if we are interested in core affective responses of how people feel during exercise (i.e., moment-to-moment ratings of pleasure–displeasure, arousal), the most suitable time to assess this is during exercise (e.g., "How do you feel right now?"). Asking people *after* a bout of exercise *about* how they *felt* during exercise requires appraisal (a defining factor of an emotion) and therefore we are no longer measuring moment-to-moment, experienced core affective responses; instead, we are measuring cognitively filtered retrospective evaluations of the exercise experience (e.g., "How did you feel while you were exercising?"). Further, care must be taken when considering the frequency and timing of assessments made during an exercise bout, especially if the intensity of exercise changes frequently, as with high-intensity interval training (Ekkekakis et al., 2023) or resistance or stretching exercise (Andrade et al., 2022; Bastos et al., 2023; Henriques et al., 2023). To continue advancing our understanding in line with contemporary dual-process theories, measuring how we feel *during* exercise seems paramount as the lived experience of how we feel will drive our future behavior decisions.

In a study exemplifying the relevance of timing, Decker and Ekkekakis (2017) assessed core affective responses before, during, and at the end of moderate-intensity and high-intensity exercise bouts. Data indicated that the start and end points of these bouts were similar in terms of affective valence; however, the journey to the end of the exercise bouts took different paths. Specifically, affective valence reported during the peaks of intensity in the high-intensity intervals was significantly lower than the corresponding timepoint for moderate-intensity continuous exercise. If only pre- and post-measures are recorded and reported, these sessions seem similar, but the affective responses recorded during the sessions show a marked difference.

Much of the work examining the timing of affective responses has been focused on cardio-based exercise (e.g., running, cycling). However, a recent consensus piece proposed an approach for assessing affective responses to resistance exercise (Andrade et al., 2022). The affective–rebound phenomenon that is evident in aerobic exercise appears less pronounced for resistance exercise, and therefore assessing affective responses immediately after a set appears more closely representative of core affective responses during resistance exercise, compared with aerobic exercise. An important caveat to this is that there is scant evidence that affective responses recorded during or after resistance exercise are related to longer-term adherence to this mode of activity.

2.2.5 Exercise Changes How We Feel

The capacity of exercise to change how we feel has long been known, but that does not equate to it being understood. Ekkekakis et al. (2018) remarked that research investigating relationships between affective responses and physical activity or exercise are at a nascent stage. Consequently, the evidence base for understanding the relationship is "fluid" (Ekkekakis et al., 2018, p. 249).

2.2.5.1 Intensity

Exercise intensity is considered to be the main driver of affective responses during exercise. Different mechanisms have been proposed to explain these changes as exercise intensity increases; for example, hypoactivation of the prefrontal cortex during high-intensity exercise (see Ekkekakis et al., 2020). While the cognitive and neural mechanisms underlying these affective changes continue to be discussed, there is a large amount of evidence demonstrating that exercise changes how we feel while we are engaged in it.

A review and meta-analyses by Niven et al. (2021) examined affective responses to high-intensity interval training and continuous moderate- and high-intensity exercise. From the pooled data for affective responses recorded during exercise, there were significantly more pleasant responses during moderate-intensity continuous exercise compared with high-intensity exercise. To further emphasize how exercise changes our feelings, the same meta-analysis found that affective responses at the end of exercise were not significantly different. Similarly, a review and meta-analysis by Hu et al. (2022) on the affective responses to sprint interval training (SIT) found that all 11 eligible studies reported a decrease in pleasure during various incarnations of SIT and an affective–rebound phenomenon upon cessation of exercise. These data demonstrate that our efforts during exercise change how we feel, and these feelings can quickly change again once we cease exercise.

While those reviews and meta-analyses have shown the negative effects on affective responses that high-intensity interval training and SIT can have, other work has demonstrated that lower intensity exercise can positively improve core affective responses. In a review of affective responses to physical activity, Ekkekakis et al. (2011) described how exercise in the moderate domain (below and up to the ventilatory threshold) is associated with increases in pleasure among most exercisers.

2.2.5.2 Extrinsic Strategies

If we acknowledge that affective responses to exercise are relevant in determining future exercise behavior, then it would seem appropriate to focus research efforts on how these affective responses can be improved. A recent review by Jones and Zenko (2023) captured studies that sought to change affective responses during exercise by altering the broader exercise environment. Jones and Zenko referred to *extrinsic strategies* as encompassing anything related to exercise outside of the FITT (frequency, intensity, time, and type) principles. These extrinsic strategies are different from intrinsic factors of exercise, such as intensity, that were discussed earlier in this chapter. Of the 125 studies included, 71% were categorized as Weak following a quality assessment. However, they suggested that several strategies had sufficient evidence to support their use in changing how people feel during exercise.

The application of music and music videos during exercise has garnered positive results in effectively enhancing pleasure across a range of exercise intensities (Bird et al., 2016; Jones et al., 2014; Karageorghis & Jones, 2014). There is some evidence that increasing the immersion in music videos (via head-mounted displays) further increased the pleasure reported during work rate standardized exercise (Jones & Ekkekakis, 2019).

Engaging in exercise outdoors has been shown to positively increase pleasure compared with exercising indoors (e.g., Krinski et al., 2017). While it is not always practical to exercise outdoors, there is consistent evidence regarding its efficacy, and it provides a low-cost, easily implementable strategy. The cognitive mechanisms underpinning the positive affective responses to outdoor exercise remain under debate, but psychological restoration (Hartig et al., 2001) is often cited when seeking to explain the effects.

While changing overall workload would fall within the FITT principles and be considered an intrinsic strategy, how the workload of the exercise session is administered would be considered an extrinsic strategy. In such studies (e.g., Hutchinson et al., 2020; Hutchinson et al., 2023), the workload was standardized and re-ordered from a low to high patterning of a typical exercise session to high to low intensity and yielded greater retrospective evaluations of the overall session, although this evidence is mixed (Kilpatrick et al., 2024; Stuntz et al., 2020). Exercising at a self-selected pace, or intensity, rather than an imposed workload is also considered an extrinsic strategy. Several studies have shown that exercising at a pace that is self-selected leads to more positive affective valence and, in turn, more physical activity in the future (e.g., Williams et al., 2016). Others have focused on affect-guided exercise prescriptions. For example, Zenko et al. (2024) found that allowing people to alternate between the highest pleasant intensity and lowest pleasant intensity resulted in greater experienced pleasure, remembered pleasure, and forecasted pleasure than high-intensity interval training and self-selected exercise. Teixeira et al. (2024) tested the effects of an individualized intensity prescription that was based on preferences for and tolerances of exercise intensity and affect-based exercise instructions (i.e., emphasizing pleasure). This individualized, pleasure-oriented exercise session resulted in greater pleasure experienced during the intervention sessions, more remembered and anticipated pleasure, and 77% greater exercise session attendance. Taken together, emphasizing pleasure as a central component of the exercise prescription seems like a promising direction.

2.2.5.3 Affect and Exercise Outside of the Laboratory

There is a growing body of work examining how exercise changes affect, and also how affect can influence exercise behavior. Using ecological momentary assessment (EMA) to capture people's feelings provides real-world insights into the relationships between affect and exercise, beyond what we can understand in the laboratory context. For example, Haas et al. (2017) tracked physical activity behavior over a ten-day period using accelerometers and measured several distinct affective states (e.g., *vigor, serenity, fatigue, anger*) and concluded that affect was more positive and less negative in the evenings on days when people were more active than usual. A systematic review of this area found strong evidence that physical activity was predictive of positive affect and energy; on the other hand, there was mixed evidence of an association between affect and subsequent physical activity (Bourke et al., 2021).

2.2.5.4 Measuring Affect Outside of the Laboratory

It should be noted here that Haas et al. (2017) and other researchers in this area have frequently adopted a distinct-states approach, rather than a dimensional approach. Rather than measure broad dimensions of affective valence and arousal, researchers have opted to assess distinct, affect-laden feeling states (e.g., *anger, happiness, excitement, nervousness, shame*). The implications of these measurement decisions are comprehensively discussed by Ekkekakis (2013). While core affective responses (e.g., pleasure–displeasure, some level of arousal) are always consciously accessible and felt (Russell, 1980; Russell & Barrett, 1999), other emotional feeling states that require cognitive appraisals are only experienced some of the time if the requisite cognitive appraisals are present (e.g., shame is experienced if one cognitively appraises themselves to be flawed, incapable, unacceptable, or desires to be unseen; Lear et al., 2022). Thus, it is likely that some feeling states, such as broad dimensional feelings aligned with core affect, will be experienced more often than others, such as those that depend upon specific cognitive appraisals and would more appropriately be characterized as emotions. This has important implications for measurement approaches that should be carefully considered when attempting to understand the research literature. For example, *shame*, *anger*, and *guilt* share a negative valence but include distinct cognitive appraisals. Many other distinct feeling states also include a negative valence. It may therefore be more appropriate to capture affective impacts of physical activity by focusing on negative and positive valence (e.g., *pleasure–displeasure, feeling good, feeling bad*), rather than attempting to isolate specific emotional states that depend on specific cognitive appraisals.

2.2.5.5 Physical Activity and Subsequent Affect

Examining how physical activity influences affect, Bourke et al. (2023) found that adolescents who engaged in greater amounts of moderate-to-vigorous physical activity (MVPA) reported more positive valence and energetic arousal. Interestingly, this was related to MVPA as part of recreational physical activity, rather than MVPA as part of active travel or household chores. Williams et al. (2016)

used EMA to explore how self-paced exercise could influence exercise adherence with affective responses as a mediating factor. Across the six-month program, data from low-active, overweight adults showed support for affective responses mediating the relationship between self-paced exercise and adherence. Specifically, more positive affective responses in an exercise session led to a longer duration for the subsequent exercise session.

Kühnhausen et al. (2013) studied the effects of physical activity on subsequent affect in children between 97 and 132 months of age. Physical activity was measured with an accelerometer, and affect was measured several times a day on dimensions of pleasantness, unpleasantness, activation, and deactivation. The researchers observed no effects of daily physical activity on daily affect. On the other hand, another study focused on children between 9 and 13 years of age and indicated that physical activity was associated with subsequent affective outcomes (Dunton et al., 2014). Similarly to Dunton et al. (2014), Ludwig and Rauch (2018) found a within-person relationship between physical activity and positive affect among preschoolers.

In a recent study of adults, physical activity measured using a smartwatch predicted more positive incidental affect (i.e., *happy, confident, content, excited*) and less negative incidental affect (i.e., *ashamed, nervous, sad, angry*) (Ruissen et al., 2022). However, these results appear to be mixed, with other studies finding that moderate-to-vigorous physical activity on one day does not predict affective outcomes the next day (Kerrigan et al., 2020).

2.2.5.6 Affect and Subsequent Physical Activity

Researchers have also examined how affect predicts physical activity behavior. Ruissen et al. (2022) observed that more negative and less positive incidental affect predicted less moderate-to-vigorous physical activity, suggesting the relation between affect and physical activity is bidirectional. Lower negative affect and lower variability in affect is also associated with more physical moderate-to-vigorous physical activity (Kerrigan et al., 2020). Liao et al. (2017) used EMA and complemented the conclusions of Rhodes and Kates (2015), finding that more energy and less negative affective states (e.g., anxious, stressed, depressed, angry) during physical activity was predictive of more moderate-to-vigorous physical activity. These results were meaningful; every one-unit increase in negative affect experienced during physical activity was associated with a decrease of 18 minutes of daily moderate-to-vigorous physical activity *per day* (Liao et al., 2017). This result, when paired with the findings from Williams et al. (2008, 2012) that a one-unit difference in affective valence experienced during exercise was associated with meaningful differences in physical activity, highlights and reinforces the importance of promoting positive and minimizing negative affective experiences during exercise.

Maher et al. (2019) combined the datasets from four EMA studies and showed that feelings of energy (arousal), but not positive affect (valence), were predictive of physical activity. This was explained in relation to self-regulatory resources, with greater feelings of energy indicating greater availability of mental resources. A study by Hevel et al. (2021) offered support for Maher et al.'s (2019) analysis by showing that greater feelings of energy, but not positive or negative affect, were related to increased standing and stepping activity in older adults. Similarly, more fatigue during physical activity has been associated with less subsequent physical activity among young adults (average age: 23 years old; Hevel & Maher, 2023). Referring to the earlier dual-process models, a key component of ART in physical inactivity and exercise (Brand & Ekkekakis, 2018) is the availability of self-control resources to overcome automatic negative affective valuations of physical activity stimulus. Therefore, these data offer some empirical support for ART.

Affectively charged motivations may provide some explanation for the relation between physical activity and affect. Do and colleagues (2022) examined affectively charged motivations (*dreading it* to *excited to do it*), pre-physical activity affect, and affective responses during physical activity (e.g., *good, exhausted, energized, miserable*). The researchers found that more positive affectively charged motivations than usual (i.e., feeling more excited to do it than usual) were associated with feeling more energized, good, thrilled, and interested during subsequent physical activity sessions (Do et al., 2022). The authors highlighted the implications of considering affectively charged motivations, which may result in more positive affective responses during exercise, and in turn more exercise behavior (Rhodes & Kates, 2015). In another study of affectively charged motivations, it was observed that affectively charged motivations fluctuate throughout the day, but the affectively charged motivations measured in the morning are more predictive of moderate-to-vigorous physical activity (Crosley-Lyons et al., 2023).

In addition, contextual and situational factors, like temperature, may moderate the relation between affect and subsequent physical activity (Timm et al., 2023). Further, the type of affective outcome may help explain some of the mixed findings (e.g., Niermann et al., 2016). A review by Liao et al. (2015) found consistent evidence of an association between physical activity and subsequent positive affect, but mixed evidence for an association between physical activity and negative affect. Kanning et al. (2015) found that physical activity predicted feelings of energy, but not valence (although older adults with lower body mass index were more likely to experience improved valence after physical activity). Wichers et al. (2012) observed an effect of physical activity on positive affect (*cheerful*, *content*, *energetic*, *enthusiastic*), but not negative affect (e.g., *lonely*, *anxious*, *guilty*, *suspicious*), and found that participants with a history of major depressive disorder experienced more rapid declines in positive affect. These findings suggest that context, situation, population, and type of outcome measured may meaningfully influence the overall study results of studies investigating the relations between physical activity and affect.

Researchers should consider whether they are interested in affect or emotion, which may be frequently changing, or more stable mood (see the three-step measurement approach described by Ekkekakis [2013] and Ekkekakis & Zenko [2016]). Further, we suggest that the specific measurement approach must be chosen carefully with a clearly articulated justification. While it is easy to hypothesize a relationship between physical activity and feeling *energetic, or positive* (outcomes aligned with the dimensions of Russell's [1980] circumplex model of affect), it is difficult to hypothesize why physical activity might make someone feel more or less *suspicious* (an outcome dependent on a very specific cognitive appraisal). This sampling of the literature indicates that measuring positive affect and negative affect using measures based on the Positive and Negative Affect Schedule (Watson et al., 1988) is common in this line of research. Researchers choosing to use measures derived from the Positive and Negative Affect Schedule in the context of daily physical activity and daily affect must also justify why they are less interested in low-arousal affective states (Ekkekakis, 2013).

2.3 Emotions

Emotions are more specific feeling states than core affect that depend on cognitive appraisal of an object or stimulus that has implications for the well-being, survival, or goals of an individual; emotions are relatively short in duration and high in intensity (Ekkekakis & Petruzzello, 2000; Ekkekakis, 2013). Researchers have investigated the effects of exercise on specific emotions (e.g., happiness; Khazaee-Pool et al., 2015), emotional states (e.g., Baumann et al., 2011), and quality of life (Marquez et al., 2020). A full treatment of the effects of exercise on states such as anxiety, distress, and well-being is beyond the scope of this chapter (see Herring et al., 2013; Ramos-Sanchez et al., 2021; Schuch et al., 2021; Wegner et al., 2014). Further, we must acknowledge the challenge of measuring distinct emotional states compared with broad dimensions of affect, especially in the context of an acute exercise session, due to the complexity of measurement choices and possibility that distinct emotional states may not reliably be experienced and therefore may not reliably be impacted (e.g., if a person does not feel angry before an exercise bout, it is not likely that exercise will have any ability to reduce anger!). For more on this, readers are encouraged to engage with Ekkekakis (2012, 2013; Ekkekakis & Zenko, 2016) and Zenko and Ladwig (2021).

2.3.1 Emotion Regulation

Emotion regulation is a concept related to coping "but refers to attempts to influence which emotions one has, when one has them, and how one experiences or expresses these emotions" (Gross, 2015, p. 5). Researchers have focused on the ability of exercise to influence emotion regulation ability, with promising results (Bernstein & McNally, 2017a, 2017b, 2018). Liu et al. (2024), for example, had participants rate the valence of facial expressions from *entirely negative* to *entirely positive* after aerobic exercise or rest. The researchers observed less positive ratings of happy facial expressions and less negative ratings of angry faces after aerobic exercise among socially anxious individuals. In a prior study on the effects of exercise on emotional face processing, Schmitt et al. (2019) analyzed the effects of low and high intensities on 21 male athletes. The researchers observed that both low- and high-intensity exercise increased positive affect as indicated by the Positive and Negative Affect Schedule (Krohne et al., 1996; Watson et al., 1988) as well as altered neural processing in response to fearful facial expressions compared with geometric shapes (e.g., circles, ellipses; Schmitt et al., 2019). Other researchers have found that acute aerobic exercise, especially if it involves coordinative control (e.g., dribbling balls), improved the ability of adolescents to label the emotional expressions of faces (Brand et al., 2019).

Improvements in emotional reactivity following acute exercise have been reported by Ligeza and colleagues (2020), who had 24 participants complete three trials in a randomized and counterbalanced order: low-intensity exercise, moderate-intensity exercise, and seated rest. Participants then viewed 300 images of pleasant and unpleasant scenes (e.g., sports, happy people vs. scenes of mutilation and sad people). The researchers analyzed event-related fields using magnetoencephalography and found that low- and moderate-intensity exercise reduced and reversed negativity biases, respectively, in comparison with the resting control condition. Similar results have been reported by Ligeza et al. (2023) for a sample of 24 healthy young adults, who demonstrated improved mood and neural emotional reactivity; among 24 adults with depression, however, mood ratings were improved, but neural emotional reactivity was not improved. These results partially contrast with earlier findings by Brush et al. (2020), who observed that 30 minutes of aerobic exercise (compared with rest) enhanced positive emotional reactivity and that the effect was not influenced by severity of depressive symptoms. Another study by Brush and colleagues (2021) concluded that aerobic exercise improved positive emotional reactivity among participants who had never been depressed, but not depressed individuals. This later research by Brush and colleagues, along with Ligeza et al. (2023), suggests that an acute bout of exercise may not have a reliable impact on positive emotional reactivity among people with depression and impaired mood reactivity or a history of depression.

In addition, the effects of a 12-week jogging intervention on emotion regulation have been investigated in a sample of children (8–12 years old) with autism spectrum disorder (Tse, 2020). In the intervention group, children participated in 12 weeks of jogging (four sessions per week and 30 minutes per session) in a school setting. The primary caregiver of each child completed assessments of emotion regulation and emotional and behavioral functioning, which were found to be improved following the intervention. A non-peer-reviewed preprint presents preliminary meta-analytic evidence that suggests exercise has medium-sized, positive effects on emotion regulation abilities and emotion regulation strategies (Liu et al., 2022). Further, a narrative review on the effects of aerobic exercise on emotion regulation suggests that moderate-intensity exercise (e.g., 60%–70% maximum heart rate) for 20–30 minutes may be most beneficial for emotion regulation (Wang et al., 2024). Among children with attention deficit hyperactivity disorder, meta-analytic evidence suggests that exercise has a large, positive effect on emotion regulation (Song et al., 2025).

2.4 Mood

Mood disorders are common, with a 12-month prevalence of 9.9% for 18- to 64-year-old adults, and a 10.4% 12-month prevalence for 13- to 17-year-olds; major depressive disorder has a 7.1% 12-month prevalence for people 13 years and older in the United States (Kessler et al., 2012). Physical activity is associated with both better physical and mental health (Mahindru et al., 2023; Penedo & Dahn, 2005). In the context of the COVID-19 pandemic and lockdowns, those who were physically active had better mood outcomes than those who were inactive, and those who decreased their physical activity experienced worse mood outcomes (Brand et al., 2020). Lockdowns were associated with poorer mental health (Karageorghis et al., 2021).

Researchers have studied physical activity in the context of several mood states, including optimism and happiness, generally finding positive associations with physical activity (Castellanos-García et al., 2023; Fortier & Morgan, 2022; Pavey et al., 2015; Ryu et al., 2023; Trudel-Fitzgerald et al., 2019; van Woudenberg et al., 2020). Researchers have also investigated how physical activity impacts well-being (Iwon et al., 2021; Wilson et al., 2022). However, physical activity has most frequently been studied in the context of depression and depressive symptoms. In this section, we focus on the effects of physical activity on depression (also see Brush et al., 2021; Heissel et al., 2023; Ross et al., 2023).

2.4.1 Depression

Depressive symptoms and major depressive disorder are associated with reduced quality of life, low mood, or persistent low mood, and are a major contributor to the global burden of disease (Thapar et al., 2022). Rates of depression have increased among young people in recent years (Thapar et al., 2022). For a diagnosis of major depressive disorder, five or more symptoms must be present within a two-week period, with one symptom being either depressed mood or loss of interest or pleasure (Tolentino & Schmidt, 2018).

2.4.1.1 Exercise for the Treatment of Depressive Symptoms

Seminal work on the beneficial effects of exercise and depression was conducted by Blumenthal and colleagues more than 25 years ago (Blumenthal et al., 1999). In this randomized-controlled trial, it was revealed that aerobic exercise was as effective at reducing depressive symptoms as antidepressant medication or a combination of antidepressant medication and exercise behavior after a 16-week intervention. A follow-up study assessed depressive symptoms six months later and revealed that relapse rates were lowest in the exercise group (Babyak et al., 2000). In a recent systematic review and network meta-analysis, Recchia et al. (2022) compared the effects of exercise to antidepressants and the combination of antidepressants and exercise across 21 randomized-controlled trials, representing a sample of 2,551 adults with non-severe depression. Confirming the results of Blumenthal et al. (1999), the researchers found no difference between exercise vs. antidepressants vs. exercise and antidepressants, with all treatments being more effective than control conditions.

Today, many randomized controlled trials and multiple meta-analyses focusing on the effects of exercise on depression and depressive symptoms have been published, with consistent evidence in favor of exercise. Noetel and colleagues (2024) included more than 200 studies and more than 14,000 participants in a meta-analysis and found that the benefits of exercise were comparable to psychotherapy and pharmacotherapy. Rebar et al. (2015) conducted a meta-meta-analysis (i.e., a meta-analysis of multiple meta-analyses) on the effects of physical activity on depression and anxiety. For depression, the meta-meta-analysis included 92 studies and 4,310 participants. Overall, physical activity reduced depression with a medium effect size (standardized mean difference of −0.50) (Rebar et al., 2015). An umbrella review of systematic reviews and meta-analyses of randomized controlled trials, representing more than 60,000 participants, revealed an overall medium effect size (standardized mean difference of −0.43), favoring physical activity as a beneficial intervention for depressive symptoms (Singh et al., 2023). The researchers classified the evidence as "Grade A", with "consistent level 1 studies", indicating consistent evidence of the effectiveness for depression and depressive symptoms based on systematic reviews of randomized-controlled trials.

A meta-analysis focusing on adolescents included 15 studies, representing 1,331 adolescents, and revealed a medium-to-large effect on reducing depression (standardized mean difference of −0.64; Wang et al., 2022). Similarly, a meta-analysis of 24 studies ranging in duration from 8 to 32 weeks revealed a positive effect on depressive symptoms of college students (standardized mean difference of −0.63; Huang et al., 2023). A recent meta-analysis has revealed similar, medium-to-large positive effects of Baduanjin exercise on depressive symptoms among people with type II diabetes and emotional disorders (Luo et al., 2023). Baduanjin exercise includes slow movements, deep rhythmic breathing, and a meditative state (Luo et al., 2023). Meta-analytic evidence also supports favorable affective effects of acute bouts of exercise among people with depression for both indoor and outdoor activity, modalities including cycling, walking/running, and "other", and in clinical and community settings (Bourke et al., 2022). We find it interesting that the aforementioned meta-analytic evidence includes a wide range of exercise modalities, from aerobic exercise to resistance exercise, to traditional Chinese exercises.

Schuch et al. (2016) conducted a meta-analysis of randomized controlled trials and attempted to control for publication bias. The researchers focused on studies that compared exercise vs. non-active control groups. Overall, 25 studies were included in the meta-analysis with a range of effect sizes, with standardized mean differences ranging from −0.230 (in favor of the control) to 4.599 (in favor of exercise). The overall effect among the 1,487 adults included was large, with a standardized mean difference of −0.98, favoring exercise (Schuch et al., 2016). Similarly large effects in favor of exercise (standardized mean difference of −0.946) were observed in a meta-analysis of 2,264 participants and 41 studies by Heissel et al. (2023). The researchers were very clear in their conclusion that exercise "offers a further-evidence-based treatment option for the large amount of untreated individuals with depression, including individuals who refuse or cannot tolerate medication and/or psychotherapy" (Heissel et al., 2023).

2.4.1.2 Exercise for the Prevention of Depressive Symptoms

As mentioned, depression is a major contributor to the global burden of disease. While the evidence above suggests that exercise is promising for *reducing* depressive symptoms, other evidence also highlights the promising effects of exercise for *preventing* depression. In a systematic review and meta-analysis, Pearce et al. (2022) examined prospective studies comprising 191,130 participants and over two-million person years. Compared with adults who did not report any activity, adults who reported physical activity equivalent to half the recommended volume had 18% lower risk of developing depression, and adults who reported physical activity equivalent to the recommended volume had 25% lower risk of developing depression (Pearce et al., 2022). Schuch et al. (2018) conducted a meta-analysis to determine whether physical activity was associated with incident depression (i.e., the odds of developing depression). Overall, the meta-analysis included 49 prospective studies and 266,939 participants, covering 1,837,794 person years. The researchers concluded that youths, adults, and the elderly were less likely to develop depression if they were engaged in more physical activity.

2.4.1.3 Exercise Warrants Serious Consideration as a Treatment Option

Ekkekakis and Murri (2017) provided a brief overview of the effectiveness of physical activity for the treatment of major depressive disorder and noted that several countries include physical activity or exercise as part of clinical guidelines, including the United Kingdom, Scotland, the Netherlands, Australia, New Zealand, and Canada. Absent from this list was the United States. The authors argued that there is compelling evidence for neural biological effects of exercise, clear and consistent evidence for the beneficial effects of exercise, and clear indications that patients may prefer exercise as a treatment option, especially given its low cost and absence of side effects. The title of their piece was *Exercise as antidepressant treatment: Time for the transition from trials to clinic?* (Ekkekakis & Murri, 2017). Based on the evidence reviewed in this chapter and the points succinctly but thoroughly raised in their editorial (Ekkekakis & Murri, 2017), it seems the answer is clearly *yes*.

Based on these data, it is hard to disagree with the conclusion of Heissel et al. (2023). Exercise interventions are evidently effective and safe and can represent a useful option for people who prefer exercise, do not want antidepressants or other therapies, cannot tolerate antidepressants or other therapies, do not benefit from antidepressants or other therapies, or cannot access antidepressants or other therapies, a problem that seems especially prevalent in the United States (Olfson et al., 2016; Zhdanava et al., 2021).

When designing physical activity programs, interventionists can apply several principles from exercise psychology. Experts from Sports Medicine Australia and the Australian Psychological Society have recognized the importance of physical activity for mental health (including but not limited to depression), recommending (a) that physical activity be designed to promote adherence and enjoyment, (b) delivering physical activity that satisfies autonomy, competence, and relatedness, (c) creating physical activity with positive social environments, (d) creating opportunities for physical activity in natural settings, and (e) promoting physical activity in leisure or transportation (e.g., commuting to work) (Vella et al., 2023).

2.5 Implications

2.5.1 *Physical Activity and Affect*

There are several implications of the existing work on physical activity, affect, emotion, and moods. For affect, researchers and practitioners should consider the following. First, the link between exercise intensity and affective responses is clear (e.g., Ekkekakis et al., 2011); researchers have investigated methods for enhancing affective responses (e.g., Jones & Zenko, 2023), and researchers have linked affective responses to exercise with future exercise behavior (e.g., Rhodes & Kates, 2015). Recent interventions aimed at promoting physical activity and exercise engagement through modified affective responses are promising (Teixeira et al., 2024). Researchers could build upon what is currently known to determine if long-term exercise behavior can be enhanced by maximizing pleasure and minimizing displeasure. Ideally, this line of research will include diverse and longitudinal outcomes, such as laboratory assessed fitness, self-reported exercise behavior, and physical activity behavior measure using accelerometers. Second, researchers should continue utilizing EMA to evaluate how real-world affect influences physical activity behavior and how physical activity behavior influences subsequent affective outcomes. Third, researchers should focus on the measurement of appropriate affective constructs to help clarify the mixed findings in the extant literature. Fourth, researchers should determine the importance of affective responses and outcomes in diverse populations and constructs. Authors have suggested not only focusing on valence, but also distinct anticipated emotions, such as pride, shame, satisfaction, and disappointment (Feil et al., 2022). The importance of affective responses for predicting subsequent physical activity may differ based on a variety of factors, such as valence and appraisal of experienced and anticipated affect and emotion, self-control resources, age, personality, or the individual's need for affect (Maio & Esses, 2001).

2.5.2 Physical Activity and Emotion

It seems clear that physical activity may enhance emotion regulation and emotional reactivity (Liu et al., 2022), although this may vary based on population (e.g., individuals with depression vs. individuals without a history of depression). Investigators can continue to study how individual differences influence emotional outcomes of exercise and conduct longitudinal studies to investigate the long-term effects of exercise on emotion regulation and emotional reactivity across diverse populations. The study of emotions and emotion regulation in physical activity, sport, and exercise psychology can be advanced using qualitative approaches (Tamminen & Bennett, 2017) as well as new theoretical developments, research with diverse populations, and applied research focused on enhancing emotion regulation and how emotion regulation is related to performance and other outcomes (Tamminen et al., 2022).

2.5.3 Physical Activity, Depressive Symptoms, and Depression

Evidence from randomized-controlled trials and meta-analyses are consistent in the conclusion that physical activity and exercise is effective for preventing and treating depression and depressive symptoms. Experts are clear that physical activity and exercise should be seriously considered as treatment options (Ekkekakis & Murri, 2017) and have outlined principles to incorporate physical activity into mental health treatment settings (Vella et al., 2023).

2.6 Conclusion

From the evidence reviewed in this chapter, it is clear that physical activity has a complex interaction with affect, emotion, and moods, serving as a correlate, predictor, and outcome. Researchers and practitioners alike should thoughtfully consider the affective impact of physical activity and aim to (a) carefully consider measurement approaches (see Ekkekakis, 2013) and (b) work to enhance the affective quality of physical activity and exercise experiences. Evidence suggests that researchers and practitioners should promote positive affective exercise experiences. In addition, researchers can build upon the foundational evidence reviewed in this chapter focused on the emotional and mood impact of physical activity.

Physical activity may be used to enhance emotion regulation. Finally, it seems obvious at this point—based on decades of consistent evidence from randomized-controlled trials, meta-analyses, and meta-meta-analyses—but physical activity can have a beneficial effect on mood, depression, and depressive symptoms; work can continue on how to effectively change practice to ensure greater use of physical activity as treatment for depressive symptoms. Taken together, this chapter has provided an overview of how affect is related to physical activity and how physical activity itself can be used to create a more affectively rich life experience.

References

Anderson, R. J., Boulby, A., & Dewhurt, S. A. (2023). "I'm just not feeling it": Affective processing of episodic physical activity memories differs between physically active and inactive individuals. *Psychology of Sport and Exercise, 68*, 102475. https://doi.org/10.1016/j.psychsport.2023.102475

Andrade, A. J., Ekkekakis, P., Evmenenko, A., Monteiro, D., Rodrigues, F., Cid, L., & Teixeira, D. S. (2022). Affective responses to resistance exercise: Toward a consensus on the timing of assessments. *Psychology of Sport and Exercise, 62,* 102223. https://doi.org/10.1016/j.psychsport.2022.102223

Ajzen, I. (1991). The theory of planned behavior. *Organizational Behavior and Human Decision Processes, 50*(2), 179–211. https://doi.org/10.1016/0749-5978(91)90020-T

Babyak, M., Blumenthal, J. A., Herman, S., Khatri, P., Doraiswamy, M., Moore, K., Craighead, W. E., Baldewicz, T. T., & Krishnan, K. R. (2000). Exercise treatment for major depression: Maintenance of therapeutic benefit at 10 months. *Psychosomatic Medicine, 62*(5), 633–638. https://doi.org/10.1097/00006842-200009000-00006

Bastos, V., Rodriguez, F., Davis, P., & Teixeira, D. S. (2023). Assessing affective valence and activation in resistance training with the feeling scale and the felt arousal scale: A systematic review. *PLoS ONE, 18*, e0294529. https://doi.org/10.1371/journal.pone.0294529

Baumann, F. T., Zopf, E. M., Nykamp, E., Kraut, L., Schüle, K., Elter, T., Fauser, A. A., & Bloch, W. (2011). Physical activity for patients undergoing an allogeneic hematopoietic stem cell transplantation: Benefits of a moderate exercise intervention. *European Journal of Haematology, 87*(2), 148–156. https://doi.org/10.1111/j.1600-0609.2011.01640.x

Bernstein, E. E., & McNally, R. J. (2017a). Acute aerobic exercise hastens emotional recovery from a subsequent stressor. *Health Psychology, 36(*6), 560–567. https://psycnet.apa.org/doi/10.1037/hea0000482

Bernstein, E. E., & McNally, R. J. (2017b). Acute aerobic exercise helps overcome emotion regulation deficits. *Cognition and Emotion, 31*(4), 834–843. https://doi.org/10.1080/02699931.2016.1168284.

Bernstein, E. E., & McNally, R. J. (2018). Exercise as a buffer against difficulties with emotion regulation: A pathway to emotional wellbeing. *Behaviour Research and Therapy, 209,* 29–36. https://doi-org/10.1016/j.brat.2018.07.010

Bird, J. M., Hall, J., Arnold, R., Karageorghis, C. I., & Hussein, A. (2016). Effects of music and music-video on core affect during exercise at the lactate threshold. *Psychology of Music, 44*(6), 1471–1487. https://doi.org/10.1177/0305735616637909

Blumenthal, J. A., Babyak, M. A., Moore, K. A., Craighead, W. E., Herman, S., Khatri, P., Waugh, R., Napolitano, M. A., Forman, L. M., Appelbaum, M., Doraiswamy, P. M., & Krishnan, K. R. (1999). Effects of exercise training on older patients with major depression. *Archives of Internal Medicine, 159*(19), 2349–2356. https://doi.org/10.1001/archinte.159.19.2349

Bourke, M., Hilland, T. A., & Craike, M. (2021). A systematic review of the within-person association between physical activity and affect in children's and adolescents' daily lives. *Psychology of Sport and Exercise, 51,* 101825. https://doi.org/10.1016/j.psychsport.2020.101825

Bourke, M., Hilland, T. A., & Craike, M. (2023). Domain specific association between physical activity and affect in adolescents' daily lives: An ecological momentary assessment study. *Psychology & Health, 38*(3), 369–388. https://doi.org/10.1080/08870446.2021.1965603

Bourke, M., Patten, R. K., Klamert, L., Klepac, B., Dash, S., & Pascoe, M. C. (2022). The acute affective response to physical activity in people with depression: A meta-analysis. *Journal of Affective Disorders, 311,* 353–363. https://doi.org/10.1016/j.jad.2022.05.089

Brand, R., & Cheval, B. (2019). Theories to explain exercise motivation and physical inactivity: Ways of expanding our current theoretical perspective. *Frontiers in Psychology, 10*, 1147. https://doi.org/10.3389/fpsyg.2019.01147

Brand, R., & Ekkekakis, P. (2018). Affective–Reflective Theory of physical inactivity and exercise. *German Journal of Exercise and Sport Research, 48*(1), 48–58. https://doi.org/10.1007/s12662-017-0477-9

Brand, R., & Ekkekakis, P. (2021). Exercise behavior change revisited: Affective-reflective theory. In Z. Zenko & L. Jones (Eds.), *Essentials of exercise and sport psychology: An open access textbook* (pp. 62–92). Society for Transparency, Openness, and Replication in Kinesiology. https://doi.org/10.51224/B1004

Brand, S., Gerber, M., College, F., Holsboer-Trachsler, E., Pühse, U., & Ludyga, S. (2019). Acute exercise and emotion recognition in young adolescents. *Journal of Sport and Exercise Psychology, 41*, 129–136. https://doi.org/10.1123/jsep.2018-0160

Brand, R., Sudeck, G., & Ekkekakis, P. (2025). Affective experiences from exercise. Youth-adult differences and prediction of exercise behavior. *Psychology of Sport and Exercise, 76*, 102755. https://doi.org/10.1016/j.psychsport.2024.102755

Brand, R., Timme, S., & Nosrat, S. (2020). When pandemic hits: Exercise frequency and subjective well-being during COVID-19 pandemic. *Frontiers in Psychology, 11*, 570567. https://doi.org/10.3389/fpsyg.2020.570567

Brush, C. J., Burani, K., Schmidt, K. M., Santopetro, N. J., & Hajcak, G. (2021). The impact of a single session of aerobic exercise on positive emotional reactivity in depression: Insight into individual differences from the late positive potential. *Behaviour Research and Therapy, 144*, 103914. https://10.1016/j.brat.2021.103914

Brush, C. J., Foti, D., Bocchine, A. J., Muniz, K. M., Gooden, M. J., Spaeth, A. M., Miller, M. W., & Alderman, B. Aerobic exercise enhances positive emotional reactivity in individuals with depressive symptoms: Evidence from neural responses to reward and emotional content. *Mental Health and Physical Activity, 19*, 100339. https://doi.org/10.1016/j.mhpa.2020.100339

Castellanos-García, P., Lera-López, F., & Sánchez-Santos, J. M. (2023). Light, moderate and vigorous physical activities: New insights into a virtuous circle with happiness. *European Journal of Sport Science, 23*(7), 1345–1355. https://doi.org/10.1080/17461391.2022.2089053

Cheval, B., & Boisgontier, M. P. (2021). The theory of effort minimization in physical activity. *Exercise and Sport Sciences Reviews, 49(*3), 168–178. https://doi.org/10.1249/JES.0000000000000252

Clore, G. L., & Ortony, A. (2000). Cognition in emotion: Always, sometimes, or never? In R. D. Lane & L. Nadel (Eds.), *Cognitive neuroscience of emotion* (pp. 24–61). Oxford University Press.

Conroy, D. E., & Berry, T. R. (2017). Automatic affective evaluations of physical activity. *Exercise and Sport Sciences Reviews, 45*(4), 230–237. https://doi.org/10.1249/jes.0000000000000120

Crosley-Lyons, R., Do, B., Hewus, M., & Dunton, G. F. (2023). An ecological momentary assessment study of affectively-charged motivational states and physical activity. *Psychology of Sport and Exercise, 67,* 102423. https://doi.org/10.1016/j.psychsport.2023.102423

Decker, E. S., & Ekkekakis, P. (2017). More efficient, perhaps, but at what price? Pleasure and enjoyment responses to high-intensity interval exercise in low-active women with obesity. *Psychology of Sport and Exercise, 28*, 1–10. https://doi.org/10.1016/j.psychsport.2016.09.005

Do, B., Rhodes, R. E., Kanning, M., Hewus, M., & Dunton, G. F. (2022). Examining whether affectively-charged motivations predict subsequent affective response during physical activity: An ecological momentary assessment study. *Frontiers in Sports and Active Living, 4*, 1029144. https://doi.org/10.3389/fspor.2022.1029144

Dukes, D., Abrams, K., Adolphs, R., Ahmed, M. E., Beatty, A., Berridge, K. C., Broomhall, S., Brosch, T., Campos, J. J., Clay, Z., Clément, F., Cunningham, W. A., Damasio, A., Damasio, H., D'Arms, J., Davidson, J. W., de Gelder, B., Deonna, J., de Sousa, R., … Sander, D. (2021). The rise of affectivism. *Nature Human Behaviour, 5*(7), 816–820. https://doi.org/10.1038/s41562-021-01130-8

Dunton, G. F., Huh, J., Leventhal, A. M., Riggs, N., Hedeker, D., Spruijt-Metz, D., & Pentz, M. A. (2014). Momentary assessment of affect, physical feeling states, and physical activity in children. *Health Psychology, 33*(3), 255–263. https://doi.org/10.1037/a0032640

Ekkekakis, P. (2003). Pleasure and displeasure from the body: Perspectives from exercise. *Cognition & Emotion, 17*(2), 213–239. https://doi.org/10.1080/02699930302292

Ekkekakis, P. (2009). The Dual-Mode Theory of affective responses to exercise in metatheoretical context: II. Bodiless heads, ethereal cognitive schemata, and other improbable dualistic creatures, exercising. *International Review of Sport and Exercise Psychology, 2*(2), 139–160. https://doi.org/10.1080/17509840902829323

Ekkekakis, P. (2012). Affect, mood, and emotion. In G. Tenenbaum, R. C. Eklund, & A. Kamata (Eds.), *Measurement in sport and exercise psychology* (pp. 321–332). Human Kinetics. https://doi.org/10.5040/9781492596332.ch-028

Ekkekakis, P. (2013). *The measurement of affect, mood, and emotion: A guide for health-behavioral research.* Cambridge University Press. https://doi.org/10.1017/CBO9780511820724

Ekkekakis, P. (2017). People have feelings! Exercise psychology in paradigmatic transition. *Current Opinion in Psychology, 16*, 84–88. https://doi.org/10.1016/j.copsyc.2017.03.018

Ekkekakis, P., & Brand, R. (2019). Affective responses to and automatic affective valuations of physical activity: Fifty years of progress on the seminal question in exercise psychology. *Psychology of Sport and Exercise, 42*, 130–137. https://doi.org/10.1016/j.psychsport.2018.12.018

Ekkekakis, P., & Dafermos, M. (2012). Exercise is a many-splendored thing, but for some it does not feel so splendid: Staging a resurgence of hedonistic ideas in the quest to understand exercise behavior. In E. O. Acevedo (Ed.), *The Oxford handbook of exercise psychology* (pp. 295–333). Oxford University Press. https://doi.org/10.1093/oxfordhb/9780195394313.013.0016

Ekkekakis, P., Hartman, M. E., & Ladwig, M. A. (2020). Affective responses to exercise. In G. Tenenbaum, R. C. Eklund, & N. Boiangin (Eds.), *Handbook of sport psychology: Social perspectives, cognition, and applications* (4th ed., pp. 233–253). John Wiley & Sons, Inc. https://doi.org/10.1002/9781119568124.ch12

Ekkekakis, P., Hartman, M. E., & Ladwig, M. A. (2023). A methodological checklist for studies of pleasure and enjoyment responses to high-intensity interval training: Part II. Intensity, timing of assessments, data modeling, and interpretation. *Journal of Sport and Exercise Psychology, 45*, 92–109. https://doi.org/10.1123/jsep.2022-0029

Ekkekakis, P., & Murri, M. B. (2017). Exercise as antidepressant treatment: Time for the transition from trials to clinic? *General Hospital Psychiatry, 49,* A1–A5. https://doi.org/10.1016/j.genhosppsych.2017.11.004

Ekkekakis, P., Parfitt, G., & Petruzzello, S. J. (2011). The pleasure and displeasure people feel when they exercise at different intensities: Decennial update and progress towards a tripartite rationale for exercise intensity prescription. *Sports Medicine, 41*(8), 641–671. https://doi.org/10.2165/11590680-000000000-00000

Ekkekakis, P., & Petruzzello, S. J. (2000). Analysis of the affect measurement conundrum in exercise psychology I. Fundamental issues. *Psychology of Sport and Exercise, 1*, 71–88. https://doi.org/10.1016/S1469-0292(00)00010-8

Ekkekakis, P., & Zenko, Z. (2016). Measurement of affective responses to exercise: From "affectless arousal" to "the most well-characterized" relationship between the body and affect. In H. L. Meiselman (Ed.), *Emotion measurement* (pp. 299–321). Woodhead Publishing. https://doi.org/10.1016/B978-0-08-100508-8.00012-6

Ekkekakis, P., Zenko, Z., Ladwig, M. A., & Hartman, M. E. (2018). Affect as a potential determinant of physical activity and exercise: Critical appraisal of an emerging research field. In D. M. Williams, R. E. Rhodes, & M. T. Conner (Eds.), *Affective determinants of health behavior* (pp. 237–261). Oxford University Press. https://doi.org/10.1093/oso/9780190499037.003.0011

Ekkekakis, P., Zenko, Z., & Vazou, S. (2021). Do you find exercise pleasant or unpleasant? The Affective Exercise Experiences (AFFEXX) questionnaire. *Psychology of Sport and Exercise, 55,* 101930. https://doi.org/10.1016/j.psychsport.2021.101930

Feil, K., Fritsch, J., Weyland, S., Warmbrunn, U., & Jekauc, D. (2023). The role of anticipated affect in the context of physical activity: A scoping review. *International Review of Sport and Exercise Psychology,* 1–33. https://doi.org/10.1080/1750984X.2023.2275249

Feil, K., Weyland, S., Fritsch, J., Wäsche, H., & Jekauc, D. (2022). Anticipatory and anticipated emotions in regular and non-regular exercisers – A qualitative study. *Frontiers in Psychology, 13*, 929380. https://doi.org/10.3389/fpsyg.2022.929380

Fortier, M. S., & Morgan, T. L. (2022). How optimism and physical activity interplay to promote happiness. *Current Psychology, 41*, 8559–8567. https://doi.org/10.1007/s12144-020-01294-y

Garcia-Hermoso, A., López-Gil, J. F., Ramírez-Vélez, R., Alonso-Martínez, A. M., Izquierdo, M., & Ezzatvar, Y. (2023). Adherence to aerobic and muscle-strengthening activities guidelines: A systematic review and meta-analysis of 3.3 million participants across 32 countries. *British Journal of Sports Medicine, 57*(4), 225–229. https://doi.org/10.1136/bjsports-2022-106189

Gross, J. J. (2015). Emotion regulation: Current status and future prospects. *Psychological Inquiry, 26*(1), 1–26. https://doi.org/10.1080/1047840X.2014.940781

Haas, P., Schmid, J., Stadler, G., Reuter, M., & Gawrilow, C. (2017). Zooming into daily life: Within-person associations between physical activity and affect in young adults. *Psychology and Health, 32*(5), 588–604. https://doi.org/10.1080/08870446.2017.1291943

Hartig, T., Kaiser, F. G., & Bowler, P. A. (2001). Psychological restoration in nature as a positive motivation for ecological behavior. *Environment and Behavior, 33*(4), 590–607. https://doi.org/10.1177/00139160121973142

Heissel, A., Heinen, D., Brokmeier, L. L., Skarabis, N., Kangas, M., Vancampfort, D., Stubbs, B., Firth, J., Ward, P. B., Rosenbaum, S., Hallgren, M., & Schuch, F. (2023). Exercise as medicine for depressive symptoms? A systematic review and meta-analysis with meta-regression. *British Journal of Sports Medicine, 57*(16), 1049–1057. https://doi.org/10.1136/bjsports-2022-106282

Henriques, L., Ekkekakis, P., Bastos, V., Rodrigues, F. Monteiro, D., & Teixeira, D. S. (2023). Affective responses to stretching exercises: Exploring the timing of assessments. *Psychology of Sport and Exercise, 69*, 102490. https://doi.org/10.1016/j.psychsport.2023.102490

Herring, M. P., Lindheimer, J. B., & O'Connor, P. J. (2013). The effects of exercise training on anxiety. *American Journal of Lifestyle Medicine, 8*(6), 388–403. https://doi.org/10.1177/1559827613508542

Hevel, D. J., Dunton, G. F., & Maher, J. P. (2021). Acute bidirectional relations between affect, physical feeling states, and activity-related behaviors among older adults: An ecological momentary assessment study. *Annals of Behavioral Medicine, 55*(1), 41–54. https://doi.org/10.1093/abm/kaaa027

Hevel, D. J, & Maher, J. P. (2023). Affective responses during physical activity predicting same day and next day physical activity in emerging adulthood: An ecological momentary assessment study. *Psychology & Health, 40*(5), 765–782. https://doi.org/10.1080/08870446.2023.2254987

Hu, M., Jung, M. E., Nie, J., & Kong, Z. (2022). Affective and enjoyment responses to sprint interval training in healthy individuals: A systematic review and meta-analysis. *Frontiers in Psychology, 13,* 820228. https://doi.org/10.3389/fpsyg.2022.820228

Huang, X., Wang, Y., & Zhang, H. (2023). Effects of physical exercise intervention on depressive and anxious moods of college students: A meta-analysis of randomized controlled trials. *Asian Journal of Sport and Exercise Psychology, 3*(3), 206–221. https://doi.org/10.1016/j.ajsep.2023.01.001

Hutchinson, K. C., Jones, L., Ekkekakis, P., Cheval, B., Brand, R., Salvatore, G. M., Adler, S., & Luo, Y. (2023). Affective responses to increasing- and decreasing-intensity resistance training protocols. *Journal of Sport and Exercise Psychology, 45*(3), 121–137. https://doi.org/10.1123/jsep.2022-0243

Hutchinson, J. C., Zenko, Z., Santich, S., & Dalton, P. C. (2020). Increasing the pleasure and enjoyment of exercise: A novel resistance-training protocol. *Journal of Sport and Exercise Psychology, 42*(2), 143–152. https://doi.org/10.1123/jsep.2019-0089

Iwon, K., Skibinska, J., Jasielska, D., & Kalwarczyk, S. (2021). Elevating subjective well-being through physical exercises: An intervention study. *Frontiers in Psychology, 12*, 702678. https://doi.org/10.3389/fpsyg.2021.702678

Jones, L., & Ekkekakis, P. (2019). Affect and prefrontal hemodynamics during exercise under immersive audiovisual stimulation: Improving the experience of exercise for overweight adults. *Journal of Sport and Health Science*, *8*(4), 325–338. https://doi.org/10.1016/j.jshs.2019.03.003

Jones, L., Karageorghis, C. I., & Ekkekakis, P. (2014). Can high-intensity exercise be more pleasant? Attentional dissociation using music and video. *Journal of Sport and Exercise Psychology, 36*(5), 528–541. https://doi.org/10.1123/jsep.2013-0251

Jones, L., & Zenko, Z. (2021). Strategies to facilitate more pleasant exercise experiences. In Z. Zenko & L. Jones (Eds.), *Essentials of exercise and sport psychology: An open access textbook* (pp. 242–270). Society for Transparency, Openness, and Replication in Kinesiology. https://doi.org/10.51224/B1011

Jones, L., & Zenko, Z. (2023). A systematic narrative review of extrinsic strategies to improve affective responses to exercise. *Frontiers in Sports and Active Living, 5*, 1186986. https://doi.org/10.3389/fspor.2023.1186986

Kanning, M., Ebner-Priemer, U., & Schlicht, W. (2015). Using activity triggered e-diaries to reveal the associations between physical activity and affective states in older adult's daily living. *International Journal of Behavioral Nutrition and Physical Activity, 12,* 111. https://doi.org/10.1186/s12966-015-0272-7

Karageorghis, C. I., Bird, J. M., Hutchinson, J. C., Hamer, M., Delevoye-Turrell, Y. N., Guérin, S. M. R., Mullin, E. M., Mellano, K. T., Parsons-Smith, R. L., Terry, V. R., & Terry, P. C. (2021). Physical activity and mental well-being under COVID-19 lockdown: A cross-sectional multination study. *BMC Public Health, 21*(1), 988. https://doi.org/10.1186/s12889-021-10931-5

Karageorghis, C. I., & Jones, L. (2014). On the stability and relevance of the exercise heart rate–music-tempo preference relationship. *Psychology of Sport and Exercise, 15*(3), 299–310. https://doi.org/10.1016/j.psychsport.2013.08.004

Kerrigan, S. G., Schumacher, L., Manasse, S. M., Loyka, C., Butryn, M. L., & Forman, E. M. (2020). The association between negative affect and physical activity among adults in behavioral weight loss treatment. *Psychology of Sport and Exercise, 47*, 101507. https://doi.org/10.1016/j.psychsport.2019.03.010

Kessler, R. C., Petukhova, M., Sampson, N. A., Zaslavsky, A. M., & Wittchen, H.-U. (2012). Twelve-month and lifetime prevalence and lifetime morbid risk of anxiety and mood disorders in the United States. *International Journal of Methods in Psychiatric Research, 21*(3), 169 184. https://doi.org/10.1002/mpr.1359

Khazaee-Pool, M., Sadeghi, R., Majlessi, F., & Rahimi Foroushani, A. (2015). Effects of physical exercise programme on happiness among older people. *Journal of Psychiatric and Mental Health Nursing, 22*(1), 47–57. https://doi.org/10.1111/jpm.12168

Kilpatrick, M. W., Mastrofini, G. F., Sheriff, P. P., McCluggage, C. L., Korte, S., & Zenko, Z. (2024). Examining the effects of increasing then decreasing exercise intensity within a session of aerobic exercise. *Psychology of Sport and Exercise, 73,* 102637. https://doi.org/10.1016/j.psychsport.2024.102637

Krinski, K., Machado, D. G. S., Lirani, L. S., DaSilva, S. G., Costa, E. C., Hardcastle, S. J., & Elsangedy, H. M. (2017). Let's walk outdoors! Self-paced walking outdoors improves future intention to exercise in women with obesity. *Journal of Sport and Exercise Psychology, 39*(2), 145–157. https://doi.org/10.1123/jsep.2016-0220

Krohne, H. W., Egloff, B., Kohlmann, C. W., & Tausch, A. (1996). Untersuchungen mit einer deutschen version der "Positive and Negative Affect Schedule" (PANAS). *Diagnostica*, *42*, 139–56.

Kühnhausen, J., Leonhardt, A., Dirk, J., & Schmiedek, F. (2013). Physical activity and affect in elementary school children's daily lives. *Frontiers in Psychology, 4*, 456. https://doi.org/10.3389/fpsyg.2013.00456

Kurth, J. D., Klenosky, D. B., Kao, S.-C., & Ruiz, Y. (2023). Factors impacting the anticipated pleasure of potential physical activity experiences: A conjoint investigation across involvement segments. *International Journal of Sport and Exercise Psychology, 22*(5), 1128–1143. https://doi.org/10.1080/1612197X.2023.2199762

Kwan, B. M., Stevens, C. J., & Bryan, A. D. (2017). What to expect when you're exercising: An experimental test of the anticipated affect-exercise relationship. *Health Psychology, 36*(4), 309–319. https://doi-org.falcon.lib.csub.edu/10.1037/hea0000453

Lear, M. K., Lee, E. B., Smith, S. M., & Luoma, J. B. (2022). A systematic review of self-report measures of generalized shame. *Journal of Clinical Psychology, 78*(7), 1288–1330. https://doi-org.falcon.lib.csub.edu/10.1002/jclp.23311

Liao, Y., Chou, C. P., Huh, J., Leventhal, A., & Dunton, G. (2017). Associations of affective responses during free-living physical activity and future physical activity levels: An ecological momentary assessment study. *International Journal of Behavioral Medicine, 24*(4), 513–519. https://doi.org/10.1007/s12529-016-9626-z

Liao, Y., Shonkoff, E. T., & Dunton, G. F. (2015). The acute relationships between affect, physical feeling states, and physical activity in daily life. A review of current evidence. *Frontiers in Psychology, 6*, 1975. https://doi.org/10.3389/fpsyg.2015.01975

Ligeza, T. S., Maciejcyk, M., Wyczesany, M., Wagner, H., Roesmann, K., & Junghofer, M. (2020). Acute aerobic exercise enhances pleasant compared to unpleasant visual scene processing. *Brain and Cognition, 143,* 105595. https://doi.org/10.1016/j.bandc.2020.105595

Ligeza, T. S., Maciejczyk, M., Wyczesany, M., & Junghofer, M. (2023). The effects of a single aerobic exercise session on mood and neural emotional reactivity in depressed and healthy young adults: A late positive potential study. *Psychophysiology, 60*(1), e14137. https://doi.org/10.1111/psyp.14137

Liu, J., Dong, Y., Zhang, Z., Rui, A., Lu, Y., & Kang, G. (2024). Acute aerobic exercise modulates facial emotion evaluation in socially anxious individuals. *International Journal of Sport and Exercise Psychology, 22*(9), 2182–2195. https://doi.org/10.1080/1612197X.2023.2275656

Liu, J., Gao, S., & Zhang, L. (2022). Effects of physical exercises on emotion regulation: A meta-analysis. *MedRxiv.* https://doi.org/10.1101/2022.07.04.22277120

Ludwig, K., & Rauch, W., A. (2018). Associations between physical activity, positive affect, and self-regulation during preschoolers' everyday lives. *Mental Health and Physical Activity, 15,* 63–70. https://doi.org/10.1016/j.mhpa.2018.07.002

Luo, X., Zhao, M., Zhang, Y., & Zhang, Y. (2023). Effects of baduanjin exercise on blood glucose, depression and anxiety among patients with Type III diabetes and emotional disorders: A meta-analysis. *Complementary Therapies in Clinical Practice, 50,* 101702. https://doi.org10.1016/j.ctcp.2022.101702

Maher, J. P., Dzubur, E., Nordgren, R., Huh, J., Chou, C.-P., Hedeker, D., & Dunton, G. F. (2019). Do fluctuations in positive affective and physical feeling states predict physical activity and sedentary time? *Psychology of Sport and Exercise, 41*, 153–161. https://doi.org/10.1016/j.psychsport.2018.01.011

Maier, S. U., Makwana, A. B., & Hare, T. A. (2015). Acute stress impairs self-control in goal-directed choice by altering multiple functional connections within the brain's decision circuits. *Neuron, 87*(3), 621–631. https://doi.org/10.1016/j.neuron.2015.07.005

Maio, G. R., & Esses, V. M. (2001). The need for affect: Individual differences in the motivation to approach or avoid emotions. *Journal of Personality, 69*(4), 583–615. https://doi-org.falcon.lib.csub.edu/10.1111/1467-6494.694156

Magnan, R. E., Shorey Fennell, B. R., & Brady, J. M. (2017). Health decision making and behavior: The role of affect-laden constructs. *Social and Personality Psychology Compass, 11*(8), e12333. https://doi.org/10.1111/spc3.12333

Mahindru, A., Patil, P., & Agrawal, V. (2023). Role of physical activity on mental health and well-being: A review. *Cureus, 15*(1), e33475. https://doi-org.falcon.lib.csub.edu/10.7759/cureus.33475

Marquez, D. X., Aguiñaga, S., Vásquez, P. M., Conroy, D. E., Erickson, K. I., Hillman, C., Stillman, C. M., Ballard, R. M., Sheppard, B. B., Petruzzello, S. J., King, A. C., & Powell, K. E.

(2020). A systematic review of physical activity and quality of life and well-being. *Translational Behavioral Medicine, 10*(5), 1098–1109. https://doi-org10.1093/tbm/ibz198

Nieves, J., & Zenko, Z. (2023). Motivational correlates of exercise behavior among college students. *Communications in Kinesiology, 1*(5). https://doi.org/10.51224/cik.2023.47

Niven, A., Laird, Y., Saunders, D. H., & Phillips, S. M. (2021). A systematic review and meta-analysis of affective responses to acute high intensity interval exercise compared with continuous moderate- and high-intensity exercise. *Health Psychology Review, 15*(4), 540–573. https://doi.org/10.1080/17437199.2020.1728564

Niermann, C. Y. N., Hermann, C., von Haaren, B., van Kann, D., & Woll, A. (2016). Affect and subsequent physical activity: An ambulatory assessment study examining the affect-activity association in a real-life context. *Frontiers in Psychology, 7*, 677. https://doi.org/10.3389/fpsyg.2016.00677

Noetel, M., Sanders, T., Gallardo-Gómez, D., Taylor, P., Del Pozo Cruz, B., van den Hoek, D., Smith, J. J., Mahoney, J., Spathis, J., Moresi, M., Pagano, R., Pagano, L., Vasconcellos, R., Arnott, H., Varley, B., Parker, P., Biddle, S., & Lonsdale, C. (2024). Effect of exercise for depression: Systematic review and network meta-analysis of randomised controlled trials. *BMJ*, *384*, e075847. https://doi.org/10.1136/bmj-2023-075847

Olfson, M., Blanco, C., & Marcus, S. C. (2016). Treatment of adults depression in the United States. *JAMA Internal Medicine, 176*(10), 1482–1491. https://doi.org/10.1001/jamainternmed.2016.5057

Pavey, T. G., Burton, N. W., & Brown, W. J. (2015). Prospective relationships between physical activity and optimism in young and mid-aged women. *Journal of Physical Activity and Health, 12*(7), 915–923. https://doi.org/10.1123/jpah.2014-0070

Pearce, M., Garcia, L., Abbas, A., Strain, T., Schuch, F. B., Golubic, R., Kelly, P., Khan, S., Utukuri, M., Laird, Y., Mok, A., Smith, A., Tainio, M., Brage, S., & Woodcock, J. (2022). Association between physical activity and risk of depression: A systematic review and meta-analysis. *JAMA Psychiatry, 79*(6), 550–559. https://doi.org/10.1001/jamapsychiatry.2022.0609

Penedo, F. J., & Dahn, J. R. (2005). Exercise and well-being: A review of mental and physical health benefits associated with physical activity. *Current Opinion in Psychiatry, 18*(2), 189–193. https://doi.org/10.1097/00001504-200503000-00013

Piva, T., Zerbini, V., Ekkekakis, P., Vazou, S., Belvederi Murri, M., Raisi, A., Menegatti, E., Grazzi, G., Mazzoni, G., & Mandini, S. (2025). Affective exercise experiences predict physical activity behaviour in cardiac outpatients within a home-based cardiac rehabilitation programme. *Journal of Sports Sciences, 43*(14), 1345–1354. https://doi.org/10.1080/02640414.2025.2500768

Posner, J., Russell, J. A., & Peterson, B. S. (2005). The circumplex model of affect: An integrative approach to affective neuroscience, cognitive development, and psychopathology. *Development and Psychopathology, 17*(3), 715–734. https://doi.org/10.1017/S0954579405050340

Prochaska, J. O., & DiClemente, C. C. (1983). Stages and processes of self-change of smoking: Toward an integrative model of change. *Journal of Consulting and Clinical Psychology, 51*(3), 390–395. https://doi.org/10.1037/0022-006X.51.3.390

Ramos-Sanchez, C. P., Schuch, F. B., Seedat, S., Louw, Q. A., Stubbs, B., Rosenbaum, S., Firth, J., van Winkel, R., & Vancampfort, D. (2021). The anxiolytic effects of exercise for people with anxiety and related disorders: An update of the available meta-analytic evidence. *Psychiatry Research*, *302*, 114046. https://doi.org/10.1016/j.psychres.2021.114046

Rebar, A. L., Alfrey, K.-L., & Gardner, B. (2021). Theories of physical activity motivation. In Z. Zenko & L. Jones (Eds.), *Essentials of exercise and sport psychology: An open access textbook* (pp.15–36). Society for Transparency, Openness, and Replication in Kinesiology. https://doi.org/10.51224/B1002

Rebar, A. L., Stanton, R., Geard, D., Short, C., Duncan, M. J., & Vandelanotte, C. (2015). A meta-meta-analysis of the effect of physical activity on depression and anxiety in non-clinical adult populations. *Health Psychology Review, 9*(3), 366–378. https://doi.org/10.1080/17437199.2015.1022901

Recchia, F., Leung, C. K., Chin, E. C., Fong, D. Y., Montero, D., Cheng, C. P., Yau, S. Y., & Siu, P. M. (2022). Comparative effectiveness of exercise, antidepressants and their combination in treating non-severe depression: A systematic review and network meta-analysis of randomised controlled trials. *British Journal of Sports Medicine*, *56*(23), 1375–1380. https://doi.org/10.1136/bjsports-2022-105964

Rhodes, R. E., & Kates, A. (2015). Can the affective response to exercise predict future motives and physical activity behavior? A systematic review of published evidence. *Annals of Behavioral Medicine*, *49*(5), 715–731. https://doi.org/10.1007/s12160-015-9704-5

Rhodes, R. E., McEwan, D., & Rebar, A. L. (2019). Theories of physical activity behaviour change: A history and synthesis of approaches. *Psychology of Sport and Exercise, 42*, 100–109. https://doi.org/10.1016/j.psychsport.2018.11.010

Ross, R. E., VanDerwerker, C. J., Saladin, M. E., & Gregory, C. M. (2023). The role of exercise in the treatment of depression: Biological underpinnings and clinical outcomes. *Molecular Psychiatry, 28,* 298–328. https://doi.org/10.1038/s41380-022-01819-w

Ruissen, G. R., Beauchamp, M. R., Puterman, E., Zumbo, B. D., Rhodes, R. E., Hives, B. A., Shapre, B. M., Vega, J., Low, C. A., & Wright, A. G. C. (2022). Continuous-time modeling of the bidirectional relationship between incidental affect and physical activity. *Annals of Behavioral Medicine, 56*(12), 1284–1299. https://doi.org/10.1093/abm/kaac024

Russell, J. A. (1980). A circumplex model of affect. *Journal of Personality and Social Psychology, 39*(6), 1161–1178. https://doi.org/10.1037/h0077714

Russell, J. A., & Barrett, L. F. (1999). Core affect, prototypical emotional episodes, and other things called emotion: Dissecting the elephant. *Journal of Personality and Social Psychology, 76*(5), 805. https://doi.org/10.1037/0022-3514.76.5.805

Ryu, R. H., Larsen, B., LaCroix, A., Nguyen, S., Posis, A. I. B., Schumacher, B. T., Danhauer, S. C., Tindle, H. A., & Bellettiere, J. (2023). Associations of physical activity and sedentary behavior with optimism and positive affect in older women. *Journal of Happiness Studies, 24,* 717–743. https://doi.org/10.1007/s10902-022-00612-4

Schmitt, A., Martin, J. A., Rojas, S., Vafa, R., Scheef, L., Strüder, H. K., & Boecker, H. (2019). Effects of low- and high-intensity exercise on emotional face processing: An fMRI face-matching study. *Social Cognitive and Affective Neuroscience*, *14*(6), 657–665. https://doi.org/10.1093/scan/nsz042

Schuch, F. B., Stubbs, B., & Kandola, A. (2021). Physical activity and exercise for the prevention and management of anxiety. In Z. Zenko & L. Jones (Eds.), *Essentials of exercise and sport psychology: An open access textbook* (pp. 369–384). Society for Transparency, Openness, and Replication in Kinesiology. https://doi.org/10.51224/B1016

Schuch, F. B., Vancampfort, D., Richards, J., Rosenbaum, S., Ward, P. B., & Stubbs, B. (2016). Exercise as a treatment for depression: A meta-analysis adjusting for publication bias. *Journal of Psychiatric Research, 77,* 42–51. https://doi.org/10.1016/j.jpsychires.2016.02.023

Schuch, F. B., Vancampfort, D., Firth, J., Rosenbaum, S., Ward, P. B., Silva, E. S., Hallgren, M., Ponce De Leon, A., Dunn, A. L., Deslandes, A. C., Fleck, M. P., Carvalho, A. F., & Stubbs, B. (2018). Physical activity and incident depression: A meta-analysis of prospective cohort studies. *The American Journal of Psychiatry, 175*(7), 631–648. https://doi.org/10.1176/appi.ajp.2018.17111194

Sheppard, K. E., & Parfitt, G. (2008). Acute affective responses to prescribed and self-selected exercise intensities in young adolescent boys and girls. *Pediatric Exercise Science, 20*(2), 129–141. https://doi.org/10.1123/pes.20.2.129

Singh, B., Olds, T., Curtis, R., Dumuid, D., Virgara, R., Watson, A., Szeto, K., O'Connor, E., Ferguson, T., Eglitis, E., Miatke, A., Simpson, C. E., & Maher, C. (2023). Effectiveness of physical activity interventions for improving depression, anxiety and distress: An overview of systematic reviews. *British Journal of Sports Medicine, 57*(18), 1203–1209. https://doi.org/10.1136/bjsports-2022-106195

Song, Y., Jia, S., Wang, X., Wang, A., Ma, T., Li, S., Chen, J., Guo, Z., Ding, F., Ren, Y., & Qin, M. (2025). Effects of physical exercise on anxiety depression and emotion regulation in children with attention deficit hyperactivity disorder: A systematic review and meta-analysis. *Frontiers in Pediatrics, 12*, 1479615. https://doi.org/10.3389/fped.2024.1479615

Stevens, C. J., Baldwin, A. S., Bryan, A. D., Conner, M., Rhodes, R. E., & Williams, D. M. (2020). Affective determinants of physical activity: A conceptual framework and narrative review. *Frontiers in Psychology, 11*, 568331. https://doi.org/10.3389/fpsyg.2020.568331

Stuntz, C. P., Grosshans, M., Boghosian, R., Brendel, A., & Williamson, M. S. (2020). Exert more and feel better, not worse? Examining links among challenges in exertion, feelings of accomplishment, and feeling states. *Psychology of Sport and Exercise, 48*, 101567. https://doi.org/10.1016/j.psychsport.2020.101657

Tamminen, K. A., & Bennett, E. V. (2017). No emotion is an island: An overview of theoretical perspectives and narrative research on emotions in sport and physical activity. *Qualitative Research in Sport, Exercise, and Health, 9*(2), 183–199. https://doi.org/10.1080/2159676X.2016.1254109

Tamminen, K., Wolf, S. A., Dunn, R., & Bissett, J. E. (2022). A review of the interpersonal experience, expression, and regulation of emotions in sport. *International Review of Sport and Exercise Psychology*. https://doi.org/10.1080/1750984X.2022.2132526

Teixeira, D. S., Bastos, V., Andrade, A. J., Palmeira, A. L., & Ekkekakis, P. (2024). Individualized pleasure-oriented exercise sessions, exercise frequency, and affective outcomes: A pragmatic randomized controlled trial. *International Journal of Behavioral Nutrition and Physical Activity, 21*, 85. https://doi.org/10.1186/s12966-024-01636-0

Thapar, A., Eyre, O., Patel, V., & Brent, D. (2022). Depression in young people. *The Lancet, 400*(10352), 617–631. https://doi.org/10.1016/S0140-6736(22)01012-1

Timm, I., Reichert, M., Ebner-Priemer, U. W., & Giurgiu, M. (2023). Momentary within-subject associations of affective states and physical behavior are moderated by weather conditions in real life: An ambulatory assessment study. *International Journal of Behavioral Nutrition and Physical Activity, 20*, 117. https://doi.org/10.1186/s12966-023-01507-0

Tolentino, J. C., & Schmidt, S. L. (2018). DSM-5 Criteria and depression severity: Implications for clinical practice. *Frontiers in Psychiatry, 9*, 450. https://doi.org/10.3389/fpsyt.2018.0045

Tse, A. C. Y. (2020). Brief Report: Impact of a physical exercise intervention on emotion regulation and behavioral functioning in children with autism spectrum disorder. *Journal of Autism and Developmental Disorders, 50*, 4191–4198. https://10.1007/s10803-020-04418-2

Trudel-Fitzgerald, C., James, P., Kim, E. S., Zevon, E. S., Grodstein, F., & Kubzansky, L. D. (2019). Prospective associations of happiness and optimism with lifestyle over up to two decades. *Preventive Medicine, 126*, 105754. https://doi.org/10.1016/j.ypmed.2019.105754

van Woudenberg, T. J., Bevelander, K. E., Burg, W. J., & Buijzen, M. (2020). The reciprocal effects of physical activity and happiness in adolescents. *International Journal of Behavioral Nutrition and Physical Activity, 17*, 147. https://doi.org/10.1186/s12966-020-01058-8

Vella, S. A., Aidman, E., Teychenne, M., Smith, J. J., Swann, C., Rosenbaum, S., White, R. L., & Lubans, D. R. (2023). Optimising the effects of physical activity on mental health and wellbeing: A joint consensus statement from Sports Medicine Australia and the Australian Psychological Society. *Journal of Science and Medicine in Sport, 26*(2), 132–139. https://doi.org/10.1016/j.jsams.2023.01.001

Wang, X., Cai, Z.-D., Jing, W.-T., Fang, Y.-Y., Sun, W.-X., & Xing, W. (2022). Systematic review and meta-analysis of the effects of exercise on depression in adolescents. *Child and Adolescent Psychiatry and Mental Health, 16*, 16. https://doi.org/10.1186/s13034-022-00453-2

Wang, X., Liu, T., Jin, X., & Zhou, C. (2024). Aerobic exercise promotes emotion regulation: A narrative review. *Experimental Brain Research, 242*, 783–796. https://doi.org/10.1007/s00221-024-06791-1

Watson, D., Clark, L. A., & Tellegen, A. (1988). Development and validation of brief measures of positive and negative affect: The PANAS scales. *Journal of Personality and Social Psychology, 54*(6), 1063–1070. https://doi.org/10.1037/0022-3514.54.6.1063

Wegner, M., Helmich, I., Machado, S., Nardi, A. E., Arias-Carrion, O., & Buddle, H. (2014). Effects of exercise on anxiety and depression disorders: Review of meta-analyses and neurobiological mechanisms. *CNS & Neurological Disorders – Drug Targets, 13*(6), 1002–1014. https://doi.org/10.2174/1871527313666140612102841

Welch, A. S., Hulley, A., Ferguson, C., & Beauchamp, M. R. (2007). Affective responses of inactive women to a maximal incremental exercise test: A test of the dual-mode model. *Psychology of Sport and Exercise, 8*(4), 401–423. https://doi.org/10.1016/j.psychsport.2006.09.002

Wichers, M., Peeters, F., Rutten, B. P. F., Jacobs, N., Derom, C., Thiery, E., Delespaul, P., & van Os, J. (2012). A time-lagged momentary assessment study on daily life physical activity and affect. *Health Psychology, 31*(2), 135–144. https://doi.org/10.1037/a0025688

Williams, D. M., Dunsiger, S., Ciccolo, J. T., Lewis, B. A., Albrecht, A. E., & Marcus, B. H. (2008). Acute affective response to a moderate-intensity exercise stimulus predicts physical activity participation 6 and 12 months later. *Psychology of Sport and Exercise, 9*(3), 231–245. https://doi-org.falcon.lib.csub.edu/10.1016/j.psychsport.2007.04.002

Williams, D. M., Dunsiger, S., Emerson, J. A., Gwaltney, C. J., Monti, P. M., & Miranda, R. (2016). Self-paced exercise, affective response, and exercise adherence: A preliminary investigation using ecological momentary assessment. *Journal of Sport and Exercise Psychology, 38*(3), 282–291. https://doi.org/10.1123/jsep.2015-0232

Williams, D. M., Dunsiger, S., Jennings, E. G., & Marcus, B. H. (2012). Does affective valence during and immediately following a 10-min walk predict concurrent and future physical activity? *Annals of Behavioral Medicine, 44*(1), 43–51. https://doi.org/10.1007/s12160-012-9362-9

Williams, D. M., & Rhodes, R. E. (2023). Guidelines for assessment of affect-related constructs. *Frontiers in Psychology, 14*, 1253477. https://doi.org/10.3389/fpsyg.2023.1253477

Wilson, O. W. A., Whatman, C., Walters, S., Keung, S., Enari, D., Rogers, A., Millar, S.-K., Ferkins, L., Hinckson, E., HJapeta, J., Sam, M., & Richards, J. (2022). The value of sport: Wellbeing benefits of sport participation during adolescence. *International Journal of Environmental Research and Public Health, 19*, 8579. https://doi.org/10.3390/ijerph19148579

Zenko, Z., Hall, E. E., & Bixby, W. R. (2024). The effects of affect-guided interval training on pleasure, enjoyment, and autonomy: A registered report. *Psychology of Sport and Exercise, 73*, 102611. https://doi.org/10.1016/j.psychsport.2024.102611

Zenko, Z., & Ladwig, M. A. (2021). Affective responses to exercise: Measurement considerations for practicing professionals. In Z. Zenko & L. Jones (Eds.), *Essentials of exercise and sport psychology: An open access textbook* (pp. 271–293). Society for Transparency, Openness, and Replication in Kinesiology. https://doi.org/10.51224/B1012

Zhdanava, M., Pilon, D., Ghelerter, I., Chow, W., Joshi, K., Lefebvre, P., & Sheehan, J. J. (2021). The prevalence and national burden of treatment-resistant depression and major depressive disorder in the United States. *The Journal of Clinical Psychiatry, 82*(2), 20m13699. https://doi.org/10.4088/JCP.20m13699

3

EXERCISE AND ANXIETY

The Impacts of Yoga

Kimberlee B. Bonura and I-Hua Chu

3.1 Preface

Anxiety disorders are among the world's most common mental disorders. It was estimated that about 4% of the global population at any given time has an anxiety disorder (GBD Results Tool, 2019). The prevalence of anxiety disorders ranges from 5.3% in Indo/Asian (e.g., India, China, and Japan) and African countries to 10.4% in Western Europe and North American countries (Baxter et al., 2013). Furthermore, anxiety disorders are associated with 10.4% of the Disability Adjusted Life Years lost due to mental, neurological, and substance-use disorders, and account for 1.1% of the global burden of disease (Alonso et al., 2018).

Individuals with an anxiety disorder may have symptoms such as fear, feeling irritable or restless, having a sense of impending danger or panic, and trouble concentrating or making decisions. Other somatic symptoms may include nausea or abdominal distress, heart palpitations, sweating, trembling, and trouble sleeping (Buckworth et al., 2013). As these symptoms involve the cardiovascular, gastrointestinal, or nervous systems, if anxiety is present in excess or for extended periods of time, it may lead to other health issues such as hypertension (Yan et al., 2015), coronary artery disease (Celano et al., 2016), and dementia (Gulpers et al., 2016). Therefore, anxiety disorders can cause great suffering for patients and place huge burdens on their families and societal resources (Kariuki-Nyuthe & Stein, 2015).

Current treatment options for anxiety disorders include pharmacotherapy and psychotherapy. In patients who show only little or no treatment response to pharmaco- and/or psychotherapy, further therapies, such as electroconvulsive therapy, vagus nerve stimulation, repetitive transcranial magnetic stimulation, and deep brain stimulation, may be considered (Kar & Sarkar, 2016). However, only 20% of people with an anxiety disorder seek treatment from health care services,

DOI: 10.4324/9781003517474-5

and only a proportion of those who seek help receive adequate treatment (Sartori & Singewald, 2019). Moreover, substantial issues remain regarding treatment non-compliance, incomplete response, and relapse (Sartori & Singewald, 2019). Taken together, there is still a need for the development of other alternative or adjunct therapies in the treatment of anxiety disorders.

Yoga, a form of mind-body practice, has received considerable attention for its therapeutic effects over the past decades (West et al. 2004). Regular yoga practice has been shown to reduce levels of perceived stress (Chong et al., 2011; Sharma, 2014), anxiety (Chu et al., 2015; Michalsen et al., 2012), and depression (Chu et al., 2017; Uebelacker et al., 2010), as well as improve quality of sleep (Panjwani et al., 2021) and quality of life (Cramer et al., 2017). There are a variety of different yoga styles or "schools" that put varying focus on physical and mental practices. While some yoga styles focus only on meditation or breathing practices, other styles emphasize intensive physical activity (Cramer et al., 2018). In the Western context, a yoga class typically includes practices of physical postures (asanas), breathing techniques (pranayama), meditation/mindfulness, and relaxation (De Michelis, 2005). It was reported that one of the main reasons people practice mind-body therapies such as yoga is to treat anxiety (Barnes et al., 2008).

Dysfunctional breathing (e.g., hyperventilation and unexplained dyspnea) is a hallmark of anxiety disorders (Banushi et al., 2023). Therefore, targeting dysfunctional breathing is expected to have therapeutic benefits for treating anxiety. Breathing practices within yoga, also referred to as pranayama, involve voluntarily changing the pattern, rate, and depth of breathing (Banushi et al., 2023). Pranayama has been shown to improve symptoms of anxiety, depression, as well as reduce levels of stress (Brown et al., 2013; Leyro et al., 2021). Among the various forms of breathing practices, controlled breathing and diaphragmatic breathing have shown the most benefits for patients with anxiety (Chandla et al., 2013; Chen et al., 2017; Valenza et al., 2014). Yogic breathing was also linked to improved symptoms of anxiety and depression, and enhanced stress tolerance and well-being (Brown & Gerbarg, 2005a,b). Many people also use meditation as an alternative or complementary approach to reduce stress and anxiety (Goyal et al., 2014). Meditation programs vary in several ways and the meditative techniques emphasize mindfulness, concentration, and automatic self-transcendence (Goyal et al., 2014). Meditation training is also an integrated part of many mind-body practices such as mindfulness-based stress reduction, yoga, qigong, and Tai Chi (Chen et al., 2012). A previous review indicated that mindfulness meditation programs had moderate evidence of improved anxiety, depression, and pain (Goyal et al., 2014). Another meta-analysis of randomized controlled trials also demonstrated some efficacy of meditative techniques in reducing symptoms of anxiety (Chen et al., 2012).

Yoga programs generally include the practice of breathing techniques (pranayama), meditation, and physical postures (asanas). Therefore, it is plausible to consider yoga as a viable complementary or alternative approach for treating anxiety. This chapter will focus on the impacts of yoga practice on anxiety. The existing evidence from previous systematic review and meta-analysis will be presented, followed by a detailed discussion of the most recent research on this topic. Plausible mechanisms of action, study limitations, and directions for future research will also be discussed.

3.2 Previous Evidence

A number of systematic reviews and meta-analyses have been published on the topic of yoga and anxiety. Sharma and Haider (2013) conducted a systematic review of the effect of yoga as an alternative and complementary therapy for patients suffering from anxiety. This review included 27 studies published between January 2010 and May 2012. The majority of these studies discussed anxiety disorders as a comorbidity to a number of other diseases and disorders, such as depression, cancer, fibromyalgia, menstrual disorder, restless leg syndrome, and schizophrenia. Of the remaining studies, two studies consisted of participants suffering from anxiety, and four studies included healthy participants with no history of psychiatric disorders. Among these studies, 19 demonstrated a significant reduction in state and/or trait anxiety post yoga intervention. The most common yoga style practiced was Hatha yoga, followed by Iyengar yoga. Sudarshan Kriya Yoga, which incorporates rhythmic breathing techniques, and yoga Nidra, a deep relaxation technique, were performed in other studies. The remaining studies incorporated mindfulness-based stress reduction, various techniques, and unspecified yoga techniques. The duration of yoga intervention ranged from one session to seven months, and the yoga classes were offered, on average, twice weekly for 20–120 minutes per session. The majority of studies indicated that in-class training with an instructor was more effective in reducing symptoms of anxiety as compared with home practice, and that 2–3 months of regular yoga practice is necessary to show significant improvements (Sharma & Haider, 2013).

Hofmann and colleagues (2016) conducted a meta-analysis on the effect of Hatha yoga on anxiety. Seventeen interventional studies with a total of 501 participants were examined. Nine studies examined the effect of Hatha yoga on anxiety in a sample with medical conditions, such as multiple sclerosis, cancer, fibromyalgia, type 2 diabetes mellitus, and panic disorder. The remaining studies included healthy participants with normal to elevated levels of anxiety. On average, the treatment duration was 8.69 weeks, and session frequency was 2.25 times per week. Most of the studies included the practice of postures and breathing techniques in yoga sessions. Seven studies reported the use of meditation, five studies reported using relaxation techniques, and two studies included the practice of mindfulness and awareness/acceptance exercises. The results of the meta-analysis provide support for Hatha yoga as a strategy to reduce symptoms of anxiety, and more yoga practices (i.e., more hours of practice and higher frequency) were associated with greater benefits. In addition, individuals with elevated levels of anxiety benefited the most; the treatment effects were not moderated by study year, gender, presence of a medical disorder, or age. The authors suggested that combining Hatha yoga with other strategies, such as cognitive and behavioral techniques, seems warranted for treating anxiety (Hofmann et al., 2016).

In 2018, Cramer and colleagues (2018) published a systematic review and meta-analysis of randomized controlled trials on the effectiveness and safety of yoga for anxiety. A total of eight randomized controlled trials with 319 participants were included in the qualitative synthesis, and six studies were included in the quantitative synthesis (meta-analysis). Five studies included patients with a diagnosis of anxiety disorder of any kind, generalized anxiety disorder, snake phobia, or anxiety neurosis. The remaining studies included individuals with unspecific or specific (examination-related) anxiety without a formal diagnosis of anxiety disorder. Most of the studies used multicomponent yoga interventions, including physical postures, breathing techniques, and/or meditation. One study used meditation only. Yoga was compared with passive control (no specific treatment) in three studies and to active control (mainly relaxation) in five studies. The results of the meta-analyses revealed small short-term effects of yoga on the severity of anxiety compared with no treatment, and large effects compared with active controls. However, no group differences in remission rates were found in the meta-analysis. While the subgroup analyses revealed similar treatment effects for individuals with elevated levels of anxiety without a formal diagnosis, no effects were found for patients with anxiety disorders diagnosed by *Diagnostic and Statistical Manual* (*DSM*) criteria. Only three studies reported safety-related data, and the results indicated that yoga was not associated with increased injuries or increased anxiety symptoms. The findings of this systematic review and meta-analysis suggest that yoga might be an effective and safe intervention for individuals with elevated levels of anxiety. However, the evidence for the effects of yoga on clinically diagnosed anxiety disorders was inconclusive (Cramer et al., 2018).

Recently, Ali and colleagues (2023) conducted a systematic review of quantitative and qualitative results of randomized-controlled trials assessing the effect of yoga in women with post-traumatic stress disorder (PTSD). Thirteen studies with a total of 496 female participants were included in this review. These studies consisted of six original randomized-controlled trials, four secondary analyses of randomized-controlled trials, and three qualitative studies. Most studies use Trauma-Sensitive Hatha Yoga as an intervention. The control intervention varied as assessment only (passive control), stretch and tone, seminar, daily exchange, and cognitive processing therapy (CPT). In a Trauma-Sensitive Hatha Yoga session, lower-intensity moderations were made to the yoga techniques to prevent the reemerging of trauma and to create a safe place for the PTSD participants, allowing them to choose if they want to proceed with the intervention while they navigate the emerging of any favorable and unfavorable bodily responses (Ali et al., 2023; Kelly et al., 2021). The average duration of yoga intervention was 11.2 weeks, and most studies offered yoga classes once weekly for 60 minutes per session. Most of the studies showed that yoga is effective in improving PTSD symptoms and those of related conditions, such as depression, emotional regulation, mindfulness, and drug and alcohol use. In addition, yoga seems to be as effective as gold standard CPT, and as an adjuvant treatment, yoga may be more beneficial for those with fewer adult interpersonal traumas. Yoga also provides profound benefits in treatment-resistant PTSD. These findings suggest that yoga is a feasible and acceptable adjuvant or alternative treatment for PTSD (Ali et al., 2023).

Another recent study provided an updated review exploring the effect of yoga on anxiety in adults (Laban-Sharman et al., 2023). This review included seven studies that were published in 2019 or later. These studies included four randomized controlled trials, one longitudinal study, and two pre- and post-intervention comparisons. Three studies consisted of participants with a diagnosis of anxiety in accordance with the *DSM V* criteria, and four studies included healthy participants. The yoga style practiced in these studies included Hatha, Yin, Kundalini, and Vinyasa. The findings from these studies revealed that not all yoga styles were effective in treating anxiety. Marshall et al. (2020) compared two styles of yoga and found that while Hatha yoga was effective in reducing symptoms of anxiety, Vinyasa yoga was not. Moreover, both Hatha yoga (Brenes et al., 2018) and Kundalini yoga (Simon et al., 2021) were shown to be as effective as cognitive-behavioral therapy for the treatment of anxiety. Yin yoga was also found to be effective in reducing symptoms of anxiety. In conclusion, the authors indicated that the evidence for the effect of yoga on anxiety remains inconclusive and suggested that well-designed studies that focused on specific types of anxiety and yoga styles are warranted (Laban-Sharman et al., 2023).

Results from yoga practice may even be immediate, and after just one session of mindful exercise (including Feldenkrais and yoga), participants experienced improved mood, including reduced depressive mood and state anxiety (Netz & Lidor, 2003). Yoga breathing may be useful for restoring a sense of control when an individual is confronted by an anxiety-inducing trigger (Brown & Gerbarg, 2005a,b). Yoga's effectiveness in reducing anxiety may be due to its capacity for lowering excitability and increasing concentration and self-control (Sharma, Yadava, & Hooda, 2005). Sugiura (2004) reported that yoga meditation could benefit the prevention of daily anxieties and found an inverse relationship between worry-proneness and the "detached objectivity," which is associated with mindfulness meditation.

Prior specific research shows the benefits of yoga for anxiety across a variety of chronic and acute conditions, including clinical anxiety (Miller et al., 1995) and context-specific anxiety (such as examination anxiety, Broota & Sanghvi, 1994; and Malathi et al., 1999). Long-term yoga practitioners have lower levels of both state and trait anxiety than do non-yoga practitioners (Venkatesh et al., 1994). In one study, outpatients with anxiety neurosis, who were provided with yoga training five days per week for three months, showed significant improvement (Sahasi et al., 1989). In another study, one hour of yoga practice for 15 days reduced anxiety levels in participants with anxiety, although not in individuals with minimal initial anxiety (Bhushan & Sinha, 2001). In yet another study, an intensive 15-day yoga experience living in a yoga ashram reduced anxiety and depression levels for patients with gastrointestinal disturbances (Mishra & Sinha, 2001). Research studies have demonstrated the benefits of yoga for reducing anxiety symptoms in specific populations, including older adults (Allen & Steinkohl, 1987), AIDS and HIV patients (Bonadies, 2004), individuals with asthma (Goyeche et al., 1982), organ-transplant recipients (Kreitzer et al., 2005), psychiatric patients (Lavey et al., 2005), individuals with irritable bowel syndrome (Taneja et al., 2004), and children with ADHD (Harrison et al., 2004).

3.2.1 Contraindications

While yoga does show potential for reducing anxiety symptoms, Brown and Gerbarg (2005b) indicated that anxious patients need preparation before beginning yoga training. Patients who have a history of hyperventilation and panic attacks may become fearful when asanas and breathing techniques increase their breathing rate. These patients should be informed that yoga is a controlled form of breathing, which should not trigger panic, and should be monitored carefully during practice. Also, anxious patients should be taught how to slow down breathing, to breathe gently, and not to exhale too forcefully during cyclical breathing. Furthermore, yoga's potential for reducing clinical anxiety may be limited by patient characteristics. Girodo (1974) suggested that yoga is useful for anxiety patients with a short history of illness but may be less effective for patients with a long history of anxiety. Finally, Norton and Johnson (1983) reported that different relaxation methods might be more effective for different types of anxiety. They compared the effects of progressive relaxation and Agni Yoga on somatic and cognitive anxiety forms in 40 moderately snake-phobic subjects. They concluded that progressive relaxation was more effective at reducing somatic anxiety, and that the yoga intervention showed slightly more effect in reducing cognitive anxiety. Norton and Johnson indicated that because anxiety comprises cognitive, somatic, and behavioral components, "specifically tailoring a treatment to a person's type of anxiety may not only improve general treatment outcome, but also produce more synchronous change in the three dimensions of anxiety" (p. 214). Further research as to how specific yoga practices and forms impact specific types of anxiety, and potential contraindications and precautions, is needed.

3.2.2 Research Limitations

The previous evidence provides support for the beneficial effects of yoga on anxiety. However, some limitations are constantly mentioned in these reviews. The common factors that compromise the findings of systematic studies on yoga and anxiety are small sample sizes and a lack of rigorous research designs. More well-controlled studies are needed to better demonstrate the therapeutic effects of yoga for anxiety

(Cramer et al., 2018; Laban-Sharman et al., 2023; Hofmann et al., 2016). Other factors include a lack of clear diagnostic criteria, lack of clinical diagnosis at baseline, lack of blinding, heterogeneity of anxiety type, heterogeneity of yoga styles, and inadequate description of yoga sessions (Cramer et al., 2018; Laban-Sharman et al., 2023). In addition, women were over-represented in most studies. The average study sample consisted of 75.5% female participants (Hofmann et al., 2016). A higher risk of bias in previous studies is another common limitation mentioned in the reviews (Cramer et al., 2018; Laban-Sharman et al., 2023; Hofmann et al., 2016). Moreover, the mechanism through which yoga improves anxiety symptoms is understudied.

Yoga is a multicomponent practice that contains postures, breathing, meditation, and mindfulness. Further studies are required to better understand the active ingredients in yoga for anxiety (Hofmann et al., 2016). The evidence for the effect of yoga on anxiety will be greatly improved if the aforementioned limitations are better addressed in future research.

3.3 Updated Evidence

According to the 2022 "Yoga in the World" survey, commissioned by The Yoga Alliance (2023), an international registry of yoga teachers, in 2022, 38.4 million Americans (approximately 11% of the population) practiced yoga at least once. According to the same survey, across the ten countries included (the United States, the United Kingdom, Germany, Brazil, China, India, United Arab Emirates, Kenya, Nigeria, and Chile), more than 50% of yoga practitioners in eight of ten countries said that relieving stress was the primary motivator for yoga practice (in Brazil and Chile, the primary motivator was to improve overall health, with stress relief/reduction coming in second place out of eight possible motivators). According to another 2022 survey, two-thirds (66%) of adults aged 50–80 have used at least one form of integrative medicine as preventative care or medical treatment; 24% of adults surveyed had specifically used yoga as part of their medical or preventive care (Malani et al., 2022). However, the same study found that only one-fifth of those individuals using complementary care actually discuss these practices, and potential implications, with their primary care provider.

Together, these survey results indicate that (1) the population of individuals practicing yoga continues to grow, (2) that many, or even most, people who come to integrative care, such as yoga, do so for mental and physical health benefits, and (3) individuals practicing yoga for mental health and anxiety reduction may not be discussing this use, and its potential benefits and/or contraindications, with their doctors or therapists. It is important for researchers and practitioners to fully understand the empirical evidence supporting the use of yoga for specific health conditions, such as anxiety, to understand potential limitations and contraindications, and to consider strategies for improving the integration of mindfulness-based practices into medical care, so that patients are more comfortable discussing the use of yoga with their doctors and therapists.

Empirical investigation of the use of yoga for anxiety continues to grow. For instance, a quick search via Google Scholar identified more than 280 peer-reviewed studies with the words "yoga" and "anxiety" in their titles published between 2020 and January of 2024. In comparison, from 2000 until 2019, there were only 513 peer-reviewed studies with the words "yoga" and anxiety in their titles, and from the beginning of time until 1999, there were only 34 studies meeting these same criteria. Similarly, from 2020 to 2023, the US National Institutes of Health issued grants for more than 90 funded studies that, in some way, included yoga as an intervention and anxiety as a measured outcome. We are still at the beginning of our understanding of the implications and mechanisms of yoga to improve mental health outcomes, such as anxiety.

Cole et al. (2021) conducted a meta-analysis of 14 articles and found that yoga was more effective than aerobic exercise in reducing anxiety symptoms, which further points to the breathwork and self-control components of yoga as key mechanisms in improving mental health and reducing exercise. Research studies and research reviews since 2020 have considered the impact of yoga on specific populations. For instance, a 2020 review assessed 27 studies investigating the use of yoga in children and adolescents (James-Palmer et al., 2020). They found that many studies had weak to moderate methodological quality, but generally showed reduction in both anxiety and depression, regardless of youth health status and the details of the intervention. In a study in rural United States, Shreve et al. (2021) found that just ten minutes of yoga per day reduced anxiety in children aged eight to ten in only eight weeks. This kind of brief intervention offers insight into the ways in which yoga may be effectively used as public health interventions in school and community-based settings.

Gonzalez et al. (2021) reviewed 16 studies and reported that yoga helped reduce self-reported depression and anxiety symptoms in individuals with cancer. In an original intervention focused on women with breast cancer, Liu and collaborators (2022) found that mindfulness-based yoga helped reduce both anxiety and depression during chemotherapy. In an original intervention with 59 healthy pregnant women, Kundarti et al. (2020) found that weekly 90-minute yoga sessions reduced state and trait anxiety measures and also blood plasma cortisol levels and led to improved sleep quality reports. Chandrababu et al. (2023) completed a meta-analysis of 17 studies, including more than 1,200 patients, and reported that after cardiovascular surgery, yoga interventions reduced anxiety, pain, and stress biomarkers. They report that yoga is an effective adjunct to care, and like most researchers, they indicate the need for more rigorous empirical research into the use and mechanisms of yoga in health care.

Deveci and collaborators (2023) conclude after a review of 64 studies, which included a meta-analysis of 7 studies meeting inclusion criteria, that while yoga does provide statistically significant benefits in reducing anxiety, poor study design impacts a great deal of yoga research, and the type of yoga intervention may be an important factor to consider. Therefore, in the next part of this section, we will discuss yoga variations and their potential impact on the use of yoga in mental health and anxiety reduction.

3.4 Yoga Variations

While a traditional yoga practice would include a balance of all eight components as outlined by Patanjali, modern yoga has evolved into different schools or styles. Generally, modern Western context and yoga classes focus on asana, pranayama, dharana, and dhyana (respectively, physical postures, breath control, concentration, and meditation); some fitness-style yoga classes may focus entirely on asana, to the exclusion of all other components (Horrigan, 2004). Table 3.1 provides a review of common modern yoga styles, with key considerations and contraindications.

There are also many variations within asana practice. More than 800,000 yoga postures have been identified, and of the 84 postures that are most common across schools of yoga, there are numerous variations (Raub, 2002). Therefore, while all yoga practices are considered yoga, there are significant differences between the types. "Each of these approaches represents a distinct intervention, in the same way that psychodynamic, cognitive-behavioral, and interpersonal therapies each involve different approaches to psychotherapy" (Bower et al., 2005, p. 166).

In addition to the differences across yoga styles, there are differences among yoga teachers. Although the Yoga Alliance, an international organization that upholds yoga teacher training standards, provides a registry of trained yoga instructors and yoga teacher training programs, there are currently no requirements for licensure as a yoga instructor at the state or national level in the United States. Though the 2002 report of the White House Commission on Complementary and Alternative Medicine (CAM; U.S. Department of Health and Human Services, 2002) included an investigation of yoga, its effectiveness, and the training standards proposed by Yoga Alliance, no national standards were established. The quality of yoga instruction may vary widely, from a self-proclaimed yoga teacher to a yoga teacher who has received training, undertaken supervised teaching experience, and achieved national certification and registration. These variations in instructional quality may impact the effectiveness of yoga interventions.

In addition to the differences in yoga style and quality of yoga instruction – yet related to each – is the location of the yoga intervention. There are marked differences in the yoga that is practiced at a yoga studio, a fitness center, and a medical center. Yoga teachers in each of these environments are likely to have undergone different levels and different types of training. Fitness center yoga teachers are often fitness instructors (aerobics, personal trainers, etc.) who have undergone brief specialty workshops in yoga postures. These individuals may have little or no basis in yoga theory, meditation, or philosophy. Yoga studio teachers often have a background in yoga theory and traditional yoga practice but may not have the specific healthcare training needed to work with individuals who need modifications due to mental or physical health conditions. Yoga instructors in medical settings,

TABLE 3.1 Common Yoga Styles

Hatha Yoga	A general term reflecting a traditional yoga practice with slow, relaxed movement and a focus on breathing. Appropriate for most populations.
Chair or Seated Yoga	An adapted yoga practice, based on Hatha yoga, in which participants sit on chairs rather than the floor and have the chair available for support during standing practice. Appropriate for most populations, including children of all ages, older adults, and individuals with limited mobility or health conditions that prevent getting up and down from the floor. Also accessible for workplace and school-based yoga classes.
Iyengar Yoga	A precise form of yoga that focuses on specific body alignment, slow movement, and endurance. Appropriate for most populations.
Mindfulness-Based Stress Reduction	The MBSR approach combines gentle Hatha yoga and mindfulness meditation. MBSR is very appropriate for new yoga practitioners and provides a comprehensive approach to mind-body wellness and stress management. Appropriate for most populations.
Restorative Yoga	Yoga practice focused on soothing and supportive yoga postures. This practice usually involves the use of yoga props (bolsters, straps, pillows, blankets, and small foam blocks) to support the individual in holding a yoga posture for a longer period of time (as much as 15 minutes) while relaxing and consciously breathing. Appropriate for most populations.
Viniyoga	Gentle yoga practice in which the breath and the physical poses are synchronized. Viniyoga is personalized to the individual practitioner. Appropriate for most populations.
Kundalini Yoga	A yoga practice that focuses on energy work, including breathing practices and flowing, repetitive movement. Some group Kundalini classes include jumping, vigorous activity, and breath-holding poses. This may or may not be appropriate for older adults and individuals with mobility limitations, depending on the instructor's teaching style and focus; inquire with the instructor about specific health concerns.
Vinyasa, Power, and Ashtanga Yoga	Vigorous yoga practices based on fast movement, high-intensity exercise, and building of strength and flexibility. Requires precise movement to prevent injury, so generally not appropriate for younger children or individuals with attentional concerns. May or may not be appropriate for older adults and individuals with mobility limitations, depending on the instructor's teaching style and focus; inquire with the instructor about specific health concerns.
Hot Yoga	Vigorous yoga practices following specific protocols with little room for modification or variation, practiced in a room heated to above 100°F. Contraindicated for individuals with a variety of health conditions exacerbated by heat, including heart conditions, skin conditions, and breathing conditions.

such as hospital-based classes, may have targeted training in teaching yoga to individuals with health or psychological conditions. As well, the location of the yoga class impacts variables such as the duration of each class (traditional studio-based yoga classes are often 90 minutes long and include a 15-minute meditation; fitness center classes are often 50 or 60 minutes long, and include minimal or no meditation), the available equipment, presence or absence of background music, presence or absence of mirrors, even the apparel of the instructor and the participants. All the variations could potentially affect the outcomes of a yoga intervention, and therefore, must be considered when comparing studies about yoga outcomes on mental health.

3.5 Implications

It is important to assess the potential applications of yoga therapy for psychological disorders such as anxiety, because individuals prefer to use self-help techniques than to seek professional treatments for dealing with these disorders (Jorm et al., 1997). In one survey, 55% of respondents had used alcohol to relax, 55% had used pain relievers, and 50% had engaged in physical activities (including yoga), compared with only 35% who consulted a general practitioner or 4% who received psychotherapy (Jorm et al., 2000). Further, caution must be utilized when including yoga in treatment protocols for psychiatric disorders. Both the yoga techniques and the yoga teacher should be thoroughly assessed. Brown and Gerbarg (2005b) caution that bipolar patients, especially those with predominantly manic symptoms, may attempt to use certain breathing techniques for self-stimulation, and warn that only experienced yoga teachers, working in conjunction with a therapist, should work with bipolar II patients.

A collaborative relationship between yoga professionals and mental health care professionals is needed to support safe yoga practice with effective psychological outcomes. Mental health practitioners interested in the use of yoga as an adjunct to care should seek out relationships with certified yoga instructors who have substantive training both in yoga and in special needs and common conditions of children and families. Further, healthcare professionals who intend to recommend yoga as a supportive self-care tool for their patients should have at least minimal experience with yoga themselves; they should try various yoga instructors in their locale to better make recommendations as to appropriate yoga venues. In addition, certain research journals, such as the *Journal of Alternative and Complementary Medicine* and the *International Journal of Yoga Therapy*, provide good sources of peer-reviewed yoga research to support ongoing professional development and understanding of the potential applications of yoga in the promotion of physical health and psychological well-being.

Additionally, the increased interest in the use of yoga and other CAM techniques as medical interventions has led to more targeted research and publications. Mental health and medical professionals interested in the use of yoga for anxiety should identify peer-reviewed articles, as well as current grant reports, focused on the use of yoga for anxiety in their target population. For instance, the primary author of this chapter has published peer-reviewed articles about the use of yoga and mindfulness strategies by military populations (Bonura & Fountain, 2020), by pregnant women (Bonura, 2014, 2017, 2018; Bonura et al., 2016), and among older adults (Bonura, 2011; Bonura & Pargman, 2009; Bonura & Tenenbaum, 2014). Population-specific articles, such as these, may be particularly useful to practitioners working to integrate yoga into mental and medical health care for their patients.

Some yoga teachers may not have the appropriate training or experience to collaborate in educational and clinical settings, so mental health providers should consider interviewing potential candidates as to their training and teaching experiences. Table 3.2 offers strategies to consider when collaborating with yoga instructors or referring clients/patients to yoga instruction or yoga therapy. Table 3.3 reviews two key credentialing bodies for yoga instructors. In addition to the websites of these organizations, yoga instructors may be identified through flyers and classes in stand-alone yoga centers; in fitness centers, community facilities such as recreation centers, libraries, and educational centers; and in medical facility wellness programs.

TABLE 3.2 Guidelines for Medical and Mental Health Professionals: Integrating Yoga into Practice

Foundational Activities	• Establish relationships with trained yoga instructors who have experience in clinical settings. See Table 3.3 for more information about credentialing bodies for yoga instructors. • Gain at least basic familiarity with yoga. Attend a few classes with yoga teachers to identify individuals in your area to whom you feel comfortable referring. • Review the published medical literature on yoga, such as *the International Journal of Yoga Therapy*.
Patient Interaction	• Discuss complementary and alternative therapies with your clients/patients to ensure you are fully informed of their self-care decisions. • Suggest yoga as a gentle exercise option for clients/patients who have not been active or who are interested in increasing their physical activity. • Provide clients/patients with basic guidelines about the potential benefits of yoga for their health and psychological condition. Remind them to discuss any contraindications with their potential yoga instructor. Empower patients with information that will allow them to make good decisions about physical activity and self-care.

TABLE 3.3 Yoga Teacher Credentialing Bodies

Registered Yoga Teacher – The Yoga Alliance	Completed a yoga teacher training course. The Registered Yoga Teacher credential from The Yoga Alliance (www.yogaalliance.org) indicates a minimum level of training and ongoing yoga teacher continuing education. The Yoga Alliance website offers a location-specific search tool.
Certified Yoga Therapist – The International Association of Yoga Therapy	If the instructor uses yoga in a therapeutic framework, the individual should also have training in yoga therapy and be Certified by the International Association of Yoga Therapists (www.iayt.org). The International Association of Yoga Therapists website offers a search tool.

3.6 Conclusion

Yoga is an effective complementary approach for both health maintenance and preventative care. Yoga has been demonstrated to reduce symptoms of anxiety and can be a useful long-term practice to improve mental health. Yoga has the potential to be even more effective when consciously and systematically integrated into an individual's overall self-care, medical, and mental healthcare program, through deliberate and open dialogue among patients, healthcare professionals, and yoga professionals.

References

Ali, M., Oble, M. J. P., Sonia, S. N., George, S., Shahi, S. R., Ali, Z., Abaza, A., Jamil, A., Gutlapalli, S. D., & Khan, S. (2023). A systematic review of quantitative and qualitative results of randomized controlled trials assessing the effect of yoga in adult women with post-traumatic stress disorder: What is known so far. *Cureus, 15*(10), e47765. https://doi.org/10.7759/cureus.47765

Allen, K. S., & Steinkohl, R. P. (1987). Yoga in a geriatric mental clinic. *Activities, Adaptation & Aging, 9*, 61–68.

Alonso, J., Liu, Z., Evans-Lacko, S., Sadikova, E., Sampson, N., Chatterji, S., Abdulmalik, J., Aguilar-Gaxiola, S., Al-Hamzawi, A., Andrade, L. H., Bruffaerts, R., Cardoso, G., Cia, A., Florescu, S., de Girolamo, G., Gureje, O., Haro, J. M., He, Y., de Jonge, P., Karam, E. G., … WHO World Mental Health Survey Collaborators (2018). Treatment gap for anxiety disorders is global: Results of the World Mental Health Surveys in 21 countries. *Depression and Anxiety, 35*(3), 195–208. https://doi.org/10.1002/da.22711

Banushi, B., Brendle, M., Ragnhildstveit, A., Murphy, T., Moore, C., Egberts, J., & Robison, R. (2023). Breathwork interventions for adults with clinically diagnosed anxiety disorders: A scoping review. *Brain Sciences, 13*(2), 256. https://doi.org/10.3390/brainsci13020256

Barnes, P. M, Bloom, B, Nahin, R. L. (2008 Dec 10). Complementary and alternative medicine use among adults and children: United States, 2007. *National Health Statistics Report*, (12), 1–23. PMID: 19361005.

Baxter, A. J., Scott, K. M., Vos, T., & Whiteford, H. A. (2013). Global prevalence of anxiety disorders: A systematic review and meta-regression. *Psychological Medicine, 43*(5), 897–910. https://doi.org/10.1017/S003329171200147X

Bhushan, S., & Sinha, P. (2001). Yoganidra and management of anxiety and hostility. *Journal of Indian Psychology, 19*, 44–49.

Bonadies, V. (2004). A yoga therapy program for AIDS-related pain and anxiety: Implications for therapeutic recreation. *Therapeutic Recreation Journal, 38*, 148–166.

Bonura, K. B. (2011). The psychological benefits of yoga practice for older adults: Evidence and guidelines. *International Journal of Yoga Therapy*, 21, 129–142. https://doi.org/10.17761/ijyt.21.1.j4l1204h12535874

Bonura, K. B. (2014). Yoga mind while expecting: The psychological benefits of prenatal yoga practice. *International Journal of Childbirth Education, 29*(4), 49–54.

Bonura, K. B. (2017). Growing fit together: Including social support in prenatal and postnatal fitness. *International Journal of Childbirth Education, 32*(3), *21–25.*

Bonura, K. B. (2018). Just breathe: Mindfulness as pain management in pregnancy. *International Journal of Childbirth Education*, *33*(1), 6–9.

Bonura, K. B., & Fountain, D. M. (2020). From “Hooah” to “Om”: Mindfulness practices for a military population. *Journal of Social, Behavioral, and Health Sciences, 14*, 183–194. https://doi.org/10.5590/JSBHS.2020.14.1.13

Bonura, K. B., & Pargman, D. (2009). The Effects of yoga versus exercise on stress, anxiety, and depression in older adults. *International Journal of Yoga Therapy, 19*, 79–89. https://doi.org/10.17761/ijyt.19.1.r4hw87m5x2171588

Bonura, K. B., Spadaro, N. I. M, & Thornton, R. W. (2016). Mindful fitness: Guidelines for prenatal ractice. *International Journal of Childbirth Education, 31*, 14–17.

Bonura, K. B., & Tenenbaum, G. (2014). Effects of yoga on psychological health in older adults. *Journal of Physical Activity and Health, 11*, 1334–1341. https://doi.org/10.1123/jpah.2012-0365

Brenes, G. A., Divers, J., Miller, M. E., & Danhauer, S. C. (2018). A randomized preference trail of cognitive-behavioral therapy and yoga for the treatment of worry in anxious older adults. *Contemporary Clinical Trials Communications, 10*, 169–176. https://doi.10.1016/j.conctc.2018.05.002

Broota, A., & Sanghvi, C. (1994). Efficacy of two relaxation techniques in examination anxiety. *Journal of Personality & Clinical Studies, 10*, 29–35.

Brown, R. P., & Gerbarg, P. L. (2005a). Sudarshan kriya yogic breathing in the treatment of stress, anxiety, and depression: Part I – Neurophysiological model. *Journal of Alternative and Complementary Medicine, 11*, 189–201. https://doi.org/10.1089/acm.2005.11.189

Brown, R.P., & Gerbarg, P. L. (2005b). Sudarshan kriya yogic breathing in the treatment of stress, anxiety, and depression: Part II-clinical applications and guidelines. *Journal of Alternative and Complementary Medicine, 11*, 711–717. https://doi.org/10.1089/acm.2005.11.711

Brown, R. P., Gerbarg, P. L., & Muench, F. (2013). Breathing practices for treatment of psychiatric and stress-related medical conditions. *The Psychiatric Clinics of North America, 36*(1), 121–140. https://doi.org/10.1016/j.psc.2013.01.001

Bower, J. E., Woolery, A., Sternlieb, B., & Garet, D. (2005). Yoga for cancer patients and survivors. *Cancer Control: Journal of the Moffitt Cancer Center, 12*, 165–171.

Buckworth, J., Dishman, R. K., O’Connor, P. J., & Tomporowski, P. D. (2013). *Exercise psychology* (2nd ed.). Human Kinetics. https://doi.org/10.5040/9781492595502

Celano, C. M., Daunis, D. J., Lokko, H. N., Campbell, K. A., & Huffman, J. C. (2016). Anxiety disorders and cardiovascular disease. *Current Psychiatry Reports*, *18*(11), 101. https://doi.org/10.1007/s11920-016-0739-5

Chandla, S. S., Sood, S., Dogra, R., Das, S., Shukla, S. K., & Gupta, S. (2013). Effect of short-term practice of pranayamic breathing exercises on cognition, anxiety, general well being and heart rate variability. *Journal of the Indian Medical Association, 111*(10), 662–665.

Chandrababu, R., Ramesh, J., Jagadeesh, N., Guo, P., Reddy, G., & Hayter M (2023). Effects of yoga on anxiety, pain, inflammatory and stress biomarkers in patients undergoing cardiac surgery: A systematic review and meta-analysis. *Complementary Therapies in Clinical Practice, 53*, 101798. https://doi.org/10.1016/j.ctcp.2023.101798

Chen, K. W., Berger, C. C., Manheimer, E., Forde, D., Magidson, J., Dachman, L., & Lejuez, C. W. (2012). Meditative therapies for reducing anxiety: A systematic review and meta-analysis of randomized controlled trials. *Depression and Anxiety*, *29*(7), 545–562. https://doi.org/10.1002/da.21964

Chen, Y. F., Huang, X. Y., Chien, C. H., & Cheng, J. F. (2017). The effectiveness of diaphragmatic breathing relaxation training for reducing anxiety. *Perspectives in Psychiatric Care*, *53*(4), 329–336. https://doi.org/10.1111/ppc.12184

Chong, C. S., Tsunaka, M., Tsang, H. W., Chan, E. P., & Cheung, W. M. (2011). Effects of yoga on stress management in healthy adults: A systematic review. *Alternative Therapies in Health and Medicine*, *17*(1), 32–38.

Chu, I. H., Lin, Y. J., Wu, W. L., Chang, Y. K., & Lin, I. M. (2015). Effects of yoga on heart rate variability and mood in women: A randomized controlled trial. *Journal of Alternative and Complementary Medicine*, *21*(12), 789–795. https://doi.org/10.1089/acm.2015.0138

Chu, I. H., Wu, W. L., Lin, I. M., Chang, Y. K., Lin, Y. J., & Yang, P. C. (2017). Effects of yoga on heart rate variability and depressive symptoms in women: A randomized controlled trial. *Journal of Alternative and Complementary Medicine*, *23*(4), 310–316. https://doi.org/10.1089/acm.2016.0135

Cole, A., Pearson, T., & Knowlton, M. (2021). Comparing aerobic exercise with yoga in anxiety reduction: An integrative review. *Issues in Mental Health Nursing, 43*, 282–287.

Cramer, H., Lauche, R., Klose, P., Lange, S., Langhorst, J., & Dobos, G. J. (2017). Yoga for improving health-related quality of life, mental health and cancer-related symptoms in women diagnosed with breast cancer. *The Cochrane Database of Systematic Reviews*, *1*(1), CD010802. https://doi.org/10.1002/14651858.CD010802.pub2

Cramer, H., Lauche, R., Anheyer, D., Pilkington, K., de Manincor, M., Dobos, G., & Ward, L. (2018). Yoga for anxiety: A systematic review and meta-analysis of randomized controlled trials. *Depression and Anxiety*, *35*(9), 830–843. https://doi.org/10.1002/da.22762

De Michelis, E. (2005). *A history of modern yoga: Patanjali and Western esotericism*. Continuum International Publishing Group.

Laban-Sharman, A., Deveci, M., & Laban-Sharman, R. (2023). Systematic review to explore the effect of yoga on anxiety in adults. *Mental Health: Global Challenges Journal*, *6*(1), 39–46. https://doi.org/10.56508/mhgcj.v6i1.150

GBD Results Tool. (2019). In: *Global Health Data Exchange* [website]. Seattle: Institute for Health Metrics and Evaluation, (https://vizhub.healthdata.org/gbd-results?params=gbd-api-2019-permalink/716f37e05d94046d6a06c1194a8eb0c9, accessed 5 September 2023).

Girodo, M. (1974). Yoga meditation and flooding in the treatment of anxiety neurosis. *Journal of Behavior Therapy & Experimental Psychiatry, 5*, 157–160. https://doi.org/10.1016/0005-7916(74)90104-9

Gonzalez, M., Pascoe, M, Yang., G., de Manicor, M., Grant, S., Lacey, J., Firth, J., & Sarris. J. (2021). Yoga for depression and anxiety symptoms in people with cancer: A systematic review and meta-analysis. *Psycho-Oncology, 30*, 1196–1208. https://doi.org/10.1002/pon.5671

Goyal, M, Singh, S, Sibinga, E. M, Gould, N. F, Rowland-Seymour, A, Sharma, R, Berger, Z, Sleicher, D, Maron, D. D, Shihab, H. M, Ranasinghe, P. D, Linn, S, Saha, S, Bass, E. B, & Haythornthwaite, J. A. (2014 Mar). Meditation programs for psychological stress and well-being: a systematic review and meta-analysis. *JAMA International Medicine*,

174(3), 357–68. doi: 10.1001/jamainternmed.2013.13018. PMID: 24395196; PMCID: PMC4142584.

Goyeche, J. R., Abo, Y., & Ikemi, Y. (1982). Asthma: The yoga perspective: II. Yoga therapy in the treatment of asthma. *Journal of Asthma, 19*, 189–201.

Gulpers, B., Ramakers, I., Hamel, R., Köhler, S., Oude Voshaar, R., & Verhey, F. (2016). Anxiety as a predictor for cognitive decline and dementia: A systematic review and meta-analysis. *The American Journal of Geriatric Psychiatry*, *24*(10), 823–842. https://doi.org/10.1016/j.jagp.2016.05.015

Harrison, L. J., Manocha, R., & Rubia, K. (2004). Sahaja yoga meditation as a family treatment programme for children with attention deficit-hyperactivity disorder. *Clinical Child Psychology & Psychiatry, 9*, 479–497.

Hofmann, S. G., Andreoli, G. Carpenter, J. K., & Curtiss, J. (2016). Effect of Hatha yoga on anxiety: A meta-analysis. *Journal of Evidence-Based Medicine, 9*(3), 116–124. https://doi.org/10.1111/jebm.12204

Horrigan, B. (2004). Richard Freeman on yoga as a path to physical and spiritual health. *Alternative Therapies, 10*, 65–72.

James-Palmer, A, Anderson, E. Z., Zucker, L., Kofman, Y., & Daneault, J.-F. (2020). Yoga as an intervention for the reduction of symptoms of anxiety and depression in children and adolescents: A systematic review. *Frontiers in Pediatrics, 8*. https://doi.org/10.3389/fped.2020.00078

Jorm, A. F., Korten, A. E., & Jacomb, P. A. (1997). "Mental health literacy": A survey of the public's ability to recognise mental disorders and their beliefs about the effectiveness of treatment. *Medical Journal of Australia, 166*(4), 182–186. https://doi.org/10.5694/j.1326-5377.1997.tb140071.x

Jorm, A. F., Medway, J., & Christensen, H. (2000). Public beliefs about the helpfulness of interventions for depression: Effects on actions taken when experiencing anxiety and depression symptoms. *Australian and New Zealand Journal of Psychiatry, 166*, 182–186. https://doi.org/ 10.1080/j.1440–1614.2000.00761.x

Kar, S. K., & Sarkar, S. (2016). Neuro-stimulation techniques for the management of anxiety disorders: An update. *Clinical Psychopharmacology and Neuroscience*, *14*(4), 330–337. https://doi.org/10.9758/cpn.2016.14.4.330

Kariuki-Nyuthe, C., & Stein, D. J. (2015). Anxiety and related disorders and physical illness. In N. Sartorius (Ed.), *Comorbidity of mental and physical disorders* (pp. 81–87). Karger.

Kelly, U., Haywood, T., Segell, E., & Higgins, M. (2021). Trauma-sensitive yoga for post-traumatic stress disorder in women veterans who experienced military sexual trauma: Interim results from a randomized controlled trial. *Journal of Alternative and Complementary Medicine, 27*(S1), S45–S59. https://doi.org/10.1089/acm.2020.0417

Kreitzer, M. J., Gross, C. R., Ye, X., Russas, V., & Treesak, C. (2005). Longitudinal impact of mindfulness meditation on illness burden in solid-organ transplant recipients. *Progress in Transplantation, 15*, 166–172. https://doi.org/10.1177/152692480501500210

Kundarti, F., Titisari, I., Sepdianto, T, Karnasih, I., & Sugijati, S. (2020). The effect of prenatal yoga on anxiety, cortisol, and sleep quality. *International Journal of Pharmaceutical Research, 12*, 2268–2276. https://doi.org/10.31838/ijpr/2020.12.03.315

Lavey, R., Sherman, T., Mueser, K. T., Osborne, D. D., Currier, M., & Wolfe, R. (2005). The effects of yoga on mood in psychiatric inpatients. *Psychiatric Rehabilitation Journal, 28*, 399–402. https://doi.org/10.2975/28.2005.399.402

Leyro, T. M., Versella, M. V., Yang, M. J., Brinkman, H. R., Hoyt, D. L., & Lehrer, P. (2021). Respiratory therapy for the treatment of anxiety: Meta-analytic review and regression. *Clinical Psychology Review, 84*, 101980. https://doi.org/10.1016/j.cpr.2021.101980

Liu, W., Liu, J., Ma, L., & Chen, J. (2022). Effect of mindfulness yoga on anxiety and depression in early breast cancer patients received adjuvant chemotherapy: A randomized clinical trial. *Journal of Cancer Research and Clinical Oncology, 148*, 2549–2560 https://doi.org/10.1007/s00432-022-04167-

Malani, P., Kullgren, J., Solway, E., Masciasz, R., Singer, D., Kirch, M., & Smith, E. (2022). *National poll on healthy aging: Use of and interest in integrative medicine strategies.* https://deepblue.lib.umich.edu/documents

Malathi, A., Damodaran, A., Shah, N., Patil, N., & Marathe, A. (1999). Self-actualization and practice of yoga. *NIMHANS Journal, 17*(1), 39–44.

Marshall, M., McClanahan, M., McArthur Warren, S., Rogers, R., & Ballmann, C. (2020). A comparison of the acute effects of different forms of yoga on physiological and psychological stress: A pilot study. *International Journal of Environmental Research and Public Health, 17*(17), 6090. https://doi.org/10.3390/ijerph17176090

Michalsen, A., Jeitler, M., Brunnhuber, S., Lüdtke, R., Büssing, A., Musial, F., Dobos, G., & Kessler, C. (2012). Iyengar yoga for distressed women: A 3-armed randomized controlled trial. *Evidence-Based Complementary and Alternative Medicine: eCAM, 2012*, 408727. https://doi.org/10.1155/2012/408727

Miller, J. J., Fletcher, K., & Kabat-Zinn, J. (1995). Three-year follow-up and clinical implications of a mindfulness-based stress reduction intervention in the treatment of anxiety disorders. *General Hospital Psychiatry, 17*, 192–200. https://doi.org/10.1016/0163-8343(95)00025-m

Mishra, M., & Sinha, R. K. (2001). Effect of yogic practices on depression and anxiety. *Journal of Projective Psychology & Mental Health, 3*(1), 23.

Netz, Y., & Lidor, R. (2003). Mood alterations in mindful versus aerobic exercise modes. Journal of Psychology: Interdisciplinary & Applied, 137, 405–419.

Norton, G. R., & Johnson, W. E. (1983). A comparison of two relaxation procedures for reducing cognitive and somatic anxiety. *Journal of Behavior Therapy & Experimental Psychiatry, 14*, 209–214. https://doi.org/10.1016/0005-7916(83)90050-2

Panjwani, U., Dudani, S., & Wadhwa, M. (2021). Sleep, cognition, and yoga. *International Journal of Yoga, 14*(2), 100–108. https://doi.org/10.4103/ijoy.IJOY_110_20

Raub, J. A. (2002). Psychophysiologic effects of Hatha yoga on musculoskeletal and cardiopulmonary function: A literature review. *Journal of Alternative and Complementary Medicine, 8*, 797–812. https://doi.org/10.1089/10755530260511810

Sahasi, G., Mohan, D., & Kacker, C. (1989). Effectiveness of yogic techniques in the management of anxiety. *Journal of Personality & Clinical Studies, 5*, 51–55.

Sartori, S. B., & Singewald, N. (2019). Novel pharmacological targets in drug development for the treatment of anxiety and anxiety-related disorders. *Pharmacology & Therapeutics, 204*, 107402. https://doi.org/10.1016/j.pharmthera.2019.107402

Sharma, M. (2014). Yoga as an alternative and complementary approach for stress management: A systematic review. *Journal of Evidence-Based Complementary & Alternative Medicine*, *19*(1), 59–67. https://doi.org/10.1177/2156587213503344

Sharma, M., & Haider, T. (2013). Yoga as an alternative and complementary therapy for patients suffering from anxiety: A systematic review. *Journal of Evidence-Based Complementary & Alternative Medicine, 18*(1), 15–22. https://doi.org/10.1177/2156587212460046

Sharma, N. R., Yadava, A., & Hooda, D. (2005). Effect of yoga on psycho-physical functions. Journal of Indian Psychology, 23, 37–42.

Shreve, M., Scott, A., McNeill, C., & Washburn, L. (2021). Using yoga to reduce anxiety in children: Exploring school-based yoga among rural third- and fourth-grade students. *Journal of Pediatric Health Care, 35*(1), 42–52. https://doi.org/10.1016/j.pedhc.2020.07.008

Simon, N. M., Hofmann, S. G., Rosenfield, D., Hoeppner, S. S., Hoge, E. A., Bui, E., & Khalsa, S. B. S. (2021). Efficacy of yoga vs cognitive behavioral therapy vs stress education for the treatment of generalized anxiety disorder: A randomized clinical trial. *JAMA Psychiatry, 78*(1), 13–20. https://doi.org/10.1001/jamapsychiatry.2020.2496

Sugiura, Y. (2004). Detached mindfulness and worry: a meta-cognitive analysis. *Personality and* Individual Differences, 37, 169–179.

Taneja, I., Deepak, K. K., Poojary, G., Acharya, I. N., Pandey, R. M., & Sharma, M. P. (2004). Yogic versus conventional treatment in diarrhea-predominant irritable bowel syndrome: A randomized control study. *Applied Psychophysiology & Biofeedback, 29*, 19–33. https://doi.org/10.1023/b:apbi.0000017861.60439.95

Uebelacker, L. A., Epstein-Lubow, G., Gaudiano, B. A., Tremont, G., Battle, C. L., & Miller, I. W. (2010). Hatha yoga for depression: Critical review of the evidence for efficacy, plausible mechanisms of action, and directions for future research. *Journal of Psychiatric Practice, 16*(1), 22–33. https://doi.org/10.1097/01.pra.0000367775.88388.96

U.S. Department of Health and Human Services. (2002). *White House Commission on Complementary and Alternative Medicine Policy: Final Report.* U.S. Department of Health and Human Services.

Valenza, M. C., Valenza-Peña, G., Torres-Sánchez, I., González-Jiménez, E., Conde-Valero, A., & Valenza-Demet, G. (2014). Effectiveness of controlled breathing techniques on anxiety and depression in hospitalized patients with COPD: A randomized clinical trial. *Respiratory Care, 59*(2), 209–215. https://doi.org/10.4187/respcare.02565

Venkatesh, S., Pal, M., Negi, B. S., & Varma, V. K. (1994). A comparative study of yoga practitioners and controls on certain psychological variables. *Indian Journal of Clinical Psychology, 21*, 22–27.

West, J., Otte, C., Geher, K., Johnson, J., & Mohr, D. C. (2004). Effects of Hatha yoga and African dance on perceived stress, affect, and salivary cortisol. *Annals of Behavioral Medicine, 28*(2), 114–118. https://doi.org/10.1207/s15324796abm2802_6

Yan, J., Pan, Y., Cai, W., et al, (2015). Association between anxiety and hypertension: a systematic review and meta-analysis of epidemiological studies. NDT, 11, 1121. https://doi.org/10.2147/NDT.S77710

Yoga Alliance. (2023). *Yoga in the world study.* https://blog.yogaalliance.org/2023/11/15/press-release-yoga-in-the-world-research-study/

4

EFFECT OF HIGH-INTENSITY INTERVAL TRAINING ON EXECUTIVE FUNCTION

A Review

Jing-Yi Ai, Chen-Sin Hung, Brandon L. Alderman, Marius Brazaitis, and Yu-Kai Chang

4.1 Introduction

Executive function refers to higher-order cognitive processes that enable individuals to regulate thoughts, behaviors, and emotions in goal-directed ways. Executive functioning encompasses three core domains, including inhibitory control, working memory, and cognitive flexibility (Diamond, 2013, 2020). Inhibitory control allows individuals to regulate attention, behavior, and emotions by suppressing automatic or distracting responses. Working memory enables the temporary storage and manipulation of information for tasks such as reasoning and problem-solving. Cognitive flexibility allows individuals to shift perspectives, adjust strategies, and adapt to changing environments (Miyake et al., 2000). Executive function is vital for learning, social functioning, emotional regulation, and mental health, and predicts long-term academic achievement and developmental outcomes (Schäfer et al., 2024). However, these cognitive processes naturally decline with age and have been implicated in neurodegenerative diseases such as Alzheimer's disease. This highlights the importance of interventions to maintain or improve executive function.

Physical activity is a well-established, non-pharmacological method for enhancing cognitive function, particularly executive function. Aerobic and resistance exercise have shown consistent cognitive benefits in both healthy (Ye et al., 2024) and clinical populations (Huang et al., 2023; Liang, Li et al., 2022; Sung et al., 2022). However, researchers continue to actively explore diverse exercise modalities, such as blood flow restriction training (Sugimoto et al., 2021) and multi-componentexercise(Liang,Qiuetal.,2022),tomaximizeexercisebenefits.High-intensity interval training (HIIT), consisting of alternating short periods (seconds to minutes) of high-intensity exercise (intensity ≥ anaerobic threshold or maximal

DOI: 10.4324/9781003517474-6

lactate steady state) with brief recovery periods or low-intensity activity (Cadenas-Sanchez et al., 2024), has gained attention for its efficiency and potential cognitive effects. Compared with traditional moderate-intensity continuous training (MICT), HIIT offers comparable or superior health benefits, including improved cardiorespiratory fitness, enhanced metabolic health, and optimized body composition (Laursen & Jenkins, 2002). This characteristic makes HIIT a potential strategy to overcome the "lack of time", a common barrier to exercise in modern society.

HIIT may enhance executive function through several mechanisms. From a physiological perspective, HIIT significantly enhances cardiorespiratory fitness, increases capillary density and mitochondrial oxidative capacity, and improves oxygen and nutrient supply to the brain (Rajizadeh et al., 2024). It also increases brain-derived neurotrophic factor (BDNF) and potentially promotes the sensitivity of BDNF receptors, which supports neuronal health and synaptic plasticity, thereby enhancing executive function (Ahmadi et al., 2025). Neuroimaging studies suggest HIIT may directly affect the structure and function of executive function-related brain regions such as the prefrontal cortex, optimizing the efficiency and connectivity patterns of neural networks (Kao et al., 2018). Although these findings provide a theoretical foundation and preliminary evidence for HIIT as an effective intervention to enhance executive function, the specific mechanisms and dose–response relationships remain to be fully understood.

Notably, existing research regarding the effects of HIIT on executive function remains relatively fragmented, with limited synthesis across exercise parameters (e.g. intensity, duration, frequency). Additionally, HIIT may have differential effects on the executive function subdomains, and it is important to determine whether individual characteristics (e.g., age, medical conditions) moderate the effects of HIIT. This chapter aims to address these gaps by systematically reviewing the effects of HIIT on each executive function component, identifying optimal exercise training parameters, and highlighting population-specific characteristics to provide an integrated reference for future research and practical applications.

4.2 Effects of HIIT on Different Domains of Executive Function

4.2.1 Overview of HIIT

HIIT is characterized by short-duration, high-intensity exercise performed at approximately 85%–95% of heart rate peak (HR peak). It involves short burst of vigorous exercise (20–30 seconds to several minutes) alternated with recovery periods of low-intensity exercise or complete passive rest (1–2 minutes), typically with a specified number of sets and multiple cycles (Batacan et al., 2017). HIIT sessions generally last between 10 and 30 minutes, yet its benefits can equal those of MICT and sometimes results in superior advantages (Wewege et al., 2017). Furthermore, HIIT offers high flexibility, and can include various modalities such as running, cycling, swimming, resistance training, or circuit-style workouts, and can be adjusted according to individual fitness levels. Due to its efficiency and adaptability, HIIT has received widespread attention in fitness and exercise science fields in recent years.

Common HIIT formats include protocols such as Tabata training and the Wingate test. Tabata training, proposed by Japanese scientist Izumi Tabata, consists of 20 seconds of extremely high-intensity exercise (e.g., all-out sprinting) alternated with 10 seconds of rest, repeated for 8 cycles, with a total duration of only 4 minutes. Tabata training has been proven to significantly improve both aerobic and anaerobic capacity (Tabata et al., 1996). Additionally, the Wingate test is a classic laboratory HIIT protocol, typically comprising 30-second all-out sprints with 4-minute rest periods, repeated for 4–6 sets, primarily used to assess changes in anaerobic capacity. These training protocols are all designed based on the alternation between high-intensity exercise and intermittent recovery, but their specific exercise parameters (e.g., exercise duration, intensity, and work-to-rest ratio) can be adjusted according to individual needs and goals (Kilpatrick et al., 2014). The diversity and adaptability of HIIT enable it to accommodate the needs of different populations, benefiting everyone from athletes to sedentary individuals. In summary, HIIT, as an efficient and highly flexible training modality, is being widely applied across different populations and has been extensively researched.

4.2.2 HIIT and Executive Function

Executive function, as an integrated system of higher-order cognitive control, encompasses multiple distinct core domains. Research indicates that HIIT positively influences executive function, though its effects on various domains of executive function show some differences. The following sections will examine the impact of HIIT on inhibitory control, working memory, and cognitive flexibility, the three core domains of executive function.

Inhibitory control refers to an individual's ability to suppress interfering stimuli or automatic responses (Diamond, 2013, 2020). A systematic review indicated that acute HIIT effectively enhances inhibitory abilities in children, adolescents, and young adults. Specifically, individuals demonstrated better reaction times and accuracy on cognitive tasks following HIIT training, indicating temporary enhancement in their ability to inhibit interfering information (Hsieh et al., 2021). Additionally, long-term HIIT intervention studies similarly support its positive impact on inhibitory control. Specifically, Hsieh et al. (2021) also noted that long-term HIIT training effectively improves inhibitory control in children. In college students, 12 weeks of twice-weekly HIIT-produced significant gains in inhibitory control, with effects emerging as early as 6 weeks (Wang et al., 2023). These studies suggest both transient and cumulative benefits of HIIT for inhibitory control.

Working memory involves the short-term maintenance and manipulation of information, forming the foundation for complex cognitive tasks (Diamond,

2013, 2020). Working memory improvements following HIIT are most evident in younger populations. Acute bouts of cycling-based HIIT enhance working memory in young adults (Gökçe et al., 2024), although age may moderate these effects. In middle-aged adults, high-intensity circuit training has produced mixed results, with some studies indicating no benefit or even temporary declines (Gmiat et al., 2017). Concerning the long-term effects of HIIT on working memory, systematic reviews indicate that HIIT interventions can benefit working memory, particularly in children (Hsieh et al., 2021). Additionally, a study on adolescents showed that six weeks of HIIT training improved their working memory (Moreau et al., 2017). However, current research examining the long-term effects of HIIT on working memory primarily focuses on children and adolescents, and more longitudinal data are needed to determine the effects in older adults.

Cognitive flexibility is a more complex aspect of executive function, requiring the ability to switch flexibly between different tasks or mental states (Diamond, 2013, 2020). Evidence for the effects of HIIT on cognitive flexibility is more variable. Acute HIIT improves task-switching and adaptability in young adults, particularly with protocols like sprint-based or boxing-style workouts (Kujach et al., 2019; Solianik et al., 2021). However, not all studies replicate these findings. For example, Schwarck et al. (2019) found no significant gains in executive function (and cognitive flexibility) after a single session of HIIT. In contrast, older adults and stroke survivors show more robust responses to long-term HIIT, with lasting improvements in cognitive flexibility reported up to 12 months post-intervention. A randomized controlled trial involving older adults found that after 6 weeks of HIIT, participants' cognitive flexibility significantly improved, while no such benefits were observed in moderate-intensity aerobic and resistance training groups (Mekari et al., 2020). Furthermore, Gjellesvik et al. (2021) examined the impact of 8 weeks of HIIT among stroke survivors, and found HIIT training to significantly improve cognitive flexibility, which persisted for 12 months, supporting the potential for longer term neuroadaptive changes. These findings suggest that cognitive flexibility may be more responsive to HIIT in populations with baseline deficits. In general, while acute HIIT may yield mixed outcomes in younger populations, its potential to elicit meaningful and enduring improvements in cognitive flexibility appears especially promising for older adults and those with neurological impairments.

4.2.3 Summary

Based on the collective evidence presented above, HIIT positively impacts all three EF domains, but the magnitude and consistency of effects differ. For inhibitory control, both acute and long-term HIIT interventions consistently showed improvements across multiple age groups, with effects becoming noticeable after six weeks of training. Working memory benefits are largely observed in youth and developing populations, while older adults remain understudied. In terms of cognitive flexibility, research showed the most variable responses to HIIT interventions. Acute HIIT appeared beneficial for young adults, while long-term benefits were inconsistent across populations. Notable improvements were observed in older adults and stroke patients, with benefits persisting up to 12 months, yet studies with adolescents and younger adults showed minimal effects. Thus, cognitive flexibility appears sensitive to population-specific factors such as age and clinical status. In summary, HIIT most consistently improved inhibitory control, benefited working memory primarily in developing populations, and enhanced cognitive flexibility mainly in older adults and specific clinical populations. These findings support the tailoring of HIIT interventions based on cognitive targets and individual characteristics.

4.3 HIIT Exercise Parameter Settings

4.3.1 Exercise Frequency and Type

Training frequency is a central factor in determining HIIT's impact on executive function. For example, Wang et al. (2023) found that college students completing two HIIT sessions per week over 12 weeks exhibited greater improvements in inhibitory control, working memory, and cognitive flexibility than those training once weekly. This finding provides preliminary evidence of a dose–response effect for HIIT training frequency, suggesting that moderately increasing training frequency may enhance its effects on executive function. Although many studies have adopted a three-times per-week model, a clear dose–response relationship has yet to be established through a systematic meta-analysis. Nonetheless, current findings suggest that a frequency of at least two sessions per week may be a critical threshold for eliciting executive function benefits.

HIIT can be implemented through a range of exercise types, provided the target intensity is achieved. In existing literature, besides common HIIT protocols, including Tabata training (Tabata et al., 1996) and the Wingate test (Burgomaster et al., 2008), aerobic-based formats, such as stationary cycling, shuttle runs, and sprint intervals, are most commonly used (Kao et al., 2017; Kujach et al., 2019; Moreau et al., 2017). Resistance-based HIIT, incorporating movements like push-ups, planks, and squats, has also demonstrated efficacy (Gmiat et al., 2017). Some interventions combine aerobic and resistance elements into circuit-style protocols (Ludyga et al., 2019). Importantly, HIIT modality can be tailored to population-specific needs. For example, game-based HIIT has proven to be effective for children with attention deficit hyperactivity disorder (ADHD) (Sun et al., 2022; Sun et al., 2024). Additionally, aquatic HIIT has reduced joint stress in older adults without compromising cognitive outcomes (Kwok et al., 2024). In summary, provided that exercise intensity reaches target heart rate zones, HIIT training can be adjusted and modified to offer considerable flexibility while maintaining its efficacy.

4.3.2 Session Duration and Program Length

Session duration, defined as the actual time spent in high-intensity exercise, excluding rest periods or low-intensity recovery exercise (Sabag et al., 2022), is a key factor in overall exercise volume. Generally, low exercise volume is defined as session lengths lasting less than 15 minutes, while high exercise volume refers to those lasting longer than 15 minutes. While no direct comparisons of different session lengths have been conducted, systematic reviews indicate that sessions lasting 11–30 minutes tend to yield positive cognitive effects (Ai et al., 2021). This duration strikes a balance between sufficient physiological stimulation and manageable training volume.

Additionally, program length also appears to influence cognitive outcomes. Specifically, Liu et al. (2024) reported that HIIT interventions improved executive function across durations, but gains in processing speed were only observed after interventions lasting more than eight weeks. These findings suggest a possible threshold for cumulative neural adaptations and underscore the value of sustained engagement. Thus, for optimal cognitive outcomes, interventions should be conducted for at least eight weeks, although meaningful effects may emerge earlier for certain EF domains.

4.3.3 Work-to-Recovery Ratio

A unique aspect of HIIT is the manipulation of the work-to-recovery time ratio. This ratio can significantly affect physiological stress and cognitive outcomes. For instance, shorter rest intervals (e.g., a 3:1 work-to-recovery ratio) enhanced VO_2max compared with a 2:1 ratio among collegiate judo athletes (Zhang et al., 2024). Smilios et al. (2018) similarly indicated that with fixed exercise times, shorter recovery periods increase cardiovascular and metabolic stress, and further activate anaerobic glycolysis, suggesting athletes can use this approach to elicit a greater overall physiological challenge. Regarding cognitive effects, Ai et al. (2021) observed positive effects across various ratios. However, it should be noted that this conclusion was based on calculating the percentage of positive results rather than direct statistical testing, so caution is warranted when interpreting these findings. Zhao et al. (2022) found that a 1:1 ratio most effectively elevated BDNF levels in young adults, which may mediate cognitive enhancement. Ludyga et al. (2019) similarly reported superior improvements in inhibitory control among children who engaged in 1:1 HIIT protocols compared with those with longer recovery intervals. These results tentatively support a 1:1 ratio as optimal for cognitive benefit, although more direct comparisons are needed.

4.3.4 Summary

Optimal HIIT protocols for executive function likely involve a combination of key parameters. Training at least twice weekly, using sessions of 11–30 minutes in duration, sustained over a minimum of 8 weeks, and employing a 1:1 work-to-recovery ratio may yield the greatest cognitive benefits. The modality of HIIT should be adapted to suit specific populations and individual preferences to ensure safety, accessibility, and adherence. These parameter settings provide a flexible yet evidence-informed framework for designing HIIT programs aimed at enhancing executive function.

4.4 Differences in HIIT Effects on Executive Function Across Populations

4.4.1 Healthy Populations

Due to its efficiency and broad adaptability, HIIT has been widely investigated in healthy individuals across the lifespan. In young children, acute HIIT interventions have repeatedly demonstrated short-term enhancements in inhibitory control (Cooper et al., 2016; Lambrick et al., 2016; Ludyga et al., 2019). These improvements likely reflect transient gains in attentional focus and response suppression following elevated arousal and neurochemical release. However, effects on other EF domains such as working memory and cognitive flexibility remain less studied in this age group. For adolescents, both acute and chronic HIIT interventions suggest benefits primarily for inhibitory control and working memory. Programs ranging from four to eight weeks have produced significant improvements, particularly when implemented during school hours or as part of structured physical education (Moreau et al., 2017; Tottori et al., 2019). Cognitive flexibility, however, has not consistently improved in this population, with Costigan et al. (2016) reporting no significant changes following an eight-week intervention.

In young adults, acute HIIT has shown consistent effects on inhibitory control and some benefits for cognitive flexibility depending on task complexity and timing post-exercise (Hashimoto et al., 2018; Kujach et al., 2020). Yet, findings are not uniform: (Schwarck et al., 2019) observed no measurable executive function changes following a single HIIT session. Chronic HIIT interventions in this age group are generally associated with positive cognitive effects, although outcomes vary based on baseline fitness, training parameters, and cognitive assessment tools. Notably, few studies directly compare HIIT with other forms of exercise in this demographic.

In middle-aged and older adults, research remains limited but promising. Connolly et al. (2017) observed improvements in working memory after 12 weeks of HIIT in middle-aged adults, indicating potential for protective cognitive effects. Among older adults, Coetsee and Terblanche (2017) reported no significant changes in inhibitory control after 16 weeks of training, suggesting that age-related physiological changes or task sensitivity may moderate responsiveness. Overall, more data are needed to clarify age-related differences, particularly in acute response patterns and long-term neural adaptations.

In summary, HIIT appears most effective for enhancing inhibitory control across all healthy age groups. Working memory benefits are more pronounced in younger individuals, and cognitive flexibility may require longer interventions or target populations with greater neurocognitive plasticity. These findings point to the importance of developmentally tailored HIIT protocols and further investigation into measurement sensitivity and intervention design.

4.4.2 Clinical Populations

The benefits of HIIT are not limited to healthy individuals; a growing body of research has explored its cognitive effects in clinical populations. In individuals with neurodevelopmental conditions, such as ADHD, both acute and chronic HIIT have been shown to enhance executive function. For instance, LaCount et al. (2022) observed improvements in cognitive performance following a single HIIT session in young adults with ADHD. Game-based HIIT formats have been particularly effective in children, improving inhibitory control while also boosting engagement and compliance (Sun et al., 2024). Cancer-related cognitive impairment (CRCI) is another area where HIIT shows promise. Northey et al. (2019) found that a 12-week HIIT intervention improved executive function in breast cancer survivors undergoing or recovering from treatment. These findings are especially relevant given the lack of non-pharmacological options for managing CRCI and the physiological challenges many cancer patients face. Considering that cancer treatments such as chemotherapy may lead to cognitive decline, HIIT, as a safe and effective intervention approach, provides a new option for enhancing executive function during cancer treatment.

HIIT has also demonstrated efficacy in individuals recovering from cerebrovascular diseases. Gjellesvik et al. (2021) reported significant gains in cognitive flexibility after an eight-week HIIT intervention, with effects persisting for up to one year. These lasting improvements suggest the potential for neuroplastic changes, which may be critical for cognitive recovery post-stroke. In patients with multiple sclerosis (MS), even brief HIIT programs appear to provide cognitive benefits. Zimmer et al. (2017) showed that even a three-week protocol-led measurable improvements in executive function. Considering the fatigue and mobility limitations common in MS, HIIT's efficiency and adaptability may make it particularly well suited for this group.

Collectively, these findings indicate that HIIT can be a viable and effective intervention for enhancing executive function in clinical populations. These findings not only expand the application scope of HIIT but also provide new evidence supporting non-pharmacological treatments for executive function disorders. Tailoring protocols to meet physical and cognitive needs of patients, by modifying intensity or session format, can help maximize both safety and impact. Future research should explore long-term cognitive outcomes and examine how HIIT interacts with concurrent treatments or rehabilitation strategies.

4.4.3 Summary

HIIT demonstrates broad applicability across age groups and clinical populations, though effects vary by executive function domain and individual characteristics. In healthy populations, inhibitory control consistently benefits from HIIT, while working memory and cognitive flexibility exhibit age-dependent responsiveness. In clinical populations, tailored HIIT interventions have improved executive function in individuals with ADHD, cancer, stroke, and MS. These results support HIIT as a flexible and efficient strategy to promote cognitive health. However, to optimize effectiveness, future research should continue refining exercise protocols, expand trials in underrepresented groups, and explore neurophysiological mechanisms underlying observed behavioral changes.

4.5 Conclusion

This chapter synthesized current evidence on the cognitive effects of HIIT, with a particular focus on executive function and its three core domains: inhibitory control, working memory, and cognitive flexibility. Our review indicates that HIIT, as a time-efficient and adaptable exercise modality, consistently improves inhibitory control and shows promising but more variable effects on working memory, and demonstrates potential to enhance cognitive flexibility, especially in older adults and clinical populations.

The cognitive benefits of HIIT appear to be influenced by multiple factors, including training frequency, session duration, intervention length, and work-to-recovery ratios. Evidence supports that training at least twice per week, for 11–30 minutes per session, over a period of at least eight weeks, using a 1:1 work-to-recovery ratio, may provide optimal conditions for cognitive enhancement. While no universal protocol applies across all contexts, the flexibility of HIIT allows for customization based on individual and group needs. Interventions ranging from game-based formats for children with ADHD to aquatic protocols for older adults exemplify this adaptability.

Physiological and neurological mechanisms help explain the observed benefits of HIIT. Enhancements in cardiorespiratory fitness and vascular function increase cerebral perfusion and nutrient delivery, while elevated levels of neurotrophic factors like BDNF support neural plasticity and synaptic function. These adaptations likely converge in executive function-related brain regions, such as the prefrontal cortex, facilitating improvements in cognitive control and processing efficiency. However, further studies employing neuroimaging and electrophysiological techniques are necessary to confirm these pathways and quantify their contribution.

The effects of HIIT also vary across populations. In healthy individuals, inhibitory control appears to benefit most consistently, while working memory improvements are more evident in children and adolescents, and cognitive flexibility gains are more pronounced in older adults. Clinical populations, including individuals with ADHD, cancer, stroke, and MS, have shown measurable improvements in executive function following appropriately tailored HIIT interventions. These findings underscore the importance of precision in exercise prescription, ensuring that HIIT protocols align with the cognitive, physical, and motivational needs of the target population.

Despite encouraging findings, several research gaps remain. First, the heterogeneity in study designs, EF measurement tools, and exercise protocols limits direct comparisons and generalizability. Second, few studies have examined long-term maintenance of cognitive benefits or conducted head-to-head comparisons between HIIT and other exercise modalities. Third, more research is needed on sex differences, individual variability in responsiveness, and potential synergistic effects of combining HIIT with cognitive training or behavioral interventions. Finally, greater use of mechanistic tools such as neuroimaging, heart rate variability, and blood biomarkers could help elucidate how HIIT translates into cognitive gains.

In conclusion, HIIT offers a promising, scalable, and efficient strategy for promoting executive function across a broad spectrum of individuals. As global aging and cognitive impairment become increasingly pressing public health concerns, HIIT may represent a valuable tool in the prevention and management of cognitive decline. Continued research should aim to refine protocols, expand applicability to diverse populations, and bridge the gap between physiological mechanisms and cognitive outcomes. With thoughtful application and ongoing investigation, HIIT could become a cornerstone of evidence-based interventions for cognitive health in the years to come.

References

Ahmadi, S., Bélanger, M., O'Brien, M. W., Registe, P. P. W., Dupuy, O., & Mekari, S. (2025). Acute effects of high-intensity interval training and moderate-intensity continuous training on executive functions in healthy older adults. *Scientific Reports*, *15*(1), 6749. https://doi.org/10.1038/s41598-025-91833-z

Ai, J. Y., Chen, F. T., Hsieh, S. S., Kao, S. C., Chen, A. G., Hung, T. M., & Chang, Y. K. (2021). The effect of acute high-intensity interval training on executive function: A systematic review. *International Journal of Environmental Research and Public Health*, *18*(7), 3593. https://doi.org/10.3390/ijerph18073593

Batacan, R. B., Duncan, M. J., Dalbo, V. J., Tucker, P. S., & Fenning, A. S. (2017). Effects of high-intensity interval training on cardiometabolic health: A systematic review and meta-analysis of intervention studies. *British Journal of Sports Medicine*, *51*(6), 494–503. https://doi.org/10.1136/bjsports-2015-095841

Burgomaster, K. A., Howarth, K. R., Phillips, S. M., Rakobowchuk, M., Macdonald, M. J., McGee, S. L., & Gibala, M. J. (2008). Similar metabolic adaptations during exercise after low volume sprint interval and traditional endurance training in humans. *The Journal of Physiology*, *586*(1), 151–160. https://doi.org/10.1113/jphysiol.2007.142109

Cadenas-Sanchez, C., Fernandez-Rodriguez, R., Martinez-Vizcaino, V., de los Reyes Gonzalez, N., Lavie, C. J., Galán-Mercant, A., & Jimenez-Pavon, D. (2024). A systematic review and cluster analysis approach of 103 studies of high-intensity interval training on cardiorespiratory fitness. *European Journal of Preventive Cardiology*, *31*(4), 400–411. https://doi.org/10.1093/eurjpc/zwad309

Coetsee, C., & Terblanche, E. (2017). The effect of three different exercise training modalities on cognitive and physical function in a healthy older population. *European Review of Aging and Physical Activity*, *14*, 13. https://doi.org/10.1186/s11556-017-0183-5

Connolly, L. J., Bailey, S. J., Krustrup, P., Fulford, J., Smietanka, C., & Jones, A. M. (2017). Effects of self-paced interval and continuous training on health markers in women. *European Journal of Applied Physiology*, *117*, 2281–2293.

Cooper, S. B., Bandelow, S., Nute, M. L., Dring, K. J., Stannard, R. L., Morris, J. G., & Nevill, M. E. (2016). Sprint-based exercise and cognitive function in adolescents. *Preventive Medicine Reports*, *4*, 155–161. https://doi.org/10.1016/j.pmedr.2016.06.004

Costigan, S. A., Eather, N., Plotnikoff, R. C., Hillman, C. H., & Lubans, D. R. (2016). High-intensity interval training for cognitive and mental health in adolescents. *Medicine & Science in Sports & Exercise*, *48*(10), 1985–1993. https://doi.org/10.1249/MSS.0000000000000993

Diamond, A. (2013). Executive functions. *Annual Review of Psychology*, *64*(1), 135–168.

Diamond, A. (2020). Executive functions. In Anne Gallagher, Christine Bulteau, David Cohen, & Jacques L. Michaud (eds.), *Handbook of clinical neurology* (Vol. 173, pp. 225–240). Elsevier.

Gjellesvik, T. I., Becker, F., Tjønna, A. E., Indredavik, B., Lundgaard, E., Solbakken, H., Brurok, B., Tørhaug, T., Lydersen, S., & Askim, T. (2021). Effects of high-intensity interval training after stroke (the HIIT stroke study) on physical and cognitive function: A multicenter randomized controlled trial. *Archives of Physical Medicine and Rehabilitation*, *102*(9), 1683–1691.

Gmiat, A., Micielska, K., Kozłowska, M., Flis, D. J., Smaruj, M., Kujach, S., Jaworska, J., Lipińska, P., & Ziemann, E. (2017). The impact of a single bout of high intensity circuit training on myokines' concentrations and cognitive functions in women of different age. *Physiology & Behavior*, *179*, 290–297. https://doi.org/10.1016/j.physbeh.2017.07.004

Gökçe, E., Adıgüzel, E., Koçak, Ö. K., Kılınç, H., Langeard, A., Boran, E., & Cengiz, B. (2024). Impact of acute high-intensity interval training on cortical excitability, M1-related cognitive functions, and myokines: A randomized crossover study. *Neuroscience*, *551*, 290–298. https://doi.org/10.1016/j.neuroscience.2024.05.032

Hashimoto, T., Tsukamoto, H., Takenaka, S., Olesen, N. D., Petersen, L. G., Sørensen, H., Nielsen, H. B., Secher, N. H., & Ogoh, S. (2018). Maintained exercise-enhanced brain executive function related to cerebral lactate metabolism in men. *The FASEB Journal*, *32*(3), 1417–1427. https://doi.org/10.1096/fj.201700381RR

Hsieh, S. S., Chueh, T. Y., Huang, C. J., Kao, S. C., Hillman, C., Chang, Y. K., & Hung, T. M. (2021). Systematic review of the acute and chronic effects of high-intensity interval training on executive function across the lifespan. *Journal of Sports Sciences, 39*(1), 10–22. https://doi.org/10.1080/02640414.2020.1803630

Huang, H., Jin, Z., He, C., Guo, S., Zhang, Y., & Quan, M. (2023). Chronic exercise for core symptoms and executive functions in ADHD: A meta-analysis. *Pediatrics*, *151*(1), e2022057745. https://doi.org/10.1542/peds.2022-057745

Kao, S. C., Drollette, E. S., Ritondale, J. P., Khan, N., & Hillman, C. H. (2018). The acute effects of high-intensity interval training and moderate-intensity continuous exercise on declarative memory and inhibitory control. *Psychology of Sport and Exercise*, *38*, 90–199. https://doi.org/10.1016/j.psychsport.2018.05.011

Kao, S. C., Westfall, D. R., Soneson, J., Gurd, B., & Hillman, C. H. (2017). Comparison of the acute effects of high-intensity interval training and continuous aerobic walking on inhibitory control. *Psychophysiology*, *54*(9), 1335–1345. https://doi.org/10.1111/psyp.12889

Kilpatrick, M. W., Jung, M. E., & Little, J. P. (2014). High-intensity interval training: A review of physiological and psychological responses. *ACSM's Health & Fitness Journal*, *18*(5), 11–16. https://doi.org/10.1249/FIT.0000000000000067

Kujach, S., Olek, R. A., Byun, K., Suwabe, K., Sitek, E. J., Ziemann, E., Laskowski, R., & Soya, H. (2019). Acute sprint interval exercise increases both cognitive functions and peripheral neurotrophic factors in humans: The possible involvement of lactate. *Frontiers in Neuroscience*, *13*, 1455. https://doi.org/10.3389/fnins.2019.01455

Kujach, S., Olek, R. A., Byun, K., Suwabe, K., Sitek, E. J., Ziemann, E., Laskowski, R., & Soya, H. (2020). Acute sprint interval exercise increases both cognitive functions and peripheral neurotrophic factors in humans: The possible involvement of lactate. *Frontiers in Neuroscience*, *13*, 1455. https://doi.org/10.3389/fnins.2019.01455

Kwok, M. M., Ng, S. S., Myers, J., & So, B. C. (2024). Aquatic high-intensity interval deep water running influence on cardiometabolic health and cognitive psychological responses in women. *Medicine and Science in Sports and Exercise*, *56*(11), 2203–2210. https://doi.org/10.1249/MSS.0000000000003500

LaCount, P. A., Hartung, C. M., Vasko, J. M., Serrano, J. W., Wright, H. A., & Smith, D. T. (2022). Acute effects of physical exercise on cognitive and psychological functioning in college students with Attention-Deficit/Hyperactivity Disorder. *Mental Health and Physical Activity*, *22*, 100443. https://doi.org/10.1016/j.mhpa.2022.100443

Lambrick, D., Stoner, L., Grigg, R., & Faulkner, J. (2016). Effects of continuous and intermittent exercise on executive function in children aged 8–10 years. *Psychophysiology*, *53*(9), 1335–1342. https://doi.org/10.1111/psyp.12688

Laursen, P. B., & Jenkins, D. G. (2002). The scientific basis for high-intensity interval training: Optimising training programmes and maximising performance in highly trained endurance athletes. *Sports Medicine*, *32*(1), 53–73. https://doi.org/10.2165/00007256-200232010-00003

Liang, X., Li, R., Wong, S. H., Sum, R. K., Wang, P., Yang, B., & Sit, C. H. (2022). The effects of exercise interventions on executive functions in children and adolescents with autism spectrum disorder: A systematic review and meta-analysis. *Sports Medicine*, *52*(1), 75–88. https://doi.org/10.1007/s40279-021-01545-3

Liang, X., Qiu, H., Wang, P., & Sit, C. H. P. (2022). The impacts of a combined exercise on executive function in children with ADHD: A randomized controlled trial. *Scandinavian Journal of Medicine & Science in Sports*, *32*(8), 1297–1312. https://doi.org/https://doi.org/10.1111/sms.14192

Liu, K., Zhao, W., Li, C., Tian, Y., Wang, L., Zhong, J., Yan, X., Wang, Y., Wang, L., & Wang, H. (2024). The effects of high-intensity interval training on cognitive performance: A systematic review and meta-analysis. *Scientific Reports*, *14*(1), 32082. https://doi.org/10.1038/s41598-024-83802-9

Ludyga, S., Pühse, U., Lucchi, S., Marti, J., & Gerber, M. (2019). Immediate and sustained effects of intermittent exercise on inhibitory control and task-related heart rate variability in adolescents. *Journal of Science and Medicine in Sport*, *22*(1), 96–100. https://doi.org/10.1016/j.jsams.2018.05.027

Mekari, S., Neyedli, H. F., Fraser, S., O'Brien, M. W., Martins, R., Evans, K., Earle, M., Aucoin, R., Chiekwe, J., Hollohan, Q., Kimmerly, D. S., & Dupuy, O. (2020). High-intensity interval training improves cognitive flexibility in older adults. *Brain Sciences*, *10*(11), 796. https://doi.org/10.3390/brainsci10110796

Miyake, A., Friedman, N. P., Emerson, M. J., Witzki, A. H., Howerter, A., & Wager, T. D. (2000). The unity and diversity of executive functions and their contributions to complex "Frontal Lobe" tasks: A latent variable analysis. *Cognitive Psychology*, *41*(1), 49–100. https://doi.org/10.1006/cogp.1999.0734

Moreau, D., Kirk, I. J., & Waldie, K. E. (2017). High-intensity training enhances executive function in children in a randomized, placebo-controlled trial. *eLife*, *6*, e25062. https://doi.org/10.7554/eLife.25062

Northey, J. M., Pumpa, K. L., Quinlan, C., Ikin, A., Toohey, K., Smee, D. J., & Rattray, B. (2019). Cognition in breast cancer survivors: A pilot study of interval and continuous exercise. *Journal of Science and Medicine in Sport*, *22*(5), 580–585. https://doi.org/https://doi.org/10.1016/j.jsams.2018.11.026

Rajizadeh, M. A., Khoramipour, K., Joukar, S., Darvishzadeh-Mahani, F., Iranpour, M., Bejeshk, M. A., & Zaboli, M. D. (2024). Lung molecular and histological changes in type 2 diabetic rats and its improvement by high-intensity interval training. *BMC Pulmonary Medicine*, *24*(1), 37. https://doi.org/10.1186/s12890-024-02840-1

Sabag, A., Barr, L., Armour, M., Armstrong, A., Baker, C. J., Twigg, S. M., Chang, D., Hackett, D. A., Keating, S. E., & George, J. (2022). The effect of high-intensity interval training vs moderate-intensity continuous training on liver fat: A systematic review and meta-analysis. *The Journal of Clinical Endocrinology & Metabolism*, *107*(3), 862–881. https://doi.org/10.1210/clinem/dgab795

Schäfer, J., Reuter, T., Leuchter, M., & Karbach, J. (2024). Executive functions and problem-solving—The contribution of inhibition, working memory, and cognitive flexibility to science problem-solving performance in elementary school students. *Journal of Experimental Child Psychology*, *244*, 105962. https://doi.org/10.1016/j.jecp.2024.105962

Schwarck, S., Schmicker, M., Dordevic, M., Rehfeld, K., Müller, N., & Müller, P. (2019). Inter-individual differences in cognitive response to a single bout of physical exercise-A randomized controlled cross-over study. *Journal of Clinical Medicine*, *8*(8), 1101. https://doi.org/10.3390/jcm8081101

Smilios, I., Myrkos, A., Zafeiridis, A., Toubekis, A., Spassis, A., & Tokmakidis, S. P. (2018). The effects of recovery duration during high-intensity interval exercise on time spent at high rates of oxygen consumption, oxygen kinetics, and blood lactate. *The Journal of Strength & Conditioning Research*, *32*(8), 2183–2189. https://doi.org/10.1519/jsc.0000000000001904

Solianik, R., Bružas, V., Mockus, P., Vadopalas, K., & Streckis, V. (2021). Acute effects of high-intensity interval training on cognition and retinal microcirculation in experienced amateur boxers. *The Journal of Sports Medicine and Physical Fitness*, *61*(6), 867–873. https://doi.org/10.23736/s0022-4707.20.11352-5

Sugimoto, T., Suga, T., Tomoo, K., Dora, K., Mok, E., Tsukamoto, H., Takada, S., Hashimoto, T., & Isaka, T. (2021). Blood flow restriction improves executive function after walking. *Medicine & Science in Sports & Exercise*, *53*(1), 131–138. https://doi.org/10.1249/mss.0000000000002446

Sun, F., Chow, G. C. C., Yu, C. C. W., Ho, Y. F., Liu, D., Wong, S. H. S., Siu, P. M. F., Cooper, S. B., & Jenkins, D. (2022). Effect of game-based high-intensity interval training program on the executive function of children with ADHD: Protocol of a randomized controlled trial. *PLoS One*, *17*(7), e0272121. https://doi.org/10.1371/journal.pone.0272121

Sun, F., Fang, Y., Ho, Y. F., Chow, G. C.-C., Yang, Y., Huang, K., Yu, C. C.-W., Liu, D., Wong, S. H.-S., & Siu, P. M.-F. (2024). Effectiveness of a game-based high-intensity interval training on executive function and other health indicators of children with

ADHD: A three-arm partially-blinded randomized controlled trial. *Journal of Exercise Science & Fitness*, *22*(4), 408–416. https://doi.org/10.1016/j.jesf.2024.09.001

Sung, M. C., Ku, B., Leung, W., & MacDonald, M. (2022). The effect of physical activity interventions on executive function among people with neurodevelopmental disorders: A meta-analysis. *Journal of Autism and Developmental Disorders*, *52*(3), 1030–1050. https://doi.org/10.1007/s10803-021-05009-5

Tabata, I., Nishimura, K., Kouzaki, M., Hirai, Y., Ogita, F., Miyachi, M., & Yamamoto, K. (1996). Effects of moderate-intensity endurance and high-intensity intermittent training on anaerobic capacity and VO~ 2~ m~ a~ x. *Medicine and Science in Sports and Exercise*, *28*, 1327–1330.

Tottori, N., Morita, N., Ueta, K., & Fujita, S. (2019). Effects of high intensity interval training on executive function in children aged 8–12 years. *International Journal of Environmental Research and Public Health*, *16*(21), 4127. https://doi.org/10.3390/ijerph16214127

Wang, X., Liu, Z., Zhang, H., & Ji, C. (2023). Effects of high-intensity interval training on executive functions in college students: Evidence from different doses. *Brain Sciences*, *13*(4), 571. https://www.mdpi.com/2076-3425/13/4/571

Wewege, M., Van Den Berg, R., Ward, R., & Keech, A. (2017). The effects of high-intensity interval training vs. moderate-intensity continuous training on body composition in overweight and obese adults: A systematic review and meta-analysis. *Obesity Reviews*, *18*(6), 635–646. https://doi.org/10.1111/obr.12532

Ye, M., Song, T., Xia, H., Hou, Y., & Chen, A. (2024). Effects of aerobic exercise on executive function of healthy middle-aged and older adults: A systematic review and meta-analysis. *International Journal of Nursing Studies*, *160*, 104912. https://doi.org/10.1016/j.ijnurstu.2024.104912

Zhang, Z., Xie, L., Ji, H., Chen, L., Gao, C., He, J., Lu, M., Yang, Q., Sun, J., & Li, D. (2024). Effects of different work-to-rest ratios of high-intensity interval training on physical performance and physiological responses in male college judo athletes. *Journal of Exercise Science & Fitness*, *22*(3), 245–253. https://doi.org/https://doi.org/10.1016/j.jesf.2024.03.009

Zhao, K., Hu, Z., Wang, T., Tian, L., Wang, M., Liu, R., Zuo, C., & Jihua, W. (2022). Acute effects of two different work-to-rest ratio of high-intensity interval training on brain-derived neurotrophic factor in untrained young men. *Frontiers in Physiology*, *13*, 988773. https://doi.org/10.3389/fphys.2022.988773

Zimmer, P., Bloch, W., Schenk, A., Oberste, M., Riedel, S., Kool, J., Langdon, D., Dalgas, U., Kesselring, J., & Bansi, J. (2017). High-intensity interval exercise improves cognitive performance and reduces matrix metalloproteinases-2 serum levels in persons with multiple sclerosis: A randomized controlled trial. *Multiple Sclerosis Journal*, *24*(12), 1635–1644. https://doi.org/10.1177/1352458517728342

PART 3

Exercise and Self-Experiences

5

PHYSICAL ACTIVITY AND BODY IMAGE

Christy Greenleaf, Maria Fernanda Laus, and Caitlyn Hauff

5.1 Preface

Body image has long been a research topic of interest within sport and exercise psychology, in part because the body is the vehicle through which one engages in and experiences physical activity. The scientific study of the body image–physical activity relationship provides critical insights into individual and societal well-being, informs interventions, and drives health initiatives. Understanding this relationship allows researchers and professionals to address the complex interactions between body image and physical activity, leading to better physical and mental health outcomes for individuals and communities. The social significance of the associations between body image and physical activity is also important because it influences various aspects of individual and public health, from physical and emotional well-being to physical fitness and overall quality of life. By studying this relationship, individuals, healthcare professionals, and policymakers can develop strategies and interventions that promote healthier body image perceptions and increased participation in physical activity, ultimately leading to a happier and healthier society.

Body image is a multidimensional construct that includes cognitive, affective, perceptual, and behavioral components related to one's bodily appearance and function with positive and negative facets (Cash & Smolak, 2011). The cognitive dimension of body image refers to a person's thoughts and beliefs about their body (Cash, 2012), for instance, internalization of body ideals, psychological investment in appearance, and body satisfaction. Affective body image is a person's emotions and feelings about their body. Social physique anxiety is a form of affective body image (Leary, 1992). Cognitive and affective body image are the most common dimensions assessed in research. Perceptual body image refers to the mental

DOI: 10.4324/9781003517474-8

representation of one's bodily appearance and function and is often studied by exploring discrepancies between a person's perceived and actual characteristics of the body (Cash & Smolak, 2011; Cash et al., 1991). The behavioral dimension of body image refers to the actions a person takes directed toward their body, such as appearance management, and body surveillance (Fredrickson & Roberts, 1997; Holland & Tiggemann, 2016). Behavioral body image is shaped by the cognitive, affective, and perceptual dimensions. All four dimensions of body image are associated with physical activity as antecedents, correlates, and consequences.

To date, negative body image, such as body dissatisfaction and social physique anxiety, has been much of the focus; however, more recently, researchers have begun studying positive body image, such as body appreciation and body functionality (Tylka & Wood-Barcalow, 2015; Tylka, 2018). Tylka and Wood-Barcalow (2015), in their seminal conceptualization of positive body image, suggest that it includes body appreciation, body acceptance and love, broad conceptualizations of beauty, adaptive investments in appearance, inner positivity, and using a body-protective perspective to filter information. It is important to highlight, however, that positive body image is not on the same spectrum as negative body image, nor should it be represented as low levels of negative body image (Tylka & Wood-Barcalow, 2015). Indeed, Tylka and colleagues frequently advocate that positive body image must be acknowledged as more than just not having negative features. In this sense, interventions aimed at reducing negative body image will not result in simultaneous enhancements in positive body image. Thus, as a multifaceted construct, positive body image offers a unique way of approaching the study of body image and physical activity, distinct from a more traditional emphasis on negative body image. Indeed, both positive and negative aspects of body image are associated with physical activity (Sabiston et al., 2019).

Research on body image and physical activity has generally been atheoretical in nature, which is important to be mindful of as we review and synthesize the literature. In Sabiston et al.'s (2019) scoping review, over 65% of studies failed to report a theoretical rationale or basis. In studies reporting a theoretical foundation, Sociocultural Theory (Thompson et al., 1999), Objectification Theory (Fredrickson & Roberts, 1997), and Self-Determination Theory (Deci & Ryan, 2001, 2002) were the most frequently used frameworks. Social Cognitive Theory (Bandura, 1991), the Exercise and Self-Esteem Model (EXSEM, Sonstroem, Harlow, & Josephs, 1994; Sonstroem & Morgan, 1989), and Social Comparison Theory (Festinger, 1954) were used infrequently. Given the value of theoretically grounded research in developing a more sophisticated and systematic understanding of the association between body image and physical activity, this is certainly an area in need of additional attention.

Historically, the focus on body image and physical activity research has been centered on the experiences of White, college-age females (Kling et al., 2019), thus in this chapter, we will consider the experiences of more diverse individuals as available in the literature, acknowledging that body image is not a one-size-fits-all concept. Social identities, including gender, age, race and ethnicity, and disability, all play a crucial role in shaping how we perceive and interact with our bodies. As such, this chapter (a) summarizes previous evidence from systematic reviews and meta-analyses, (b) presents recent evidence on possible moderators of the body image–physical activity relationship, including gender, race and ethnicity, age, and disability, and (c) offers implications for future research.

5.2 Previous Evidence from Systematic Reviews and Meta-Analyses

In this section, we synthesize findings derived from systematic reviews and meta-analyses exploring the issue within apparently healthy populations, special populations (such as cancer patients and survivors), and across a range of demographic characteristics, including age and gender. First, we explore the overall relationship between physical activity and body image. Second, we provide an overview of the meta-analyses and reviews conducted focused on special populations. Subsequently, we summarize details on the site, study type, participant demographics, and the aspect of body image being evaluated. Finally, we conclude with a concise summary of the results (see Table 5.1) and identify limitations and gaps in the literature to date.

The search was conducted on key databases and studies were required to meet the following inclusion criteria: (a) being either a systematic review or a meta-analysis; (b) being written in English; and (c) being published no later than September 2023. The search terms employed encompassed keywords such as *body image*, *body dissatisfaction*, *exercise*, *physical activity*, *physical exercise*, *meta-analysis*, and *systematic review*. It is worth noting that studies used varied operational definitions of physical activity and exercise. We excluded studies that focused exclusively on sport participation and athletes. Eighteen studies fit the criteria and were selected for inclusion in this section (Babic et al., 2014; Bassett-Gunter et al., 2017; Burkhardt & Brennan, 2012; Campbell & Hausenblas, 2009; Duijts et al., 2011; Hausenblas & Fallon, 2006; Kerner et al., 2022; King et al., 2020; Koch et al., 2014; Langelier et al., 2019; Lewis-Smith et al., 2018; Matheson et al., 2025; Panão & Carraça, 2020; Reel et al., 2007; Sabiston et al., 2019; SantaBarbara et al., 2017; Srismith et al., 2020; Sun et al., 2018).

5.2.1 Relationship between Physical Activity and Body Image

Meta-analyses and systematic reviews provide consistent results: (a) individuals who are more physically active also have more positive body image and less negative body image, (b) physical activity interventions improve body image, and (c) there are few differences in the associations between physical activity and body image across gender and age (Bassett-Gunter et al., 2017; Campbell & Hausenblas,

TABLE 5.1 Review and Meta-Analytic Article Summary

Authors (Year)	*Journal*	*Review/ Meta*	*Population*	*Studies Included*[a]	*Study Designs Included*	*Moderators*	*Conclusions*
Babic et al. (2014)	*Sports Medicine*	R & MA	Youth; Girls & Boys	111 students (review); 64 studies (meta-analysis); physical activity studies	Cross-sectional, experimental, longitudinal	Age (younger > older) Sex NS	Weak effect; younger participants had stronger associations; no gender or study design moderation effects
Bassett-Gunter et al. (2017)	*Body Image*	MA	Boys and Men	36 studies; physical activity studies	Controlled interventions, single-group interventions, correlational	Age (middle > younger and older) Intensity (less intense > more intense; limited # studies) Mode NS	Medium effect; significant effects for adult males (weak for adolescents and older men), low and moderate intensity PA, aerobic and resistance PA; general and body satisfaction measures
Burkhardt & Brennan (2012)	*Arts & Health*	R	Youth; Males & Females	Seven studies; recreational dance interventions	Control trials, cohort studies, case-control studies, cross-sectional studies with control group		Limited evidence of dance intervention positively influencing body image

Campbell & Hausenblas (2009)	*Journal of Health Psychology*	MA	Youth & Adults; Males & Females	57 studies; exercise interventions	Control trials	Gender, Race, Weight NS Age (older > younger) Duration, Length of int, Mode, Intensity NS Frequency (more frequent > less frequent)	Small effect; exercise intervention positively influenced body image
Duijts et al. (2011)	*Psycho-Oncology*	MA	Breast Cancer Patients & Survivors; Females	Seven studies; exercise interventions	RCTs		Small effect; exercise intervention positively influenced body image

(*Continued*)

TABLE 5.1 (Continued)

Authors (Year)	*Journal*	*Review/ Meta*	*Population*	*Studies Included*[a]	*Study Designs Included*	*Moderators*	*Conclusions*
Hausenblas & Fallon (2006)	*Psychology & Health*	MA	Youth & Adults; Males & Females	121 studies; exercise studies	Correlational, single-group interventions, controlled intervention	Gender (females > males) Age (younger > older) Mode (aer + ana > aer or ana) Duration, Length, Frequency NS Intensity (more intense > less intense)	Small to medium effects; exercisers had more positive body image than non-exercisers; exercise interventions resulted in improved body image
Kerner et al. (2022)	*European Physical Education Review*	R	Youth	19 studies; physical education-based studies	Qualitative, mixed method, RCTs, non-controlled trials		Evidence of positive association between physical education physical activity interventions and improved body image

King et al. (2020)	*Mental Health & Physical Activity*	R & MA	Youth with Obesity; Boys & Girls	17 studies; Physical activity interventions	Case-control studies, non-controlled trials, randomized controlled trial, and non-RCT trials	Age NS Intervention design NS Change in weight NS	Medium effect; No significant moderators (intervention content, duration, age, study setting, inclusion of a behavioral component)
Koch et al. (2014)	*The Arts in Psychotherapy*	MA	Youth & Adults; Males and Females	Six studies; dance movement interventions	Controlled trials (dance movement therapy and dance)		Small effect; dance interventions positively influenced body image
Langelier et al. (2019)	*Psycho-Oncology*	R	Men with Prostate Cancer	Six studies; movement-based interventions	RCTs and qualitative		Physical activity positively associated with improved body image

(*Continued*)

TABLE 5.1 (Continued)

Authors (Year)	*Journal*	*Review/ Meta*	*Population*	*Studies Included*[a]	*Study Designs Included*	*Moderators*	*Conclusions*
Lewis-Smith et al. (2018)	*Psycho-Oncology*	R	Women Treated for Breast Cancer	Seven studies; physical activity interventions	Controlled trials		Some evidence that physical activity intervention benefited body image primarily among women who had completed active treatment
Matheson et al. (2025)	*International Review of Sport and Exercise Psychology*	R & MA	Girls and Women	29 studies; movement-based interventions	RCTs	Age (middle > younger and older)	Small effect; no significant ES at follow-up; most studies tested PA → BI (not much bidirectional research)
Reel et al. (2007)	*Psychological Report*	MA	Adults	35 studies; exercise studies	Control trials, no control trials, correlational, cross-sectional	Gender (single sex > mixed) Age (younger > older) Mode (ana > aer)	Medium effect; exercise positively associated with body image

					Frequency (mor frequent > less frequent) Intensity (more intense > less intense) Length NS	
Sabiston et al. (2019)	*Psychology of Sport & Exercise*	R	Youth and adults; males & females	210 studies; physical activity studies		Engagement in physical activity positively associated with positive body image and negatively associated with negative body image for males and females across a variety of ages

(*Continued*)

TABLE 5.1 (Continued)

Authors (Year)	*Journal*	*Review/ Meta*	*Population*	*Studies Included*[a]	*Study Designs Included*	*Moderators*	*Conclusions*
SantaBarbara et al. (2017)	*Journal of Strength & Conditioning Research*	R	Adults; males & females	11 studies; resistance training interventions	Control and no control trials		Most study results showed positive impact of resistance training on body image; authors noted poor study quality and methodological limitations
Srismith et al. (2020)	*Frontiers in Psychiatry*	R	Adults; clinical, sub-clinical, not clinical eating disorder symptomatology	34 studies; physical activity interventions	Longitudinal, quasi-experimental, and control trials		Positive impact of physical activity intervention on body image across most studies
Sun et al. (2018)	*European Journal of Obstetrics & Gynecology and Reproductive Biology*	R & MA	Adults; pregnant women	Four studies; physical activity studies	Cohort studies		Physical activity positively associated with body image satisfaction

[a] Number of studies reported reflects number of studies included that examined physical activity – body image associations. Some reviews and meta-analyses included studies that used psychoeducational interventions and/or explored multiple outcomes.

2009; Hausenblas & Fallon, 2006; Matheson et al., 2025; Reel et al., 2007). For example, in a seminal meta-analysis, Hausenblas and Fallon (2006) examined results from 121 published and unpublished studies. Significant small effect sizes indicated both correlational and causal associations. Moreover, the positive impact of exercise on body image was consistent across all age groups, benefiting both men and women. Similarly, the results of Reel and colleagues' (2007) meta-analysis of 35 studies provided evidence of associations between physical activity and body image across age groups for both men and women.

Meta-analyses of single-sex studies (Bassett-Gunter et al., 2017; Matheson et al., 2025) also indicate positive relationships between physical activity and body image across age. Further, in research summaries of studies with youth participants, the general conclusions reflect positive associations between physical activity and body image. Babic et al.'s (2014) meta-analysis of 64 studies, for instance, found a significant effect size for the association between physical activity and body image, and gender did not moderate the association. More recently, Kerner et al. (2022), in a review of 19 studies, also found positive associations between physical education-based physical activity interventions and improved body image among both boys and girls.

Results of meta-analyses seem to indicate that the mode and intensity of physical activity may play a role in the physical activity–body image association; however, trends are not completely clear. Both Hausenblas and Fallon (2006) and Reel et al. (2007) found that anaerobic activity, such as strength training (perhaps in combination with aerobic) and higher intensity activity, may benefit body image above aerobic activity alone and lower intensity activity. Bassett-Gunter et al.'s (2017) meta-analysis on studies including only boys and men, on the other hand, found stronger effects at lower intensities and that exercise mode did not moderate the association. Reel et al. (2007) and Campbell and Hausenblas (2009) also found that physical activity frequency was a significant moderator. More recently, one review focused on the effect of 11 resistance training interventions and concluded that most studies showed positive effects on body image, yet the authors noted that study quality was a concern (SantaBarbara et al., 2017).

Besides mode and intensity, exercise motivations also appear to play an important role in body image. Panão and Carraça's (2020) systematic review found that positive body image was linked to autonomous motivations (e.g., pleasure, health, well-being) and health-focused physical activity, while engaging in exercise for appearance-related reasons was associated with more negative body image. That is, exercising to lose weight, improve body tone, and improve attractiveness is more related to body image concerns (e.g., dissatisfaction and body image anxiety), which can be explained by the theories of Objectification (Fredrickson & Roberts, 1997) and Self-determination (Deci & Ryan, 2001, 2002).

Several research summaries reflect an expanding focus on specific populations, including individuals with cancer (Duijts et al., 2011; Langelier et al., 2019; Lewis-Smith et al., 2018), adults with disordered eating (Srismith et al., 2020), pregnant women (Sun et al., 2018), and youth with overweight and obesity (King et al., 2020).

5.2.1.1 Individuals with Cancer

Duijts and colleagues (2011) conducted a comprehensive meta-analysis aimed at quantifying the impact of behavioral techniques and physical exercise on psychosocial well-being, including body image, among women with breast cancer. Seven studies specifically investigated the effect of physical exercise on body image. The outcomes revealed statistically significant results regarding the impact of physical exercise interventions on body image. Lewis-Smith et al. (2018) completed a review of 21 articles that included 7 physical activity interventions for women who had received treatment for breast cancer. Four of the seven physical activity interventions positively impacted body image post-intervention. The authors note that most of the participants who engaged in the physical activity interventions had completed active treatment for their breast cancer. They concluded that this was likely due to physical limitations experienced during active treatment.

Langelier et al. (2019) completed a systematic review of six studies using movement-based interventions in men with prostate cancer. Physical activity was associated with improved body image, and the authors highlighted the impact of physical activity on developing a physique aligned with a masculine ideal as being central to the participants' experiences. Men who participated in group-based and supervised physical activities seemed to experience the greatest benefit. Additionally, men who had completed treatment or were undergoing treatment benefited from movement-based interventions.

5.2.1.2 Individuals with Eating Disorders and Disordered Eating

Srismith et al. (2020) completed a systematic review of longitudinal physical activity intervention studies with adult male and female participants to explore if individuals with sub-clinical and clinical eating disorders differed from non-eating disordered adults. The review included 14 strength training, 13 aerobic, and 3 mixed activity intervention studies. Structured longitudinal physical activity interventions had positive impacts on body image, but no conclusions regarding physical activity intervention impact on participants with clinical or sub-clinical eating symptoms were drawn due to study quality. The authors suggest the need for additional high-quality intervention studies with sub-clinical and clinical samples sensitive to the complexities of body image among such populations and the need for a more multifaceted assessment of body representations that may be relevant within disordered eating populations.

5.2.1.3 Pregnant Women

Sun et al. (2018) analyzed four cohort studies with pregnant women. Women who engaged in more physical activity also had more positive body image. The authors noted that the trimester was a significant moderator; however, they cautioned that additional research is needed due to the small number of studies included.

In addition, the measurement of body image in the four studies included in this meta-analysis was general in nature and not specific to pregnant women. Future research exploring body image and physical activity among pregnant women may benefit from more specialized measurement of body image.

5.2.1.4 Youth with Obesity

King and colleagues (2020) conducted a meta-analysis and review of 17 physical activity intervention studies among children and adolescents enrolled in obesity treatment. Results indicated a medium effect size for physical activity interventions on body image improvement. Moderators, including participant age, study setting, and study duration, were not significant. Improvements in body image were found regardless of changes in body weight; thus the authors conclude that psychological health can be improved via physical activity without weight loss among youth with obesity.

5.2.2 Characteristics of Studies: Location, Study Type, Population, and Body Image Assessment

Regarding the site of research, most studies to date were conducted in the United States, followed by various European countries, including the United Kingdom, Germany, Norway, Turkey, Italy, Sweden, and Switzerland. Comparatively, a smaller number of studies were conducted in Canada and Australia, with only a few carried out in Asian countries. Studies also showed that, over the past decades, different approaches have been used to investigate the impact of physical exercise on body image. While several studies adopted a correlational design, other authors found that experimental, pre–post-test, or experimental control designs were prevalent. Several authors noted that although it is hypothesized that there is a bidirectional association between physical activity and body image, the majority of studies have tested the association in one direction; that is, the impact of physical activity on body image.

Most studies were carried out with female populations, followed by both sexes. The meta-analyses also revealed that research was typically constrained to adults, with a scarcity of studies involving younger or older individuals. Moreover, there has been a lack of attention to participants' race/ethnicity, socioeconomic status, gender and sexual identity, and disability status as only a limited number of studies have explored the impact of these variables on the relationship between physical activity and body image. Additionally, only a small number of studies have considered the body mass index (BMI) of participants, and even fewer have examined their body composition, including their percentage of body fat or fat-free mass.

In summary, previous research has consistently demonstrated the positive impact of physical exercise on body image for individuals of all ages, regardless of gender. Nevertheless, conflicting outcomes have arisen concerning various factors, such as the type of exercise (aerobic vs. anaerobic; appearance-focused vs. non-appearance-focused; endurance, etc.), intensity, and frequency. Additionally, inconsistencies have been identified regarding the magnitude of the effect based on participants' age or BMI.

5.3 Updated Evidence

The most recent, relevant research on the relationship between physical activity and body image indicates a more specific focus on understanding the complexities of hypothesized moderators of the relationship and more recent developments around holistic forms of movement and body image. Studies that focused on sport involvement are not included in this review as sports are distinct, socially constructed practices that are beyond the scope of this chapter.

5.3.1 Social Identities, Body Image, and Physical Activity

5.3.1.1 Gender

As reflected in the results of meta-analytic and systematic review studies, gender-related patterns of difference in the associations between physical activity and body image do not seem to be evident. Rather, similar patterns of physical activity – body image associations are seen in studies of boys and men compared with girls and women. For example, Sabiston and colleagues (2022), in a five-year longitudinal study of 776 adolescents in Canada, found that negative affective body image, such as body shame, was related to lower levels of physical activity among both boys and girls. There was no gender-related difference in that association. Sánchez-Miguel et al. (2021) similarly found no gender differences in the association between body dissatisfaction and physical activity among 2026 adolescents in Spain.

Although patterns of difference associated with gender seem to be fairly limited, research has often focused primarily on girls and women. This trend is not too surprising given that girls and women (a) often experience sociocultural appearance-related pressures to achieve a thin body (Grogan, 2021), (b) report high rates of body dissatisfaction (Massey-Stokes et al., 2023), and (c) have low rates of physical activity (Guthold et al., 2018) compared with males. It is likely that social norms around gender are important in understanding how people experience their bodies in and through physical activity. These experiences in physical activity may be associated with both positive and negative body image. As noted, meta-analytic research clearly documents the positive effects of physical activity on girls' and women's body image (e.g., Matheson et al., 2025). Yet, for some, engagement in physical activity is associated with negative body image in complex ways. Pila et al. (2021), for example, in a prospective study of 206 adolescent girls in Canada, found that girls' experiences of body shame were associated with lower levels of physical activity, whereas anticipation of body shame was associated with higher levels of physical activity. It may be that physical activity is seen as a strategy for achieving a more idealized physique, thus reducing negative body image, yet the experience within a physical activity setting may highlight and exacerbate body distress.

More recent work has adopted a broadened perspective beyond an assumption of the thin ideal with a recognition that female bodies come in a variety of shapes and sizes. As an example, Laus et al. (2022) found that women engaged in CrossFit ($n = 56$) and weight training ($n = 62$) did not report any greater concerns about muscularity than non-active women ($n = 74$) in Brazil. They concluded that exposure to fitness settings supportive of weight training may challenge social norms around muscularity for women. Moreover, women achieving muscularity and strength via physical activity have been a focus of recent qualitative research. In a study of eight female powerlifters in Australia, Kelly et al. (2023) revealed the empowering experiences women had through strength training with a focus on developing muscularity. Women reported that they emphasized body functionality, experienced embodiment, rejected social body ideals, pushed back against self-objectification, adopted a flexible and compassionate approach toward themselves and their bodies, and participated in communities that support body positivity through engagement in strength training. Similarly, Walters and Hefferon (2020) interviewed 12 women from New Zealand, United States, and United Kingdom who reported having a positive body image and engaging in strength training. Participants indicated that strength training improved their body image through increasing appreciation for their bodies and functionality and rejecting social pressures to conform to a thin ideal.

A focus on muscularity as an outcome resulting from exercise, long outside of the social norm for females, is a central goal for males. Indeed, males may experience a drive for muscularity that contributes to pathogenic exercise behaviors, such as excessive exercise or obligatory exercise, in the quest for a socially ideal physique (Liu et al., 2019; Tod & Edwards, 2015). For instance, a study of 278 male weightlifters in Taiwan found that body dissatisfaction was associated with exercise dependence and that drive for muscularity mediated the association (Liu et al., 2019). Moreover, in a study of 326 sexual minority men in the United States, Brewster et al. (2017) found that drive for muscularity was associated with compulsive exercise. For some men, exercise may lessen body concerns. In a study of 21 men in the United States who reported symptoms of muscle dysmorphia, SantaBarbara et al. (2023) found acute improvements in state body image after completing moderate and vigorous resistance training. In one of the few studies to explore the physical activity – body image relationship among transgender individuals, Teti et al. (2020) interviewed 16 transmasculine adolescents in the Midwest United States. Participants reported using physical activity, sometimes excessive, as a method for developing a more muscular and masculine physique to lessen body dissatisfaction and distress.

It can be seen from the studies described above that issues related to male body image may possess nuances distinct from those observed among females. For example, Objectification Theory (e.g., Oehlhof et al., 2009) and sociocultural models (e.g., Frederick, Tylka et al., 2022) are applicable to both men and women; however, they manifest differently across genders. This distinction has prompted researchers to move beyond scales originally designed and validated for women, developing measures tailored to address the specific concerns of men. Thus, it becomes imperative that studies use appropriate tools for the target audience to accurately assess the constructs under evaluation and not draw misguided conclusions about how men and women experience their body image.

5.3.1.2 Age and Life Stages

Meta-analytic research, along with individual studies, indicates that the associations between physical activity and body image are similar across age groups (e.g., Babic et al., 2014; Bassett-Gunter et al., 2017; Campbell & Hausenblas, 2009; Hausenblas & Fallon, 2006; Sabiston et al., 2019). Developmental and societal pressures, however, may differ across the lifespan. As such, in a study of Italian men and women between 50 and 98 years, Federici et al. (2019) found positive associations between physical activity and body image across all age groups of older adults. Additionally, in a qualitative study examining body image across the lifespan in 16 males and 15 females in Sweden, participants noted that positive body image developed as a result of gaining a sense of agency, which was frequently related to being successful in physical activity contexts (Gattario & Frisén, 2019). Furthermore, self-care was an important part of maintaining positive body image in emerging adulthood, and physical activity was noted as a prominent self-care strategy. Fougner and colleagues (2019) noted similar trends in interviews with 16 women in Norway between the ages 70 and 85. Participants suggested that being able to maintain physical functioning was a way to create body autonomy, which in turn helped develop feelings of accomplishment. Being able to engage in exercise allowed these women to identify themselves as powerful, which not only enhanced self-image but also countered traditional aging stereotypes (Fougner et al., 2019).

Exercise and physical activity experiences across the lifespan appear to aid in the development and maintenance of positive body image. However, it can be useful to consider how age and gender may intersect to differentially influence the experiences people have in their bodies and in physical activity across the lifespan. As previously noted, for girls and women, the thin ideal internalization is often the leading standard of beauty for bodies, with much attention being focused on obtaining a slender, yet slightly toned build and maintaining the look of youth, despite moving through the aging process (Bozsik et al., 2018; Hockey et al., 2021; Myers & Crowther, 2007). Although this ideal is often unrealistic to obtain, sociocultural pressures continue to impose and encourage this standard of beauty, resulting in body dissatisfaction that tends to continue across the lifespan (Cameron et al., 2019; Pruis & Janowsky, 2010; Quittkat et al., 2019; Tiggemann, 2004; Tiggemann & McCourt, 2013).

Navigating body image changes across the lifespan can be difficult for women, as different stages of life can amplify unique feelings of negative body image associated with physical and psychosocial development. For example, adolescent and young adult women often experience pressures related to appearance and perceived attractiveness as they seek romantic partners and social acceptance by peers, and these pressures can be exacerbated by body-related comparisons driven by social media engagement (Fardouly & Vartanian, 2016; Holland & Tiggemann, 2016). Pregnancy and postpartum are also periods where women might experience extreme changes in the body, and often, these changes can result in negative body image as the body moves away from the ideal standard of beauty and frustration occurs when one's body does not "bounce back" after moving through pregnancy (Hodgkinson et al., 2014). For instance, Raspovic et al. (2020), in a qualitative study, including 21 mothers in Australia (0–5 years postpartum), found that participants described complex and varied relationships between body image and physical activity. The authors noted that experiences of body image-related distress seemed connected to maladaptive exercise and health, whereas body appreciation was connected to more adaptive physical activity.

Beyond pregnancy, women's body image in middle and late adulthood is complex and differs from the ideals once experienced at younger ages (Kilpela et al., 2015). As women's bodies age, individuals are forced to navigate new body-related challenges, including muscle mass changes, loss or graying of hair, changes in skin tone and texture, weight distribution fluctuations, and frustration with mobility (Hockey et al., 2021; Kilpela et al., 2015). Despite these changes in the body, older women may focus less on self-objectification compared with younger women and have higher levels of body appreciation (Tiggemann & McCourt, 2013). Hockey and colleagues (2021) also noted trends in body appreciation as women aged, suggesting that a shift may occur during the aging process where body functionality, over appearance, becomes the priority, particularly as sociocultural pressures for thinness decrease (Hockey et al., 2021; Tiggemann & McCourt, 2013).

Much of the literature on body image across the lifespan focuses on women, and it is well documented that women across the lifespan experience higher rates of poor body image than men (Quittkat et al., 2019; Tiggemann, 2004). Like women, body dissatisfaction in men remains relatively stable across the lifespan (Quittkat et al., 2019), with dissatisfaction mainly stemming from weight gain during the aging process (Keel et al., 2007) and perceived loss of muscularity, which often results in muscle dysmorphia and related concerns of losing one's masculine physique (Karazsia et al., 2017). Bennett et al. (2020) interviewed 28 men of diverse ethnicities and sexual orientations, of ages 65–83 in Canada, and found that men indicated overall appreciation for their health and bodies but acknowledged challenges associated with physical changes in their bodies and weight as they age. Physical activity was seen as a mechanism for weight management and coping with unwanted physical changes.

In one study exploring lifespan developmental tasks and men's body image, Malik et al. (2021) interviewed 14 men in England between the ages of 45 and 67 years. The men reflected on their lives and indicated that during preadolescence, they experienced few body image disturbances and focused on sport participation. During adolescence and young adulthood, the men reported being more aware of their bodies as they became interested in developing romantic relationships and social acceptance. As men moved into early middle age, they focused more on their families and paid little attention to their bodies, with little time for exercise. Some men also reported experiencing divorce and a sense of panic over their physique as they contemplated dating. A focus on body functionality and a move toward body acceptance was experienced as men moved into later middle age. Malik et al. (2021) provide insight into how developmental life stages of boys and men relate to body image; the connection to participation in physical activity needs further attention. More longitudinal research is needed in this area as nuances related to body image and physical activity in males across the lifespan are somewhat unexamined.

5.3.1.3 Race/Ethnicity

The possible influence of race and ethnicity on the associations between physical activity and body image has received little attention in research literature. Evidence does indicate that participation in physical activity varies between racial and ethnic groups. In the United States, for example, non-Hispanic Black and Hispanic adults have the highest rates of inactivity (Centers for Disease Control and Prevention, 2022). Previous research has also indicated possible race-based differences in body image (Grabe & Hyde, 2006; Wildes, Emery, & Simons, 2001). Frederick, Crerand et al. (2022) reported data from a large sample of White, Black, Hispanic, and Asian men and women in the United States and found that race influences the associations between sociocultural pressures, internalization of idealized appearance, body surveillance, and body image. The patterns were somewhat different for men and women. For instance, Asian women were more strongly impacted by media pressures around a thin ideal than other groups of women, and Black women's body image was negatively influenced more strongly by body surveillance than other groups. For men in the sample, body surveillance was also negatively associated with body image. However, Olson et al. (2020) in a large study of 2,212 adults in the United States found few race-based differences in body shape concerns. Although some race-related patterns in physical activity and in body image are found in the literature, it is not clear if, or how, the nature of the relationship between engaging in physical activity and body image differs based on race or ethnicity.

Race-based sociocultural norms, racialized media representations, and experiences of racial discrimination may influence how individuals experience their bodies within physical activity settings. For example, in a girls' physical activity participatory action project, ten Black and African American girl leaders in the

United States shared that they perceived the ideal body as "slim-thick" (i.e., exaggerated hourglass shape) (Chard et al., 2020), which differs from the "thin ideal" often cited in body image work. Moreover, some work suggests that Black individuals have different views of the cultural relevance of physical activity. Hughes (2021) found that among 31 Black American women in the United States, a larger, more curvaceous physique was desirable, and some felt that exercise, while having health benefits, moved their body away from that ideal. Lowy et al. (2021) have called for an increased and informed effort to use culturally sensitive approaches in research addressing body image among Black women. Their advocacy also seems relevant in considering efforts to understand the body image–physical activity relationship experienced by Black and other racial and ethnic minority groups.

5.3.1.4 Disability

Disability often is associated with assumed negative body image; however, Martin (2018) suggests that a multitude of factors, including disability type, severity, and visibility, along with other sociocultural identities, such as gender and race, likely influence associations between disability and body image. In addition, individuals living with disabilities have lower rates of physical activity compared with individuals without disabilities. Indeed, Ginis et al. (2021) estimate that globally, people with disabilities are 16%–62% less likely to achieve recommended levels of physical activity compared with people without disability. Yet, the extent to which disability moderates the association between physical activity and body image is unclear.

A focus on body functionality seems particularly salient within the study of disability, body image, and physical activity. Alleva et al. (2014) suggest body functionality acts as a mechanism to counteract negative body image. Body functionality focuses on the process of how a body moves or functions and what it can do, versus examining the body as an object or how it appears, particularly regarding societal standards for attractiveness (Alleva et al., 2014; Alleva et al., 2016). It is interesting to examine body functionality as a mechanism for body image improvement in the context of individuals with physical disabilities, as physical limitations and constraints might exist because of a disability. In line with this notion, individuals with disabilities note that while their bodies might function differently, they are still functioning, and thus, the idea of body functionality needs to be fluid to encompass the variety of ways a body can function (Rice et al., 2021; Thomas et al., 2019). Indeed, Alleva and Tylka (2021) note the value of physical activity in enhancing perceived body functionality.

To date, research on disability and body image with active populations has tended to focus on sport engagement (e.g., Paillard, 2018; Sousa et al., 2009), which is beyond the scope of this chapter. The limited research on physical activity and body image among adults with disability is consistent with other research, indicating positive associations between physical activity and body image. Bailey and colleagues (2015), for instance, examined body image in a cohort of nine individuals with spinal cord injuries in the United States. Despite some of the physical limitations that existed with their disability, participants in this study noted numerous factors that supported their positive body image experiences, including body acceptance, body appreciation, gratitude, and appreciation for functionality (Bailey et al., 2015). Specifically, some participants noted that gaining back strength and functionality of different body parts contributed to feeling pride and positive emotions toward one's body, and that exercise played a role in that experience. It is important to recognize that much research surrounding body image situates the individual in a "normal" body and while this type of body might be reflective of most of the population, it ignores a subset of the population who are born with physical disabilities and will never inhabit society's definition of a "normal" body (Rice et al., 2021).

For individuals with physical disabilities, body image fluctuates on a continuum from positive to negative and seems to vary daily (Bailey et al., 2015; Thomas et al., 2019). Appearance concerns can occur when individuals compare their limited bodies to those of individuals who are considered able-bodied, and often, this comparison can result in negative body image (Galli et al., 2016; Thomas et al., 2019). A focus on body functionality can also result in negative body image when the focus remains solely on what the body can do and how it functions for a "normal" body. Future research in body image and disability must focus on the lived experiences of individuals existing in different bodies and recognize that functionality is dynamic and multifaceted. Thomas and colleagues (2019) also suggest that research in this area focus on what they have termed functional-aesthetic body image to capture the overlap between function and appearance in individuals with physical disabilities. Functional-aesthetic body image recognizes that body image concerns may result from how a person perceives others are looking at them while they complete functional tasks, such as eating or utilizing mobility aids. This may also be a relevant concept to consider within physical activity settings where individuals with disability may engage in different ways or use different techniques than individuals without physical disability. The creation of this concept centers on the understanding that body functionality must co-exist with body image for individuals with physical disabilities because function is part of their overall outward appearance and thus, it will impact how they view themselves and how others view them (Thomas et al., 2019).

5.3.2 *Mindful and Appreciative Approaches to Movement and Body*

Recent research has begun exploring mindful approaches to movement and the body (e.g., Balciuniene et al., 2021). As examples, intuitive exercise (Reel, Galli et al., 2016) and attunement with exercise (AWE; Calogero et al., 2019) are mindful approaches to movement that seem to positively benefit bodily experiences within physical activity. Intuitive exercise entails focusing on personal cues rather than rigid exercise routines, relying on body trust and mindful engagement in exercise (Reel, Lee et al., 2016). Calogero et al. describe AWE as physical activity experiences in which one feels at one with, and a sense of care for, one's body. The foundation of AWE is a sense of physical and psychosocial safety, upon which the process of attunement can be engaged and ultimately culminates in experiences of joy during activity. Greenleaf and Hauff (2019) suggest that physical activity environments can be shaped to support mindful movement by focusing on embodying experiences such as connection to the self and body.

These types of mindful and appreciative physical activity experiences are thought to benefit body image (e.g., Cox & McMahon, 2019). For example, Balciuniene et al. (2021) conducted an eight-week intervention entailing cognitive behavioral therapy and mindful movement with female Lithuanian university students. The mindful movement component was conducted in a body-friendly environment without "fitspiration" images, recovery and relaxation for self-care after exercise, and instructors who wore loose-fitting clothing. Results indicated that the intervention decreased body image concerns among women in the intervention group. In addition, specific forms of physical activity, such as yoga, may be particularly salient in efforts to improve body image via mindful movement (e.g., Cox & McMahon, 2019; Cox et al., 2022; Mahlo & Tiggemann, 2016; Neumark-Sztainer et al., 2018; Webb et al., 2022). Finally, positive shifts toward body appreciation also have been represented in the literature recently and promote body positivity, body inclusivity, weight neutrality, and body acceptance (e.g., Pellizzer & Wade, 2023).

5.4 Implications

As highlighted in the chapter, research has primarily centered on exploring aspects of negative body image in female university students and younger adults, which has limited our understanding of the association between physical activity and body image across a more diverse population, including individuals of varying ages, socioeconomic backgrounds, ethnicities, and disabilities/specific health conditions. Additionally, it is important to acknowledge that when studying body image, researchers must consider its multidimensional nature. Most studies have concentrated on assessing body dissatisfaction while neglecting other facets of body image, including its positive dimension. Also, there is noticeable confusion in the use of appropriate terms, such as studies assessing body dissatisfaction and concluding that exercise has a significant effect on "positive body image". Finally, while most studies have assessed the impact of physical activity on body image, the opposite direction remains relatively unexplored. This is unfortunate because exercise motivation is recognized as a powerful moderator in the binomial relationship between body image and physical exercise.

In this chapter, we presented intersections of body image with numerous psychosocial factors, but the question that remains is "Where do we go from here?"

As society continues to evolve and change, so too, do viewpoints regarding body image. Despite the steady understanding that internal and external factors affect the way we view and accept our bodies, it is important to continue exploring this complex relationship to develop new prevention and intervention strategies that might impact the adverse physical and psychological outcomes associated with negative body image.

Future directions in this area of research include unpacking the nuances of the social media world and how interacting with social media content (either as a consumer or as a creator) may impact body image and one's engagement in physical activity experiences. Harriger and colleagues (2023) recently published an opinion piece regarding the most urgent areas of research with social media and body image. Of those factors mentioned, understanding the dynamic nature of social media has posed a significant problem for researchers, as social media platforms tend to engage users in different ways, and thus, measuring social media "use" and its effects has become difficult. In line with this, Harriger et al. (2023) also suggest that many of our theoretical frameworks surrounding the interaction of social media and body image may only capture one facet of body image, missing several complex relationships that occur as the user dynamically participates in social media engagement.

Tylka and colleagues (2023) outline some of the existing moderator, mediator, and predictor variables that occur within the current scope of body image literature and how these variables might benefit from a theoretical refresh to fully capture the experience one has on social media. These variables include elements such as exposure to appearance-based versus non-appearance-based social media, appearance pressures due to interacting with social media content, user engagement (i.e., serving as a creator or consumer), and investment in social media usage (Tylka et al., 2023). Many of these factors have been situated in current theoretical frameworks (e.g., Social Comparison Theory, Objectification Theory), yet researchers are now calling for new models that combine layers of these theories to fully capture the influence of social media on body image (Harriger et al., 2023; Tylka et al., 2023). For example, Rodgers and Laveway (2022) developed the "theory of development of critical body awareness" on social media, which seeks to capture how one's motivation to use social media and their investment in social media might influence how they navigate and perceive different types of messaging. Rodgers and Laveway (2022) ultimately suggest that the impact of social media on an individual's body image will be driven by how that person situates themselves in body liberation and body neutrality.

Despite the emergence of new frameworks such as this, these theories remain untested and lack validity at this point in time. The positive of a framework like "theory of development of critical body awareness" on social media is that it looks at social media as an experience, rather than assuming that social media operates in the same way as traditional media (e.g., television, magazines). There are still many unknowns about the world of social media, particularly regarding its influence across the age spectrum, and this will be a critical area to explore moving forward, especially as social media can have a powerful impact on physical activity engagement and the perception one has of themselves if identifying as an "exerciser".

Another area of exploration within body image research includes examining the impact of the body positivity movement on body image. At its core, body positivity emerged as a movement meant to challenge the perspective of the thin ideal, encouraging individuals to respect and celebrate bodies of all shapes and sizes and focus on functionality of the body as opposed to appearance (Sastre, 2014). Although the "thin ideal" remains the predominate body ideal in Western cultures, movements like Health At Every Size® (Association for Size Diversity and Health, n.d.), which encourage weight neutrality by prioritizing health and wellness over dieting and weight loss, are gaining popularity and attention in the research literature (e.g., Adams et al., 2022; Dimitrov et al., 2022; O'Hara et al., 2021). Further, as advocates for body-inclusive fitness, such as Ragen Chastain (n.d., https://danceswithfat.org/) and Louise Green (n.d., www.bigfitgirl.com), gain influence and call for celebrating bodies for their functionality and respecting bodies of varying shapes and sizes within fitness environments, rigid appearance-related norms around assumed body ideals, health, and fitness may be challenged.

While the focus on body positivity and weight neutrality has yielded positive outcomes associated with body image (e.g., Cohen et al., 2019; Tylka & Wood-Barcalow, 2015), there are critics to these movements, making arguments that (1) body positivity glorifies overweight and obesity and (2) body positivity still centers itself on appearance, creating a new layer of pressure if an individual does not love their body (Cohen et al., 2021). While some researchers have sought to debunk these claims (e.g., Alleva & Tylka, 2018), future research in this area is warranted, particularly the exploration of the role of objectification in the body positivity movement (Cohen et al., 2021). Hockey and colleagues (2021) also suggest that recent feminist movements have shifted the value placed on women away from appearance and toward other characteristics like intelligence and work ethic. Although still theoretical in nature, changing societal norms that promote body inclusivity and worth based on intrinsic characteristics may result in enhanced body image and more positive and empowering physical activity engagement.

5.5 Conclusion

The association, both correlational and causal, between physical activity and body image is well documented across a variety of populations and sociodemographic groups, yet continuing to build the literature in this area is critical. Moving forward, researchers should examine new theoretical frameworks, expand research into different populations (e.g., minority populations, LGBTQIA+), and consider longitudinal and multimethod approaches to understanding more of the complexities of people's experiences of their bodies and physical activity. Addressing body image and fostering a healthy relationship with physical activity can lead to substantial improvements in psychological and physical health. Building a more diverse and theoretically grounded research base can support efforts among exercise psychology professionals to accept and embrace diverse body types and encourage inclusive participation in physical activities so that we create a more equitable and supportive society.

References

Adams, V., Gladden, A., & Craddock, J. (2022). Perceptions of health among black women in emerging adulthood: Alignment with a Health at Every Size perspective. *Journal of Nutrition Education and Behavior*, *54*(10), 916–924. https://doi.org/10.1016/j.jneb.2022.07.004

Alleva, J. M., Martijn, C., Jansen, A., & Nederkoorn, C. (2014). Body language: Affecting body satisfaction by describing the body in functionality terms. *Psychology of Women Quarterly, 38*(2), 181–196. https://doi.org/10.1177/0361684313507897

Alleva, J. M., & Tylka, T. L. (2021). Body functionality: A review of the literature. *Body Image*, *36*, 149–171. https://doi.org/10.1016/j.bodyim.2020.11.006

Alleva, J. M., & Tylka, T. L. (2018). Muttarak's study design cannot support the link between the body-positive movement and overweight or obesity. *Obesity*, *26*(10), 1527–1529. https://doi.org/10.1002/oby.22281

Alleva, J. M., Veldhuis, J., & Martijn, C. (2016). A pilot study investigating whether focusing on body functionality can protect women from the potential negative effects of viewing thin ideal media images. *Body Image, 17*, 10–13. https://doi.org/10.1016/j.bodyim.2016.01.007

Association for Size Diversity and Health. (n.d.). *HAES® principles*. https://asdah.org/haes/

Babic, M. J., Morgan, P. J., Plotnikoff, R. C., Lonsdale, C., White, R. L., & Lubans, D. R. (2014). Physical activity and physical self-concept in youth: Systematic review and meta-analysis. *Sports Medicine*, *44*, 1589–1601. https://doi.org/10.1007/s40279-014-0229-z

Bailey, K. A., Gammage, K. L., van Ingen, C., & Ditor, D. S. (2015). "It's all about acceptance": A qualitative study exploring a model of positive body image for people with spinal cord injury. *Body Image, 15*, 24–34. https://doi.org/10.1016/j.bodyim.2015.04.010

Balciuniene, V., Jankauskiene, R., & Baceviciene, M. (2021). Effect of an education and mindfulness-based physical activity intervention for the promotion of positive body image in Lithuanian female students. *Eating and Weight Disorders-Studies on Anorexia, Bulimia and Obesity*, *27*, 563–577. https://doi.org/10.1007/s40519-021-01195-4

Bandura, A. (1991). Social cognitive theory of self-regulation. *Organizational Behavior and Human Decision Processes*, *50*, 248–287. https://doi.org/10.1016/0749-5978(91)90022-L

Bassett-Gunter, R., McEwan, D., & Kamarhie, A. (2017). Physical activity and body image among men and boys: A meta-analysis. *Body Image*, *22*, 114–128. https://doi.org/10.1016/j.bodyim.2017.06.007

Bennett, E. V., Hurd, L. C., Pritchard, E. M., Colton, T., & Crocker, P. R. (2020). An examination of older men's body image: How men 65 years and older perceive, experience, and cope with their aging bodies. *Body Image*, *34*, 27–37. https://doi.org/10.1016/j.bodyim.2020.04.005

Bozsik, F., Whisenhunt, B. L., Hudson, D. L., Bennett, B., & Lundgren, J. D. (2018). Thin is in? Think again: The rising importance of muscularity in the thin ideal female body. *Sex Roles, 79*, 609–615. https://doi.org/10.1007/s11199-017-0886-0

Brewster, M. E., Sandil, R., DeBlaere, C., Breslow, A., & Eklund, A. (2017). "Do you even lift, bro?" Objectification, minority stress, and body image concerns for sexual minority men. *Psychology of Men & Masculinity*, *18*(2), 87. https://doi.org/10.1037/men0000043

Burkhardt, J., & Brennan, C. (2012). The effects of recreational dance interventions on the health and well-being of children and young people: A systematic review. *Arts & Health*, *4*(2), 148–161. https://doi.org/10.1080/17533015.2012.665810

Calogero, R. C., Tylka, T. L., Hartman McGilley, B., & Pedroddy-Stump, K. N. (2019). Attunement with exercise (AWE). In T. L. Tylka & N. Piran (Eds.), *Handbook of positive body image and embodiment* (pp. 80–90). Oxford University Press.

Cameron, E., Ward, P., Mandville-Anstey, S. A., & Coombs, A. (2019). The female aging body: A systematic review of female perspectives on aging, health, and body image. *Journal of Women & Aging, 31*(1), 3–17. https://doi.org/10.1080/08952841.2018.1449586

Campbell, A., & Hausenblas, H. A. (2009). Effects of exercise interventions on body image: A meta-analysis. *Journal of Health Psychology*, *14*(6), 780–793. https://doi.org/10.1177/13591053093389

Cash, T. F. (2012). Cognitive-behavioral perspectives on body image. In T. F. Cash (Ed.), *Encyclopedia of body image and human appearance* (pp. 334–342). Elsevier Academic Press.

Cash, T. F., & Smolak, L. (Eds.). (2011). *Body image: A handbook of science, practice, and prevention*. Guilford Press.

Cash, T. F., Wood, K. C., Phelps, K. D., & Boyd, K. (1991). New assessments of weight-related body image derived from extant instruments. *Perceptual and Motor Skills, 73*(1), 235–241. https://doi.org/10.2466/pms.1991.73.1.2

Centers for Disease Control and Prevention. (2022). *Adult physical inactivity prevalence maps by race/ethnicity*. https://www.cdc.gov/physicalactivity/data/inactivity-prevalence-maps/index.html

Chard, C. A., Nelson, D. S., Walters, K. A., Pollard, N., Pollard, N., Pollard, N., Gomez, K., Smith, D., Jenkins, N., Muwwakkil, S., Garland, C., Fard, A., & Fields, M. J. (2020). An inclusive approach to exploring perceptions of body image, self-esteem, and physical activity among Black and African-American girls: Smart Fit Girls Melanin Magic. *Journal of Park & Recreation Administration*, *38*(3). https://doi.org/10.18666/JPRA-2019-9710

Chastain, R. (n.d.) *Dances with fat*. https://danceswithfat.org/

Cohen, R., Newton-John, T., & Slater, A. (2021). The case for body positivity on social media: Perspectives on current advances and future directions. *Journal of Health Psychology,26*(13), 2365–2373. https://doi.org/10.1177/1359105320912

Cohen, R., Irwin, L., Newton-John, T., & Slater, A. (2019). # bodypositivity: A content analysis of body positive accounts on Instagram. *Body Image, 29,* 47–57. https://doi.org/10.1016/j.bodyim.2019.02.007

Cox, A. E., & McMahon, A. K. (2019). Exploring changes in mindfulness and body appreciation during yoga participation. *Body Image*, *29*, 118–121. https://doi.org/10.1016/j.bodyim.2019.03.003

Cox, A. E., Ullrich-French, S., Cook-Cottone, C., Tylka, T. L., & Neumark-Sztainer, D. (2022). Examining the effects of mindfulness-based yoga instruction on positive embodiment and affective responses. In C. Cook-Cottone, A. E. Cox, D. Neumark-Sztainer, & T. L. Tylka (Eds.), *Yoga for positive embodiment in eating disorder prevention and treatment* (pp. 155–172). Routledge.

Deci, E. L., & Ryan, R. M. (2001). *Self-determination theory: An approach to human motivation and personality*. https://www.psych.rochester.edu/SDT/theory.html.

Deci, E. L., & Ryan, R. M. (2002). *Handbook of self-determination*. University of Rochester.

Dimitrov Ulian, M., Pinto, A. J., Morais Sato, P. D., Benatti, F. B., Lopes de Campos-Ferraz, P., Coelho, D., Roble, O. J., Sabatini, F., Perez, I., Aburad, L., Vessoni, A., Fernandez Unsain, R., Macedo Rogero, R., Sampaio, G., Gualano, B., & Scagliusi, F. B. (2022). Health at Every Size®-based interventions may improve cardiometabolic risk and quality of life even in the absence of weight loss: An ancillary, exploratory analysis of the health and wellness in obesity study. *Frontiers in Nutrition*, *9*, 598920. https://doi.org/10.3389/fnut.2022.598920

Duijts, S. F., Faber, M. M., Oldenburg, H. S., Van Beurden, M., & Aaronson, N. K. (2011). Effectiveness of behavioral techniques and physical exercise on psychosocial functioning and health-related quality of life in breast cancer patients and survivors—a meta-analysis. *Psycho-Oncology*, *20*(2), 115–126. https://doi.org/10.1002/pon.1728

Fardouly, J., & Vartanian, L. R. (2016). Social media and body image concerns: Current research and future directions. *Current Opinion in Psychology, 9*, 1–5. https://doi.org/10.1016/j.copsyc.2015.09.005

Federici, A., Marini, C. F., Lucertini, F., Zoffoli, L., Fanelli, V., Capriotti, A., & Shoaei, V. (2019). The effect of physical activity on the perception of body image and well-being during aging. *Journal of Physical Education and Sport*, *19*, 1341–1348. https://doi.org/10.7752/jpes.2019.s4194

Festinger, L. (1954). A theory of social comparison processes. *Human Relations*, *7*, 117–140. https://doi.org/10.1177/001872675400700202

Fougner, M., Bergland, A., Lund, A., & Debesay, J. (2019). Aging and exercise: Perceptions of the active lived-body. *Physiotherapy Theory and Practice*, *35*(7), 651–662. https://doi.org/10.1080/09593985.2018.1456584

Frederick, D. A., Crerand, C. E., Brown, T. A., Perez, M., Best, C. R., Cook-Cottone, C. P., Compte, E. J., Convertino, L., Gordon, A. R., Malcarne, V. L., Nagata, J. M., Parent, M. C., Pennesi, J.-L., Pila,E. Rodgers, R. F., Schaefer, L. M., Kevin Thompson, J., Tylka, T. L., & Murray, S. B. (2022). Demographic predictors of body image satisfaction: The US Body Project I. *Body Image*, *41*, 17–31. https://doi.org/10.1016/j.bodyim.2022.01.011

Frederick, D. A., Tylka, T. L., Rodgers, R. F., Convertino, L., Pennesi, J. L., Parent, M. C., Brown, T. A., Compte, E. J., Cook-Cottone, C. P., Crerand, C. E., Malcarne, V. L., Nagata, J. M., Perez, M., Pila, E., Schaefer, L. M., Kevin Thompson, J., & Murray, S. B. (2022). Pathways from sociocultural and objectification constructs to body satisfaction among men: The US Body Project I. *Body Image*, *41*, 84–96. https://doi.org/10.1016/j.bodyim.2022.02.001

Fredrickson, B. L., & Roberts, T. A. (1997). Objectification theory: Toward understanding women's lived experiences and mental health risks. *Psychology of Women Quarterly, 21*(2), 173–206. https://doi.org/10.1111/j.1471-6402.1997.tb0010

Galli, N., Reel, J. J., Henderson, H., & Detling, N. (2016). An investigation of body image in athletes with physical disabilities. *Journal of Clinical Sport Psychology, 10*(1), 1–18. https://doi.org/10.1123/JCSP.2015-0018

Gattario, K. H., & Frisén, A. (2019). From negative to positive body image: Men's and women's journeys from early adolescence to emerging adulthood. *Body Image, 28*, 53–65. https://doi.org/10.1016/j.bodyim.2018.12.002

Ginis, K. A. M., van der Ploeg, H. P., Foster, C., Lai, B., McBride, C. B., Ng, K., Pratt, M., Shirazipour, C. H., Smith, B., Vásquez, P. M., & Heath, G. W. (2021). Participation of people living with disabilities in physical activity: A global perspective. *The Lancet*, *398*(10298), 443–455. https://doi.org/10.1016/S0140-6736(21)01164-8

Grabe, S., & Hyde, J. S. (2006). Ethnicity and body dissatisfaction among women in the United States: A meta-analysis. *Psychological Bulletin*, *132*(4), 622. https://doi.org/10.1037/0033-2909.132.4.622

Green, L. (n.d.) *Big fit girl*. https://www.bigfitgirl.com

Greenleaf, C., & Hauff, C. (2019). Environments that cultivate embodiment through mindful movement. In T. L. Tylka and N. Piran (Eds.), *Handbook of positive body image: Constructs, protective factors, and interventions* (pp. 118–128). Oxford University Press.

Grogan, S. (2021). *Body image: Understanding body dissatisfaction in men, women and children*. Routledge.

Guthold, R., Stevens, G. A., Riley, L. M., & Bull, F. C. (2018). Worldwide trends in insufficient physical activity from 2001 to 2016: A pooled analysis of 358 population-based surveys with 1· 9 million participants. *The Lancet Global Health*, *6*(10), e1077–e1086. https://doi.org/10.1016/S2214-109X(18)30357-7

Harriger, J. A., Thompson, J. K., & Tiggemann, M. (2023). TikTok, TikTok, the time is now: Future directions in social media and body image. *Body Image, 44*, 222–226. https://doi.org/10.1016/j.bodyim.2023.01.005

Hausenblas, H. A., & Fallon, E. A. (2006). Exercise and body image: A meta-analysis. *Psychology and Health*, *21*(1), 33–47. https://doi.org/10.1080/14768320500105270

Hockey, A., Milojev, P., Sibley, C. G., Donovan, C. L., & Barlow, F. K. (2021). Body image across the adult lifespan: A longitudinal investigation of developmental and cohort effects. *Body Image, 39*, 114–124. https://doi.org/10.1016/j.bodyim.2021.06.007

Hodgkinson, E. L., Smith, D. M., & Wittkowski, A. (2014). Women's experiences of their pregnancy and postpartum body image: A systematic review and meta-synthesis. *BMC Pregnancy and Childbirth, 14*(1), 1–11. https://doi.org/10.1186/1471-2393-14-330

Holland, G., & Tiggemann, M. (2016). A systematic review of the impact of the use of social networking sites on body image and disordered eating outcomes. *Body Image, 17*, 100–110. https://doi.org/10.1016/j.bodyim.2016.02.008

Hughes, E. (2021). "I'm supposed to be thick": Managing body image anxieties among Black American women. *Journal of Black Studies*, *52*(3), 310–330. https://doi.org/10.1177/002193472097244

Karazsia, B. T., Murnen, S. K., & Tylka, T. L. (2017). Is body dissatisfaction changing across time? A cross-temporal meta-analysis. *Psychological Bulletin, 143*(3), 293–320. https://doi.org/10.1037/bul0000081

Keel, P. K., Baxter, M. G., Heatherton, T. F., & Joiner Jr, T. E. (2007). A 20-year longitudinal study of body weight, dieting, and eating disorder symptoms. *Journal of Abnormal Psychology, 116*(2), 422–432. https://doi.org/10.1037/0021-843X.116.2.422

Kelly, E. L., Minehan, M., & Pumpa, K. (2023). Maximal strength training as a pathway to positive body image: A qualitative exploration of the experiences of female powerlifters. *Women in Sport and Physical Activity Journal*, *1*, 1–9. https://doi.org/10.1123/wspaj.2022-0088

Kerner, C., Prescott, A., Smith, R., & Owen, M. (2022). A systematic review exploring body image programmes and interventions in physical education. *European Physical Education Review*, *28*(4), 942–967. https://doi.org/10.1177/1356336X22109731

Kilpela, L. S., Becker, C. B., Wesley, N., & Stewart, T. (2015). Body image in adult women: Moving beyond the younger years. *Advances in Eating Disorders: Theory, Research and Practice, 3*(2), 144–164. https://doi.org/10.1080/21662630.2015.1012728

King, J. E., Jebeile, H., Garnett, S. P., Baur, L. A., Paxton, S. J., & Gow, M. L. (2020). Physical activity based pediatric obesity treatment, depression, self-esteem and body image: A systematic review with meta-analysis. *Mental Health and Physical Activity*, *19*, 100342. https://doi.org/10.1016/j.mhpa.2020.100342

Kling, J., Kwakkenbos, L., Diedrichs, P. C., Rumsey, N., Frisen, A., Brandao, M. P., Silva, A. G., Dooley, B., Rodgers, R. F., & Fitzgerald, A. (2019). Systematic review of body image measures. *Body Image, 30*, 170–211. https://doi.org/10.1016/j.bodyim.2019.06.006

Koch, S., Kunz, T., Lykou, S., & Cruz, R. (2014). Effects of dance movement therapy and dance on health-related psychological outcomes: A meta-analysis. *The Arts in Psychotherapy*, *41*(1), 46–64. https://doi.org/10.1016/j.aip.2013.10.004

Langelier, D. M., D'Silva, A., Shank, J., Grant, C., Bridel, W., & Culos-Reed, S. N. (2019). Exercise interventions and their effect on masculinity, body image, and personal identity in prostate cancer—A systematic qualitative review. *Psycho-Oncology*, *28*(6), 1184–1196. https://doi.org/10.1002/pon.5060

Laus, M. F., Junqueira, A. C. P., Almeida, S. S., Costa, T. M. B., & Swami, V. (2022). Body image, muscle dysmorphia, and muscularity concerns: A comparison of CrossFit athletes, weight-trainers, and non-athletes. *Motricidade*, *18*(1), 50–60. https://doi.org/10.6063/motricidade.25584

Leary, M. R. (1992). Self-presentational processes in exercise and sport. *Journal of Sport and Exercise Psychology, 14*, 339–351. https://doi.org/10.1123/jsep.14.4.339

Lewis-Smith, H., Diedrichs, P. C., Rumsey, N., & Harcourt, D. (2018). Efficacy of psychosocial and physical activity-based interventions to improve body image among women treated for breast cancer: A systematic review. *Psycho-Oncology*, *27*(12), 2687–2699. https://doi.org/10.1002/pon.4870

Liu, H. Y., Chang, C. C., Gill, D. L., Wu, S. C., & Lu, F. J. (2019). Male weight trainers' body dissatisfaction and exercise dependence: Mediating role of muscularity drive. *Psychological Reports*, *122*(6), 2137–2154. https://doi.org/10.1177/0033294118805010

Lowy, A. S., Rodgers, R. F., Franko, D. L., Pluhar, E., & Webb, J. B. (2021). Body image and internalization of appearance ideals in Black women: An update and call for culturally-sensitive research. *Body Image*, *39*, 313–327. https://doi.org/10.1016/j.bodyim.2021.10.005

Mahlo, L., & Tiggemann, M. (2016). Yoga and positive body image: A test of the Embodiment Model. *Body Image*, *18*, 135–142. https://doi.org/10.1016/j.bodyim.2016.06.008

Malik, M., Grogan, S., Cole, J., & Gough, B. (2021). Men's reflections on their body image at different life stages: A thematic analysis of interview accounts from middle-aged men. *Journal of health psychology*, *26*(8), 1222–1232. https://doi.org/10.1177/135910531987164

Martin, J. J. (2018). *Handbook of disability sport and exercise psychology*. Oxford University Press.

Massey-Stokes, M., Golman, M., Quezada Ochoa, A., Stokes, A., & Robert-McComb, J. J. (2023). Body image throughout the lifespan. In J. J. Robert-McComb, M. Zumwalt, & M. Fernandez-del-Valle (Eds.), *The active female: Health issues throughout the lifespan* (pp. 25–54). Springer International Publishing.

Matheson, E. L., Schneider, J., Gentili, C., Tinoco, A., Silva-Breen, H., White, P., LaVol, N. M., & Diedrichs, P. C. (2025). A systematic review and meta-analysis of interventions that target the intersection of body image and movement among girls and women. *International Review of Sport and Exercise Psychology, 18*, 467–502. https://doi.org/10.1080/1750984X.2023.2258379

Myers, T. A., & Crowther, J. H. (2007). Sociocultural pressures, thin-ideal internalization, self objectification, and body dissatisfaction: Could feminist beliefs be a moderating factor? *Body Image, 4*(3), 296–308. https://doi.org/10.1016/j.bodyim.2007.04.001

Neumark-Sztainer, D., Watts, A. W., & Rydell, S. (2018). Yoga and body image: How do young adults practicing yoga describe its impact on their body image? *Body Image*, *27*, 156–168. https://doi.org/10.1016/j.bodyim.2018.09.001

O'Hara, L., Ahmed, H., & Elashie, S. (2021). Evaluating the impact of a brief Health at Every Size®-informed health promotion activity on body positivity and internalized weight-based oppression. *Body Image*, *37*, 225–237. https://doi.org/10.1016/j.bodyim.2021.02.006

Oehlhof, M. E. W., Musher-Eizenman, D. R., Neufeld, J. M., & Hauser, J. C. (2009). Self-objectification and ideal body shape for men and women. *Body Image*, *6*(4), 308–310. https://doi.org/10.1016/j.bodyim.2009.05.002

Olson, K. L., Lillis, J., Panza, E., Wing, R. R., Quinn, D. M., & Puhl, R. R. (2020). Body shape concerns across racial and ethnic groups among adults in the United States: More similarities than differences. *Body Image*, *35*, 108–113. https://doi.org/10.1016/j.bodyim.2020.08.013

Paillard, A. (2018). Can practising sport activities improve body image in people with physical disabilities? *International Physical Medicine and Rehabilitation*, *3*(1/0008), 101–102. https://doi.org/10.15406/ipmrj.2018.03.00083

Panão, I., & Carraça, E. V. (2020). Effects of exercise motivations on body image and eating habits/behaviours: A systematic review. *Nutrition & Dietetics, 77,* 41–59. https://doi.org/10.1111/1747-0080.12575

Pila, E., Gilchrist, J. D., Huellemann, K. L., Adam, M. E., & Sabiston, C. M. (2021). Body surveillance prospectively linked with physical activity via body shame in adolescent girls. *Body Image*, *36*, 276–282. https://doi.org/10.1016/j.bodyim.2021.01.002

Pellizzer, M. L., & Wade, T. D. (2023). Developing a definition of body neutrality and strategies for an intervention. *Body Image*, *46*, 434–442. https://doi.org/10.1016/j.bodyim.2023.07.006

Pruis, T. A., & Janowsky, J. S. (2010). Assessment of body image in younger and older women. *The Journal of General Psychology: Experimental, Psychological, and Comparative Psychology, 137*(3), 225–238. https://doi.org/10.1080/00221309.2010.484446

Quittkat, H. L., Hartmann, A. S., Düsing, R., Buhlmann, U., & Vocks, S. (2019). Body dissatisfaction, importance of appearance, and body appreciation in men and women over the lifespan. *Frontiers in Psychiatry, 10*, 864. https://doi.org/10.3389/fpsyt.2019.00864

Raspovic, A. M., Prichard, I., Yager, Z., & Hart, L. M. (2020). Mothers' experiences of the relationship between body image and exercise, 0–5 years postpartum: A qualitative study. *Body Image*, *35*, 41–52. https://doi.org/10.1016/j.bodyim.2020.08.003

Reel, J. J., Greenleaf, C., Baker, W. K., Aragon, S., Bishop, D., Cachaper, C., Handwerk, P., Locicero, J., Rathburn, L., Reid, W. K., & Hattie, J. (2007). Relations of body concerns and exercise behavior: A meta-analysis. *Psychological Reports*, *101*(3), 927–942. https://doi.org/10.2466/pr0.101.3.927-942

Reel, J. J., Galli, N., Miyairi, M., Voelker, D., & Greenleaf, C. (2016). Development and validation of the intuitive exercise scale. *Eating Behaviors*, *22*, 129–132. https://doi.org/10.1016/j.eatbeh.2016.06.013

Reel, J. J., Lee, J. J., & Bellows, A. (2016). Integrating exercise and mindfulness for an emerging conceptual framework: The intuitive approach to prevention and health promotion (IAPHP). *Eating Disorders*, *24*(1), 90–97. https://doi.org/10.1080/10640266.2015.1118951

Rice, C., Riley, S., LaMarre, A., & Bailey, K. A. (2021). What a body can do: Rethinking body functionality through a feminist materialist disability lens. *Body Image, 38*, 95–105. https://doi.org/10.1016/j.bodyim.2021.03.014

Rodgers, R. F., & Laveway, K. (2022). Social media use, body image and eating disorders. In A. House & C. Brennan (Eds.), *Social media and mental health*. Cambridge University Press.

Sabiston, C. M., Doré, I., Lucibello, K. M., Pila, E., Brunet, J., Thibault, V., & Bélanger, M. (2022). Body image self-conscious emotions get worse throughout adolescence and relate to physical activity behavior in girls and boys. *Social Science & Medicine*, *315*, 115543. https://doi.org/10.1016/j.socscimed.2022.115543

Sabiston, C. M., Pila, E., Vani, M., & Thogersen-Ntoumani, C. (2019). Body image, physical activity, and sport: A scoping review. *Psychology of Sport and Exercise*, *42*, 48–57. https://doi.org/10.1016/j.psychsport.2018.12.010

Sánchez-Miguel, P. A., Sevil-Serrano, J., Sanchez-Oliva, D., Vaquero-Solis, M., & Tapia-Serrano, M. A. (2021). Does gender moderate the relationship between physical activity and body dissatisfaction among adolescents? *Journal of Gender Studies*, *30*(6), 676–686. https://doi.org/10.1080/09589236.2021.1937078

SantaBarbara, N. J., Whitworth, J. W., & Ciccolo, J. T. (2017). A systematic review of the effects of resistance training on body image. *The Journal of Strength & Conditioning Research*, *31*(10), 2880–2888. https://doi.org/10.1519/JSC.0000000000002135

SantaBarbara, N. J., Nosrat, S., Whitworth, J. W., & Ciccolo, J. T. (2023). Acute psychological effects of resistance exercise in men with symptoms of muscle dysmorphia: A pilot study. *The Journal of Strength & Conditioning Research*, *37*(2): 277–283. https://doi.org/10.1519/JSC.0000000000003615

Sastre, A. (2014). Towards a radical body positive: Reading the online "body positive movement". *Feminist Media Studies*, *14*(6), 929–943. https://doi.org/10.1080/14680777.2014.883420

Sonstroem, R. J., Harlow, L. L., & Josephs, L. (1994). Exercise and self-esteem: Validity of model expansion and exercise associations. *Journal of Sport & Exercise Psychology*, *16*, 29–42. https://doi.org/10.1123/jsep.16.1.29

Sonstroem, R. J., & Morgan, W. P. (1989). Exercise and self-esteem: Rationale and model. *Medicine and Science in Sport and Exercise*, *21*, 329–337.

Sousa, A. I., Corredeira, R., & Pereira, A. L. (2009). The body in persons with an amputation. *Adapted Physical Activity Quarterly, 26*(3), 236–258. https://doi.org/10.1123/apaq.26.3.236

Srismith, D., Wider, L. M., Wong, H. Y., Zipfel, S., Thiel, A., Giel, K. E., & Behrens, S. C. (2020). Influence of physical activity interventions on body representation: A systematic review. *Frontiers in Psychiatry*, *11*, 99. https://doi.org/10.3389/fpsyt.2020.00099

Sun, W., Chen, D., Wang, J., Liu, N., & Zhang, W. (2018). Physical activity and body image dissatisfaction among pregnant women: A systematic review and meta-analysis of cohort studies. *European Journal of Obstetrics & Gynecology and Reproductive Biology*, *229*, 38–44. https://doi.org/10.1016/j.ejogrb.2018.07.021

Teti, M., Bauerband, L. A., Rolbiecki, A., & Young, C. (2020). Physical activity and body image: Intertwined health priorities identified by transmasculine young people in a non-metropolitan area. *International Journal of Transgender Health*, *21*(2), 209–219. https://doi.org/10.1080/26895269.2020.1719950

Thomas, E. V., Warren-Findlow, J., Webb, J. B., Quinlan, M. M., Laditka, S. B., & Reeve, C. (2019). "It's very valuable to me that I appear capable": A qualitative study exploring relationships between body functionality and appearance among women with visible physical disabilities. *Body Image, 30*, 81–92. https://doi.org/10.1016/j.bodyim.2019.05.007

Thompson, J. K., Heinberg, L. J., Altabe, M., & Tantleff-Dunn, S. (1999). *Exacting beauty: Theory, assessment, and treatment of body image disturbance*. American Psychological Association.

Tiggemann, M. (2004). Body image across the adult life span: Stability and change. *Body Image, 1*(1), 29–41. https://doi.org/10.1016/S1740-1445(03)00002-0

Tiggemann, M. & McCourt, A. (2013). Body appreciation in adult women: Relationships with age and body satisfaction. *Body Image, 10*(4), 624–627. https://doi.org/10.1016/j.bodyim.2013.07.003

Tod, D., & Edwards, C. (2015). A meta-analysis of the drive for muscularity's relationships with exercise behaviour, disordered eating, supplement consumption, and exercise dependence. *International Review of Sport and Exercise Psychology, 8*(1), 185–203. https://doi.org/10.1080/1750984X.2015.1052089

Tylka, T. L. (2018). Overview of the field of positive body image. In E. A. Daniels, M. M. Gillen, & C. H. Markey (Eds.), *Body positive: Understanding and improving body image in science and practice* (pp. 6–33). Cambridge University Press.

Tylka, T. L., Rodgers, R. F., Calogero, R. M., Thompson, J. K., & Harriger, J. A. (2023). Integrating social media variables as predictors, mediators, and moderators within body image frameworks: Potential mechanisms of action to consider in future research. *Body Image, 44*, 197–221. https://doi.org/10.1016/j.bodyim.2023.01.004

Tylka, T. L., & Wood-Barcalow, N. L. (2015). What is and what is not positive body image? Conceptual foundations and construct definition. *Body Image*, *14*, 118–129. https://doi.org/10.1016/j.bodyim.2015.04.001

Walters, R., & Hefferon, K. (2020). 'Strength becomes her'–resistance training as a route to positive body image in women. *Qualitative Research in Sport, Exercise and Health, 12*(3), 446–464. https://doi.org/10.1080/2159676X.2019.1634127

Webb, J. B., Padro, M. P., Thomas, E. V., Davies, A. E., Etzel, L., Rogers, C. B., & Heredia, N. I. (2022). Yoga at every size: A preliminary evaluation of a brief online size-inclusive yoga and body gratitude journaling intervention to enhance positive embodiment in higher weight college women. *Frontiers in Global Women's Health*, *3*, 852854. https://doi.org/10.3389/fgwh.2022.852854

Wildes, J. E., Emery, R. E., & Simons, A. D. (2001). The roles of ethnicity and culture in the development of eating disturbance and body dissatisfaction: A meta-analytic review. *Clinical Psychology Review*, *21*(4), 521–551. https://doi.org/10.1016/S0272-7358(99)00071-9

6

WEIGHT-RELATED STIGMA IN PHYSICAL ACTIVITY SPACES

Trauma and Demotivation in Higher-Weight Individuals

Garcia Ashdown-Franks, Angela Meadows, Eva Pila

6.1 Introduction

For individuals across the weight spectrum, physical activity offers much promise in the prevention and treatment of mental health concerns in both adults and youngsters (Biddle et al., 2019; Schuch & Vancampfort, 2021), as well as the promotion of psychological well-being (Marquez et al., 2020). However, at a population level, there is an inverse relationship between body mass index (BMI) and physical activity behavior (Bennie et al., 2019; NHS Digital, 2023; Ren et al., 2024), such that higher-weight individuals may engage in insufficient levels of physical activity to attain mental health benefits. These lower levels of physical activity engagement are particularly concerning since higher-weight individuals also experience greater prevalence of mental health concerns than normative-weight individuals (Daly et al., 2020; Kokka et al., 2023; Rajan & Menon, 2017). While most public health efforts focus on using physical activity as a method of "obesity prevention and treatment," there is ample evidence that physical activity has mental health benefits across the weight spectrum (Hamer et al., 2009), not necessitating weight loss to attain psychological benefit. As such, there have been calls to increase access to physical activity participation for higher-weight individuals, without a focus on weight management (Bombak, 2014; Mansfield & Rich, 2013; Pickett & Cunningham, 2017b). In a critical review of the current state of research, this chapter will examine how weight stigma impedes physical activity participation and quality experiences in higher-weight individuals, contributing to health inequities in this population. This chapter will also outline a series of evidence-based recommendations for targeting weight stigma in physical activity contexts and improving the physical activity experiences of higher-weight individuals.

DOI: 10.4324/9781003517474-9

6.2 Defining Weight Stigma

Weight stigma can be defined as the societal devaluation of people based solely on their weight or body size. While weight stigma manifests as negative beliefs, attitudes, and treatment of higher-weight people, stigma is fundamentally a mark of otherness or deviance, labeling a group of people as being outside of acceptable society (Goffman, 1963). That is, the issue of weight stigma is not simply about the behavior of prejudiced individuals that can be solved at an interpersonal level; rather experiences of weight stigma are a *consequence* of being regarded as unequal in society. Because weight stigma is culturally entrenched, it is pervasive through all aspects of everyday life (for a review, see Puhl & Heuer, 2009). Consequently, in addition to being stigmatized by others, some higher-weight people internalize these beliefs and values and apply them to themselves (i.e., internalized weight stigma), which is associated with concomitant decrements in self-worth (Durso & Latner, 2008). Internalized weight stigma is distinct from negative body image and negative body- and weight-related perceptions and experiences (Meadows & Higgs, 2020), as it incorporates an element of shame aligned with societal beliefs about weight controllability and one's inability to adhere to societal norms and expectations about weight (Townend, 2009). While individuals across the weight spectrum often report negative weight-related experiences in physical activity (e.g., receive negative commentary regarding their weight, experience shame and guilt about their weight; Ashdown-Franks et al., 2022; Huellemann et al., 2024; Sabiston et al., 2020; Vani et al., 2020), the lived experience and implications differ for those in normative and non-normative bodies (Meadows et al., 2017), and the mechanisms of action in predicting physical activity outcomes are also likely to differ (Meadows & Bombak, 2019). As such, this chapter will focus on studies that explore the association between weight stigma and physical activity in higher-weight samples or conduct analyses by weight status.[1]

Additionally, we will use the term "higher-weight" when describing larger bodies in general, rather than the medicalized terms "overweight" and "obese," in line with recommendations from weight-related social justice organizations, researchers, and health professionals advocating for the avoidance of pathologizing terminology as one avenue to reduce weight stigma in academic and professional domains (Meadows & Daníelsdóttir, 2016). Consistently, "normative-weight" in the sense of socially acceptable, will be used in place of "normal weight" to describe people whose bodies are not in the upper two BMI categories. When necessary to use the BMI categories in describing particular studies, these will be placed in inverted commas to indicate contestation of the medicalization of body weight and the social construction of the disease narrative.

6.3 Anti-Fat Attitudes in Physical Activity Spaces

A considerable body of evidence now exists documenting widespread weight stigma in the physical activity domain, including anti-fat attitudes held and perpetuated by physical activity professionals (e.g., fitness trainers, physical education [PE] teachers, kinesiology, and exercise science pre-service and professionals). For example, strong explicit and implicit anti-fat attitudes have been noted in both current (Dimmock et al., 2009; Fontana et al., 2018; Robertson & Vohora, 2008) and future (Alameida & Whitehead, 2015; Chambliss et al., 2004; Fontana et al., 2013; Langdon et al., 2016; Sartore & Cunningham, 2007) fitness professional. Such attitudes encompass both emotional responses such as dislike and disgust, and endorsement of negative stereotypes, for example, that higher-weight people are weak-willed and lazy. Interestingly, witnessing higher-weight people engaging in physical activity (i.e., countering the stereotype that they were lazy) did not change these attitudes or beliefs (Dimmock et al., 2009). Class instructors may stigmatize fat bodies, using the fear of becoming fat or the imperative to "burn it off" as a desirable end goal to "motivate" class participants (Kenen, 1987; Packer, 1989; Souza & Ebbeck, 2018). Many gyms use anti-fat messaging in their advertising and promotional campaigns, suggesting that only a thin body is acceptable and that the goal of physical activity is to achieve this normative appearance (Argüelles et al., 2022; Myre et al., 2020), and some gyms have gone so far as to use explicit anti-fat humor (AdWeek, 2010; Murphy, 2017; Schlossberg, 2016). As Rinaldi and colleagues (2020) eloquently note, "Exercise facilities, then, take on a double purpose: they function both to exclude and to prevent the existence of fat bodies" (p. 46).

Some studies have compared exercise professionals with non-exercise professionals (e.g., PE versus math teachers) and noted significantly higher levels of explicit and implicit anti-fat attitudes in the physical activity domain (Carmona-Márquez et al., 2021). Similar results have been found in PE or sport and exercise students compared with students from non-exercise-related majors (Greenleaf et al., 2008; Lau et al., 2018; Lynagh et al., 2015; O'Brien et al., 2007). Importantly, when comparing PE students and psychology students at the beginning and toward the end of their degrees, not only did PE students have higher explicit and implicit anti-fat bias than psychology students at baseline, but their negative implicit attitudes worsened over the course of their training (O'Brien et al., 2007). This amplification of fatphobia during training is unlikely to change while exercise science students are taught by professors with high levels of anti-fat bias themselves (Fontana et al., 2017), and the curriculum focuses on an anti-obesity rhetoric and positions higher-weight status as a problem requiring intervention (Norman & Petherick, 2016; Quennerstedt et al., 2021; Tinning, 1985 as cited in Pausé, 2019). Interventions that focus on changing beliefs about the supposed controllability of body weight are often quite effective in their stated goal, raising awareness that higher-weight status is not simply a matter of willpower and hard work, but are mostly unsuccessful in changing anti-fat attitudes (Daníelsdóttir et al., 2010), likely because although trying to alleviate "blame," they nevertheless continue to problematize fatness (Brochu, 2023).

Despite this, many fitness professionals consider themselves to be unbiased, often providing relatively neutral answers to explicit questions about anti-fat attitudes while nevertheless displaying bias on implicit measures (e.g., Alameida & Whitehead, 2015; Dimmock et al., 2009; Fontana et al. 2013). Further, awareness of the impact of weight stigma is lacking. For example, in a qualitative study of 27 physiotherapists, participants expressed a range of anti-fat attitudes and labeled higher-weight patients as difficult to treat, yet believed higher-weight patients are not affected by stigma (Setchell et al., 2016). Conversely, when patients were interviewed about their experiences in physiotherapy with participants reporting experiencing weight stigma both from the environment and from the practitioners themselves (Setchell et al., 2015). Relatedly, evidence from the wider healthcare literature suggests that patients pick up on subtle cues from providers and that practitioner biases, including implicit biases, have a negative impact on the clinical relationship, clinical outcomes, and patient well-being (Phelan et al., 2015; Zestcott et al., 2016). Thus, while a couple of studies have reported no evidence that anti-fat attitudes translated into differing clinical treatment (Setchell et al., 2014) or fitness plan prescriptions (Fontana et al., 2018) based on weight status, it would be naive to think that negative attitudes are not picked up by clients.

Similar to research in physical activity providers, frequent exercisers may also contribute to hostile physical activity environments. Quantitative data from a large UK study found that frequent exercisers (over eight hours per week) reported more explicit anti-fat attitudes than people who exercised less than three hours per week (Flint et al., 2015). Focus groups with people who met the recommended guidelines for physical activity through gyms, exercise classes, sports, or outdoor activities such as running, identified shocking levels of explicit weight stigma, with participants overtly mocking, dehumanizing, and harassing higher-weight exercisers, and described enacting stigma toward them as both common and acceptable (Flint & Reale, 2018).

6.4 Experienced Weight Stigma in Physical Activity Spaces

It should therefore come as no surprise that higher-weight exercisers report frequent negative experiences in physical activity contexts, including being stared at, photographed, humiliated, and verbally and physically abused (Argüelles et al., 2022; Bombak, 2015; Ellison, 2009; Harjunen, 2019; Rocha & Winton, 2016). Others report being treated differently by fitness instructors (Argüelles et al., 2022; Myre et al., 2020; Pickett & Cunningham, 2018) and coaches (Ashdown-Franks et al., 2022; Goe, 2021; Nguyen, 2012; Thedinga et al., 2021), with some being literally excluded from their sport.

This phenomenon is not limited to adults. Childhood experiences of weight stigma during PE and extra-curricular sporting endeavors have been well documented, with students reporting both overt fat shaming and bullying and reduced expectations of teachers and peers (Ashdown-Franks et al., 2022; Faith et al., 2002; Li & Rukavina, 2012; Sykes & McPhail, 2008; Trout & Graber, 2009). Lack of awareness or response, and even complicity, further compounded the trauma experienced by youngsters in these settings (e.g., Li & Rukavina, 2012). Practices involving weighing and measurement reinforce the surveillance and disciplining of fat bodies and are perceived by higher-weight children as humiliating and othering (Ashdown-Franks et al., 2022; Sykes & McPhail, 2008); while all children may be subjected to these practices, in an environment where fatness is explicitly stigmatized, the lived experience of weighing for a higher-weight child is not the same as that of a normative-weight child who is not the target of blame and shame from themselves and others. Summarizing participants' recall of their PE experiences, Sykes and McPhail (2008) concluded that "fat phobia created extremely difficult situations that demanded constant psychic/emotional work, provided pitiful opportunities for learning, and numerous alienating and traumatic movement experiences" (p. 68).

6.5 Impact of Weight Stigma on Physical Activity Outcomes

Research has explored the impact of experienced and internalized weight stigma on a variety of physical activity variables, including attitudes toward physical activity (e.g., Cheng et al., 2019; Myre et al., 2020); preference for different types of physical activity (e.g., Myre et al., 2020; Schvey et al., 2017; Thedinga et al., 2021); and physical activity intentions (e.g., Gallardo et al., 2020; Pearl, Dovidio et al., 2015; Seacat & Mickelson, 2009; Vartanian et al., 2018). Due to space limitations, we will focus predominantly on four key outcomes: physical activity behavior, affective experiences of physical activity, and two psychological predictors of physical activity behavior: exercise self-efficacy and exercise motivation.

6.5.1 Physical Activity Behavior

A recent review of the relationship between weight stigma and physical activity identified 29 studies in adults and 9 in youngsters (Pearl et al., 2021); however, only 16 of the adult studies were restricted to higher-weight participants, and only two of those in youngsters. Of the studies that included weight-diverse samples, most did not distinguish effects by weight status. On the whole, results showed negative impact of all forms of weight stigma on physical activity outcomes (Pearl et al., 2021). Overall, and across the weight spectrum, having ever had experiences of weight-related stigma or teasing was linked with less physical activity behavior, compared with never having had these experiences, and especially with lower duration (e.g., Boros et al., 2017) and frequency of moderate- or high-intensity physical activity (e.g., Jackson & Steptoe, 2017; Phibbs et al., 2019). These findings have been largely supported across ethnicity and cultures (e.g., Cheng et al., 2019; Gallardo et al., 2020; Gerend et al., 2023; Lessard et al., 2021), and age spectrum (e.g., Bombak et al., 2024; Jackson & Steptoe, 2017; Pearl et al., 2021), although some differences were evident by gender (e.g., Gerend et al., 2023; Sattler et al., 2018; Udo et al., 2016), most likely as a result of different societal expectations for men's and women's bodies.

Of the studies on internalized weight stigma, about half reported direct, significant associations with reduced physical activity, while internalized weight stigma was also found to mediate the associations between stigmatizing experiences and physical activity, such that experienced stigma was linked with higher internalized stigma, which, in turn, predicted lower engagement in physical activity (e.g., Pearl, Puhl et al., 2015).

Some studies did not find direct associations between weight stigma and physical activity but identified indirect effects, via depression (e.g., Storch et al., 2007), reduced self-efficacy and greater perceived barriers (e.g., Feig et al., 2020), and motivation to avoid exercise (e.g., Han et al., 2018; Vartanian & Novak, 2011). Others found no relationship at all (Carels et al., 2019; Puhl et al., 2019). A handful of studies identified a small increase in physical activity following exposure to stigma (e.g, Pearl, Dovidio et al., 2015; Udo et al., 2016); possible explanations for this finding will be discussed further below. It is worth noting that the validity of many measures of weight stigma – whether they are accurately capturing stigma experiences – has been questioned (e.g., Lindloff & Meadows, 2023). This contention is supported by studies that utilize ecological momentary assessment to capture stigma experiences in real time, rather than by survey recollection, and suggest that weight stigma is often a daily experience for many higher-weight individuals (Seacat et al., 2016; Vartanian et al., 2018). One such study reported that the more frequently people experience weight stigma on a given day, the less motivated they were to exercise (or diet/lose weight) at the end of the day, an effect that was mediated by reductions in positive affect (Vartanian et al., 2018).

In addition, the longitudinal relationship between weight stigma and physical activity and sport (dis)engagement are also well-evidenced. Qualitative studies have repeatedly noted that weight-stigmatizing experiences earlier in life can lead to activity and sport disengagement later in life (Ashdown-Franks et al., 2022 Myre et al., 2020). Another interview study found that in order to avoid weight-stigmatizing experiences in the gym, some 'obese' gym-users purposely self-excluded themselves from the gym entirely, or from specific aspects of the gym experience, such as social or group-based exercise (Thedinga et al., 2021). Collectively, research suggests that exclusion can either result in individuals exercising on their own and thus not reaping the social support benefits that come from social exercise or fully excluding themselves and not being able to enjoy the benefits that come from being active at all.

6.5.2 Exercise Self-Efficacy

Perceived self-efficacy represents an individual's beliefs in their ability to successfully complete a given task (Bandura, 1997), and exercise self-efficacy is an important psychological factor related to engagement in and maintenance of physical activity (Bauman et al., 2012; McAuley & Blissmer, 2000; Williams & French, 2011). Much of the health promotion research in this area focuses on self-regulatory capacity, which assesses an individual's perceived ability to persevere in the face of barriers and challenges (Williams & Rhodes, 2016); regulatory self-capacity therefore applies more to the maintenance aspect of exercise behavior than to initial engagement. Both experienced and internalized weight stigma have been linked with lower exercise self-regulatory capacity (Feig et al., 2020; Ievers-Landis et al., 2019; Pearl, Puhl et al., 2015).

In contrast, competence assesses an individual's perceived ability to successfully complete the task itself; if people feel a particular undertaking is beyond their capabilities, many will choose not to spend time and effort on an activity that they consider to be futile (Bandura, 1997). Scholars have proposed that this perception of competence may be most profoundly influenced by weight stigma and likely to have the most pronounced impact on physical activity behavior in higher-weight individuals (Meadows & Bombak, 2019). In the absence of positive "enactive mastery experience" (Bandura, 1997, p. 80), individuals will be deprived of opportunities to develop this self-efficacy and come to incorporate their competence in a given domain into their sense of identity. Meadows and Bombak (2019) present a recursive model outlining the direct and indirect routes via which weight stigma may negatively impact exercise self-efficacy, exercise identity development, and engagement in physical activity behavior (Figure 6.1).

In this model, the direct route between experienced weight stigma and physical activity behavior can be driven by past negative, even traumatic, experiences during physical activity. Some of these experiences are overt, including being called names, bullied, and openly mocked for actual or perceived lack of athletic prowess in PE classes (Li & Rukavina, 2012; Sykes & McPhail, 2008; Trout &

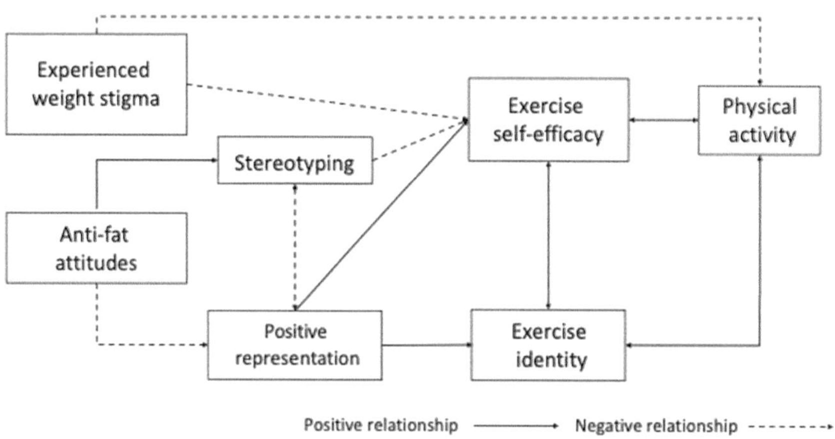

FIGURE 6.1 Proposed Dual-Pathway Relationship Between Weight Stigma and Physical Activity *From Meadows & Bombak,* 2019; reprinted with permission.

Graber, 2009). Others are more subtle, such as teachers holding lower expectations of higher-weight students, believing them to be less fit and healthy than slimmer children (Greenleaf & Weiller, 2005; Myre et al., 2020; Trout & Graber, 2009), even more so for higher-weight girls than boys (Peterson et al., 2012). In an experimental study, German PE teachers gave lower grades to a student for a particular gymnastics maneuver, depending on whether the student was described as "overweight" or "normal weight," and these judgments were driven by the teacher's agreements with stereotypes of higher-weight people (Glock & Schuchart, 2021).

It is well documented that teacher-expectation effects have an impact on subsequent student performance, including in PE (Trouilloud et al., 2002; Trouilloud et al., 2006). This effect is partially mediated by students' own perceived competence (Trouilloud et al., 2006). It is further known that students from vulnerable or stigmatized groups are more susceptible to teacher-expectation effects (Madon et al., 1997). In both quantitative (Gallardo et al., 2020; Greenleaf et al., 2014; Losekam et al., 2010; Maïano et al., 2018) and qualitative (Bauer et al., 2004; Li & Rukavina, 2012) studies in children, both overt and subtle physical activity-related weight-stigmatizing experiences are linked with lower self-perceived physical capabilities and concomitant reduction in physical activity behavior, with effects often lasting through to adulthood (Rice, 2007; Schmalz, 2010; Sykes & McPhail, 2008; Thedinga et al., 2021). Thus, higher-weight youngsters learn that their bodies preclude their successful engagement in physical activity and do not belong in the physical activity domain, impairing the development of a physical activity identity, which, in turn, may curtail opportunities to further develop self-efficacy and active identities, resulting in a vicious circle.

Stereotypes also play a role in the indirect route, whereby the perception that an active body is necessarily a thin body results in the non-provision of exercise apparel and equipment suitable for larger bodies (Chastain, 2014; Christel et al., 2016; Greenleaf et al., 2020; Marks, 2013; Lewis & Van Puymbroeck, 2008), reinforcing the message that fat bodies do not belong in these spaces and potentially creating a self-fulfilling prophecy. The resultant lack of visibility of higher-weight bodies in these spaces may also contribute to the indirect effects of weight stigma on physical activity.

In the absence of exercise self-efficacy developed by learned competence, an alternative route to developing self-efficacy is via exposure to role models; seeing somebody like you succeed in a domain where your group is under-represented can lead to the development of vicarious self-efficacy (Bandura, 1997). In a meta-analysis of exercise self-efficacy interventions, those based on vicarious experiences were highly effective at increasing participants' perceived self-efficacy for physical activity (Ashford et al., 2010). However, due to widespread societal weight stigma, the availability of positive active higher-weight role models is sometimes limited and attempts to rectify this situation are sometimes criticized as "glorifying obesity," the curious implication being that seeing a higher-weight person enjoying physical activity is more likely to encourage other people to be fat than it is to encourage them to be active (Meadows & Bombak, 2019). Indeed, higher-weight fitness professionals have been deemed not to be good role models by PE professors (Fontana et al., 2017), students (Greenleaf et al., 2008; Sartore & Cunningham, 2007), qualified exercise professionals (Hare et al., 2000), employers (Poole, 2002), and potential clients (Myre et al., 2020).

Yet, considerable anecdotal evidence speaks to the effectiveness of having access to plus-size active role models for promoting engagement in physical activity (Meadows & Bombak, 2019) and an interview study with body-positive yoga instructors supports the idea that the presence of a non-stereotypical body at the front of the classroom sends a profound message of inclusivity; they note that their classes are frequently weight-diverse – it is not only higher-weight people who are sometimes alienated in physical activity spaces (Pickett & Cunningham, 2017a). In another study, undergraduates enrolled in on-campus yoga classes were randomized to view a 20-minute online yoga instruction session, with either a higher-weight or a normative-weight instructor (Pickett & Cunningham, 2018). After following the workout, participants completed a series of questionnaire measures, including identification with the instructor and intentions to continue with yoga. Interestingly, while higher-weight participants identified more strongly with the higher-weight instructor, normative-weight participants identified equally with both instructors. Further, identification with instructor was linked with future yoga intentions (Pickett & Cunningham, 2018). In a study of women who had engaged in a wide range of individual and group physical activity and sports in the previous year, perceived body-inclusivity of their physical activity environment was positively associated with physical activity identity and with self-rated health. Importantly, the relationship between body-inclusivity and physical activity identity was only statistically significant in higher-weight women (Cunningham & Pickett, 2020).

Another experimental study randomized higher-weight inactive women to view an inspirational story of a woman taking up a new hobby (running or learning a language) in middle age, accompanied by a photo of either a higher-weight or normative-weight role model engaged in that activity (Meadows, 2024). Participants identified more strongly with the higher-weight model, which indirectly, via feeling more inspired, predicted higher levels of exercise self-efficacy, lower exercise-related body self-conscious emotions (e.g., embarrassment, shame), and greater self-reported likelihood of initiating exercise in the next three months. Participants in the fat-active role model condition were also more likely to provide an email address and request information about beginning exercise (Meadows, 2024).

Thus, through a series of direct and indirect effects, higher-weight adults and children may be deprived of opportunities to develop exercise self-efficacy, which, in turn, teaches them that bodies like theirs do not belong in physical activity spaces, and that a fit and active body is, by definition, a slim body. It is through these mechanisms that Meadows and Bombak (2019) propose that it is notably more difficult for a higher-weight person to develop a robust exercise identity.

6.5.3 Affective Experiences

Affective experiences of physical activity are consistently shown to predict future exercise behavior across a variety of populations and cultural contexts (Ekkekakis & Dafermos, 2012; Rhodes et al., 2009). Both a history of weight-related teasing by others (Boros et al., 2017) and weight-related self-stigma (Mensinger & Meadows, 2017) have been linked with lower exercise enjoyment in weight-diverse female college students and higher-weight women enrolled in a healthy living trial, respectively. Unsurprisingly, weight-related teasing experienced *during* physical activity has also been linked with reduced enjoyment of sports in youngsters (Faith et al. 2002; Gallardo et al., 2020). Mensinger and Meadows (2017) also found that participants low in internalized weight stigma increased engagement in physical activity after the six-month trial, whereas the effect was muted in those high in self-stigma. Indeed, in a sample of low-active higher-weight participants in a six-month healthy living program, reductions in self-stigma were associated with increases in exercise enjoyment, which, in turn predicted greater engagement in physical activity (Mensinger & Meadows, 2017).

In a separate study of low-active, higher-weight adults signing up for a weight-loss intervention, participants completed a 30-minute supervised session of moderate-intensity treadmill walking; their heart rate was measured every minute and their rate of perceived exertion every five minutes (Olson et al., 2021). Higher levels of internalized weight stigma were linked with greater perceived exertion during exercise, controlling for BMI. Further, elevations in heart rate during exercise were linked with greater positive affect in participants low in self-stigma but with greater negative affect in participants high in self-stigma; that is, higher internalized weight stigma was associated with finding the physical experience of exercise more strenuous and unpleasant (Olson et al., 2021). This finding is likely linked with the phenomenon of stereotype threat, whereby holders of a salient social identity are aware that their behavior is observable by others and may reinforce negative stereotypes about their social group. The visible physiological manifestations of an exercising body – increased heart rate, sweating, and so on may be perceived as evidence of fitness and health in a slim body, but could be perceived as evidence of low fitness and lack of personal responsibility in a higher-weight person. Thus, for an individual with higher levels of self-stigma, being seen exercising, with the physiological response that entails, may intensify their sense of shame (Meadows & Bombak, 2019). Thus, interventions that target both weight stigma in physical activity contexts and internalized weight stigma may have positive effects on exercise outcomes.

6.5.4 Exercise Motivation

According to the organismic integration mini-theory of self-determination (Deci & Ryan, 1985), behavior is driven by different types of motivation, which can be

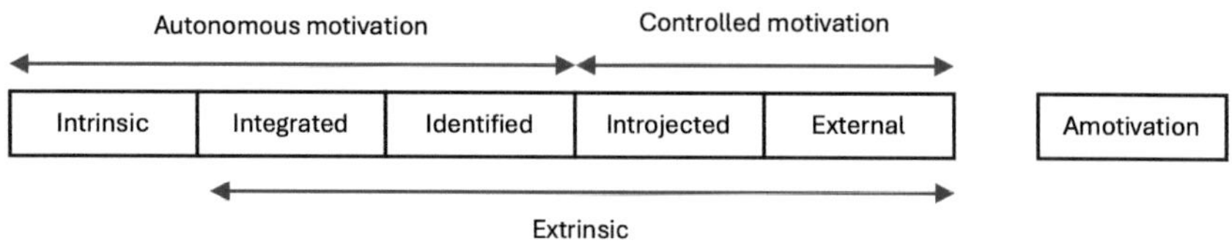

FIGURE 6.2 Continuum of Autonomous and Controlled Motivation.

imagined on a continuum from most to least autonomous (Figure 6.2). At one end, intrinsic motivation involves engaging in an activity entirely for its own benefits, such as enjoyment or to develop a sense of achievement. In contrast, extrinsic motivation involves benefits, or the absence of negative outcomes, that extend beyond participation *per se*. Extrinsic motivation can be either self- or other-driven. Next on the continuum, and also autonomous forms of motivation, are integrated and identified regulation. Integrated regulation involves a behavior being incorporated into one's sense of self, whereas identified regulation involves an activity being personally important and valuable. Unsurprisingly, autonomous forms of motivation are strongly linked to holding an exercise identity (Rhodes et al., 2016).

At the other end of the continuum are introjected and external regulation, which are other-directed (controlled) rather than self-directed (autonomous). Introjected regulation involves doing an activity out of a sense of guilt or obligation or to avoid negative judgment, for example, whereas external regulation, the least autonomous, involves engaging in an activity because others instruct or require you to do so. The absence of any motivation – amotivation – involves total disengagement from a domain (Deci & Ryan, 1985). Type of motivation is important to consider because different types of motivation are differentially associated with a variety of downstream outcomes. With respect to physical activity, autonomous motivation is associated with greater enjoyment, better psychological well-being, and improved long-term engagement, whereas the reverse is true for controlled motivation, including being active to achieve weight and/or appearance goals (Homan & Tylka, 2014; Raedeke et al., 2007; Strelan et al., 2003; Teixeira et al., 2012).

Unfortunately, much of the research on weight stigma and exercise motivation is atheoretical. One of the first studies to test this relationship empirically demonstrated that experienced weight stigma was linked with an increased desire to *avoid* exercise (Vartanian & Shaprow, 2008), which was more pronounced in the subset of participants in the 'overweight' or 'obese' BMI categories (personal correspondence). Stigma was a stronger predictor of motivation to avoid exercise than was age, BMI, self-esteem, or body dissatisfaction. Further, avoidance motivation was negatively associated with moderate- and vigorous-intensity physical activity, but not mild-intensity activity. One plausible explanation for this finding is that the measure used to assess avoidance motivation was created for the study and focused predominantly on embarrassment and public activities. It is possible that stigma indirectly predicts motivation to avoid *public* exercise, such as swimming, running, or going to a gym, but may not be linked with motivation to exercise more generally (Myre et al., 2020; Thedinga et al., 2021); however, solo exercise undertaken, for example, in the privacy of one's own home, may be less likely to involve higher-intensity forms of exercise.

Other studies use generic items, such as "How motivated are you to exercise?" that can tell us something about levels of motivation, but not what type of motivation, or combine items assessing both autonomous and controlled motivation (e.g., Han et al., 2018; Pearl, Dovidio et al., 2015; Vartanian et al., 2018), perhaps explaining contradictory findings and making interpretation difficult. However, a few studies have explored physical activity motivation using a self-determination theory framework that allows for a more nuanced understanding of the processes involved.

In one experimental study in a weight-diverse community sample, stigmatizing experiences were linked to greater controlled motivation, as well as higher body dissatisfaction and drive for thinness; the effects weakened (although remaining statistically significant) when controlling for BMI, suggesting that the effects of stigma are more pronounced in higher-weight participants (Pearl, Dovidio et al., 2015). None of these variables was linked with autonomous motivation; however, self-esteem was associated with greater autonomous motivation to exercise. Interestingly, controlled motivation was significantly linked with both higher exercise intentions and higher exercise avoidance, but was unrelated to actual exercise behavior, whereas autonomous motivation was linked with lower avoidance, higher intentions, more frequent physical activity (Pearl, Dovidio et al., 2015). On the other hand, a study in a weight-diverse student sample found that weight-related social control, i.e., others urging you to eat less or exercise more, was associated with less overall physical activity, even controlling for objective and self-classified weight status, and the effect was strongest when the source of control was parents (Brunson et al. 2014).

In another study with a weight-diverse sample recruited through an online survey panel, higher BMI was linked with greater belief that the public considers higher-weight people to be both immoral and incompetent, and to greater fears of condemnation and internalized weight stigma, which, in turn, were linked with lower autonomous motivation and greater controlled motivation and amotivation to exercise (Täuber et al., 2018).

In contrast, in a weight-diverse student sample, internalized weight stigma was not associated with intrinsic, identified, or external motivation to exercise, but was positively associated with higher introjected motivation, although the effect was significant only in participants who self-classified as "overweight" (Ali & Meadows, 2022). Experienced weight stigma was not associated with autonomous motivation but was linked with increased controlled motivation and amotivation. Interestingly, in the "overweight" participants only, size-acceptance beliefs (the belief that diversity in body size is normal and that all bodies should be celebrated) were linked to reduced external and amotivation, suggesting a possible protective effect (Ali & Meadows, 2022). Thus, far from contentions that stigma has a positive effect and "acceptance" of larger bodies may result in fewer health behaviors, the reverse may be true (Blake et al., 2013; Dickins et al., 2011).

In one of the few studies to consider the effects of stigma on men and women separately, 439 adults enrolling in a 12-month weight-loss trial reported prior weight stigma experiences, exercise motivation, and self-reported walking, moderate- and vigorous-intensity physical activity (Sattler et al., 2018). Both BMI and stigma experiences were linked with reduced autonomous motivation. However, in men, prior stigma experiences were directly linked with *higher* self-reported walking and vigorous-intensity physical activity; in contrast, there was no direct effect of stigma on exercise behavior for women; rather, stigma was linked with reduced autonomous motivation, which, in turn was linked to *lower* levels of exercise at all intensities. The opposing nature of these effects canceled each other out, such that neither BMI nor stigma experiences were significantly correlated with exercise behavior in the full-sample analysis, highlighting the importance of studying mechanisms as well as simple relationships.

Finally, in an experimental study of "overweight" junior school students between the ages of 9 and 12, participants played an exergame on the Nintendo Wii in which both visual and social cues were used to stimulate a weight-related stigma effect (Li et al., 2014). Students were randomly assigned to be represented either by a slim or an "overweight" avatar. Additionally, half of the children were asked their height and weight, making their weight salient. This latter manipulation has been used to engender stereotype threat related to exercise (Seacat & Mickelson, 2009). Interestingly, performance on the game was slightly improved under the threat conditions, suggesting an initial spurt of excitement and/or challenge to counter negative expectations; however, both the heavier avatar and the weight-salience manipulation resulted in more negative attitudes to exercise and reduced intrinsic motivation, measured after playing the game, indicating any beneficial effects are short-term, and longer-term implications are less likely to be positive (Li et al. 2014).

In an interesting experimental study, exercise science students were presented with a hypothetical client who displayed either autonomous or controlled motivation for beginning exercise and was also either higher-weight or normative-weight, and their own motivations for working with this client and the approach they would take were examined (Ntoumanis et al., 2018). A main effect of weight was found such that students presented with a higher-weight client had lower autonomous and higher controlled motivation to work with them, compared with a normative-weight client. Students also preferred more controlling behaviors in their approach to working with higher-weight clients but more autonomy-supporting behaviors for working with normative-weight clients (Ntoumanis et al., 2018). These findings have profound implications for the working relationship between exercise professionals and higher-weight clients, for the clients' experiences of these interactions, and for the likely longer-term effects of these sessions on clients' relationship with exercise.

Two experimental studies have explored the impact on exercise motivation of countering the status quo by using fat-positive or weight-neutral images. In the role model study described above (Meadows, 2024), participants were also asked to write about how they imagined their future self one year hence. Participants who had read about the woman starting running both mentioned exercise more than those who had read about the language learner, but those who had seen the normative-weight active role model used more words related to weight and appearance, whereas those who had seen the higher-weight active role model used more words related to empowerment. Further, those viewing the higher-weight active role model used more positive and fewer negative words, whereas the reverse was true for those viewing the normative-weight model (Meadows, 2024). And in an experimental study of the impact of viewing weight-inclusive versus more traditional "fitspiration" images, participants in the weight-neutral condition reported greater increases in fitness/health motivation whereas those in the fit-normative condition exhibited greater increases in weight or appearance motivation. No differences emerged by participant weight status (Wood & Pila, 2022). Thus, emerging evidence provides support for the impact of positive representation of higher-weight exercisers on psychological correlates of physical activity.

6.6 Addressing Weight Stigma in Physical Activity Environments

To reduce weight stigma in physical activity environments, the following recommendations require concurrent implementation: (1) increase knowledge and awareness among researchers and practitioners on the evidence that challenges the dominant weight-centric paradigm that underpins current physical activity promotion approaches; (2) create weight-inclusive fitness spaces; and (3) implement effective weight stigma education and reduction interventions for physical activity providers and advocates.

6.6.1 Increase Knowledge of Criticism of Weight-Centric Approaches to Physical Activity

Widespread misconceptions about the relationship between weight and health underpin much of the rampant weight stigma in physical activity contexts. Extensive evidence now attests that weight cannot be equated with health (for reviews, see Calogero et al., 2019; Hunger et al., 2020; O'Hara & Taylor, 2018; Tylka et al., 2014). Briefly, higher weight is not consistently linked to poor health (e.g., Flegal et al., 2013; Matheson et al., 2012), in particular when accounting for confounding variables such as fitness levels (Barry et al., 2014) and weight stigma (Muennig, 2008). Indeed, weight stigma is an independent predictor of physical and psychological ill-health and early mortality in higher-weight people, even controlling for BMI (Hatzenbuehler et al., 2009; Sutin et al., 2015; Udo et al., 2016; Vadiveloo &

Mattei, 2017). The relationship between weight and health is U-shaped, with the lowest long-term health risks being observed in the "overweight" BMI category (Flegal et al., 2013). Further, body weight is only partially under individual control (Rosenbaum & Leibel, 2010; Sumithran & Proietto, 2013; Tremblay et al., 2013), and intentional weight-loss attempts are more likely to lead to subsequent weight gain than to permanent weight loss (Mann et al., 2007; Rothblum, 2018). Additionally, repeated weight control efforts worsen metabolic health and long-term health outcomes (for reviews, see Bhammar & Gaesser, 2014; Montani et al., 2015; Zhang et al., 2019). Importantly, a meta-analysis of randomized controlled trials of weight-neutral versus weight-loss-focused health interventions found that the weight-neutral interventions were at least as effective at improving physical, psychological, and behavioral health outcomes as those focused on weight loss, with noticeably lower attrition rates (Dugmore et al., 2020).

Health improvements noted in short-term studies of weight-loss interventions are not linked to amount of weight lost, but are more closely linked to increases in physical activity (Tomiyama et al., 2013); unfortunately, weight-focused health promotion that prescribes physical activity for its weight-loss benefits means that when weight inevitably rebounds (Rosenbaum & Leibel, 2010; Sumithran & Proietto, 2013; Tremblay et al., 2013), physical activity behavior is frequently discontinued (Bombak, 2015; Thomas et al., 2015), risking the loss of associated health benefits. In addition to the many other benefits of physical activity, maintaining a reasonable level of cardiorespiratory fitness also attenuates the weight–health relationship; that is, although higher-weight status is often linked with poor health outcomes, this is not true for individuals who engage in regular physical activity – those who are "fat and fit" enjoy similar health outcomes to those who are thin and fit, and better outcomes than those who are thin yet unfit (Barry et al., 2014). As physical activity behavior is significantly more malleable and under personal control than is body weight, increasing physical activity levels is a more achievable target for improving individual and population health than is the pursuit of weight loss (Meadows, 2014). Importantly, despite its undoubted benefits for almost all aspects of physical and psychological health and well-being, physical activity is largely ineffective for driving weight loss (Meadows, 2014; Shaw et al., 2006; Wu et al., 2009), at least at levels that are safe and feasible for most people. Thus, the weight-inclusive approach involves promoting physical activity for its own benefits, not as a means to effect weight loss.

Fortunately, given the physical and psychological health benefits of physical activity occur independent of weight loss (Bacon & Aphramor, 2011; Barry et al., 2014; Bombak, 2014; Tomiyama et al., 2013; Watkins et al., 2014), it is entirely possible to remove the focus on weight management from physical activity spaces, and critical thinkers have been encouraging such a move for some time, not only to encourage more positive experiences for all bodies in physical activity spaces, but on fundamental ethical grounds (e.g., Evans, 2003; Mansfield & Rich, 2013; Norman & Petherick, 2016; Powell, 2016, Tinning, 1985, as cited in Pausé, 2019).

Given the mass of evidence challenging the weight-centric health paradigm, much of which has been available for decades (O'Hara & Taylor, 2018), it is nearly incomprehensible that mainstream curricula continue to promote this approach. The "war on obesity" has evolved with considerable industry pressure and advocacy and continues to influence health policy to this day (Bombak et al., 2022). It is often taken for granted that physical activity professionals are in the job of promoting weight management, and yet the harms of doing so are immense, both in terms of physical activity experiences but also on the harms caused to health by the fight against "obesity" (Gard & Wright, 2005; Hunger et al., 2020; O'Hara & Taylor, 2018). It has even been argued that promotion of a weight-centered health paradigm contravenes many of the articles in the Universal Declaration of Human Rights and is a serious breach of professional conduct (O'Hara & Gregg, 2012). As such, it becomes critical that physical activity researchers, educators, and providers are aware of the consequences of weight-centric paradigms in physical activity, critically evaluate widespread rhetoric that equates weight with health, and increase awareness of weight-inclusive approaches to physical activity.

6.6.2 Creating Weight-Inclusive Physical Activity Environments

At its simplest, weight-inclusive physical activity environments can be defined as those where the physical activity access and experience of all participants is the same, irrespective of weight. Researchers, practitioners, and users of fitness facilities have made a range of suggestions for creating such spaces, from the interpersonal to the structural (Bombak, 2015; Pickett & Cunningham, 2017b; Pickett & Cunningham, 2018; Souza & Ebbeck, 2018; Watkins et al., 2014; Zuest et al., 2021). Recommendations include hiring of diverse instructors and other staff; training for staff on inclusivity and weight-neutral fitness supported by explicit codes of conduct; positive representations of diverse body sizes in displayed artwork and advertising; clothing (where sold) available in a wider range of sizes; size-appropriate equipment, furniture, and changing rooms; removal of scales and promotional materials related to weight loss; removal of (or facing away from) mirrors. While implementation of weight-inclusive practices in physical activity environments is scarce, researchers have begun to assess and evaluate the extent to which virtual (e.g., online fitness classes) and physical spaces (e.g., YMCAs in Southwestern Ontario) are weight-inclusive (Sutton et al., 2023).

Interpersonally, weight-inclusive physical activity environments ought to focus on (i) not making assumptions about clients' motivations, experience, or ability; (ii) not participating in dialog that perpetuates primacy of certain body types over others, even when the clients hold such beliefs, and refraining from promotion or celebration of weight loss, delivery of diet programs, or body surveillance practices such as weighing and body composition analysis; (iii) focusing on the intrinsic and health benefits of physical activity unrelated to changing body size and using language that doesn't devalue certain bodies or levels of ability; (iv) respecting and promoting clients' autonomy and agency in shaping their own relationship with their bodies and how they move; and (v) building inclusive communities that create a sense of collective identity, built on acceptance and celebration of diversity and shared goals of embodied empowerment (Pickett & Cunningham, 2017a; Stevens et al., 2017). Beyond fitness centers, a sense of community is consistently reported as helping to drive engagement and persistence in sports and exercise despite exposure to weight stigma from others (Bell et al., 2023; Burns-Ardolino, 2019; Chase, 2008; Hill et al., 2016; Myre et al., 2022; Sampson, 2019; Sniezek, 2019).

Introduction of such measures can be implemented at the level of the fitness professional, even if a facility remains aligned with more traditional practices; however, a non-inclusive facility will remain a potentially unsafe space for many clients. True culture change will require a multi-pronged approach (Zuest et al., 2021). Researcher partnerships with physical activity institutions that are committed to offering equitable participation opportunities for higher-weight clients (e.g., YMCA Canada), may be a promising avenue for real-world implementation (Sutton et al., 2023). Notably, improvements do not need to be time-consuming or costly. In a study of fitness professionals and past and current gym members, education of fitness professionals was rated as the single most important strategy in making fitness centers more inclusive to higher-weight members, more important than changing the physical environment, having a code of conduct, or range of fitness offerings (Souza & Ebbeck, 2018).

A number of online and in-person weight-inclusive programs and facilities for adults and youngsters have now been created (see, e.g., Korbines, 2018; Miller et al., 2024; Sutton et al., 2024). Extensive qualitative data support the need for and success of these approaches in terms of client experiences, psychological well-being, and enjoyment of and commitment to physical activity (Cunningham & Woods, 2011; Ellison, 2009; Myre et al., 2022; Pickett & Cunningham, 2017a; Watkins et al., 2014). However, the emergence of weight-inclusive physical activity options is relatively new, and quantitative research evaluating their impact on physical activity outcomes remains limited (for exceptions, see Cunningham & Pickett, 2020; Watkins et al., 2014). To date, most weight-inclusive physical activity offerings remain in virtual spaces. Researchers have recently identified over 60 weight-inclusive physical activity platforms, which offer a range of activities (e.g., yoga, weight training, dance), showcase body and weight diversity, use weight-inclusive language, and center physical activity that is focused on bodily attunement and enjoyment (Sutton et al., 2024). Future research is needed to evaluate the uptake of these virtual services and their effects on participant physical activity and mental health.

6.6.3 Reducing Anti-Fat Bias in Fitness Professionals

Many interventions have been developed that aim to reduce anti-fat bias in healthcare and fitness professionals, mostly by focusing on the complexity of body weight control with the goal of reducing attributions of responsibility and blame. Despite being relatively successful in increasing knowledge about the limited personal controllability of weight, most have been largely ineffective at improving underlying anti-fat biases, and some have even increased weight stigma in their targets (Alberga et al., 2016; Daníelsdóttir et al., 2010; Schneider et al., 2024). It has been argued that interventions to reduce individual levels of weight stigma are likely to be ineffective in a societal context where higher-weight bodies remain pathologized and devalued – meaningful reductions in anti-fat attitudes will require a structural shift away from a weight-focused health paradigm (Brochu, 2023; Calogero et al., 2019; Hunger et al., 2020; Mansfield & Rich, 2013).

In an effort to create more effective anti-fat bias reduction interventions, a recently developed two-hour self-paced online course entitled "Weight-Inclusive Thinking for Fitness Spaces" (WIT FITS) also included components to raise awareness of the prevalence and harms of weight stigma, address misconceptions about the relationship between weight and health, recognize the value of size diversity, and considerations of weight inclusivity in physical activity spaces (Zuest et al., 2024). In a test of this intervention, fitness professionals were randomized to complete either the WIT FITS program or the Motivation to Move program, a communication course for fitness professionals focusing on assessing stage of change for increasing physical activity, enhancing intrinsic motivation for change, motivational interviewing, and aspects of inclusivity, without directly addressing weight stigma. Compared with the control group, the WIT FITS participants had greater improvements in all aspects of weight stigma (Zuest et al., 2024), which was maintained at three-month follow-up (Fogaça et al., 2024). The program has also received buy in from instructors and managers, with many reporting intended behavioral change at the personal and structural levels (Lee et al., 2024).[2] In addition to stand-alone interventions, it is imperative to partner with community and national stakeholders to conduct scalable weight-inclusive implementation projects at multiple organizational levels (e.g., individual training for fitness providers, professional development training for organizational leaders, changes to policies and physical spaces). Researchers have just begun to partner with national organizations to implement and evaluate large-scale anti-fat bias interventions in fitness professionals, within existing equity, diversity, and inclusion frameworks, which will be delivered alongside structural and organizational commitments to weight-inclusive physical activity (Pila et al., 2022).

6.7 Conclusion

In light of the qualitative and quantitative evidence summarized herein, it is incontrovertible that weight stigma in higher-weight individuals is a key barrier to accessing, engaging, and attaining the mental health benefits associated with physical activity. The current pervasive weight-centric approach to physical activity is psychologically harmful for individuals across the weight spectrum, but even more so for those facing broader societal marginalization and oppression, such as higher-weight individuals. The adoption of weight-inclusive physical activity paradigms addresses an ethical imperative to 'do not harm' in the delivery and implementation of physical activity for higher-weight individuals, while also making physical activity more universally accessible and psychologically beneficial across the weight spectrum. To change the traditional weight-centric approach to physical activity, researchers are urged to rigorously test weight-inclusive physical activity interventions and consequent effects on physical activity and mental health, and physical activity practitioners are encouraged to adopt weight-inclusive practices to support quality participation experiences among higher-weight individuals.

Notes

1 It should be noted that a surprising amount of weight stigma research is conducted in predominantly normative-weight samples. While insights can be gained from such research, care should be taken in interpretation of findings.
2 WIT FITS is currently available for free by contacting the study authors.

References

AdWeek. (2010, January 6). *Gym ad's recycled fatties joke offends again.* https://www.adweek.com/creativity/gym-ads-recycled-fatties-joke-offends-again-13209/

Alameida, M., & Whitehead, J. (2015). Comparing levels of anti-fat bias between American and Mexican athletes and undergraduate physical education and exercise science students. *Physical Educator*, *72*(5), 1–22. https://doi.org/10.18666/TPE-2015-V72-I5-4668

Alberga, A. S., Pickering, B. J., Hayden, K. A., Ball, G. D. C., Edwards, A., Jelinski, S., Nutter, S., Sharma, A. M., & Russell-Mayhew, S. (2016). Weight bias reduction in health professionals: A systematic review. *Clinical Obesity*, *6*(3), 175–188. https://doi.org/10.1111/cob.12147

Ali, Y., & Meadows, A. (2022, July 14–15). *Motivations to exercise: The good, the bad, and the ugly* [Conference presentation]. In *8th Annual International Weight Stigma Conference*, Berlin, Germany. https://doi.org/10.31076/2022.p15

Argüelles, D., Pérez-Samaniego, V., & López-Cañada, E. (2022). "Do you find it normal to be so fat?" Weight stigma in obese gym users. *International Review for the Sociology of Sport*, *57*(7), 1095–1116. https://doi.org/10.1177/10126902211056867

Ashdown-Franks, G., Meadows, A., & Pila, E. (2022). "Negative things that kids should never have to hear": Exploring women's histories of weight stigma in physical activity. *Journal of Sport and Exercise Psychology*, *44*(1), 1–13. https://doi.org/10.1123/jsep.2021-0139

Ashford, S., Edmunds, J., & and French, D. P. (2010). What is the best way to change self-efficacy to promote lifestyle and recreational physical activity? A systematic review with meta-analysis. *British Journal of Health Psychology*, *15*(2), 265–288. https://doi.org/10.1348/135910709X461752

Bacon, L., & Aphramor, L. (2011). Weight science: Evaluating the evidence for a paradigm shift. *Nutrition Journal*, *10*, Article no. 9. https://doi.org/10.1186/1475-2891-10-9

Bandura, A. (1997). *Self-efficacy: The exercise of control.* W. H. Freeman & Company.

Barry, V. W., Baruth, M., Beets, M. W., Durstine, J. L., Liu, J., & Blair, S. N. (2014). Fitness vs. fatness on all-cause mortality: A meta-analysis. *Progress in Cardiovascular Diseases*, *56*, 382–390. https://doi.org/10.1016/j.pcad.2013.09.002

Bauer, K. W., Yang, Y. W., & Bryn Austin, S. (2004). "How can we stay healthy when you're throwing all of this in front of us?" Findings from focus groups and interviews in middle schools on environmental influences on nutrition and physical activity. *Health Education & Behavior*, *31*(1), 34–46. https://doi.org/10.1177/1090198103255372

Bauman, A. E., Reis, R. S., Sallis, J. F., Wells, J. C., Loos, R. J., Martin, B. W., & Lancet Physical Activity Series Working Group. (2012). Correlates of physical activity: Why are some people physically active and others not? *Lancet*, *380*(9838), 258–271. https://doi.org/10.1016/S0140-6736(12)60735-1

Bell, D., Rahman, S., & Rochon, R. (2023). (Trans)forming fitness: Intersectionality as a framework for resistance and collective action. *Frontiers in Sport and Active Living, 5*, Article no. 944782. https://doi.org/10.3389/fspor.2023.944782

Bennie, J. A., De Crocker, K., Teychenne, M. J., Brown, W. J., & Biddle, S. J. H. (2019). The epidemiology of aerobic physical activity and muscle-strengthening activity guideline adherence among 383,928 U.S. adults. *International Journal of Behavioral Nutrition and Physical Activity*, *16*, 34. https://doi.org/10.1186/s12966-019-0797-2

Bhammar, D. M., & Gaesser, G. A. (2014). Health risks associated with weight cycling. In E. Glovsky (Ed.), *Wellness not weight: Motivational interviewing and health at every size* (pp. 83–92). Cognella Academic Publishing.

Biddle, S. J. H., Ciaccioni, S., Thomas, G., & Vergeer, I. (2019). Physical activity and mental health in children and adolescents: An updated review of reviews and an analysis of causality. *Psychology of Sport & Exercise*, *42*, 146–155. https://doi.org/10.1016/j.psychsport.2018.08.011

Blake, C. E., Hébert, J. R., Lee, D., Adams, S. A., Steck, S. E., Sui, X., Kuk, J. L., Baruth, M., & Blair, S. N. (2013). Adults with greater weight satisfaction report more positive health behaviors and have better health status regardless of BMI. *Journal of Obesity*, *2013*, Article no. 291371. https://doi.org/10.1155/2013/291371

Bombak, A. E. (2014). Obesity, health at every size, and public health policy. *American Journal of Public Health*, 104(2), e60–e67. https://doi.org/10.2105/AJPH.2013.301486.

Bombak, A. E. (2015). Obese persons' physical activity experiences and motivations across weight changes: A qualitative exploratory study. *BMC Public Health*, *15*, Article no. 1129. https://doi.org/10.1186/s12889-015-2456-0

Bombak, A. E., Adams, L., & Thille, P. (2022). Drivers of medicalization in the Canadian Adult Obesity Clinical Practice Guidelines. *Canadian Journal of Public Health*, *113*, 743–748. https://doi.org/10.17269/s41997-022-00662-4

Bombak, A. E., Chinho, N., Thomson, L., Burk, C., Akhter, S., O'Keefe, K., & Turner, L. (2024). Bright-siding stigma: Older adults' experiences at a higher weight in Atlantic Canada. *Health*, *29*(2), 236–257. Advance online publication. https://doi.org/10.1177/13634593241238869

Boros, P., Fontana, F., & Mack, M. (2017). A comparison of physical activity engagement and enjoyment in female college students with and without a history of weight-related teasing. *College Student Journal*, *51*(3), 444–449.

Brochu, P. M. (2023). Testing the effectiveness of a weight bias educational intervention among clinical psychology trainees. *Journal of Applied Social Psychology*, *53*(3), 231–241. https://doi.org/10.1111/jasp.12653

Brunson, J. A., Øverup, C. S., Nguyen, M.-L., Novak, S. A., & Smith, C. V. (2014). Good intentions gone awry? Effects of weight-related social control on health and wellbeing. *Body Image*, *11*, 1–10. https://doi.org/10.1016/j.bodyim.2013.08.003

Burns-Ardolino, W. (2019). Badass Athena triathletes: Athletic performativity and embodiment. *Fat Studies*, *8*(3), 240–258. https://doi.org/10.1080/21604851.2019.1546517

Calogero, R. M., Tylka, T. L., Mensinger, J. L., Meadows, A., & Daníelsdóttir, S. (2019). Recognizing the fundamental right to be a fat. A weight-inclusive approach to size acceptance and healing from sizcism. *Women & Therapy*, *42*(1–2), 22–44. https://doi.org/10.1080/02703149.2018.1524067

Carels, R. A., Rossi, J., Solar, C., & Selensky, J. C. (2019). An ecological momentary assessment of weight stigma among weight loss participants. *Journal of Health Psychology*, *24*(9), 1155–1166. https://doi.org/10.1177/1359105317692855

Carmona-Márquez, J., Sierra-Robles, A., Sánchez-García, M., García-Rodríguez, P., Munoz-Silva, A., Arbinaga, F., & Tornero-Quinones, I. (2021). Anti-fat bias in secondary school teachers: Are physical education teachers more biased than mathematics teachers? *European Physical Education Review*, *27*(1), 168–184. https://doi.org/10.1177/1356336X20932187

Chambliss, H. O., Finley, C. E., & Blair, S. N. (2004). Attitudes toward obese individuals among exercise science students. *Medicine & Science in Sports & Exercise*, *36*(3), 468–474. https://doi.org/10.1249/01.mss.0000117115.94062.e4

Chase, L. F. (2008). Running big: Clydesdale runners and technologies of the body. *Sociology of Sport Journal*, *25*, 130–147. https://doi.org/10.1123/ssj.25.1.130

Chastain, R. (2014. September 27). Gearing up – plus size workout clothes. *IronFat*. https://ironfatblog.wordpress.com/2014/09/27/gearing-up-plus-size-workout-clothes/

Cheng, O. Y., Yam, C. L. Y., Cheung, N. S., Lee, P. L. P., Ngai, M. C., & Lin, C.-Y. (2019). Extended theory of planned behavior on eating and physical activity. *American Journal of Health Behavior*, *43*(3), 569–581. https://doi.org/10.5993/AJHB.43.3.11

Christel, D. A., O'Donnell, N. H., & Bradley, L. A. (2016). Coping by crossdressing: An exploration of exercise clothing for obese heterosexual women. *Fashion and Textiles*, *3*(1), Article no. 11. https://doi.org/10.1186/s40691-016-0063-z

Cunningham, G. B., & Pickett, A. C. (2020). The importance of perceived body-inclusiveness among physically active women in larger bodies. *Sex Roles*, *83*, 754–762. https://doi.org/10.1007/s11199-020-01139-9

Cunningham, G. B., & Woods, J. (2011). For the health of it: Advertisement message and attraction to fitness clubs. *American Journal of Health Studies*, *26*(1), 4–9.

Daly, M., Robinson, E., & Sutin, A. R. (2020). Perceived overweight and suicidality among US adolescents from 1999 to 2017. *International Journal of Obesity*, *44*, 2075–2079 https://doi.org/10.1038/s41366-020-0620-9

Daníelsdóttir, S., O'Brien, K. S., & Ciao, A. (2010). Anti-fat prejudice reduction: A review of published studies. *Obesity Facts*, *3*, 47–58. https://doi.org/10.1159/000277067

Deci, E. L., & Ryan, R. M. (1985). *Intrinsic motivation and self-determination in human behavior*. Springer. https://doi.org/10.1007/978-1-4899-2271-7

Dickins, M., Thomas, S. L., King, B., Lewis, S., & Holland, K. (2011). The role of the Fatosphere in fat adults' responses to obesity stigma: A model of empowerment without a focus on weight loss. *Qualitative Health Research*, *21*(12), 1679–1691. https://doi.org/10.1177/1049732311417728

Dimmock, J. A., Hallett, B. E., & Grove, J. R. (2009). Attitudes toward overweight individuals among fitness center employees: An examination of contextual effects. *Research Quarterly for Exercise and Sport*, *80*(3), 641–647. https://doi.org/10.1080/02701367.2009.10599603

Dugmore, J. A., Winten, C. G., Niven, H. E., & Bauer, J. (2020). Effects of weight-neutral approaches compared with traditional weight-loss approaches on behavioral, physical, and psychological health outcomes: A systematic review and meta-analysis. *Nutrition Reviews*, *78*(1), 39–55. Https://doi.org/10.1093/nutrit/nuz020

Durso L. E., & Latner J. D. (2008). Understanding self-directed stigma: Development of the Weight Bias Internalization Scale. *Obesity*, *16*(S2), S80–S86. https://doi.org/10.1038/oby.2008.448

Ekkekakis, P., & Dafermos, M. (2012). Exercise is a many-splendored thing, but for some it does not feel so splendid: Staging a resurgence of hedonistic ideas in the quest to understand exercise behavior. In E. O. Acevedo (Ed.), *The Oxford handbook of exercise psychology* (pp. 295–333). Oxford University Press.

Ellison, J. (2009). Not Jane Fonda: Aerobics for fat women only. In E. Rothblum and S. Solovay (Eds.), *The fat studies reader* (pp. 312–319). New York University Press.

Evans, J. (2003). Physical education and health: A polemic; or 'let them eat cake.' *European Physical Education Review*, *9*(1), 87–101. https://doi.org/10.1177/1356336X03009001182

Faith, M. S., Leone, M. A., Ayers, T. S., Heo, M., & Pietrobelli, A. (2002). Weight criticism during physical activity, coping skills, and reported physical activity in children. *Pediatrics*, *110*, Article no. e23. https://doi.org/10.1542/peds.110.2.e23

Feig, E. H., Amonoo, H. L., Onyeaka, H. K., Romero, P. M., Kim, S., & Huffman, J. C. (2020). Weight bias internalization and its association with health behaviour adherence after bariatric surgery. *Clinical Obesity*, *10*, Article no. e12361. https://doi.org/10.1111/cob.12361

Flegal, K. M., Kit, B. K., Orpana, H., & Graubard, B. I. (2013). Association of all-cause mortality with overweight and obesity using standard body mass index categories: A systematic review and meta-analysis. *Journal of the American Medical Association*, *309*(1), 71–82. https://doi.org/10.1001/jama.2012.113905

Flint, S. W., Hudson, J., & Lavallee, D. (2015). UK adults' implicit and explicit attitudes towards obesity: A cross-sectional study. *BMC Obesity*, *2*(1), Article no. 31. https://doi.org/10.1186/s40608-015-0064-2

Flint, S. W., & Reale, S. (2018). Weight stigma in frequent exercisers: Overt, demeaning and condescending. *Journal of Health Psychology*, *23*(5), 710–719. https://doi.org/10.1177/1359105316656232

Fogaça, J. L., Zuest, L., Lee, S., Squires, N., & Clifford, D. (2024). Weight Inclusive Thinking for Fitness Spaces (WIT FITS): A three-month follow-up of a weight stigma intervention for exercise professionals. *Recreational Sports Journal*, *48*(2), 132–145. Advance online publication. https://doi.org/10.1177/15588661241244771

Fontana, F., Bopes, J., Bendixen, S., Speed, T., George, M., & Mack, M. (2018). Discrimination against obese exercise clients: An experimental study of personal trainers. *International Journal of Exercise Science*, *11*(5), 116–128.

Fontana, F., Furtado, O., Jr., Marston, R., Mazzardo, O., & Gallagher, J. D. (2013). Anti-fat bias among physical education teachers and majors. *Psychology*, *70*, 15–31.

Fontana, F., Furtado, O., Jr., Mazzardo, O., Jr., Hong, D., & de Campos, W. (2017). Anti-fat bias by professors teaching physical education majors. *European Physical Education Review*, *23*(1), 127–138. https://doi.org/10.1177/1356336X16643304

Gallardo, L. O., Abarca-Sos, A., & Moreno Doña, A. (2020). Expectancy-value model related to physical activity behaviors in Chilean and Spanish Adolescents. *International Journal of Environmental Research and Public Health*, *17*, Article no. 8219. https://doi.org/10.3390/ijerph17218219

Gard, M., & Wright, J. (2005). *The obesity epidemic: Science, morality and ideology*. Routledge/Taylor & Francis Group.

Gerend, M. A., Zetrenne, S., Sutin, A. R., Naar, S., & Maner, J. K. (2023). Weight discrimination and health risk behavior in racial, ethnic, and sexual minority adults. *Annals of Behavioral Medicine*, *57*(7), 571–581. https://doi.org/10.1093/abm/kaad003

Goe, K. (2021, October 25). Women athletes allege body shaming within Oregon Ducks track and field program. *Oregon Live.* https://www.oregonlive.com/trackandfield/2021/10/women-athletes-allege-body-shaming-within-oregon-ducks-track-and-field-program.html

Glock, S., & Schuchart, C. (2021). Stereotypes about overweight students and their impact on grading among physical education teachers. *Social Psychology of Education*, *24*(5), 1193–1208. https://doi.org/10.1007/s11218-021-09649-4

Goffman, E. (1963). *Stigma. Notes on the management of spoiled identity*. Penguin Books.

Greenleaf, C., Hauff, C., Klos, L., & Serafin, G. (2020). "Fat people exercise too!": Perceptions and realities of shopping for women's plus-size exercise apparel. *Clothing and Textiles Research Journal*, *38*(2), 75–89. https://doi.org/10.1177/0887302X19878507

Greenleaf, C., Martin, S. B., & Rhea, D. (2008). Fighting fat: How do fat stereotypes influence beliefs about physical education? *Obesity, 16*(S2), S53–S59. https://doi.org/10.1038/oby.2008.454

Greenleaf, C., Petrie, T. A., & Martin, S. B. (2014). Relationship of weight-based teasing and adolescents' psychological well-being and physical health. *Journal of School Health*, *84*(1), 49–55. https://doi.org/10.1111/josh.12118

Greenleaf, C., & Weiller, K. (2005). Perceptions of youth obesity among physical educators. *Social Psychology of Education*, *8*(4), 407–423. https://doi.org/10.1007/s11218-005-0662-9

Hamer, M., Stamatakis, E., & Steptoe, A. (2009). Dose-response relationship between physical activity and mental health: The Scottish Health Survey. *British Journal of Sports Medicine*, *43*, 1111–1114. https://doi.org/10.1136/bjsm.2008.046243

Han, S., Agostini, G., Brewis, A. A., & Wutich, A. (2018). Avoiding exercise mediates the effects of internalized and experienced weight stigma on physical activity in the years following bariatric surgery. *BMC Obesity*, *5*, Article no. 18, https://doi.org/10.1186/s40608-018-0195-3

Hare, S. W., Price, J. H., Flynn, M. G., & King, K. A. (2000). Attitudes and perceptions of fitness professionals regarding obesity. *Journal of Community Health*, *25*(1), 5–21. https://doi.org/10.1023/a:1005170600319

Harjunen, H. (2019). Exercising exclusions: Space, visibility, and monitoring of the exercising fat female body. *Fat Studies*, *8*(2), 173–186. https://doi.org/10.1080/21604851.2019.1561101

Hatzenbuehler, M. L., Keyes, K. M., & Hasin, D. S. (2009). Associations between perceived weight discrimination and the prevalence of psychiatric disorders in the general population. *Obesity*, *17*, 2033–2039. https://doi.org/10.1038/oby.2009.131

Hill, J., Sandford, R., & Enright, E. (2016). 'It has really amazed me what my body can now do': Boundary work and the construction of a body-positive dance community. *Sport in Society*, *19*(5), 667–679. https://doi.org/10.1080/17430437.2015.1073946

Homan, K. J., & Tylka, T. L. (2014). Appearance-based exercise motivation moderates the relationship between exercise frequency and positive body image. *Body Image*, *11*, 101–108. https://doi.org/10.1016/j.bodyim.2014.01.003

Huellemann, K. L., Ens, G., Gray, E., Osa, M. L., & Pila, E. (2024). "If I talk about it, I'm weak, and I'm supposed to be strong": Experiences of body-related shame in women athletes. *International Journal of Sport and Exercise Psychology. Advance online publication*, *22*(7), 1819–1842. https://doi.org/10.1080/1612197X.2023.2238277

Hunger, J. M., Smith, J. P., & Tomiyama, A. J. (2020). An evidence-based rationale for adopting weight-inclusive health policy. *Social Issues and Policy Review*, *14*(1), 73–107. https://doi.org/10.1111/sipr.12062

Ievers-Landis, C. E., Dykstra, C., Uli, N., & O'Riordan, M. A. (2019). Weight-related teasing of adolescents who are primarily obese: Roles of sociocultural attitudes towards appearance and physical activity self-efficacy. *International Journal of Environmental Research and Public Health*, *16*(9), Article no. 1540. https://doi.org/10.3390/ijerph16091540

Jackson, S. E., & Steptoe, A. (2017). Association between perceived weight discrimination and physical activity: A population-based study among English middle-aged and older adults. *BMJ Open*, *7*(3), Article no. e014592. https://doi.org/10.1136/bmjopen-2016-014592

Kenen, R. H. (1987). Double messages, double images: Physical fitness, self-concepts, and women's exercise classes. *Journal of Physical Education, Recreation & Dance*, *58*(6), 74–79. https://doi.org/10.1080/07303084.1987.10609581

Kokka, I., Mourikis, I., & Bacopoulou, F. (2023). Psychiatric disorders and obesity in childhood and adolescence: A systematic review of cross-sectional studies. *Children*, *10*, 285. https://doi.org/ 10.3390/children10020285

Korbines, L. (2018). *An intervention to promote physical activity through creation of body-size inclusive spaces* [Master of Public Health dissertation, University of Washington]. https://foodsystems.uw.edu/wp-content/uploads/2020/09/Korbines_Leilah_SUM_2018-Capstone-Report-.pdf

Langdon, J., Rukavina, P. B., & Greenleaf, C. (2016). Predictors of obesity bias among exercise science students. *Advances in Physiology Education*, *40*(2), 157–164. https://doi.org/10.1152/advan.00185.2015

Lau, W. C. P., Leung, B. W. C., Pitkethly, A., Ransdell, L. B. (2018). Do physical education teachers and general teachers differ in their implicit anti-fat bias? *Sport International, 55*(1), 27–37.

Lee, S., Zuest, L., Fogaça, J. L., Squires, N. D., Balam, C., & Clifford, D. E. (2024). An interdisciplinary collaboration to reduce weight stigma among exercise professionals, *Journal of Physical Education, Recreation & Dance*, *95*(5), 28–33, https://doi.org/10.1080/07303084.2024.2319533

Lessard, L. M., Puhl, R. M., Himmelstein, M. S., Pearl, R. L. and Foster, G. D. (2021). Eating and exercise-related correlates of weight stigma: A multinational investigation. *Obesity*, *29*, 966–970. https://doi.org/10.1002/oby.23168

Lewis, S. T., & Van Puymbroeck, M. (2008). Obesity-stigma as a multifaceted constraint to leisure. *Journal of Leisure Research*, *40*(4), 574–588. https://doi.org/10.1080/00222216.2008.11950153

Li, B. J., Lwin, M. O., & Jung, Y. (2014). Wii, myself, and size: The influence of proteus effect and stereotype threat on overweight children's exercise motivation and behaviour in exergames. *Games for Health Journal*, *3*(1), 40–48. https://doi.org/10.1089/g4h.2013.0081

Li, W., & Rukavina, P. B. (2012). The nature, occurring contexts, and psychological implications of weight-related teasing in urban physical education programs. *Research Quarterly for Exercise and Sport*, *83*(2), 308–317. https://doi.org/10.5641/027013612800745130

Lindloff, M., & Meadows, A. (2023). Assessment of weight-related stigmatisation. In A. Meule (Ed.), *Assessment of eating behavior* (pp. 221–237). European Association of Psychological Assessment book series. Hogrefe.

Losekam, S., Goetzky, B., Kraeling, S., Rief, W., & Hilbert, A. (2010). Physical activity in normal-weight and overweight youth: Associations with weight teasing and self-efficacy. *Obesity Facts, 3*(4), 239–244. https://doi.org/10.1159/000319433

Lynagh, M., Cliff, K., & Morgan, P. J. (2015). Attitudes and beliefs of nonspecialist and specialist trainee health and physical education teachers toward obese children: Evidence for "anti-fat" bias. *Journal of School Health*, *85*(9), 595–603. https://doi.org/10.1111/josh.12287

Madon, S., Jussim, L., & Eccles, J. (1997). In search of the powerful self-fulfilling prophecy. *Journal of Personality and Social Psychology*, *72*(4), 791–809. https://doi.org/10.1037//0022-3514.72.4.791

Maïano, C., Lepage, G., Aimé, A., ASPQ Team, & Morin, A. J. S. (2018). Perceived weight-related victimization and physical activity outcomes among adolescents with overweight and obesity: Indirect role of perceived physical abilities and fear of enacted stigma. *Psychology of Sport and Exercise*, *34*, 70–78. https://doi.org/10.1016/J.PSYCHSPORT.2017.08.007

Mann, T., Tomiyama, A. J., Westling, E., Lew, A. M., Samuels, B., & Chatman, J. (2007). Medicare's search for effective obesity treatments: Diets are not the answer. *American Psychologist*, *62*(3), 220–233. https://doi.org/10.1037/0003-066x.62.3.220

Mansfield, L., & Rich, E. (2013). Public health pedagogy, border crossings and physical activity at every size. *Critical Public Health*, *23*(3), 356–370. https://doi.org/10.1080/09581596.2013.783685

Marks, H. (2013, August 6). Fat shaming or smart marketing? Why Lululemon (and others) don't sell plus sizes. *Bust.com*. https://bust.com/fat-shaming-or-smart-marketing-why-lululemon-and-others-dont-sell-plus-sizes/

Marquez, D. X., Aguiñaga, S., Vásquez, P. M., Conroy, D. E., Erickson, K. I., Hillman, C., Stillman, C. M., Ballard, R. M., Bloodgood Sheppard, B., Petruzzello, S. J., King, A. C., & Powell, K. E. (2020). A systematic review of physical activity and quality of life and wellbeing. *Translational Behavioral Medicine*, *10*, 1098–1109. https://doi.org/10.1093/tbm/ibz198

Matheson, E. M., King, D. E., & Everett, C. J. (2012). Healthy lifestyle habits and mortality in overweight and obese individuals. *Journal of the American Board of Family Medicine*, *25*(1), 9–15. https://doi.org/10.3122/jabfm.2012.01.110164

McAuley, E., & Blissmer, B. (2000). Self-efficacy determinants and consequences of physical activity. *Exercise and Sport Sciences Reviews*, *28*(2), 85–88.

Meadows, A. (2014). Fat and fit: Possible, probable, protective? In R Chastain (Ed.), *The politics of size: Perspectives from the Fat-Acceptance Movement*. Praeger/ABC-Clio (pp. 1–14). https://www.researchgate.net/publication/296331024

Meadows, A. (2024, June 16–17). *Anything she can do: The effectiveness of fat role models in promoting physical activity in sedentary higher-weight women* [Conference presentation]. In *10th Annual International Weight Stigma Conference*, Colchester, UK. https://doi.org/10. 31076/2025.o16

Meadows, A., & Bombak, A. E. (2019). Yes, we can (no, you can't): Weight stigma, exercise self-efficacy, and active fat identity development. *Fat Studies, 8*(2), 135–153. https://doi.org/10.1080/21604851.2019.1550303

Meadows, A., & Daníelsdóttir, S. (2016). What's in a word? On weight stigma and terminology. *Frontiers in Psychology*, *7*, Article no. 1527. https://doi.org/10.3389/fpsyg.2016.01527

Meadows, A., Daníelsdóttir, S., Calogero, R., & O'Reilly, C. (2017). Why fat suits do not advance the scientific study of weight stigma. *Obesity*, 25(2), 275. https://doi.org/10.1002/oby.21742

Meadows, A., & Higgs, S. (2020). A bifactor analysis of the Weight Bias Internalization Scale: What are we really measuring? *Body Image*, *33*, 137–151. https://doi.org/10.1016/j.bodyim.2020.02.013

Mensinger, J. L., & Meadows, A. (2017). Internalized weight stigma mediates and moderates physical activity outcomes during a healthy living program for women with high body mass index. *Psychology of Sport and Exercise*, *30*, 64–72. https://doi.org/10.1016/j.psychsport.2017.01.010

Miller, K. K., Hooper, L., & Kaja, S. M. (2024). Move and Thrive: Development of an adolescent friendly and inclusive online fitness resource. *Health Promotion Practice*. Advance online publication. https://doi.org/10.1177/15248399241245055

Montani, J.-P., Schutz, Y., & Dulloo, A. G. (2015). Dieting and weight cycling as risk factors for cardiometabolic diseases: Who is really at risk? *Obesity Reviews*, *16*, 7–18. https://doi.org/10.1111/obr.12251

Muennig, P. (2008). The body politic: The relationship between stigma and obesity-associated disease. *BMC Public Health*, *8*, Article no. 128. https://doi.org/10.1186/1471-2458-8-128

Murphy, S. (2017, January 26). *These disturbing, shaming advertisements prove that gyms get body positivity all wrong*. https://hellogiggles.com/lifestyle/body-shaming-gym-advertisements/

Myre, M., Glenn, N. M., & Berry, T. R. (2020). Exploring the impact of physical activity-related weight stigma among women with self-identified obesity. *Qualitative Research in Sport, Exercise and Health*, *13*(4), 586–603. https://doi.org/10.1080/2159676X.2020.1751690

Myre, M., Glenn, N. M., & Berry, T. R. (2022). Experiences of size inclusive physical activity settings among women with larger bodies. *Research Quarterly for Exercise and Sport*, *94*(2), 351–360. https://doi.org/10.1080/02701367.2021.1983515

Nguyen, C. (2012, September 7). Taylor Townsend dispute: USTA cuts funding until No. 1 junior loses weight. *Sports Illustrated.* https://www.si.com/tennis/2012/09/07/taylor-townsend-usta-controversy

NHS Digital. (2023). *Health Survey for England, 2021 Part 2*. https://digital.nhs.uk/data-and-information/publications/statistical/health-survey-for-england/2021-part-2

Norman, M., & Petherick, L. 2016. The enemy within: Teaching "hard knowledge" about "soft bodies" in a kinesiology faculty. In E. Cameron and C. Russell (Eds.), *The fat pedagogy reader: Challenging weight-biased oppression through critical education* (pp. 91–100). Peter Lang.

Ntoumanis, N., Guerrero, M. D., Gadeke, C., & Thøgersen-Ntoumani, C. (2018). Do exerciser weight status and perceived motivation predict instructors' motivation and beliefs about the exerciser? A test of motivation contagion effects. *Body Image*, *26*, 10–18. https://doi.org/10.1016/j.bodyim.2018.05.001

O'Brien, K. S., Hunter, J. A., & Bank, M. (2007). Implicit anti-fat bias in physical educators: Physical attributes, ideology and socialization. *International Journal of Obesity, 31*(2), 308–314. https://doi.org/10.1038/sj.ijo.0803398

O'Hara, L., & Gregg, G. (2012). Human rights casualties from the "war on obesity": Why focusing on body weight is inconsistent with a human rights approach to health. *Fat Studies*, *1*(1), 32–46. https://doi.org/10.1080/21604851.2012.627790

O'Hara, L., & Taylor, J. (2018). What's wrong with the 'war on obesity'? A narrative review of the weight-centered health paradigm and development of the 3C framework to build critical competency for a paradigm shift. *SAGE Open*, *8*(2). https://doi.org/10.1177/2158244018772888

Olson, K. L., Goldstein, S. P., Wing, R. R., Williams, D. M., Demos, K. E., & Unick, J. L. (2021). Internalized weight bias is associated with perceived exertion and affect during exercise in a sample with higher body weight. *Obesity Science and Practice*, *7*, 405–414. https://doi.org/10.1002/osp4.494

Packer, J. (1989). The role of stigmatization in fat people's avoidance of physical exercise. *Women & Therapy*, *8*(3), 49–63. https://doi.org/10.1300/J015V08N03_07

Pausé, C. (2019). (Can we) get together? Fat kids and physical education. *Health Education Journal*, *78*(6), 662–669. https://doi.org/10.1177/0017896919846182

Pearl, R. L., Dovidio, J. F., Puhl, R. M., & Brownell, K. D. (2015). Exposure to weight-stigmatizing media: Effects on exercise intentions, motivation, and behaviour. *Journal of Health Communication*, *20*(9), 1004–1013. https://doi.org/10.1080/10810730.2015.1018601

Pearl, R. L., Puhl, R. M., & Dovidio, J. F. (2015). Differential effects of weight bias experiences and internalization on exercise among women with overweight and obesity. *Journal of Health Psychology*, *20*(12), 1626–1632. https://doi.org/10.1177/1359105313520338

Pearl, R. L., Wadden, T. A., & Jakicic, J. M. (2021). Is weight stigma associated with physical activity? A systematic review. *Obesity*, *29*(12), 1994–2012. https://doi.org/10.1002/oby.23274

Peterson, J. L., Puhl, R. M., & Luedicke, J. (2012). An experimental assessment of physical educators' expectations and attitudes: The importance of student weight and gender. *Journal of School Health*, *82*(9), 432–440. https://doi.org/10.1111/j.1746-1561.2012.00719.x

Phelan, S. M., Burgess, D. J., Yeazel, M. W., Hellerstedt, W. L., Griffin, J. M., & van Ryn, M. (2015). Impact of weight bias and stigma on quality of care and outcomes for patients with obesity. *Obesity Reviews*, *16*(4), 319–326. https://doi.org/10.1111/obr.12266

Phibbs, S., Thorburn, S., & Branscum, A. J. (2019). Is weight discrimination associated with physical activity among middle aged and older adults? *Journal of Primary Prevention*, *40*(3), 279–295. https://doi.org/10.1007/s10935-019-00546-3

Pickett, A. C., & Cunningham, G. B. (2017a). Creating inclusive physical activity spaces: The case of body-positive yoga. *Research Quarterly for Exercise and Sport*, *88*(3), 329–338. https://doi.org/10.1080/02701367.2017.1335851

Pickett, A. C., & Cunningham, G. B. (2017b). Physical activity for every body: A model for managing weight stigma and creating body-inclusive spaces, *Quest*, *69*(1), 19–36. https://doi.org/10.1080/00336297.2016.1145129

Pickett, A. C., & Cunningham, G. B. (2018). Body weight stigma in physical activity settings. *American Journal of Health Studies*, *33*(1), 21–29. https://doi.org/10.47779/ajhs.2018.53

Pila, E., Doherty, A., Sandmeyer-Graves, A., Maharaj, A., Sabiston, C., Hallward, L., & Calogero, R. (2022). *Weight-inclusive physical activity for girls and women: Co-developing resources to change the physical activity landscape in Canada*. https://www.sshrc-crsh.gc.ca/results-resultats/recipients-recipiendaires/2021/pdg-sdp-eng.aspx

Poole, O. (2002, May 9). Victory for "too fat" fitness instructor. *The Telegraph*. https://www.telegraph.co.uk/news/worldnews/northamerica/usa/1393682/Victory-for-too-fat-fitness-instructor.html

Powell, D. (2016). Schools and the 'war against obesity'. *New Zealand Physical Educator*, *49*(3), 4–5.

Puhl, R. M., & Heuer, C. A. (2009). The stigma of obesity: A review and update. *Obesity*, *17*(5), 941–964. https://doi.org/10.1038/oby.2008.636

Puhl, R. M., Himmelstein, M. S., Pearl, R. L., Wojtanowski, A. C., & Foster, G. D. (2019). Weight stigma among sexual minority adults: Findings from a matched sample of adults engaged in weight management. *Obesity*, *27*(11), 1906–1915. https://doi.org/10.1002/oby.22633

Quennerstedt, M., Barker, D., Johansson, A., & Korp, P. (2021). The relation between teaching physical education and discourses on body weight – An integrative review of research. *Curriculum Studies in Health and Physical Education*, *12*(3), 287–305. https://doi.org/10.1080/25742981.2021.1894407

Raedeke, T. D., Focht, B. C., & Scales, D. (2007). Social environmental factors and psychological responses to acute exercise for socially physique anxious females. *Psychology of Sport and Exercise*, *8*, 463–476. https://doi.org/10.1016/j.psychsport.2006.10.005

Rajan, T. M., & Menon, V. (2017). Psychiatric disorders and obesity: A review of association studies. *Journal of Postgraduate Medicine*, *63*(3), 182–190. https://doi.org/10.4103/jpgm.JPGM_712_16

Ren, Z., Zhang, Y., Drenowatz, C., Eather, N., Hong, J., Wang, L., Yan, J., & Chen, S. (2024). How many adults have sufficient muscle-strengthening exercise and the associated factors: A systematic review consisting of 2,629,508 participants. *Journal of Exercise Science & Fitness*, *22*, 359–368. https://doi.org/10.1016/j.jesf.2024.06.002

Rhodes, R. E., Fiala, B., & Conner, M. (2009). Affective judgments and physical activity: A review and meta-analysis. *Annals of Behavioral Medicine*, *38*, Article no. 180e204. https://doi.org/10.1007/s12160-009-9147-y

Rhodes, R. E., Kaushal, N., & Quinlan, A. (2016). Is physical activity a part of who I am? A review and meta-analysis of identity, schema and physical activity. *Health Psychology Review*, *10*(2), 204–225. https://doi.org/10.1080/17437199.2016.1143334

Rice, C. (2007). Becoming "the fat girl": Acquisition of an unfit identity. *Women's Studies International Forum*, *30*(2), 158–174. https://doi.org/10.1016/J.WSIF.2007.01.001

Rinaldi, J., Rice, C., Kotow, C., & Lind, E. (2020). Mapping the circulation of fat hatred. *Fat Studies*, *9*(1), 37–50. https://doi.org/10.1080/21604851.2019.1592949

Robertson, N., & Vohora, R. (2008). Fitness vs. fatness: Implicit bias towards obesity among fitness professionals and regular exercisers. *Psychology of Sport and Exercise, 9*(4), 547–557. https://doi.org/10.1016/j.psychsport.2007.06.002

Rocha, V., & Winton, R. (2016, July 19). How 'fat shaming' on Snapchat turned into a criminal investigation. *Los Angeles Times*. https://www.latimes.com/local/lanow/la-me-fat-shaming-playboy-model-20160718-snap-story.html

Rosenbaum, M., & Leibel, R. L. (2010). Adaptive thermogenesis. *International Journal of Obesity*, *34*, S47–S55. https://doi.org/10.1038/ijo.2010.184

Rothblum, E. D. (2018). Slim chance for permanent weight loss. *Archives of Scientific Psychology*, *6*, 63–69. https://doi.org/10.1037/arc0000043

Sabiston, C. M., Lucibello, K. M., Kuzmochka-Wilks, D., Koulanova, A., Pila, E., Sandmeyer-Graves, A., & Maginn, D. (2020). What's a coach to do? Exploring coaches' perspectives on body image in girls sport. *Psychology of Sport and Exercise*, *48*, Article no. 101669. https://doi.org/10.1016/j.psychsport.2020.101669

Sampson, A. (2019). *Empowering the plus size body using dance as therapy* (Publication No. 29) [Expressive Therapies Capstone Theses, Lesley University.] https://digitalcommons.lesley.edu/expressive_theses/229

Sartore, M. L., & Cunningham, G. B. (2007). Weight discrimination, hiring recommendations, person–job fit, and attributions: Fitness-industry implications. *Journal of Sport Management*, *21*, 172–193. https://doi.org/10.1123/jsm.21.2.172

Sattler, K. M., Deane, F. P., Tapsell, L., & Kelly, P. J. (2018). Gender differences in the relationship of weight-based stigmatisation with motivation to exercise and physical activity in overweight individuals. *Health Psychology Open*, *5*(1). https://doi.org/10.1177/2055102918759691

Schlossberg, M. (2016, August 18). A major gym chain is under fire after an actress called out its fat-shaming ads. https://uk.businessinsider.com/golds-gym -fat-shaming-ad-causes-controversy-2016–8?r=US&IR=T

Schmalz, D. L. (2010). 'I feel fat': Weight-related stigma, body esteem, and BMI as predictors of perceived competence in physical activity. *Obesity Facts*, *3*(1), 15–21. https://doi.org/10.1159/000273210

Schneider, J., Tinoco, A., Scott, B., Witcomb, G. L., Matheson, E. L., & Diedrichs, P. C. (2024). *A systematic review of interventions that aim to reduce implicit and explicit weight biases among fitness professionals*. [Manuscript submitted for publication]. Centre for Appearance Research, University of the West of England.

Schuch, F. B., & Vancampfort, D. (2021). Physical activity, exercise, and mental disorders: It is time to move on. *Trends in Psychiatry and Psychotherapy*, *43*(3), 177–184. https://doi.org/10.47626/2237-6089-2021-0237

Schvey, N. A., Sbrocco, T., Bakalar, J. L., Ress, R., Barmine, M., Gorlick, J., Pine, A., Stephens, M., & Tanofsky-Kraff, M. (2017). The experience of weight stigma among gym members with overweight and obesity. *Stigma and Health*, *2*(4), 292–306. https://doi.org/10.1037/sah0000062

Seacat, J. D., Dougal, S. C., & Roy, D. (2016). A daily diary assessment of female weight stigmatization. *Journal of Health Psychology*, *21*(2), 228–240. https://doi.org/10.1177/1359105314525067

Seacat, J. D., & Mickelson, K. D. (2009). Stereotype threat and the exercise/dietary health intentions of overweight women. *Journal of Health Psychology*, *14*(4), 556–567. https://doi.org/10.1177/1359105309103575

Setchell, J., Watson, B. M., Gard, M., & Jones, L. (2016). Physical therapists' ways of talking about overweight and obesity: Clinical implications. *Physical Therapy*, *96*(6), 865–875. https://doi.org/10.2522/ptj.20150286

Setchell, J., Watson, B. M., Jones, L., & Gard, M. (2015). Weight stigma in physiotherapy practice: Patient perceptions of interactions with physiotherapists. *Manual Therapy*, *20*(6), 835–841. https://doi.org/10.1016/j.math.2015.04.001

Setchell, J., Watson, B. M., Jones, L., Gard, M., & Briffa, K. (2014). Physiotherapists demonstrate weight stigma: A cross-sectional survey of Australian physiotherapists. *Journal of Physiotherapy*, *60*(3), 157–162. https://doi.org/10.1016/j.jphys.2014.06.020

Shaw, K. A., Gennat, H. C., O'Rourke, P., & Del Mar, C. (2006). Exercise for overweight or obesity. *Cochrane Database of Systematic Reviews*, *4*, Article no. CD003817. https://doi.org/10.1002/14651858.CD003817.pub3

Sniezek, T. (2019): Running while fat: How women runners experienceand respond to size discrimination. *Fat Studies*, *10*(1), 64–77. https://doi.org/10.1080/21604851.2019.1671135

Souza, B. J., & Ebbeck, V. (2018). Perspectives on increasing positive attitudes toward larger members in fitness centers. *Journal of Applied Sport Psychology*, *30*(1), 96–118. https://doi.org/10.1080/10413200.2017.1337822

Stevens, M., Rees, T., Coffee, P., Steffens, N. K., Haslam, S. A., & Polman, R. (2017). A social identity approach to understanding and promoting physical activity. *Sports Medicine*, *47*(10), 1911–1918. https://doi.org/10.1007/s40279-017-0720-4

Storch, E. A., Milsom, V. A., DeBraganza, N., Lewin, A. B., Geffken, G. R., & Silverstein, J. H. (2007). Peer victimization, psychosocial adjustment, and physical activity in overweight and at-risk-for-overweight youth. *Journal of Pediatric Psychology*, *32*(1), 80–89. https://doi.org/10.1093/jpepsy/jsj113

Strelan, P., Mehaffey, S. J., & Tiggemann, M. (2003). Self-objectification and esteem in young women: The mediating role of reasons for exercise. *Sex Roles*, *48*(1–2), 89–95. https://doi.org/10.1023/A:1022300930307

Sumithran, P., & Proietto, J. (2013). The defence of body weight: A physiological basis for weight regain after weight loss. *Clinical Science*, *124*(4), 231–241. https://doi.org/10.1042/CS20120223

Sutin, A. R., Stephan, Y., & Terracciano, A. (2015). Weight discrimination and risk of mortality. *Psychological Science*, *26*(11), 1803–1811. https://doi.org/10.1177/0956797615601103

Sutton, M., Stanley, S., Doherty, A., Driediger, M., Calogero, R. M., Maharaj, A., Meadows, A., Sabiston, C., & Pila, E. (2024). *Weight-inclusive physical activity resources: A systematic evaluation of online content* [Manuscript in preparation]. School of Kinesiology, Western University.

Sutton, M., Stanley, S., & Pila, E. (2023). Evaluating weight inclusivity in physical activity: Environmental scans of virtual resources and physical spaces. *Journal of Exercise, Movement, and Sport*, *54*(1), Article no. 3157. https://www.scapps.org/jems/index.php/1/article/view/3157

Sykes, H., & McPhail, D. (2008). Unbearable lessons: Contesting fat phobia in physical education. *Sociology of Sport Journal*, *25*(1), 66–96. https://doi.org/10.1123/ssj.25.1.66

Täuber, S., Gausel, N., & Flint, S. W. (2018). Weight bias internalization: The maladaptive effects of moral condemnation on intrinsic motivation. *Frontiers in Psychology*, *9*, Article no. 1836. https://doi.org/10.3389/fpsyg.2018.01836

Teixeira, P. J., Carraça, E. V., Markland, D., Silva, M. N., & Ryan, R. M. (2012). Exercise, physical activity, and self-determination theory: A systematic review. *International Journal of Behavioral Nutrition and Physical Activity*, *9*(1), 78. https://doi.org/10.1186/1479-5868-9-78

Thedinga, H. K., Zehl, R., & Thiel, A. (2021). Weight stigma experiences and self-exclusion from sport and exercise settings among people with obesity. *BMC Public Health*, *21*, 565. https://doi.org/10.1186/s12889-021-10565

Thomas, D. M., Kyle, T. K., & Stanford, F. C. (2015). The gap between expectations and reality of exercise-induced weight loss is associated with discouragement. *Preventive Medicine*, *81*, 357–360. https://doi.org/10.1016/j.ypmed.2015.10.001

Tomiyama, A. J., Ahlstrom, B., & Mann, T. (2013). Long-term effects of dieting: Is weight loss related to health? *Social and Personality Psychology Compass, 7*(12), 861–877. https://doi.org/10.1111/spc3.12076

Townend, L. (2009). The moralizing of obesity: A new name for an old sin? *Critical Social Policy*, *29*(2), 171–190. https://doi.org/10.1177/0261018308101625

Tremblay, A., Royer, M.-M., Chaput, J.-P., & Doucet, É. (2013). Adapative thermogenesis can make a difference in the ability of obese individuals to lose body weight. *International Journal of Obesity*, *37*, 759–764. https://doi.org/10.1038/ijo.2012.124

Trouilloud, D. O., Sarrazin, P. G., Martinek, T. J., & Guillet, E. (2002). The influence of teacher expectations on student achievement in physical education classes: Pygmalion revisited. *European Journal of Social Psychology*, *32*, 591–607. https://doi.org/10.1002/ejsp.109

Trouilloud, D., Sarrazin, P., Bressouz, P., & Bois, J. (2006). Relation between teachers' early expectations and students' later perceived competence in physical education classes: Autonomy-supportive climate as a moderator. *Journal of Educational Psychology*, *98*(1), 75–86. https://doi.org/10.1037/0022-0663.98.1.75

Trout, J., & Graber, K. C. (2009). Perceptions of overweight students concerning their experiences in physical education. *Journal of Teaching in Physical Education*, *28*(3), 272–292. https://doi.org/10.1123/jtpe.28.3.272

Tylka, T. L., Annunziato, R. A., Burgard, D., Daníelsdóttir, S., Shuman, E., Davis, C., & Calogero, R. M. (2014). The weight-inclusive versus weight-normative approach to health. Evaluating the evidence for prioritizing well-being over weight loss. *Journal of Obesity*, 2014, Article no. 983495. https://doi.org/10.1155/2014/983495

Udo, T., Purcell, K., & Grilo, C. M., (2016). Perceived weight discrimination and chronic medical conditions in adults with overweight and obesity. *International Journal of Clinical Practice, 70*(12), 1003–1011. https://doi.org/10.1111/ijcp.12902

Vadiveloo, M., & Mattei, J. (2017). Perceived weight discrimination and 10-year risk of allostatic load among US adults. *Annals of Behavioral Medicine*, *51*, 94–104. https://doi.org/10.1007/s12160-016-9870-0

Vani, M. F., Pila, E., deJonge, M., Solomon-Krakus, S., & Sabiston, C. M. (2020). 'Can you move your fat ass off the baseline?' Exploring the sport experiences of adolescent girls with body image concerns. *Qualitative Research in Sport, Exercise and Health, 13*(4), 671–689. https://doi.org/10.1080/2159676X.2020.1771409

Vartanian, L. R., & Novak, S. A. (2011). Internalized societal attitudes moderate the impact of weight stigma on avoidance of exercise. *Obesity, 19*(4), 757–762. https://doi.org/10.1038/oby.2010.234

Vartanian, L. R., Pinkus, R. T., & Smyth, J. M. (2018). Experiences of weight stigma in everyday life: Implications for health motivation. *Stigma and Health, 3*(2), 85–92. https://doi.org/10.1037/sah0000077

Vartanian, L. R., & Shaprow, J. G. (2008). Effects of weight stigma on exercise motivation and behavior: A preliminary investigation among college-aged females. *Journal of Health Psychology, 13*(1), 131–138. https://doi.org/10.1177/1359105307084318

Watkins, P. L., Ebbeck, V., & Levy, S. S. (2014). Overcoming weight bias: Promoting physical activity and psychosocial health. *Ethnicity and Inequalities in Health and Social Care*, *7*(4), 187–197. https://doi.org/10.1108/EIHSC-11-2013-0043

Williams, S. L., & French, D. P. (2011). What are the most effective intervention techniques for changing physical activity self-efficacy and physical activity behaviour—And are they the same? *Health Education Research*, 26(2), 308–322. https://doi.org/10.1093/her/cyr005

Williams, D. M., & Rhodes, R. E. (2016). The confounded self-efficacy construct: Conceptual analysis and recommendations for future research. *Health Psychology Review*, *10*(2), 113–128. https://doi.org/10.1080/17437199.2014.941998

Wood, M., & Pila, E. (2022). Investigating the effects of fit-normative and weight-inclusive Instagram images on women's exercise motivations. *Body Image*, *41*, 460–471. https://doi.org/10.1016/j.bodyim.2022.04.003

Wu, T., Gao, X., Chen, M., & van Dam, R. M. (2009). Long-term effectiveness of diet-plus-exercise interventions vs. diet-only interventions for weight loss: A meta-analysis. *Obesity Reviews*, *10*(3), 313–323. https://doi.org/10.1111/j.1467-789X.2008.00547.x

Zestcott, C. A., Blair, I. V., & Stone, J. (2016). Examining the presence, consequences, and reduction of implicit bias in health care: A narrative review. *Group Processes & Intergroup Relations*, *19*(4), 528–542. https://doi.org/10.1177/1368430216642029

Zhang, Y., Hou, F., Li, J., Yu, H., Li, L., Hu, S., Shen, G., & Yatsuya, H. (2019). The association between weight fluctuation and all-cause mortality: A systematic review and meta-analysis. *Medicine*, *98*(42), Article no. e17513. https://doi.org/10.1097/MD.0000000000017513

Zuest, L., Lee, S., Fogaça, J., Squires, N., & Clifford, D. E. (2024). WIT FITS: Effects of weight stigma intervention on exercise professionals' attitudes toward fatness: A randomized controlled trial. *Recreational Sports Journal*, *48*(1), 3–13. https://doi.org/10.1177/15588661231219098

Zuest, L., Lee, S.-M., Leedeman, J., Li, S., & Clifford, D. E. (2021). Promoting body size diversity in university recreation centers. *Quest*, *73*(4), 357–374. https://doi.org/10.1080/00336297.2021.1970594

PART 4

Exercise and Specific Topics

7

THE EFFECT OF PHYSICAL ACTIVITY ON SLEEP

Szilvia Boros, Nikoletta Barka, and Feifei Wang

7.1 Preface

Physical activity is one of the major types of recreational or leisure-time activities. Although physical activity is a structured, planned form of movement, where in most cases, the frequency, duration, and intensity of exercise are defined. The main purpose is more about maintaining health and well-being. Elite sport is based on preparation for competitions and competitive events as well.

Regarding the WHO (World Health Organization) Guidelines on physical activity and sedentary behavior for health promotion and health maintenance, it is advised to have 150–300 minutes/week aerobic physical activity at a moderate-intensity level, or 75–150 minu tes/week at a vigorous intensity level (Bull et al., 2020). For additional health benefits, it is recommended to include muscle-strengthening exercise at least twice a week. Sedentary adults should focus on incorporating some physical activity without concern for duration and gradually increase the time, frequency, and ultimately the intensity. For older adults and the elderly, it is important to engage in multicomponent exercise for the development of balance and muscle coordination with a focus on fall prevention.

According to present knowledge, good sleep quality is fundamental to well-being and known to be influenced by biological factors and lifestyle. The benefits of physical exercise have been examined from both biological and physiological perspectives. However, the prevalence of sleep loss is increasing nowadays (Ferrie et al., 2011). Insufficient sleep and irregular sleep–wake patterns are frequently documented in younger adolescents, presented alarmingly in college population (Lund & Prichard, 2010). Impaired sleep quality is adversely associated with neuro-cognitive and academic performance (Curcio et al., 2006). And, poor sleep quality is negatively associated with academic performance in adolescents

DOI: 10.4324/9781003517474-11

from middle school through the college years (Wolfson & Carskadon, 2003). Despite the biological necessity of sleep, it has been traded off in modern societies to accommodate social and work schedules. Sufficient sleep is important to personal achievements (Ahrberg et al., 2012).

Sleep quality has a critical role in promoting health. Researchers over the past decade have documented that sleep disturbance has a powerful influence on the risk of medical illnesses, including cardiovascular disease and cancer, and the incidence of depression (Garbarino et al., 2021; Irwin, 2016; Liu et al., 2021; Muscogiuri et al., 2020). To benefit health, Centers for Disease Control and Prevention (CDC) recommends a variety of physical activities from moderate to vigorous intensities with a wide range of activities. Existing evidence considered physical activity as an effective, nonpharmacological approach to improve sleep.

Meditative Movement Therapy (MMT) and relaxation endorsed by the European Sleep Research Society have been recognized as potential contributors to the improvement of poor sleep quality (Riemann et al., 2017). Yoga, along with tai-chi and chi-kung commonly acknowledged as forms of MMT (Larkey et al., 2009), has found widespread adoption in both the modern Eastern and Western hemispheres in various manifestations. With numerous styles such as Tibetan, Iyengar, and Hatha Yoga, each can be characterized as a mindful form of physical activity. The combination of yoga asana, pranayama, and meditation is identified as a form of body-mind therapy based on movements (Jeter et al., 2015; Neuendorf et al., 2015). Contemporary yoga practices are often labeled as MPY (Modern Postural Yoga), highlighting the emphasis on asana and breath control (Lindsay, 2013; Shaw & Kaytaz, 2021). Further, physical exercise – especially MMT – is recommended as an alternative or complementary approach to existing therapies for sleep problems (Baglioni et al., 2020; Yang et al., 2012).

The intensity of physical activity (PA) is related to how hard our body works while doing that activity. In accordance with the CDC and American College of Sports Medicine guidelines, moderate activity is defined as below 3.0–6.0 exercise metabolic rates (METs) (3.5–7 kcal/min), and vigorous activity is defined as greater than 6.0 METs (more than 7 kcal/min) (Ainsworth et al., 1993). Existing review demonstrates that moderate physical exercise benefits sleep quality in all age groups in healthy population, given that physical intensity is better acknowledged and implemented (Wang & Boros, 2021). Evidence from cross-sectional studies indicated that physically active adolescents have more favorable sleep quality than those who are physically inactive (King et al., 2008; Park, 2014). There was evidence supporting that evening exercise may positively affect sleep, but vigorous exercise might impair sleep-onset latency and total sleep time (Stutz, 2019).

The purpose of this chapter is to explore the impact of leisure-time physical activity on sleep quality. Additionally, we are curious about how elite sport can affect sleep quality. We can defer the questions: Is there a certain type of PA that might enhance sleep more effectively than others? How can we characterize the most suitable type of activity and exercise intensity concerning sleep health for various age categories and health conditions?

7.2 Previous Evidence

It is generally thought that physical exercise constitutes a therapeutic behavior that promotes sleep (Yang et al., 2012; Youngstedt, 2005). We now know that the quantity and/or quality of sleep is involved in the manifestation of various alterations in physical exercise functions. Leisure-time physical exercise contributes to increased total energy expenditure (Tremblay et al., 2007). Moreover, it was demonstrated that PA can improve neuro-psychological performance and subjective sleep quality in older adults (Benloucif et al., 2004). Rapid eye movement (REM) sleep is considered a sensitive marker of the exercise effects on sleep. Exercise is significantly correlated with the decrease of REM sleep (Oda & Shirakawa, 2014), which explained the mechanism of PA effect on sleep. Both vigorous and moderate activities may be beneficial to metabolic issues among middle-aged populations (Rennie et al., 2003). It revealed that participating in an exercise training program has positive effects on sleep quality in middle-aged and older adults (Yang et al., 2012). In this regard, this would indicate that physical exercise may elicit larger changes in sleep. Given that age is likely an important mediating factor influencing the intensity of physical exercise, it is important to examine the incidental effect of age. The aging populations face a high prevalence of physical disability. It has been examined that poor physical function is associated with sleep fragmentation in older women (Goldman et al., 2007) and hypoxia in older men (Dam et al., 2008). However, the interaction of age in the functioning of physical intensities of sleep requires more exploration.

There is a growing research interest in the effects of PA on sleep quality in the recent decade. Existing evidence showed that regular PA can improve sleep quality and duration (Brupbacher et al., 2021; Rosa et al., 2021; Xie et al., 2021). Adults who performed a minimum of 30 minutes exercise a day slept an average of 15 minutes longer than those who did not (Baron et al., 2013). PA was shown to be helpful in reducing sleep disorders, such as insomnia, daytime sleepiness, and sleep apnea (Hartescu et al., 2015; McClain et al., 2014; Van Offenwert et al., 2019). A meta-analysis systematically investigated the magnitude and moderate effects of PA on sleep, which revealed that acute exercise has small beneficial effects on total sleep time, sleep-onset latency, sleep efficiency, and a moderate beneficial effect on wake time after sleep onset, and a small effect on REM sleep (Kredlow et al., 2015).

The effect of PA on sleep has always been proposed to be influenced by moderators. In general, sleep-onset latency slightly increases with age, sleep latency, percentages of stage 1 and stage 2 significantly increased with age while the percentage of REM sleep decreased in adults (Ohayon et al., 2004). Age was found to have a significantly less beneficial effects of exercise on the sleep-onset latency among older individuals (Kredlow et al., 2015). In contrast, the benefits of regular exercise did not vary by sex and for one variable (sleep-onset latency), appeared to be stronger for younger than older individuals (Kredlow et al., 2015). The effect sizes for physical exercises modified by age associations with different sleep parameters are still unclear. Additionally, very few studies examined the effect of ethnicity on polysomnographic sleep parameters (Baldwin et al., 2010).

7.2.1 PA Types and Sleep Quality

PA has been widely studied in scientific research for its role in promoting health conditions. Trials of physical exercise on sleep quality were diverse; nevertheless, more positive results were received from previous studies despite the types and dedicated samples. Physical exercise is supposed to benefit sleep quality in a wide spectrum of exercise types. An increase of walking distance by 500 steps per week showed a positive effect in improving sleep quality on postmenopausal women (Tadayon et al., 2016). Not only in postmenopausal women, but also in secondary school students, walking exercise showed significant improvement of subjective sleep quality (Baldursdottir et al., 2017). Moreover, a real-world study added additional evidence that daily walking exercise is beneficial to improve subjective sleep quality in people who are both physically active and non-active (Hori et al., 2016). Aerobic exercises, such as tai-chi and home exercise, were examined within community-dwelling elderly in a randomized-controlled trial, and exercisers reported better sleep quality than non-exercisers (Brandão et al., 2018; Kashefi et al., 2014; Nguyen & Kruse, 2012). Rather than slow movement exercise, participation of moderate-intensity physical activities (e.g. included roller skating, cycling, baseball, and walking/running) launched in college students (nine exercisers and ten non-exercisers), indicated that participation in such a program improves sleep (Hurdiel et al., 2017). Physical exercise may partially improve sleep components. Evidence showed that home-based 30-min pilates exercises also significantly improved subjective sleep quality, sleep latency, daytime dysfunction, and global Pittsburgh Sleep Quality Index score, but not sleep duration, habitual sleep efficiency, and sleep disturbance (Ashrafinia et al., 2014). The implementation of physical exercise needs to take participants' age and health status into consideration. Intensity and duration of PA for sleep benefits are under discussion.

Even though more positive results were found in most articles, negative or novel results still existed. A floor-seated exercise program conducted in 77 old participants (between 71 and 85 years) found no significant effect on sleep quality (Choi, 2018). As illustrated from a cross-sectional study launched in the low socioeconomic status urban areas, decreased PA may be associated with poor sleep (Greever et al., 2017; Wu et al., 2015). It has been suggested that PA may be a modifiable risk factor to improve sleep (Greever et al., 2017).

7.2.2 PA Intensity and Sleep Quality

PA interventions that showed positive results were mostly moderate exercise or moderate to vigorous exercise. There were ambiguous data illustrating the effect of acute exercise on sleep and sleep disorders (Morita et al., 2017; Passos et al., 2010). In a cross-sectional study covering participants from 23 countries, it was demonstrated that there was no association between vigorous PA and sleep quality and quantity (Pengpid & Peltzer, 2018). A qualitative study examined the effects of acute exercise on sleep; however, it found no effect of vigorous PA on sleep quality (Myllymäki et al., 2011). Nevertheless, there were findings that did not support the result. For instance, among people with insomnia, acute morning exercise turned out to improve nocturnal sleep quality in individuals with difficulty initiating sleep (Morita et al., 2017). In addition, it was indicated that increased PA is favorably associated with restoring sleep, and vigorous PA levels tend to be a better predictor for good sleep than moderate PA (Lang et al., 2013). To our best acknowledgment, the number of studies defining the effect of vigorous PA on sleep quality is limited.

Moderate physical activities were more popular in scientific research as a physiotherapy method to improve sleep quality. It is a good idea to discuss the effects of physical intensity and duration on sleep quality. A cross-sectional study showed that neither intensity nor duration of PA was associated with sleep quality or quantity (Kakinami et al., 2017). It was highly suggested that regular moderate-intensity exercise program improves self-rated sleep quality in older adults with moderate sleep complaints (King et al., 2020). According to the results illustrated above, it is reasonable to assume that physical intensity may be related to sleep quality, which still needs more evidence (Kredlow et al., 2015). Sleepiness was suggested to be associated with age in daytime workers (Åkerstedt et al., 2017).

Cultural and religious beliefs may influence beliefs of sleep since it was predicted that spiritual and religious activity was associated with different components of sleep quality (Yang et al., 2008). There were few scientific data addressed how physical exercise duration is sufficient in terms of moderate activity, which, as a specific aspect, has not yet been explicitly investigated in scientific research. Physical exercise is subjective and individual; in this context, people are free to carry out any kind of activities.

7.3 Updated Evidence

In regular leisure-time PA, each training session or competition triggers an acute stress reaction. After the sport session, the body endeavors to restore homeostasis as quickly as possible. The more trained we are, the faster and easier the balance is restored. The body responds to a series of training through adaptation. Compensatory mechanisms lead to a more favorable resting state.

Walking is recognized as sustainable exercise that does not need professional instructions to perform, making it a viable option for public health promotion. Research has shown that walking enhances the restoration of autonomic control during night-time sleep (Gladwell et al., 2016). A before- and after comparison related to forest walking supported the idea that forest walking improved nocturnal sleep conditions among a community-based sample of people with sleep complaints (Li, 2023; Morita et al., 2011). Meta-analyses have highlighted the benefits of moderate-intensity walking for clinical patients (Tang et al., 2019), and moderate-intensity walking exercise has shown efficacy in improving sleep (Chiu et al., 2015). Brisk walking lasting for at least 20 min is associated with less subsequent sleep difficulties (Chen et al., 2018), and it is recommended to add a walking exercise program to the daily program for elderly population (Karimi et al., 2016; Storer et al., 2023). There was only one randomized-controlled trial examining on walking and light exposure, which stated that walking showed no significant effect on improving sleep disorder (McCurry et al., 2011).

The number of studies examining the effect of cycling and sleep quality is limited. One study investigated the impact of a six, once-daily bouts of aerobic cycling exercise on subjective and objective sleep quality metrics. The results indicated that cycling exercise exhibited improvements in sleep duration ($p = 0.008$) and sleep efficiency ($p = 0.023$) (McCartney et al., 2021). In another study examining the effect of various cycling intensities on sleep-related parameters in healthy young adults, ten recreationally trained male volunteers reported better sleep efficiency ($p < 0.05$). However, no significant differences were found regarding sleep-onset latency and bedtime duration ($p > 0.05$) (Vlahoyiannis et al., 2021). It is important to note that mountain bikers reported significantly more tiredness (tired/energetic visual analog scale) on each night of cycling ($p < 0.01$) and reported more wakeups during the night (double the number of times) ($p < 0.001$) (Murphy et al., 2011).

Additionally, there are also many recreational PA types that may benefit sleep quality, such as judo and ball games (soccer, volleyball, handball, and basketball) (Rosa et al., 2021).

A recent systematic review of 19 studies examining the impact of yoga on women's sleep quality and severity of insomnia, compelling evidence was revealed for the positive effects of yoga on sleep-related issues (Wang et al., 2020). In a clinical trial that comparing yoga practitioners with participants engaged in passive stretching, postmenopausal women experienced a significant reduction in insomnia when practicing yoga (Afonso et al., 2012; Kim et al., 2020). Furthermore, for breast cancer patients, regular yoga practice (2–3 times a week, lasting 6–8 weeks) appears to be an effective intervention for treating insomnia (Zhu et al., 2023).

There are other body-mind exercises such as Baduanjin (a form of martial art consisting of eight sequential movements involving body and trunk, limb, and eye movements matching with breathing) and tai-chi (consists of a series of gentle physical activities that incorporate element and meditation, body awareness, imagery, and abdominal breathing), which have been extensively discussed. For instance, a randomized trial involving community-dwelling elderly people reported significant improvements in overall sleep quality after 24 weeks of 5 sessions/week, each lasting 45-minutes of Baduanjin exercise, compared with those randomized to control group (sleep quality endpoint-to-baseline change $= -2.6 \pm 4.0$ vs. -0.5 ± 4.2, time × group interaction $p = 0.007$) (Fan et al., 2020). Additionally, twenty randomized-controlled studies, encompassing 1,703 patients from five countries, revealed that tai-chi also has a positive effect on improving sleep quality (Li et al., 2020).

Dance movement practice is a type of art therapy that has been entrenched in modern culture for 70 years (Millman et al., 2021). Dance is a PA medium that can provide discrete and precise exercise prescriptions. Dancing or aerobic dancing is becoming a trendy intervention method nowadays, especially in Asia (He et al., 2021). Evidence of the relationship between dancing and sleep quality is only reported in several randomized trials; no systematic review or meta-analysis is available as of the written date of this chapter). A randomized-controlled trial of dance-training program conducted with 67 women reported a significant improvement in sleep quality ($p < 0.05$) (Serrano-Guzmán et al., 2016). A recent study of an aerobic dancing program was published in 2023, which was a randomized-controlled trial with older adults. The participants in the intervention group demonstrated a significantly greater improvement in terms of general sleep quality (β, −1.74; 95% CI, −3.41 to −0.08; p =0.04), sleep latency (β, −0.19; 95% CI, −0.37 to −0.02; p =0.03), sleep duration (β, 0.51; 95% CI, 0.24 to 0.99; p = 0.04), sleep efficiency (β, 0.11; 95% CI, 0.07 to 1.12; p = 0.04), and cognitive function (β, 1.64; 95% CI, 0.43 to 2.86; p = 0.008) compared with the control group over the pre–post-test periods (Song, 2024).

The association between aquatic exercise and sleep quality has only been sporadically studied. The most recent studies on aquatic treatment and sleep quality among musculoskeletal patients were published in recent years (Bravo et al., 2024; So et al., 2021). Aquatic exercise therapy refers to the application of aquatic properties to design a therapy program to improve patient functionality. Water is an environment that, due to its properties, provides the opportunity for the patient to undertake global activity and to apply physiotherapy (Zamunér et al., 2019). In recent decades, aquatic therapy studies have been conducted and have shown beneficial effects on physical fitness and wellness (Lima et al., 2013). In 2021, an aquatic exercise program involving a total of 30 adults examined its effects. The results showed that the intervention group had a significantly longer total true sleep time (by 27.6 minutes, p = 0.006) and greater sleep efficiency (+3.01%, p = 0.005) than the control group (So et al., 2021).

The association between late-night PA and sleep quality has not reached consensus. Meta-analyses on the effects of exercise on sleep published to date have also not definitively answered whether exercise performed close to bedtime has a negative impact on sleep (Kredlow et al., 2015). Generally, exercising at night as part of good sleep hygiene is not traditionally recommended, and American Academy of Sleep Medicine suggests that late-night exercise may be one possible cause of sleep difficulties (Sateia, 2014). Increasingly, new studies report negative effects of late-night PA on sleep quality. For instance, a systematic review and meta-analysis in 2019, which analyzed 11,717 references indicated that evening exercise significantly increased REM latency (+7.7 min; p = 0.032) and slow-wave sleep (+1.3 percentage points [pp]; p = 0.041), but it decreased stage 1 sleep (−0.9 pp; p = 0.001) (Stutz, 2019). In a late-night exercise study with 11 young adults, applying acute PA starting approximately at 21:00 hours found no differences in actigraphic or subjective sleep quality (Myllymäki et al., 2011). A cross-sectional study from Saudi Arabia indicated that evening vigorous (r = 0.25, p = 0.038) and moderate (r = 0.30, p = 0.025) physical exercise sessions lasting >90 min had a significant positive correlation with poor sleep quality (Alkhaldi et al., 2023).

The association, including low-intensity and less-structured activity such as gardening, has not yet been explicitly investigated. Gardening, involving indoor or outdoor planting and gardening activities, has been recognized as an intervention (Spano et al., 2020). Gardening activities might exhibit the better healing effect on the elderly, providing a reference for organizing different programs in residential facilities and adult day-care services. An empirical study with 24 participants engaging in gardening activities showed that sleep quality significantly improved after a six-week course of gardening activities (Shen et al., 2022). A pilot study invited patients with sleep disturbance and/or agitation to participate in a five-week gardening intervention by using a sleep diary. The results emphasized the effectiveness of gardening for improving sleep (Lee & Kim, 2008). An updated systematic review supported positive association between gardening or green space exposures and sleep quality and quantity (Shin et al., 2020).

7.4 Implications

There is a growing research interest in the effects of PA on sleep, including moderate and/or vigorous, indoor and/or outdoor activities. A great heterogeneity of studies have reported the effectiveness of PA on sleep quality. Existing evidence has been conducted in various settings with participants in different health statuses; continuously updated findings would enrich the topic of PA and sleep quality. With the agreement of WHO PA recommendations, any type of recreational PA could be a good choice for improving sleep quality, such as walking types:

- moderate-intensity walking
- brisk walking
- forest walking.

The recommended duration of moderate walking is at least 20–30 minutes/day. Walking can be advised for all age groups, especially younger and older adults, postmenopausal women, the elderly, as well as clinical patients.

Meditative movement therapies, such as yoga, tai-chi, and even Baduanjin might be one of the most tolerable and useful activity types for postmenopausal women, as well as patients with insomnia. Dance therapy and aquatic training might be effective in improving sleep health as well.

As a residential facility for the elderly population, five to six weeks of gardening activities might be implemented as a nonpharmacological therapy in everyday life.

Evening or late-night exercise has no convincing favorable impact on sleep quality; therefore, it should be done with caution. The type, duration, and intensity of PA might depend upon individual requirements and preferences.

7.5 Conclusion

The connection between physical intensity and sleep quality lacks sufficient experimental evidence. Although there are some convincing results that demonstrate the beneficial effects of PA on sleep health, such as moderate-intensity walking, brisk walking or forest walking might be useful especially for elderly people. Ambiguous data exists regarding the impact of acute exercise on sleep and sleep disorders, and there is limited evidence supporting the notion that vigorous PA benefits sleep quality.

This study underscores that moderate PA is beneficial for sleep quality across all age groups in healthy population, provided that the physical intensity is well acknowledged. However, available data do not strongly support the idea of gender influencing the interaction during physical exercise. Physical exercise is subjective and individual, allowing individuals the freedom to engage in various activities. Given the subjective nature of physical exercise, qualitative recommendations and guidelines are deemed essential.

References

Afonso, R. F., Hachul, H., Kozasa, E. H., Oliveira, D. de S., Goto, V., Rodrigues, D., Tufik, S., & Leite, J. R. (2012). Yoga decreases insomnia in postmenopausal women: A randomized clinical trial. *Menopause (New York, N.Y.)*, *19*(2), Article 2. https://doi.org/10.1097/gme.0b013e318228225f

Ahrberg, K. Dresler, M., Niedemaier, S., Steiner, A., & Gensel, L. (2012). The interaction between sleep quality and academic performance. *Journal of Psychiatric Research*, *12*, 1618–1622. https://doi.org/10.1016/j.jpsychires.2012.09.008

Ainsworth, B. E., Haskell, W. L., Leon, A. S., Jacobs, D. R., Montoye, H. J., Sallis, J. F., & Paffenbarger, R. S. (1993). Compendium of physical activities: Classification of energy costs of human physical activities. *Medicine and Science in Sports and Exercise*, *25*(1), 71–74. https://doi.org/10.1249/00005768-199301000-00011

Åkerstedt, T., Hallvig, D., & Kecklund, G. (2017). Normative data on the diurnal pattern of the Karolinska Sleepiness Scale ratings and its relation to age, sex, work, stress, sleep quality and sickness absence/illness in a large sample of daytime workers. *Journal of Sleep Research*, *26*(5), Article 5. https://doi.org/10.1111/jsr.12528

Alkhaldi, E. H., Battar, S., Alsuwailem, S. I., Almutairi, K. S., Alshamari, W. K., & Alkhaldi, A. H. (2023). Effect of nighttime exercise on sleep quality among the general population in Riyadh, Saudi Arabia: A cross-sectional study. *Cureus*, *15*(7), Article 7. https://doi.org/10.7759/cureus.41638

Ashrafinia, F., Mirmohammadali, M., Rajabi, H., Kazemnejad, A., Sadeghniiathaghighi, K., Amelvalizadeh, M., & Chen, H. (2014). The effects of Pilates exercise on sleep quality in postpartum women. *Journal of Bodywork and Movement Therapies*, *18*(2), Article 2. https://doi.org/10.1016/j.jbmt.2013.09.007

Baglioni, C., Bostanova, Z., Bacaro, V., Benz, F., Hertenstein, E., Spiegelhalder, K., Rücker, G., Frase, L., Riemann, D., & Feige, B. (2020). A systematic review and network meta-analysis of randomized controlled trials evaluating the evidence base of melatonin, light exposure, exercise, and complementary and alternative medicine for patients with insomnia disorder. *Journal of Clinical Medicine*, *9*(6), Article 6. https://doi.org/10.3390/jcm9061949

Baldursdottir, B., Taehtinen, R. E., Sigfusdottir, I. D., Krettek, A., & Valdimarsdottir, H. B. (2017). Impact of a physical activity intervention on adolescents' subjective sleep quality: A pilot study. *Global Health Promotion*, *24*(4), Article 4. https://doi.org/10.1177/1757975915626112

Baldwin, C. M., Ervin, A.-M., Mays, M. Z., Robbins, J., Shafazand, S., Walsleben, J., & Weaver, T. (2010). Sleep disturbances, quality of life, and ethnicity: The sleep heart health study. *Journal of Clinical Sleep Medicine*, *6*(2), 176–183. https://doi.org/10.5664/jcsm.27768

Baron, K. G., Reid, K. J., & Zee, P. C. (2013). Exercise to improve sleep in insomnia: Exploration of the bidirectional effects. *Journal of Clinical Sleep Medicine: JCSM: Official Publication of the American Academy of Sleep Medicine*, *9*(8), 819–824. https://doi.org/10.5664/jcsm.2930

Benloucif, S., Orbeta, L., Ortiz, R., Janssen, I., Finkel, S. I., Bleiberg, J., & Zee, P. C. (2004). Morning or evening activity improves neuropsychological performance and subjective sleep quality in older adults. *Sleep*, *27*(8), Article 8.

Brandão, G. S., Callou, A. A., Brandão, G. S., Silva, A. S., & Urbano, J. J. (2018). The effect of home-based exercise in sleep quality and excessive daytime sleepiness in elderly people: A protocol of randomized controlled clinical trial. *Manual Therapy, Posturology & Rehabilitation Journal*, *16*(577), 1–6. https://doi.org/10.17784/mtprehabjournal.2018.16.577

Bravo, C., Rubí-Carnacea, F., Colomo, I., Sánchez-de-la-Torre, M., Fernández-Lago, H., & Climent-Sanz, C. (2024). Aquatic therapy improves self-reported sleep quality in fibromyalgia patients: A systematic review and meta-analysis. *Sleep and Breathing, 28*, 565–583. https://doi.org/10.1007/s11325-023-02933-x

Brupbacher, G., Gerger, H., Zander-Schellenberg, T., Straus, D., Porschke, H., Gerber, M., von Känel, R., & Schmidt-Trucksäss, A. (2021). The effects of exercise on sleep in unipolar depression: A systematic review and network meta-analysis. *Sleep Medicine Reviews*, *59*, 101452. https://doi.org/10.1016/j.smrv.2021.101452

Bull, F. C., Al-Ansari, S. S., Biddle, S., Borodulin, K., Buman, M. P., Cardon, G., Carty, C., Chaput, J.-P., Chastin, S., Chou, R., Dempsey, P. C., DiPietro, L., Ekelund, U., Firth, J., Friedenreich, C. M., Garcia, L., Gichu, M., Jago, R., Katzmarzyk, P. T., … Willumsen, J. F. (2020). World Health Organization 2020 guidelines on physical activity and sedentary behaviour. *British Journal of Sports Medicine*, *54*(24), 1451–1462. https://doi.org/10.1136/bjsports-2020-102955

Chen, L.-J., Fox, K. R., Sun, W.-J., Tsai, P.-S., Ku, P.-W., & Chu, D. (2018). Associations between walking parameters and subsequent sleep difficulty in older adults: A 2-year follow-up study. *Journal of Sport and Health Science*, *7*(1), Article 1. https://doi.org/10.1016/j.jshs.2017.01.007

Chiu, H.-Y., Huang, H.-C., Chen, P.-Y., Hou, W.-H., & Tsai, P.-S. (2015). Walking improves sleep in individuals with cancer: A meta-analysis of randomized, controlled trials. *Oncology Nursing Forum*, *42*(2), Article 2. https://doi.org/10.1188/15.ONF.E54-E62

Choi, M.-J. (2018). The effects of floor-seated exercise program on physical fitness, depression, and sleep in older adults: A cluster randomized controlled trial. *International Journal of Gerontology*, *12*, Article 12.

Curcio, G., Ferrara, M., & Gennaro, L. D. (2006). Sleep loss, learning capacity and academic performance. *Sleep Medicine Reviews*, *10*(5), 323–337. https://doi.org/10.1016/j.smrv.2005.11.001

Dam, T.-T. L., Ewing, S., Ancoli-Israel, S., Ensrud, K., Redline, S., Stone, K., & Osteoporotic Fractures in Men Research Group. (2008). Association between sleep and physical function in older men: The osteoporotic fractures in men sleep study. *Journal of the American Geriatrics Society*, *56*(9), Article 9. https://doi.org/10.1111/j.1532-5415.2008.01846.x

Fan, B., Song, W., Zhang, J., Er, Y., Xie, B., Zhang, H., Liao, Y., Wang, C., Hu, X., Mcintyre, R., & Lee, Y. (2020). The efficacy of mind-body (Baduanjin) exercise on self-reported sleep quality and quality of life in elderly subjects with sleep disturbances: A randomized controlled trial. *Sleep & Breathing = Schlaf & Atmung*, *24*(2), Article 2. https://doi.org/10.1007/s11325-019-01999-w

Ferrie, J. E., Kumari, M., Salo, P., Singh-Manoux, A., & Kivimäki, M. (2011). Sleep epidemiology—A rapidly growing field. *International Journal of Epidemiology*, *40*(6), 1431–1437. https://doi.org/10.1093/ije/dyr203

Garbarino, S., Lanteri, P., Bragazzi, N. L., Magnavita, N., & Scoditti, E. (2021). Role of sleep deprivation in immune-related disease risk and outcomes. *Communications Biology*, *4*(1), Article 1. https://doi.org/10.1038/s42003-021-02825-4

Gladwell, V. F., Kuoppa, P., Tarvainen, M. P., & Rogerson, M. (2016). A lunchtime walk in nature enhances restoration of autonomic control during night-time sleep: Results from a preliminary study. *International Journal of Environmental Research and Public Health*, *13*(3), Article 3. https://doi.org/10.3390/ijerph13030280

Goldman, S. E., Stone, K. L., Ancoli-Israel, S., Blackwell, T., Ewing, S. K., Boudreau, R., Cauley, J. A., Hall, M., Matthews, K. A., & Newman, A. B. (2007). Poor sleep is associated with poorer physical performance and greater functional limitations in older women. *Sleep*, *30*(10), 1317–1324. https://doi.org/10.1093/sleep/30.10.1317

Greever, C. J., Ahmadi, M., Sirard, J., & Alhassan, S. (2017). Associations among physical activity, screen time, and sleep in low socioeconomic status urban girls. *Preventive Medicine Reports*, *5*, 275–278. https://doi.org/10.1016/j.pmedr.2017.01.014

Hartescu, I., Morgan, K., & Stevinson, C. D. (2015). Increased physical activity improves sleep and mood outcomes in inactive people with insomnia: A randomized controlled trial. *Journal of Sleep Research*, *24*(5), 526–534. https://doi.org/10.1111/jsr.12297

He, X., Ng, M. S. N., Wang, X., Guo, P., Li, L., Zhao, W., Zhang, M., & So, W. K. W. (2021). A dance program to manage a fatigue-sleep disturbance-depression symptom cluster among breast cancer patients receiving adjuvant chemotherapy: A feasibility study. *Asia-Pacific Journal of Oncology Nursing*, *8*(3), Article 3. https://doi.org/10.4103/2347-5625.308677

Hori, H., Ikenouchi-Sugita, A., Yoshimura, R., & Nakamura, J. (2016). Does subjective sleep quality improve by a walking intervention? A real-world study in a Japanese workplace. *BMJ Open*, *6*(10), Article 10. https://doi.org/10.1136/bmjopen-2016-011055

Hurdiel, R., Watier, T., Honn, K., Pezé, T., Zunquin, G., & Theunynck, D. (2017). Effects of a 12-week physical activities programme on sleep in female university students. *Research in Sports Medicine (Print)*, *25*(2), Article 2. https://doi.org/10.1080/15438627.2017.1282354

Irwin, M. R. (2016). Why sleep is important for health: A psychoneuroimmunology perspective. *Annual Review of Psychology, 66*, 143–72. https://doi.org/10.1146/annurev-psych-010213–115205.

Jeter, P. E., Slutsky, J., Singh, N., & Khalsa, S. B. S. (2015). Yoga as a therapeutic intervention: A bibliometric analysis of published research studies from 1967 to 2013. *Journal of Alternative and Complementary Medicine*, *21*(10), 586–92. https://doi.org/10.1089/acm.2015.0057

Kakinami, L., O'Loughlin, E. K., Brunet, J., Dugas, E. N., Constantin, E., Sabiston, C. M., & O'Loughlin, J. (2017). Associations between physical activity and sedentary behavior with sleep quality and quantity in young adults. *Sleep Health*, *3*(1), Article 1. https://doi.org/10.1016/j.sleh.2016.11.001

Karimi, S., Soroush, A., Towhidi, F., Makhsosi, B. R., Karimi, M., Jamehshorani, S., Akhgar, A., Fakhri, M., & Abdi, A. (2016). Surveying the effects of an exercise program on the sleep quality of elderly males. *Clinical Interventions in Aging*, *11*, 997–1002. https://doi.org/10.2147/CIA.S106808

Kashefi, Z., Mirzaei, B., & Shabani, R. (2014). The effects of eight weeks selected aerobic exercises on sleep quality of middle-aged non-athlete females. *Iranian Red Crescent Medical Journal*, *16*(7), Article 7. https://doi.org/10.5812/ircmj.16408

Kim, H., Kim, J., Ju, H. J., Jang, B. J., Wang, T. K., & Kim, Y. I. (2020). Effect of forest therapy for menopausal women with insomnia. *International Journal of Environmental Research and Public Health*, *17*(18), Article 18. https://doi.org/10.3390/ijerph17186548

King, A. C., Pruitt, L. A., Woo, S., Castro, C. M., Ahn, D. K., Vitiello, M. V., Woodward, S. H., & Bliwise, D. L. (2008). Effects of moderate-intensity exercise on polysomnographic and subjective sleep quality in older adults with mild to moderate sleep complaints. *The Journals of Gerontology, Series A: Biological Sciences and Medical* Sciences, *63*(9), 997–1004. https://doi.org/10.1093/gerona/63.9.997

Kredlow, M. A., Capozzoli, M. C., Hearon, B. A., Calkins, A. W., & Otto, M. W. (2015). The effects of physical activity on sleep: A meta-analytic review. *Journal of Behavioral Medicine*, *38*(3), 427–449. https://doi.org/10.1007/s10865-015-9617-6

Lang, C., Brand, S., Feldmeth, A. K., Holsboer-Trachsler, E., Pühse, U., & Gerber, M. (2013). Increased self-reported and objectively assessed physical activity predict sleep quality among adolescents. *Physiology & Behavior*, *120*, 46–53. https://doi.org/10.1016/j.physbeh.2013.07.001

Larkey, L., Jahnke, R., Etnier, J., & Gonzalez, J. (2009). Meditative movement as a category of exercise: Implications for research. *Journal of Physical Activity & Health*, *6*(2), 230–238.

Lee, Y., & Kim, S. (2008). Effects of indoor gardening on sleep, agitation, and cognition in dementia patients—A pilot study. *International Journal of Geriatric Psychiatry*, *23*(5), Article 5. https://doi.org/10.1002/gps.1920

Li, H., Chen, J., Xu, G., Duan, Y., Huang, D., Tang, C., & Liu, J. (2020). The effect of Tai Chi for improving sleep quality: A systematic review and meta-analysis. *Journal of Affective Disorders*, *274*, 1102–1112. https://doi.org/10.1016/j.jad.2020.05.076

Li, Q. (2023). New concept of forest medicine. *Forests*, *14*(5), Article 5. https://doi.org/10.3390/f14051024

Lima, T. B., Dias, J. M., Mazuquin, B. F., da Silva, C. T., Nogueira, R. M. P., Marques, A. P., Lavado, E. L., & Cardoso, J. R. (2013). The effectiveness of aquatic physical therapy in the treatment of fibromyalgia: A systematic review with meta-analysis. *Clinical Rehabilitation*, *27*(10), Article 10. https://doi.org/10.1177/0269215513484772

Lindsay, K. (2013). Spiritual authenticity in a secular context: How modern postural yoga is searching for legitimacy in all the wrong places. *The Arbutus Review*, *4*(1), 108–127. https://journals.uvic.ca/index.php/arbutus/article/view/12686

Liu, X., Chen, B., Huang, Z., Duan, R., Li, H., Xie, L., Wang, R., Li, Z., Gao, Y., Zheng, Y., & Su, W. (2021). Effects of poor sleep on the immune cell landscape as assessed by single-cell analysis. *Communications Biology*, *4*(1), Article 1. https://doi.org/10.1038/s42003-021-02859-8

Lund, H. G., & Prichard, J. R. (2010). Sleep patterns and predictors of disturbed sleep in a large population of college students. *Journal of Adolescent Health*, *46*(2), 124–132. https://doi.org/10.1016/j.jadohealth.2009.06.016.

McCartney, D., Isik, A. D., Rooney, K., Arnold, J. C., Bartlett, D. J., Murnion, B., Richards, E., Arkell, T. R., Lintzeris, N., & McGregor, I. S. (2021). The effect of daily aerobic cycling exercise on sleep quality during inpatient cannabis withdrawal: A randomised controlled trial. *Journal of Sleep Research*, *30*(3), e13211. https://doi.org/10.1111/jsr.13211

McClain, J. J., Lewin, D. S., Laposky, A. D., Kahle, L., & Berrigan, D. (2014). Associations between physical activity, sedentary time, sleep duration and daytime sleepiness in US adults. *Preventive Medicine*, *66*, 68–73. https://doi.org/10.1016/j.ypmed.2014.06.003

McCurry, S. M., Pike, K. C., Vitiello, M. V., Logsdon, R. G., Larson, E. B., & Teri, L. (2011). Increasing walking and bright light exposure to improve sleep in community-dwelling persons with Alzheimer's disease: Results of a randomized, controlled trial. *Journal of the American Geriatrics Society*, *59*(8), Article 8. https://doi.org/10.1111/j.1532-5415.2011.03519.x

Millman, L. S. M., Terhune, D. B., Hunter, E. C. M., & Orgs, G. (2021). Towards a neurocognitive approach to dance movement therapy for mental health: A systematic review. *Clinical Psychology & Psychotherapy*, *28*(1), 24–38. https://doi.org/10.1002/cpp.2490

Morita, E., Imai, M., Okawa, M., Miyaura, T., & Miyazaki, S. (2011). A before and after comparison of the effects of forest walking on the sleep of a community-based sample of people with sleep complaints. *BioPsychoSocial Medicine*, *5*, 13. https://doi.org/10.1186/1751-0759-5-13

Morita, Y., Sasai-Sakuma, T., & Inoue, Y. (2017). Effects of acute morning and evening exercise on subjective and objective sleep quality in older individuals with insomnia. *Sleep Medicine*, *34*, 200–208. https://doi.org/10.1016/j.sleep.2017.03.014

Murphy, S. P., Fuller, A., Bentley, A. J., & Avidon, I. (2011). The effects of three days of submaximal-intensity mountain biking on sleep. *South African Sports Medicine Association*, *23*(1), Article 1.

Muscogiuri, G., Tuccinardi, D., Nicastro, V., Barrea, L., Colao, A., & Savastano, S. (2020). Sleep disturbances: One of the culprits of obesity-related cardiovascular risk? *International Journal of Obesity Supplements*, *10*(1), Article 1. https://doi.org/10.1038/s41367-020-0019-z

Myllymäki, T., Kyröläinen, H., Savolainen, K., Hokka, L., Jakonen, R., Juuti, T., Martinmäki, K., Kaartinen, J., Kinnunen, M.-L., & Rusko, H. (2011). Effects of vigorous late-night exercise on sleep quality and cardiac autonomic activity. *Journal of Sleep Research*, *20*(1 Pt 2), Article 1 Pt 2. https://doi.org/10.1111/j.1365-2869.2010.00874.x

Neuendorf, R., Wahbeh, H., Chamine, I., Yu, J., Hutchison, K., & Oken, B. S. (2015). The effects of mind-body interventions on sleep quality: A systematic review. *Evidence-Based Complementary and Alternative Medicine: eCAM*, *2015*, 902708. https://doi.org/10.1155/2015/902708

Nguyen, M. H., & Kruse, A. (2012). A randomized controlled trial of Tai chi for balance, sleep quality and cognitive performance in elderly Vietnamese. *Clinical Interventions in Aging*, *7*, 185–190. https://doi.org/10.2147/CIA.S32600

Oda, S., & Shirakawa, K. (2014). Sleep onset is disrupted following pre-sleep exercise that causes large physiological excitement at bedtime. *European Journal of Applied Physiology*, *114*(9), Article 9. https://doi.org/10.1007/s00421-014-2873-2

Ohayon, M. M., Carskadon, M. A., Guilleminault, C., & Vitiello, M. V. (2004). Meta-analysis of quantitative sleep parameters from childhood to old age in healthy individuals: Developing normative sleep values across the human lifespan. *Sleep*, *27*(7), 1255–1273. https://doi.org/10.1093/sleep/27.7.1255

Park, S. (2014). Associations of physical activity with sleep satisfaction, perceived stress, and problematic Internet use in Korean adolescents. *BMC Public Health*, *14*, 1143.

Passos, G. S., Poyares, D., Santana, M. G., Garbuio, S. A., Tufik, S., & Mello, M. T. (2010). Effect of acute physical exercise on patients with chronic primary insomnia. *Journal of Clinical Sleep Medicine: JCSM: Official Publication of the American Academy of Sleep Medicine*, *6*(3), Article 3.

Pengpid, S., & Peltzer, K. (2018). Vigorous physical activity, perceived stress, sleep and mental health among university students from 23 low- and middle-income countries. *International Journal of Adolescent Medicine and Health*, *32*(2), Article 2. https://doi.org/10.1515/ijamh-2017-0116

Rennie, K. L., McCarthy, N., Yazdgerdi, S., Marmot, M., & Brunner, E. (2003). Association of the metabolic syndrome with both vigorous and moderate physical activity. *International Journal of Epidemiology*, *32*(4), Article 4. https://doi.org/10.1093/ije/dyg179

Riemann, D., Baglioni, C., Bassetti, C., Bjorvatn, B., Dolenc Groselj, L., Ellis, J. G., Espie, C. A., Garcia-Borreguero, D., Gjerstad, M., Gonçalves, M., Hertenstein, E., Jansson-Fröjmark, M., Jennum, P. J., Leger, D., Nissen, C., Parrino, L., Paunio, T., Pevernagie, D., Verbraecken, J., … Spiegelhalder, K. (2017). European guideline for the diagnosis and treatment of insomnia. *Journal of Sleep Research*, *26*(6), Article 6. https://doi.org/10.1111/jsr.12594

Rosa, C. C., Tebar, W. R., Oliveira, C. B. S., Farah, B. Q., Casonatto, J., Saraiva, B. T. C., & Christofaro, D. G. D. (2021). Effect of different sports practice on sleep quality and quality of life in children and adolescents: Randomized clinical trial. *Sports Medicine - Open*, *7*(1), Article 1. https://doi.org/10.1186/s40798-021-00376-w

Sateia, M. J. (2014). International classification of sleep disorders-third edition: Highlights and modifications. *Chest*, *146*(5), Article 5. https://doi.org/10.1378/chest.14-0970

Serrano-Guzmán, M., Valenza-Peña, C. M., Serrano-Guzmán, C., Aguilar-Ferrándiz, E., Valenza-Demet, G., & Villaverde-Gutiérrez, C. (2016). Effects of a dance therapy programme on quality of life, sleep and blood pressure in middle-aged women: A randomised controlled trial. *Medicina Clinica*, *147*(8), Article 8. https://doi.org/10.1016/j.medcli.2016.06.030

Shaw, A., & Kaytaz, E. S. (2021). Yoga bodies, yoga minds: Contextualising the health discourses and practices of modern postural yoga. *Anthropology & Medicine*, *28*(3), 279–296. https://doi.org/10.1080/13648470.2021.1949943

Shen, J.-L., Hung, B.-L., & Fang, S.-H. (2022). Horticulture therapy affected the mental status, sleep quality, and salivary markers of mucosal immunity in an elderly population. *Scientific Reports*, *12*(1), Article 1. https://doi.org/10.1038/s41598-022-14534-x

Shin, J. C., Parab, K. V., An, R., & Grigsby-Toussaint, D. S. (2020). Greenspace exposure and sleep: A systematic review. *Environmental Research*, *182*, 109081. https://doi.org/10.1016/j.envres.2019.109081

So, B. C. L., Kwok, S. C., & Lee, P. H. (2021). Effect of aquatic exercise on sleep efficiency of adults with chronic musculoskeletal pain. *Journal of Physical Activity and Health*, *18*(9), 1037–1045. https://doi.org/10.1123/jpah.2020-0476

Song, D. (2024). Effect of an aerobic dancing program on sleep quality for older adults with mild cognitive impairment and poor sleep: A randomized controlled trial. *Journal of the American Medical Directors Association*, *25*(3), 494–499. https://doi.org/10.1016/j.jamda.2023.09.020

Spano, G., D'Este, M., Giannico, V., Carrus, G., Elia, M., Lafortezza, R., Panno, A., & Sanesi, G. (2020). Are community gardening and horticultural interventions beneficial for psychosocial well-being? A meta-analysis. *International Journal of Environmental Research and Public Health*, *17*(10), Article 10. https://doi.org/10.3390/ijerph17103584

Storer, T. W., Pahor, M., Woodhouse, L. J., Lachman, M. E., & Fielding, R. A. (2023). Exercise and behavior: adjuncts to pro-myogenic compounds for enhancing mobility in older adults. *The Journals of Gerontology: Series A*, *78*(Supplement_1), 61–66. https://doi.org/10.1093/gerona/glad041

Stutz, J. (2019). Effects of evening exercise on sleep in healthy participants: A systematic review and meta-analysis. *Sports Medicine*, *49*, 269–287.

Tadayon, M., Abedi, P., & Farshadbakht, F. (2016). Impact of pedometer-based walking on menopausal women's sleep quality: A randomized controlled trial. *Climacteric: The Journal of the International Menopause Society*, *19*(4), Article 4. https://doi.org/10.3109/13697137.2015.1123240

Tang, M.-F., Chiu, H.-Y., Xu, X., Kwok, J. Y., Cheung, D. S. T., Chen, C.-Y., & Lin, C.-C. (2019). Walking is more effective than yoga at reducing sleep disturbance in cancer patients: A systematic review and meta-analysis of randomized controlled trials. *Sleep Medicine Reviews*, *47*, 1–8. https://doi.org/10.1016/j.smrv.2019.05.003

Tremblay, M. S., Esliger, D. W., Tremblay, A., & Colley, R. (2007). Incidental movement, lifestyle-embedded activity and sleep: New frontiers in physical activity assessment. *Canadian Journal of Public Health = Revue Canadienne De Sante Publique*, *98*(Suppl 2), S208–S217.

Van Offenwert, E., Vrijsen, B., Belge, C., Troosters, T., Buyse, B., & Testelmans, D. (2019). Physical activity and exercise in obstructive sleep apnea. *Acta Clinica Belgica*, *74*(2), 92–101. https://doi.org/10.1080/17843286.2018.1467587

Vlahoyiannis, A., Aphamis, G., Eddin, D. A., & Giannaki, C. D. (2021). The effect of evening cycling at different intensities on sleep in healthy young adults with intermediate chronobiological phenotype: A randomized, cross-over trial. *Journal of Sports Sciences*, *39*(2), Article 2. https://doi.org/10.1080/02640414.2020.1812194

Wang, F., & Boros, S. (2021). The effect of physical activity on sleep quality: A systematic review. *European Journal of Physiotherapy*, *23*(1), 11–18. https://doi.org/10.1080/21679169.2019.1623314

Wang, W.-L., Chen, K.-H., Pan, Y.-C., Yang, S.-N., & Chan, Y.-Y. (2020). The effect of yoga on sleep quality and insomnia in women with sleep problems: A systematic review and meta-analysis. *BMC Psychiatry*, *20*(1), Article 1. https://doi.org/10.1186/s12888-020-02566-4

Wolfson, A. R., & Carskadon, M. A. (2003). Understanding adolescents' sleep patterns and school performance: A critical appraisal. *Sleep Medicine Reviews*, *7*(6), Article 6. https://doi.org/10.1053/smrv.2002.0258

Wu, X., Tao, S., Zhang, Y., Zhang, S., & Tao, F. (2015). Low physical activity and high screen time can increase the risks of mental health problems and poor sleep quality among Chinese college students. *PLoS One*, *10*(3), Article 3. https://doi.org/10.1371/journal.pone.0119607

Xie, Y., Liu, S., Chen, X.-J., Yu, H.-H., Yang, Y., & Wang, W. (2021). Effects of exercise on sleep quality and insomnia in adults: A systematic review and meta-analysis of randomized controlled trials. *Frontiers in Psychiatry*, *12*, 664499. https://doi.org/10.3389/fpsyt.2021.664499

Yang, P.-Y., Ho, K.-H., Chen, H.-C., & Chien, M.-Y. (2012). Exercise training improves sleep quality in middle-aged and older adults with sleep problems: A systematic review. *Journal of Physiotherapy*, *58*(3), 157–163. https://doi.org/10.1016/S1836-9553(12)70106-6

Yang, J.-Y., Huang, J.-W., Kao, T.-W., Peng, Y.-S., Lu, C.-S., Chen, D.-L., Yang, C.-S., Yang, C.-C., Tsai, D.-M., Liao, C.-S., Chang, H.-W., Wu, W.-C., Wu, M.-S., Wu, K.-D., Chang, C.-J., Tsai, T.-J., & Chen, W.-Y. (2008). Impact of spiritual and religious activity on quality of sleep in hemodialysis patients. *Blood Purification*, *26*(3), Article 3. https://doi.org/10.1159/000118845

Youngstedt, S. D. (2005). Effects of exercise on sleep. *Clinics in Sports Medicine*, *24*(2), 355–365. https://doi.org/10.1016/j.csm.2004.12.003

Zamunér, A. R., Andrade, C. P., Arca, E. A., & Avila, M. A. (2019). Impact of water therapy on pain management in patients with fibromyalgia: Current perspectives. *Journal of Pain Research*, *12*, 1971–2007. https://doi.org/10.2147/JPR.S161494

Zhu, J., Chen, X., Zhen, X., Zheng, H., Chen, H., Chen, H., Liao, H., Zhu, J., Wang, C., Zheng, Z., Chen, R., & Wang, Y. (2023). Meta-analysis of effects of yoga exercise intervention on sleep quality in breast cancer patients. *Frontiers in Oncology*, *13*, 1146433. https://www.frontiersin.org/articles/10.3389/fonc.2023.1146433

8

OPTIMAL EXPERIENCE IN EXERCISE

A Flow Perspective

Patricia C. Jackman, Rebecca M. Hawkins, Christian Swann, and Scott G. Goddard

8.1 Preface

What is it that makes life worth living? How do people, groups, and communities thrive? These are the types of questions that Martin Seligman and Mihaly Csikszentmihalyi (2000) suggested researchers in the field of psychology should invest more effort into finding answers to when they called for the development of the field of positive psychology at the turn of the millennium. Seligman and Csikszentmihalyi (2000) noted that a focus on the science of positive subjective experiences, individual traits, and group processes was not new, but these areas had received relatively little attention when taking into consideration the size and composition of the field of psychology more broadly. Indeed, they argued that psychological research and theories developed up to that point were mainly pathological in their focus and had been underpinned largely by a medical model, a core assumption of which was that the primary role of psychology was to remediate damage. In contrast, a central mission of researchers and practitioners interested in positive psychology is to develop and apply psychological theory and research that focuses on optimal human functioning and supporting individuals, groups, and communities to flourish (Seligman & Csikszentmihalyi, 2000). A positive psychology approach, therefore, centralises understanding what makes life most worth living and what enables humans to thrive (American Psychological Association, 2023).

A key construct in the field of positive psychology that has received considerable attention in exercise is the subjective experience of flow. Flow was first defined and conceptualised by Csikszentmihalyi (1975) and has been labelled by some as "the archetype of positive affective experiences" (Maltagliati et al., 2022, p. 4). Flow is described as a harmonious and intrinsically rewarding psychological state that is characterised by deep absorption in what one is doing, a distinct feeling

DOI: 10.4324/9781003517474-12

of control, and the sense that everything comes together and "clicks", even in difficult scenarios (Csikszentmihalyi, 2002). Flow has been regarded as a state "intimately associated with motivation and enjoyment" (Jackson, 2014, pp. 117–118) and proposed as a valuable way to promote adherence to exercise (Petosa & Holtz, 2013). Empirical evidence also demonstrates positive associations between flow and a range of psychological and behavioural outcomes, including greater: positive post-exercise feelings (Karageorghis et al., 2000); physical self-concept (Martin et al., 2010); intentions to be physically active (Franco et al., 2017); and long-term physical activity (Elbe et al., 2016). As outcomes like these are likely to be highly desirable for many people, the development of interventions that can promote the occurrence of flow states and help exercisers to attain this intrinsically rewarding state more frequently could be valuable (e.g., Jackman, Hawkins et al., 2019).

Flow has been conceptualised traditionally as a combination of nine dimensions (Csikszentmihalyi, 2002). Componential measures based on this nine-dimensional conceptualisation have been developed to assess the intensity of flow in specific activities (i.e., flow intensity—Flow State Scale-2—Jackson & Eklund, 2002) and the frequency of flow in general in a particular domain or activity (i.e., dispositional flow—Dispositional Flow Scale-2—Jackson & Eklund, 2002). These measures have been used widely with exercising populations (see Jackman, Hawkins et al., 2019 and Jackman, Dargue et al., 2021 for systematic reviews) and in contexts beyond exercise (Moneta, 2021). According to Nakamura and Csikszentmihalyi (2002), the nine dimensions can be divided into three proximal conditions of flow (i.e., perceived balance between challenge and skills, clear goals, unambiguous feedback) and six characteristics of flow (i.e., concentration on the task at hand, action-awareness merging, sense of control, loss of self-consciousness, transformation of time, autotelic experience). Nakamura and Csikszentmihalyi (2002) proposed that an individual will enter flow—and thus experience the characteristics of flow—if the proximal conditions of flow are achieved. A key quality of the flow experience is that it is, as Csikszentmihalyi (1975) termed it, an 'autotelic' experience. This infers that flow states have experiential and motivational properties—they are enjoyable in the moment (experiential) and should motivate individuals to want to engage in that task again once finished (motivational—Csikszentmihalyi, 1975; Landhäuβer & Keller, 2012). Despite the widespread adoption of the nine-dimensions framework—both in exercise and non-exercise contexts—this conceptualisation has been critiqued in recent years (e.g., Hassmén et al., 2016; Moran & Toner, 2017).

With the continued advances in knowledge and understanding of flow in exercise lately, it is timely and valuable to take stock of developments in this field and to consider how research in this area can move forward meaningfully in the years to come. In this chapter, we will first provide a summary of existing literature on flow in exercise based on previous systematic reviews published in the field. Subsequently, we will offer a detailed discussion of recent and relevant research on flow in exercise, which will include key findings, limitations of studies conducted to date, and future research directions. Based on the evidence that exists, we will propose a series of implications for researchers and for exercisers, exercise psychology practitioners, exercise professionals, and organisations committed to improving people's experiences in exercise. Finally, we will conclude by briefly summarising key points in this chapter and take the opportunity to reflect on the field of flow research in exercise.

8.2 Previous Evidence from Systematic Reviews

In recent years, several systematic reviews have provided insights into flow in exercise and physical activity (Goddard, Stevens, Jackman et al., 2023; Jackman, Hawkins et al., 2019; Jackman, Dargue et al., 2021). The only systematic review specifically focused on flow in exercise settings synthesised evidence from 26 studies involving 4,478 participants (Jackman, Hawkins et al., 2019). Relatedly, Goddard, Stevens, Jackman et al. (2023) reviewed evidence on flow interventions in exercise *and* sport, while Jackman, Dargue et al. (2021) synthesised findings about flow among young people in physical activity, physical education, and sport. In the following sections, we summarise key findings on flow in exercise from relevant reviews of literature in terms of the: (a) conceptualisation of flow in exercise; (b) methods used to study flow in exercise; (c) antecedents and/or correlates of flow in exercise; (d) interventions and proposed mechanisms to facilitate flow in exercise; and (e) outcomes associated with flow in exercise.

8.2.1 Conceptualisation of Flow

Within quantitative studies identified by Jackman, Hawkins et al. (2019), the nine-dimensions framework (Csikszentmihalyi, 2002) was the dominant conceptual perspective adopted by researchers (n = 17/25; 68%). Although several other conceptual models were cited, these models were either influenced by, or broadly reconciled with, the nine-dimensions framework (Csikszentmihalyi, 2002). Despite the widespread adoption of Csikszentmihalyi's (2002) framework or other comparable conceptualisations, the only qualitative study in the review (Swann et al., 2019) offered a somewhat different perspective. Grounded in data generated via event-focused interviews (see Jackman et al., 2022 for an overview) conducted with exercisers within two days of rewarding exercise activities on average, Swann et al. (2019) reported that the experiences of flow described could be organised into 12 characteristics: absence of negative thoughts; absorption; altered perceptions; automatic skill execution; confidence; ease/reduced effort; effortless attention; enjoyment; feeling in control; optimal arousal; motivation for more; and positive, in-the-moment feedback. Although many of these characteristics were similar to the nine-dimensions framework (Csikszentmihalyi, 2002), this description of flow generated by Swann et al. (2019) in the integrated model of flow and clutch states in exercise offered a different perspective to the traditional nine-dimensions conceptualisation. Moreover, Swann et al. (2019) also reported that the conceptualisation of flow included some characteristics shared with a second, overlapping phenomenon, termed a clutch state. Jackman, Hawkins et al. (2019) concluded that there were a number of conceptual issues with flow research in exercise, including: large heterogeneity in the conceptualisation of flow in quantitative research; the dominance of a conceptualisation (i.e., nine-dimensions framework; Csikszentmihalyi, 2002) that has been the subject of significant critique; and that none of the measures used to study flow in exercise were developed based on descriptions of flow generated specifically within exercise. As a result of these conceptual issues, the ability to amalgamate findings and draw firm conclusions in this field remains limited.

8.2.2 Methods Used to Study Flow in Exercise

A clear lack of methodological diversity was evident in studies on flow in exercise reviewed by Jackman, Hawkins et al. (2019), with 24 of the 26 studies (92.31%) employing quantitative designs and only a single study using qualitative (Swann et al., 2019) or mixed methods designs (Lee et al., 2016), respectively. Within the quantitative studies, there was considerable diversity in the flow measures used, with 18 psychometric tools used in 25 studies. Examination of the psychometric properties and reporting of measures used also revealed several issues, including that researchers had utilised measures that had shown an inadequate model fit and that had not been tested psychometrically (Jackman, Hawkins et al., 2019). Furthermore, Jackman, Hawkins et al. (2019) highlighted issues with studies that used validated measures of flow, with many of these studies not using the full contents of measures and/or not reporting the reliability of measures that were used. As most studies used measures based on the nine-dimensions framework (Csikszentmihalyi, 2002), a conceptualisation of flow that was not developed based on the experiences of exercisers, this also raises some questions about evidence generated in studies that have used measures based on this conceptualisation. Overall, Jackman, Hawkins et al. (2019) suggested that there was significant room to improve the quantitative measurement of flow in exercise and to expand qualitative and mixed methods research in this area.

8.2.3 Antecedents and/or Correlates of Flow in Exercise

Although a relatively high proportion of quantitative studies (60%) reported antecedents or correlates of flow in exercise, the synthesis of findings within several themes revealed equivocal or negligible relationships (Jackman, Hawkins et al., 2019). For instance, there was mixed or limited evidence of relationships between flow intensity and physiological correlates (e.g., VO2 metabolic equivalent of the task), gender, and age (Jackman, Hawkins et al., 2019). In contrast, there was some evidence that more experienced exercisers were more likely to report higher flow intensity in circuit training (Grove & Lewis, 1996) and tai chi (Iida & Oguma, 2013). In terms of dispositional flow, Jackman, Hawkins et al. (2019) found no cross-study evidence regarding antecedents or correlates, making it difficult to draw conclusions. Consistent with the assumption that flow is an intrinsically rewarding experience (Csikszentmihalyi, 2002), Ersöz and Eklund (2017) reported that intrinsic regulation (i.e., people choose to engage in the activity because of pure interest) was the only one of the six motivation regulations proposed within organismic integration theory (Deci & Ryan, 2000) that was significantly and positively associated with all nine dimensions of dispositional flow. In sum, there was a lack of robust, cross-study evidence for antecedents or correlates of flow in exercise, which Jackman, Hawkins et al. (2019) reported made it difficult to draw firm conclusions.

8.2.4 Interventions and Proposed Mechanisms to Produce Flow in Exercise

Theoretical explanations and robust interventions for the occurrence of flow in exercise were lacking in the previous review of flow in exercise (Jackman, Hawkins et al., 2019). Jackman, Hawkins et al. (2019) noted that although several experimental studies had measured flow in exercise-based studies, flow tended to be assessed as a secondary outcome, rather than the primary focus of the intervention. Further, researchers rarely offered explicit rationales or proposed mechanisms explaining how and why different intervention strategies might facilitate flow. Thus, of the interventions that have attempted to induce flow to date in exercise, none had been developed based on empirical findings (i.e., concerning flow occurrence) or an explanatory theory (Jackman, Hawkins et al., 2019).

In terms of experimental studies on flow in exercise, there is some evidence to suggest that exposure to virtual stimuli during exergaming could be associated with higher scores on some dimensions of flow compared with traditional exercise (e.g., Barry et al., 2016; Monedero et al., 2017; Robinson et al., 2015). However, as most studies that examined flow in exergaming did not assess or analyse flow at a global level (i.e., they focused only on specific dimensions), this made it difficult to conclude that virtual stimuli were associated with greater flow intensity (Jackman, Hawkins et al., 2019). Several studies also found that different design features in exergames produced different levels of flow intensity (e.g., Bronner et al., 2013, 2015; Lee et al., 2018), but there was significant variation in the measures of flow used and the design features tested, making it difficult to arrive at firm conclusions. Beyond exergaming, there was evidence that exercising with music was associated with significantly higher flow intensity in treadmill walking/running compared with a no-music condition (Karageorghis et al., 2008; Karageorghis & Jones, 2014).

Whereas the foregoing studies employed experimental designs, Swann et al. (2019) explored exercisers' experiences of flow qualitatively and offered some tentative suggestions on potential mechanisms that could underpin the occurrence of flow in exercise. Swann et al. (2019) reported that within exercise contexts involving flexible outcomes, exploration, and novelty/variation, flow was proposed to occur through a series of five steps. This process of flow occurrence was reported to be instigated by a positive event, which provided the exercisers with positive feedback that subsequently enhanced their confidence. In turn, this confidence was purported to encourage them to challenge themselves and to set 'open goals' (i.e., non-specific and phrased in an exploratory way, with measurable parameters, producing graded rather than succeed-or-fail outcomes—see Swann et al., 2025 for a review), which aided the transition into flow. Although offering potential insights into mechanisms underpinning the occurrence of flow, these findings were only based on a single study. Nevertheless, Jackman, Hawkins et al. (2019) suggested that the findings could offer researchers avenues to develop interventions grounded in empirical data on flow in exercise in the future.

8.2.5 Outcomes Associated with Flow in Exercise

A range of outcomes have been identified as being positively related to flow in exercise, albeit the evidence is only drawn from single studies and thus requires further development. In aerobic dance exercisers, Karageorghis et al. (2000) reported significant, moderate-to-strong, positive associations between flow intensity and post-exercise feelings of positive engagement, revitalisation, and tranquillity. Using a qualitative approach, Swann et al. (2019) identified a range of positive consequences after experiences of flow in exercise, which included a sense of achievement, confidence, energy, intrinsic motivation, and positive mood and emotions. Iida and Oguma (2014) reported that flow intensity in tai chi experts was positively related to the sense of coherence in a single tai chi class one year later. Furthermore, these authors also found that flow intensity was significantly and positively associated with 'ikigai' (Iida & Oguma, 2013), an indicator of well-being in Japanese culture (Sone et al., 2008). Finally, Martin et al. (2010) found a small-to-moderate relationship between dispositional flow in physical activity and both general physical self-concept and physical activity self-concept in school pupils. Together, this evidence suggests flow has been related to a range of positive psychological outcomes in exercisers, but further studies using more advanced study designs are needed to form stronger conclusions about the outcomes elicited by flow states in exercise.

8.3 Update on Evidence

The following section presents an overview and update of the latest research evidence on flow in the context of exercise, extending beyond the existing evidence reported in recent systematic reviews above. While Csikszentmihalyi's (2002) nine dimensions have traditionally been the primary framework for understanding flow in the context of optimal exercise experiences, further evidence has accumulated supporting the integrated model of flow and clutch states (Swann et al., 2019). To illustrate the advances that have been made by researchers adopting these different conceptualisations, our discussion of recent research developments is separated into nine-dimensional and integrated model perspectives. Further, we provide an overview of the measurement challenges and possible solutions for assessments of flow in exercise. Lastly, we outline the limitations of research in this field and recommend directions for future studies.

8.3.1 Recent Evidence from a Nine-Dimensional Perspective

The nine-dimensional framework continues to be a popular conceptual framework for flow research in exercise. Since the most recent systematic reviews, several studies have adopted the nine-dimensions conceptualisation of flow (e.g., Meggs & Chen, 2021), assessed flow using measures based on this conceptualisation (e.g., Flow State Scale [FSS]; Ditchburn et al., 2020); or reported that experiences described by participants in exercise resonated with Csikszentmihalyi's conceptualisation of flow (e.g., Hall & Noonan, 2023). Given the conceptual issues previously highlighted in research on flow in exercise (Goddard, Stevens, Jackman et al., 2023; Jackman, Hawkins et al., 2019; Jackman, Dargue et al., 2021)—many of which are specific to the nine dimensions (see Swann et al., 2018)—the continued use of this framework underscores its enduring influence on the field.

Exergaming remains an activity associated with flow in exercise. For example, similar to previous studies of exergaming (e.g., Barry et al., 2016), the effects of a virtual reality exergaming system (IREX) were compared with traditional gym-based exercise across time (Ditchburn et al., 2020). Ditchburn et al. (2020) reported significant increases in eight of nine flow dimensions across time for both groups, with the largest effect on the perception of feedback. Notably, only significant between-group differences were found for concentration on the task at hand, which was greater for those assigned to the traditional gym-based exercise group (Ditchburn et al., 2020), indicating minimal differences between traditional gym-based exercise and exergaming in enhancing specific flow dimensions. Furthermore, flow was not analysed at a global level, making it difficult to determine whether changes occurred in flow intensity over time (Ditchburn et al., 2020). Therefore, exergaming is still an area of interest for those seeking to promote flow during exercise, but there is much that remains to be understood about which stimuli and game designs are most effective.

Recent research underpinned by the nine dimensions has begun to examine the effects of mindfulness on flow in exercise. Mindfulness has been a popular strategy used in previous flow interventions in sport: mindfulness-based interventions comprised nine out of the 29 (31.03%) flow intervention studies reviewed by Goddard, Stevens, Jackman et al. (2023). Despite this, Meggs and Chen (2021) were the first to examine the effects of mindfulness on flow in exercise. Using a brief (15-minute) mindfulness intervention, Meggs and Chen (2021) assessed physical exertion and flow among sedentary adults during a cycling task. Flow was measured using a 13-item variation of the short-form FSS (which normally includes nine items—one item per dimension; Jackson et al., 2008) that included only three subscales (fluency of performance, absorption by activity, and perceived importance). A significant difference between the control and experimental conditions was found for the absorption by activity subscale; however, no significant differences between conditions were reported for fluency of performance or perceived importance of the exercise. In addition, similar to mindfulness-based flow interventions in sport (Goddard, Stevens, Jackman et al., 2023), the rationale linking mindfulness to the occurrence of flow was unclear. Meggs and Chen (2021) suggested that mindfulness training emphasises the present moment and a non-judgemental acceptance of internal and external experiences, which are similar to the flow dimensions of concentration on the task at hand and the merging of action and awareness outlined by Csikszentmihalyi (2002). However, concentration on the task at hand and merging of action and awareness are characteristics of the nine dimensions of flow rather than 'conditions' that result in its occurrence. Overall, only three subscales were used to capture what is typically nine dimensions of flow, and significant changes were only observed in absorption. Combined with the somewhat unclear rationale linking mindfulness to flow occurrence, we suggest further evidence is required to support the assertion that mindfulness training can facilitate flow during exercise.

More broadly, recent studies of flow in exercise based on the nine-dimensions perspective succumb to similar critiques directed at existing studies (Goddard, Stevens, Jackman et al., 2023; Jackman, Hawkins et al., 2019; Jackman, Dargue et al., 2021). That is, these studies use componential quantitative assessments of flow that do not adequately capture the full extent of flow experiences, especially when global scales are not reported (e.g., Ditchburn et al., 2020), or capture only some of the nine dimensions (e.g., Meggs & Chen, 2021; see below for a further discussion of measurement challenges). Further, the theoretical explanation of flow remains unclear (e.g., the proximal conditions of flow are often confused with characteristics), making it difficult to structure exercise activities or interventions in ways that might promote the occurrence of flow. It could be that these studies did not adequately address some of the key limitations outlined in previous research, as they were not solely focused on flow as an outcome. To illustrate, in addition to flow, Ditchburn et al. (2020) examined the effects of exergaming on pain, postural control, and technology acceptance, while Meggs and Chen (2021) examined the effects of mindfulness on psychophysiological exertion. Nevertheless, there is limited evidence from the nine-dimensional perspective to suggest that understanding of how to promote flow in exercise is advancing.

8.3.2 Recent Evidence from an Integrated Model Perspective

The perspective on flow presented within the integrated model of flow and clutch states (Swann et al., 2019) differs from previous perspectives that regard flow as the sole psychological state underpinning optimal experiences during exercise (e.g., nine dimensions—Csikszentmihalyi, 2002). Since the introduction of the integrated model in exercise, several studies adopting this perspective have been conducted on flow in running (Goddard et al., 2024; Goddard, Stevens, & Swann, 2023; Jackman, Hawkins et al., 2021; Jackman et al., 2023). Jackman, Hawkins et al. (2021), for example, explored the self-regulatory (i.e., thoughts, feelings, and actions that are pre-planned and adjusted to achieve goals; Zimmerman, 2000) and metacognitive processes (i.e., planning, monitoring, or reviewing one's cognitions) involved in the rewarding experiences of recreational runners. To achieve this, event-focused interviews were conducted with 16 runners following a positive, rewarding recreational run. Aligning with the integrated model, participants reported both flow and clutch experiences during these runs. The forethought phase for flow experiences offered insights into factors reported by runners to facilitate flow states, which included having intrinsic experiential motives for running (e.g., autonomy, experience simulation, exploration, novelty, relatedness, restoration, variety), pursuing non-specific or flexible goals, being optimally challenged, not feeling under pressure, and running in pleasant weather conditions or on a scenic route. During the monitoring phase (i.e., attending and responding to internal and external stimuli), the runners reported a low perception of effort and direction of their attention to the route rather than a device (e.g., a watch), which contributed to altered perceptions of time. Consistent with other reports of flow (e.g., Swann et al., 2019), participants described effortlessness and comfort, feelings of ease, confidence, and satisfaction, all of which were reported to lead to a pleasant experience and motivation to continue the running task.

In addition, Jackman, Hawkins et al. (2021) reported that the runners did not describe the use of cognitive strategies aimed at enhancing self-regulatory control over one's thoughts, feelings, and/or performance (e.g., technique, pacing, or self-talk) when recounting their flow experiences. Instead, these runners spoke about how active distractions, such as music, and involuntary distractions, like scenic natural environments, helped to limit conscious thoughts of running, which in turn appeared to help them to remain in flow (Jackman, Hawkins et al., 2021). The benefits of music reported by these runners resonate with findings from previous experimental research in treadmill walking/running, which found greater flow intensity in music versus no-music conditions (Karageorghis et al., 2008; Karageorghis & Jones, 2014). In addition to lending further support to propositions within the integrated model, Jackman, Hawkins et al. (2021) provided several key insights that extended current understanding of flow during exercise. First, participants reported setting non-specific goals (in addition to open goals) before the run, and after a sequence of positive events, feedback, and challenge appraisal (as proposed in the integrated model). Second, participants reported that changes in metacognitive processes (e.g., from perceptions of ease to difficulty; and from recognising that self-regulatory control was unnecessary to feeling that it was needed) could contribute to the disruption of flow. Third, findings concerning cognitive strategy use during flow offer preliminary evidence to suggest that interventions relying on active self-regulatory strategies (e.g., mindfulness; Meggs & Chen, 2021) might potentially hinder one's attempts to experience flow during exercise.

Extending their earlier work on self-regulatory aspects of flow in exercise, Jackman et al. (2023) used a sociological phenomenological lens to emphasise the embodied pleasures of running as described by participants during flow (Jackman, Hawkins et al., 2021). In the past, researchers have highlighted that physical and embodied aspects of flow have tended to be overlooked in flow research, especially within literature that adopts the traditional (and cognitively focused) nine-dimensional conceptualisation of flow (see Jackman, Lane et al., 2019; Swann et al., 2015). The findings were presented as three main themes. The first theme, *running feels like it should*, offered an embodiment perspective on the feelings of relative effortlessness (i.e., less effort required than anticipated) reported by the runners during flow. Using Leder's (1990) concepts of bodily dys-appearance (i.e., the body is to the foreground of our conscious mind) and dis-appearance (i.e., the body is largely absent from the conscious mind) to interpret the runners' accounts, Jackman et al. (2023) reported that the mild discomfort and stiffness experienced in the warm-up phase (i.e., the body had dys-appeared) became backgrounded (i.e., the body dis-appeared) as they began to 'switch off' from 'controlling' their running technique (and entered flow). The second theme, *sensory engagements*, captured the sense of mind–body–world interconnectedness (primarily with outdoor environments), as well as auditory pleasures, during flow. The third theme, *time out*, involved detaching from performance metrics (i.e., not monitoring their run with a phone or watch) and illustrated the enjoyment linked to the runners' surprise at the discrepancy between the actual and perceived clock time. The study provided new conceptual and methodological perspectives on the lived experience of flow in running by offering unique insights into the deeply embodied and sensory nature of flow, which is often overlooked in flow literature.

Researchers using the integrated model have also developed nuanced insights into possible flow intervention strategies for exercisers. For example, Goddard, Stevens, and Swann (2023) used a combination of event-focused and career-based interviews to examine runners' perspectives on factors facilitating or inhibiting flow experiences and how these factors could inform potential intervention strategies. Aligning with core principles of the integrated model (Swann et al., 2019), 14 runners identified strategies that should be incorporated into flow interventions, which included creating an exploratory or novel context, setting open-ended goals, providing positive feedback that exceeds expectations, and ensuring that attention is directed towards pleasant aspects of the run (e.g., aesthetically pleasing environment, enjoyable music). Runners also identified strategies that should be avoided, including evaluative contexts, setting specific goals, quantitative feedback, and focusing on disruptive stimuli and bodily sensations. Of note, many of these proposed intervention strategies overlap with self-regulatory processes reported to facilitate flow during rewarding recreational runs (e.g., exploration, non-specific goals, not monitoring a device;

Jackman, Hawkins et al., 2021), yet perhaps contradict proximal conditions of flow proposed in the nine-dimensions framework (Csikszentmihalyi, 2002). For example, 'clear goals' may be misconstrued as the need for specific goals, which appear to be more conducive to the occurrence of clutch states rather than flow (Jackman, Hawkins et al., 2021; Swann et al., 2019).

Building on these insights, Goddard et al. (2024) developed and evaluated a flow intervention grounded in the integrated model of flow and clutch states, which aimed to promote flow through open goals, exploratory contexts, positive feedback, and attentional focus strategies. A preliminary evaluation indicated that participants reported increases in flow intensity across the laboratory-based running sessions, with qualitative findings supporting the value of exploratory, flexible, and intrinsically motivated approaches to promoting flow (Goddard et al., 2024). However, as participants reported flow and clutch states in both the intervention and control conditions, these findings highlight the complexities of inducing flow in exercising tasks. Thus, although the flow intervention developed by Goddard et al. (2024) was based on runners' perspectives and the integrated model provides a strong foundation, further refinement and extension of these strategies are needed in future intervention development and evaluation efforts.

8.3.3 Measurement Challenges

Measuring flow has consistently been a challenge. Researchers interested in flow have developed various measurement tools over the past 40 years, with suggestions that a "gold measurement standard for flow has yet to be achieved" (Moneta, 2021, p. 2). Flow in exercise has typically been measured via questionnaires that adopt a componential approach and thus include subscales for each of the proposed characteristics of flow—often the nine dimensions of flow (Csikszentmihalyi, 2002)—plus a cumulative global flow score (e.g., Jackson & Eklund, 2002). Interpreting componential measures of flow is challenging because changes observed in some, but not all dimensions, are unlikely to represent the full extent of a flow experience, and it is assumed that all dimensions of flow are weighted equally. For example, Meggs and Chen (2021) reported an increase in absorption, but this subscale alone does not represent a flow experience. Likewise, high scores on two or three dimensions but no changes to other dimensions could still result in changes to global scores. Nonetheless, issues related to the measurement of flow are not limited to exercise (see Moneta, 2021, for an expanded discussion).

Evidence indicating that flow and clutch are distinct—yet overlapping—psychological states (Jackman, Hawkins et al., 2021; Swann et al., 2019) may further exacerbate the limitations of traditional flow measures. For example, in sport, Jackman et al. (2017) reported that different quantitative measures of flow (i.e., the Flow Questionnaire [FQ] and FSS-2) were unable to discriminate between episodes of flow and clutch states reported by athletes. This limitation is likely because the FQ and FSS-2 were developed based on Csikszentmihalyi's nine-dimensional framework, which researchers have suggested likely contains components of both flow and clutch states (Jackman et al., 2017; Swann et al., 2018). Despite the limitations of the traditional componential measure of flow experiences, they are still widely used in flow research, as evidenced by the large number of total citations for FSS publications (e.g., Khoo et al., 2021), and ongoing translation of these scales into alternative languages for use in sport and exercise (e.g., Garcia et al., 2022).

In contrast, a recent study provided preliminary validation of a quantitative measure of flow that accounts for the overlapping clutch state (Flow-Clutch-Scale [FCS]; Swann et al., 2022). This measure of flow is based on a synthesised version of the integrated model, which has reconciled the findings of studies examining flow and clutch across both sport and exercise. The FCS allows respondents to indicate whether they experienced a flow-like or clutch-like state during an activity (i.e., a categorical measure), before answering a range of items related to the various aspects of each respective state (i.e., a continuous measure). The responses are divided into four subscales: two relating to flow, one relating to clutch, and one overlapping (i.e., absorption; Swann et al., 2022). Similar to the development of the integrated model, the development of the FCS was data-driven, meaning that exploratory factor analysis was initially conducted to identify an appropriate factor structure, followed by confirmatory factor analysis to test this structure. Nevertheless, the FCS requires further validation (e.g., predictive validity, test–retest reliability) and it is currently recommended that quantitative data from this scale be supplemented with qualitative data to interpret the participant's experience of the relevant state (i.e., flow or clutch).

The difficulties with measuring flow quantitatively have often led researchers to suggest the use of qualitative methods to study this experience, although qualitative studies on flow in exercise have only begun to emerge in recent years. This contrasts with sport, where interviews have been widely used for several decades (see Swann et al., 2012 for a systematic review). Traditionally, researchers have used what have been termed 'career-based interviews' to investigate flow, which involve participants reflecting upon previous experiences regardless of when it occurred (e.g., months or years prior; Swann et al., 2016). In contrast, event-focused interviews are conducted soon after specific events or episodes in which a target phenomenon, such as flow, might have occurred (Jackman et al., 2022). Event-focused interviews possess three defining features: (a) participants are sampled based on pre-determined criteria for the occurrence of an event (i.e., a phenomenon); (b) the interview takes place soon after that event; and (c) the researchers seek to elicit rich, detailed, and chronological descriptions of that event. Event-focused interviews were first used to explore the psychological states underpinning exceptional golf performances (Swann et al., 2016) and studies using this novel method have generated new insights into flow (and clutch states) in exercise (Goddard, Stevens, & Swann, 2023; Jackman, Hawkins et al., 2021; Jackman et al., 2023; Swann et al., 2019). Based on the advances in understanding developed through event-focused interview studies on flow in exercise, the adoption of this method in future research could help to further progress the field.

Finally, a common feature of the aforementioned methods used to study flow is that they have generally been used to collect data *after* an individual has completed an exercise activity. Indeed, only one study identified in the systematic review of flow in exercise by Jackman, Hawkins et al. (2019) asked participants to complete measures *during* an exercise activity (Grove & Lewis, 1996). To capture repeated, real-time data on people's subjective experiences (including flow) in their daily lives, Csikszentmihalyi and Larson (1987) developed the experience sampling method (ESM). In a traditional ESM study, participants are signalled (e.g., by a beeper or notification on a mobile device) at random intervals over a period of time (e.g., one week) to complete a brief questionnaire, which could elicit information about the activity they are completing and include a measure of flow. Despite the potential benefits of obtaining in the-moment, self-report data on flow in exercise, there are practical challenges with using such a methodology in this setting; for example, it might not be feasible to disrupt someone during an exercise activity (see Jackman et al., 2022, for a discussion). Nevertheless, we suggest that researchers might consider pragmatic ways to collect data in situ during activities to generate a novel understanding of the dynamics of flow over time (e.g., changes in intensity, transitions between flow and other states) in exercise activities. For instance, real-time assessments (e.g., written or verbal reports) might be possible in exercise activities that have scheduled breaks (e.g., circuit classes) or those in which momentary assessments are less likely to interfere with performance (e.g., exercising on a stationary indoor bike).

8.3.4 Limitations

Despite the recent advances in flow research in exercise, there are several limitations that need to be addressed. For instance, substantially less research has focused on flow in exercise compared with sport. As such, there is a smaller evidence base from which to draw conclusions about flow states in exercise, and it should not be assumed that findings regarding flow in sport can be easily translated to flow in exercise. Similarly, since the systematic reviews of flow in exercise, there has been limited diversity in the specific exercise activities involved in research, particularly with respect to research underpinned by the integrated model. To illustrate, the updated evidence provided in this chapter was derived from studies with exergaming and traditional gym-based exercise (Ditchburn et al., 2020), stationary cycling (Meggs & Chen, 2021), and three studies involving running (Goddard, Stevens, & Swann, 2023; Jackman, Hawkins et al., 2021; Jackman et al., 2023). Additionally, there is a distinct lack of qualitative studies on flow in exercise, which is problematic given that qualitative methods—when done well—can provide rich and detailed insights into subjective experiences (Sparkes & Smith, 2014). Lastly, research conducted to date on flow in exercise has tended to focus on early- and middle-aged adults, thus adopting a somewhat narrow perspective on flow across the life course.

8.3.5 Future Directions

Considering the limitations of flow research in exercise, we suggest that a more diverse approach is required. First, future studies on flow in exercise should consider a broader array of exercise activities. For example, Swann et al. (2019) reported flow experiences across diverse exercises (e.g., yoga, swimming, running, surfing, weight training, hiking, half ironman, and indoor climbing), and similar studies are required to broaden understanding of flow across different activities. Second, future studies should also recruit more diverse samples. For instance, further studies are warranted to explore the flow experiences of young people and older adults. In addition, researchers should also direct further attention towards cultural aspects of flow and seek to understand the experiences of minoritised groups. Third, additional qualitative studies on flow in exercise could help to advance the field and continue to enrich one's understanding of the experience of flow in this domain. Finally, intervention studies that test strategies based on empirical data generated about the occurrence of flow in exercise (e.g., Goddard, Stevens, & Swann, 2023; Jackman, Hawkins et al., 2021; Swann et al., 2019) could help the field to develop stronger recommendations on how to promote flow in this setting.

8.4 Implications

Although we acknowledge that further development of the flow literature is necessary before more robust recommendations can be advanced, we offer several implications for practice. We divide our recommendations based on whether they are intended for (a) exercisers or (b) exercise psychologists, professionals, and/or organisations (e.g., gyms, physical activity groups, social running clubs).

8.4.1 Implications for Exercisers

Based on contemporary perspectives on flow in exercise, we offer several suggestions for exercisers to promote flow. First, intrinsic motivation is integral to flow (Csikszentmihalyi, 2002) and having motives focused on the experience of exercise could help to promote flow (Jackman, Hawkins et al., 2021). For example, exercisers could seek exploration, novelty, or variety in exercise tasks/sessions, or approach exercise as an activity that provides a chance for experiential stimulation (e.g., "I want to enjoy this run"), mental or physical restoration, and/or relatedness (e.g., a social opportunity). Second, within such contexts, there is consistent qualitative evidence in exercising populations that points towards the benefits of non-specific goals for flow (Goddard, Stevens, & Swann, 2023; Jackman, Hawkins et al., 2021; Swann et al., 2019). Although some of this research suggests such goals are set during an activity following several other processes (i.e., after a positive event, positive feedback, confidence builds, challenge appraisal—Swann et al., 2019), recreational runners have reported setting non-specific goals prior to activities (Jackman, Hawkins et al., 2021). Thus, exercisers could benefit from setting goals that are devoid of a specific, quantifiable outcome (e.g., not having a pace goal), and that allow room for flexibility in goal setting in at least some part of their programme (e.g., in repetitions, time, pace, duration). Third, exercising in a way that is free of pressure/expectation, which can be aided by being less concerned with achieving specific targets, and under circumstances of optimal challenge (i.e., those that closely match or are within one's capabilities) could also be beneficial. Finally, during flow, exercisers might benefit from distraction rather than active self-regulation, as efforts to increase cognitive control might, counterproductively, disrupt flow (Birrer et al., 2020; Jackman, Hawkins et al., 2021). Based on research with recreational runners (Jackman, Hawkins et al., 2021), we suggest that exercisers might benefit from active distraction (e.g., listening to music; conversing; switching off from conscious, self-regulatory thought over movements) and involuntary distraction (e.g., scenic distractions, mind wandering).

8.4.2 Implications for Exercise Psychologists, Professionals, and Organisations

Although there is scant evidence on how exercise psychologists, professionals, and organisations can promote flow in exercise, we draw upon existing literature to illustrate how they can support their efforts to experience flow. First, exercise professionals and organisations might consider how exploration, novelty, and variety could be built into exercisers' activities. For example, in a circuit session, an exercise professional could vary tasks, integrate new exercises, or allow attendees to explore within an activity (e.g., explore range of motion that can be reached in a move). Likewise, exercise psychologists and professionals could engage in conversation with exercisers about their 'why' for engaging in exercise and support them in the development of intrinsic motives that centre on the experience of (rather than accomplishment within) exercise. Second, exercise psychologists, professionals, and organisations should be aware of the potential benefits of using non-specific goals and adopt a flexible approach to goal setting. These approaches could be added to the repertoire of goal-setting approaches that are used with exercisers. Third, exercise professionals and organisations should seek to create exercise environments that are task-oriented and focus on individual mastery (e.g., "that was a really good set of lifts") rather than introducing comparison with others within a group. Such an approach will also provide an opportunity for exercisers to build confidence and perceive that a task is optimally challenging, both of which can help to promote flow (Jackman, Hawkins et al., 2021; Swann et al., 2019).

Finally, exercise professionals and organisations might consider how they can create scenarios that enable exercisers to refrain from engaging effortful, cognitive control that could prevent or disrupt flow. For recreational runners, monitoring information on their watch, higher perceptions of effort, discomfort, fatigue, increased heart rate, more intense breathing, and temperature changes were reported to elicit changes in metacognitive feelings (i.e., how people think about their thoughts—e.g., feelings of difficulty, feeling of knowing that you need to engage control), affective responses (i.e., less pleasure), and motivation (i.e., motivation to continue lowers), which subsequently disrupted flow and resulted in increased use of active self-regulatory strategies to cope with these responses (Jackman, Hawkins et al., 2021). Consequently, we suggest strategies that can support active distraction or involuntary distraction to be implemented could be useful. For instance, an exercise professional or organisation could design activities to include music, enable conversation between exercisers, or take place in a scenic location, while exercise psychologists could encourage exercisers to initiate these actions themselves.

8.5 Conclusion

The occurrence of flow in exercise could have multiple benefits for exercisers, including for their experiences within exercise and their desire to re-engage in exercise again in future. In this chapter, we provided a contemporary review of flow research in exercise. We highlighted core findings from recent systematic reviews of this growing literature and summarised more recent findings in this area. We discussed and critiqued different conceptual perspectives on flow and offered suggestions on how researchers might move forward with research in this field and address the limitations of previous research in the area. Based on the evidence generated to date, we offered suggestions on how exercisers might be able to facilitate flow states and how exercise psychologists, professionals, and organisations can help them to achieve this. It is key that future research involves the designing, testing, and refinement of evidence-informed interventions to enable researchers to more confidently suggest strategies that could help exercisers to experience flow. By doing so, this can help the field to get closer to reaching the potential of flow states in exercise and, ultimately, help exercisers to experience this rewarding psychological state more consistently.

References

American Psychological Association. (2023). Positive psychology. In *APA Dictionary of Psychology*. https://dictionary.apa.org/

Barry, G., van Schaik, P., MacSween, A., Dixon, J., & Martin, D. (2016). Exergaming (XBOX Kinect™) versus traditional gym-based exercise for postural control, flow and technology acceptance in healthy adults: A randomised controlled trial. *BMC Sports Science, Medicine and Rehabilitation*, *8*, 25. https://doi.org/10.1186/s13102-016-0050-0

Birrer, D., Jackman, P. C., & Latinjak, A. T. (2020). Contesting the role of self-talk in sport psychology in views of mindfulness, flow, and mind wandering. In A. Latinjak & A. Hatzigeorgiadis (Eds.), *Self-talk in sport* (pp. 201–217). Routledge.

Bronner, S., Pinsker, R., & Adam Noah, J. (2015). Physiological and psychophysiological responses in experienced players while playing different dance exer-games. *Computers in Human Behavior*, *51*, 34–41. https://doi.org/10.1016/j.chb.2015.04.047

Bronner, S., Pinsker, R., & Noah, J. A. (2013). Energy cost and game flow of 5 exer-games in trained players. *American Journal of Health Behavior*, *37*(3), 369–380. https://doi.org/10.5993/AJHB.37.3.10

Csikszentmihalyi, M. (1975). *Beyond boredom and anxiety*. Jossey-Bass.

Csikszentmihalyi, M. (2002). *Flow: The classic work on how to achieve happiness*. Rider.

Csikszentmihalyi, M., & Larson, R. (1987). Validity and reliability of the experience-sampling method. *The Journal of Nervous and Mental Disease, 175*(9), 526–536.

Deci, E. L., & Ryan, R. M. (2000). The "what" and "why" of goal pursuits: Human needs and the self-determination of behavior. *Psychological Inquiry*, *11*(4), 227–268. https://doi.org/10.1207/S15327965PLI1104_01

Ditchburn, J.-L., van Schaik, P., Dixon, J., MacSween, A., & Martin, D. (2020). The effects of exergaming on pain, postural control, technology acceptance and flow experience in older people with chronic musculoskeletal pain: A randomised controlled trial. *BMC Sports Science, Medicine & Rehabilitation*, *12*(1), 63. https://doi.org/10.1186/s13102-020-00211-x

Elbe, A.-M., Barene, S., Strahler, K., Krustrup, P., & Holtermann, A. (2016). Experiencing flow in a workplace physical activity intervention for female health care workers: A longitudinal comparison between Football and Zumba. *Women in Sport and Physical Activity Journal*, *24*(1), 70–77. https://doi.org/10.1123/wspaj.2015-0011

Ersöz, G., & Eklund, R. C. (2017). Behavioral regulations and dispositional flow in exercise among American college students relative to stages of change and gender. *Journal of American College Health*, *65*(2), 94–102. https://doi.org/10.1080/07448481.2016.1239203

Franco, E., Coterón, J., Gómez, V., & Pérez-Tejero, J. (2017). The role of dispositional flow's dimensions in the prediction of intention to be physically active in adolescents. *Universitas Psychologica*, *16*(4), 1–11. https://doi.org/10.11144/Javeriana.upsy16-4.rdfd

Garcia, W. F., Nascimento Junior, J. R. A., Mizoguchi, M. V., Brandão, M. R. F., & Fiorese, L. (2022). Transcultural adaptation and psychometric support for a Brazilian Portuguese version of the Flow State Scale (FSS-2). *Perceptual and Motor Skills*, *129*(3), 800–815. https://doi.org/10.1177/00315125221093917

Goddard, S. G., Stevens, C. J., Jackman, P. C., & Swann, C. (2023). A systematic review of flow interventions in sport and exercise. *International Review of Sport and Exercise Psychology*, *16*(1), 657–692. https://doi.org/10.1080/1750984X.2021.1923055

Goddard, S. G., Stevens, C. J., & Swann, C. (2023). Exploring runners' perspectives of potential strategies for flow interventions. *Journal of Applied Sport Psychology*, *35*(3), 455–477. https://doi.org/10.1080/10413200.2022.2046205

Goddard, S. G., Stevens, C. J., & Swann, C. (2024). A flow intervention for runners: Mixed-method evaluation. *Sport, Exercise, and Performance Psychology*, *13*(2), 144–161. https://doi.org/10.1037/spy0000340

Grove, J. R., & Lewis, M. A. E. (1996). Hypnotic susceptibility and the attainment of flow-like states during exercise. *Journal of Sport and Exercise Psychology*, *18*(4), 380–391. https://doi.org/10.1123/jsep.18.4.380

Hall, F. C., & Noonan, R. J. (2023). A qualitative study of how and why gym-based resistance training may benefit women's mental health and wellbeing. *Performance Enhancement and Health*, *11*(3), 100254. https://doi.org/10.1016/j.peh.2023.100254

Hassmén, P., Keegan, R., & Piggott, D. (2016). *Rethinking sport and exercise psychology research*. Palgrave Macmillan. https://doi.org/10.1057/978-1-137-48338-6

Iida, K., & Oguma, Y. (2013). Relationships between flow experience, ikigai, and sense of coherence in tai chi practitioners: *Holistic Nursing Practice*, *27*(5), 260–267. https://doi.org/10.1097/HNP.0b013e31829b9199

Iida, K., & Oguma, Y. (2014). The relationship between flow experience and sense of coherence: A 1-year follow-up study. *Holistic Nursing Practice*, *28*(2), 91–97. https://doi.org/10.1097/HNP.0000000000000018

Jackman, P. C., Allen-Collinson, J., Ronkainen, N., & Brick, N. (2023). Feeling good, sensory engagements, and time out: Embodied pleasures of running. *Qualitative Research in Sport, Exercise and Health, 15*(4), 467–480. https://doi.org/10.1080/2159676X.2022.2150674

Jackman, P. C., Hawkins, R. M., Whitehead, A. E., & Brick, N. E. (2021). Integrating models of self-regulation and optimal experiences: A qualitative study into flow and clutch states in recreational distance running. *Psychology of Sport and Exercise, 57*, 102051. https://doi.org/10.1016/j.psychsport.2021.102051

Jackman, P. C., Crust, L., & Swann, C. (2017). Systematically comparing methods used to study flow in sport: A longitudinal multiple-case study. *Psychology of Sport and Exercise, 32*, 113–123. https://doi.org/10.1016/j.psychsport.2017.06.009

Jackman, P. C., Dargue, E. J., Johnston, J. P., & Hawkins, R. M. (2021). Flow in youth sport, physical activity, and physical education: A systematic review. *Psychology of Sport and Exercise, 53*, 101852. https://doi.org/10.1016/j.psychsport.2020.101852

Jackman, P. C., Hawkins, R. M., Crust, L., & Swann, C. (2019). Flow states in exercise: A systematic review. *Psychology of Sport and Exercise, 45*, 101546. https://doi.org/10.1016/j.psychsport.2019.101546

Jackman, P. C., Lane, A., Fitzpatrick, G., & Swann. C. (2019). Exploring bodily sensations experienced during flow states in professional national hunt jockeys: A connecting analysis. *Qualitative Research in Sport, Exercise and Health, 11*(1), 92–105. https://doi.org/10.1080/2159676X.2017.1380693

Jackman, P. C., Schweickle, M. J., Goddard, S. G., Vella, S. A., & Swann, C. (2022). The event-focused interview: What is it, why is it useful, and how is it used? *Qualitative Research in Sport, Exercise and Health, 14*(2), 167–180. https://doi.org/10.1080/2159676X.2021.1904442

Jackson, S. A., & Eklund, R. C. (2002). Assessing flow in physical activity: The Flow State Scale-2 and Dispositional Flow Scale-2. *Journal of Sport and Exercise Psychology*, *24*(2), 133–150. https://doi.org/10.1123/jsep.24.2.133

Jackson, S. A., Martin, A. J., & Eklund, R. C. (2008). Long and short measures of flow: The construct validity of the FSS-2, DFS-2, and new brief counterparts. *Journal of Sport and Exercise Psychology*, *30*(5), 561–587. https://doi.org/10.1123/jsep.30.5.561

Jackson, S. (2014). Flow. In R. M. Ryan (Ed.), *The Oxford handbook of human motivation* (pp. 127–140). Oxford University Press.

Karageorghis, C. I., & Jones, L. (2014). On the stability and relevance of the exercise heart rate–music-tempo preference relationship. *Psychology of Sport and Exercise*, *15*(3), 299–310. https://doi.org/10.1016/j.psychsport.2013.08.004

Karageorghis, C. I., Jones, L. I., & Stuart, D. (2008). Psychological effects of music tempi during exercise. *International Journal of Sports Medicine*, *29*(7), 613–619. https://doi.org/10.1055/s-2007-989266

Karageorghis, C. I., Vlachopoulos, S. P., & Terry, P. C. (2000). Latent variable modelling of the relationship between flow and exercise-induced feelings: An intuitive appraisal perspective. *European Physical Education Review*, *6*(3), 230–248. https://doi.org/10.1177/1356336X000063002

Khoo, S., Ansari, P., & Morris, T. (2021). Sport and exercise psychology research from the Asian and South Pacific region: A bibliometric analysis. *Asian Journal of Sport and Exercise Psychology*, *1*(1), 21–29. https://doi.org/10.1016/j.ajsep.2021.03.003

Landhäußer, A., & Keller, J. (2012). Flow and its affective, cognitive, and performance-related consequences. In S. Engeser (Ed.), *Advances in flow research* (pp. 65–86). Springer.

Leder, D. (1990). *The absent body*. University of Chicago Press.

Lee, M., Suh, D., Son, J., Kim, J., Eun, S.D., Yoon, B. Patient perspectives on virtual reality-based rehabilitation after knee surgery: Importance of level of difficulty. J Rehabil Res Dev. 2016;53(2):239–52. doi: 10.1682/JRRD.2014.07.0164. PMID: 27149529.

Lee, S., Myers, N. D., Park, T., Hill, C. R., & Feltz, D. L. (2018). An exploratory study on the Köhler Effect and flow in long-term exergaming. *Simulation & Gaming*, *49*(5), 538–552. https://doi.org/10.1177/1046878118776043

Maltagliati, S., Sarrazin, P., Fessler, L., Lebreton, M., & Cheval, B. (2022). Why people should run after positive affective experiences instead of health benefits. *Journal of Sport and Health Science*, *13*(4), 445–450. https://doi.org/10.1016/j.jshs.2022.10.005

Martin, A. J., Liem, G. A. D., Coffey, L., Martinez, C., Parker, P. P., Marsh, H. W., & Jackson, S. A. (2010). What happens to physical activity behavior, motivation, self-concept, and flow after completing school? A longitudinal study. *Journal of Applied Sport Psychology, 22*(4), 437–457. https://doi.org/10.1080/10413200.2010.495699

Meggs, J., & Chen, M. (2021). The effect of a brief-mindfulness intervention on psychophysiological exertion and flow-state among sedentary adults. *Perceptual and Motor Skills*, *128*(3), 1078–1090. https://doi.org/10.1177/0031512520984422

Monedero, J., Murphy, E. E., & O'Gorman, D. J. (2017). Energy expenditure and affect responses to different types of active video game and exercise. *PLoS One*, *12*(5), e0176213. https://doi.org/10.1371/journal.pone.0176213

Moneta, G. B. (2021). On the conceptualization and measurement of flow. In C. Peifer & S. Engeser (Eds.), *Advances in flow research* (2nd ed., pp. 31–69). Springer. https://doi.org/10.1007/978-3-030-53468-4

Moran, A., & Toner, J. (2017). *A critical introduction to sport psychology* (3rd ed.). Routledge. https://doi.org/10.4324/9781315657974

Nakamura, J., & Csikszentmihalyi, M. (2002). The concept of flow. In C. R. Snyder & J. L. Shane (Eds.), *Handbook of positive psychology* (pp. 89–105). Oxford University Press.

Petosa, R. L., & Holtz, B. (2013). Flow for exercise adherence: Testing an intrinsic model of health behavior. *American Journal of Health Education*, *44*(5), 273–277. https://doi.org/10.1080/19325037.2013.811364

Robinson, J., Dixon, J., Macsween, A., van Schaik, P., & Martin, D. (2015). The effects of exergaming on balance, gait, technology acceptance and flow experience in people with multiple sclerosis: A randomized controlled trial. *BMC Sports Science, Medicine and Rehabilitation*, *7*(1), 8. https://doi.org/10.1186/s13102-015-0001-1

Seligman, M. E. P., & Csikszentmihalyi, M. (2000). Positive psychology: An introduction. *American Psychologist, 55*(1), 5–14. https://doi.org/10.1037/0003-066X.55.1.5

Sone, T., Nakaya, N., Ohmori, K., Shimazu, T., Higashiguchi, M., Kakizaki, M., Kikuchi, N., Kuriyama, S., & Tsuji, I. (2008). Sense of life worth living (ikigai) and mortality in Japan: Ohsaki Study. *Psychosomatic Medicine*, *70*(6), 709–715. https://doi.org/10.1097/PSY.0b013e31817e7e64

Sparkes, A. C., & Smith, B. (2014). *Qualitative research methods in sport, exercise and health*. Routledge.

Swann, C., Keegan, R., Crust, L., & Piggott, D. (2016). Psychological states underlying excellent performance in professional golfers: "Letting it happen" vs. "making it happen." *Psychology of Sport and Exercise*, *23*, 101–113. https://doi.org/10.1016/j.psychsport.2015.10.008

Swann, C., Crust, L., Keegan, R., Piggott, D., & Hemmings, B. (2015). An inductive exploration into the flow experiences of European Tour golfers. *Qualitative Research in Sport, Exercise and Health*, *7*(2), 210–234. https://doi.org/10.1080/2159676X.2014.926969

Swann, C., Driscoll, J., Goddard, S. G., Willis, R., Schweickle, M. J., Ribeiro, I. A. F., Gatt, M., Jackman, P. C., & Vella, S. A. (2022). The Flow-Clutch Scale: Development and preliminary validation in sport and exercise. *Psychology of Sport and Exercise*, *58*, 102066. https://doi.org/10.1016/j.psychsport.2021.102066

Swann, C., Goddard, S. G., Schweickle, M. J., Hawkins, R. M., Williamson, O., Gargioli, D., Clarke, M. M., Jackman, P. C., & Vella, S. A. (2025). Defining open goals for the promotion of health behaviours: A critical conceptual review. *Health Psychology Review, 19*(2), 344–367. https://doi.org/10.1080/17437199.2025.2467695

Swann, C., Jackman, P. C., Schweickle, M. J., & Vella, S. A. (2019). Optimal experiences in exercise: A qualitative investigation of flow and clutch states. *Psychology of Sport and Exercise, 40*, 87–98. https://doi.org/10.1016/j.psychsport.2018.09.007

Swann, C., Keegan, R. J., Piggott, D., & Crust, L. (2012). A systematic review of the experience, occurrence, and controllability of flow states in elite sport. *Psychology of Sport and Exercise*, *13*(6), 807–819. https://doi.org/10.1016/j.psychsport.2012.05.006

Swann, C., Piggott, D., Schweickle, M., & Vella, S. A. (2018). A review of scientific progress in flow in sport and exercise: Normal science, crisis, and a progressive shift. *Journal of Applied Sport Psychology*, *30*(3), 249–271. https://doi.org/10.1080/10413200.2018.1443525

Zimmerman, B. J. (2000). Attaining self-regulation: A social cognitive perspective. In M. Boekaerts, P. R. Pintrich, & M. Zeidner (Eds.), *Handbook of self-regulation* (pp. 13–39). Academic Press. https://doi.org/10.1016/B978-012109890-2/50031-7

9

HARMONIZING BODY AND MIND

Music-Related Applications for Exercise and Mental Health

Garry Kuan, Costas I. Karageorghis, and Peter C. Terry

9.1 Preface

Despite the numerous health benefits associated with maintaining regular exercise, it remains an irregular behavior among large swaths of population in industrialized nations (Strain et al., 2024). Epidemiological studies, for example, indicate that most adolescents and adults do not meet recommended levels of exercise (WHO, 2022). The issue of physical inactivity is multifaceted and appears to be relatively unmalleable when considering the multifarious efforts of practitioners and researchers to change its trajectory (Ekkekakis et al., 2016; 2020). The phenomenon referred to widely as the 'revolving door' (Dishman, 2001) highlights a prevalent trend, wherein most individuals embarking on a physical exercise program tend to discontinue within the initial three months (Kohl III et al., 2019). This trend stands out as one of the most disconcerting aspects of physical inactivity (Ekkekakis et al., 2020).

For individuals to realize the full benefits of physical activity, they need to engage on a regular and frequent basis. There has, accordingly, been a heightened focus on the psychological factors that pertain to exercise adherence (Ekkekakis et al., 2020). Exercise has been defined as any form of structured, repetitive physical activity with the primary or intermediate objective of improving or sustaining physical fitness (Brand & Ekkekakis, 2018). The subdisciplines of exercise psychology and health psychology have grappled with the issue of adherence for over five decades, without any noticeable improvement at a population level (Ekkekakis, 2023).

9.2 Theoretical Perspectives

To address the general lack of adherence, researchers have focused primarily on cognitive variables, such as self-efficacy and self-set goals (see Brand & Ekkekakis,

DOI: 10.4324/9781003517474-13

2018; Ekkekakis et al., 2020). However, in recent years, they have also started to examine the importance of affective variables, such as enjoyment and pleasure (Pottratz et al., 2021; Terry et al., 2020). Beyond the ventilatory threshold (VT), the exercise intensity at which breathing becomes labored, perceptions of physical fatigue and negative emotions typically ensue (Chang et al., 2019; Rhodes et al., 2019). This can discourage further involvement and pose a threat to exercise motivation and future intentions (Brand & Ekkekakis, 2018).

One approach to counteracting the adverse effects of physical inactivity on health is the enhancement of motivation to participate in exercise. Motivation constitutes a cornerstone within the realm of exercise psychology (Rhodes & Kates, 2015). The field faces a significant challenge in its ongoing pursuit of strategies to improve exercise participation and levels of physical activity. Greater understanding of the fundamental drivers of human behavior can light a path toward more effective interventions. In line with psychological or motivational hedonism, individuals typically seek pleasurable experiences while avoiding unpleasant ones (Rozin, 1999).

Brand and Ekkekakis (2018) asserted that negative affective valence during exercise reflects some kind of suffering, particularly for people who are obese, sedentary, or categorized as 'low-active'. This can influence deliberative reasoning about exercise engagement and effort, and bear direct influence on behavior through behavioral urges. Over the past decade, several research groups have focused on the use of music in the context of exercise and sport (Karageorghis et al., 2018b, 2021b; Marques et al., 2024; Terry et al., 2020). Based on a meta-analytic review of 139 studies (Terry et al., 2020), it was suggested that the judicious application of music has multiple benefits, such as enhancing affective responses, improving physical performance, reducing perceived exertion, and promoting greater physiological efficiency. Moreover, such benefits tend to be more pronounced in exercise compared with sport settings (Terry et al., 2020).

The presence of music can help offset the potentially deleterious influence of interoceptive signals of fatigue and lead to a reduction in perceived exertion (Karageorghis et al., 2021b). This can promote longer exercise sessions and, from a public health perspective, greater adherence to a prescribed physical activity regimen, with the attendant physical and mental health benefits (Hutchinson et al., 2018; Stork et al., 2019). Notably, the benefits of music in terms of reducing perceived exertion tend to be greater at low-to-moderate exercise intensities (see Terry et al., 2020), because interoceptive cues can become overwhelming during high-intensity exercise (Ekkekakis et al., 2020). Research has shown that *attentional switching* tends to occur beyond VT, meaning that exercisers struggle to focus on external cues (dissociation) and are 'forced' to focus on internal, fatigue-related cues (association; see Karageorghis & Jones, 2014).

Certain theoretical perspectives on exercise motivation, which emphasize the significance of affect, feelings, and emotions, include models that conceptualize human behavior as both intuitive and influential (e.g., Brand & Ekkekakis,

2018). However, such perspectives have received relatively little attention from researchers. Lewin (1951) introduced force-field analysis, a conceptual framework that captures both the propelling and inhibiting factors associated with transitioning from one behavior to another. Lewin's framework is relevant to addressing physical inactivity, particularly when considering an individual who is hesitant to transition from their current sedentary state to a more active lifestyle. Ostensibly, the sedentary individual does not modify their behavior and engage in exercise because restraining forces (e.g., previous unpleasant affective experiences of physical activity) are equal to, or greater than, driving forces (e.g., the desire to lead a healthier lifestyle).

9.3 Music in the Exercise Domain

The sound that we experience as music requires the careful organization of elements such as melody, harmony, rhythm, timbre, dynamics, and tempo. In an exercise context, given the ease with which it can be manipulated, tempo has been one of the most researched elements (see e.g., Jones et al., 2024). According to Stanovich (2008), the preference for music tempo is a higher-order construct that involves making choices and evaluative judgments. This construct underscores the cognitive processes that individuals engage in when determining which music tempo might optimize their exercise experience. In addition to tempo preference, several other constructs have been identified as relevant when examining the broader impact of music use in exercise contexts. For example, positive affective valence reflects the pleasurable feelings associated with music, which can be relevant in motivating individuals to engage in physical activity (Jones et al., 2024). This emotional positivity can serve to amplify the enjoyment of a workout, encouraging longer and more frequent bouts of exercise.

Research shows that music can enhance physical performance by providing rhythmic cues that improve coordination and timing during physical activity, thereby facilitating more efficient execution of movements (e.g., Bacon et al., 2012). Additionally, music has been shown to reduce perceived exertion, enabling individuals to deal with the fatigue and discomfort that can typify a workout. If the primary aim of listening to music during workouts is to enhance enjoyment (e.g., Jones & Zenko, 2021), then tempo plays a key role, given the degree to which it can regulate affective arousal (Karageorghis et al., 2011). Most research examining the relationship between exercise intensity and music-tempo preference has used familiar, lyrical music. Recent work by Jones et al. (2024) found no relationship between exercise intensity and preferred tempo when using unfamiliar, non-lyrical music.

It has been suggested that the listener's level of arousal and the environment in which they hear music can influence their choice of music tempo (Berlyne, 1973; Karageorghis, 2017). Therefore, when the listener is experiencing a high degree of stimulation, such as during high-intensity exercise, they tend to choose music of a faster tempo (i.e., > 130 bpm). Additionally, certain activities or conditions, like sprint intervals on a cycle ergometer, require heightened levels of psychomotor arousal, and fast, exhilarating music may enhance performance as a consequence (see e.g., Stork et al., 2019).

9.3.1 Mechanisms Underlying the Effects of Music in Exercise

Pinpointing the exact mechanisms by which music influences the exercise experience is challenging and, to date, understanding of such mechanisms is incomplete. Although study of the neural mechanisms underlying the effects of music during exercise has attracted the attention of researchers during the past two decades (for a review, see Karageorghis et al., 2018a), there are challenges involved in studying brain activity during movement, as many data-capture techniques become impractical when motion is present (e.g., *f*MRI). Additionally, exercise causes regional changes in blood volume, making it difficult to detect the subtle hemodynamic changes associated with the effects of music on outcomes such as affective state and attentional focus (Karageorghis, 2020). The effects of music on exercise performance are multifaceted and influenced by a variety of mechanisms. As we established earlier, during exercise, attention shifts toward fatigue-related cues, as the brain's ability to interpret sensory inputs decreases (Bigliassi, 2015). Moreover, the benefits of music in terms of psychological and psychophysical outcomes seem to diminish as exercise intensity increases, seemingly due to forced shifts in attentional focus (Bigliassi, 2015; Karageorghis et al., 2025).

Juslin (2013) put forward a theoretical framework that outlines eight psychological mechanisms through which music influences human emotions. One such mechanism is the brain stem reflex, which triggers reactions based on the basic auditory features of music. The reflex works by alerting the listener to an imminent or significant event. For example, loud, up-tempo music immediately stimulates the listener by engaging the central nervous system, regardless of how the music is later perceived (see Van Dyck, 2019 for a review). Such stimulation results in increased body temperature, skin conductance, heart rate, blood pressure, and muscle tension (Chapados & Levitin, 2008). Conversely, soft, slow music reduces sympathetic arousal, achieved by, for example, mimicking soothing natural sounds such as cooing, purring, and maternal vocalizations (Chanda & Levitin, 2013).

The propensity for music to stimulate arousal becomes particularly salient when high levels of psychomotor activation are needed, such as during supramaximal exercise (Karageorghis, 2020). This pertains to the biomusicological mechanism of *rhythmic entrainment*, wherein movements and physiological rhythms, such as heart rate and respiration, display a tendency to entrain (align) with the rhythmic aspects of music. It is common, therefore, for people to prefer faster tempi when engaging in vigorous exercise (Jones et al., 2024). Furthermore, it has been shown that engaging with music during exercise can engender small improvements in physiological efficiency (Terry et al., 2020). Although the mechanisms for this benefit are not well understood, at least two explanations have been advanced.

First, synchronizing movement patterns with a musical beat helps in regulating breathing patterns and, by extension, improving blood flow. Second, synchronous music reduces the need for micro-adjustments to movement patterns during exercise (e.g., stride rate during running; see Terry et al., 2012). In combination, these two mechanisms may serve to reduce oxygen consumption for equivalent workloads (Bacon et al., 2012; Terry et al., 2020).

According to Scherer and Zentner (2001), music can serve as a catalyst for emotional connections, potentially mediated by subcortical systems. Appraisal theory posits that an individual's subjective evaluation of an experience shapes their emotional response to music during physical exercise (Scherer, 1999). Juslin (2013) introduced the concept of *evaluative conditioning*, which involves repeatedly pairing a specific piece of music with other stimuli that carry either positive or negative emotional significance. For example, after frequently hearing a specific track during an enjoyable exercise class, one might develop a strong emotional association with that class. This is an instance of classical conditioning, where an emotionally neutral conditioned stimulus (music) becomes capable of eliciting the same feelings as a positively charged unconditioned stimulus (the enjoyment of the exercise class).

The hormonal system is also relevant when exercising to music. Music listening during exercise modifies hormonal responses, particularly in the hypothalamus pituitary axis (Arazi et al., 2015). While performing high-intensity activity, listening to fast-paced music has been found to raise salivary cortisol levels and promote rhythmic movement, both of which have potential uses in exercise and sport (Arazi et al., 2015). The impact of music on the heart varies according to whether the music has relaxing or arousing qualities (see e.g., Copeland & Franks, 1991). Research has shown that music listening can enhance various aspects of the exercise experience, conferring a range of positive affective and perceptual outcomes (Karageorghis et al., 2021b; Terry et al., 2020). The cognitive process that underlies the psychological impacts of auditory and visual inputs is frequently referred to as *attentional dissociation* (Hutchinson & Karageorghis, 2013). This concerns the propensity of stimuli, including music and video, to divert attention away from internal, fatigue-related cues and toward external cues, lowering effort-related sensations, and their corresponding negative influence on affect.

According to theorists, when the signal strength of physiological feedback is potent, the inhibitory capacity of music will be diminished at higher exercise intensities (Ekkekakis et al., 2020; Tenenbaum & Hutchinson, 2007). However, empirical work has shown that affective stimuli, such as music, continue to bear influence on how people feel and how they interpret the feelings of physical effort and tiredness, even during high-intensity exercise (Bigliassi et al., 2016; Hutchinson & Karageorghis, 2013). Moreover, neurophysiological studies that have used electroencephalography (EEG) have shown that music reduces brain connectivity between the frontal and central regions of the cortex (also known as the sensorimotor regions), a phenomenon linked to decreased exercise consciousness (see e.g., Bigliassi et al., 2017).

Music with a strong rhythm, a 'happy' harmonic structure and familiar melodies can serve to distract individuals from feelings of fatigue and discomfort, effectively lowering perceived exertion and promoting greater exercise enjoyment (Karageorghis et al., 2021b). The psychological effects of music, such as the enhancement of affective valence and stress reduction, have a bearing on individuals' habitual behavior and overall mental health as they engage in exercise. Listening to music during workouts not only gives physical performance a boost but can also influence emotional states in a positive manner, creating a synergistic effect that supports both cardiometabolic health and mental well-being (Hutchinson et al., 2018). This harmonious relationship between body and mind underscores the potential of music-related applications as a valuable strategy in the pursuit of healthier lifestyles (Terry et al., 2020).

9.3.2 Music Use Prior to Exercise

The beneficial impact of music prior to exercise has garnered significant research attention, particularly regarding its potential to enhance performance through various psychological and psychophysiological mechanisms (e.g., Delleli et al., 2023; Smirmaul, 2016). Prior studies have adopted a dichotomy represented by stimulative and sedative music, with a focus on how music with such qualities can influence an individual's level of activation and subsequent performance outcomes (e.g., Karageorghis et al., 2018d).

Studies examining the effects of music used before exercise frequently focus on its use as a stimulant or auditory prime (Karageorghis, 2020). For example, Karageorghis et al. (2018d) investigated the effects of fast/loud music on grip strength, with results showing that participants exhibited lower grip strength performance when exposed to calming music, compared with stimulating music. A limitation of such research is that simple motor tasks have been used, leaving question marks regarding how music might influence more complex forms of psychomotor performance. Nonetheless, it has been important in this literature for researchers to adopt a systematic approach and to orientate investigations toward internally valid approaches prior to pursuing more ecologically valid protocols.

Similar to grip strength, the bench press is a simple motoric task that has been examined with reference to pretask music. Ballmann et al. (2021) used a bench press task in which one set of repetitions at 75% of one-repetition maximum was performed to failure. The authors recruited resistance-trained participants ($N = 10$) to minimize learning effects. Additionally, they standardized the sound intensity, although the exact decibel level was not reported. Their findings showed that compared with a no-music control, self-selected lyrical music (> 120 bpm) significantly increased the number of bench press repetitions ($d = 0.98$), barbell power ($d = 0.79$), and barbell velocity ($d = 0.72$). Moreover, a post-task measure of state motivation, using a visual analogue scale, showed higher motivation scores in response to pretask music ($d = 0.93$). Such findings are indicative of a potentially strong ergogenic effect associated with the use of self-selected, pretask music for an anaerobic task performed to exhaustion.

The findings of a recent meta-analysis indicated that listening to music prior to exercise can yield small but statistically significant improvements in exercise performance, including enhancements in relative mean power and reductions in fatigue-related symptoms (Delleli et al., 2023). Specifically, this analysis showed a moderate effect on relative peak power and a strong positive effect on subjective feelings of well-being following exercise. However, Smirmaul (2016) highlighted that investigations into the effects of pretask music often lack systematic organization and methodological rigor, resulting in inconclusive findings regarding its potential ergogenic benefits. Despite such limitations, there is evidence to suggest that pretask music may have a more pronounced effect on short-duration tasks, such as sprints or other anaerobic activities, where heightened emotional and/or physiological arousal has the potential to enhance performance (Smirmaul, 2016).

9.3.3 Music Use During Exercise

The dual-mode theory of exercise-related affect (Ekkekakis, 2003), which postulates interindividual variability in the interpretation of physiological symptoms during strenuous exercise, can be linked to the affective benefits associated with music use during both low- and moderate-intensity exercise (Terry et al., 2020). Previous research (e.g., Hutchinson & Karageorghis, 2013) has shown that the presence of music appears to limit the degree to which fatigue-related symptoms enter focal awareness.

Other submaximal and performance-to-exhaustion activities, such as swimming, cycling, and rowing, may benefit from the use of synchronous music (Terry et al., 2012). Regarding performance-to-exhaustion and oxygen consumption, neutral music has proven to be just as effective as motivational music, although typically it has not yielded the same psychological benefits (e.g., Karageorghis et al., 2013; Terry et al., 2012). Thus, the perceived motivational aspects of music may be of lesser importance when compared with factors such as the prominence of the beat and the extent to which participants are able to synchronize their movements with the tempo (Karageorghis et al., 2010). Compared with neutral music and no music, motivational music has been associated with more positive affective states (Karageorghis et al., 2009; Terry et al., 2012). Due to the variety of musical selections employed, it is difficult to pinpoint whether extramusical elements (e.g., associations) or musical components (e.g., tempo, lyrics) were responsible for the more positive affective responses. Additionally, in the Terry et al. (2012) study, motivational music was linked to the lowest blood lactate levels, while neutral music was associated with the lowest oxygen consumption. Although the reduction in oxygen consumption by 1.0–2.7% falls within the physiological testing error margin of ±3%, the trend toward positive effects remained, suggesting that music can have a modest yet meaningful impact on physiological efficiency.

A growing body of empirical research indicates that exercising while listening to music might improve the exercise experience (Karageorghis et al., 2018a; Karageorghis & Priest, 2012; Kuan, 2023). For example, it can help to control negative emotions (Juslin, 2013), induce positive emotions such as happiness and liveliness (Levitin et al., 2018), promote dissociation (Hutchinson & Karageorghis, 2013), and used as a rhythmic stimulus to regulate movement (Karageorghis et al., 2019). The metronomic qualities of music render it a particularly useful tool in regulating movement or modulating the rate of movement (e.g., in switching from low to high intensity in a Zumba class). Music seems to influence the interpretation of fatigue at low-to-moderate exercise intensities (Karageorghis, 2020) but appears to be ineffectual during supramaximal exercise protocols (see Karageorghis et al., 2025).

Hutchinson et al. (2018) explored the impact of self-selected music on affect-regulated exercise intensity and remembered pleasure. Participants first completed a maximal exercise test to determine their individual VTs. They then engaged in two treadmill exercise trials at an intensity corresponding to a Feeling Scale value of +3 (*good*). The results indicated that participants chose an exercise intensity that exceeded their VT during the affect-regulated sessions and exercised more intensely with music than without, all while maintaining a 'good' feeling (Hutchinson et al., 2018). Additionally, participants found the music session to be more pleasurable in retrospect when compared with the no-music session. These findings illustrate the ergogenic effects and psychological benefits of music during affect-regulated exercise (Hutchinson et al., 2018).

Although such self-selected music protocols can yield quite impressive effects and even lead to the suggestion that music-related applications might be a panacea in the face of declining levels of physical activity, they do not come without significant methodological limitations. For example, participant self-selection creates fertile ground for Hawthorne and experimenter effects (see e.g., Terry et al., 2020). The selections that participants make can vary greatly in their psychoacoustic properties (cf. Biagini et al., 2012; Stork et al., 2015), meaning that there is inherently a source of potential error. Moreover, self-selection affords participants a sense of autonomy, and so researchers cannot be sure that it is the music per se influencing participants' ability to exercise choice. However, a large meta-analysis, which summarized 219 performance effects, indicated that across the literature, the ergogenic effect of music in exercise-related tasks was significant although small in magnitude ($g = 0.31$; Terry et al., 2020).

Karageorghis et al. (2025) explored the effects of in-task asynchronous music and respite-active music (i.e., music used during active recovery between bouts of high-intensity exercise) on various psychological, psychophysical, and physiological outcomes. The music interventions only influenced state motivation, which was significantly higher in the fast-tempo–medium-tempo condition compared with the no-music control ($d = 0.49$), and the standard deviation of the time between normal heartbeats (SDNN) component of heart rate variability (HRV), which was significantly lower in the fast-tempo–no-music condition compared with the control ($d = 0.32$).

Other recent findings suggest that the most effective music choices are associated with higher scores for affective valence and arousal, lower perceived exertion, and greater levels of dissociation (Hutchinson et al., 2018; Terry et al., 2020). Drawn from Karageorghis and Jones's (2014) study, Figure 9.1 illustrates the effect of fast-tempo music on associative and dissociative attentional focus across six exercise intensities (40%–90% of maximal heart rate reserve [maxHRR]). At low, moderate, and high intensities, fast music increased dissociative thoughts while reducing associative ones. Exercise with music prompts an 'attentional shift' (indicated by the arrow in Figure 9.1), causing the transition from dissociation to association to occur at around 80% of maxHRR with music, compared with about 70% of maxHRR without music.

The influence of music, music video, and 360-degree video with music was investigated by Bird et al. (2019) in relation to affective and perceptual responses both during and immediately after cycle ergometer exercise at VT. Their results showed that the 360-degree video with music elicited the most positive affective valence, the

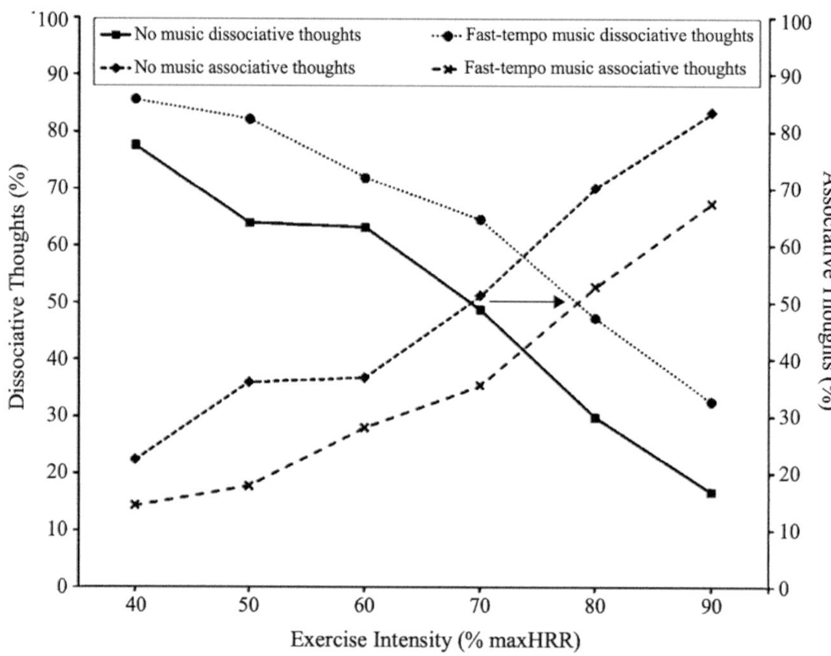

FIGURE 9.1 Comparison of State Attention Scores across all Exercise Intensities between No-Music Control and Fast-Tempo Music Conditions.

Note: Reproduced with permission from Elsevier; from Karageorghis & Jones, 2014; permission conveyed through Copyright Clearance Center.

greatest perceived activation, the most dissociative thoughts, and the highest ratings of perceived enjoyment. The authors recommended that audiovisual stimuli, such as a 360-degree video with music, be considered by practitioners as a means to promote more pleasurable exercise experiences. A limitation of immersive technologies, such as a 360-degree video and virtual reality (VR), is that the headsets feel uncomfortable when levels of perspiration are high (e.g., in hot and humid conditions).

Park et al. (2020) conducted an acute gait trial involving older adults with Parkinson's disease. They reported that patients exhibited increased gait velocity, stride length, peak arm swing velocity, and arm swing range of motion when walking to pleasant music cues, compared with baseline, walking to unpleasant music, or walking to isochronous cues. The findings suggest that increasing familiarity and personalization with music stimulation may enhance emotional responses and foster a motivational state that encourages engagement in physical activity. To optimize musical enjoyment, the researchers allowed participants to select their own music, which enabled personalization of the experience. It is important to note that generalizing these findings to the broader population of individuals with Parkinson's disease may be challenging, as the participants exhibited relatively mild symptoms.

9.3.4 *Music Use After Exercise*

Research on the use of music after exercise is a recent area of investigation (Jia et al., 2016; Karageorghis et al., 2018c), and its full potential for enhancing recovery remains underexplored. Karageorghis (2020) described the primary post-task application of music as a form of a 'recuperative' application. This approach aims to use music to positively influence hemodynamic and cardiovascular recovery, as well as mitigate the negative emotional states often induced by high-intensity interval training (HIIT). For instance, Karageorghis et al. (2018c) employed recuperative music to expedite the recovery process during a 30-minutes period following exhaustive exercise on a cycle ergometer. This type of music can facilitate both active (movement-based) and passive (static) relaxation, with the intention of leaving the exerciser feeling both refreshed and revitalized (Terry & Karageorghis, 2011).

Recuperative music playlists are typically characterized by a gradual decrease in tempo, ranging from approximately 90 beats per minute (bpm) to 60 bpm, which corresponds to the resting heart rate of most fit individuals. Karageorghis et al. (2021a) used a within-subject design to evaluate the effects of respite-active music during 8 × 60-s efforts on a cycle ergometer with 90 seconds of active recovery. The respite-active music was applied after the first 15 seconds of each recovery period. Participants listened to either a medium-tempo playlist, a fast-tempo playlist, or no music. Both music conditions led to increased dissociation (notably only during recovery) and enhanced recalled pleasure. Notably, medium-tempo music improved affective valence during both the supramaximal exercise bouts and the recovery phases (see Figure 9.2). Furthermore, medium-tempo music lowered the rating of perceived exertion, although data regarding heart rates were inconclusive.

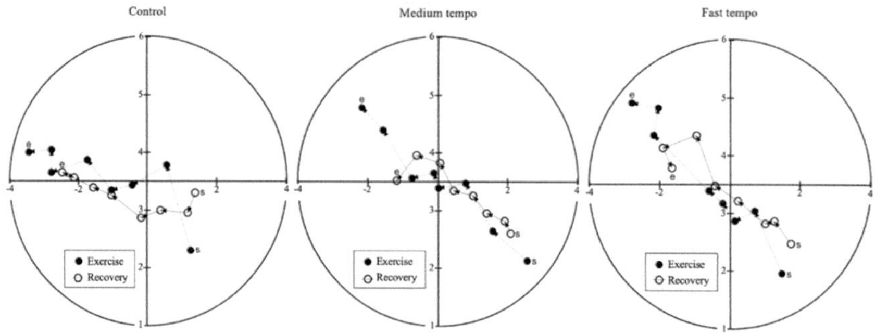

FIGURE 9.2 Feeling Scale (*x*-axis) and Felt Arousal Scale (*y*-axis) Scores Plotted on the Circumplex Model of Affect for Three Conditions. The Arrows Denote the 'affective journey' through the Eight Stages of the HIIT Protocol. The First Stage Is Indicated with an 's' and the Final Stage with an 'e'.

Note: Reproduced with permission from Elsevier; from Karageorghis et al. (2021a); permission conveyed through Copyright Clearance Center.

One limitation of the study, as noted by Karageorghis et al. (2021a), was the absence of music during the supramaximal exercise bouts, which reduces the ecological validity of the findings since music is typically present throughout an exercise session in real-world settings. Another limitation was the study's use of an unconventional 90-second active recovery period for HIIT, chosen to leverage the biomusicological principle of entrainment, which may not accurately reflect typical training practices.

As a follow-up study, Karageorghis et al. (2025) investigated the effects of active-respite music on the psychological, psychophysical, and psychophysiological responses of recreationally active individuals during 8 × 60 seconds all-out efforts on a cycle ergometer with 75 seconds of active recovery. The results showed that the music manipulations during supramaximal exercise and active recovery had no significant effect on remembered pleasure or exercise enjoyment, as measured by the Physical Activity Enjoyment Scale (PACES), in contrast to the findings of Karageorghis et al. (2021a). However, the researchers found that a condition with music throughout, comprising fast-tempo music for supramaximal exercise bouts and medium-tempo music for periods of active recovery, led to higher state motivation when compared with a no-music control. Interestingly, Jones et al. (2020) found that music throughout the HIIT protocol led to higher PACES scores and remembered pleasure scores. In the Karageorghis et al. (2025) study, the perceived unpleasantness of the HIIT protocol might have been so intense that the musical manipulations were ineffectual.

Calming music can have restorative effects after moderate-intensity and high-intensity exercise (Jing & Xudong, 2008). For example, a shift in autonomic balance toward parasympathetic predominance (i.e., through reduced heart rate, lower blood pressure, and muscle relaxation) in healthy people might underlie the calming effects of music. Jia et al. (2016) also demonstrated that calming music lowered cortisol levels immediately after brief, high-intensity exercise. By way of contrast, listening to stimulative music after working out causes cortisol levels to rise and therefore is contraindicated because it thwarts the gradual return of physiological systems toward homeostasis (see Karageorghis et al., 2018c). Accordingly, there is an emerging body of evidence to suggest that music can alter autonomic nervous system function immediately after exercise.

Exercise is known to increase sympathetic nervous system activity, which can persist for 15 minutes post-recovery. However, aerobic exercise performed below the anaerobic threshold significantly reduces parasympathetic activity without increasing sympathetic activity (Jia et al., 2016). Other research has shown that listening to music before and after exercise, rather than during, increases sympathetic activity (Tan et al., 2014). Such findings suggest that music could serve as an effective method for enhancing post-exercise parasympathetic reactivation, ultimately leading to enhanced recovery and reduced cardiac stress following exercise. Jia et al. (2016) were the first to investigate the impact of music on orthostatic tolerance, the ability to maintain stable blood pressure and adequate blood flow to the brain and other vital organs when moving from a lying or sitting position to a standing position, both with and without exercise. Their results indicated that neither music nor exercise significantly affected the heart rate, systolic blood pressure, or HRV indices in the orthostatic test. There is, nonetheless, a growing body of evidence suggesting that the use of post-task music for both active and passive recovery can have beneficial effects (see Karageorghis et al., 2020).

9.4 Music, Exercise, and Mental Health

The importance of music in promoting physical and mental health is receiving increased recognition (Jones et al., 2024). Research in clinical settings supports the notion that music influences neurochemical changes associated with reward, motivation, pleasure, stress, arousal, immunity, and social connection (Chanda & Levitin, 2013; Quan et al., 2025). Music can enhance affective responses to exercise, which hold implications for long-term participation (Jones et al., 2024). During exercise at low-to-moderate intensities, music can serve as an effective distraction from the physical discomfort that is typically experienced (Brandt & Razon, 2019).

The integration of music into exercise routines has demonstrated benefits for participation and mental health (see e.g., Zhou et al., 2021). Research indicates that music can bear influence on emotional and neurochemical responses, promoting a positive mindset that is broadly conducive to physical activity participation (Jones et al., 2024). The rhythmic and motivational qualities of music can facilitate psychological readiness and thus help individuals in transitioning from a sedentary to an active state (Loizou & Karageorghis, 2015; Smirmaul, 2016). Music enhances the enjoyment of exercise, serving as a distraction from discomfort and promoting lower exercise consciousness, which can lead to increased adherence (Brandt & Razon, 2019; Chanda & Levitin, 2013). Well-selected music not only elevates the exercise experience but also has the potential to mitigate feelings of anxiety and depression, thus enhancing an overall sense of well-being (Karageorghis & Priest, 2012).

Exercise has also been shown to be an effective treatment for mental health conditions such as depression, anxiety, and stress reduction (Giménez-Meseguer et al., 2020). The American Psychiatric Association (2022) defines a mental disorder as "…a syndrome characterized by clinically significant disturbance in an individual's cognition, emotion regulation, or behavior that reflects a dysfunction in the psychological, biological, or developmental processes underlying mental functioning" (p. 14). Such disturbances can lead to significant distress or impairment in crucial areas of functioning, including social, educational, occupational, family, or personal life (Druss et al., 2009). The relationships between music, exercise participation, and mental health are well-established, as engaging in physical activity can help mitigate the negative effects associated with mental health conditions, such as anxiety and depression. Incorporating music into exercise routines enhances motivation and enjoyment, leading to more consistent participation. Research shows that preferred music enhances affective states and reduces perceived exertion, thus enabling individuals to reap the diverse benefits of physical activity engagement (Terry et al., 2020).

There has been increased interest in the potentially positive effects of physical activity on cognitive function (Da Costa et al., 2017) and overall life satisfaction (Nani et al., 2017). The cognitive benefits of exercise are especially valuable for individuals struggling with mental health issues, as physical activity is linked to improvements in executive function, memory, and attention. Additionally, enhanced life satisfaction often arises from the social interactions fostered by group exercise settings, countering feelings of isolation and contributing to emotional well-being. By using music as an integral part of the exercise experience, individuals not only improve physical fitness but also address the psychological barriers associated with common mental health conditions (Kuan, 2023).

Recently, Quan et al. (2025) compared the effectiveness of aerobic exercise with music, aerobic exercise without music, and dance on cognitive function in adults with mild cognitive impairment. Using Bayesian meta-analyses, they showed that aerobic exercise with music exhibited the highest probability of being most effective in improving global cognition, executive function, and processing speed. These authors support the notion that incorporating music into exercise magnifies the cognitive benefits for people with mild cognitive impairment. Moreover, they made an important contribution to this literature with a Music Exercise Synergy Model that seeks to explain the cognitive benefits of combining exercise with music.

Among non-clinical populations, listening to music during exercise has been shown to boost state motivation, enhance affective states, and reduce anxiety, ultimately rendering the experience more enjoyable and engaging (Karageorghis & Priest, 2012). Additionally, music has a propensity to improve endurance, control the rate of movement, and divert attention from physical discomfort, leading to longer and more immersive exercise experiences that further enhance mental well-being. In post-task applications, music has been shown to facilitate relaxation and enhance recovery, lowering stress levels after exercise and boosting mood (Karageorghis & Priest, 2012). By linking music with exercise, individuals can not only improve their physical fitness but also mitigate the deleterious effects of common mental health conditions.

State anxiety can have a detrimental effect on participation in exercise activities (Giménez-Meseguer et al., 2020). Listening to music has been shown to be effective in managing pre-exercise anxiety and reducing exercise-related fatigue, resulting in improved relaxation and a reduced heart rate after exercise (Kuan et al., 2018). Moreover, depression is a common psychological disorder that can severely inhibit exercise participation, even though there is emerging evidence to suggest that regular exercise can provide an effective antidote (Kvam et al., 2016). Music interventions have been found to upregulate energy levels and downregulate negative emotions, offering exercisers a means by which to cope with underlying psychological factors that might serve to inhibit exercise participation (Ford & Arvinen-Barrow, 2019).

Numerous studies have shown that exercise is an effective supplementary treatment for anxiety (Asmundson et al., 2013; Gaudlitz et al., 2023; Utschig et al., 2013). Notably, exercise has been found to be nearly as effective as medication and psychotherapy for treating anxiety. For example, individuals with panic disorders and mild to severe agoraphobia experienced significant anxiolytic effects after just eight weeks of aerobic exercise, which also enhanced the efficacy of cognitive-behavioral therapy (CBT; Gaudlitz et al., 2015). Thus, aerobic exercise may serve as a valuable adjunct therapy to improve CBT outcomes. Furthermore, exercise can be regarded as a supportive therapy for individuals with panic disorders, regardless of the presence of agoraphobia, as it offers additional benefits for both physical and mental health (Gaudlitz et al., 2015).

Listening to music has been shown to engage various brain regions associated with emotions, memory, and reward, leading to positive mood changes and relaxation (Saarikallio, 2017). Current research indicates that music can influence brain activity and improve emotional states during exercise, offering important mental health benefits and supporting exercise endurance (Stewart & Irons, 2018). By incorporating music into their routines, exercisers can potentially mitigate the negative effects of anxiety, depression, and exercise-induced discomfort, ultimately promoting improved physical performance and psychological well-being.

Active participation in music-making activities such as singing, playing instruments, or engaging in music therapy has been linked to improved cognitive function, increased self-esteem, and enhanced social connections, all of which contribute to mental well-being (Shu-Ya & Chun-Fei, 2020; Silverman, 2021). Music therapy, in particular, has emerged as a structured intervention that uses musical experiences to address psychological, emotional, and social needs, offering a non-invasive and holistic approach to mental health treatment (Silverman, 2019). By incorporating music into mental health interventions, individuals can harness its potential to promote relaxation, self-expression, and emotional healing, fostering a harmonious balance between mind and body (Silverman, 2019; Thomas, 2020). Thus, by enhancing mood, lowering stress levels, and creating a positive training environment, listening to music while exercising not only enhances physical performance but also has the potential to confer benefits for mental health.

9.5 Directions for Future Work

Studies addressing music-related applications have delivered new insights regarding how music can affect emotions, physical performance, and the overall exercise experience (Giménez-Meseguer et al., 2020; Karageorghis & Priest, 2012; Terry et al., 2020). Even though studies to date have shown that music can increase motivation, reduce perceived exertion, and boost endurance in physical tasks, several related areas remain underexplored. Researchers might focus on the methodical examination of the effects of musical qualities, conducting longitudinal studies, examining individual variability (e.g., hormonal cycles), clarifying mechanistic pathways, using technology (e.g., that facilitates auditory-motor synchronization), working with a variety of demographic and individual difference factors, and applying research results in real-world scenarios. Through the advancement of knowledge regarding the intricate relationship between music and exercise, researchers will be able to formulate evidence-based plans with a view to maximizing exercise participation, adherence, and mental health.

Future research could explore a range of music interventions, such as respite-active music (Karageorghis et al., 2021a, 2025), over extended periods to better understand the connection between exercise behaviors and measures of mental health. There is a notable lack of studies in this area within the exercise psychology literature (Terry et al., 2020). Moreover, through systematically investigating how variations in musical elements (e.g., tempo, syncopation, lyrical content, and harmony) influence mental health outcomes, such as mood, anxiety, and depression disorders, researchers can offer deeper insights into the optimal use of music before, during, and after exercise.

Clarifying the underlying physiological and psychological mechanisms by which music influences exercise performance requires more mechanistic studies (Bigliassi et al., 2018; Terry et al., 2020). Researchers can identify the neural pathways and physiological processes involved in the music–exercise nexus by using neuroimaging techniques, physiological monitoring, and psychophysiological assessments. The incorporation of technological tools, including wearable technology and smartphone apps, offers tantalizing prospects in terms of customized music-based exercise routines. Researchers can maximize the impact of music interventions by using algorithms that customize music playlists to individual preferences, workout objectives, and real-time physiological reactions. Furthermore, additional research is necessary to fully understand the music aesthetics and how these mediate responses during exercise. Comprehending ways in which individual difference factors, cultural background, and musical background influence the efficacy of music-related applications can help in customizing fitness regimens to meet individual preferences and goals.

9.6 Conclusions

The use of music in the exercise domain has gained significant traction over the past 40 years. Over the last 20 years, there have been notable theoretical advancements, and more recently, models have emerged to offer guidance for both researchers and practitioners (e.g., Bird & Karageorghis, 2020; Karageorghis, 2016; Quan et al., 2025). Such models present a set of testable hypotheses that serve as the foundation for future research endeavors. This chapter illustrates how the judicious use of music can improve exercise-related affect, lower perceived exertion, and engender an ergogenic effect during exercise-related tasks. As an intervention, music is accessible, effective, and low cost. This chapter has offered insights into the use of music before, during, and after exercise. Most scientific research has focused on the application of music during exercise, whether in a synchronous or asynchronous mode.

Key findings include that music reduces perceived exertion at low-to-moderate exercise intensities but does not have the same effect at high intensities (i.e., beyond VT). Well-chosen music can enhance exercise-related affect across a range of exercise intensities (e.g., Hutchinson et al., 2015; Jones et al., 2014), and research is beginning to elucidate the cerebral mechanisms that underlie the music–affect connection during exercise (e.g., Bigliassi et al., 2016, 2017). Music can also provide a mild ergogenic or performance-enhancing effect across a broad range of physical tasks (e.g., Karageorghis, 2020; Terry et al., 2020), and there is growing evidence supporting the use of post-exercise music for both active and passive recovery (Jia et al., 2016; Karageorghis et al., 2018c, 2021a).

Although there is a great deal of evidence to suggest that exercising while listening to preferred music is the best approach toward promoting a positive mental state and engendering an ergogenic effect, it is encouraging to note that a wide range of music, preferred or otherwise, can still yield benefits for exercisers (Terry et al., 2020). Moreover, the findings of several experimental studies show how music in combination with video or VR can improve exercise-related affect (e.g., Bird et al., 2019, 2021, 2024). The emergence of new technologies both for the delivery of music and for the assessment of how it influences people during exercise, means that the study of music in exercise and mental health is an adventure happening all around us right now.

References

American Psychiatric Association. (2022). *Diagnostic and statistical manual of mental disorders* (5th ed., text rev.). https://doi.org/10.1176/appi.books.9780890425787

Arazi, H., Asadi, A., & Purabed, M. (2015). Physiological and psychophysical responses to listening to music during warm-up and circuit-type resistance exercise in strength trained men. *Journal of Sports Medicine*, *1*, Article e389831. https://doi.org/10.1155/2015/389831

Asmundson, G. J., Fetzner, M. G., DeBoer, L. B., Powers, M. B., Otto, M. W., & Smits, J. A. (2013). Let's get physical: A contemporary review of the anxiolytic effects of exercise for anxiety and its disorders. *Depression and Anxiety*, *30*(4), 362–373. https://onlinelibrary.wiley.com/doi/abs/10.1002/da.22043

Bacon, C., Myers, T., & Karageorghis, C. (2012). Effect of music-movement synchrony on exercise oxygen consumption. *The Journal of Sports Medicine and Physical Fitness, 52*(4), 359–365. PMID: 22828457

Ballmann, C. G., Favre, M. L., Phillips, M. T., Rogers, R. R., Pederson, J. A., & Williams, T. D. (2021). Effect of pre-exercise music on bench press power, velocity, and repetition volume. *Perceptual and Motor Skills*, *128*(3), 1183–1196. https://doi.org/10.1177/0031512521100240

Berlyne, D. E. (1973). Aesthetics and psychobiology. *Journal of Aesthetics and Art Criticism*, *31*(4), 177–184. https://doi.org/10.2307/429334

Biagini, M. S., Brown, L. E., Coburn, J. W., Judelson, D. A., Statler, T. A., Bottaro, M., ... & Longo, N. A. (2012). Effects of self-selected music on strength, explosiveness, and mood. *The Journal of Strength & Conditioning Research*, *26*(7), 1934–1938. https://doi.org/10.1519/JSC.0b013e318237e7b3

Bigliassi, M. (2015). Use the brain: Complementary methods to analyse the effects of motivational music. *Frontiers in Human Neuroscience*, *9*, Article e508. https://doi.org/10.3389/fnhum.2015.00508

Bigliassi, M., Karageorghis, C. I., Bishop, D. T., Nowicky, A. V., & Wright, M. J. (2018). Cerebral effects of music during isometric exercise: An *f*MRI study. *International Journal of Psychophysiology*, *133*, 131–139. https://doi.org/10.1016/j.ijpsycho.2018.07.475

Bigliassi, M., Karageorghis, C. I., Nowicky, A. V., Orgs, G., & Wright, M. J. (2016). Cerebral mechanisms underlying the effects of music during a fatiguing isometric ankle-dorsiflexion task. *Psychophysiology*, *53*(10), 1472–1483. https://doi.org/10.1111/psyp.12693

Bigliassi, M., Karageorghis, C. I., Wright, M. J., Orgs, G., & Nowicky, A. V. (2017). Effects of auditory stimuli on electrical activity in the brain during cycle ergometry. *Physiology & Behavior*, *177*, 135–147. https://doi.org/10.1016/j.physbeh.2017.04.023

Bird, J. M., & Karageorghis, C. I. (2020). A grounded theory of music-video use in an exercise facility. *Research Quarterly for Exercise and Sport*, *91*(3), 445–459. https://doi.org/10.1080/02701367.2019.1680788

Bird, J. M., Karageorghis, C. I., Baker, S. J., & Brookes, D. A. (2019). Effects of music, video, and 360-degree video on cycle ergometer exercise at the ventilatory threshold. *Scandinavian Journal of Medicine & Science in Sports*, *29*(8), 1161–1173. https://doi.org/10.1111/sms.13453

Bird, J. M., Karageorghis, C. I., Baker, S. J., Brookes, D. A., & Nowicky, A. V. (2021). Ready exerciser one: Effects of music and virtual reality on cycle ergometer exercise. *British Journal of Health Psychology*, *26*(1), 15–32. https://doi.org/10.1111/bjhp.12445

Bird, J. M., Karageorghis, C. I., Jones, L., Harris, D. J., Alharbi, M., & Vine, S. J. (2024). Beyond rubik: The embodiment–presence–interactivity cube applied to exercise. *Psychology of Sport and Exercise*, *74*, 102684. https://doi.org/10.1016/j.psychsport.2024.102684

Brand, R., & Ekkekakis, P. (2018). Affective–reflective theory of physical inactivity and exercise. *German Journal of Exercise and Sport Research*, *48*(1), 48–58. https://doi.org/10.1007/s12662-017-0477-9.

Brandt, N., & Razon, S. (2019). Effect of self-selected music on affective responses and running performance: Directions and implications. *International Journal of Exercise Science, 12*(5), 310–323. https://doi.org/10.70252/HWOL5013

Chanda, M. L., & Levitin, D. J. (2013). The neurochemistry of music. *Trends in Cognitive Sciences*, *17*(4), 179–193. https://doi.org/10.1016/j.tics.2013.02.007

Chang, Y. K., Chen, F. T., Kuan, G., Wei, G. X., Chu, C. H., Yan, J., Chen, A. G., & Hung, T. M. (2019). Effects of acute exercise duration on the inhibition aspect of executive function in late middle-aged adults. *Frontiers in Aging Neuroscience*, *11*, Article e227. https://doi.org/10.3389/fnagi.2019.00227.

Chapados, C., & Levitin, D. J. (2008). Cross-modal interactions in the experience of musical performances: Physiological correlates. *Cognition*, *108*(3), 639–651. https://doi.org/10.1016/j.cognition.2008.05.008

Copeland, B. L., & Franks, B. D. (1991). Effects of types and intensities of background music on treadmill endurance. *The Journal of Sports Medicine and Physical Fitness*, *31*(1), 100–103. PMID: 1861474

Da Costa, K. G., Barbieri, J., Hohl, R., Costa, E., & Fontes, E. (2017). Exercise training improves cardiorespiratory fitness and cognitive function in individuals with substance use disorders: A pilot study. *Sport Sciences for Health*, *13*, 437–441. https://doi.org/10.1007/s11332-016-0338-1

Delleli, S., Ouergui, I., Ballmann, C. G., Messaoudi, H., Trabelsi, K., Ardigò, L. P., & Chtourou, H. (2023). The effects of pre-task music on exercise performance and associated psycho-physiological responses: A systematic review with multilevel meta-analysis of controlled studies. *Frontiers in Psychology*, *14*, Article e1293783. https://doi.org/10.3389/fpsyg.2023.1293783

Dishman, R. K. (2001). The problem of exercise adherence: Fighting sloth in nations with market economies. *Quest*, *53*(3), 279–294. https://doi.org/10.1080/00336297.2001.10491745

Druss, B. G., Hwang, I., Petukhova, M., Sampson, N. A., Wang, P. S., & Kessler, R. C. (2009). Impairment in role functioning in mental and chronic medical disorders in the United States: Results from the National Comorbidity Survey Replication. *Molecular Psychiatry*, *14*(7), 728–737. https://doi.org/10.1038/mp.2008.13

Ekkekakis, P. (2003). Pleasure and displeasure from the body: Perspectives from exercise. *Cognition and Emotion*, *17*(2), 213–239. https://doi.org/10.1080/02699930302292

Ekkekakis, P. (2023). Physical activity as a mental health intervention in the era of managed care. In P. Ekkekakis (Ed.), *Routledge handbook of physical activity and mental health*. (pp. 1–32). Routledge. https://doi.org/10.4324/9781003423430

Ekkekakis, P., Hartman, M. E., & Ladwig, M. A. (2020). Affective responses to exercise. In G. Tenebaum, & R. C. Eklund (Eds.). *Handbook of sport psychology* (4th ed., pp. 231–253). Wiley. https://doi.org/10.1002/9781119568124.ch12

Ekkekakis, P., Vazou, S., Bixby, W., & Georgiadis, E. (2016). The mysterious case of the public health guideline that is (almost) entirely ignored: Call for a research agenda on the causes of the extreme avoidance of physical activity in obesity. *Obesity Reviews*, *17*(4), 313–329. https://doi.org/10.1111/obr.12369

Ford, J., & Arvinen-Barrow, M. (2019). Exploring the use of psychological skills training interventions in a music domain: A systematic review. *Medical Problems of Performing Artists*, *34*(4), 222–229. https://doi.org/10.21091/mppa.2019.4033

Gaudlitz, K., Plag, J., Dimeo, F., & Ströhle, A. (2015). Aerobic exercise training facilitates the effectiveness of cognitive behavioral therapy in panic disorder. *Depression and Anxiety*, *32*(3), 221–228. https://doi.org/10.1002/da.22337

Gaudlitz, K., von Lindenberger, B.-L., Zschucke, E., & Ströhle, A. (2023). Mechanisms underlying the relationship between physical activity and anxiety: Human data. In P. Ekkekakis (Ed.), *Routledge handbook of physical activity and mental health* (pp. 117–129). Routledge. https://doi.org/10.4324/9781003423430

Giménez-Meseguer, J., Tortosa-Martínez, J., & Cortell-Tormo, J. M. (2020). The benefits of physical exercise on mental disorders and quality of life in substance use disorders patients. Systematic review and meta-analysis. *International Journal of Environmental Research and Public Health*, *17*(10), Article e3680. https://doi.org/10.3390/ijerph17103680

Hutchinson, J. C., & Karageorghis, C. I. (2013). Moderating influence of dominant attentional style and exercise intensity on responses to asynchronous music. *Journal of Sport & Exercise Psychology*, *35*(6), 625–643. https://doi.org/10.1123/jsep.35.6.625

Hutchinson, J. C., Karageorghis, C. I., & Jones, L. (2015). See hear: Psychological effects of music and music-video during treadmill running. *Annals of Behavioral Medicine*, *49*(2), 199–211. https://doi.org/10.1007/s12160-014-9647-2

Hutchinson, J. C., Jones, L., Vitti, S. N., Moore, A., Dalton, P. C., & O'Neil, B. J. (2018). The influence of self-selected music on affect-regulated exercise intensity and remembered pleasure during treadmill running. *Sport, Exercise, and Performance Psychology*, *7*(1), 80–92. https://doi.org/10.1037/spy0000115

Jia, T., Ogawa, Y., Miura, M., Ito, O., & Kohzuki, M. (2016). Music attenuated a decrease in parasympathetic nervous system activity after exercise. *PLoS One*, *11*(2), Article e0148648. https://doi.org/10.1371/journal.pone.0148648

Jing, L., & Xudong, W. (2008). Evaluation on the effects of relaxing music on the recovery from aerobic exercise-induced fatigue. *The Journal of Sports Medicine and Physical Fitness*, *48*(1), 102–106. PMID: 18212717

Jones, L., Karageorghis, C. I., & Ekkekakis, P. (2014). Can high-intensity exercise be more pleasant? Attentional dissociation using music and video. *Journal of Sport and Exercise Psychology*, *36*(5), 528–541. https://doi.org/10.1123/jsep.2013-0251

Jones, L., Karageorghis, C., Ker, T., Rushton, C., Stephenson, S., & Wheeldon, I. (2024). The exercise intensity–music-tempo preference relationship: A decennial revisit. *Psychology of Sport and Exercise*, *74*, Article e102644. https://doi.org/10.1016/j.psychsport.2024.102644

Jones, L., Stork, M. J., & Oliver, L. S. (2020). Affective responses to high-intensity interval training with continuous and respite music. *Journal of Sports Sciences*, *38*(24), 2803–2810. https://doi.org/10.1080/02640414.2020.1801324

Jones, L., & Zenko, Z. (2021). Strategies to facilitate more pleasant exercise experiences. In Z. Zenko & L. Jones (Eds.), *Essentials of exercise and sport psychology: An open access textbook* (pp. 242–270). Society for Transparency, Openness, and Replication in Kinesiology. https://doi.org/10.51224/B1000

Juslin, P. N. (2013). From everyday emotions to aesthetic emotions: Towards a unified theory of musical emotions. *Physics of Life Reviews*, *10*(3), 235–266. https://doi.org/10.1016/j.plrev.2013.05.008

Karageorghis, C. I. (2016). The scientific application of music in exercise and sport: Towards a new theoretical model. In A. M. Lane (Ed.), *Sport and exercise psychology* (2nd ed., pp. 274–320). Taylor & Francis.

Karageorghis, C. I. (2017). *Applying music in exercise and sport*. Human Kinetics.

Karageorghis, C. I. (2020). Music-related interventions in the exercise domain: A theory-based approach. In G. Tenenbaum & R. C. Eklund (Eds.), *Handbook of sport psychology* (4th ed., pp. 929–949). Wiley. https://doi.org/10.1002/9781119568124.ch45

Karageorghis, C. I., Bigliassi, M., Guérin, S. M., & Delevoye-Turrell, Y. (2018a). Brain mechanisms that underlie music interventions in the exercise domain. *Progress in Brain Research*, *240*, 109–125. https://doi.org/10.1016/bs.pbr.2018.09.004

Karageorghis, C. I., Bigliassi, M., Tayara, K., Priest, D.-L., & Bird, J. M. (2018b). A grounded theory of music use in the psychological preparation of academy soccer players. *Sport, Exercise, and Performance Psychology*, *7*(2), 109–127. https://doi.org/10.1037/spy0000110

Karageorghis, C. I., Bruce, A. C., Pottratz, S. T., Stevens, R. C., Bigliassi, M., & Hamer, M. (2018c). Psychological and psychophysiological effects of recuperative music postexercise. *Medicine & Science in Sports & Exercise, 50*(4), 739–746. https://doi.org/10.1249/MSS.0000000000001497

Karageorghis, C. I., Cheek, P., Simpson, S. D., & Bigliassi, M. (2018d). Interactive effects of music tempi and intensities on grip strength and subjective affect. *Scandinavian Journal of Medicine & Science in Sports*, *28*(3), 1166–1175. https://doi.org/10.1111/sms.12979

Karageorghis, C. I., Guérin, S. M., Fessler, L., Howard, L. W., Pinto, C., Ojuri, O., Kuan, J., & Samwell-Nash, K. G. (2025). One-HIIT wonder: Can music make high-intensity interval training more pleasant? *Psychology of Sport and Exercise*, *76*, Article e102717, 1–38. ISSN: 1469-0292. https://doi.org/10.1016/j.psychsport.2024.102717

Karageorghis, C. I., Hutchinson, J. C., Bigliassi, M., Watson, M. P., Perry, F. A., Burges, L. D., Melville-Griffiths, T., & Gomes-Baho, T. J. (2019). Effects of auditory-motor synchronization on 400-m sprint performance: An applied study. *International Journal of Sports Science & Coaching*, *14*(6), 738–748. https://doi.org/10.1177/1747954119879359

Karageorghis, C. I., Hutchinson, J. C., Jones, L., Farmer, H. L., Ayhan, M. S., Wilson, R. C., Rance, J., Hepworth, C. H., & Bailey, S. G. (2013). Psychological, psychophysical, and ergogenic effects of music in swimming. *Psychology of Sport and Exercise*, *14*(4), 560–568. https://doi.org/10.1016/j.psychsport.2013.01.009

Karageorghis, C. I., & Jones, L. (2014). On the stability and relevance of the exercise heart rate–music-tempo preference relationship. *Psychology of Sport and Exercise*, *15*(3), 299–310. https://doi.org/10.1016/j.psychsport.2013.08.004

Karageorghis, C. I., Jones, L., Howard, L. W., Thomas, R. M., Moulashis, P., & Santich, S. J. (2021a). When it HIITs, you feel no pain: Psychological and psychophysiological effects of respite–active music in high-intensity interval training. *Journal of Sport & Exercise Psychology*, *43*(1), 41–52. https://doi.org/10.1123/jsep.2019-0335

Karageorghis, C. I., Jones, L., Priest, D.-L., Akers, R. I., Clarke, A., Perry, J. M., Reddick, B. T., Bishop, D. T., & Lim, H. B. (2011). Revisiting the relationship between exercise heart rate and music tempo preference. *Research Quarterly for Exercise and Sport*, *82*(2), 274–284. https://doi.org/10.1080/02701367.2011.10599755

Karageorghis, C. I., Kuan, G., & Schiphof-Godart, L. (2021b). Music in sport: From conceptual underpinnings to applications. In Z. Zenko & L. Jones (Eds.), *Essentials of exercise and sport psychology: An open access textbook* (pp. 530–564). Society for Transparency, Openness, and Replication in Kinesiology. https://doi.org/10.51224/B1023

Karageorghis, C. I., Mouzourides, D. A., Priest, D.-L., Sasso, T. A., Morrish, D. J., & Walley, C. L. (2009). Psychophysical and ergogenic effects of synchronous music during treadmill walking. *Journal of Sport & Exercise Psychology*, *31*(1), 18–36. https://doi.org/10.1123/jsep.31.1.18

Karageorghis, C. I., & Priest, D.-L. (2012). Music in the exercise domain: A review and synthesis (Part I). *International Review of Sport and Exercise Psychology*, *5*(1), 44–66. https://doi.org/10.1080/1750984X.2011.631026

Karageorghis, C. I., Priest, D., Williams, L., Hirani, R., Lannon, K., & Bates, B. (2010). Ergogenic and psychological effects of synchronous music during circuit-type exercise. *Psychology of Sport and Exercise*, *11*(6), 551–559. https://doi.org/10.1016/j.psychsport.2010.06.004

Kohl III, H. W., Murray, T. D., & Salvo, D. (2019). *Foundations of physical activity and public health*. Human Kinetics.

Kuan, G. (2023). The effect of music listening on athletes' anxiety, depression, and pain: A mini review. *The Asian Journal of Kinesiology*, *25*(2), 19–25. https://doi.org/10.15758/ajk.2023.25.2.19

Kuan, G., Morris, T., Kueh, Y. C., & Terry, P. C. (2018). Effects of relaxing and arousing music during imagery training on dart-throwing performance, physiological arousal indices, and competitive state anxiety. *Frontiers in Psychology*, *9*, 14. https://doi.org/10.3389/fpsyg.2018.00014

Kvam, S., Kleppe, C. L., Nordhus, I. H., & Hovland, A. (2016). Exercise as a treatment for depression: A meta-analysis. *Journal of Affective Disorders*, *202*, 67–86. https://doi.org/10.1016/j.jad.2016.03.063

Levitin, D. J., Grahn, J. A., & London, J. (2018). The psychology of music: Rhythm and movement. *Annual Review of Psychology*, *69*, 51–75. https://doi.org/10.1146/annurev-psych-122216-011740

Lewin, K. (1951). Field theory in social science: Selected theoretical papers. *Harper Google Scholar*, *2*, 1–346. https://books.google.com.au/books/about/Field_theory_in_social_science.html?id=PzMYAAAAIAAJ&redir_esc=y

Loizou, G., & Karageorghis, C. (2015). Effects of psychological priming, video, and music on anaerobic exercise performance. *Scandinavian Journal of Medicine & Science in Sports*, *25*(6), 909–920. https://doi.org/10.1111/sms.12391

Marques, M., Henrique, N., Takito, M., & Franchini, E. (2024). Effects of music on perceptive and performance responses during high-intensity exercise: A systematic review. *Sport Sciences for Health*, *20*, 727–738. https://doi.org/10.1007/s11332-024-01189-6

Nani, S., Matsouka, O., Tsitskari, E., & Avgerinos, A. (2017). The role of physical activity in life happiness of Greek drug abusers participating in a treatment program. *Sport Sciences for Health*, *13*, 25–32. https://doi.org/10.1007/s11332-016-0345-2

Park, K. S., Hass, C. J., Patel, B., & Janelle, C. M. (2020). Musical pleasure beneficially alters stride and arm swing amplitude during rhythmically-cued walking in people with Parkinson's disease. *Human Movement Science*, *74*, e102718. https://doi.org/10.1016/j.humov.2020.102718

Pottratz, S. T., Hutchinson, J. C., Karageorghis, C. I., Mullin, E. M., & Zenko, Z. (2021). Prime movers: Effects of subliminal primes, music, and music video on psychological responses to exercise. *Annals of Behavioral Medicine*, *55*(2), 112–122. https://doi.org/10.1093/abm/kaaa036

Quan, Y., Lo, C. Y., Wolff, L., Wang, J., Olsen, K. N., & Thompson, W. F. (2025). Cognitive benefits of music in aerobic exercise: Evidence from a Bayesian network meta-analysis in adults with mild cognitive impairment. *Archives of Gerontology and Geriatrics*, *134*, Article e105848. https://doi.org/10.1016/j.archger.2025.105848

Rhodes, R. E., Gray, S. M., & Husband, C. (2019). Experimental manipulation of affective judgments about physical activity: A systematic review and meta-analysis of adults. *Health Psychology Review*, *13*(1), 18–34. https://doi.org/10.1080/17437199.2018.1530067

Rhodes, R. E., & Kates, A. (2015). Can the affective response to exercise predict future motives and physical activity behavior? A systematic review of published evidence. *Annals of Behavioral Medicine*, *49*(5), 715–731. https://doi.org/10.1007/s12160-015-9704-5

Rozin, P. (1999). Preadaptation and the puzzles and properties of pleasure. In D. Kahneman, E. Diener & N. Schwarz (Eds.). *Well-being: The foundations of hedonic psychology* (pp. 109–133). Sage.

Smirmaul, B. P. (2016). Effect of pre-task music on sports or exercise performance. *The Journal of Sports Medicine and Physical Fitness*, *57*(7–8), 976–984. https://doi.org/10.23736/s0022-4707.16.06411-2

Saarikallio, S. (2017). Musical identity in fostering emotional health. In R. MacDonald, D. J. Hargreaves, & D. Miell (Eds.), *Handbook of musical identities* (pp. 602–623). Oxford University Press. https://doi.org/10.1093/acprof:oso/9780199679485.003.0033

Scherer, K. R. (1999). Appraisal theory. In T. Dalgleish & M. J. Power (Eds.), *Handbook of cognition and emotion* (pp. 637–663). Wiley. https://doi.org/10.1002/0470013494

Scherer, K. R., & Zentner, M. R. (2001). Emotional effects of music: Production rules. In P. N. Juslin & J. A. Sloboda (Eds.), *Music and emotion: Theory and research* (pp. 361–392). Oxford University Press. https://doi.org/10.1093/oso/9780192631886.001.0001

Shu-Ya, C., & Chun-Fei, C. (2020). Effects of an active music therapy program on functional fitness in community older adults. *Journal of Nursing Research*, *28*(5), Article e111. https://doi.org/10.1097/JNR.0000000000000391

Silverman, M. J. (2019). Music therapy and therapeutic alliance in adult mental health: A qualitative investigation. *Journal of Music Therapy*, *56*(1), 90–116. https://doi.org/10.1093/jmt/thy019

Silverman, M. J. (2021). Music-based emotion regulation and healthy and unhealthy music use predict coping strategies in adults with substance use disorder: A cross-sectional study. *Psychology of Music*, *49*(3), 333–350. https://doi.org/10.1177/0305735619854529

Stanovich, K. E. (2008). Higher-order preferences and the Master Rationality Motive. *Thinking & Reasoning*, *14*(1), 111–127. https://doi.org/10.1080/13546780701384621

Stewart, D. E., & Irons, J. Y. (2018). Music, public health, and health promotion: Can music be a social determinant of health? In N. Sunderland, N. Lewandowski, D. Bendrups, & B. L. Bartleet (Eds.), *Music, health and wellbeing* (pp. 17–31). Palgrave Macmillan. https://doi.org/10.1057/978-1-349-95284-7_2

Stork, M. J., Karageorghis, C. I., & Martin Ginis, K. A. (2019). *Let's Go*: Psychological, psychophysical, and physiological effects of music during sprint interval exercise. *Psychology of Sport and Exercise*, *45*, Article e101547. https://doi.org/10.1016/j.psychsport.2019.101547

Stork, M. J., Kwan, M. Y., Gibala, M. J., & Martin Ginis, K. A. (2015). Music enhances performance and perceived enjoyment of sprint interval exercise. *Medicine & Science in Sports & Exercise*, *47*(5), 1052–1060. https://doi.org/10.1249/MSS.0000000000000494

Strain, T., Flaxman, S., Guthold, R., Semenova, E., Cowan, M., Riley, L. M., Bull, F. C., Stevens, G. A., & Country Data Author Group. (2024). National, regional, and global trends in insufficient physical activity among adults from 2000 to 2022: A pooled analysis of 507 population-based surveys with 5.7 million participants. *The Lancet Global Health*, *12*(8), e1232–e1243. https://doi.org/10.1016/s2214-109x(24)00150-5

Tan, F., Tengah, A., Nee, L. Y., & Fredericks, S. (2014). A study of the effect of relaxing music on heart rate recovery after exercise among healthy students. *Complementary Therapies in Clinical Practice*, *20*(2), 114–117. https://doi.org/10.1016/j.ctcp.2014.01.001

Tenenbaum, G., & Hutchinson, J. C. (2007). A social-cognitive perspective of perceived and sustained effort. In G. Tenenbaum & R. C. Eklund (Eds.), *Handbook of sport psychology* (3rd ed., pp. 560–577). Wiley. https://doi.org/10.1002/9781118270011.ch25

Terry, P. C., & Karageorghis, C. I. (2011). Music in sport and exercise. In T. Morris, & P. C. Terry (Eds.). *The new sport and exercise psychology companion* (pp. 359–380). Fitness Information Technology.

Terry, P. C., Karageorghis, C. I., Curran, M. L., Martin, O. V., & Parsons-Smith, R. L. (2020). Effects of music in exercise and sport: A meta-analytic review. *Psychological Bulletin*, *146*(2), 91–117. https://doi.org/10.1037/bul0000216

Terry, P. C., Karageorghis, C. I., Mecozzi Saha, A., & D'Auria, S. (2012). Effects of synchronous music on treadmill running among elite triathletes. *Journal of Science and Medicine in Sport, 15*(1), 52–57. https://doi.org/10.1016/j.jsams.2011.06.003

Thomas, N. (2020). Community-based referential music making with limited-resource adolescents: A pilot study. *Music Therapy Perspectives*, *38*(2), 112–118. https://doi.org/10.1093/mtp/miaa016

Van Dyck, E. (2019). Musical intensity applied in the sports and exercise domain: An effective strategy to boost performance? *Frontiers in Psychology*, *10*, Article e1145. https://doi.org/10.3389/fpsyg.2019.01145

Utschig, A. C., Otto, M. W., Powers, M. B., & Smits, J. A. (2013). The relationship between physical activity and anxiety and its disorders. In P. Ekkekakis, D. B. Cook, L. L. Craft, S. N. Culos-Reed, J. L. Etnier, M. Hamer, K. A. Martin Ginis, J. Reed, J. A. J. Smits, & M. Ussher (Eds.), *Routledge handbook of physical activity and mental health* (pp. 105–116). Routledge. https://doi.org/10.4324/9780203132678

World Health Organization. (2022). *Global status report on physical activity 2022: Country profiles*. World Health Organization. https://www.who.int/teams/health-promotion/physical-activity/global-status-report-on-physical-activity-2022

Zhou, Z., Zhou, R., Wei, W., Luan, R., & Li, K. (2021). Effects of music-based movement therapy on motor function, balance, gait, mental health, and quality of life for patients with Parkinson's disease: A systematic review and meta-analysis. *Clinical Rehabilitation*, *35*(7), 937–951. https://doi.org/10.1177/0269215521990526

PART 5

Exercise and Applications around the World

10

PROMOTING MENTAL HEALTH THROUGH PHYSICAL ACTIVITY IN SUB-SAHARAN AFRICA

Medina Srem-Sai, Jacob Owusu Sarfo, and John Elvis Hagan Jnr

10.1 Preface

MH has received increasing global attention in the past decade and is currently at the forefront through its promotion against the prevention and treatment of mental illnesses by the United Nations' Sustainable Development Goals (World Health Organization, 2017). According to Sankoh et al. (2018), MH conditions seem to be gaining much attention in Africa. Available scholarly records suggest that between 2000 and 2015, Africa's population increased by 49%, yet the years lost to disability because of mental and substance use disorders increased by 52%. By 2015, the impact of mental health challenges had accounted for 17.9 million years lost to disability. With the continent's population projected to double in the three decades ahead, the burden on its young population, who are already besieged with significant livelihood challenges, is likely to worsen. It is anticipated that this cohort will encounter numerous psychological challenges as they strive to overcome these life challenges.

PA promotion has been identified as an important strategy for improving mental health globally, with increasingly strong research evidence on the usefulness of PA on MH and well-being across both non-clinical (Rebar et al., 2015) and clinical (Bailey et al., 2018; Rosenbaum et al., 2015) populations. Previous research evidence has shown the role of PA as a protective factor against the risk of developing mental health conditions (Schuch et al., 2018; Stubbs et al., 2018). Scientific evidence has proven that PA is related to favourable mental health outcomes, including age-related cognitive decline (Colcombe & Kramer, 2003), anxiety (Taylor, 2000), enduring fatigue (Puetz et al., 2006), improved psychological well-being (Bize et al., 2007), minimal symptoms of depression (Rethorst et al., 2009), self-esteem (Spence et al., 2005), and sleep (Youngstedt & Kline, 2006). It has also been documented that people with MH conditions like depression are less likely to complete

DOI: 10.4324/9781003517474-15

a set of prescribed PA and rather engage more in sedentary behaviours by health agencies (Firth et al., 2019; Schuch et al., 2018; Vancampfort et al., 2017).

Despite this growing evidence of PA on MH, there remains a translational gap, especially in low- to middle-income countries like sub-Saharan Africa. For many sub-Saharan African countries, MH issues remain the least priority for policymakers. The morbidity and disability caused by mental illness usually receive limited attention from stakeholders. MH services are rarely developed, with many countries in the region having no mental health policies, interventions, research programmes, or action plans (Okasha, 2002).

As often ignored, addressing this translation gap requires the identification of how contextual and personal factors affect behavioural engagement and potential intervention programmes. The translational evidence in the PA and MH areas is significantly lacking in the region. Although there is increasing evidence that individuals with MH challenges are less active than the general population (Schuch et al., 2017), the underlying mechanisms of how MH issues affect individuals' psychological processes to begin and maintain PA are not clearly understood (Farholm & Sørensen, 2016; Roessler et al., 2017).

Clarifying these mechanisms of PA on MH is key for designing appropriate evidence-based intervention programmes to provide lasting MH benefits (Taylor & Faulkner, 2008). By ignoring this approach to evidence, developing nations would risk wasting already limited resources and time in an attempt to fit mismatched interventions across populations with unique characteristics.

The rationale for this conceptualised review is to highlight reflections on PA and MH by providing researchers, service providers, practitioners, and policymakers with insights on how this available evidence could inform applied practice and intervention and highlight existing knowledge gaps as strategic directions for future research.

10.2 Context-Specific MH and PA

Engagement in PA usually occurs in different socio-cultural and organisational contexts, with varied individual and group practices (Werneck et al., 2018). Although previous research on PA and MH conditions is limited, there is strong research evidence that suggests that context may moderate the relationship between PA and MH issues like depression and/or related MH challenges (Vittengl, 2021). Previous studies have already shown that leisure-time PA is inversely related to depressive symptoms (White et al., 2017). Similarly, PA during leisure and with family, compared to during cooking, work, and travel, was associated with mental well-being among adults in Scotland (Mason et al., 2016). Further, some leisure activities (e.g., aerobics, gym work, popular sports engagement), compared to household chores, predicted lower mental health load among adults in the United States (Chekroud et al., 2018). Other evidence in Japan showed that PA during leisure, compared to work or walking to and from work, was a somewhat stronger negative predictor of the development of depressive symptoms among employees in Japan. However, PA was measured differently across contexts, making direct comparisons somewhat unclear (Kuwahara et al., 2015). With so many structural and logistical inadequacies (e.g., restricted neighbourhood walkability), including cultural barriers (e.g., masculinity–femininity norms) in many sub-Saharan African countries, the baseline information on PA is lacking or non-existent. Some specific populations are especially concerning, as PA engagement is significantly lower among girls/women, older adults, people with disabilities, obese individuals, rural populations, and individuals with less or no education as well as income. Hence, individuals with MH challenges serve as a critical population of which sedentariness may cause further increases in morbidity, mortality, and healthcare expenditures.

10.3 Previous Evidence from Reviews on MH and PA in SSA

In SSA, there is a dearth of research on the role of PA in MH despite evidence suggesting its significant benefits (Peltzer, 2010). The limited number of studies exploring this relationship underscores the need for more comprehensive research in the prevention and management of mental health problems in SSA. Researchers in the region have studied the relationship between MH and PA (Adeniyi et al., 2011; Osei, 2024), with several examples of these studies conducted in locations like Ghana (Asare & Danquah, 2015; Osei, 2024), Kenya (Peltzer, 2010), Namibia (Zealand, 2008), Nigeria (Adeniyi et al., 2011; Ugwueze et al., 2021), Senegal (Peltzer, 2010), South Africa (Nwosu, 2018), Uganda (Peltzer, 2010), and Zambia (Peltzer, 2010).

In a survey among eight countries, Peltzer (2010) noted that only 14.2% of participants were frequently physically active (at least 60 minutes per day, five or more days a week) during leisure time, with boys being more active than girls. The study reported again that Ugandan and Kenyan students had the highest rates of physical activity (17.7% and 16.0%, respectively), while Zambian and Senegalese students had the lowest (9.0% and 10.9%, respectively). There was a significant association between leisure-time PA and the frequency of alcohol consumption as well as higher socioeconomic status. Further, leisure-time sedentary behaviour (spending five or more hours sitting on a usual day) was strongly associated with all substance use variables.

Additionally, Asare and Danquah (2015) observed that regular participation in PAs significantly reduced symptoms of anxiety and depression in Ghana. In Namibia, Zealand (2008) similarly provided insights into the MH benefits of PA among adolescents. The study revealed that PA not only improved physical health but also significantly enhanced mental well-being through the process of improving self-esteem. Thus, these studies align with broader findings that suggest PA serves as a protective factor against MH disorders in SSA. In South Africa, Nwosu's (2018) study on the role of PA in managing MH conditions among patients in psychiatric facilities observed that those who participated in regular physical activities reported lower levels of depressive symptoms and improved self-esteem. Additionally, Ugwueze et al. (2021) also highlighted that structured exercise programmes could benefit persons with MH issues as a form of adjunctive treatment in Nigerian healthcare settings.

There is scientific evidence that has shown PA to alleviate cognitive deficits, which are often untreated yet significantly impact long-term functioning (Vancampfort et al., 2017). Notwithstanding the positive impact of PA on mental well-being, a systematic review by Vancampfort et al. (2017) noted a low integration of PA within MH policies across countries in SSA. In their review, the authors observed that although 69% of nations in SSA have a working mental health policy, only 2 out of 22 policies included explicit recommendations for physical activity. This evidence indicates a significant policy support gap for PA as a therapeutic preventive and rehabilitative intervention. Consequently, incorporating PA interventions in the treatment of individuals with MH issues could lessen mental, physical, and social burdens, support functional recovery, and reduce disability (Nwosu, 2018; Osei, 2024; Vancampfort et al., 2017).

10.4 Practical Implications of MH through PA Promotion

The findings from the existing literature have several implications for promoting PA as a means to improve MH in SSA (Asare & Danquah, 2015; Osei, 2024; Vancampfort et al., 2017). Interventions in SSA should be culturally sensitive and tailored to guarantee their acceptance and feasibility for the target population. Also, community-based programmes should involve local leaders and stakeholders to enhance participation and sustainability (Seekles et al., 2023). Further, school-based programmes should be prioritised to promote improved MH outcomes among adolescents. Integrating PA into the school curriculum will help schools in SSA provide a structured and supportive school environment for students and teachers to engage in physical activity programmes to enhance their MH outcomes.

10.5 Public Policy

Active PA engagement may play a significant role in easing symptoms of MH conditions such as anxiety, depression, and other related disorders. Hence, policymakers in MH within SSA should recognise the importance of PA for MH. As observed by Vancampfort et al. (2017), the low integration of PA in SSA MH policies calls for urgent policy action. Policies in SSA should promote the development of neighbourhood infrastructure, such as parks and recreational facilities, which can facilitate PA participation. Moreover, policies that address socioeconomic barriers, such as providing affordable access to sports facilities and keep-fit clubs, can enhance participation among disadvantaged populations. Additionally, healthcare policies should also incorporate PA into MH treatment. Policies regarding training mental healthcare professionals should recommend curriculums that value PA as part of holistic MH care for patients with MH conditions.

10.6 Future Research

To solve the challenges in the dearth of research on the role of PA in MH (Peltzer, 2010), there is a need for more high-quality research on the relationship between these constructs in SSA. Future studies should focus on conducting randomised controlled trials with larger sample sizes and longer intervention durations to provide more robust evidence. Also, research should focus on the mechanisms through which PA affects MH and the effective types and intensities of physical activity for different populations. Studies could also address the challenges faced by populations in SSA in relation to PA participation. Understanding the cultural, psychological, social, and economic factors that influence PA can inform the development of targeted interventions that are more likely to be successful.

Although there is enough evidence on the association between PA and MH, there are still many areas that warrant further inquiry for better clarity through rigorous research designs like randomised, case-control, and population-based studies. Well-designed studies to answer the under-listed questions might be very useful in addressing issues related to PA and MH:

- What are the relative contributions of the numerous psychological and physiological pathways of PA to enhance MH?
- How do PA recommendations vary across specific populations, such as people with disabilities, children, adolescents, and older adults?
- What are the long-term impacts of regular PA on the risk of developing MH disorders?
- When and how could PA be integrated into the therapeutic protocol of individuals with MH conditions relative to other treatment routines, which may include medication and psychotherapy?

10.7 Conclusion

While research has already been done in PA on MH, its translational use in MH promotion, rehabilitation, and treatment from an applied perspective to date is sparse. It will be crucial to incorporate these ideas into existing MH services driven by updated scientific evidence. There is growing interest in how individuals with MH conditions can begin and sustain PA. What is unclear is how much and the type of support is required and provided by whom? It would be desirable to help the regularity, sufficiency, and maintenance in PA to elicit significant positive effects on MH. These questions pose major challenges in translating research efforts to ecological settings to help persons in need.

Addressing these challenges requires reliable empirical evidence from translational and mediational research across different geographical settings, viable data collection methods, and study designs. Promoting this research agenda through both qualitative and quantitative methods in sub-Saharan Africa to unknot the effects of PA on specific areas in MH would be worthwhile for sustainable intervention programmes. The former approach offers valuable in-depth information on how regular PA affects psychosocial mediators and MH, and explains unforeseen impacts and distinctive outcomes; the latter strategy quantifies the mediating processes and assesses their statistical reliability and rigorousness.

In conclusion, the existing literature provides strong evidence that PA can significantly improve MH outcomes in SSA. Systematic reviews, meta-analyses, and scoping reviews highlight the benefits of PA in reducing symptoms of depression and anxiety among various populations. However, more high-quality research is needed to understand the underlying mechanisms and address barriers to participation. Policymakers and practitioners are encouraged to prioritise person-centred, culturally sensitive, community-based, school-based interventions, and integrate PA into national health policies and programmes to promote MH in SSA.

Bibliography

Adeniyi, A. F., Okafor, N. C., & Adeniyi, C. Y. (2011). Depression and physical activity in a sample of Nigerian adolescents: Levels, relationships and predictors. *Child and Adolescent Psychiatry and Mental Health*, *5*, 16. https://doi.org/10.1186/1753-2000-5-16

Asare, M., & Danquah, S. A. (2015). The relationship between physical activity, sedentary behaviour and mental health in Ghanaian adolescents. *Child and Adolescent Psychiatry and Mental Health*, *9*, 11. https://doi.org/10.1186/s13034-015-0043-x

Bailey, A. P., Hetrick, S. E., Rosenbaum, S., Purcell, R., Parker, A. G. (2018). Treating depression with physical activity in adolescents and young adults: A systematic review and meta-analysis of randomized controlled trials. *Psychological Medicine, 48*(7), 1068–1083. https://doi.org/10.1017/s0033291717002653

Bize, R., Johnson, J. A., & Plotnikoff, R. C. (2007). Physical activity level and health-related quality of life in the general adult population: A systematic review. *Preventive Medicine*, *45*(6), 401–415. https://doi.org/10.1016/j.ypmed.2007.07.017

Chekroud, S. R., Gueorguieva, R., Zheutlin, A. B., Paulus, M., Krumholz, H. M., Krystal, J. H., & Chekroud, A. M. (2018). Association between physical exercise and mental health in 1·2 million individuals in the USA between 2011 and 2015: A cross-sectional study. *The Lancet Psychiatry, 5*, 739–746. https://doi.org/10.1016/S2215-0366(18)30227-X

Colcombe, S., & Kramer, A. F. (2003). Fitness effects on the cognitive function of older adults: A meta-analytic study. *Psychological Science*, *14*(2), 125e130. https://doi.org/10.1111/1467-9280.t01-1-01430

Farholm, A., & Sørensen, M. (2016). Motivation for physical activity and exercise in severe mental illness: A systematic review of intervention studies. *International Journal of Mental Health Nursing, 25*(3), 194–205. https://doi.org/10.1111/inm.12214

Faulkner, G., & Biddle, S. J. H. (2004). Exercise and depression: Considering variability and contextuality. *Journal of Sport & Exercise Psychology, 26*(1), 3–18. https://doi.org/10.1123/jsep.26.1.3

Firth, J., Siddiqi, N., Koyanagi, A., Siskind, D., Rosenbaum, S., Galletly, C., Allan, S., Caneo, C., Carney, R., Carvalho, A. F., Chatterton, M. L., Correll, C. U., Curtis, J., Gaughran, F., Heald, A., Hoare, E., Jackson, S. E., Kisely, S., Lovell, K., … Stubbs, B. (2019). The lancet psychiatry commission: A blueprint for protecting physical health in people with mental illness. *The Lancet. Psychiatry*, *6*(8), 675–712. https://doi.org/10.1016/S2215-0366(19)30132-4

Kuwahara, K., Honda, T., Nakagawa, T., Yamamoto, S., Akter, S., Hayashi, T., & Mizoue, T. (2015). Associations of leisure-time, occupational, and commuting physical activity with risk of depressive symptoms among Japanese workers: A cohort study. *International Journal of Behavioral Nutrition and Physical Activity, 12*, 119. https://doi.org/10.1186/s12966-015-0283-4

Mason, P., Curl, A., & Kearns, A. (2016). Domains and levels of physical activity are linked to adult mental health and wellbeing in deprived neighbourhoods: A cross-sectional study. *Mental Health and Physical Activity, 11*, 19–28. https://doi.org/ 10.1016/j.mhpa.2016.07.001

Maxwell, J. A. (2004). Causal explanation, qualitative research, and scientific inquiry in education. *Educational Researcher*, *33*(2), 3–11. https://doi.org/10.3102/0013189X033002003

Nwosu, C. O. (2018). The relationship between employment and mental and physical health in South Africa. *Development Southern Africa*, *35*(2), 145–162. https://doi.org/10.1080/0376835X.2017.1392847

Okasha, A. (2002). Mental health in Africa: The role of the WPA. *World Psychiatry*, *1*(1), 32.

Osei, E. (2024). Impact of physical activity on mental health among adolescents in Ghana. *European Journal of Health Sciences*, *10*(4), 15–26. https://doi.org/10.47672/ejhs.2188

Peltzer, K. (2010). Leisure time physical activity and sedentary behavior and substance use among in-school adolescents in eight African countries. *International Journal of Behavioral Medicine*, *17*(4), 271–278. https://doi.org/10.1007/s12529-009-9073-1

Puetz, T. W., O'Connor, P. J., & Dishman, R. K. (2006). Effects of chronic exercise on feelings of energy and fatigue: A quantitative synthesis. *Psychological Bulletin*, *132*(6), 866–876. https://doi.org/10.1037/0033-2909.132.6.866

Rebar, A. L., Stanton, R., Geard, D., Short, C., Duncan, M. J., & Vandelanotte, C. (2015). A meta-meta-analysis of the effect of physical activity on depression and anxiety in non-clinical adult populations. *Health Psychology Review,* 9(3), 366–378. https://doi.org/10.1080/17437199.2015.1022901

Rethorst, C. D., Wipfli, B. M., & Landers, D. M. (2009). The anti-depressive effects of exercise: A meta-analysis of randomized trials. *Sports Medicine*, *39*(6), 491–511. https://doi.org/10.2165/00007256-200939060-00004

Roessler, K. K., Bramsen, R. H., Dervisevic, A., & Bilberg, R. (2017). Exercise based interventions for alcohol use disorder: A comment on motivational aspects of participation. *Scandinavian Journal of Psychology*, *58*(1), 23–28. https://doi.org/10.1111/sjop.12334

Rosenbaum, S., Tiedemann, A., Ward, P. B., Curtis, J., & Sherrington, C. (2015). Physical activity interventions: An essential component in recovery from mental illness. *British Journal of Sports Medicine*, *49*(24), 1544–1545. https://doi.org/10.1136/bjsports-2014-094314

Sankoh, O., Sevalie, S., & Weston, M. (2018). Mental health in Africa. *The Lancet. Global Health.* 6(9), 954–955. https://doi.org/10.1016/s2214-109x(18)30303-6

Schuch, F. B., Vancampfort, D., Firth, J., Rosenbaum, S., Ward, P. B., Silva, E. S., Hallgren, M., Ponce De Leon, A., Dunn, A. L., Deslandes, A. C., Fleck, M. P., Carvalho, A. F., & Stubbs, B. (2018). Physical activity and incident depression: A meta-analysis of prospective cohort studies. *American Journal of Psychiatry, 175*, 631–648. https://doi.org/10.1176/appi.ajp.2018.17111194

Schuch, F., Vancampfort, D., Firth, J., Rosenbaum, S., Ward, P., Reichert, T., Bagatini, N. C., Bgeginski, R., & Stubbs, B. (2017). Physical activity and sedentary behavior in people with major depressive disorder: A systematic review and meta-analysis. *Journal of Affective Disorders*, *210*, 139–150. https://doi.org/10.1016/j.jad.2016.10.050

Seekles, M., Twagira, F., Alam, A., & Obasi, A. (2023). Promotive and preventive interventions for adolescent mental health in Sub-Saharan Africa: A combined scoping and systematic review. *BMJ Public Health*, *1*(1), e000037. https://doi.org/10.1136/bmjph-2023-000037

Spence, J. C., McGannon, K. R., & Poon, P. L. (2005). The effect of exercise on global self-esteem: A quantitative review. *Journal of Sport & Exercise Psychology, 27*, 311–334. https://doi.org/10.1123/JSEP.27.3.311

Stubbs, B., Vancampfort, D., Firth, J., Solmi, M., Siddiqi, N., Smith, L., Carvalho, A. F., & Koyanagi, A. (2018). Association between depression and smoking: A global perspective from 48 low- and middle-income countries. *Journal of Psychiatric Research, 103*, 142–149. https://doi.org/10.1016/j.jpsychires.2018.05.018

Taylor, A. H. (2000). Physical activity, anxiety, and stress. In S. J. H. Biddle, K. R. Fox, & S. H. Boucher (Eds.), *Physical activity and psychological well-being* (pp. 130e153). Routledge London.

Taylor, A. H., & Faulkner, G. (2008). Inaugural editorial. *Mental Health & Physical Activity*, *1*, 1–8.

Ugwueze, F. C., Agbaje, O. S., Umoke, P. C. I., & Ozoemena, E. L. (2021). Relationship between physical activity levels and psychological well-being among male university students in South East, Nigeria: A cross-sectional study. *American Journal of Men's Health*, *15*(2), 15579883211008337. https://doi.org/10.1177/15579883211008337

Vancampfort, D., Stubbs, B., De Hert, M., du Plessis, C., Gbiri, C. A. O., Kibet, J., Wanyonyi, N., & Mugisha, J. (2017). A systematic review of physical activity policy recommendations and interventions for people with mental health problems in Sub-Saharan African countries. *Pan African Medical Journal*, *26*, 104. https://doi.org/10.11604/pamj.2017.26.104.10051

Vittengl, J. R. (2021). Does context moderate physical activity's relations with depression?: A cross-sectional study. *Mental Health and Physical Activity, 20*, 100374. https://doi.org/10.1016/j.mhpa.2020.100374

Werneck, A. O., Oyeyemi, A. L., & Silva, D. R. (2018). Physical activity and depression: Is 150 min/week of moderate to vigorous physical activity a necessary threshold for decreasing risk of depression in adults? Different views from the same data. *Social Psychiatry and Psychiatric Epidemiology, 53*, 323–324. https://doi.org/10.1007/ s00127-018-1490–5

White, R. L., Babic, M. J., Parker, P. D., Lubans, D. R., Astell-Burt, T., & Lonsdale, C. (2017). Domain-specific physical activity and mental health: A meta-analysis. *American Journal of Preventive Medicine, 52*, 653–666. https://doi.org/10.1016/j. amepre.2016.12.008

World Health Organization. (2017). *Mental health included in the UN Sustainable Development Goals*.

Youngstedt, S. D., & Kline, C. E. (2006). Epidemiology of exercise and sleep. *Sleep and Biological Rhythms*, *4*(3), 215–221. https://doi.org/10.1111/j.1479-8425.2006.00235.x

Zealand, D. (2008). Physical activity and self-esteem: A Namibian youth perspective. *Trends Psychiatry Psychotherapy, 43*(3). https://doi.org/10.47626/2237-6089-2021-0237

11

PROMOTING MENTAL HEALTH THROUGH PHYSICAL ACTIVITY AND SPORT IN OCEANIA

Stewart A. Vella, Caitlin Liddelow, Matthew J. Schweickle, Kurtis Pankow and Jordan T. Sutcliffe

11.1 Preface

The personal and economic costs of mental disorders are astronomical. A total of over 400 million disability-adjusted life years were attributable to mental disorders globally in 2019 (Arias et al., 2022) – approximately 16% of the global total of disability-adjusted life years. This costs the global economy approximately US$5 trillion (Arias et al., 2022). In Oceania, approximately 12% of all disability-adjusted life years are attributable to mental disorders with an associated economic burden of over 5% of total gross domestic product (Arias et al., 2022). This is in addition to the substantial personal, emotional and social costs of mental disorders, which can be both lifelong and debilitative. These personal and economic costs underscore the urgency to implement effective interventions for the promotion and protection of mental health globally.

Sport and physical activity have been promoted as potentially engaging and effective means to promote mental health and well-being, prevent mental health problems and treat mental disorders (Firth et al., 2020; Stubbs et al., 2018; Swann et al., 2018). For example, the European Psychiatry Association and the International Organization of Physical Therapists in Mental Health have published guidance on the use of physical activity in the treatment of mental illness (Stubbs et al., 2018). Similarly, there have been calls for systematic and actionable guidelines to promote mental health and prevent mental health problems within recreational sport systems globally (Vella & Swann, 2021). For example, in Australia, childhood maltreatment is responsible for over 1.8 million preventable cases of mental disorders (Grummitt et al., 2024), with urgent action needed to address childhood maltreatment and mental ill-health in the environments where young people spend their time. Sport participation is one of the most popular and time-consuming

DOI: 10.4324/9781003517474-16

activities for children and young people in Oceania and globally (Hulteen et al., 2017), making it a key area to target to improve children's and young people's mental health outcomes. Moreover, sport participation in Australia and elsewhere has been reported to have alarmingly high rates of maltreatment, including psychological abuse (Pankowiak et al., 2023). As such, mental health guidelines for sport are also urgently needed.

This chapter will address the evidence-based ways in which sport and physical activity can be used to promote mental health and well-being and prevent mental health disorders with a focus on major initiatives underway in Oceania. To do so, we will treat sport and physical activity separately, although sport is a subset of the broader category of physical activity (Khan et al., 2012). Specifically, we will exemplify initiatives specific to physical activity by reference to a joint consensus statement between Sports Medicine Australia and the Australian Psychological Society on optimising the effects of physical activity on mental health and well-being. We will then exemplify sport-based initiatives by using the Australian mental health guidelines for recreational sport as a case study of mental health promotion through sport. For both examples, we will provide a summary of the existing literature, followed by a detailed discussion of the two specific initiatives, including their key findings and limitations. Finally, we will articulate some of the major implications that stem from each approach. We deal first with physical activity, followed by sport participation.

11.2 Optimising the Effects of Physical Activity on Mental Health and Well-Being

11.2.1 A Summary of Existing Literature

Over recent decades, physical activity has become an increasingly accepted intervention to promote mental health and well-being (Firth et al., 2020). It has also become increasingly accepted as a treatment for mental health disorders (Rosenbaum et al., 2014). For example, there is strong evidence that engaging in physical activity can be beneficial in reducing the symptoms of both depression and anxiety (McDowell et al., 2019; Schuch et al., 2016). As a result, practitioners such as psychologists, general practitioners and other allied health professionals are being guided to promote physical activity as a strategy to enhance mental health and well-being (e.g., Stubbs et al., 2018). To guide their prescriptions for physical activity, most practitioners rely on the relevant physical activity guidelines.

Physical activity guidelines are evidence-based recommendations for the minimum frequency, intensity and duration of physical activity necessary for health benefits. Physical activity guidelines have been developed and endorsed by the World Health Organization (2020). In addition, many countries around the world have endorsed their own set of national physical activity guidelines. For example, Australia has endorsed national physical activity guidelines for children and young people, adults and older adults (e.g., Australian Government Department of Health, 2021).

More recently, countries such as Australia and Canada have updated their physical activity guidelines and moved towards a set of 24-hour movement guidelines that incorporate recommendations for physical activity, sedentary behaviour and sleep (Tremblay et al., 2016).

All physical activity guidelines globally focus on the frequency, intensity, duration and type of activity that should be undertaken for health benefits. For example, the World Health Organization's physical activity guidelines for adults (2020) stipulate that

> Adults should do at least 150–300 minutes of moderate-intensity aerobic physical activity; or at least 75–150 minutes of vigorous-intensity aerobic physical activity; or an equivalent combination of moderate- and vigorous-intensity activity throughout the week, for substantial health benefits.

Similarly, the Australian Physical Activity Guidelines stipulate that

> Adults should be active most days, preferably every day. Each week, adults should do either: 2.5 to 5 hours of moderate intensity physical activity – such as a brisk walk, golf, mowing the lawn or swimming; 1.25 to 2.5 hours of vigorous intensity physical activity – such as jogging, aerobics, fast cycling, soccer or netball; or, an equivalent combination of moderate and vigorous activities.
>
> *(Australian Government Department of Health, 2021)*

Such recommendations are based on an extensive evidence base which has been regularly reviewed and updated over the last decade during the process of writing physical activity guidelines (e.g. Warburton et al., 2010).

11.2.2 The Most Recent and Relevant Research

The exclusive focus of physical activity guidelines on the frequency, duration and intensity of physical activity for health benefits implies that the benefits derived from physical activity are mostly physiological in nature. However, this may not be the case when it comes to the mental health benefits of physical activity (e.g., White et al., 2017). For example, in a review of the mechanisms through which physical activity may enhance mental health, Lubans et al. (2016) hypothesised three major categories of potential mechanisms: neurobiological mechanisms, psychosocial mechanisms, and behavioural mechanisms. Neurobiological mechanisms improve mental health via changes in the structural and functional composition of the brain such as increased volume and activation of grey matter, as well as the release of endogenous opioids and their interaction with neurotransmitter systems. Psychosocial mechanisms include greater social interaction, enhanced mood and emotions, and better physical self-concept. Behavioural mechanisms include better quality and quantity of sleep, as well as enhanced coping and self-regulation skills.

An acknowledgement of the diversity of mechanisms through which physical activity may provide mental health benefits extends the focus from the quantitative characteristics of physical activity (its frequency, intensity and duration) towards some of the qualitative characteristics of physical activity. As noted by Teychenne et al. (2020):

> given that evidence has shown that the relationship between physical activity and mental health/ill-health is likely to, in part, be influenced by contextual factors across the lifespan (e.g. domain of physical activity), there is a need to extend the focus/scope of existing physical activity guidelines to ensure they effectively address mental health.
>
> *(p. 1).*

The contextual or qualitative characteristics of physical activity include, but are not limited to, the type of activity, the way in which it is delivered, the social and physical environment in which it takes place, and the domain of life in which it occurs (Vella et al., 2023). A recent systematic review of reviews identified that variations in the contextual factors of physical activity can enhance the effect of physical activity on mental health and well-being (Vella et al., 2023).

Vella et al. (2023) have defined five distinct contextual factors that may influence the mental health outcomes of physical activity. These are: (1) the type of physical activity (e.g., aerobic versus resistance exercise, or sport participation); (2) the quality of the delivery of physical activity (e.g., instructional style, mode of delivery, supervised versus self-initiated physical activity); (3) the social environment in which physical activity is undertaken (e.g., group or team versus individual participation, participation with friends); (4) the physical environment in which physical activity is undertaken (e.g., indoor vs. outdoor environments; green or blue space vs. man-made environments); and (5) the domain of life in which physical activity occurs (e.g., leisure time versus occupational physical activity).

With regard to the type of physical activity, there is consistent evidence across systematic reviews and meta-analyses that many different types of physical activity can facilitate mental health benefits. These include aerobic, resistance (Gordon et al., 2017, 2018), high-intensity interval training (Martland et al., 2020), mind-body exercise such as yoga and pilates (Brinsley et al., 2021; Fleming & Herring, 2018) and sport (Eime et al., 2013). Further, these types of activities also have an effect on a broad range of mental health outcomes among the general population, and among people with clinical and sub-clinical mental health disorders. This led Vella et al. (2023) to conclude that

> the type of physical activity likely has no meaningful effect on mental health independent of its quantitative characteristics (i.e., its frequency, intensity, and duration) or other contextual factors such as the social and physical environment. As such, the type of physical activity (to optimise mental health benefits)

> should be selected based on personal preference and other factors which are likely to lead to greater long-term adherence and better mental health.
>
> *(p. 135)*

Evidence from coaching in youth sports, as well as the delivery of physical education lessons suggests that the delivery (i.e., instructional or pedagogical style, coaching behaviours) of organised physical activity has an impact on mental health outcomes. This may also extend to the level of supervision (i.e., supervised or self-initiated) and delivery mode (e.g., face-to-face, online live or pre-recorded). For example, there is extensive evidence on the benefits of appropriate motivational climates and autonomy-supportive environments on mental health and well-being in sport and physical education (Occhino et al., 2014; Saugy et al., 2020; Solmi et al., 2022). Indeed, this is consistent with several psychological frameworks which hypothesise that leader behaviours that satisfy one's need for social connection, autonomy, self-acceptance, environmental mastery and purpose in life, can lead to improvements in mental health and well-being (Deci & Ryan, 2002; Nicholls, 1984; Ryff & Keyes, 1995).

Increased social connection is one key mechanism through which physical activity may influence mental health (Lubans et al., 2016). In regard to physical activity, social interactions and interpersonal relationships have been studied in the form of constructs such as social support, social connection and social networks – which have been shown to mediate the effects of physical activity on mental health (Conley et al., 2020; Oberle et al., 2019). Underpinning this hypothesis is a range of consistent findings such as the benefits of team sport participation over and above those of participation in individual sports (Eime et al., 2013). Further, those who undertake at least some of their physical activity with others have lower odds of experiencing depressive symptoms than those who complete all their physical activity alone (Teychenne et al., 2020). Importantly, undertaking physical activity with others may even enhance the beneficial effects of other contextual factors such as being physically active outside in green or blue space (Wicks et al., 2022). As such, social support during physical activity can strengthen the beneficial effects on depression and distress (Gyasi, 2019; Moya et al., 2021). The conclusion is that the quality of social interactions during physical activity strengthens mental health outcomes. Social interactions may also improve mental health by facilitating increased adherence to physical activity over time.

In regard to the physical environment in which physical activity takes place, the simplest and most common distinction is between physical activity undertaken indoors and outdoors. On this distinction, there is consistent evidence that physical activity undertaken outdoors has a larger beneficial effect on a range of mental health outcomes, when compared with physical activity undertaken indoors (Wicks et al., 2022). However, further distinctions can be made with regard to outdoor environments, and include green space (e.g., parks and reserves), blue space (i.e., environments that include water) or man-made and urban structures. Evidence is emerging that demonstrates that green and blue spaces have greater benefits for mental health – including depression, anxiety, vigour and affect – when compared with man-made environments (Wicks et al., 2022). Indeed, some theoretical frameworks have emerged and can explain such findings, including 'Stress Recovery Theory' and 'Attention Restoration Theory' (Frumkin et al., 2017). Although robust evidence is still emerging in this field, there is some reason to conclude that natural environments have greater benefits for mental health than indoor environments when it comes to physical activity.

Typically, the domain of physical activity refers to a life domain such as leisure time (i.e., free time), active transport (i.e., being physically active in order to travel somewhere), domestic (e.g., household activities), occupational (e.g., being active for work) and school (e.g., during physical education, recess or lunch times). There is good evidence to suggest that the domain of life in which physical activity is undertaken can influence mental health outcomes (White et al., 2017). Of all domains, only leisure-time physical activity has been consistently associated with better mental health outcomes. This suggests that physical activity undertaken during leisure time may be most optimal for mental health promotion. While the exact reason for this is somewhat unclear, it could be that leisure-time physical activity is voluntary in nature whereby one is free to choose if and when to be physically active, which activity to do, where to do it and with whom to do it. In this way, leisure-time physical activity may serve to optimise the effects of physical activity on mental health by allowing individuals to choose the most beneficial contextual factors for themselves, thereby maximising motivation, enjoyment, self-efficacy and social support.

Limitations of this body of research exist. The major limitation is that studies have rarely made direct comparisons between aspects within a given contextual factor. More high-quality studies are needed to compare the various derivatives of contextual factors in order to have greater confidence in the ways that physical activity is prescribed to optimise mental health. For example, studies that compare physical activity in blue versus green versus man-made environments can shed light on the most influential physical environment in which to undertake physical activity. Similarly, studies that compare physical activity undertaken in various life domains or different social environments are also needed.

11.2.3 Implications

The implication of this body of research related to the contextual factors of physical activity is that they are important considerations when seeking to optimise the effects of physical activity on mental health. Consideration should be given to each contextual factor as an addition to those quantitative aspects of physical activity prescribed in physical activity guidelines. To guide practitioners in doing so, the Australian Psychological Society and Sports Medicine Australia produced a joint consensus statement to help guide practitioners – including psychologists and other sports practitioners – as to the ways in which physical activity could be undertaken to optimise its impact on mental health and well-being. In that statement, the five contextual factors of physical activity were addressed via distinct recommendations. Those recommendations are as follows (quoted from Vella et al., 2023, p. 137):

1 Type of physical activity: Activity selection be guided by factors associated with adherence and enjoyment as opposed to any specific type. Practitioners should also focus on factors such as access, client/patient preference and physical activity history.
2 Delivery of physical activity: Facilitators (i.e., teachers, coaches, instructors, practitioners) deliver organised physical activity sessions using an instructional style that satisfies individuals' basic psychological needs, most importantly the need for autonomy and social connection. At a minimum, design principles for such instructional style should include engaging participants' perspectives/preferences, offering choice and minimising pressure. We also recommend the use of supervised physical activity sessions for clinical populations, which appear to be more beneficial than unsupervised sessions.
3 Social environment: Engaging in some physical activity with others who provide support, facilitate positive interactions or make people feel valued, so long as it does not undermine a preference to be active alone.
4 Physical environment: Where possible and appropriate, some physical activity be undertaken outside in pleasant natural environments (e.g., green or blue spaces).
5 Domain: At least some physical activity is undertaken during leisure time, where possible prioritising activities one enjoys or personally chooses to undertake.

11.2.4 Conclusion

Physical activity is an evidence-based way to promote mental health and prevent mental health problems. The focus of physical activity guidelines has been solely on the quantitative aspects of physical activity, including its frequency, intensity and duration. However, the contextual factors of physical activity – the type of activity, its delivery, social environment, physical environment and the domain of life in which it is undertaken – all influence mental health outcomes. A greater focus on these factors is needed in research and in practice. To bring a focus to these contextual factors and optimise the mental health benefits of physical activity, the Australian Psychological Society and Sports Medicine Australia delivered a set of recommendations to guide practitioners in the prescription of physical activity for mental health. On this basis, practitioners are recommended to prescribe: A type of physical activity that one enjoys and can adhere to over the long term; at least some physical activity with valued others; at least some physical activity in natural spaces; at some physical activity during leisure time; and, the delivery of physical activity to meet psychological needs. A greater focus on comparing and contrasting aspects of these contextual factors of physical activity is needed.

11.3 Optimising the Effects of Sport Participation on Mental Health and Well-Being

11.3.1 *A Summary of the Existing Literature*

There has been a growing focus on the promotion of mental health and the prevention of mental health problems in organised sports over recent years. A plethora of evidence has emerged to suggest that, on balance, participation in organised sports is associated with better mental health and well-being, when compared with dropout or nonparticipation (Eime et al., 2013; Panza et al., 2020). There is also some evidence that the amount of time spent in sport is related to lowered symptoms of mental health problems (Panza et al., 2020). Team sports participation has been consistently shown to be associated with greater mental health benefits than individual sports (Eime et al., 2013); however, this distinction may be rather arbitrary given that most individual sports are largely undertaken in groups (Panza et al., 2020). There is also some suggestion that the benefits of sports may differ by sex (Panza et al., 2020).

Despite the consistency of the evidence base, there are some legitimate criticisms of the current state of knowledge. Primarily, the reliance on cross-sectional and longitudinal cohort studies precludes any causal assertions with regard to the role of sport in the promotion of mental health (Vella, 2019). For instance, there is evidence to suggest that the relationship between sport participation and mental health is bidirectional in nature, with young people who report better mental health being more likely to participate in sport over time, and vice versa (Vella et al., 2017). At the very least these findings suggest that the relationship between sport participation and mental health is more complex than a simple, causal relationship. In addition, even if the relationship between sports participation and mental health was causal, it is unclear exactly what mechanisms are responsible for driving such benefits. Physical activity, social interaction, being outside in green and blue space, as well as learning skills such as emotion regulation could all be possible mechanisms through which sport can lead to better mental health. However, the vast difficulties in obtaining causal evidence preclude robust evidence upon which to test such hypotheses (Vella, 2019). Furthermore, there is some difficulty in measuring sport participation. There are various measures available which may result in variations in the effect of sport participation, and range from dichotomous items regarding participation, time spent in sport, the number of teams participated on and estimates of total sport participation. Reconciling these discrepancies is an important step in providing a consistent evidence base on the influence of sport participation on mental health.

There is also evidence of substantial harms associated with participation in organised sports. In an Australian sample of youth sport participants, 82% reported being the victim of some form of interpersonal violence (Pankowiak et al., 2023). The most commonly reported form of interpersonal violence was psychological abuse at 76%. These levels are alarming because of their magnitude, but also because of the severe consequences associated with psychological abuse, and the consistency with which these rates are reported worldwide. For example, in a sample of Canadian youth sport participants, the rate of reported psychological abuse was 54% (Parent et al., 2023). Rates of reported abuse were high, including those perpetrated by coaches (41%), peers (38%) and parents (25%). Therefore, sports organisations must look for prevent the onset of mental health problems in sport through coordinated policy and practice action.

11.3.2 The Most Recent and Relevant Research

In 2016, a review of sports organisations' websites showed that there was little being done in Australia in the area of mental health and sport (Liddle et al., 2017). In addition, where there was action being taken, it was rarely evidence-informed and also lacked evidence in regard to its efficacy or effectiveness (Liddle et al., 2017). However, in recent years, much has changed in this regard. For example, global events such as the Rugby League World Cup 2021/2022 had an official 'Mental Fitness Charter' with targeted population-wide benefits for mental health on the back of coordinated actions during the tournament. At a national level, governing bodies such as the Australian Football League have also put a Mental Fitness Charter in place, which includes a 'quick win action plan' for community AFL clubs (Hall et al., 2024). The Western Australian government has put a Mental Health and Wellbeing Community Sport Framework in place (n.d.), while the South Australian Government has developed a Mental Fitness Charter for Sport (2022). Such actions have added to the toolkit available to community sports clubs in Australia to enable them to take action on mental health. However, many states and national sports organisations still lack relevant and actionable guidance that will allow community sports organisations to promote mental health and well-being and prevent the onset of mental health problems.

To provide such guidance, recent calls have been made to provide clear and actionable guidelines for the promotion and protection of mental health in recreational sports. In order to do so, a system-based approach is needed (Vella et al., 2022). A system-based approach recognises the role of all components within the sports system, including national sports organisations and government bodies, community sport organisations, regional governing and administrative bodies and individuals such as coaches, parents and participants. Central to a systems-based approach is the consensus that the role of sport organisations is (alongside the provisions of sporting programmes) to promote mental health and well-being and prevent mental health problems (Vella et al., 2022). Once such a consensus is in place, coordinated action among all components of the system is necessary to achieve meaningful change. While governing bodies have begun to put in place things such as Mental Fitness Charters, community sports clubs report being under-resourced, under-trained and lacking the knowledge to put in place even basic strategies to provide a safe and healthy environment for all participants (Finch & Donaldson, 2010).

One way of achieving system-wide consensus and change is through the implementation of mental health guidelines. Guidelines in the form of position statements, position stands and consensus statements have become common in the field of mental health and sport. In a recent review and meta-synthesis, a number of key areas that were addressed by a growing number of mental health guidelines in sport were articulated (Vella et al., 2021). Those areas include having a written mental health plan, the provision of mental health care, putting athlete support systems in place and dealing with high-risk events. To supplement these findings, a Delphi study of Australian experts led to eight key recommendations concerning mental health promotion in community sport (Liddelow et al., 2024). First, mandatory mental health literacy training was recommended for all adults who work with young people. Second, mandatory mental health literacy training was recommended for those people in the sports organisation who occupy a role of mental health officer (or similar). Third, community sports organisations should offer non-mandatory mental health literacy training to all members. Fourth, sports clubs are recommended to normalise conversations about mental health and provide a safe space for those conversations to occur. Fifth, the sports environment should be free from psychological harm. Sixth, sports organisations should foster a well-being-enhancing environment that includes physical activity, social connection and inclusivity. Seventh, evidence-based approaches to coaching are recommended to be offered to all coaches. Finally, adults involved in community sports clubs need to know how to recognise and refer individuals to appropriate mental health service providers.

The key limitation to this line of research is the lack of involvement of key stakeholders in the process of articulating recommendations for action on mental health. For example, participants, coaches and administrators have rarely been included in the development of such recommendations, in favour of expert opinion. For any form of mental health guideline to be actionable and effective, it must be appropriate for the prevailing culture of sports, be actionable within the resources and programming available to sports clubs and organisations and incorporate sports clubs' preferences and capabilities with regard to their implementation (Donaldson et al., 2012).

11.3.3 Implications

In addressing the limitations of previous research, a co-design process was undertaken in order to write National Mental Health Guidelines for Community Sport in Australia (Liddelow et al., 2022). The guidelines were developed based on a foundation of evidence-synthesis of existing mental health position statements and intervention in community sport (Vella et al., 2021; Sutcliffe et al., 2024), expert opinion (Liddelow et al., 2024) and key stakeholder involvement via focus groups that included participants, parents, officials and administrators. In total, nine guidelines were developed to promote mental health and prevent mental health problems (Vella et al., 2025). These guidelines are that:

1 Promoting Well-Being: Community sport organisations demonstrate a commitment to enhancing the well-being of everybody involved in the club.
2 Reducing Mental Health Stigma: Community sport organisations demonstrate an ongoing commitment to promoting positive attitudes about mental health.
3 Promoting Coach Development: Community sport organisations support their coaches to participate in ongoing coach development in methods that promote safe/supportive coaching.
4 Increasing Mental Health Literacy: Community sport organisations demonstrate a commitment to enhancing the mental health literacy of their key stakeholders.
5 Locating Appropriate Help: Community sport organisations need to demonstrate an awareness on what appropriate mental health services are available and how to access them.
6 Responding to a Mental Health Emergency: Community sport organisations have a plan for how to respond to an identified mental health emergency (e.g., risk or suicide or harm to self/others).
7 Responding to Major Events that May Impact Mental Health: Community sport organisations have a plan for how to respond to major events or critical incidents that may impact the psychological well-being of their members.
8 Implementing a Mental Health Champion: Community sport organisations and clubs have a mental health champion who actively oversees and contributes to the implementation of the mental health guidelines.
9 Developing a Mental Health Action Plan: Community sport organisations have a completed up-to-date mental health action plan outlining how they will prevent, promote and respond to mental health and well-being in sport.

These guidelines have been tested via focus groups with key stakeholders from community sporting clubs in Australia, but need to be further tested for their feasibility of implementation and their impact on a suite of outcomes, including mental health. It is imperative that such initiatives gather robust evidence for their effectiveness (or otherwise), which should include evidence as to the ability of community sport organisations to implement the guidelines, the resources needed to do so, the effectiveness of implementation efforts in promoting mental health and preventing mental health problems within the sport organisation, and the broader intended and unintended consequences of implementation for things such as club culture.

11.3.4 Conclusion

Globally, participation in recreational sports is high, and is particularly high across high income countries (Aubert et al., 2020). While sport participation is, on balance, associated with better mental health and well-being, the causal mechanisms are not well understood. In addition, there are obvious harms associated with participation in organised recreational sports that include alarmingly high rates of psychological and other abuses. To enable community sport organisations to fulfil their promise in promoting mental health and preventing the onset of mental health problems, a participatory approach to developing a set of national mental health guidelines was undertaken in Australia. The final set of nine guidelines contained recommendation in the areas of: Promoting Well-Being; Reducing Mental Health Stigma; Promoting Coach Development; Increasing Mental Health Literacy; Locating Appropriate Help; Responding to a Mental Health Emergency; Responding to Major Events that May Impact Mental Health; Implementing a Mental Health Champion; and, Developing a Mental Health Action Plan (Vella et al., 2025). These guidelines require further testing, especially around their implementation and the effects of implementation efforts on intended and unintended outcomes. However, the guidelines present a novel, unifying framework through which to promote mental health and well-being in community sports in Australia.

References

Arias, D., Saxena, S., & Verguet, S. (2022). Quantifying the global burden of mental disorders and their economic value. *EClinicalMedicine*, *54*, 101675. https://doi.org/10.1016/j.eclinm.2022.101675

Aubert, S., Aucouturier, J., Vanhelst, J., Fillon, A., Genin, P., Ganière, C., … & Thivel, D. (2020). France's 2018 report card on physical activity for children and youth: Results and international comparisons. *Journal of Physical Activity and Health*, *17*(3), 270–277. https://doi.org/10.1123/jpah.2019-0241

Australian Government Department of Health. (2021). *Australia's physical activity and sedentary behaviour guidelines: Fact sheet: Adults (18–64 years)*.

Brinsley, J., Schuch, F., Lederman, O., Girard, D., Smout, M., Immink, M. A., … & Rosenbaum, S. (2021). Effects of yoga on depressive symptoms in people with mental disorders: A systematic review and meta-analysis. *British Journal of Sports Medicine*, *55*(17), 992–1000. https://doi.org/10.1136/bjsports-2019-101242

Conley, M. I., Hindley, I., Baskin-Sommers, A., Gee, D. G., Casey, B. J., & Rosenberg, M. D. (2020). The importance of social factors in the association between physical activity and depression in children. *Child and Adolescent Psychiatry and Mental Health*, *14*, 28. https://doi.org/10.1186/s13034-020-00335-5

Deci, E. L., & Ryan, R. M. (Eds.). (2002). *Handbook of self-determination research*. University Rochester Press.

Donaldson, A., Leggett, S., & Finch, C. F. (2012). Sports policy development and implementation in context: Researching and understanding the perceptions of community end-users. *International Review of the Sociology of Sport*, *47*(6), 743–760. https://doi.org/10.1177/1012690211422009

Eime, R. M., Young, J. A., Harvey, J. T., Charity, M. J., & Payne, W. R. (2013). A systematic review of the psychological and social benefits of participation in sport for children and adolescents: Informing development of a conceptual model of health through sport.

International Journal of Behavioral Nutrition and Physical Activity, *10*, 98. https://doi.org/10.1186/1479-5868-10-98

Finch, C. F., & Donaldson, A. (2010). A sports setting matrix for understanding the implementation context for community sport. *British Journal of Sports Medicine*, *44*(13), 973–978. https://doi.org/10.1136/bjsm.2008.056069

Firth, J., Solmi, M., Wootton, R. E., Vancampfort, D., Schuch, F. B., Hoare, E., ... & Stubbs, B. (2020). A meta-review of "lifestyle psychiatry": The role of exercise, smoking, diet and sleep in the prevention and treatment of mental disorders. *World Psychiatry*, *19*(3), 360–380. https://doi.org/10.1002/wps.20773

Fleming, K. M., & Herring, M. P. (2018). The effects of pilates on mental health outcomes: A meta-analysis of controlled trials. *Complementary Therapies in Medicine*, *37*, 80–95. https://doi.org/10.1016/j.ctim.2018.02.003

Frumkin, H., Bratman, G. N., Breslow, S. J., Cochran, B., Kahn Jr, P. H., Lawler, J. J., ... & Wood, S. A. (2017). Nature contact and human health: A research agenda. *Environmental Health Perspectives*, *125*(7), 075001. https://doi.org/10.1289/EHP1663

Gordon, B. R., McDowell, C. P., Hallgren, M., Meyer, J. D., Lyons, M., & Herring, M. P. (2018). Association of efficacy of resistance exercise training with depressive symptoms: Meta-analysis and meta-regression analysis of randomized clinical trials. *JAMA Psychiatry*, *75*(6), 566–576. https://doi.org/10.1001/jamapsychiatry.2018.0572

Gordon, B. R., McDowell, C. P., Lyons, M., & Herring, M. P. (2017). The effects of resistance exercise training on anxiety: A meta-analysis and meta-regression analysis of randomized controlled trials. *Sports Medicine*, *47*, 2521–2532. https://doi.org/10.1007/s40279-017-0769-0

Grummitt, L., Baldwin, J. R., Lafoa'i, J., Keyes, K. M., & Barrett, E. L. (2024). Burden of mental disorders and suicide attributable to childhood maltreatment. *JAMA Psychiatry*, *81*(8), 782–788. https://doi.org/10.1001/jamapsychiatry.2024.0804

Gyasi, R. M. (2019). Social support, physical activity and psychological distress among community-dwelling older Ghanaians. *Archives of Gerontology and Geriatrics*, *81*, 142–148. https://doi.org/10.1016/j.archger.2018.11.016

Hall, K., Harris, E., Couston, N., Godfrey, S., & Hoare, E. (2024). *AFL Mental Fitness Charter 2024–2027*. Australian Football League.

Hulteen, R. M., Smith, J. J., Morgan, P. J., Barnett, L. M., Hallal, P. C., Colyvas, K., & Lubans, D. R. (2017). Global participation in sport and leisure-time physical activities: A systematic review and meta-analysis. *Preventive Medicine*, *95*, 14–25. https://doi.org/10.1016/J.YPMED.2016.11.027

Khan, K. M., Thompson, A. M., Blair, S. N., Sallis, J. F., Powell, K. E., Bull, F. C., & Bauman, A. E. (2012). Sport and exercise as contributors to the health of nations. *The Lancet*, *380*(9836), 59–64. https://doi.org/10.1016/S0140-6736(12)60865-4

Liddelow, C., Schweickle, M. J., Sutcliffe, J. T., Swann, C., Keegan, R., Rice, S., Okely, A. D., & Vella, S. A. (2022). Protocol for national mental health guidelines for community sport in Australia. *BMJ Open Sport & Exercise Medicine*, *8*(4), e001426. https://doi.org/10.1136/bmjsem-2022-001426

Liddelow, C., Schweickle, M. J., Sutcliffe, J. T., Swann, C., Keegan, R., Rice, S., Okely, A. D., & Vella, S. A. (2024). Defining the scope and content of mental health guidelines for community sport in Australia: A Delphi study. *Psychology of Sport and Exercise*, *70*, 102553. https://doi.org/10.1016/j.psychsport.2023.102553

Liddle, S. K., Deane, F. P., & Vella, S. A. (2017). Addressing mental health through sport: A review of sporting organizations' websites. *Early Intervention in Psychiatry*, *11*(2), 93–103. https://doi.org/10.1111/eip.12337

Lubans, D., Richards, J., Hillman, C., Faulkner, G., Beauchamp, M., Nilsson, M., ... & Biddle, S. (2016). Physical activity for cognitive and mental health in youth: A systematic review of mechanisms. *Pediatrics*, *138*(3), e20161642. https://doi.org/10.1542/peds.2016-1642

Martland, R., Mondelli, V., Gaughran, F., & Stubbs, B. (2020). Can high-intensity interval training improve physical and mental health outcomes? A meta-review of 33 systematic reviews across the lifespan. *Journal of Sports Sciences*, *38*(4), 430–469. https://doi.org/10.1080/02640414.2019.1706829

McDowell, C. P., Dishman, R. K., Gordon, B. R., & Herring, M. P. (2019). Physical activity and anxiety: A systematic review and meta-analysis of prospective cohort studies. *American Journal of Preventive Medicine*, *57*(4), 545–556. https://doi.org/10.1016/j.amepre.2019.05.012

Moya, C. A. M., Soares, F. C., Lima, R. A., de Barros, M. V. G., & Bezerra, J. (2021). Depressive symptoms in older adults: The role of physical activity and social support. *Trends in Psychiatry and Psychotherapy*, *43*(3), 185–192. https://doi.org/10.47626/2237-6089-2020-0093

Nicholls, J. G. (1984). Achievement motivation: Conceptions of ability, subjective experience, task choice, and performance. *Psychological Review*, *91*(3), 328–346. https://doi.org/10.1037/0033-295X.91.3.328

Oberle, E., Ji, X. R., Guhn, M., Schonert-Reichl, K. A., & Gadermann, A. M. (2019). Benefits of extracurricular participation in early adolescence: Associations with peer belonging and mental health. *Journal of Youth and Adolescence*, *48*, 2255–2270. https://doi.org/10.1007/s10964-019-01110-2

Occhino, J. L., Mallett, C. J., Rynne, S. B., & Carlisle, K. N. (2014). Autonomy-supportive pedagogical approach to sports coaching: Research, challenges and opportunities. *International Journal of Sports Science & Coaching*, *9*(2), 401–415. https://doi.org/10.1260/1747-9541.9.2.401

Pankowiak, A., Woessner, M. N., Parent, S., Vertommen, T., Eime, R., Spaaij, R., ... & Parker, A. G. (2023). Psychological, physical, and sexual violence against children in Australian community sport: Frequency, perpetrator, and victim characteristics. *Journal of Interpersonal Violence*, *38*(3–4), 4338–4365. https://doi.org/10.1177/08862605221114155

Panza, M. J., Graupensperger, S., Agans, J. P., Doré, I., Vella, S. A., & Evans, M. B. (2020). Adolescent sport participation and symptoms of anxiety and depression: A systematic review and meta-analysis. *Journal of Sport and Exercise Psychology*, *42*(3), 201–218. https://doi.org/10.1123/jsep.2019-0235

Parent, S., Clermont, C., Radziszewski, S., Vertommen, T., & Dion, J. (2023). Child maltreatment and links with experiences of interpersonal violence in sport in a sample of Canadian adolescents. *Social Sciences*, *12*(6), 336. https://doi.org/10.3390/socsci12060336

Rosenbaum, S., Tiedemann, A., Sherrington, C., Curtis, J., & Ward, P. B. (2014). Physical activity interventions for people with mental illness: A systematic review and meta-analysis. *The Journal of Clinical Psychiatry*, *75*(9), 14465. https://doi.org/10.4088/JCP.13r08765

Ryff, C. D., & Keyes, C. L. M. (1995). The structure of psychological well-being revisited. *Journal of Personality and Social Psychology*, *69*(4), 719–727. https://doi.org/10.1037/0022-3514.69.4.719

Saugy, J. J., Drouet, O., Millet, G. P., & Lentillon-Kaestner, V. (2020). A systematic review on self-determination theory in physical education. *Translational Sports Medicine*, *3*(2), 134–147. https://doi.org/10.1002/tsm2.121

Schuch, F. B., Vancampfort, D., Richards, J., Rosenbaum, S., Ward, P. B., & Stubbs, B. (2016). Exercise as a treatment for depression: A meta-analysis adjusting for publication bias. *Journal of Psychiatric Research*, *77*, 42–51. https://doi.org/10.1016/j.jpsychires.2016.02.023

Solmi, M., Radua, J., Olivola, M., Croce, E., Soardo, L., Salazar de Pablo, G., … & Fusar-Poli, P. (2022). Age at onset of mental disorders worldwide: Large-scale meta-analysis of 192 epidemiological studies. *Molecular Psychiatry*, *27*, 281–295. https://doi.org/10.1038/s41380-021-01161-7

Sport SA. (2022). *Mental fitness charter*. Sport SA.

SportWest. (n.d.). *Mental health and wellbeing community sport framework*. SportWest.

Stubbs, B., Vancampfort, D., Hallgren, M., Firth, J., Veronese, N., Solmi, M., … & Kahl, K. G. (2018). EPA guidance on physical activity as a treatment for severe mental illness: A meta-review of the evidence and Position Statement from the European Psychiatric Association (EPA), supported by the International Organization of Physical Therapists in Mental Health (IOPTMH). *European Psychiatry*, *54*, 124–144. https://doi.org/10.1016/j.eurpsy.2018.07.004

Sutcliffe, J. T., Graupensperger, S., Schweickle, M. J., Rice, S. M., Swann, C., & Vella, S. A. (2024). Mental health interventions in non-elite sport: A systematic review and meta-analysis. *International Review of Sport and Exercise Psychology*, *17*(1), 319–342. https://doi.org/10.1080/1750984X.2021.2001839

Swann, C., Telenta, J., Draper, G., Liddle, S., Fogarty, A., Hurley, D., & Vella, S. (2018). Youth sport as a context for supporting mental health: Adolescent male perspectives. *Psychology of Sport and Exercise*, *35*, 55–64. https://doi.org/10.1016/j.psychsport.2017.11.008

Teychenne, M., White, R. L., Richards, J., Schuch, F. B., Rosenbaum, S., & Bennie, J. A. (2020). Do we need physical activity guidelines for mental health: What does the evidence tell us? *Mental Health and Physical Activity*, *18*, 100315. https://doi.org/10.1016/j.mhpa.2019.100315

Tremblay, M. S., Carson, V., Chaput, J. P., Connor Gorber, S., Dinh, T., Duggan, M., … & Zehr, L. (2016). Canadian 24-hour movement guidelines for children and youth: An integration of physical activity, sedentary behaviour, and sleep. *Applied Physiology, Nutrition, and Metabolism*, *41*, S311–S327. https://doi.org/10.1139/apnm-2016-0151

Vella, S. A. (2019). Mental health and organized youth sport. *Kinesiology Review*, *8*(3), 229–236. https://doi.org/10.1123/kr.2019-0025

Vella, S. A., Aidman, E., Teychenne, M., Smith, J. J., Swann, C., Rosenbaum, S., … & Lubans, D. R. (2023). Optimising the effects of physical activity on mental health and wellbeing: A joint consensus statement from Sports Medicine Australia and the Australian Psychological Society. *Journal of Science and Medicine in Sport, 26*(2), 132–139. 10.1016/j.jsams.2023.01.001

Vella, S. A., Cliff, D. P., Magee, C. A., & Okely, A. D. (2014). Sports participation and parent-reported health-related quality of life in children: Longitudinal associations. *The Journal of Pediatrics*, *164*(6), 1469–1474. https://doi.org/10.1016/j.jpeds.2014.01.071

Vella, S. A., Liddelow, C., Rice, S. M., Keegan, R., Hall, K., Jones, M. A., Lubans, D., McLeod, S., Okely, A. D., Olive, L. S., Purcell, R., Reece, L. J., Rosenbaum, S., Schweickle, M. J., Singh, K., Stewart, D., Stimpson, L., Sutcliffe, J. T., Teychenne, M., … Swann, C. (2025). The development of Australian mental health guidelines for community sport. *British Journal of Sports Medicine*, *59*(9), 659–666. https://doi.org/10.1136/bjsports-2024-108749

Vella, S. A., Sutcliffe, J. T., Fernandez, D., Liddelow, C., Aidman, E., Teychenne, M., … & Lubans, D. R. (2023). Context matters: A review of reviews examining the effects of contextual factors in physical activity interventions on mental health and wellbeing. *Mental Health and Physical Activity, 25*, 100520. https://doi.org/10.1016/j.mhpa.2023.100520

Vella, S. A., Schweickle, M. J., Sutcliffe, J., Liddelow, C., & Swann, C. (2022). A systems theory of mental health in recreational sport. *International Journal of Environmental Research and Public Health*, *19*(21), 14244. https://doi.org/10.3390/ijerph192114244

Vella, S. A., Schweickle, M. J., Sutcliffe, J. T., & Swann, C. (2021). A systematic review and meta-synthesis of mental health position statements in sport: Scope, quality and future directions. *Psychology of Sport and Exercise*, *55*, 101946. https://doi.org/10.1016/j.psychsport.2021.101946

Vella, S. A., & Swann, C. (2021). Time for mental healthcare guidelines for recreational sports: A call to action. *British Journal of Sports Medicine*, *55*(4), 184–185. https://doi.org/10.1136/bjsports-2019-101591

Vella, S. A., Swann, C., Allen, M. S., Schweickle, M. J., & Magee, C. A. (2017). Bidirectional associations between sport involvement and mental health in adolescence. *Medicine and Science in Sports and Exercise*, *49*(4), 687–694. https://doi.org/10.1249/MSS.0000000000001142

Warburton, D. E., Charlesworth, S., Ivey, A., Nettlefold, L., & Bredin, S. S. (2010). A systematic review of the evidence for Canada's Physical Activity Guidelines for Adults. *International Journal of Behavioral Nutrition and Physical Activity*, *7*, 39. https://doi.org/10.1186/1479-5868-7-39

White, R. L., Babic, M. J., Parker, P. D., Lubans, D. R., Astell-Burt, T., & Lonsdale, C. (2017). Domain-specific physical activity and mental health: A meta-analysis. *American Journal of Preventive Medicine*, *52*(5), 653–666. https://doi.org/10.1016/j.amepre.2016.12.008

Wicks, C., Barton, J., Orbell, S., & Andrews, L. (2022). Psychological benefits of outdoor physical activity in natural versus urban environments: A systematic review and meta-analysis of experimental studies. *Applied Psychology: Health and Well-Being*, *14*(3), 1037–1061. https://doi.org/10.1111/aphw.12353

World Health Organization. (2020). *WHO guidelines on physical activity and sedentary behaviour.* World Health Organization.

12

PROMOTING MENTAL HEALTH THROUGH PHYSICAL ACTIVITY AND EXERCISE IN ASIA

Fenghua Sun, Claudia Ming Yu Wong, Yan Shi, and Simon B. Cooper

12.1 Preface

According to the World Health Organization (WHO), mental health is defined as "a state of well-being in which an individual realizes his or her abilities, copes with the normal stresses of life, works productively, and is able to contribute to his or her community" while encompassing multiple conditions (WHO, 2019a). Nowadays mental health issue is considered an important and increasing public health problem, which causes a wide range of personal and societal influences. Mental health conditions, especially depression, cause 800,000 suicidal deaths per year globally, having suicidal death ranking as the fourth most common cause of death among people of ages 15–29. Moreover, preventable physical diseases cause severe burden to people with serious mental health conditions, resulting in early death (WHO, 2019b). Despite the fact that the majority of mental health conditions can be effectively managed at a reasonable cost, there is still a significant gap between the required care provided and those actively accessed, as well as the effective coverage of mental health condition treatment given in most of the less developed countries, resulting in a large amount of unmet need for treating mental health problems. Hence, the WHO has emphasized the need to raise awareness of mental health care and treatment, acknowledging the important role of mental health in reaching sustainable development goals, as well as supporting novel research in creating effective therapies and interventions in dealing with emergent mental illness issues globally.

Many different strategies have been proposed to treat mental illness issues in the literature. According to the WHO's Optimal Mix of Service Pyramid Framework (WHO, 2007), self-care is considered the fundamental service needed in dealing with mental health issues, and it is also classified as having the highest frequency of

DOI: 10.4324/9781003517474-17

need. Given that self-care is one of the most numerous cares in this WHO pyramid framework, it encourages individuals to manage their mental health problems by themselves through acquiring knowledge regarding the negative effects of being mentally unhealthy, developing stress management and coping skills, having the ability to discuss emotional problems with others, as well as having a help-seeking behavior. In other words, self-care aims to facilitate people's autonomy in taking care of themselves, as well as fostering the need to enhance people's ability to care about their own mental health status. The self-caring activities were summarized by the Self-Care Matrix (El-Osta et al., 2019). According to this matrix, there are seven pillars of self-care activities as the micro-perspective, including (i) knowledge and health literacy, (ii) mental well-being, self-awareness, and agency, (iii) physical activity (PA), (iv) healthy eating, (v) risk avoidance and mitigation, (vi) good hygiene, and (vii) the rational use of products and services. These activities, in other words, are person-centered activities that facilitate self-caring. Apart from health literacy as mentioned by the WHO, PA, mental well-being, and self-awareness are all considered as self-care activities.

In recent years, "Exercise is Medicine" (Thompson et al., 2020) has been widely discussed and promoted. Frequent PA has been suggested to aid in the management and prevention of non-communicable diseases. PA may lower blood pressure, support healthy body weight, and enhance subjective well-being, mental health, and quality of life. However, the WHO reported that 81% of adolescents and one in four adults do not get enough PA or exercise in the globe, especially under rapid economic development, causing shifting transportation patterns, the reliance on technology, and living patterns. It is believed that the elevated degrees of inactivity have detrimental effects on health care systems, the environment, economic growth, the well-being of communities, and the overall quality of life. The benefits of PA on various mental health outcomes have been extensively researched and discussed, in particular, in the post-COVID-19 era, adhering to healthy lifestyle behaviors and maintaining positive mental health has been considered as a big challenge. Engaging in regular PA is known to release dopamine and serotonin, which we call "happy chemicals", that make people feel happy and confident thus improving mental well-being. Hence, PA is "great for your body, great for your mind" (WHO, 2022).

With the increasing prevalence of discourse surrounding mental health issues and the widely documented benefits of PA or exercise on psychological well-being, this chapter aims to provide an overview on how various aspects of mental health have been achieved through PA or exercise among Asian populations. In this chapter, we focus on the Asia populations of children, adolescents, adults, and elderly, while illustrating the updated evidence of the effect of PA or exercise on reducing mental illness (majorly focusing on depression, anxiety, post-traumatic stress disorder [PTSD], and dissociation) and enhancing positive well-being (mainly including self-efficacy, self-confidence, mindfulness, and resilience). Additionally, the potential benefits of traditional mind-body exercise and/or mindfulness on mental health issues are also discussed. Thus, this chapter provides researchers, practitioners, and educators with an overall picture of the intimate association between PA/exercise and mental health among Asia populations.

12.2 Previous Evidence

12.2.1 Children and Adolescents

In recent years, numerous systematic reviews and meta-analytical studies have investigated the associations between mental health and PA. However, varying conclusions have emerged with respect to different age groups. More participation in PA has been suggested to support children and adolescents' current and future mental health. For instance, a recent systematic review (Hale et al., 2021) concluded that, among adolescents, PA is effective in improving psychological well-being including self-esteem, self-concept, self-efficacy, self-image, and quality of life. However, for reducing psychological ill-being such as depression, anxiety, stress, or negative affect, the evidence is less clear. Some similar findings were also presented in another meta-analysis (Neill et al., 2020), in which PA intervention shows no overall effect on anxiety, depression, and stress outcomes in adolescents. Consistently, another recent systematic review observed that 4 out of 13 studies reported no association between PA and psychological health (Okuyama et al., 2021). Such conclusions should be explained with caution because of the relatively low quality of intervention and varied methodologies employed in the literature. In one systematic review (Ahmed et al., 2021) that investigated the benefits of PA interventions among Asian children and adolescents, it was concluded that PA intervention studies in Asian children are of relatively low number, low-methodological quality, and small sample size. Of the included studies, 70% of them adopted school-based PA interventions, whereas only half were randomized controlled trials (RCTs). Therefore, for future Asian researchers, well-designed PA interventions are needed to inform evidence-based strategies to enhance PA engagements among children and adolescents in Asia.

From another standpoint, heightened focus is warranted on effective PA interventions and health promotion strategies to improve the mental health of Asian children and adolescents, as academic stress in Asian countries is relatively high. Evidence from systematic reviews (Rodriguez-Ayllon et al., 2019; Zhang et al., 2017; Zhu et al., 2019) proved that academic stress is associated with anxiety and depression among children and adolescents. One study (Liu et al., 2018) that did comparisons across provinces and among subgroups in China has elucidated that elevated academic stress levels may exhibit a direct correlation with increased anxiety and depression among children and adolescents. Additionally, a separate Chinese study (Zhu et al., 2017) has underscored the adverse impact of academic stress on both the PA levels and sleep patterns of adolescents. Moreover, another Chinese study (X. Zhu et al., 2021) has demonstrated a positive relationship between reduced academic stress, enhanced mental health, and increased levels of PA.

Therefore, academic stress warrants further increased attention when designing and implementing effective PA interventions, health promotion, and policy strategies to enhance the mental health of children and adolescents in Asia.

12.2.2 Adults

For young adults, one recent systematic review (Pan et al., 2022) focuses on Chinese college students and shows that academic pressure, facilities constraints, and lack of professional exercise guidance are the main cause young people lack time for PA participation. Therefore, for this specific age group, these factors should be carefully considered when investigating the benefits of PA interventions on their mental health. For adult groups in general, most of the available systematic reviews explored the benefit of plaza dance and traditional Chinese mind-body exercise, such as Tai Chi or Baduanjin. Plaza dance is a popular form of PA among adults in China. One recent systematic review and meta-analysis on plaza dance in China included 25 studies in review and 17 in meta-analysis, and the results show that plaza dance improved psychological well-being (life satisfaction, energy, happiness, positive affect, and self-esteem) and reduced psychological ill-being (depression, anxiety, hostility, and anger) (Bai et al., 2022). Another popular form of PA is traditional Chinese mind-body exercise, which contains both PA and mindfulness elements. One recent systematic review and meta-analysis (Dong et al., 2024) has revealed that participating in traditional Chinese exercise (Baduanjin or Taichi) had better effects on anxiety and depression in adults who did not participate in exercise or other forms of exercise compared with control groups. Similarly, another systematic review and meta-analysis showed that Baduanjin is beneficial for quality of life and sleep quality, while most of the studies included are conducted in China (Zou et al., 2017). The positive effect of traditional Chinese mind-body exercise on mental health was not only observed in healthy adults but also in patients. One meta-analytical study (Wang et al., 2015) summarized 60 RCT studies with 4,311 patients with chronic diseases and concluded that traditional Chinese mind-body exercise can significantly improve quality of life and reduce depression. Consistently, two recent systematic reviews and meta-analysis research mainly involved studies conducted in Asia (Kong et al., 2022; Zou et al., 2018), which also observed the benefits of traditional Chinese mind-body exercise such as Baduanjin in reducing depression and anxiety symptoms and improving psychological well-being among adult population with illness. Therefore, when targeting the mental health of adult population, traditional Chinese mind-body exercises deserve further attention as they place greater emphasis on regulating breathing, cultivating a clear state of mindfulness, and achieving musculoskeletal relaxation, aiming to optimize both physical and mental health when compared with conventional exercises.

12.2.3 Elderly

Research studies on PA and mental health of the Asian elderly were conducted in different ways and revealed various outcomes, yet only two reviews solely focused on

Asian/Chinese older adults (Ou et al., 2022; Wong, Ou, Chung et al., 2023). Recent reviews on the PA and mental health of older adults, which included both Asian and non-Asian population studies, have been focused on the relationship between PA and depression, as well as PA and cognitive function (Choo et al., 2020; Kim et al., 2022; Xu et al., 2023). They mainly divided PA into aerobic exercise and resistance training, as well as with a special focus on Chinese traditional mind-body exercise (Wu et al., 2022), like Tai Chi, Qigong, and Wuqinxi. The review indicated that both aerobic exercise and resistance training foster a positive impact on the cognitive function of older adults, yet the two types of exercise impose no differences on the level of effect (Xu et al., 2023). Moreover, general aerobic exercise and traditional Chinese mind-body exercises provide similar influences on the sleep quality and mental well-being of older adults (Wu et al., 2022). Tai Chi specifically showed well-documented evidence of its effect on the depressive symptoms and quality of life of older adults (Choo et al., 2020; Wang et al., 2020; Zhang et al., 2019). This may be due to the mindfulness effect of Tai Chi in cultivating mental concentration on breathing, body movement, and muscle relaxation in older adults, thus leading to a positive effect on their mental well-being (Birdee et al., 2009). In another review (Zhang et al., 2019), the team has illustrated a relatively comprehensive summary of the effect of Tai Chi intervention, which indicated its effect on reducing negative emotions, anxiety, and depression, while the older age imposed a moderating effect on these casual relationships too. Apart from the general aerobic exercises and the traditional Chinese mind-body exercises, it is surprising that there were two reviews on dance intervention among older adults. A dance intervention review, not limited to the Asian population, showed improvement in physical health and emphasized the need for analysis of dance on mental health among older adults (Hwang & Braun, 2015). However, plaza dance is considered as a community-based emerging aerobic exercise in China. Despite there being a lack of systematic exercise design protocol for plaza dance, it was possible to retrieve 24 papers in regard to examining the effect of plaza dance on older adults' physical and mental health. Plaza dance has been tested and shown a positive effect on self-esteem, well-being, emotions, and quality of life (Ou et al., 2022). Additionally, a meta-analysis on serious games intervention, in other words, activities conducted with digital devices/video games, indicated that digital games for PA (i.e. Wii Fit), digital games for cognitive function (i.e. touch controller-applied games), and digital games for both (i.e. electronic steps pads and Nintendo) had a significant effect on reducing depression in older adults, regardless of duration and dose of games (Kim et al., 2022). As a result, research on PA in older adults has built a solid foundation on its effect on enhancing cognition, depression, and well-being, thus enabling to achieve active aging (Liu et al., 2023).

12.3 Updated Evidence

When addressing the impact of PA on the mental health of children and adolescents, it is imperative to acknowledge Coronavirus Disease 2019 (COVID-19) as a catalyst for significant disruptions within the global social framework. The period from 2020 to 2022 witnessed widespread school closures, government-imposed activity limitations, and reduced social interactions for children and adolescents. These restrictive measures had a negative impact on the PA levels of children and adolescents. Recent studies have shown that low PA has been a significant concern during the COVID-19 pandemic, with almost one-third of youth having very low PA levels even in year 3 of the pandemic (Ravens-Sieberer et al., 2023). The COVID-19 pandemic has led to a substantial decline in the mental health of children and adolescents, with an increase in mental health problems and a decrease in health-related quality of life compared with pre-pandemic levels (Harrison et al., 2022; Jo et al., 2023; Paunova-Markova et al., 2023).

COVID-19 pandemic has also led to a significant impact on mental health in the adult population. Anxiety and depression levels were found to be significantly higher in adults with low PA levels during the pandemic (Wut et al., 2023). Meanwhile, for those who keep adequate PA as part of a healthy lifestyle, they may have a beneficial effect on their mental health during the COVID-19 outbreak, potentially reducing anxiety and depression levels (Wut et al., 2023). After the pandemic, PA also plays a crucial role in reducing the risk of long COVID and its associated symptoms, meanwhile maintaining an active lifestyle for both physical and mental well-being among adults (Feter et al., 2023; Zheng et al., 2025).

According to the statistics provided by the World Population Prospect 2022 (United Nations Department of Economic and Social Affairs, 2022), the prevalence of the aging population has been seriously affecting the globe with 2.1 million people expected to reach the age of 60 by 2050. Although the majority are in good health, many are susceptible to mental health issues like anxiety and depression, as well as other mental and cognitive disabilities that require long-term care, which increases the financial and social burden of the community. Moreover, the COVID-19 pandemic has had a detrimental impact on the mental health of older adults, leading to severe mental health issues such as loneliness, anxiety, and fear of disease and death (Ashiq et al., 2023). Social isolation and loneliness during quarantine and hospitalization have significantly affected the mental well-being of the elderly population (Sadatnia et al., 2023). As a result, PA, as a self-caring approach, to influencing older adults' mental well-being is essential.

12.3.1 Depression and Anxiety

Plenty of research has been done in Asia, especially in China, Korea, and Japan to investigate the protective effects of PA on depression and anxiety caused by the COVID-19 pandemic.

Regular epidemic prevention and control measures, such as lockdowns and social distancing protocols during COVID-19, may have disrupted the daily routines of children and adolescents, leading to feelings of uncertainty and stress, which could have contributed to the development of depression and anxiety. Children and adolescents are suggested to have at least one hour of moderate to vigorous PA every day, according to the WHO guideline (WHO, 2020). However, restrictions on outdoor activities and limited access to sports facilities during the pandemic have reduced opportunities for PA of children and adolescents significantly. Cross-sectional studies proved that during the pandemic, due to lower PA levels, children and adolescents (Li & Wang, 2023) were at a higher risk of experiencing mental health issues such as depression and anxiety. One Chinese interventional study highlighted that even a PA program slightly lower than the recommended PA guideline level could bring significant mental health benefits and help alleviate symptoms of depression and anxiety in children and adolescents during and after the pandemic (Dong & Dou, 2023). Consequently, enhancing PA holds significance for the promotion of mental well-being among children and adolescents, particularly in the context of the pandemic and its aftermath.

Two recent studies have also documented the beneficial impact of PA interventions in alleviating negative and detrimental emotions among Chinese adults and college students amidst the COVID-19 pandemic (Qin et al., 2020; Jiang et al., 2021). A certain amount of PA during pandemic has a positive effect on improving the depression, anxiety, anger, and panic of college students (Jiang et al., 2021). Another interesting study among Chinese college students found that specific types of PA, such as stretching and resistance training, were correlated with lower anxiety and depression, while household chores and activities negatively correlated with depression (Xiang et al., 2020).

Large-scale research has been done on Korean and Japanese adults, indicating that exercise frequency has been restricted by social distancing during COVID-19 and was associated with depression and thus associated with various physical factors, like physical fatigue, poor sleeping quality, and appetite loss (Jung, 2023; Nishida et al., 2023). Longitudinal studies, targeting Korean and Chinese, have found a significant link between depression and physical as well as cognitive frailty. As age advances, the severity of this association increases. Therefore, identifying protective and risk factors and promoting preventive measures that enhance health outcomes is crucial (Lee et al., 2023; Yuan et al., 2023).

PA is also highly related to older adults' health-related quality of life, including their physical function, physical health, vitality, bodily pain, and other psychosocial factors. Hence, research indicated that depression partially mediated the relationship between various intensities of PA and physical and mental components of health-related quality of life. It emphasized higher levels of moderate and vigorous intensity PA were associated with lower depression and higher health-related quality of life involving physical and mental components (Li et al., 2024). It was summarized that perceived stress, limited PA, and perceived health status were associated with depression and health-related quality of life (Jang & Yang, 2023). Moreover, the residential greenness was shown to facilitate older adults' long-term greenness exposure, thus affecting PA and leading to the reduction of depression symptoms (Wang et al., 2024). Hence, PA was generally found to protect against depression and anxiety.

12.3.2 PSTD and Dissociation

Depression and anxiety have been seen as common mental illnesses around the globe, and PA has been proven as a "medicine". However, PTSD and dissociation are also considered common mental disorders, especially after experiencing traumatic events (Bryant, 2019), which would potentially cause stress, anxiety, and fear, as well as tend to overlap with other mental disorders, including depression (Sareen, 2014). Therefore, it is worth discussing the impact of PA on reducing PTSD and dissociation symptoms.

It is surprising that individual studies specifying the relationship between PA and PTSD among Asian children, adolescents, and older adults are lacking, while systematic reviews have reflected the association across all age groups, mainly of ages 18–78 (Björkman & Ekblom, 2022; Sabri et al., 2023; Wang et al., 2023). They summarized that exercise can be an effective facilitator in PTSD treatment. It might be because PTSD brings about numerous biological effects, such as those involving neuropathology, immunological, endocrinological, and physiological functions. They cause unpleasant thoughts, feelings, dreams about trauma, and withdrawal, thus affecting the amygdala and hippocampus in regulating stress and emotional responses. Research indicated that hippocampal volume and connectivity can be improved by 2% through exercise, thus reducing PTSD symptoms (Erickson et al., 2011; Leavitt et al., 2014). Hence, PA plays a significant role in reducing PTSD (Wang et al., 2023). Specifically, a systematic review study on mind-body exercises with Chinese databases indicated that mind-body exercises provide strong evidence of their effectiveness on PTSD symptoms and PTSD patients (L. Zhu et al., 2021). Given the lack of intervention evidence among Chinese and Asian children, adolescents, and older adults, various forms of PA intervention targeting PTSD symptoms in children and older adult patients should be promoted.

12.3.3 Self-Confidence and Self-Efficacy

The importance of self-confidence and self-efficacy in well-being has been unshakably evidenced, such as in enhancing exercise performances, and self-esteem, as well as reducing negative thoughts and emotions. A recent study conducted among Chinese adolescents shows that PA can significantly positively predict the subjective well-being of adolescents, with the mediating effect of self-efficacy (Yao et al., 2023).

Self-confidence, self-efficacy, mastery, and psychological control were observed to significantly improve through the maintenance of self-regulation, self-judgment, and self-discipline during PA engagement, particularly in recent studies conducted amid the COVID-19 outbreak. Engaging in home-based exercise emerged as a primary approach to bolster individuals' sense of control, diverting them from negative thoughts and rumination within the pandemic context (Matias et al., 2020). The mechanism might be that establishing a consistent home-based exercise routine can create a sense of order and reliability in an otherwise unpredictable and rapidly changing environment. This structured regimen promotes feelings of self-control and self-efficacy in managing daily activities and time effectively (Ryan & Deci, 2017). Moreover, engaging in home-based exercise during the pandemic empowers individuals to take control of their physical fitness regimen, granting them autonomy and decision-making authority regarding the type, intensity, and duration of their workouts. By actively choosing to engage in home-based exercise, individuals experience a sense of personal empowerment and agency, reinforcing the perception of control over their own health and well-being (Matias et al., 2020), and in this way building up their self-confidence and efficacy.

Research studies among Korean older adults indicated that the most influencing factors on successful and healthy aging were self-esteem, self-achievement, self-efficacy, interpersonal relationships, and leisure activities; while they negatively correlated with loneliness and depression (Han et al., 2015; Hyun Cha et al., 2012; Kim et al., 2022). PA is always being seen as a lifelong supplement for healthy aging, to improve diabetes, osteoporosis, depression, and other physical and mental-related illnesses. Asian-based research studies sufficiently indicated the association between PA and older adults' self-efficacy, with exercise self-efficacy in particular. Self-efficacy is stated as a fundamental idea of developing thriving and effective habits, in which individuals have the confidence in their capacity to execute self-monitoring, self-regulation, and behavior modification, to maintain a persistent effort toward success. Limited self-efficacy and competence were seen as barriers in achieving health behaviors among older adults (Huang et al., 2022). Therefore, adherence to PA and a healthy lifestyle are expected to enhance physical skills executing confidence and general self-efficacy (Stahl et al., 2020; Zhu et al., 2022). There was also Chinese-specific dance intervention, Guazhuang Dance, which showed a positive effect on improving older adults' subjective well-being through the mediation effect of self-efficacy (Y. Lin et al., 2022). It is noteworthy that healthy lifestyle behavior interventions should not be restricted by PA alone but not be limited to psychological variables add-ons, such as empowerment interventions that include lifestyle medication psychoeducation sessions and group discussions beyond exercise training. The eight-week empowerment intervention on healthy lifestyle behavior was shown to enhance perceived health, PA, as well as exercise self-efficacy (Chang et al., 2013). Given the significance of the psychoeducation elements within the intervention, it raised the importance of health literacy and e-health literacy among Chinese and Asian older adults in gaining self-efficacy in engaging in healthy lifestyle behavior. Research studies indicated that the older adults' level of literacy in acknowledging the importance of healthy lifestyle behaviors and self-care agencies could highly enhance older adults' level of self-efficacy in disease and health-related self-management, such as better decision-making for disease risk self-assessment and self-monitoring of physical status and sustaining a health status (Du et al., 2023; Wu et al., 2022). Given the importance of exercise self-efficacy, the Self-efficacy for Exercise Scale for older adults was translated and well-validated among Korean and Chinese participants (Choi et al., 2015; Lee et al., 2009).

12.3.4 Resilience and Mindfulness

Resilience denotes an individual's capacity to adapt to and recover from adversity, trauma, threats, and stressful events, while also promoting environmental adaptability, mental rehabilitation, and emotional relief (Windle, 2011). In recent years especially after the COVID-19 pandemic, cultivating resilience and mindfulness has been a promising way to fight against stress and promote both physical and mental health. Recent evidence found that PA positively impacts adolescents' resilience levels (Guo & Liang, 2023; H. Lin et al., 2022), and the resilience and self-esteem mediate PA's impact on adaptation (H. Lin et al., 2022). Similar finding was also reported among Korean adolescents (Ji-Hang, 2022), in which regular PA was suggested to contribute to the development of effective stress-coping mechanisms such as seeking social support and problem-solving skills. Resilience also plays a mediating role in the relationship between PA and academic stress, i.e., higher levels of resilience resulting from PA can help mitigate the negative effects of academic stress on students. In another Korean study, high PA level groups exhibited high levels of resilience, emphasizing the importance of engaging in vigorous PAs for promoting resilience in Korean adolescent boys (Eun-Jung, 2022). A recent Singapore study also found that engaging in PAs, such as sports and exercise, was found to be associated with higher resilience levels among adolescents during the COVID-19 pandemic (Moosa et al., 2023). Active participation in PA, especially during times of crisis like the COVID-19 outbreak, may contribute to building resilience and enhancing coping mechanisms among adolescents, potentially improving their overall well-being and mental health (Moosa et al., 2023).

Mindfulness-based training has been suggested to enhance emotional regulation skills, leading to better coping mechanisms and reduced psychological distress in children and adolescents, especially those facing physical health challenges (Hughes et al., 2023). Within the Asian context, mind-body exercises blending elements of mindfulness and PA emerge as prevalent interventions for children and adolescents, particularly those with special educational needs. A recent systematic review underscored the efficacy of mind-body programs in benefiting children and adolescents diagnosed with attention-deficit/hyperactivity disorder (ADHD). Such interventions demonstrated positive effects in reducing ADHD symptoms, addressing behavioral challenges, enhancing executive function, bolstering mental well-being, and increasing academic performance (Fang et al., 2024). Notably, a significant portion of the studies reviewed examining mind-body exercises were carried out in Asia, with Tai Chi, Baduanjin, and Qigong emerging as the main forms of exercises within these programs (Fang et al., 2024). However, a single study highlighted the intricacies associated with examining the effect of Tai Chi or Qigong on the mental well-being of children and adolescents, presenting a notable challenge in research endeavors. This systematic review encompassed a spectrum of findings regarding the effects of Tai Chi and Qigong on the mental health outcomes of children and adolescents. A majority of the studies reviewed reported positive enhancements in mental health, a subset conveyed neutral findings, but a noteworthy study detailing a decline in psychological health and well-being within this demographic (Riskowski & Almeheyawi, 2019). These contrasting outcomes underscore the complexity inherent in assessing the impact of mind-body exercises on the mental health of children and adolescents, thereby underscoring the imperative for further comprehensive investigations.

In Asians, although most of the studies focusing on resilience, mindfulness, and mind-body exercise were conducted among older adults or adults with physical or mental health conditions, there were several studies that explored the impact of PA among general adult populations. One recent cross-sectional study found the mediating role of resilience in the relationships of PA and mindful self-awareness among Taiwanese young adults in university (Liao et al., 2023). Building resilience, therefore, may be a crucial factor in enhancing the positive effects of PA and mindful self-awareness. Numerous reviews and original studies have extensively documented the positive impact of mind-body exercise on health conditions and the overall quality of life in adult populations (Lee et al., 2022). However, the majority of these studies are predominantly conducted in China, showcasing the significant contribution of Chinese researchers in this field (Lee et al., 2022). Among all the mind-body exercises, Qigong, such as Baduanjin, involves gentle movements, breathing techniques, and meditation, is a suitable light to moderate PA among adults. Qigong not only trains the mind and body for healing, promoting physical well-being, but also may offer a safe and low-cost intervention for reducing perceived stress and depressive symptoms among adults (Cheung et al., 2019).

Asian older adults have perceived the aging experiences consisting of "slowing down", "relationship harmony", "social connectedness", "keep moving", and "keep learning" as important themes, in which indicating the continued adaptation of self-determination, self-management, and resilience as the essential approaches in coping with negative thoughts due to frailty, aging, and the declining of physical health (Shiraz et al., 2020). Frailty is also considered as a factor in affecting older adults' resilience to stressors, hence a higher level of resilience is significantly associated with successful aging. Research studies among Asian older adults indicated the mediation effect of resilience and physical health on the association between loneliness and depression, as well as the mediation effect of resilience on the association between PA and perceived mental and physical health (Kukihara et al., 2018; Lim et al., 2022). They all evidenced the effect of resilience on benefiting older adults' physical and mental health, especially in minimizing loneliness and depression, as well as strengthening successful aging. One recent study also revealed that the level of resilience of Hong Kong's older adults was significantly influenced by exercise self-efficacy, healthy lifestyle behaviors, social networking, and leisure activities (Wong, Ou, & Man Leung, 2023). Regarding the theme of "slowing down" and self-management, resilience connects to the need for awareness and mindfulness. Various types of traditional Chinese mind-body exercises, like Tai Chi, Baduanjin, and Qigong, were shown to improve older adults' mental and physical health (Wong, Ou, & Man Leung, 2023). Plenty of reviews and studies documented the effect of Qigong/Taichi on mind-body health benefits, including benefiting the immune system, lowering blood pressure, offering higher vital capacity (Su & Zhao, 2021), reducing depressive symptoms and fatigue, and improving the quality of life (Leung et al., 2021). Most importantly, mindfulness meditation interventions alone showed greater influences on Asian older adults' depression, compared to that of other nationalities (Reangsing et al., 2022). While, long-term mindfulness meditation training has a greater effect on the life quality, nervous system, and brain connectivity of older adults, only combining it with PA showed a greater effect on physical fitness (Tang et al., 2020).

12.4 Implications

Evidence from recent systematic reviews and original studies regarding the impact of PA on the mental health of children and adolescents in Asia presents a complex picture. The discourse surrounding the therapeutic impact of PA in addressing common mental illnesses such as depression and anxiety, as well as aspects of mental well-being such as self-confidence and self-efficacy, has been suggested especially in recent years after the COVID-19 pandemic. While there are clear indications of its positive effects on psychological well-being, particularly in areas like self-esteem and self-efficacy, the relationship between PA and reducing psychological ill-being such as depression and anxiety appears less straightforward. The body of research pertaining to resilience and mindfulness presents notable advantages within the context of Asia, with a predominant concentration of studies emanating from Asia. It is also imperative to extend this discussion to encompass PTSD and dissociation, which are prevalent after traumatic events and often co-occur with other mental disorders, compounding the challenges faced by individuals. However, there is a dearth of focused studies exploring the relationship between PA and PTSD among Asian population especially children and adolescents. Variations in findings across studies underscore the influence of factors such as intervention quality, methodology, and regional context. Notably, the scarcity of high-quality studies focusing on Asian children and adolescents suggests a critical need for well-designed interventions and high-quality research methodologies to inform strategies that effectively enhance PA engagement in this population. Addressing these research gaps is crucial for developing tailored interventions that support the mental well-being of children and adolescents, particularly in the Asian context.

Conversely, in the domain of adult populations, the focal point of research predominantly pertains to individuals grappling with both physical and mental illnesses. PA in adults, specifically highlighting plaza dance and traditional Chinese mind-body exercises such as Tai Chi or Qigong, reveals promising insights into the psychological benefits of these practices. Studies predominantly conducted in China showcase the positive effects of plaza dance and traditional Chinese exercises on psychological well-being and the reduction of mental health issues like depression and anxiety. This presents a compelling argument for the integration of traditional Chinese mind-body exercises into interventions targeting the adult population, highlighting their unique focus on mindfulness, relaxation, and mental health benefits. Leveraging the therapeutic potential of these practices may offer a comprehensive approach to optimizing both physical and mental well-being in adults, particularly those in Asia and beyond. Consequently, a compelling call to action emerges, advocating for future studies to pivot toward encompassing the general adult population and promoting widespread engagement with mind-body exercises. This shift in research focus has the potential to yield valuable insights and interventions that cater to the broader demographic, aligning with the overarching goal of advocating for holistic well-being in diverse populations.

The illustration of PA as self-caring and self-management activities, the updated findings have provided important insights into the implications of promoting mental well-being among the Asian older adult population through mind-body exercises. In particular, Tang et al.'s (2020) research indicated exercise improves physical fitness while mindfulness meditation induces central nervous system plasticity. These two strategies underlie their respective functions. Hence, the results imply that combining mindfulness meditation training and physical training may improve the aging population's health and quality of life. Incorporating mindfulness training techniques that emphasize bodily awareness, deep breathing, and being in the present can optimize the advantages of PA for psychological wellness in general and illnesses like depression and PTSD in particular, as well as building resilience to difficulties, stress management, and self-confidence—all of which may have a good impact on mental illness. It is also believed that healthcare professionals should have a thorough understanding of the traits of different types of older adults (i.e. living alone older adults, active older adults, and those with disabilities) and focus more on issues related to the needs, the enablers, and factors related to health behaviors. While mindfulness-integrated PAs are considered as cost-effective, they can be person-tailored and accessible for healthcare practitioners to support the holistic health of Asian seniors. Beyond that, research studies with RCTs should stick to the rigorous process of intervention program design, with the provision of an in-depth explanation of the methods and intervention items included to enhance the solidarity of the program implication and representativeness.

12.5 Conclusion

The main findings of this review chapter are to highlight the huge potential for PA to be used in enhancing mental health and well-being, particularly in Asian populations. The evidence reviewed here suggests that PA has a positive effect on the management of mental health conditions such as anxiety, depression, and PTSD; alongside a positive effect on the development of aspects of mental well-being, such as self-confidence, self-efficacy, and resilience. In particular, the mediating effect of age has been considered by discussing the effects of PA in children/adolescents, adults, and the elderly separately. The latest evidence in each of these areas in Asian populations has been reviewed, and recommendations for future research have been made; in particular, the need for (i) more high-quality, well-designed, and well-controlled studies in Asian populations, and (ii) more studies specifically in adult populations. Nonetheless, this chapter provides encouraging evidence for the role of PA in promoting mental health and well-being in different populations.

References

Ahmed, K. R., Uddin, R., Kolbe-Alexander, T. L., & Khan, A. (2021). The effectiveness of physical activity interventions in Asian children and adolescents: A systematic review. *Public Health*, *194*, 48–59.

Ashiq, U., Abbas, N., Sajid, I. U., & Shafiq, M. (2023). Effects of covid-19 on mental health of older adults: Study based on perceptions and experiences of adults suffered from Covid-19. *Pakistan Journal of Medical & Health Sciences*, *17*(3), 64–64.

Bai, Z., Li, Y., Yang, Y., Xie, C., Zhu, Z., Xu, Y., & Bai, R. (2022). The effectiveness of plaza dancing on psychological well-being and ill-being: A systematic review and meta-analysis. *Frontiers in Psychology*, *13*, 864327.

Birdee, G. S., Wayne, P. M., Davis, R. B., Phillips, R. S., & Yeh, G. Y. (2009). T'ai chi and qigong for health: Patterns of use in the United States. *The Journal of Alternative and Complementary Medicine*, *15*(9), 969–973.

Björkman, F., & Ekblom, Ö. (2022). Physical exercise as treatment for PTSD: A systematic review and meta-analysis. *Military Medicine*, *187*(9–10), e1103–e1113.

Bryant, R. A. (2019). Post-traumatic stress disorder: A state-of-the-art review of evidence and challenges. *World Psychiatry*, *18*(3), 259–269.

Chang, A. K., Fritschi, C., & Kim, M. J. (2013). Sedentary behavior, physical activity, and psychological health of Korean older adults with hypertension: Effect of an empowerment intervention. *Research in Gerontological Nursing*, *6*(2), 81–88.

Cheung, D. S. T., Deng, W., Tsao, S.-W., Ho, R. T. H., Chan, C. L. W., Fong, D. Y. T., Chau, P. H., Hong, A. W. L., Fung, H. Y. K. Y., & Ma, J. L. C. (2019). Effect of a qigong intervention on telomerase activity and mental health in Chinese women survivors of intimate partner violence: A randomized clinical trial. *JAMA Network Open*, *2*(1), e186967–e186967.

Choi, M., Ahn, S., & Jung, D. (2015). Psychometric evaluation of the Korean version of the Self-Efficacy for Exercise Scale for older adults. *Geriatric Nursing*, *36*(4), 301–305.

Choo, Y. T., Jiang, Y., Hong, J., & Wang, W. (2020). Effectiveness of Tai Chi on quality of life, depressive symptoms and physical function among community-dwelling older adults with chronic disease: A systematic review and meta-analysis. *International Journal of Nursing Studies*, *111*, 103737.

Dong, J., Wang, D., Li, H., & Ni, H. (2024). Effects of different Chinese traditional exercises on sleep quality and mental health of adults: Systematic review and meta-analysis. *Sleep and Breathing*, *28*(1), 29–39.

Dong, R. b., & Dou, K. y. (2023). Changes in physical activity level of adolescents and its relationship with mental health during regular COVID-19 prevention and control. *Brain and Behavior*, *13*(9), e3116.

Du, S., Tian, L., Tian, Y., Feng, Z., & Wang, Y. (2023). The role of self-efficacy and self-care agency as mediating factors in the link between health literacy and health-promoting lifestyle among older adults post covid 19 era: A multiple mediator model. *Geriatric Nursing*, *54*, 252–257.

El-Osta, A., Webber, D., Gnani, S., Banarsee, R., Mummery, D., Majeed, A., & Smith, P. (2019). The self-care matrix: A unifying framework for self-care. *SelfCare Journal, 10*(3), 38–56.

Erickson, K. I., Voss, M. W., Prakash, R. S., Basak, C., Szabo, A., Chaddock, L., Kim, J. S., Heo, S., Alves, H., & White, S. M. (2011). Exercise training increases size of hippocampus and improves memory. *Proceedings of the National Academy of Sciences*, *108*(7), 3017–3022.

Eun-Jung, K., Young, Ho, So. (2022). Difference of resilience according to stages of exercise behavior change and physical activity in male high school students. *Journal of Sport and Leisure Studies*, *1*, 215–225.

Fang, Y., Liu, J., Zhang, B., Lau, M., Ho, Y. F., Yang, Y., Shi, Y., Poon, E. T. C., Tse, A. C. Y., & Sun, F. (2024). A systematic review of the benefits and mechanisms of family-based mind-body therapy programs targeting families of children and adolescents with attention-deficit/hyperactivity disorder. *Journal of Social and Personal Relationships, 41*(8), 2219–2250.

Feter, N., Caputo, E., Delpino, F., Leite, J., da Silva, L., de Almeida Paz, I., Rocha, J. S., Vieira, Y., Schröeder, N., & da Silva, C. (2023). Physical activity and long COVID: Findings from the prospective study about mental and physical health in adults cohort. *Public Health*, *220*, 148–154.

Guo, L., & Liang, L. (2023). Physical activity as a causal variable for adolescent resilience levels: A cross-lagged analysis. *Frontiers in Psychology*, *14*, 1095999.

Hale, G. E., Colquhoun, L., Lancastle, D., Lewis, N., & Tyson, P. J. (2021). Physical activity interventions for the mental health and well-being of adolescents–a systematic review. *Child and Adolescent Mental Health*, *26*(4), 357–368.

Han, K., Lee, Y., Gu, J., Oh, H., Han, J., & Kim, K. (2015). Psychosocial factors for influencing healthy aging in adults in Korea. *Health and Quality of life Outcomes*, *13*, 1–10.

Harrison, L., Carducci, B., Klein, J. D., & Bhutta, Z. A. (2022). Indirect effects of COVID-19 on child and adolescent mental health: An overview of systematic reviews. *BMJ Global Health*, *7*(12), e010713.

Huang, Z., Ho, J. S., Ven Yap, Q., Chan, Y. H., Tan, S. Y., Ya, N. K. S., Low, L. P., Tan, H. C., Koh, W. P., & Chua, T. S. J. (2022). Patterns of motivators and barriers to heart health behaviors among adults with behavior-modifiable cardiovascular risk factors: A population-based survey in Singapore. *PLoS One*, *17*(1), e0262752.

Hughes, O., Shelton, K. H., Penny, H., & Thompson, A. R. (2023). Living with physical health conditions: A systematic review of mindfulness-based interventions for children, adolescents, and their parents. *Journal of Pediatric Psychology*, *48*(4), 396–413.

Hwang, P. W.-N., & Braun, K. L. (2015). The effectiveness of dance interventions to improve older adults' health: A systematic literature review. *Alternative Therapies in Health and Medicine*, *21*(5), 64.

Hyun Cha, N., Ju Seo, E., & Sok, S. R. (2012). Factors influencing the successful aging of older Korean adults. *Contemporary Nurse*, *41*(1), 78–87.

Jang, S., & Yang, E. (2023). Sleep, physical activity, and sedentary behaviors as factors related to depression and health-related quality of life among older women living alone: A population-based study. *European Review of Aging and Physical Activity*, *20*(1), 6.

Ji-Hang, L. (2022). The mediated effects of resilience on the relations between physical activity and academic stress in middle and high school students. *Journal of Sport and Leisure Studies*, *10*, 377–387.

Jiang, Y., Pu, Y., & Zhao, Y. (2021). Analysis of college students' home exercise and mental state during the Novel Corona Pneumonia Epidemic. In *2021 2nd Asia-Pacific Conference on Image Processing, Electronics and Computers*, Dalian, China.

Jo, E., Seo, K., Nam, B., Shin, D., Kim, S., Jeong, Y., Kim, A., & Kim, Y. (2023). Deterioration of mental health in children and adolescents during the COVID-19 pandemic. *Journal of the Korean Academy of Child and Adolescent Psychiatry*, *34*(1), 21.

Jung, H. (2023). Mental health status of individuals with diabetes in Korea before and during the COVID-19 pandemic: A comparison of data from the Korean national health and nutrition examination surveys of 2018–2019 and 2020–2021. *BMJ Open*, *13*(10), e074080.

Kim, Y., Hong, S., & Choi, M. (2022). Effects of serious games on depression in older adults: Systematic review and meta-analysis of randomized controlled trials. *Journal of Medical Internet Research*, *24*(9), e37753.

Kong, L., Ren, J., Fang, S., He, T., Zhou, X., & Fang, M. (2022). Effects of traditional Chinese mind-body exercise-Baduanjin for type 2 diabetes on psychological well-being: A systematic review and meta-analysis. *Frontiers in Public Health*, *10*, 923411.

Kukihara, H., Yamawaki, N., Ando, M., Tamura, Y., Arita, K., & Nakashima, E. (2018). The mediating effects of resilience, morale, and sense of coherence between physical activity and perceived physical/mental health among Japanese community-dwelling older adults: A cross-sectional study. *Journal of Aging and Physical Activity*, *26*(4), 544–552.

Leavitt, V., Cirnigliaro, C., Cohen, A., Farag, A., Brooks, M., Wecht, J., Wylie, G., Chiaravalloti, N., DeLuca, J., & Sumowski, J. (2014). Aerobic exercise increases hippocampal volume and improves memory in multiple sclerosis: Preliminary findings. *Neurocase*, *20*(6), 695–697.

Lee, L.-L., Perng, S.-J., Ho, C.-C., Hsu, H.-M., Lau, S.-C., & Arthur, A. (2009). A preliminary reliability and validity study of the Chinese version of the self-efficacy for exercise scale for older adults. *International Journal of Nursing Studies*, *46*(2), 230–238.

Lee, S. H., Jeon, Y., Huang, C.-W., Cheon, C., & Ko, S.-G. (2022). Qigong and tai chi on human health: An overview of systematic reviews. *The American Journal of Chinese Medicine*, *50*(8), 1995–2010.

Lee, T., Chung, J., Song, K., & Ji, Y. (2023). Prevalence and associated factors of cognitive frailty in community-dwelling older adults: Results from the Korean longitudinal study of aging. *International Journal of Older People Nursing*, *18*(6), e12576.

Leung, K.-C. W., Yang, Y.-J., Hui, S. S.-C., & Woo, J. (2021). Mind-body health benefits of traditional Chinese qigong on women: A systematic review of randomized controlled trials. *Evidence-Based Complementary and Alternative Medicine*, *2021*(1), 7443498.

Li, S., & Wang, Y. (2023). Cross-lagged analysis of the relationship between risk perception, physical activity, and adolescent mental health. *International Journal of Health Sciences*, *7*(S1), 1977–1987.

Li, X., Wang, P., Jiang, Y., Yang, Y., Wang, F., Yan, F., Li, M., Peng, W., & Wang, Y. (2024). Physical activity and health-related quality of life in older adults: Depression as a mediator. *BMC Geriatrics*, *24*(1), 26.

Liao, Y.-C., Huang, T.-Y., Lin, S.-H., Wu, C.-H., Chang, K.-T., Hsieh, S., Lin, S.-H., Goh, J.O.S., & Yang, C.-T. (2023). Mediating role of resilience in the relationships of physical activity and mindful self-awareness with peace of mind among college students. *Scientific Reports*, *13*(1), 10386.

Lim, Y. M., Baek, J., Lee, S., & Kim, J. S. (2022). Association between loneliness and depression among community-dwelling older women living alone in South Korea: The mediating effects of subjective physical health, resilience, and social support. *International Journal of Environmental Research and Public Health*, *19*(15), 9246.

Lin, H., Wang, B., Hu, Y., Song, X., & Zhang, D. (2022). Physical activity and interpersonal adaptation in Chinese adolescents after COVID-19: The mediating roles of self-esteem and psychological resilience. *Psychological Reports*, *127*(3), 1156–1174.

Lin, Y., Zhao, B., & Ma, X. (2022). The Influence of Guozhuang Dance on the subjective well-being of older adults: The chain mediating effect of group identity and self-efficacy. *International Journal of Environmental Research and Public Health*, *19*(21), 14545.

Liu, H., Shi, Y., Auden, E., & Rozelle, S. (2018). Anxiety in rural Chinese children and adolescents: Comparisons across provinces and among subgroups. *International Journal of Environmental Research and Public Health*, *15*(10), 2087.

Liu, Y., Verma, R., & Theng, Y.-L. (2023). Determining factors on active aging in Asia and Oceania: A systematic review. *Aging*, 77–111.

Matias, T., Dominski, F. H., & Marks, D. F. (2020). Human needs in COVID-19 isolation. *Journal of Health Psychology*, *25*(7), 871–882.

Moosa, A. S., Ng, D. X., Aau, W. K., Goy, W. T. T., Yang, C. R., Sim, E. H. A., Wee, J. D., & Tan, N. C. (2023). Resilience and coping behaviour among adolescents in a high-income city-state during the COVID-19 pandemic. *Scientific Reports*, *13*(1), 4061.

Neill, R. D., Lloyd, K., Best, P., & Tully, M. A. (2020). The effects of interventions with physical activity components on adolescent mental health: Systematic review and meta-analysis. *Mental Health and Physical Activity*, *19*, 100359.

Nishida, T., Ide, Y., Honda, A., & Honda, S. (2023). Association between frequency of exercise at home and depression during the COVID-19 epidemic among Japanese community-dwelling older adults. *International Journal of Gerontology*, *17*(3), 167–171.

Okuyama, J., Seto, S., Fukuda, Y., Funakoshi, S., Amae, S., Onobe, J., Izumi, S., Ito, K., & Imamura, F. (2021). Mental health and physical activity among children and adolescents during the COVID-19 pandemic. *The Tohoku Journal of Experimental Medicine*, *253*(3), 203–215.

Ou, K.-L., Wong, M. Y. C., Chung, P. K., & Chui, K. Y. K. (2022). Effect of square dance interventions on physical and mental health among Chinese older adults: A systematic review. *International Journal of Environmental Research and Public Health*, *19*(10), 6181.

Pan, M., Ying, B., Lai, Y., & Kuan, G. (2022). Status and influencing factors of physical exercise among college students in china: A systematic review. *International Journal of Environmental Research and Public Health*, *19*(20), 13465.

Paunova-Markova, E., Alexandrova-Karamanova, A., Yordanova, T., & Mineva, K. (2023). Impact of the covid-19 pandemic on adolescent mental health and well-being. *Central European Journal of Paediatrics*, *19*(1), 54–64.

Qin, F., Song, Y., Nassis, G. P., Zhao, L., Dong, Y., Zhao, C., Feng, Y., & Zhao, J. (2020). Physical activity, screen time, and emotional well-being during the 2019 novel coronavirus outbreak in China. *International Journal of Environmental Research and Public Health*, *17*(14), 5170.

Ravens-Sieberer, U., Kaman, A., Devine, J., & Reiß, F. (2023). The COVID-19 pandemic-How did it affect the mental health of children? *Monatsschrift Kinderheilkunde*, 1–7.

Reangsing, C., Lauderman, C., & Schneider, J. K. (2022). Effects of mindfulness meditation intervention on depressive symptoms in emerging adults: A systematic review and meta-analysis. *Journal of Integrative and Complementary Medicine*, *28*(1), 6–24.

Riskowski, J. L., & Almeheyawi, R. (2019). Effects of tai chi and qigong in children and adolescents: A systematic review of trials. *Adolescent Research Review*, *4*, 73–91.

Rodriguez-Ayllon, M., Cadenas-Sánchez, C., Estévez-López, F., Muñoz, N. E., Mora-Gonzalez, J., Migueles, J. H., Molina-García, P., Henriksson, H., Mena-Molina, A., & Martínez-Vizcaíno, V. (2019). Role of physical activity and sedentary behavior in the mental health of preschoolers, children and adolescents: A systematic review and meta-analysis. *Sports Medicine*, *49*(9), 1383–1410.

Ryan, R. M., & Deci, E. L. (2017). *Self-determination theory: Basic psychological needs in motivation, development, and wellness*. Guilford publications.

Sabri, S., Rashid, N., & Mao, Z.-X. (2023). Physical activity and exercise as a tool to cure anxiety and posttraumatic stress disorder. *Mental Illness*, *2023*(1), 4294753.

Sadatnia, M., Jalali, A., Tapak, L., & Shamsaei, F. (2023). The relationship between mental health and loneliness in the elderly during the covid-19 pandemic. *Journal of Ageing and Longevity*, *3*(3), 433–441.

Sareen, J. (2014). Posttraumatic stress disorder in adults: Impact, comorbidity, risk factors, and treatment. *The Canadian Journal of Psychiatry*, *59*(9), 460–467.

Shiraz, F., Hildon, Z., & Vrijhoef, H. (2020). Exploring the perceptions of the ageing experience in Singaporean older adults: A qualitative study. *Journal of Cross-Cultural Gerontology*, *35*(4), 389–408.

Stahl, J. E., Belisle, S. S., & Zhao, W. (2020). Medical Qigong for mobility and balance self-confidence in older adults. *Frontiers in Medicine*, *7*, 559349.

Su, Z., & Zhao, J. (2021). Comparative study of the effects of Tai Chi and square dance on immune function, physical health, and life satisfaction in urban empty-nest older adults. *Frontiers in Physiology*, *12*, 721758.

Tang, Y.-Y., Fan, Y., Lu, Q., Tan, L.-H., Tang, R., Kaplan, R. M., Pinho, M. C., Thomas, B. P., Chen, K., & Friston, K. J. (2020). Long-term physical exercise and mindfulness practice in an aging population. *Frontiers in Psychology*, *11*, 358.

Thompson, W. R., Sallis, R., Joy, E., Jaworski, C. A., Stuhr, R. M., & Trilk, J. L. (2020). Exercise is medicine. *American Journal of Lifestyle Medicine*, *14*(5), 511–523.

United Nations Department of Economic and Social Affairs, Population Division. (2022). *World Population Prospect 2022: Release note about major differences in total population estimates for mid-2021 between 2019 and 2022 revisions*. https://population.un.org/wpp/assets/Files/WPP2022_Release-Note-rev1.pdf (accessed on 12 September 2023).

Wang, D., Wang, P., Lan, K., Zhang, Y., & Pan, Y. (2020). Effectiveness of Tai chi exercise on overall quality of life and its physical and psychological components among older adults: A systematic review and meta-analysis. *Brazilian Journal of Medical and Biological Research*, *53*, e10196.

Wang, P., Wang, M., Shan, J., Liu, X., Jing, Y., Zhu, H., Zheng, G., Peng, W., & Wang, Y. (2024). Association between residential greenness and depression symptoms in Chinese community-dwelling older adults. *Environmental Research*, *243*, 117869.

Wang, X., Pi, Y., Chen, B., Chen, P., Liu, Y., Wang, R., Li, X., Zhu, Y., Yang, Y., & Niu, Z. (2015). Effect of traditional Chinese exercise on the quality of life and depression for chronic diseases: A meta-analysis of randomised trials. *Scientific Reports*, *5*(1), 15913.

Wang, Z., Jiang, B., Wang, X., Li, Z., Wang, D., Xue, H., & Wang, D. (2023). Relationship between physical activity and individual mental health after traumatic events: A systematic review. *European Journal of Psychotraumatology*, *14*(2), 2205667.

WHO. (2007). *The optimal mix ofservice. Gneva, World Health Organization, 2007*. https://communitykeepers.org/wp-content/uploads/2021/04/2_Optimal-Mix-of-Services_Infosheet.pdf (accessed on 1 May 2024).

WHO. (2019a). *Mental health: Strengthening our response*. https://www.who.int/news-room/fact-sheets/detail/mental-health-strengthening-our-response (accessed on 1 May 2024).

WHO. (2019b). *The WHO special initiative for mental health (2019–2023): Universal health coverage for mental health.* https://iris.who.int/handle/10665/310981 (accessed on 1 May 2024).

WHO. (2020). *WHO guidelines on physical activity and sedentary behaviour*. https://www.who.int/publications/i/item/9789240015128. (accessed on 1 May 2024).

WHO. (2022). *Physical activity - Great for your body, great for your mind.* https://www.who.int/news-room/feature-stories/detail/physical-activity---great-for-your-body--great-for-your-mind. (accessed on 1 May 2024).

Windle, G. (2011). What is resilience? A review and concept analysis. *Reviews in Clinical Gerontology*, *21*(2), 152–169.

Wong, M. Y. C., Ou, K.-L., Chung, P. K., Chui, K. Y. K., & Zhang, C.-Q. (2023). The relationship between physical activity, physical health, and mental health among older Chinese adults: A scoping review. *Frontiers in Public Health*, *10*, 914548.

Wong, M. Y. C., Ou, K.-L., & Man Leung, K. (2023). Investigating and promoting health behaviors reactivity among Hong Kong older adults in the post-COVID-19 Era: An exploratory network analysis. *PLoS One*, *18*(11), e0293512.

Wu, Y., Wen, J., Wang, X., Wang, Q., Wang, W., Wang, X., Xie, J., & Cong, L. (2022). Associations between e-health literacy and chronic disease self-management in older Chinese patients with chronic non-communicable diseases: A mediation analysis. *BMC Public Health*, *22*(1), 2226.

Wut, T.-M., Lee, S. W., & Xu, J. (2023). Mental health of working adults during the COVID-19 pandemic: Does physical activity level matter? *International Journal of Environmental Research and Public Health*, *20*(4), 2961.

Xiang, M.-Q., Tan, X.-M., Sun, J., Yang, H.-Y., Zhao, X.-P., Liu, L., Hou, X.-H., & Hu, M. (2020). Relationship of physical activity with anxiety and depression symptoms in Chinese college students during the COVID-19 outbreak. *Frontiers in Psychology*, *11*, 582436.

Xu, L., Gu, H., Cai, X., Zhang, Y., Hou, X., Yu, J., & Sun, T. (2023). The effects of exercise for cognitive function in older adults: A systematic review and meta-analysis of randomized controlled trials. *International Journal of Environmental Research and Public Health*, *20*(2), 1088.

Yao, S.-J., Ma, Q.-S., Liu, C., Cao, D.-W., Lyu, T., & Guo, K.-L. (2023). The relationship between physical exercise and subjective well-being among Chinese junior high school students: A chain mediating model. *Frontiers in Psychology*, *13*, 1053252.

Yuan, Y., Peng, C., Burr, J. A., & Lapane, K. L. (2023). Frailty, cognitive impairment, and depressive symptoms in Chinese older adults: An eight-year multi-trajectory analysis. *BMC Geriatrics*, *23*(1), 843.

Zhang, J., Paksarian, D., Lamers, F., Hickie, I. B., He, J., & Merikangas, K. R. (2017). Sleep patterns and mental health correlates in US adolescents. *The Journal of Pediatrics*, *182*, 137–143.

Zhang, S., Zou, L., Chen, L.-Z., Yao, Y., Loprinzi, P. D., Siu, P. M., & Wei, G.-X. (2019). The effect of Tai Chi Chuan on negative emotions in non-clinical populations: A meta-analysis and systematic review. *International Journal of Environmental Research and Public Health*, *16*(17), 3033.

Zheng, C., Huang, W. Y.-J., Sun, F.-H., Wong, M. C.-S., Siu, P. M.-F., Chen, X.-K., & Wong, S. H.-S. (2025). Association of sedentary lifestyle with risk of acute and post-acute COVID-19 sequelae: A retrospective cohort study. *The American Journal of Medicine, 138*(2):298–307.e4.

Zhu, L., Li, L., Li, X.-z., & Wang, L. (2021). Effects of mind-body exercise on PTSD symptoms, depression and anxiety in PTSD patients: A protocol of systematic review and meta-analysis. *Medicine*, *100*(4), e24447.

Zhu, X., Haegele, J. A., & Healy, S. (2019). Movement and mental health: Behavioral correlates of anxiety and depression among children of 6–17 years old in the US. *Mental Health and Physical Activity*, *16*, 60–65.

Zhu, X., Haegele, J. A., Liu, H., & Yu, F. (2021). Academic stress, physical activity, sleep, and mental health among Chinese adolescents. *International Journal of Environmental Research and Public Health*, *18*(14), 7257.

Zhu, X., Haegele, J. A., Tang, Y., & Wu, X. (2017). Physical activity and sedentary behaviors of urban Chinese children: Grade level prevalence and academic burden associations. *BioMed Research International*, *2017*, 7540147.

Zhu, Z., Xu, J., Lin, Y., Chai, K., Zhou, Y., Jia, R., Ni, H., Wu, M., Wen, C., & Qiao, Y. (2022). Correlation between nutritional status and oral health quality of life, self-efficacy of older inpatients and the influencing factors. *BMC Geriatrics*, *22*(1), 280.

Zou, L., Sasaki, J. E., Wang, H., Xiao, Z., Fang, Q., & Zhang, M. (2017). A systematic review and meta-analysis of baduanjin qigong for health benefits: Randomized controlled trials. *Evidence-Based Complementary and Alternative Medicine*, *2017,* 4548706.

Zou, L., Yeung, A., Quan, X., Hui, S. S.-C., Hu, X., Chan, J. S., Wang, C., Boyden, S. D., Sun, L., & Wang, H. (2018). Mindfulness-based Baduanjin exercise for depression and anxiety in people with physical or mental illnesses: A systematic review and meta-analysis. *International Journal of Environmental Research and Public Health*, *15*(2), 321.

13

PROMOTING MENTAL HEALTH THROUGH PHYSICAL ACTIVITY

Evidence from Greece, Italy and Spain

Giampaolo Santi, Marta Duina, Dimitrios Kokaridas, Athanasios Papaioannou, Joan Pons, Marta Borrueco and Attilio Carraro

13.1 Preface

The relationship between physical activity (PA) and mental health has been explored by an increasing number of research works in recent decades (Sabe et al., 2022; Smith & Merwin, 2021; World Health Organization [WHO], 2010), and several disciplines have approached it from different perspectives (physiological, psychological, social and educational). A growing body of evidence highlights the pivotal role of exercise in preventing and managing a wide spectrum of mental health conditions, from anxiety and depression to chronic stress and cognitive decline (Anderson & Shivakumar, 2013; Biddle, 2016; Rahmati et al., 2024). Similarly, PA or exercise is often related to positive mental health states, such as increased self-esteem, body image satisfaction and satisfaction with life (Hausenblas & Fallon, 2006; Liu et al., 2015; Rejeski & Mihalko, 2001). This chapter delves into this relationship, focusing specifically on research works conducted in three countries of South Europe with rich cultural and historical ties to PA: Greece, Italy and Spain.

The Mediterranean area, which encompasses Greece, Italy and Spain among other countries, has a long-standing tradition of PA embedded in its cultural fabric (Legrand et al., 2021). From the ancient Greeks' emphasis on the harmonious development of mind and body, to the modern use of the Latin poet Giovenale's sentence *mens sana in corpore sano* (a healthy mind in a healthy body), to the contemporary popularity of outdoor pursuits and sports, physical exertion has been a cornerstone of life in these countries. However, despite this deep-rooted connection and this historical and cultural affinity for movement, these nations, like many others, are grappling with the rising prevalence of sedentary lifestyles and associated mental health challenges.

DOI: 10.4324/9781003517474-18

This chapter aims to bridge the gap between the area's historical and cultural heritage of PA and its contemporary mental health landscape. By examining the current state of PA and mental health in Greece, Italy and Spain, we seek to identify opportunities for promoting mental well-being through PA and exercise. This includes exploring the effectiveness of various exercise interventions, the role of policy and environmental factors, and the potential for leveraging cultural and historical resources to amplify the mental health benefits of PA.

It is essential to acknowledge that, while the Mediterranean area shares commonalities in its approach to PA and health, there are also significant cultural, socioeconomic and epidemiological differences among Greece, Italy and Spain. This chapter will therefore examine the unique characteristics of each country, highlighting both similarities and contrasts in the relationship between PA and mental health. Moreover, it is also important to note that these three countries only represent a portion of the broader European Mediterranean area, with North Africa and Western Asia presenting additional cultural and contextual variations.

By providing a comprehensive overview of the current evidence and practices in Greece, Italy and Spain, this chapter seeks to inform the development of effective and culturally appropriate interventions to promote mental health through PA and exercise. Ultimately, our goal is to inspire researchers, policymakers and practitioners to harness the power of PA to enhance the mental well-being of populations in the Mediterranean area and beyond.

13.2 Previous Evidence from Systematic Review and Meta-Analysis

PA practice leads to psychological and physiological benefits, thus favouring mental health. Engaging in PA is related to lower levels of anxiety and stress, as well as a lower incidence of mental disorders (Callow et al., 2020; Saxena et al., 2005; Stanton et al., 2014). Gender differences exist in this area, with women reporting higher levels of depression, stress, and anxiety compared to men (Graves et al., 2021; Seedat et al., 2009). These disparities are more evident in Europe (Mateo-Orcajada et al., 2023). Additionally, women also tend to practice less PA than men at any age (Bauman et al., 2009; Mielgo-Ayuso et al., 2016; Owen et al., 2025), and this can have an influence on gender differences in mental health outcomes.

Despite the consistent body of studies around the world connecting PA and mental health, limited systematic reviews and meta-analyses have addressed the peculiarities of Greece, Italy or Spain. An exception to this is a systematic review, involving also Italy and Spain among other European countries, focused on the benefits associated with PA in nature (Eigenschenk et al., 2019). The authors qualitatively identified six categories of benefits: physical health, mental health and well-being, education and life-long learning, active citizenship, crime reduction and reduction in anti-social behaviour. However, they also indicated the impossibility to conduct meta-analyses due to heterogeneity of measures and study designs and highlighted gaps in the literature, especially regarding the long-term effects of outdoor sports on personal and social development. The need for large, well-designed and longitudinal studies was also mentioned in conclusions. Since then, however, most of studies have been cross-sectional, with conclusions that are limited in terms of causality and long-term impacts.

A notable meta-analysis, conducted in Europe by Yuan et al. (2022) and focused on postpartum depression, demonstrated significant correlations between PA and reduced postpartum depression risk (adjusted OR = 0.85; 95% CI: 0.76–0.95; $p = 0.004$), suggesting sport activities should be prescribed as a treatment among pregnant women. In particular, the authors classified three different PA types: sport, work and household activities. They highlighted that only sport activities were associated with reduced postpartum depression symptoms (adjusted OR = 0.89, 95% CI: 0.78 to 1.00, $p < 0.001$), while the other two types of PA, on the other hand, showed contrasting results, with some even increasing the risk of postpartum depression.

More recently, Teno and colleagues (2024) systematically reviewed studies on the association between PA, sedentary behaviour and mental health in adults. Based on their review, they asserted that leisure time PA shows a stronger association with mental health, if compared to transportation or occupational PA. Despite this study is not strictly focused on European countries, it compares results for geographic region, concluding that Europeans show better mental health also in relation to transportation or occupational PA. This does not appear true for European women of low social classes that only find beneficial leisure time PA, and this is in line with Yuan and colleagues' (2022) findings.

In addition to scientific research, it is interesting to note the active role of governments and institutions in countries such as Greece, Italy and Spain in promoting PA to improve mental health. These countries have introduced public health initiatives, school programmes and even economic incentives aimed at encouraging PA participation. For example, Spain, Italy and Greece have all been involved in the *MENS – Mental European Network of Sport Events*, a project co-financed by the European Commission under the Erasmus+ Sport programme. This initiative aims to develop a documented and concrete approach to sports practice in the treatment of mental health issues. The project involved partners from several European countries and aimed to create a European network linking mental health and sports (CESIE, n.d.). Additionally, the *Let's Fit Healthy Life! The role of sport in regenerating deprived areas* project has inspired various territorial areas in these countries to implement pilot initiatives on health, promoting specific physical activities and more active lifestyles. The initiative aims to raise awareness and encourage local and regional stakeholders to adopt policies promoting and developing PA and sports at the local level (Regione Piemonte, 2019). In terms of education, the *Physical Education and Sport in Schools in Europe* report examines the approaches of Spain, Italy and Greece to the development and promotion of physical education and PA in schools, providing an overview of national strategies and large-scale initiatives in this area (European Commission, 2013). A preeminent action to promote PA among European adolescents and influence psychological variables was the IMPACT (*Identifying and Motivating Youth who mostly need Physical Activity*) project, which involved Greece, Italy and Spain among other countries (Maltagliati et al., 2023; Pons et al., 2023; Saoudi et al., 2024). The IMPACT was a European Union funded project run between 2016 and 2019 that aimed at improving attitudes towards PA and subjective well-being among adolescent students. These efforts illustrate the importance of governmental and institutional support in promoting PA as a key factor for improving public mental health.

Considering this brief overview, we think there is a need for summarising the most recent scientific research on this topic and for these geographical areas (i.e. Greece, Italy and Spain), with the aim to highlight current trends, but also gaps in the literature. The following section, therefore, aims to summarise the most recent literature that explored the relationship between PA and mental health in Greece, Italy and Spain. The paragraphs are structured to discuss research conducted in each of these three countries, highlighting the research directions that have characterised each scenario.

Some studies have been purposefully excluded from the review below, as it was not possible to distinguish between the benefits of PA and those due to other variables. For example, a few studies explored PA as a component of the 'Mediterranean lifestyle' (Fastame et al., 2015; Knox & Muros, 2017), which may also include peculiar dietary habits (i.e., 'Mediterranean diet'; Martínez-González et al., 2017). This made it difficult to distinguish between the benefits of a physically active lifestyle and those of a healthy diet. Similarly, a study was conducted among psychiatric patients and did not discern between the sole effect of PA and the effect of pharmacological treatment (Belvederi Murri et al., 2015).

13.3 Updated Evidence from Greece

Recent research in Greece was conducted during the COVID-19 pandemic. PA programmes implemented during the two quarantine periods led to a reduction in depression and anxiety (Skalidou et al., 2023), suggesting that this type of intervention should be included by the government in future emergencies. The association between PA and mental health during the COVID-19 pandemic was also studied in another investigation conducted on isolated Greek islands (Kassimi et al., 2023). Findings from this study highlighted how changes in physical and mental health were partly influenced by PA levels; however, these relationships remained unchanged despite the COVID-19 pandemic. Given the increased psychological stress during crises, PA could offer a valuable tool for reducing anxiety and promoting well-being, and investigating the long-term benefits of such programmes could help integrate them into future public health policies, ensuring accessible mental health support during emergencies. Considering that well-being and most particularly depressive symptoms during the COVID-19 period were below the threshold indicated by the WHO's guidelines, researchers recommended an increase of PA, decrease of sedentariness and improvement of eating behaviour as a priority for communities and policy makers (Morres et al., 2021).

Studies conducted prior to the pandemic supported the positive association between physical exercise and mental health in older patients with type 2 diabetes (Klinis et al., 2022) and in caregivers of people experiencing mental health issues (Zacharis et al., 2020). In these settings, physical exercise programmes can be prescribed as treatment, given their positive outcomes on both caregivers and patients with diabetes, although in this last case, a proper diet should be associated. PA exerts a favourable effect even on patients suffering a great deal of stress from serious health conditions such as cancer which creates a new reality and brings people face to face with new dilemmas and problems. Research findings also emerged supporting the beneficial effect of exercise as part of supportive group therapy interventions on psychiatric morbidity of cancer patients, especially in the field of anxiety and insomnia with positive outcomes on anger and mood (Papastergiou et al., 2018, 2020).

Research in Greece also focused on the application of adapted exercise programmes for people with psychosis combined with a token economy system approach, a behavioural therapy that uses a token as a reward for positive behaviours by the participant with schizophrenia and is given at predetermined times during the exercise programme. Target behaviours are those related to improve patients' self-care and personal hygiene skills, and their participation in daily work activities, social interaction and participation in treatment. The rewards (tokens) are given immediately to the patient as soon as he or she exhibits the desired behaviour, aiming to encourage the individual to continue pursuing this behaviour that leads to positive changes. Research-wise, the benefits of such programme in improving behavioural, health and quality of life parameters of patients with schizophrenia are reflected in published studies that also describe in detail the exercise programme for participants with psychosis (Kokaridas et al., 2013; Maggouritsa, Kokaridas, Stoforos, et al., 2014; Maggouritsa, Kokaridas, Theodorakis, et al., 2014). Moreover, Gabrščšek et al.'s (2019) subsequent study showed that goal-setting also has the potential to improve physical condition aspects and promote exercise commitment in patients with schizophrenia.

Further studies in Greece have also focused on mental health among refugees, demonstrating a link between perceived fitness, low-intensity PA and mental well-being (Filippou et al., 2024; Gerber et al., 2021). Researchers concluded that exercise can be prescribed as a form of treatment even in refugee camps, but also highlighted the need for more objective measurement of PA, such as through instrumental measures. Other studies also support the beneficial effect of exercise on mood, anxiety, self-esteem and quality of life of inmates in Greek prison settings (Psychou et al., 2019, 2021). Nevertheless, larger samples of both male and female inmates are needed in future studies to portray an overall picture of the effect of exercise interventions on improving prisoners' psychological health and coping with prison conditions.

Intervention programmes optimising the effectiveness of exercise to sustain rehabilitation efforts and skill development for individuals with substance use disorders has also been developed, encompassing goal-setting, emotional control, social interaction, communication, problem-solving, and decision-making into the context of treatment protocols (Theodorakis et al., 2024). Conclusively, researchers urged the need for new initiatives to be taken by advocating for inclusive policies, promoting community engagement and fostering collaborations across sectors.

Overall, research in Greece is consistent in highlighting positive relationships between PA levels and mental health. Several studies indicated how PA programmes or exercise can be prescribed to reduce mental illness, such as symptoms of depression in patients with major depression (Morres, Hatzigeorgiadis, Stathi, et al., 2019), with findings providing valuable evidence about the relationship between objectively measured moderate PA and lower depression in patients with major depressive disorder (Morres, Hatzigeorgiadis, Krommidas, et al., 2019). Further research should explore the effectiveness of PA programmes in increasing PA levels measured through instrumental measures, and in promoting positive mental health outcomes, including emotional, psychological and social well-being.

13.4 Updated Evidence from Italy

A vast amount of research in Italy has been conducted during the COVID-19 pandemic. Ricci and colleagues (2023) found a link between physical exercise and psychological outcomes, such as depressive and somatic symptomatology, and life satisfaction. While they did not administer any PA programme in their study, they assessed the time spent on physical exercise through self-report questionnaire. Unlike research in Greece, Ricci et al. (2023) also focused on positive aspects of mental health like satisfaction with life. Still in time of COVID-19, a comparative study between Italy and the United Kingdom (Sansone-Pollock et al., 2023) has highlighted how stricter governmental restrictions on outdoor PA (in Italy) were linked to increased levels of stress and depression. In general, the reduced amount of PA due to the COVID-19 restrictions was often found to be linked with increased stress and reduced mental health (Cerea et al., 2023), suggesting PA as a protective factor in front of stressful situations.

Italian research during the pandemic has also investigated the relationship between PA habits and exercise addiction (Ceci et al., 2023). Specifically, according to Ceci and colleagues (2023), people afraid of getting infected by the virus developed habits leading to exercise addiction. People with high exercise addiction were also more prone to perceive higher benefits from practicing PA, thus incurring a vicious cycle.

Another Italian study compared athletes and non-athletes during COVID-19 lockdowns (Elce et al., 2022). The study findings highlighted initial differences in terms of sleep and mental health, with athletes being healthier. These differences, however, were flattened during the lockdown periods suggesting that the absence of sport practice was detrimental for athletes' health. In the same period, other authors investigated gender differences and found women to be more resilient than men in coping with the decrease of PA caused by the lockdown (Orlandi et al., 2021).

Most of this research in the Italian context investigated the decrease in PA due to the COVID-19 pandemic and its association with mental health issues, such as stress, anxiety and depression. A general trend indicated an inverse relationship with reduction in PA associated with increased symptoms of mental illness (Maugeri et al., 2020). This trend emerged also in a comparative study conducted in Italy, Germany, Russia and Spain (Brailovskaia et al., 2021). Similarly, research conducted in Spain (Jiménez-Pavón et al., 2020) revealed the same trend in a specific population of older adults.

It should be noted that this relationship has also been observed before and after the pandemic, thus can be considered a general rule in Italy. Levante and colleagues (2024) for example, highlighted an association between PA habits and psychological distress among a sample of female university students, with more active students being less distressed. A similar study from Maran and colleagues (2018) explored how physical practice and wellness courses can reduce distress among police officers. Further research investigated how PA promotion interventions proposed in city parks led to a reduction in the state of tension, sadness and fatigue, and an improvement in the state of energy, serenity and vitality (Toselli et al., 2022).

Another direction of research in Italy focuses on instruments validation for psychiatric settings. Carraro and colleagues (Carraro et al., 2020, 2023), in particular, validated the M-BACK and the EMIQ-HP for use among an Italian-speaking population. The M-BACK measures the awareness of health professionals regarding the barriers, attitudes, confidence and knowledge regarding PA in psychiatric patients with metabolic syndrome. The EMIQ-HP measures the awareness of health professionals regarding the role of exercise in people with mental illness. Other studies in this direction (Bonfioli et al., 2018) explored the effectiveness of lifestyle intervention programmes for psychotic patients, demonstrating that these kinds of interventions can increase PA levels and improve their dietary habits. A previous study conducted by Carpiniello and colleagues (Carpiniello et al., 2013) also indicated the need for more research focused on identifying barriers to PA in patients with mental disorders. However, since then, not much has been done in this research direction.

Collectively, research in Italy also supported the positive relationship between PA levels and mental health. Contrary to research in Greece, which only focused on the negative aspects of mental health, Italian studies have also considered positive states, such as satisfaction with life or psychological well-being (Cerea et al., 2023; Ricci et al., 2023). Like in Greece, PA levels were generally measured through self-report measures, which underscores the importance of including more instrumental measures of PA. About the specific population investigated, no studies in Italy emerged that have explored refugees, but a relevant research direction focused on psychiatric contexts (Bonfioli et al., 2018; Carraro et al., 2020, 2023).

13.5 Updated Evidence from Spain

Research conducted during the COVID-19 home confinement in Spain (Cecchini et al., 2023) highlighted how, in the general population, higher frequency of PA was associated with sustained attention, increased alertness and enthusiasm. In the same period of time, studies among specific populations indicated consistent results (Fennell et al., 2022; Gutiérrez-Santamaría et al., 2023; Pons et al., 2020). Gutiérrez-Santamaría and colleagues (2023), for example, found that the decline in PA levels due to the quarantines led to decreased psychological well-being in cancer patients. Additionally, studies involving university students emphasised how engaging in PA during COVID-19 lockdowns helped to maintain good mental health (Fennell et al., 2022). Similarly, Pons and colleagues' (2020) study with athlete population indicated that the possibility to keep training conditions as much regular as possible was associated with better mental health.

Like in Italy, research in Spain has also focused on psychiatric settings exploring the beneficial psychological effects of exercise and behavioural counselling in outpatients with schizophrenia (Fernández-Abascal et al., 2023). After a 24-month programme, participants showed reduced waist circumference, reduced negative symptomatology, and increased motivation towards exercise. No other studies, however, followed this research direction.

Studies conducted in Spain among specific populations also indicated consistent results. Specifically, a recent study in primary care settings (Hernández-Pizarro & Maynou, 2024) concluded that the prescription of PA not only contributes to the improvement of physical health but also helps preserve mental well-being. Similarly, Denche-Zamorano and colleagues (Denche-Zamorano, Salas-Gómez, et al., 2024) identified physical inactivity as a risk factor for depression in the adult (>40 years old) and elderly population. Another study (Denche-Zamorano, García-Paniagua, et al., 2024) found that women experiencing menopause problems reported lower psychological distress and higher self-esteem when being very physically active and perceiving high social support. Moreover, consistent results emerged for Spanish adults with diabetes (Denche-Zamorano, Pisà-Canyelles, et al., 2023): in this case, higher PA levels and perceived social support were indicative of lower psychological distress and higher self-perceived health. A large-scale study conducted among informal caregivers (people acting as caregivers without having a formal role) associated a lower PA frequency with higher levels of depression and anxiety as well as increased use of antidepressants and anxiolytics (Denche-Zamorano, Rodriguez-Redondo, et al., 2023). The beneficial effect of PA and sport practice on anxiety and depressive symptoms has also been highlighted in a Spanish prison population (Penado Abilleira et al., 2023). Furthermore, consistent results also emerged for Spanish adults with anxiety disorders: in this case, higher PA levels and perceived social support were indicative of lower psychological distress and higher self-perceived health (Pereira-Payo et al., 2023).

A unique research direction followed in Spain, which has not emerged in Greece and Italy, is the study of PA and mental health in relation to the urban environment (Zijlema et al., 2024). In their study developed in Barcelona, Zijlema and colleagues (2024) concluded that the differences in terms of mental health in people living in dense urban areas are mainly due to the air pollution rather than other factors such as population density or the possibility to practice outdoor PA. This finding suggests that environmental stressors linked to urbanisation, such as exposure to fine particulate matter and noise pollution, may play a more significant role in mental well-being. Research has shown that long-term exposure to air pollution, particularly fine particulate matter, is associated with an increased risk of depression, anxiety and cognitive decline due to neuroinflammatory responses and oxidative stress (Braithwaite et al., 2019; Xu et al., 2016). A potential reason for this relationship could be that air pollution does not just have physiological effects but also contributes to psychological distress, influencing mood disorders and overall quality of life. Studies indicate that urban environments with high pollution and noise levels tend to increase stress, whereas access to green spaces and well-designed public areas can mitigate these negative effects (Lederbogen et al., 2011; Van Den Bosch & Meyer-Lindenberg, 2019). In contrast, the Mediterranean lifestyle, which often emphasises social interactions in public spaces, walkability and access to nature, might counterbalance some of the negative effects typically associated with dense urban environments. Furthermore, this lifestyle is also characterised by active living, social engagement and a diet rich in antioxidants, and therefore has been linked to lower stress levels and better mental well-being (Sidossis et al., 2024). Further studies in this direction seem needed to compare different urban environments, taking into consideration not only pollution levels but also socio-cultural aspects that shape individuals' relationships with their surroundings. Concretely, it would be valuable to extend the research beyond urban settings to rural areas, where lower pollution levels and greater exposure to natural landscapes might offer protective factors for mental health, contributing to a more comprehensive understanding of the interplay between PA, environment and psychological well-being.

In sum, research on this topic in Spain presents similar key findings and limitations when compared to Italy. A strength of Spanish research is that the positive relationship between PA levels and mental health has been established among a large variety of population samples, including women in menopause, adults with diabetes, adults with anxiety disorders, and prisoners among others. Like in Greece and Italy, also future Spanish research should focus on evaluating the effectiveness of PA programmes and increase the number of instrumental measurements of PA practice.

13.6 Implications

The examined literature consistently supports the pivotal role of PA practice and exercise in fostering mental health. However, some common limitations should be acknowledged to be addressed in future studies. First of all, gender differences have rarely been researched or included among the analyses, with the exception of Orlandi et al.'s study (2021). If it is true that women tend to be less physically active and experience poorer mental health outcomes (Bauman et al., 2009; Mateo-Orcajada et al., 2023), this must be a focal point in future investigations.

A second point that future studies should take into consideration is the adoption of instrumental measures for both PA practice (e.g., accelerometers) and psychological outcomes (e.g. muscular tension as an indicator of stress). Even though the adoption of these measurements would affect the numerosity of sample size, it is also true that most of the research in this field is affected by an overuse of self-report instruments. Increasing research in this field is adopting new technologies (Phillips et al., 2018), such as mobile apps and wearable devices, so this is a potential direction that should be taken into account.

Third, PA is strongly linked with mental health, but little is known about the intensity of PA, the duration of the intervention, the type of PA (outdoor vs indoor, individual vs group, with instructor vs without instructor). Earlier research among a population of Italian cyclists (Whitaker, 2005) highlighted the beneficial effect of vigorous PA (i.e., cycling) in elderly age on mental health outcomes. However, this study seemed to remain isolated, and no further research has explored the effects of different intensities of PA on mental health.

Finally, despite a large number of cross-sectional studies, limited research in Southern Europe has explored how PA-based interventions may improve or maintain mental health. Again, while PA levels are positively correlated with improved mental health, we probably need less cross-sectional studies and more intervention research, especially randomised-controlled trials. The aim of this would be to provide us with details about which types of interventions may help overcome barriers and facilitate PA practice among various populations.

13.7 Conclusion

In conclusion, this chapter reviewed studies focusing on PA and mental health in Greece, Italy and Spain. A notable gap of systematic reviews and meta-analysis specific for these three countries emerged from the review; however, a large number of studies, mostly cross-sectional, highlighted the relationship between PA levels and mental health outcomes in a variety of population samples. Future research directions have also been drawn and need to address: (1) gender differences, with the aim to reduce gender inequalities in mental health outcomes; (2) the use of more instrumental measurements; (3) the impact of different intensity levels and types of PAs; (4) more intervention studies, rather than cross-sectional. Following these four points, future research will provide practical and useful advice to policy makers, helping them design more effective and targeted interventions. This would strengthen the importance of integrated policies, where PA programmes may become a fundamental instrument for the prevention of mental disorders and the promotion of positive mental health states.

References

Anderson, E. H., & Shivakumar, G. (2013). Effects of exercise and physical activity on anxiety. *Frontiers in Psychiatry*, *4*, 00027. https://www.frontiersin.org/journals/psychiatry/articles/10.3389/fpsyt.2013.00027

Bauman, A., Bull, F., Chey, T., Craig, C. L., Ainsworth, B. E., Sallis, J. F., Bowles, H. R., Hagstromer, M., Sjostrom, M., Pratt, M., & The IPS Group. (2009). The international prevalence study on physical activity: Results from 20 countries. *International Journal of Behavioral Nutrition and Physical Activity*, *6*(1), 21. https://doi.org/10.1186/1479-5868-6-21

Belvederi Murri, M., Amore, M., Menchetti, M., Toni, G., Neviani, F., Cerri, M., Rocchi, M. B. L., Zocchi, D., Bagnoli, L., Tam, E., Buffa, A., Ferrara, S., Neri, M., Alexopoulos, G. S., & Zanetidou, S. (2015). Physical exercise for late-life major depression. *British Journal of Psychiatry*, *207*(3), 235–242. https://doi.org/10.1192/bjp.bp.114.150516

Biddle, S. (2016). Physical activity and mental health: Evidence is growing. *World Psychiatry: Official Journal of the World Psychiatric Association (WPA)*, *15*(2), 176–177. https://doi.org/10.1002/wps.20331

Bonfioli, E., Mazzi, M. A., Berti, L., & Burti, L. (2018). Physical health promotion in patients with functional psychoses receiving community psychiatric services: Results of the PHYSICO-DSM-VR study. *Schizophrenia Research*, *193*, 406–411. https://doi.org/10.1016/j.schres.2017.06.017

Brailovskaia, J., Cosci, F., Mansueto, G., Miragall, M., Herrero, R., Baños, R. M., Krasavtseva, Y., Kochetkov, Y., & Margraf, J. (2021). The association between depression symptoms, psychological burden caused by Covid-19 and physical activity: An investigation in Germany, Italy, Russia, and Spain. *Psychiatry Research*, *295*, 113596. https://doi.org/10.1016/j.psychres.2020.113596

Braithwaite, I., Zhang, S., Kirkbride, J. B., Osborn, D. P. J., & Hayes, J. F. (2019). Air pollution (particulate matter) exposure and associations with depression, anxiety, bipolar, psychosis and suicide risk: A systematic review and meta-analysis. *Environmental Health Perspectives*, *127*(12), 126002. https://doi.org/10.1289/EHP4595

Callow, D. D., Arnold-Nedimala, N. A., Jordan, L. S., Pena, G. S., Won, J., Woodard, J. L., & Smith, J. C. (2020). The mental health benefits of physical activity in older adults survive the COVID-19 pandemic. *The American Journal of Geriatric Psychiatry*, *28*(10), 1046–1057. https://doi.org/10.1016/j.jagp.2020.06.024

Carpiniello, B., Primavera, D., Pilu, A., Vaccargiu, N., & Pinna, F. (2013). Physical activity and mental disorders: A case-control study on attitudes, preferences and perceived barriers in Italy. *Journal of Mental Health*, *22*(6), 492–500. https://doi.org/10.3109/09638237.2013.815330

Carraro, A., Gobbi, E., Solmi, M., Watkins, A., Ward, P. B., & Rosenbaum, S. (2020). Test–retest reliability of the Italian version of the M-BACK questionnaire to assess the barriers, attitudes, confidence, and knowledge of mental health staff regarding metabolic health of psychiatric patients. *Brain and Behavior*, *10*(2), e01491. https://doi.org/10.1002/brb3.1491

Carraro, A., Gobbi, E., Stanton, R., Santi, G., & Rosenbaum, S. (2023). Psychometric properties of the Italian version of the Emiq-Hp (Exercise in Mental Illness Questionnaire-Health Professionals Version) to investigate the views of health professionals regarding exercise for treatment of mental illness. *Clinical Neuropsychiatry*, *20*(1), 55–60. https://doi.org/10.36131/cnfioritieditore20230107

Cecchini, J. A., Carriedo, A., Méndez-Giménez, A., & Fernández-Río, J. (2023). Network analysis of physical activity and depressive and affective symptoms during COVID-19 home confinement. *Global Mental Health*, *10*, e63. https://doi.org/10.1017/gmh.2023.57

Ceci, F., Di Carlo, F., Burkauskas, J., Salone, A., De Luca, I., Cicconcelli, D., Giorgetti, V., La Fratta, I., Todaro, A., Simonato, P., Martinotti, G., di Giannantonio, M., & Corazza, O. (2023). Physical activity and exercise addiction during the Covid-19 pandemic in Italy. *International Journal of Mental Health and Addiction*, *21*(6), 3678–3698. https://doi.org/10.1007/s11469-022-00815-z

Cerea, S., Pecunioso, A., Casali, N., Moro, T., Paoli, A., & Ghisi, M. (2023). How COVID-19 lockdown affected physical activity levels and wellbeing: An Italian Survey. *International Journal of Sport and Exercise Psychology*, *21*(6), 1054–1069. https://doi.org/10.1080/1612197X.2022.2098358

CESIE. (n.d.). *MENS – Mental European Network of Sport events*. https://cesie.org/project/mens/ (accessed on 21 February 2025).

Denche-Zamorano, Á., García-Paniagua, R., Pastor-Cisneros, R., Pereira-Payo, D., & Pérez Gómez, J. (2024). Influence of physical activity level and perceived social support on mental health and psychological distress in women with menopause problems. *Psychology, Health and Medicine*, *29*(8), 1493–1511. https://doi.org/10.1080/13548506.2024.2347522

Denche-Zamorano, A., Pisà-Canyelles, J., Barrios-Fernandez, S., Pastor-Cisneros, R., Adsuar, J. C., Garcia-Gordillo, M. A., Pereira-Payo, D., & Mendoza-Muñoz, M. (2023). Is psychological distress associated with self-perceived health, perceived social support and physical activity level in Spanish adults with diabetes? *Journal of Personalized Medicine*, *13*(5), 739. https://doi.org/10.3390/jpm13050739

Denche-Zamorano, A., Rodriguez-Redondo, Y., Barrios-Fernandez, S., Mendoza-Muñoz, M., Rojo-Ramos, J., Garcia-Gordillo, M. A., Adsuar, J. C., & Muñoz-Bermejo, L. (2023). Depression, anxiety and antidepressants and anxiolytics use in Spanish informal caregivers according to the physical activity frequency: EHSS 2014–2020. *Healthcare (Switzerland)*, *11*(7), 990. https://doi.org/10.3390/healthcare11070990

Denche-Zamorano, Á., Salas-Gómez, D., Parraca, J. A., Tomas-Carus, P., Adsuar, J. C., & Barrios-Fernandez, S. (2024). Relationship between depression and physical activity frequency in Spanish people with low, medium, and high pain levels. *Journal of Personalized Medicine*, *14*(8), 855. https://doi.org/10.3390/jpm14080855

Eigenschenk, B., Thomann, A., McClure, M., Davies, L., Gregory, M., Dettweiler, U., & Inglés, E. (2019). Benefits of outdoor sports for society. A systematic literature review and reflections on evidence. *International Journal of Environmental Research and Public Health*, *16*(6), 937. https://doi.org/10.3390/ijerph16060937

Elce, A., Daniele, A., Loperto, I., De Coppi, L., Sangiorgio, A., Vivona, A., Sorrentino, C., Iannaccone, S., Martiniello, L., & Nigro, E. (2022). COVID19 pandemic and physical activity: An observational study on sleep quality and anxiety. *Sports (Basel, Switzerland)*, *10*(3), 44. https://doi.org/10.3390/sports10030044

European Commission. (2013). *Physical education and sport at school in Europe*. European Commission: Education, Audiovisual and Culture Executive Agency. https://data.europa.eu/doi/10.2797/49648

Fastame, M. C., Penna, M. P., & Hitchcott, P. K. (2015). Mental health in late adulthood: What can preserve it? *Applied Research in Quality of Life*, *2014*, 459–471. https://doi.org/10.1007/s11482-014-9323-5

Fennell, C., Eremus, T., Puyana, M. G., & Sañudo, B. (2022). The importance of physical activity to augment mood during COVID-19 lockdown. *International Journal of Environmental Research and Public Health*, *19*(3), 1270. https://doi.org/10.3390/ijerph19031270

Fernández-Abascal, B., Suárez-Pinilla, M., Cobo-Corrales, C., Crespo-Facorro, B., & Suárez-Pinilla, P. (2023). Lifestyle intervention based on exercise and behavioural counselling and its effect on physical and psychological health in outpatients with schizophrenia spectrum disorders. An exploratory, pragmatic randomized clinical trial. *Schizophrenia Research*, *261*, 256–268. https://doi.org/10.1016/j.schres.2023.09.036

Filippou, K., Knappe, F., Hatzigeorgiadis, A., Morres, I. D., Tzormpatzakis, E., Havas, E., Pühse, U., Theodorakis, Y., & Gerber, M. (2024). Self-reported physical activity and mental health among asylum seekers in a refugee camp. *Journal of Physical Activity and Health*, *21*(7), 657–667. https://doi.org/10.1123/jpah.2023-0325

Gabrščček, L., Kokaridas, D., Maggouritsa, G., Loules, G., Stoforos, P., Theodorakis, Y., & Krommidas, C. (2019). The effect of a goal setting exercise program on improving upper body strength, lower extremity strength, balance and commitment to exercise of patients with schizophrenia. *European Journal of Physical Education and Sport Science*, *5*(12), 215–227. https://doi.org/10.5281/zenodo.3555581

Gerber, M., Colledge, F., de Quervain, D., Filippou, K., Havas, E., Knappe, F., Ludyga, S., Meier, M., Morres, I. D., Panagos, A., Pühse, U., Ramadan, K., Seelig, H., Theodorakis, Y., von Känel, R., & Hatzigeorgiadis, A. (2021). Effects of an exercise and sport intervention among refugees living in a Greek refugee camp on mental health, physical fitness and cardiovascular risk markers: Study protocol for the SALEEM pragmatic randomized controlled trial. *Trials*, *22*(1), 827. https://doi.org/10.1186/s13063-021-05808-2

Graves, B. S., Hall, M. E., Dias-Karch, C., Haischer, M. H., & Apter, C. (2021). Gender differences in perceived stress and coping among college students. *PLoS One*, *16*(8), e0255634. https://doi.org/10.1371/journal.pone.0255634

Gutiérrez-Santamaría, B., Castañeda-Babarro, A., Arietaleanizbeaskoa, M. S., Mendizabal-Gallastegui, N., Grandes, G., & Coca, A. (2023). Physiological and mental health changes in cancer patients during the COVID-19 state of emergency. *Sport Sciences for Health*, *19*(1), 123–130. https://doi.org/10.1007/s11332-022-01008-w

Hausenblas, H. A., & Fallon, E. A. (2006). Exercise and body image: A meta-analysis. *Psychology & Health*, *21*(1), 33–47. https://doi.org/10.1080/14768320500105270

Hernández-Pizarro, H. M., & Maynou, L. (2024). The effects of physical activity prescription on mental health: Evidence from primary care. *Economics and Human Biology*, *55*, 101432. https://doi.org/10.1016/j.ehb.2024.101432

Jiménez-Pavón, D., Carbonell-Baeza, A., & Lavie, C. J. (2020). Physical exercise as therapy to fight against the mental and physical consequences of COVID-19 quarantine: Special focus in older people. *Progress in Cardiovascular Diseases*, *63*(3), 386–388. https://doi.org/10.1016/j.pcad.2020.03.009

Kassimi, M., Karachrysafi, S., Delis, G., Kavvadas, D., & Papamitsou, T. (2023). The COVID-19 effects on isolated societies The case of the Greek island of Lemnos. *Archives of Hellenic Medicine*, *40*(3), 363–368.

Klinis, S., Symvoulakis, E. K., Stefanidou, M., Bertsias, A., Christodoulou, N., & Tsiouri, I. (2022). Self-efficacy, stress levels and daily style of living among older patients with type 2 diabetes in a rural primary care setting: A cross-sectional study. *Medicine and Pharmacy Reports*, *95*(3), 267–274. https://doi.org/10.15386/mpr-2152

Knox, E., & Muros, J. J. (2017). Association of lifestyle behaviours with self-esteem through health-related quality of life in Spanish adolescents. *European Journal of Pediatrics*, *176*(5), 621–628. https://doi.org/10.1007/s00431-017-2886-z

Kokaridas, D., Maggouritsa, G., Stoforos, P., Patsiaouras, A., Theodorakis, Y., & Diggelidis, N. (2013). The effect of a token economy system program and physical activity on improving quality of life of patients with schizophrenia: A pilot study. *American Journal of Applied Psychology*, *2*(6), 80–88. https://doi.org/10.11648/j.ajap.20130206.13

Lederbogen, F., Kirsch, P., Haddad, L., Streit, F., Tost, H., Schuch, P., Wüst, S., Pruessner, J. C., Rietschel, M., Deuschle, M., & Meyer-Lindenberg, A. (2011). City living and urban upbringing affect neural social stress processing in humans. *Nature*, *474*(7352), 498–501. https://doi.org/10.1038/nature10190

Legrand, R., Nuemi, G., Poulain, M., & Manckoundia, P. (2021). Description of lifestyle, including social life, diet and physical activity, of people ≥90 years living in Ikaria, a longevity blue zone. *International Journal of Environmental Research and Public Health*, *18*(12), 6602. https://doi.org/10.3390/ijerph18126602

Levante, A., Quarta, S., Massaro, M., Calabriso, N., Carluccio, M. A., Damiano, F., Pollice, F., Siculella, L., & Lecciso, F. (2024). Physical activity habits prevent psychological distress in female academic students: The multiple mediating role of physical and psychosocial parameters. *Heliyon*, *10*(4), e26626. https://doi.org/10.1016/j.heliyon.2024.e26626

Liu, M., Wu, L., & Ming, Q. (2015). How does physical activity intervention improve self-esteem and self-concept in children and adolescents? Evidence from a meta-analysis. *PLoS One*, *10*(8), e0134804. https://doi.org/10.1371/journal.pone.0134804

Maggouritsa, G., Kokaridas, D., Stoforos, P., Patsiaouras, A., Diggelidis, N., & Theodorakis, Y. (2014). The effect of a physical activity program on improving body cathexis and self-esteem of patients with schizophrenia. *Inquiries in Physical Education and Sport*, *12*(1), 40–51. https://doi.org/10.26253/heal.uth.ojs.ispe.2014.1416

Maggouritsa, G., Kokaridas, D., Theodorakis, I., Patsiaouras, A., Mouzas, O., Dimitrakopoulos, S., & Diggelidis, N. (2014). The effect of a physical activity programme on improving mood profile of patients with schizophrenia. *International Journal of Sport and Exercise Psychology*, *12*(3), 273–284. https://doi.org/10.1080/1612197X.2014.898968

Maltagliati, S., Papaioannou, A., Tessier, D., Carraro, A., Pons, J., Demirhan, G., Ramis, Y., Appleton, P., Martins, J., Escriva-Boulley, G., Chalabaev, A., Cheval, B., Krommidas, C., & Sarrazin, P. (2023). Antecedents and mediators of the association between adolescents' intention and physical activity: A cross-sectional study in seven European countries. *International Journal of Sport and Exercise Psychology*, 1–20. https://doi.org/10.1080/1612197X.2023.2196670

Maran, D. A., Zedda, M., & Varetto, A. (2018). Physical practice and wellness courses reduce distress and improve wellbeing in police officers. *International Journal of Environmental Research and Public Health*, *15*(4), 578. https://doi.org/10.3390/ijerph15040578

Martínez-González, M. Á., Hershey, M. S., Zazpe, I., & Trichopoulou, A. (2017). Transferability of the Mediterranean diet to non-Mediterranean countries. What is and what is not the Mediterranean diet. *Nutrients*, *9*(11), 1226. https://doi.org/10.3390/nu9111226

Mateo-Orcajada, A., González-Gálvez, N., Abenza-Cano, L., Leiva-Arcas, A., & Vaquero-Cristóbal, R. (2023). Physical activity and mental health: Examining the links between exercise, physical activity, and mental health outcomes such as stress, anxiety, and depression. In S. Amin, O. Mbah, A. Mateo-Orcajada, M. Albaladejo-Saura, & R. Vaquero-Cristóbal (Eds.), *European handbook for gender equality, equity, inclusion in sport: A perspective through the erasmus + women-up project* (pp. 91–105). Dykinson. https://doi.org/10.14679/2213

Maugeri, G., Castrogiovanni, P., Battaglia, G., Pippi, R., D'Agata, V., Palma, A., Di Rosa, M., & Musumeci, G. (2020). The impact of physical activity on psychological health during Covid-19 pandemic in Italy. *Heliyon, 6*(6), e04315. https://doi.org/10.1016/j.heliyon.2020.e04315

Mielgo-Ayuso, J., Aparicio-Ugarriza, R., Castillo, A., Ruiz, E., Ávila, J. M., Aranceta-Batrina, J., Gil, Á., Ortega, R. M., Serra-Majem, L., Varela-Moreiras, G., & González-Gross, M. (2016). Physical activity patterns of the spanish population are mostly determined by sex and age: Findings in the ANIBES study. *PLoS One*, *11*(2), e0149969. https://doi.org/10.1371/journal.pone.0149969

Morres, I. D., Galanis, E., Hatzigeorgiadis, A., Androutsos, O., & Theodorakis, Y. (2021). Physical activity, sedentariness, eating behaviour and well-being during a COVID-19 lockdown period in Greek adolescents. *Nutrients*, *13*(5), 1449. https://doi.org/10.3390/nu13051449

Morres, I. D., Hatzigeorgiadis, A., Krommidas, C., Comoutos, N., Sideri, E., Ploumpidis, D., Economou, M., Papaioannou, A., & Theodorakis, Y. (2019). Objectively measured physical activity and depressive symptoms in adult outpatients diagnosed with major depression. Clinical perspectives. *Psychiatry Research*, *280*, 112489. https://doi.org/10.1016/j. psychres.2019.112489

Morres, I. D., Hatzigeorgiadis, A., Stathi, A., Comoutos, N., Arpin-Cribbie, C., Krommidas, C., & Theodorakis, Y. (2019). Aerobic exercise for adult patients with major depressive disorder in mental health services: A systematic review and meta-analysis. *Depression and Anxiety*, *36*(1), 39–53. https://doi.org/10.1002/da.22842

Orlandi, M., Rosselli, M., Pellegrino, A., Boddi, M., Stefani, L., Toncelli, L., & Modesti, P. A. (2021). Gender differences in the impact on physical activity and lifestyle in Italy during the lockdown, due to the COVID-19 pandemic. *Nutrition, Metabolism and Cardiovascular Diseases*, *31*(7), 2173–2180. https://doi.org/10.1016/j.numecd.2021.03.011

Owen, K. B., Corbett, L., Ding, D., Eime, R., & Bauman, A. (2025). Gender differences in physical activity and sport participation in adults across 28 European countries between 2005 and 2022. *Annals of Epidemiology*, *101*, 52–57. https://doi.org/10.1016/j. annepidem.2024.12.011

Papastergiou, D., Bonotis, K., Kokaridas, D., Digelidis, N., & Patsiouras, A. (2020). Exercise effect on general health status of Greek cancer patients: Intervention effect and related comparisons. *International Journal of Caring Sciences*, *13*(1), 180.

Papastergiou, D., Kokaridas, D., Bonotis, K., Diggelidis, N., & Patsiaouras, A. (2018). Exercise, supportive group therapy, and mood profile of Greek cancer patients: Intervention effect and related comparisons. *Supportive Care in Cancer*, *26*(10), 3571–3578. https://doi.org/10.1007/s00520-018-4219-9

Penado Abilleira, M., Ríos-de-Deus, M.-P., Tomé-Lourido, D., Rodicio-García, M.-L., Mosquera-González, M.-J., López-López, D., & Gómez-Salgado, J. (2023). Relationship between sports practice, physical and mental health and anxiety–depressive symptomatology in the Spanish prison population. *Healthcare (Switzerland)*, *11*(6), 789. https://doi.org/10.3390/healthcare11060789

Pereira-Payo, D., Denche-Zamorano, Á., Mayordomo-Pinilla, N., Franco-García, J. M., Castillo-Paredes, A., Garcia-Gordillo, M. A., Rojo-Ramos, J., & Barrios-Fernández, S. (2023). Higher physical activity level and perceived social support is associated with less psychological distress in people with anxiety. *PeerJ*, *11*, e16000. https://doi.org/10.7717/peerj.16000

Phillips, S. M., Cadmus-Bertram, L., Rosenberg, D., Buman, M. P., & Lynch, B. M. (2018). Wearable technology and hysical activity in chronic disease: Opportunities and challenges. *American Journal of Preventive Medicine*, *54*(1), 144–150. https://doi.org/10.1016/j.amepre.2017.08.015

Pons, J., Ramis, Y., Alcaraz, S., Jordana, A., Borrueco, M., & Torregrossa, M. (2020). Where did all the sport go? Negative impact of COVID-19 lockdown on life-spheres and mental health of Spanish young athletes. *Frontiers in Psychology*, *11*, 611872. https://doi.org/10.3389/fpsyg.2020.611872

Pons, J., Ramis, Y., Torregrossa, M., Sarrazin, P., Maltagliati, S., Krommidas, C., Appleton, P. R., Gobbi, E., Erturan, G., Escriva–Boulley, G., Duda, J. L., Martins, J., Demirhan, G., Carraro, A., Bouglas, V., & Papaioannou, A. G. (2023). Physical education motivational climate, on the achievement goals, and intrinsic motivation of students: A multilevel approach. *International Journal of Sport and Exercise Psychology*, 1–16. https://doi.org/10.1080/1612197X.2023.2224841

Psychou, D., Kokaridas, D., Koulouris, N., Theodorakis, Y., & Krommidas, C. (2019). The effect of exercise on improving quality of life and self-esteem of inmates in Greek prisons. *Journal of Human Sport and Exercise*, *14*(2), 374–384. https://doi.org/10.14198/jhse.2019.142.10

Psychou, D., Kokaridas, D., Koulouris, N., Theodorakis, Y., Krommidas, C., & Psycho, C. (2021). Impact of exercise intervention on anxiety levels and mood profile of Greek prison inmates. *Journal of Human Sport and Exercise*, *16*(1), 147–156. https://doi.org/10.14198/jhse.2021.161.13

Rahmati, M., Lee, S., Yon, D. K., Lee, S. W., Udeh, R., McEvoy, M., Oh, H., Butler, L., Keyes, H., Barnett, Y., Koyanagi, A., Shin, J. I., & Smith, L. (2024). Physical activity and prevention of mental health complications: An umbrella review. *Neuroscience & Biobehavioral Reviews*, *160*, 105641. https://doi.org/10.1016/j.neubiorev.2024.105641

Regione Piemonte. (2019). *Let's fit healthy life! The role of sport in regenerating deprived areas*. Www.Regione.Piemonte.It. https://www.regione.piemonte.it/web/temi/fondi-progetti-europei/programmi-progetti-europei/lets-fit-healthy-life-the-role-of-sport-regenerating-deprived-areas#

Rejeski, W. J., & Mihalko, S. L. (2001). Physical activity and quality of life in older adults. *The Journals of Gerontology: Series A*, *56*(suppl_2), 23–35. https://doi.org/10.1093/gerona/56.suppl_2.23

Ricci, P., Pallocci, M., Treglia, M., Ricci, S., Ferrara, R., Zanovello, C., Passalacqua, P., & Damato, F. M. (2023). The effect of physical exercise during COVID-19 lockdown. *Healthcare (Switzerland)*, *11*(11), 1618. https://doi.org/10.3390/healthcare11111618

Sabe, M., Chen, C., Sentissi, O., Deenik, J., Vancampfort, D., Firth, J., Smith, L., Stubbs, B., Rosenbaum, S., Schuch, F. B., & Solmi, M. (2022). Thirty years of research on physical activity, mental health, and wellbeing: A scientometric analysis of hotspots and trends. *Frontiers in Public Health*, *10*, 943435. https://www.frontiersin.org/journals/public-health/articles/10.3389/fpubh.2022.943435

Sansone-Pollock, M., Mutrie, N., Guerra, C., Sechi, C., Mula, S., & Calia, C. (2023). COVID-19: Physical activity, government restrictions, and mental health in the UK and Italy. *Trends in Psychology*. https://doi.org/10.1007/s43076-023-00262-2

Saoudi, I., Sarrazin, P., Papaioannou, A. G., Krommidas, C., Borrueco, M., Gobbi, E., Martins, J., Appleton, P. R., Maltagliati, S., Erturan, G., Tessier, D., Escriva-Boulley, G., Ramis, Y., Demirhan, G., Carraro, A., Duda, J. L., Digelidis, N., Loules, G., Cheval, B., & Chalabaev, A. (2024). Economic status as a predictor of motivational and affective experiences in physical education and physical activity intentions: A cross-sectional study in six European countries. *International Journal of Sport and Exercise Psychology*, 1–23. https://doi.org/10.1080/1612197X.2024.2321346

Saxena, S., Van Ommeren, M., Tang, K. C., & Armstrong, T. P. (2005). Mental health benefits of physical activity. *Journal of Mental Health*, *14*(5), 445–451. https://doi.org/10.1080/09638230500270776

Seedat, S., Scott, K. M., Angermeyer, M. C., Berglund, P., Bromet, E. J., Brugha, T. S., Demyttenaere, K., de Girolamo, G., Haro, J. M., Jin, R., Karam, E. G., Kovess-Masfety, V., Levinson, D., Medina Mora, M. E., Ono, Y., Ormel, J., Pennell, B.-E., Posada-Villa, J., Sampson, N. A., … Kessler, R. C. (2009). Cross-national associations between gender and mental disorders in the World Health Organization World Mental Health Surveys. *Archives of General Psychiatry*, *66*(7), 785–795. https://doi.org/10.1001/archgenpsychiatry.2009.36

Sidossis, L. S., Lawson, R., Aprilakis, E., Barata, B. C., Baska, A., Beneka, A., Bird, R., Birrell, F., Chatzinikola, C., Chondronikola, M., Chrousos, G. P., Conduit, R., Constantinou, C.,

De Courten, B., Cvejic, J. H., Davis, A. M., Demetriou, C. A., Errington, L., Feehan, J., … Itsiopoulos, C. (2024). Defining the traditional Mediterranean lifestyle: Joint international consensus statement. *Lifestyle Medicine*, *5*(4), e115. https://doi.org/10.1002/lim2.115

Skalidou, S., Anestis, A., Skalidis, E., Kontaxi, O., Kyrezi, A., Konstantinou, P., & Papadimitriou, K. (2023). A repeated cross-sectional pilot study of physical activity, levels of depression and anxiety during the COVID-19 pandemic in young Greek adults. *Healthcare (Switzerland)*, *11*(18), 2493. https://doi.org/10.3390/healthcare11182493

Smith, P. J., & Merwin, R. M. (2021). The role of exercise in management of mental health disorders: An integrative review. *Annual Review of Medicine*, *72*, 45–62. https://doi.org/10.1146/annurev-med-060619-022943

Stanton, R., Happell, B., & Reaburn, P. (2014). The mental health benefits of regular physical activity, and its role in preventing future depressive illness. *Nursing: Research and Reviews*, *2014*(4), 45–53. https://doi.org/10.2147/NRR.S41956

Teno, S. C., Silva, M. N., & Júdice, P. B. (2024). Physical activity and sedentary behaviour-specific domains and their associations with mental health in adults: A systematic review. *Advances in Mental Health*, *22*(3), 738–765. https://doi.org/10.1080/18387357.2024.2324099

Theodorakis, Y., Hassandra, M., & Panagiotounis, F. (2024). Enhancing substance use disorder recovery through integrated physical activity and behavioral interventions: A comprehensive approach to treatment and prevention. *Brain Sciences*, *14*(6), 534. https://doi.org/10.3390/brainsci14060534

Toselli, S., Bragonzoni, L., Dallolio, L., Alessia, G., Masini, A., Marini, S., Barone, G., Pinelli, E., Zinno, R., Mauro, M., Astorino, G., Pilone, P. L., Galli, S., & Latessa, P. M. (2022). The effects of park based interventions on health: The Italian project "Moving Parks". *International Journal of Environmental Research and Public Health*, *19*(4), 2130. https://doi.org/10.3390/ijerph19042130

Van Den Bosch, M., & Meyer-Lindenberg, A. (2019). Environmental exposures and depression: Biological mechanisms and epidemiological evidence. *Annual Review of Public Health*, *40*(1), 239–259. https://doi.org/10.1146/annurev-publhealth-040218-044106

Whitaker, E. D. (2005). The bicycle makes the eyes smile: Exercise, aging, and psychophysical well-being in older Italian cyclists. *Medical Anthropology: Cross Cultural Studies in Health and Illness*, *24*(1), 1–43. https://doi.org/10.1080/01459740590905633

World Health Organisation (WHO). (2010). *Global recommendations on physical activity for health.* https://whqlibdoc.who.int/publications/2010/9789241599979_eng.pdf (accessed on 19 September 2022).

Xu, X., Ha, S. U., & Basnet, R. (2016). A review of epidemiological research on adverse neurological effects of exposure to ambient air pollution. *Frontiers in Public Health*, *4*, 00157. https://doi.org/10.3389/fpubh.2016.00157

Yuan, M., Chen, H., Chen, D., Wan, D., Luo, F., Zhang, C., Nan, Y., Bi, X., & Liang, J. (2022). Effect of physical activity on prevention of postpartum depression: A dose-response meta-analysis of 186,412 women. *Frontiers in Psychiatry*, *13*, 984677. https://doi.org/10.3389/fpsyt.2022.984677

Zacharis, T., Lyrakos, G., & Zisi, V. Z. (2020). Physical activity and mental health in caregivers of mental ill patients in Greece. *Journal of Human Sport and Exercise*, *15*, S848–S855. https://doi.org/10.14198/jhse.2020.15.Proc3.36

Zijlema, W., Cerin, E., Cirach, M., Bartoll, X., Borrell, C., Dadvand, P., & Nieuwenhuijsen, M. J. (2024). Cities and mental health: The role of the built environment, and environmental and lifestyle factors in Barcelona. *Environmental Pollution*, *346*, 123559. https://doi.org/10.1016/j.envpol.2024.123559

14

PROMOTING MENTAL HEALTH THROUGH PHYSICAL ACTIVITY IN LATIN AMERICAN ATHLETES

Franco Noce, José Marcelo Roffé,
Francisco Enrique García Ucha, Cristina Carvalho de Melo,
and Renato Gomes Sá de Moraes

14.1 Introduction: The Relationship between Exercise and Mental Health

The relationship between physical exercise and mental health has been the subject of growing interest in health research, with evidence pointing to the benefits of exercise for psychological well-being (Al-Qahtani et al., 2018). Promoting mental health through physical activity and exercise is gaining increasing attention in Latin America. The issue of mental health occupies a prominent place throughout society. In our view, people's awareness of the pursuit of psychological well-being has become a reason to achieve mental health.

Well-being is defined by the WHO (World Health Organization, 2025) as the state in which "a person can realize his or her own abilities and cope with factors that may disturb him or her". This leads us to think of psychological well-being as the ideal functioning of the person and is closely related to mental health, defined as "a state of well-being in which each individual develops his or her potential, can cope with the stresses of life, can work productively and profitably, and can contribute something to his or her community". There is a very close relationship between the state of mental health and personality qualities that are very evident in sport, such as self-confidence and the relationship between mental health and performance (Rice et al., 2020).

In this context, this relationship becomes even more complex and relevant, since sports practice involves significant physical and psychological demands (Rice et al., 2016). This chapter aims to deepen the understanding of the relationship between physical exercise and mental health in Latin American athletes, considering the cultural, social, and individual particularities of this group.

The scientific literature demonstrates that physical exercise acts on several neurobiological mechanisms (e.g., increasing BDNF levels and other trophic factors,

DOI: 10.4324/9781003517474-19

improving frontal lobe functions, adequate modulation of the reward system and antioxidant action, and neurotransmitter synthesis) and psychological mechanisms, promoting mental health (Fogaca, 2021; Leguizamo et al., 2021; Nicholls & Polman, 2007). The release of endorphins, reduced cortisol levels, and improved neurogenesis are some of the mechanisms proposed to explain the beneficial effects of exercise on mental health (Marcelo, 2023). Furthermore, exercise can help in the development of coping skills, emotional regulation, and self-esteem, which contributes to better psychological well-being (Brown & Fletcher, 2017; Hilpisch et al., 2024; Norris et al., 2017). Mental health in high-performance athletes is a complex phenomenon that involves a combination of internal and external factors. Cultivating passion, setting clear goals, receiving support, and adopting a growth mindset are key elements to maintaining motivation and achieving success in elite sport (Rice et al., 2016; Vella et al., 2020). As Peris-Delcampo & Roffé (2023) point out, "an athlete who has good mental health is able to be happy, enjoy what they do through good psychological well-being and deal well with the different situations, more or less stressful, that a high-level competition already involves". Furthermore, García Ucha and Nieri Romero (2023) highlight that "Sports Psychology is guided by the search for the well-being of the person". In this sense, the sports psychologist plays a fundamental role in promoting coping strategies and improving the mental well-being of athletes. Peris-Delcampo & Roffé (2023) also mention that "we are mental health agents and that before being athletes we deal with real people who, no matter how famous and millionaire they are, things happen to them as they do to any human being". This highlights the importance of considering the psychological well-being of athletes holistically, in addition to their athletic performance.

On the other hand, García Ucha and Nieri Romero (2023) highlight that "sporting success must be conceptualized as a process and not just in terms of results such as the level of the team or the fulfillment of a performance". This reinforces the idea that psychological preparation must be focused on resilience and personal growth, not just on achieving victories. It is important to note that concern for mental health and the consequences of dealing with it have led nations and governments to develop organizations such as the Pan American Health Organization, which adopt the need for physical activity as a precept in the implementation of mental health. This process has been generalized to the formation of similar institutions at the level of all nations within society, both in regional areas and in state agencies. The entire mental health movement is evident in social media posts that promote scientific events and programs related to the use of physical activity to promote mental health (Roffé et al., 2023). Initiatives emerge as campaigns or events carried out by organizations or programs at a regional or even national level.

However, the relationship between physical exercise and mental health is not linear and can be influenced by several factors. De Alvarez et al. (2016) highlight the importance of adherence to treatment to obtain the benefits of exercise.

In our presentation, we give a significant role to psychologists, since in many circumstances they are involved in providing children, adolescents, athletes, coaches, family members, and other sports participants with precautions against potential difficulties and setbacks, so that they maintain an adequate state of mental health. A first aspect to consider is to diagnose the needs of people who want to promote mental health and how they can achieve it through exercise and physical activity. This requires a psychologist or other expert to have knowledge about physical exercise and its impact on the participant's psyche to achieve their mental health.

Physical exercise is defined as planned, structured, and repetitive physical activity that aims to improve or maintain one or more components of physical fitness (Caspersen et al., 1985). Sport is a regulated and competitive physical activity. Virtually all physical activities and most sports are considered physical exercise. Physical activity can contribute to the prevention and control of many other diseases. Among them, the most important are arterial hypertension, osteoporosis, diabetes mellitus, and certain types of neoplasia, in addition to psychological problems such as anxiety, stress, and other negative psychological manifestations. On the other hand, regular physical exercise produces beneficial effects on joints, weight loss, and positive psychological effects on the health and well-being of the population. Factors such as social support, the perception of control over one's own health, and the quality of the relationship with the physical education professional can significantly influence adherence to physical training programs. In the context of athletes, pressure for results, injuries, and training load can be additional factors that influence adherence to training programs.

The COVID-19 pandemic has brought new challenges to athletes' mental health, intensifying the need for research on the role of physical exercise in this context (Budimir et al., 2021; Gurvich et al., 2021; Han et al., 2021; Leguizamo et al., 2021; Rettie & Daniels, 2021). Vancini et al. (2021) highlight the importance of physical exercise for mental well-being during periods of social isolation and uncertainty. Regular physical activity can help modulate stress and improve mood, and is especially relevant for athletes who have had their training routines interrupted.

This involves the psychologist assessing the participants' potential psychopathological problems, such as anxiety, depression, stress, and other mental disorders, and this forms the basis for developing recommendations on the types, frequency, and intensity of physical activity that are most beneficial for each individual (García Ucha & Ortiz, 2023).

The COVID-19 pandemic has also led to a shift in the perception of mental health in sports. According to Peris-Delcampo and Roffé (2023),

> the positive side of the pandemic is that the mental factor has started to gain the place it deserves. Many have started to seek us for help, something that did not happen before, and we have become more important than we were.

This recognition of the role of sports psychology has led to a greater integration of mental health support programs into athlete training.

Collaborate with fitness trainers and health professionals to confirm exercise programs that are tailored to the participant's physical capabilities and psychological needs. Programs may include relaxation exercises, breathing, yoga, walking, running, swimming, meditation, psychodrama, cognitive behavioral therapies, or any other activity acceptable to patients.

Exercise is used as a tool to improve mood, reduce stress, and increase self-esteem, all of which are crucial in the treatment of disorders such as depression and anxiety, which are more common in athletes (Chang et al., 2024). Sports psychologists, in particular, provide support and education to athletes, can help them navigate the interpersonal and team dynamics that can be intense and complicated in highly competitive environments, and can help teams establish systems of care that successfully meet the special needs of athletes (Weinberg & Gould, 2017). However, participating in physical activities is a guarantee of maintaining mental health.

Social determinants of mental health play a crucial role in the relationship between physical exercise and psychological well-being. Social inequalities, violence, and stigmatization can negatively affect mental health and hinder access to health resources (Almeida-Filho et al., 2023). For athletes, these factors may be even more relevant, as many come from marginalized communities and are exposed to higher levels of stress and pressure. Physical exercise programs should consider these issues and offer additional support for these athletes, since psychiatric disorders are a reality in the general population. Therefore, sport becomes an important tool for improving the quality of life, not only for athletes, but also for practitioners who seek to have better health (Vella et al., 2020). Regular sports practice can enhance the use of antidepressants, become a gateway to better habits (e.g., diet, sleep hygiene), in addition to saving on overall health by reducing chronic diseases and absenteeism (Didymus, 2017; Gouttebarge et al., 2021; Kim et al., 2020; Rice et al., 2016).

Suicidal behavior is a problem that has been a major concern in the Olympic Games environment due to its importance. Prevention of this circumstance should be carried out by sports psychologists and in which doctors and nurses should be incorporated with activities to be evaluated. To predict suicidal behavior in order to have time to intervene, athletes generally tend to isolate themselves from the sports system (Gouttebarge et al., 2021; McLoughlin et al., 2021; Rice et al., 2016).

Another problem with the loss of mental health is that all attempts to ensure success and happiness through doping and drug taking seem attractive to some athletes.

For all these reasons, research is currently being conducted on the effects of exercise on mental health. Studies are being conducted to examine how different types of exercise can benefit people with different psychological characteristics. The results of these investigations will allow us to recommend best practices and evidence-based guidelines for integrating exercise into mental health treatments.

The cultural diversity of Latin American athletes also influences the relationship between physical exercise and mental health. Cultural practices, values, and beliefs can shape the perception of physical exercise and the search for help for mental health problems. It is essential to consider this cultural diversity when developing mental health promotion programs for athletes. The promotion of a healthy lifestyle has contributed to the popularization of physical exercise and to the increase in consultations related to this activity, requiring up-to-date knowledge about these activities. These results are achieved through shared activities among groups of people who can become aware of the importance of participating in physical activities.

Drawing on insights from research conducted in Latin America, we explore the existing literature on mental health research, treatment adherence, and the impact of physical exercise on psychological states. Studies provide a comprehensive framework for understanding the challenges and opportunities surrounding mental health care in Latin America. These studies highlight disparities in mental health literacy, the need for improved infrastructure and policies, and the potential of physical activity as a valuable tool to promote well-being (Almeida-Filho et al., 2023; De Alvarez et al., 2016; Do Amaral Menezes et al., 2018; Marcelo, 2023; Mari et al., 2006; Moreira et al., 2022; Vancini et al., 2021).

It is possible to imagine that the actions of different organizations and institutions are present in the implementation of actions aimed at using physical activity to develop mental health. A special aspect is the role played by psychologists in shaping people's understanding of the benefits of physical activity for mental health. There is no doubt that these actions will generate new knowledge about how to apply physical activity to promote mental health and how to do so effectively, contributing to an overall improvement in emotional and physical well-being in Latin America.

The relationship between physical exercise and mental health in Latin American athletes is complex and multifaceted. The studies analyzed in this chapter highlight the importance of physical exercise for promoting psychological well-being, but they also highlight the need for an approach that considers cultural, social, and individual contexts. By investing in personalized and educational physical exercise programs, it is possible to promote the mental health of athletes and contribute to the development of healthier and more equitable societies.

14.2 Implications for Practice

Personalized programs: It is essential to develop personalized physical exercise programs, considering the individual needs and characteristics of each athlete.

Multidisciplinary support: Promoting the mental health of athletes requires a multidisciplinary approach, involving professionals from physical education, psychology, nutrition, and other areas.

Mental health education: Mental health education should be integrated into sports training programs to promote the psychological well-being of athletes and reduce the stigma associated with mental health issues. Education can address topics such as identifying signs of mental health issues, coping strategies, and the importance of seeking professional help.

Consideration of social determinants: When developing mental health promotion programs, it is essential to consider the social determinants of health and provide additional support for athletes from marginalized communities. This may include offering exercise programs in accessible locations and creating support groups for athletes facing social challenges.

14.3 Future Considerations

Research on the relationship between physical exercise and mental health in Latin American athletes is still in its infancy. More research is needed to investigate the neurobiological and psychological mechanisms underlying this relationship, as well as to assess the effectiveness of different types of interventions in different cultural and social contexts. Furthermore, it is essential to consider the perspective of athletes when developing mental health promotion programs, ensuring that their needs and expectations are met.

References

Al-Qahtani, A. M., Shaikh, M. A. K., & Shaikh, I. A. (2018). Exercise as a treatment modality for depression: A narrative review. *Alexandria Journal of Medicine*, *54*(4), 429–435. https://doi.org/10.1016/j.ajme.2018.05.004

Almeida-Filho, N., de Jesus Mari, J., & Kieling, C. (2023). A narrative historical review of psychiatric epidemiology in Brazil: Focus on social and cultural determinants of mental health. *SSM - Mental Health*, *3*(December 2022), 100212. https://doi.org/10.1016/j.ssmmh.2023.100212

Brown, D. J., & Fletcher, D. (2017). Effects of psychological and psychosocial interventions on sport performance: A meta-analysis. *Sports Medicine*, *47*(1), 77–99. https://doi.org/10.1007/s40279-016-0552-7

Budimir, S., Probst, T., & Pieh, C. (2021). Coping strategies and mental health during COVID-19 lockdown. *Journal of Mental Health*, *30*(2), 156–163. https://doi.org/10.1080/09638237.2021.1875412

Caspersen, C. J., Powell, K. E., & Christenson, G. M. (1985). Physical activity, exercise, and physical fitness: Definitions and distinctions for health-related research. *Public Health Reports*, *100*(2), 126–131. https://pubmed.ncbi.nlm.nih.gov/3920711/

Chang, C., Chu, C.-L., & Hung, T.-M. (2024). Exercise may benefit patients with schizophrenia. In R. J. Schinke & A. Quartiroli (Eds.), *Mental health in sport and physical activity* (pp. 288–302). Routledge. https://doi.org/10.4324/9781003459750

De Alvarez, P. E. S., Rosendo, E., & Alchieri, J. C. (2016). The applicability of the concept of treatment adherence in the context of the Brazilian mental health system. *Revista Da Escola de Enfermagem*, *50*(Specialissue), 53–58. https://doi.org/10.1590/S0080-623420160000300008

Didymus, F. F. (2017). Olympic and international level sports coaches' experiences of stressors, appraisals, and coping. *Qualitative Research in Sport, Exercise and Health*, *9*(2), 214–232. https://doi.org/10.1080/2159676X.2016.1261364

Do Amaral Menezes, A. L., Muller, M. R., de Andrade Soares, T. R., Figueiredo, A. P., de Moraes Correia, C. R., Corrêa, L. M., & Ortega, F. (2018). Parallels between research in mental health in Brazil and in the field of Global Mental Health: An integrative literature review. *Cadernos de Saude Publica*, *34*(11), 1–20. https://doi.org/10.1590/0102-311X00158017

Fogaca, J. L. (2021). Combining mental health and performance interventions: Coping and social support for student-athletes. *Journal of Applied Sport Psychology*, *33*(1), 4–19. https://doi.org/10.1080/10413200.2019.1648326

García Ucha, F. E., & Nieri Romero, J. C. D. (2023). La resiliencia y la resistencia en la actividad deportiva. In D. Peris-Delcampo, M. Roffé, P. Jodra, & F. García Ucha (Eds.), *Salud Mental y Psicología del Deporte: fundamentos prácticos* (pp. 133–142). Imaginante Editorial.

García Ucha, F., & Ortiz, P. (2023). Psicopatología y Deporte. In D. Peris-Delcampo, M. Roffé, P. Jodra, & F. García Ucha (Eds.), *Salud Mental y Psicología del Deporte: fundamentos prácticos* (pp. 21–30). Imaginante Editorial.

Gouttebarge, V., Bindra, A., Blauwet, C., Campriani, N., Currie, A., Engebretsen, L., Hainline, B., Kroshus, E., McDuff, D., Mountjoy, M., Purcell, R., Putukian, M., Reardon, C. L., Rice, S. M., & Budgett, R. (2021). International Olympic Committee (IOC) Sport Mental Health Assessment Tool 1 (SMHAT-1) and Sport Mental Health Recognition Tool 1 (SMHRT-1): Towards better support of athletes' mental health. *British Journal of Sports Medicine*, *55*(1), 30–37. https://doi.org/10.1136/bjsports-2020-102411

Gurvich, C., Thomas, N., Thomas, E. H. X., Hudaib, A. R., Sood, L., Fabiatos, K., Sutton, K., Isaacs, A., Arunogiri, S., Sharp, G., & Kulkarni, J. (2021). Coping styles and mental health in response to societal changes during the COVID-19 pandemic. *International Journal of Social Psychiatry*, *67*(5), 540–549. https://doi.org/10.1177/0020764020961790

Han, Q., Li, X., & Wang, Z. (2021). How should athletes coping with COVID-19: Focus on severity and sychological support. *Frontiers in Psychology*, *12*(June), 1–5. https://doi.org/10.3389/fpsyg.2021.559125

Hilpisch, C., Krüger, K., Raab, M., Wiese, L., Zentgraf, K., & Mutz, M. (2024). Burnout symptoms in elite athletes: Assessing the role of effort–reward imbalance, support and emotions. *International Review for the Sociology of Sport*, 29(7), 1054–1074. https://doi.org/10.1177/10126902241248767

Kim, S. S. Y., Hamiliton, B., Beable, S., Cavadino, A., & Fulcher, M. L. (2020). Elite coaches have a similar prevalence of depressive symptoms to the general population and lower rates than elite athletes. *BMJ Open Sport and Exercise Medicine*, *6*(1), 1–6. https://doi.org/10.1136/bmjsem-2019-000719

Leguizamo, F., Olmedilla, A., Núñez, A., Verdaguer, F. J. P., Gómez-Espejo, V., Ruiz-Barquín, R., & Garcia-Mas, A. (2021). Personality, coping strategies, and mental health in high-performance athletes during confinement derived from the COVID-19 pandemic. *Frontiers in Public Health*, *8*(January), 1–15. https://doi.org/10.3389/fpubh.2020.561198

Marcelo, F. (2023). Relationship between physical activity and mental health in adults in Brazil. *International Journal of Physical Education, Recreation and Sports*, *1*(1), 14–25. https://doi.org/10.47604/ijpers.2144

Mari, J. de J., Bressan, R. A., Almeida-Filho, N., Gerolin, J., Shara, P., & Saxena, S. (2006). Mental health research in Brazil: Policies, infrastructure, financing and human resources. *Revista de Saude Publica*, *40*(1), 161–169. https://doi.org/10.1590/S0034-89102006000100024

McLoughlin, E., Fletcher, D., Slavich, G. M., Arnold, R., & Moore, L. J. (2021). Cumulative lifetime stress exposure, depression, anxiety, and well-being in elite athletes:

A mixed-method study. *Psychology of Sport and Exercise*, *52*(April 2020), 101823. https://doi.org/10.1016/j.psychsport.2020.101823

Moreira, W. C., Sousa, A. R. de, Cardoso, R. da S. S., Queiroz, A. M. de, Oliveira, M. A. F. de, & Sequeira, C. A. da C. (2022). COVID-19 no Brasil: existem diferenças no letramento em saúde mental entre homens jovens e idosos? *Revista Latino-Americana de Enfermagem*, *30*, e3603. https://doi.org/10.1590/1518-8345.5651.3603

Nicholls, A. R., & Polman, R. C. J. (2007). Coping in sport: A systematic review. *Journal of Sports Sciences*, *25*(1), 11–31. https://doi.org/10.1080/02640410600630654

Norris, L. A., Didymus, F. F., & Kaiseler, M. (2017). Stressors, coping, and well-being among sports coaches: A systematic review. *Psychology of Sport and Exercise*, *33*, 93–112. https://doi.org/10.1016/j.psychsport.2017.08.005

Peris-Delcampo, D., & Roffé, M. (2023). ¿Qué es la salud mental y cuál es su relación en el deporte? In D. Peris-Delcampo, M. Roffé, P. Jodra, & F. García Ucha (Eds.), *Salud Mental y Psicología del Deporte: fundamentos prácticos* (pp. 9–20). Imaginante Editorial.

Rettie, H., & Daniels, J. (2021). Supplemental material for coping and tolerance of uncertainty: Predictors and mediators of mental health during the COVID-19 pandemic. *American Psychologist*, *76*(3), 427–437. https://doi.org/10.1037/amp0000710.supp

Rice, S. M., Purcell, R., De Silva, S., Mawren, D., McGorry, P. D., & Parker, A. G. (2016). The mental health of elite athletes: A narrative systematic review. *Sports Medicine*, *46*(9), 1333–1353. https://doi.org/10.1007/s40279-016-0492-2

Rice, S., Olive, L., Gouttebarge, V., Parker, A. G., Clifton, P., Harcourt, P., Llyod, M., Kountouris, A., Smith, B., Busch, B., & Purcell, R. (2020). Mental health screening: Severity and cut-off point sensitivity of the Athlete Psychological Strain Questionnaire in male and female elite athletes. *BMJ Open Sport and Exercise Medicine*, *6*(1), 1–6. https://doi.org/10.1136/bmjsem-2019-000712

Roffé, M., Camaño, D., & Primo, G. (2023). Redes sociales: efectos en deportistas y entrenadores. In D. Peris-Delcampo, M. Roffé, P. Jodra, & F. García Ucha (Eds.), *Salud Mental y Psicología del Deporte: fundamentos prácticos* (pp. 103–112). Imaginante Editorial.

Vancini, R. L., Andrade, M. S., Viana, R. B., Nikolaidis, P. T., Knechtle, B., Campanharo, C. R. V., de Almeida, A. A., Gentil, P., & de Lira, C. A. B. (2021). Physical exercise and COVID-19 pandemic in PubMed: Two months of dynamics and one year of original scientific production. *Sports Medicine and Health Science*, *3*(2), 80–92. https://doi.org/10.1016/j.smhs.2021.04.004

Vella, S. A., Swann, C., & Tamminen, K. A. (2020). Mental health in sport: An overview and introduction to the special issue. *Journal of Applied Sport Psychology*, *33*(1), 1–3. https://doi.org/10.1080/10413200.2020.1854897

Weinberg, R. S., & Gould, D. (2017). Fundamentos da Psicologia do Esporte e do Exercício. In *Sport, education and society* (Vol. 15, Issue 1). https://books.google.co.uk/books?hl=en&lr=&id=sL3tCwAAQBAJ&oi=fnd&pg=PP1&ots=g2K-IdX08y&sig=arKtRy_sE488VO9w0zkilWF-FHo&redir_esc=y#v=onepage&q&f=false%0Ahttps://books.google.com/books?id=Z0Hl-ngqL2YC&pgis=1

World Health Organization. (2025). Health and well-being. Retrieved October 12, 2025, from https://www.who.int/data/gho/data/major-themes/health-and-well-being

PART 6

Becoming an Exercise and Physical Activity Psychology Professional

15

THE ROLE OF EXERCISE PSYCHOLOGY PRACTITIONERS IN PROMOTING PHYSICAL ACTIVITY

Competence, Training and Practice

Alessandro Quartiroli, Amanda Warner and Christopher R. D. Wagstaff

15.1 Introduction

The relationship between psychological well-being and physical activity has been understood for centuries (Buckworth et al., 2013). The historical journey of exercise and psychology sciences, evolving from separate fields towards their convergence into the discipline of exercise psychology, is marked by key developments and critical moments. Initially, in the late 19th century, exercise sciences and psychology evolved independently, with the former concentrating on the physiological and biomechanical aspects of human movement and the latter on understanding human behaviour and cognition (Buckworth et al., 2013). During the 1950s and 1960s, researchers began to recognise the influence of psychological factors on athletic performance and physical health (Biddle et al., 2021). This period saw the establishment of the International Society of Sport Psychology in 1965, highlighting the growing interest in the psychological dimensions of sport (Schinke et al., 2018). By the 1970s, sport and exercise psychology was formally recognised as a distinct field within psychology, further solidified by the creation of dedicated academic programmes and journals (Aoyagi et al., 2012). The 1980s and 1990s witnessed a significant expansion of the field. The American Psychological Association recognised sport and exercise psychology as a proficiency area in 1986 with an increased focus on research on the psychological benefits of physical activity for the general population (Kornspan & Quartiroli, 2019). Today, the integration of exercise sciences and psychology reflects a comprehensive approach to health and wellness, acknowledging the critical influence of physical activity on overall well-being (Buecker et al., 2021). This evolution underscores a profound recognition of the mind-body connection, leading to enhanced strategies for health promotion, disease prevention and athletic performance (Ntoumanis et al., 2021).

DOI: 10.4324/9781003517474-21

As research has deepened our grasp of the psychological dimensions of physical activity, psychologists have increasingly applied this knowledge to foster and encourage engagement in physical activity (García-Álvarez & Faubel, 2020). Despite the growing interest among psychologists in promoting physical activity beyond athletic performance, the specifics of the role of applied exercise psychologist (AEP) and the necessary competencies for providing ethical and effective services remain unclear. In this chapter, we seek to offer some clarity and ideas for those interested in pursuing a career promoting physical activity through psychological intervention, and to highlight the importance of developing the competencies necessary to deliver ethical and effective services. We divide the chapter into three sections. First, we outline the essential competencies required to practice applied exercise psychology and offer an insight into global training and accreditation requirements. Second, we explore the practical application of these competencies. We examine how exercise psychologists leverage their skills in applied domains and discuss potential career opportunities within the field of promoting physical activity. Finally, we reflect on the challenges and opportunities of working in applied exercise psychology, and how addressing these challenges might contribute to the professionalisation of applied exercise psychology.

15.1.1 Applied Physical Activity Psychology or Applied Exercise Psychology?

There is ongoing debate in academic literature over whether the terms physical activity and exercise require differentiation to distinguish the two concepts and improve consistency in use and understanding for both practitioners and public (Dasso, 2019). International, cultural and social differences in the meanings and interpretations of labels such as sport, exercise and physical activity make universal consensus on their definition challenging (Cremades et al., 2014), especially when these labels are used interchangeably in literature (Acevedo 2012). Caspersen et al. (1985) defined physical activity as "any bodily movement produced by skeletal muscles that results in energy expenditure" (p. 126), which suggests both sport and exercise are the sub-components of physical activity. Exercise is often defined as a structured, deliberate form of physical activity (Dasso, 2019), and for some has negative or unpleasant associations (Ekkekakis et al., 2021). Physical activity, on the other hand, encompasses all forms of health-enhancing and active living behaviours such as walking short distances instead of driving (Herrmann et al., 2024). In practice, however, we observe a preference for the term 'exercise' over 'physical activity' in the discourse of diverse cultural contexts, as the global community seems more likely to use 'exercise' in everyday language (Watson, 2023). Therefore, we prefer to use the title Applied Exercise Psychologist, or AEP, when referring to the practice of promoting physical activity.

15.2 Competence, Training and Accreditation

Much attention has been given to identifying the academic standards, proficiencies and professional competencies within psychology (Fletcher & Maher, 2013; Portenga et al., 2017; Rodolfa et al., 2005) and the identity of the sport psychology profession (Wagstaff & Quartiroli, 2020). Exercise psychology, while often integrated with sport psychology, represents a distinct field, a distinction not always clearly articulated in definitions or professional titles that commonly label practitioners as sport and exercise psychologists (Wagstaff & Quartiroli, 2020). Although the identity, academic standards and professional competencies of the sport psychology profession have been extensively explored (Fletcher & Maher, 2013; Portenga et al., 2017; Rodolfa et al., 2005), similar scrutiny has not yet been applied to exercise psychology.

Sport psychologists primarily enhance athletic performance, focusing on aspects of team dynamics, motivation and athlete well-being. In contrast, exercise psychologists apply psychological principles to promote participation in physical activity, aiming to improve mental and physical health (Watson, 2023). Notably, the clientele of AEPs often includes individuals who are less likely to engage in or maintain a positive relationship with physical activity, highlighting a significant difference in the populations served compared to sport psychologists (Watson, 2023). Indeed, it could be argued that exercise psychology shares greater connections to health psychology than sport psychology (Dasso, 2019). To elaborate, both exercise and health psychology explore the psychological processes influencing and influenced by physical and mental health and lifestyle behaviours. Moreover, both fields seek understanding of how biological, psychological and social factors affect health and illness. Both fields focus on promoting healthier lifestyles and studying the psychological impacts of illness to improve health outcomes (Dasso, 2019). The overlap between health and exercise psychology is evident in interventions designed to enhance well-being and prevent disease across diverse populations. Consequently, professionals in both health and exercise psychology fields have cause to collaborate, employing psychological theories and methods to optimise individuals' physical health and overall life quality (Takemura et al., 2023).

Specialties within psychology are defined by the distinct populations they serve, the specific problems addressed, the interventions employed and the settings in which they operate (Rodolfa et al., 2005). With these criteria in mind, applied exercise psychology clearly stands apart from sport psychology. This distinction underscores the need for tailored competencies and training specific to applied exercise psychology, ensuring practitioners are equipped with the necessary skills and knowledge for effective practice. Clarifying these competencies will enable the profession to better define its scope and practice boundaries, ensuring practitioners understand the parameters within which they are trained and competent to practice and contribute to the credibility and professionalisation of the field (Rodolfa et al., 2013; Quartiroli, Harris et al., 2021).

15.2.1 Competence

Rodolfa et al. (2005) presented a cube model of competences tailored for professional psychology, recommending its application to sub-disciplines like exercise or sport psychology to guide the development of professional competencies. Despite considerable exploration of competencies for applied sport psychology practice (e.g., Durand-Bush et al., 2023; Fletcher & Maher, 2013; Portenga et al., 2017), there remains a lack of consensus and common understanding of what constitutes competence within the increasingly diverse practice fields of sport psychology and exercise psychology (Jooste et al., 2016; Sly et al., 2020). Currently, exercise psychologists are left to determine how competencies identified for sport psychologists might be applicable to their own specialisation (Shannon & Zizzi, 2017). There is, therefore, a growing need to clarify competencies specific to exercise psychologists, distinguishing them from those in sport psychology. In response to requests for unification of competency models for psychological practice, Rodolfa et al. (2013) outlined six core competency clusters for psychologists: (a) Scientific Knowledge Base, (b) Evidence-Based Decision-Making/Critical Reasoning, (c) Interpersonal and Cultural Competence, (d) Professionalism/Ethics, (e) Assessment, and (f) Intervention/Supervision/Consultation. In the following section, we explore these competency clusters in relation to the practice of exercise psychology, noting that the requirements of practice will be unique to each practitioner such that the exact nature of competencies must be tailored to each practitioner.

15.2.1.1 Scientific Knowledge Base

Applied exercise psychology practitioners need a thorough grasp of the scientific principles underlying exercise physiology, psychology and behaviour change (Shannon & Zizzi, 2017). This involves understanding the physiological and psychological impacts of exercise on both the body and mind, as well as recognising the cognitive, socio-economic and environmental factors that act as barriers to physical activity (Razon & Sachs, 2017). Additionally, a detailed knowledge of the influence of cognitive and affective processes on behaviour is crucial for effectively encouraging physical activity across various groups (Biddle et al., 2021; Teixeira et al., 2023). A profound comprehension of exercise, physical activity and the behaviour change theories associated with engaging in and maintaining an active lifestyle is crucial. This entails a solid understanding of various physical activities and familiarity with evidence-based strategies to promote physically active and healthy lifestyles (Hermann et al., 2024). Furthermore, a thorough knowledge and critical understanding of research methodologies is essential for AEPs to evaluate academic literature and incorporate research findings into their professional practices (Schinke et al., 2023).

15.2.1.2 Evidence-Based Decision-Making and Critical Reasoning

Evidence-based practice is the foundation of competence within psychology (Rodolfa et al., 2013). The field of exercise psychology and applied exercise psychology practitioners should aim to integrate and apply rigorous scientific principles to enhance the effectiveness and ethical value of the services provided to clients. In essence, and congruent with the International Society of Sport Psychology's (ISSP) position stand, AEPs must become scientist-practitioners where science and practice inform each other (Schinke et al., 2023). Practitioners combine scientific knowledge and understanding in all practice areas (Schinke et al., 2023), and the discipline must actively engage with the latest research to adapt and apply evidence-based interventions that promote physical activity and encourage healthy lifestyle behaviours (Watson, 2023). AEPs should meticulously select and critically assess up-to-date theoretical and empirical literature on exercise, health, psychology and behaviour change, ensuring their methods are supported by strong, actionable evidence (Schinke et al., 2023). Practitioners must be competent in investigative processes (including assessment, formulating and testing hypotheses, gathering evidence and data), utilising evidence to create case formulations, selecting appropriate interventions and continually evaluating treatment and interventions (Schinke et al., 2023). Further, they should demonstrate competence in consultation, working closely with clients to set realistic goals, monitor progress and make necessary adjustments to interventions (Dishman et al., 2018).

Thus, practitioners need to be proficient in employing a structured approach to integrate results from various forms of assessments, such as fitness tests or psychological evaluations, to support a systematic formulation process and the continuous refinement of strategies and enhance the effectiveness of interventions. Formulation frameworks must be adopted to consider the complexities and individualistic nature of health-related behaviours, utilising such frameworks encourages the development of appropriate strategies and interventions (Hutchison & Johnston, 2013). AEPs should clearly articulate the rationale behind their decisions, grounding them in evidence-based practices while balancing the unique needs of the client and their context (Schinke et al., 2023).

15.2.1.3 Cultural and Interpersonal Competence

Cultural competence in psychology encompasses cultural awareness, knowledge, skills, encounters and desires (Ryba et al., 2024). Awareness involves gaining insight into one's own cultural values, attitudes and biases while developing sensitivity to the diverse attitudes, values and beliefs of others (Ryba et al., 2024). Knowledge pertains to understanding the client's culture and worldviews, while skills refer to the practitioner's ability to engage with clients in a sensitive and appropriate manner (Sue et al., 2009). Cultural competence necessitates looking beyond generalisations of race, ethnicity, age, gender, sexuality or social class, and addressing occurrences of the normalisation of the dominant group which may otherwise limit the effectiveness of one's practice and intervention (Quartiroli et al., 2020; Quartiroli, Schinke et al., 2023). Quartiroli, Schinke and colleagues (2023) argue that mere knowledge and awareness of cultural differences are insufficient. Practitioners must embrace humility and reflexivity, be willing to engage in uncomfortable conversations and learn from others and each other. Embracing cultural humility encourages practitioners to move beyond mere cultural understanding, committing instead to a lifelong journey of personal accountability and advocacy against systemic barriers that affect marginalised groups (Ryba et al., 2024). However, practitioners are encouraged to go beyond humility by embracing cultural safety, which involves actively engaging in dismantling systemic barriers and addressing power imbalances faced by marginalised groups, thereby establishing genuinely inclusive practices (Ryba et al., 2024).

In practice, practitioners should aim to engage in meaningful dialogue to explore the client's complex identity of intersecting cultural influences by demonstrating humility, reflexivity and a willingness to learn to improve the quality of their interaction with clients (Ryba et al., 2024). Taking hormonal changes (such as menstruation, pregnancy and menopause) as just one arena where cultural beliefs and stigmatisation can contribute to a great diversity of lived experiences (Pao, 2023, Saglam & Orsal, 2020), it is essential for practitioners to fully understand the intersecting identities, cultural beliefs and norms in conjunction with the physiological and psychological effect of hormones on activity as part of a fully informed formulation process. Awareness of cultural intersectionality further equips practitioners to challenge practices, policies and environments where necessary to advocate for inclusivity and sensitivity for improved well-being (Quartiroli, Schinke et al., 2023).

15.2.1.4 Professionalism and Ethics

Professionalism is often highlighted as a key component of competency models and is also considered an overarching domain that encompasses other competencies (Quartiroli, Fogaça, & Wagstaff, 2023; Rodolfa et al., 2005). In psychology, professionalism has been defined as a value system that guides practitioners' conduct, behaviours and actions (Grus et al., 2018). Professionalism encompasses adherence to ethical standards, demonstrating competence and maintaining a commitment to the well-being and development of clients. Grus et al. (2018) identified the following components and associated behaviours to describe professionalism: accountability, ethical engagement, self-reflection, excellence, humanism, civility, collaboration, cultural humility, psychology's social contract with society and social responsibility (cf. Grus et al., 2018). Consistent demonstration of these standards and behaviours is essential to ensure ethical, effective, credible and trustworthy practice, ensuring client safety and well-being, enhancing the credibility of the field of exercise psychology and providing protection for both client and practitioner.

Professionalism requires congruence between the practitioner's personal values and professional values (Quartiroli, Fogaça, & Wagstaff, 2023). The integration of personal values and professional philosophy provides an opportunity for meaningful and ethical service delivery (Quartiroli, Fogaça, & Wagstaff, 2023). Professional philosophies evolve throughout the developmental phases of a career (Collins et al., 2013) and enable the practitioner to practice with congruence and authenticity, to develop and establish their own professional identity (Quartiroli,

Wagstaff, Hunter, & Martin, 2022, Quartiroli, Fogaça, & Wagstaff, 2023). It follows that AEPs must ensure they develop an understanding of their personal values and beliefs, reflect upon how their practice and behaviours align with their values to ensure they uphold their professional and ethical responsibilities to their client (Quartiroli, Harris et al., 2021).

In addition to practicing with professionalism and congruence, a competent practitioner needs to be aware of the boundaries of their training and competence to practice ethically and safely (Quartiroli, Harris et al., 2021). Ethical considerations are paramount when working with clients to promote health and well-being (Quartiroli, Harris et al., 2021), exercise practitioners have a responsibility to uphold ethical standards and maintain appropriate professional boundaries with their client (Quartiroli, Fogaça, & Wagstaff, 2023). It is essential that practitioners recognise where the boundaries of their qualification, training and competence lie and have a referral network available to them to ensure the individual receives appropriate intervention (Tod et al., 2021). Given the overlap between exercise psychology with health psychology and the growing interest in improving well-being and physical activity, it is possible that practitioners might encounter clients who require clinical support beyond the scope of their own practice (Anshel, 2005, Biddle & Fox, 1989). The practitioner must be competent in conducting the appropriate assessment of the client's needs and determining whether a referral to different practitioner (such as physiotherapist or clinical psychologist) is required (Tod et al., 2021). Making a referral is not without ethical challenges, such as balancing potential waiting lists for other health practitioners with the immediate needs of the client (Roberts et al., 2016). As well as developing their competence in identifying when a referral is required, the practitioner will also need to develop skills to appropriately support the client through the referral process (Tod et al., 2021). Finally, practitioners have an ethical mandate to ensure they are fit to practice (Quartiroli, Wagstaff, and Thelwell, 2022). This requires an understanding of how to manage the demands of the role while actively maintaining personal well-being (Quartiroli, Wagstaff, & Thelwell, 2022). Although defined in relation to sport psychologists, self-care is understood as the "purposeful engagement in activities grounded in one's values" (Quartiroli, Wagstaff, & Thelwell, 2022, p.8). Self-care is most successful when aligned with one's life values and is a personal experience which benefits both personal and professional identities, relationships and practice (Quartiroli, Etzel et al., 2019). Of all the fields of psychology, self-care is perhaps most relevant for AEPs who seek to improve the well-being and quality of life of others. A practitioner who fails to practice what they preach or consider their own well-being is unlikely to establish credibility or trust, or be considered competent by their clients (Quartiroli, Hunter, & Martin, 2022).

15.2.1.5 Assessment

The processes of assessment allow an AEP to evaluate their clients' physical and psychological health, identify risk factors for sedentary behaviours and assess readiness for change (Schneider et al., 2003). Psychological assessment must only be undertaken within the boundaries of the practitioners' expertise (Quartiroli, Harris et al., 2021) and could encompass a variety of approaches. For example, applied exercise psychology practitioners could use psychometric testing, involving the use of validated questionnaires to measure variables such as motivation, anxiety and self-efficacy. Similarly, practitioners may require a familiarity with performance-based assessments, which evaluate physical capabilities and psychological responses, including wearable technologies such as pedometers and heart rate monitors (Greiwe & Nyenhuis, 2020). Additionally, understanding and applying observational techniques, such as behavioural analysis during activity, provides insights into the psychological responses and attitudes towards physical activity, as well as perceptions of barriers towards being active (da Silva et al., 2021). Furthermore, practitioners may need to be proficient in conducting structured and semi-structured interviews to evoke a deeper exploration of personal and psychological factors that impact a client's behaviour and well-being (Sparkes & Smith, 2014). Significantly, the use of assessment tools must be grounded in evidence-based decision-making in alignment with the practitioners' professional philosophy and the needs of the client (Poczwardowski et al., 2004). The assessment process is fundamental for formulating interventions that enhance both mental and physical health, ultimately leading to improved performance and overall well-being (Watson, 2023).

Competence in assessment includes the evaluation of interventions and services to ensure the effectiveness and efficiency of psychological support provided to clients (Chandler & Donovan, 2023). This involves systematically assessing both the processes and outcomes of an intervention, utilising quantitative and qualitative measures (Toomey et al., 2020). Quantitative assessments might include questionnaires and performance metrics to objectively measure changes in psychological variables and physical performance. Qualitative evaluations, such as client interviews and feedback, provide deeper insights into the subjective experiences and perceived benefits of the interventions. AEPs must also be adept at using data analysis techniques to interpret these results, identifying trends and areas for improvement. Self-reflection serves as a useful tool for refining interventions and enhancing service delivery, ensuring that they are evidence-based, client-centred and contextually relevant (Fogaça et al., 2018). Assessment and evaluation competence must be underpinned by ethical considerations regarding informed consent, confidentiality, security and safekeeping of documentation, data and records, secure disposal of materials and results, competent and safe use of technology (Quartiroli, Harris et al., 2021).

15.2.1.6 Intervention, Supervision and Consultation

AEPs require a robust range of intervention-based competencies that align with their professional philosophy to support their clients effectively (Poczwardowski et al., 2004). These interventions span various therapeutic techniques and strategies, which will be tailored to improve physical activity and mental well-being.

AEPs may refer to theoretical frameworks such as (but not limited to) the Health Belief Model (Becker & Maiman, 1975), Theory of Planned Behaviour (Ajzen, 1985), Self-Determination Theory (Deci & Ryan, 1985) and Trans-Theoretical Model (Prochaska & DiClemente, 1982), to support clients in their journeys to improve physical activity and mental well-being (see Hagger et al., 2020). Since theoretical understanding is insufficient on its own, practitioners must ensure their interventions are grounded in evidence-based best practice, drawing on their scientific knowledge when developing a suitable framework for their intervention (Hagger et al., 2020).

Training, development and competence is underpinned by supervision as an essential component to ethical practice throughout a practitioner's career (Quartiroli, Fogaça, & Wagstaff, 2023; Zizzi & Fogaça, 2018). The supervision process is an essential component of development and ethical practice (American Psychological Association, 2017). Supervision provides opportunities for reflection, feedback, and skill development under the guidance of experienced professionals (Quartiroli, Fogaça, & Wagstaff, 2023, Zizzi & Fogaça, 2018) and plays a key role in supporting the practitioner through challenges such as making referrals, terminating a client relationship or improving service delivery (Quartiroli, Knight et al., 2019). By engaging in supervision and consultation, AEPs enhance their effectiveness and contribute to the advancement of the profession through their credibility and professionalism (Quartiroli, Fogaça, & Wagstaff, 2023). Yet, the field of applied exercise psychology is currently characterised by a lack of supervisors with experience and competence in this domain (Watson, 2023). Undertaking supervised applied practice is foundational for trainees to gain experience and develop competence (McEwan & Tod, 2015); thus, it is essential to ensure the supervisor has the appropriate skills and experience to provide effective and informed supervision (Poczwardowski et al., 2023).

15.2.2 Training, Development and Accreditation

The practice of psychology is subject to significant global variations in training pathway requirements (Quartiroli, Vosloo et al., 2021). This presents challenges when outlining pathways to professional qualification across different countries. The complexity is further compounded by the diverse legislative environments that regulate the profession internationally. Consequently, practitioners must take personal responsibility to thoroughly understand and comply with the particular requirements and regulations relevant to their regions (Cremades et al., 2014).

In this section, we provide an introduction to the general academic and professional steps practitioners worldwide should consider when embarking on their journey to become an AEP. Since specific requirements for practicing psychology vary by country, potential practitioners are advised to familiarise themselves with the qualifications and standards required in each region where they hope to work. Although we do not claim to have provided an exhaustive coverage, in Tables 15.1

and 15.2, we offer a sample of some organisations responsible for setting standards and regulating the practice and provision of sport psychology. While qualifications and professionalising pathways are essential steps toward the professionalisation of exercise psychology, they are often limited to general psychology or sport psychology. This limitation creates a lack of clarity regarding the field or the necessary competencies to work in this domain (Watson, 2023). Critically, it is important to highlight how the practice of psychology in general, and exercise psychology specifically, is not regulated in many countries, making the ethical mandate for practitioners to establish and continue their competence, development and training even more relevant (Shah et al., 2023). For example, in India, Poland and Singapore, there are no accreditation frameworks for sport and exercise psychology; the title of such a psychologist is not protected (Shah et al., 2023). In such situations, it is recommended that aspiring practitioners seek guidance from international frameworks established by international organisations such as the ISSP.

Whether following a regulated pathway or not, practitioners typically begin their training with an undergraduate degree in psychology, which introduces the foundations of the field, psychological theories and research methods. In many countries, but by no means all, graduates must then enrol in post-graduate or internship pathways designed to meet the rigorous standards set by accrediting organisations, which provide the only approved routes to practice (Cremades et al., 2014). In the United Kingdom, aspiring sport and exercise psychology practitioners have three primary training routes upon completing an accredited master's degree. These include a university-led Professional Doctorate, the British Psychological Society's Qualification in sport and exercise psychology, and the British Association of Sport and Exercise Sciences Sport and Exercise Psychology Accreditation Route. Successful completion of any of these pathways allows practitioners to register with the Health and Care Professions Council (HCPC) and practice as registered psychologists. In contrast, China employs a tiered accreditation system for sport psychologists, with the highest tier requiring a doctoral degree in sport psychology or related field, alongside meeting additional criteria regarding practice hours, research, consulting experience and passing an oral examination (Schinke et al., 2018). However, educational opportunities in sport and exercise psychology are limited globally, leading to a "scarcity and geographical concentration" of such pathways (Quartiroli, Fogaça, & Wagstaff, 2023, p. 358). As a result, many prospective psychologists seek education abroad to advance their careers (Hutter et al., 2018; Quartiroli, Vosloo et al., 2021).

Training pathways lay the groundwork for proficient practice in various professional fields (Fletcher & Maher, 2013). However, obtaining the necessary regional qualifications and securing accreditation or registration with the relevant regulatory authority does not inherently guarantee competence (Rodolfa et al., 2005). Ultimately, it is the behaviour and performance of practitioners that determine competence, rather than the achievement of educational qualifications (Wagstaff & Quartiroli, 2020). Fogaça et al. (2024) identify four phases of development experienced by sport psychology practitioners: the introduction phase, exploration phase, consolidation phase and fulfilment phase. These phases are supported by processes such as (a) learning by doing, (b) reflection, (c) supervision and (d) connections and networking with peers (Fogaça et al., 2024). Thus, development does not only occur during the formal stages of training; professional development is an ongoing journey characterised by growth in confidence, a shift in focus towards the client, increased adaptability and the development of a congruent philosophy (Fogaça et al., 2024).

Once accreditation, registration and or qualification are achieved, it remains the responsibility of the practitioner to continue to develop their competence and stay informed on regulations and advances in research in order to practice psychology legally and ethically (Quartiroli, Wagstaff et al., 2021). The 'half-life' of professional knowledge is the time it takes for half of the knowledge gained during training to be lost (Neimeyer et al., 2012), or how long before one is half as knowledgeable as when one qualified. Scholars indicated sport psychology to have a 'half-life' of ten years (Neimeyer et al., 2012; Quartiroli, Wagstaff et al., 2021). While exercise psychology was not identified as a separate field, this finding highlights the importance of ongoing development and staying informed on innovations and research.

Society special interest groups (see Tables 15.1 and 15.2 for examples) can provide useful training and networking opportunities within exercise psychology, although there remains a dominance of sport over exercise in many of these groups. We therefore welcome the creation of the Applied Psychologists in Physical Activity Network (APPAN) in the United Kingdom in 2021 for taking the lead in creating a community for applied psychologists with an interest in physical activity. APPAN offers the opportunity for exercise practitioners to learn from and contribute to the development and education of others through sharing best practice, research and networking events. Such groups have the potential to influence and develop this new domain, building recognition for the role, contributing to the growth, credibility and professionalisation of the field.

15.3 Putting It All into (Applied) Practice

The lack of experienced supervisors and fewer structured opportunities in applied exercise psychology might seem daunting for those considering it as a career. However, numerous contexts and opportunities exist where aspiring and current practitioners can apply their training and thrive professionally. This section delves into the practical application of the acquired exercise psychology knowledge and skills and discusses potential challenges that may arise when applied in service delivery. Whether a practitioner has recently commenced their professional journey, already met the entry-level requirements for their region, or has developed experience in the sport and performance context, and it is now looking into the exercise and physical activity realms, these insights may inspire individuals to seek practice-based

TABLE 15.1 Examples of National Organisations Responsible for Setting Standards, Accrediting and Regulating Psychologists by Country

Country	*Organisations Responsible for Regulation, Standards and Practice*
Australia	Australian Psychological Society is the leading professional organisation for psychologists in Australia. The Australian Psychology Accreditation Council accredits education and training programmes for psychologists and the Psychology Board of Australia (PsyBA) is the regulatory authority responsible for the registration and regulation of psychologists, including sport psychologists. https://psychology.org.au The Australian Health Practitioner Regulation Agency works in partnership with national boards to ensure registered health practitioners are suitably trained, qualified and safe to practice https://www.ahpra.gov.au
Canada	Canadian Psychological Association represents psychologists nationally in Canada. It has a dedicated Sport and Exercise section. Registration and licensure as a psychologist vary between provinces and territories. https://cpa.ca
China	Zhongguo Xinli Xuehui (中国心理学会) or Chinese Psychological Society is the primary professional organisation for psychologists in China. The Sport Psychology branch of the Chinese Sports Science Association establishes the accredited standards for sport psychology professionals.
India	Clinical Psychologists must meet regulatory and accreditation requirements set by the Rehabilitation Council of India, but no such requirements are in place to practice sport and exercise psychology. https://rehabcouncil.nic.in. Specialist organisations interested in the field of sport psychology: Sport Psychology Association of India (affiliated to the ISSP), Indian Sport Psychologists's Association.
Japan	Nihon Shinri Gakkai (日本心理学会) or Japanese Psychological Association is the main professional organisation for psychologists, setting standards, establishing guidelines for education, training and ethical practice, and a licence is required to practice as a clinical psychologist. No formal recognition or licence for sport and exercise psychology. https://psych.or.jp/english/
New Zealand	The Psychologists Board of New Zealand is the regulatory authority responsible for the oversight of registration and practice. The New Zealand Psychological Society is the professional association representing psychologists in New Zealand. Psychologist is a protected title, to practice as a sport and exercise psychologist, completion of the requirements to become a registered psychologist is recommended. https://www.psychology.org.nz Sport and Exercise Science New Zealand has developed an accreditation and quality assurance scheme for professionals working in the field of sport and exercise science.
South Africa	The Psychological Society of South Africa is the national professional association representing psychologists. Psychologists are required to be registered with the Health Professions Council of South Africa as either a clinical or counselling psychologist in order to legally practice; sport and exercise is not a recognised speciality. http://www.hpcsa.co.za

United Kingdom	To practice as a practitioner psychologist in the United Kingdom, psychologists must be registered with the Health Care Professions Council. The title Sport and Exercise Psychologist is legally protected and can only be used by individuals registered with the HCPC.
	The British Psychological Society is the main professional organisation for psychologists in the United Kingdom. Exercise psychologists may find relevant divisions such as the Division of Sport and Exercise Psychology. https://www.bps.org.uk. The British Association for Sport and Exercise Science also offers an HCPC accredited route for sport and exercise psychologists.
United States	The American Psychological Association is a prominent organisation for psychologists in the United States. Exercise psychologists may join divisions related to health psychology or sport and exercise psychology, such as Division 38 (Health Psychology) or Division 47 (Exercise and Sport Psychology). https://www.apa.org
	The Association for Applied Sport Psychology is an organisation dedicated to applied sport and exercise psychology. Membership provides access to resources and networking opportunities. https://appliedsportpsych.org
	Each state has its own specific requirements regarding who can obtain a licence to legally practice as a psychologist. Individuals should familiarise themselves with the specific laws and requirements for the state(s) they wish to practice in.

TABLE 15.2 Multinational Organisations Representing Sport and Exercise Psychologists

Organisation	*Currently Representing*
Asian South-Pacific Association of Sport Psychology https://aspasp.org	Australia, China, Fiji, Hong Kong, India, Indonesia, Iran, Iraq, Israel, Japan, Korea, Kuwait, Macau, Malaysia, Mongolia, Nepal, New Zealand, Philippines, Qatar, Saudi Arabia, Singapore, Sri Lanka, Taiwan, Thailand, and Viet Nam.
European Federation of Sport Psychology (FEPSCAC) https://fepsac.com (offers certification)	Austria, Belgium, Catalonia, Croatia, Czech Republic, Finland, France, Germany, Greece, Italy, the Netherlands, Poland, Portugal, Romania, Russia, Slovakia, Spain, Sweden, Switzerland, Turkey, United Kingdom, Europe (European Network of Young Specialists in Sport Psychology), Arab Union (Arab Association for Sport Psychology).
International Society of Sport Psychology (ISSP)	Global – registration with the ISSP recognises the practitioner has fulfilled the minimum academic and experiential standards of practice required.

experiences and tailor their professional paths (Poczwardowski et al., 2004). The dearth of literature on the practical application of research reveals a significant gap in understanding how AEPs effectively meet service delivery needs (Watson, 2023). This lack of information underscores the necessity for practitioners to be inventive, especially since positions specifically tailored to their expertise are rarely advertised. Watson (2023) stresses the importance of aligning the services offered by exercise psychologists with the actual needs and desires of potential clients, who may not fully understand the benefits these professionals can provide.

15.3.1 Applied Domains

The opportunities for AEPs to practice encompass not only physical settings or environments such as fitness centres or rehabilitation facilities. Practitioners may prefer to work in broader, more conceptual areas, influencing intervention strategies, programme development and policy decision-making. The following are a few examples of domains within which exercise psychologists might practice and populations they might serve.

15.3.1.1 Fitness Domains

Fitness environments may represent one of the more obvious settings for AEPs to practice and deliver their services. In addition to working with individual clients, there are opportunities to work with fitness professionals, exercise referral groups utilising fitness settings (see Section 3.1.4. *Clinical Domains)*, and the fitness setting provider (Meredith et al., 2019; Swedlund, 2023). Individuals who attend a fitness centre likely appreciate the benefits of being physically active but may require support with motivation, self-esteem, exercise anxiety, body image issues or adherence. AEPs have the opportunity to work individually with clients to address the complex interplay of physiological and psychological factors, influencing participation and enjoyment of physical activity (O'Neill & Kremer, 2017, Teixeira et al., 2022, 2023). Additionally, practitioners can collaborate with fitness professionals to create psychologically informed environments for clients (Swedlund, 2023). This collaboration might include offering psychoeducation on the psychological aspects of behaviour change, motivation and self-esteem to enhance client interaction and outcomes (Swedlund, 2023). Such efforts enable personal trainers, instructors and coaches to use psychologically informed techniques to influence clients' motivation, address barriers and modify negative beliefs or behaviours (Ballengee et al., 2021).

AEPs can equally promote their services to support the fitness setting provider. Fitness centres typically lose a significant proportion of their members each year (Yi et al., 2021) and invest considerable time and effort in attracting new members, even though it is more cost-effective to retain existing ones (Yi et al., 2021). Practitioners can leverage their knowledge and skills to influence the retention of new and existing members through improved contact and support from fitness professionals and support staff (Riseth et al., 2021). Many sedentary individuals self-exclude from exercising in public due to body image concerns (Thedinga et al., 2021) or perceived negative judgement (Seal et al., 2022). By understanding these barriers to participation, AEPs can advise fitness providers on creating more inclusive environments. This might involve offering stronger or larger equipment, using diverse populations in marketing materials, providing different intensity classes for beginners, and training staff on respectful and appropriate language and behaviours (Pickett & Cunningham, 2017). Additionally, the setting may benefit from the presence of AEPs providing their services directly to members and further encouraging retention. AEPs can provide guidance on overcoming the psychological challenges associated with being active, such as motivation, overcoming barriers, self-esteem and social support.

15.3.1.2 Sports Domains

Sports clubs are typically considered as centres of athletic performance, a place for those already active. Sport clubs, however, could become a setting for exercise psychology practitioners to reach fans, supporters, volunteers, parents, coaches and whole communities (Van Hoye et al., 2021). Sports clubs are often hubs for community engagement and social interaction, especially in rural areas where clubs can shape a community's identity, making them ideal settings for health and well-being interventions (Hutchesson et al., 2021). The communal and supportive environment of sports clubs, combined with the existing sense of identity associated with the club, may represent an ideal setting for implementing effective physical activity interventions. These interventions might be aimed at motivating those who would otherwise not engage in exercise towards increased activity, promoting improved well-being through education on health behaviours or training stakeholders to deliver health-promoting activities to the community (Baker et al., 2016; Johnson et al., 2020). AEPs might work with key stakeholders within the club to understand the needs of the club and community before planning and implementing appropriate interventions (Johnson et al., 2020). Sports club settings provide AEPs with an opportunity to significantly impact the health and well-being of the wider community, making these clubs exemplary venues for exercise psychology practice (Hutchesson et al., 2021).

15.3.1.3 Educational Domains

Educational experiences in schools and universities contribute to the shaping of physical activity behaviours and beliefs of young people (Ekkekakis et al., 2021). Yet, it is estimated that globally in 2016, 81% of school-going 11–17-year-olds were insufficiently physically active (Guthold et al., 2020). Sedentary lifestyles contribute to rising levels of obesity, anxiety, depression and behavioural issues in young people (Álvarez-Bueno et al., 2017). AEPs can help improve physical activity experiences in educational environments, not only for physical health but also to enhance cognitive function, academic performance and overall well-being. Given the significant amount of time students spend on educational activities, educational settings may provide ideal environments for promoting lifelong habits of physical activity for improved well-being.

In schools, AEPs can have a significant impact by designing and implementing programmes to encourage enjoyment of and participation in physical activity among children and adolescents. Understanding the physiological and psychological needs at different developmental stages will enable practitioners to tailor programmes accordingly. Authentic engagement with students is crucial to understanding their needs, beliefs and fears (Knowles et al., 2023). By working closely with students, teachers, parents and administrators, practitioners can integrate physical activity into students' daily routines, making it a natural and enjoyable part of their day. They may also develop interventions to reduce barriers to participation, such as social anxiety or lack of motivation, fostering a positive attitude towards physical activity from an early age, which can contribute to long-term health and academic success (Álvarez-Bueno et al., 2017).

In higher education, AEPs can address the unique challenges faced by young adults, who often experience significant stress during educational transitions (Parker et al., 2021). University students may struggle to balance academic demands, financial pressures and psychosocial adjustments with maintaining an active lifestyle (Parker et al., 2021). Opportunities for practice might include developing programmes promoting physical activity as a means of stress management, improving mental health and enhancing social interaction. Collaborating with university wellness centres, they may offer workshops, fitness classes or personalised exercise plans to fit around students' busy schedules. By promoting a culture of physical activity on campus, AEPs can help students develop healthy habits that can last a lifetime.

For students with special educational needs or intellectual disabilities, physical activity offers physical, psychological and social benefits (Fitzpatrick et al., 2023). However, low levels of participation among these students can result from a lack of support, knowledge, inclusivity an over-emphasis on competition, and the prevalence of stigma, exacerbating feelings of isolation and anxiety towards physical activity (Fox et al., 2019; Fitzpatrick et al., 2023). Promoting enjoyment and fun, rather than competition, can change the relationship young people have with physical activity (Fitzpatrick et al., 2023). AEPs can create adaptive physical activity programmes addressing these students' specific needs. By working with special education teachers, adapted physical activity practitioners and caregivers, they can design safe, enjoyable and accessible activities that promote physical and emotional well-being. This tailored approach ensures all students, regardless of their abilities, can engage in physical activities and enjoy a higher quality of life (Hendrix et al., 2020).

15.3.1.4 Clinical Domains

There is a wide variety of clinical environments where AEPs might utilise their skills, knowledge and competence in promoting physical activity and enhancing well-being. These include inpatient and outpatient clinics, where practitioners can work with individuals recovering from surgery or managing chronic illness, such as rehabilitation centres, oncology units, weight management clinics and community health programmes. Clinical settings provide opportunities for AEPs to play a pivotal role in fostering healthy lifestyles and supporting long-term physical and mental health outcomes.

Individuals who have experienced chronic ill-health conditions such as cancer, cardiovascular or pulmonary disease will undoubtedly experience fears regarding returning to or commencing physical activity during or after treatment (Meredith et al., 2019). Internationally, there is a low use of recommended rehabilitation services in oncology care, despite the publication of guidelines and evidence for reducing the negative effects of treatment-related symptoms through physical activity (Schneider et al., 2003; Stout et al., 2021). Those who experience injuries are similarly less likely to return to physical activity and may experience fears, doubts and anxiety regarding engagement in activity, physical therapy or exercise rehabilitation (Baez et al., 2020; Pham et al., 2023). This highlights the need for AEPs who have the skills and knowledge to support individuals throughout their treatment and recovery stages, tailoring interventions to the specific contexts and challenges faced by the individual. Individuals may require support in psychological adjustment relating to body image, self-esteem, self-concept, fear, sleep, loss of routine and social isolation (Russell, 2019; Schneider et al., 2003). AEPs are uniquely skilled to identify and help individuals process cognitive and emotional responses which can accompany chronic illness or injury by utilising their compassion, knowledge and exercise consulting skills (Meredith et al., 2019).

It is likely that working in clinical settings will involve collaboration with multi-disciplinary teams, or individual health practitioners such as physiotherapists, clinical nurse specialists, clinical psychologists, occupational therapists and many other professionals as part of a rehabilitation or programme (Crozier et al., 2020). Exercise Referral Programmes (ERPs) in the United Kingdom are a primary care physical activity intervention that promote collaboration between health professionals (e.g., GPs) and local exercise professionals (Wade et al., 2020). ERPs are typically aimed at increasing levels of physical activity by individuals with chronic illness (Wade et al., 2020), but there is little evidence to suggest these short-term interventions are effective at facilitating meaningful long-term health and well-being outcomes or behaviour change (Wade et al., 2020). It has been noted that a lack of communication and collaboration between the referring health professional and the exercise professional can result in inconsistent delivery and disparity of expectations (Crozier et al., 2020). AEPs have the opportunity to play a significant role in bridging this gap by understanding the psychological and social needs of the individual before tailoring any intervention to provide the appropriate support (Meredith et al., 2019). As well as working directly with the individual, this might also include advising the referring practitioner on the importance of psychological and social support in recovery or training the exercise professional on the psychological aspects of behaviour change and chronic illness (Crozier et al., 2020).

15.3.1.5 Corporate and Organisational Domains

Corporate and organisational domains represent another context where exercise psychology practitioners may deliver their services, whether independently or in collaboration with wellness specialist, occupational therapist and fitness practitioners. Employers are increasingly aware of the influence of employee welfare and work life balance on productivity, performance and retention with many organisations providing benefits such as access to fitness centres, health risk assessments, health screening, health coaches, smoking cessation programmes, healthy menus and cycle to work schemes (Kelly & Snow, 2019; Swift et al., 2016; Wiradendi Wolor et al., 2020).

Psychologists with the appropriate understanding of organisational management can contribute to the introduction and effectiveness of corporate well-being programmes which provide opportunities for improving the health of employees and promote healthy lifestyle choices. Working with the appropriate professionals and conducting needs assessments to understand the specific challenges faced by a corporate workforce, AEPs can tailor evidence-based interventions or expand existing programmes. Interventions might seek to increase physical activity, reduce sedentary behaviour, introduce health-supporting behaviours or improve mental well-being through individual support, group education sessions, physical activities, cognitive behavioural techniques, policy changes or incentive schemes (Kelly & Snow, 2019; Tam & Yeung, 2018). AEPs can facilitate a cultural shift in the way organisations function, for example contributing to the development of initiatives such as walking meetings, stretch breaks and lunch time walks or fitness sessions to integrate more movement into the workday (Proper & van Oostrom, 2019). These interventions not only enhance physical health but also improve concentration, reduce stress and improve well-being and staff retention (Tam & Yeung, 2018).

15.3.1.6 Community Group Domains

In addition to being able to work in a variety of environments, exercise psychology practitioners have the opportunity to work with diverse populations. AEPs can play a critical role in enhancing the physical activity levels and mental well-being of different populations such as ageing populations, people with physical disabilities and people with learning disabilities. For ageing populations, activity is crucial for preserving mobility, cognitive function, overall quality of life, and it offers an opportunity for social connection (Fakoya et al., 2020; Meredith et al., 2019). Whether working with individuals or groups (such as residential homes or community locations), AEPs can develop tailored programmes to address the specific needs of older adults, to improve both physical, mental and social outcomes (Festa et al., 2023). Interventions might focus on improving balance, strength and flexibility to reduce the risk of falls and enhance daily functioning, as well as addressing the psychological challenges of ageing and remaining active. Group sessions might provide an opportunity for social interaction and mitigate feelings of loneliness or isolation often experienced in older age (Fakoya et al., 2020).

For adults with physical or learning disabilities, AEPs can play a role in designing adaptive programmes that accommodate varying levels of ability and mobility, for improved physical and mental well-being, fostering a sense of accomplishment and independence. In addition, practitioners might work with individuals on identifying factors that inhibit their ability to participate in activities in order to develop appropriate strategies to help overcome barriers (Ginis et al., 2021). This might involve working closely with other health care professionals to ensure the availability and safety of assistive devices or modified equipment, or with fitness providers to create inclusive and accessible spaces that enable individuals to participate in group activities and benefit from improved social connection (Auger & Spencer, 2021). Inclusive and adaptive activities have a positive effect not just on the physical and psychological well-being of individuals with disabilities but can also contribute to reducing stigma and improving awareness of bias and discrimination within society (Auger & Spencer, 2021).

15.3.1.7 Public Policy

AEPs have a crucial role in promoting physical activity across the wider community, extending beyond fitness clubs and educational establishments to reach diverse populations (Drenowatz et al., 2010). They can create direct interventions for individuals or groups and advocate for policy and environmental changes to support physical activity (Oldridge-Turner et al., 2022). By working within multi-disciplinary policy-making teams, AEPs can identify social and environmental barriers to activity and develop strategies to overcome them, thereby improving levels of activity (Sallis et al., 2012). Collaborating with urban planners, architects, and community organisations, they can help design spaces that encourage physical activity and well-being, including parks, playgrounds and green spaces, ensuring these areas are safe, well-maintained and accessible (Motomura et al., 2022). AEPs might also support initiatives that promote active transportation by enhancing infrastructure and connectivity within communities, thus encouraging walking or cycling as alternatives to driving (Nieuwenhuijsen, 2020). By creating environments that facilitate physical activity, practitioners can help address the broader social determinants of health and contribute to overall community well-being. Additionally, AEPs can advocate for policy changes supporting physical activity and well-being, as well as improved inclusivity for all populations. This involves collaborating with local governments, public health organisations and other stakeholders to develop and implement policies promoting active lifestyles. For instance, the World Cancer Research Fund International's MOVING framework helps policymakers worldwide increase physical activity levels (Oldridge-Turner et al., 2022). By influencing policy, AEPs encourage the community to incorporate physical activity into their daily lives, contributing to improved well-being and health outcomes (Motomura et al., 2022).

The examples above highlight the diverse opportunities available to AEPs, ranging from working within clinical settings to developing community wellness programmes. Practitioners are encouraged to be creative and explore opportunities that align with their personal and professional values. This could involve designing tailored interventions for specific populations, such as individuals with special needs, elderly individuals or those with chronic illnesses, ensuring that the interventions meet the unique needs and goals of these groups. Additionally, collaborating with other healthcare professionals such as physical therapists, nutritionists and medical doctors can promote holistic well-being and comprehensive care. By doing so, AEPs can apply their skills and knowledge in meaningful and impactful ways, ultimately contributing to the enhancement of physical and mental health within wider communities. However, we would like to reiterate that the examples provided are not exhaustive and do not intend to be a comprehensive list but rather illustrate the breadth of possibilities within the field.

15.3.2 Challenges to Practice

In this section, we provide insights into the challenges faced by AEPs. Like their counterparts in sport psychology, exercise psychologists encounter issues such as establishing a professional identity (Quartiroli, Wagstaff, Hunter, & Martin, 2022), maintaining appropriate levels of self-care (Quartiroli, Wagstaff, & Thelwell, 2022), starting and managing a new business (Norton, 2020) and working online (Price et al., 2022). However, they also face unique challenges due to the ambiguous nature of their profession. Specifically, they must demonstrate their value in contexts where their role is often seen as unnecessary by practitioners in more traditional and established fields, establish recognition and understanding of their role and identify clients among those who show no interest in being physically active.

AEPs are uniquely positioned to offer an invaluable holistic perspective on health improvement and physical activity, setting them apart from wellness coaches, personal trainers and medical practitioners. Yet, there is a lack of awareness within the population regarding the role of exercise psychologists, the benefits of working with an applied practitioner and how to access their services (Watson, 2023). This lack of awareness poses a significant challenge for potential practitioners and limits the public's ability to seek out specialised support for mental and physical health issues related to exercise and activity. Increasing public knowledge about exercise psychology and making it easier to locate qualified professionals are essential for maximising the impact of this important field.

Raising awareness of exercise psychology and its benefits is crucial (Watson, 2023); we suggest academic research and establishing professional referral networks as two potential opportunities for doing so. High-quality case studies are required to showcase the value of AEPs by sharing practice-based evidence of interventions and establishing appropriate evaluation criteria (Watson, 2023). Networking events, conferences and workshops offer opportunities to deepen one's understanding of the profession's nuances (Quartiroli, Fogaça, & Wagstaff, 2023). Although exercise psychology draws on sport and health psychology literature, the diverse opportunities for practice with clients with unique needs are underexplored (Watson, 2023). Global professional practice development through research, collaboration and networking is essential for the field's professionalisation (Quartiroli, Fogaça, & Wagstaff, 2023).

Identifying clients who prefer not to be active might also be challenging. Collaborating with other professions can help in identifying these clients and ensuring psychologists practice within their boundaries (Quartiroli, Fogaça, & Wagstaff, 2023). Building a network of professionals, including clinical psychologists, eating disorder specialists, social workers, physiotherapists, osteopaths, personal trainers, occupational therapists, sports club leaders, community leaders, relationship counsellors, substance abuse therapists and career guidance counsellors will be beneficial (Tod et al., 2021 [1951]). These relationships not only enable AEPs to identify the most appropriate expert for their clients but also create opportunities for reciprocal referrals, increasing awareness of the services AEPs offer (Tod et al., 2021 [1951]).

15.4 Conclusion

In this chapter, we sought to outline the role of an applied exercise psychology practitioner, highlighting the competencies and training required to practice. Exercise psychology draws on evidence from health and sport psychology, yet current training pathways typically favour sport over exercise. We hope we have established the importance of tailoring one's training and development to suit the specific needs of the practitioner and their practice, highlighting the requirement for ethical practice, including the identification of practice boundaries, the need for AEPs to become scientist-practitioners, grounding decisions in evidence-based practice. Further, we have outlined the need for cultural humility in creating cultural safety in practice and the essential role supervision plays in the practitioner's ongoing development. These competencies, alongside robust and appropriate training opportunities, enable practitioners to develop professionalism and contribute to the growing credibility of our profession. The acquisition of knowledge and skills and the development of competencies is a dynamic and integrated process, each dependent upon the other for continued growth (Rodolfa et al., 2005). Regardless of specialism, psychologists should be mindful that competence and skill development extend throughout one's career, supported by training, experience, supervision and personal reflection (Quartiroli, Wagstaff et al., 2021).

Despite the challenges detailed in the previous section, this is an exciting era for AEPs. The journey to applied practice is both challenging and profoundly rewarding. Aspiring exercise psychology practitioners have an opportunity to contribute to the growth of the professional and its recognition as an essential field within psychology and health. We have detailed the need for dedication to training and development of competencies through continuous learning and refection, which will enable practitioners to have a lasting impact on individuals and the wider community. Reflecting on the diversity of opportunities in an evolving landscape of practice, the role of AEPs is more critical now than ever. The expertise developed enables the promotion of physical activity and healthier lifestyles for all populations, improving mental health and well-being alongside physical health outcomes. Challenges are encountered in any role, yet we see these as opportunities for growth, innovation and the continued development towards improved recognition of the profession. We encourage the reader to actively contribute to the growth of the profession through collaboration, networking and knowledge sharing within the growing community of AEPs, knowing that you are paving the way for future practitioners to improve physical and mental health with evidence-based psychological insight.

References

Acevedo, E. O. (2012). Exercise psychology: Understanding the mental health benefits of physical activity and the public health challenges of inactivity. In E. O. Acevedo (Ed.), *The Oxford handbook of exercise psychology* (pp. 3–8). Oxford University Press.

Ajzen, I. (1985). From intentions to actions: A theory of planned behavior. In Julius Kuhl, & Jürgen Beckmann (Eds.), *Action control: From cognition to behavior* (pp. 11–39). Springer.

Álvarez-Bueno, C., Pesce, C., Cavero-Redondo, I., Sánchez-López, M., Garrido-Miguel, M., & Martínez-Vizcaíno, V. (2017). Academic achievement and physical activity: A meta-analysis. *Pediatrics*, *140*(6), 1–14. https://doi.org/10.1542/peds.2017-1498

American Psychological Association. (2017). *Ethical principles of psychologists and code of conduct*. American Psychological Association.

Anshel, M. H. (2005). *Applied exercise psychology: A practitioner's guide to improving client health and fitness*. Springer Publishing Company.

Aoyagi, M. W., Portenga, S. T., Poczwardowski, A., Cohen, A. B., & Statler, T. (2012). Reflections and directions: The profession of sport psychology past, present, and future. *Professional Psychology: Research and Practice*, *43*(1), 32–38. https://doi.org/10.1037/a0025676

Auger, J. M., & Spencer, N. L. (2021). "Just going to a spin class": Participant experiences of inclusion within an integrated indoor cycling program. *Adapted Physical Activity Quarterly*, *38(3)*, 359–376. https://doi.org/10.1123/apaq.2020-0107

Baez, S. E., Hoch, M. C., & Hoch, J. M. (2020). Psychological factors are associated with return to pre-injury levels of sport and physical activity after ACL reconstruction. *Knee Surgery, Sports Traumatology, Arthroscopy*, *28*, 495–501. https://doi.org/10.1007/s00167-019-05696-9

Baker, C., Elizabeth, L., Crone, D., Tutton, A., & Aitken, P. (2016). Contemporary lifestyle interventions for public health–Potential roles for professional sports clubs. In S. Cotterill, N. Weston, & G. Breslin (Eds.), *Sport and exercise psychology practitioner case studies* (pp. 417–436). John Wiley & Sons.

Ballengee, L. A., Zullig, L. L., & George, S. Z. (2021). Implementation of psychologically informed physical therapy for low back pain: Where do we stand, where do we go? *Journal of Pain Research*, 3747–3757. https://doi.org/10.2147/JPR.S311973

Becker, M. H., & Maiman, L. A. (1975). Sociobehavioral determinants of compliance with health and medical care recommendations. *Medical Care*, *13*(1), 10–24. https://www.jstor.org/stable/3763271

Biddle, S. J., & Fox, K. R. (1989). Exercise and health psychology: Emerging relationships. *British Journal of Medical Psychology, 62*(3), 205–216. https://doi.org/10.1111/j.2044-8341.1989.tb02829.x

Biddle, S. J. H., Mutrie, N., Gorely, T., & Faulkner, G. (2021). *Psychology of physical activity: Determinants, well-being and interventions* (4th ed.). Routledge.

Buckworth, J., Dishman, R. K., O'Connor, P. J. O., & Tomporowski, P. D. (2013). *Exercise Psychology* (2nd ed.). Human Kinetics.

Buecker, S., Simacek, T., Ingwersen, B., Terwiel, S., & Simonsmeier, B. A. (2021). Physical activity and subjective well-being in healthy individuals: A meta-analytic review. *Health Psychology Review, 15*(4), 574–592. https://doi.org/10.1080/17437199.2020.1760728

Caspersen, C. J., Powell, K. E., & Christenson, G. M. (1985). Physical activity, exercise and physical fitness: Definitions and distinctions for health-related research. *Public Health Reports, 100*, 126–131. https://stacks.cdc.gov/view/cdc/66195/cdc_66195_DS1.pdf

Chandler, C., & Donovan, T. (2023). Effectiveness in practice. In A. Borrie, C. Chandler, A. Hooton, A. Miles, & P. Watson (Eds.), *The applied sport and exercise practitioner* (pp. 189–196). Routledge.

Collins, R., Evans-Jones, K., & O'Connor, H. L. (2013). Reflections on three neophyte sport and exercise psychologists' developing philosophies for practice. *The Sport Psychologist, 27*(4), 399–409. https://doi.org/10.1123/tsp.27.4.399

Cremades, J. G., Tashman, L. S., & Quartiroli, A. (2014). Developing the pathway to become a sport, exercise and performance psychology professional. In J. G. Cremades and L. S. Tashman (Eds.), *Becoming a sport, exercise and performance psychology professional: A global perspective* (pp. 3–11). Psychology Press.

Crozier, A., Porcellato, L., Buckley, B. J., & Watson, P. M. (2020). Facilitators and challenges in delivering a peer-support physical activity intervention for older adults: A qualitative study with multiple stakeholders. *BMC Public Health*, *20*, 1–10. https://doi.org/10.1186/s12889-020-09990-x

da Silva, P. M. R., Soares, S. H. D. S. S., Mota, J. A. P. S., Viana, P. M. M. M. G., & Carvalho, P. M. M. S. (2021). Reviving direct observation methods for physical activity behavior. *Journal of Sports Science*, *9*, 9–16. https://doi.org/ 10.17265/2332–7839/2021.01.002

Dasso, N. A. (2019, January). How is exercise different from physical activity? A concept analysis. *Nursing Forum*, *54*(1), 45–52. https://doi.org/10.1111/nuf.12296

Deci, E. L., & Ryan, R. M. (1985). *Intrinsic motivation and self-determination in human behavior*. Plenum.

Dishman, R. K., Heath, G. W., & Lee, I.-M. (2018). *Physical Activity Epidemiology* (3rd ed.). Human Kinetics.

Drenowatz, C., Eisenmann, J. C., Pfeiffer, K. A., Welk, G., Heelan, K., Gentile, D., & Walsh, D. (2010). Influence of socio-economic status on habitual physical activity and sedentary behavior in 8-to 11-year-old children. *BMC Public Health*, *10*(1), 1–11. https://www.biomedcentral.com/1471-2458/10/214

Durand-Bush, N., Baker, J., van den Berg, F., Richard, V., & Bloom, G. A. (2023). The Gold Medal Profile for Sport Psychology (GMP-SP). *Journal of Applied Sport Psychology,35*(4), 547–570. https://doi.org/10.1080/10413200.2022.2055224

Ekkekakis, P., Zenko, Z., & Vazou, S. (2021). Do you find exercise pleasant or unpleasant? The affective exercise experiences (AFFEXX) questionnaire. *Psychology of Sport and Exercise, 55*, Article 101930. https://doi.org/10.1016/j.psychsport.2021.101930

Fakoya, O. A., McCorry, N. K., & Donnelly, M. (2020). Loneliness and social isolation interventions for older adults: A scoping review of reviews. *BMC Public Health*, *20*, 1–14. https://doi.org/10.1186/s12889-020-8251-6

Festa, F., Medori, S., & Macrì, M. (2023). Move your body, boost your brain: The positive impact of physical activity on cognition across all age groups. *Biomedicines*, *11*(6), 1765, 1–27. https://doi.org/10.3390/biomedicines11061765

Fitzpatrick, B. L., Breslin, G., & Taggart, L. (2023). Developing a school-based physical activity protocol for those with intellectual disabilities. In S. Cotterill, N. Weston, & G. Brelin (Eds.), *Sport and exercise psychology practitioner case studies* (pp. 353–372). John Wiley & Sons.

Fletcher, D., & Maher, J. (2013). Toward a competency-based understanding of the training and development of applied sport psychologists. *Sport, Exercise and Performance Psychology*, *2*(4), 265–280. https://doi.org/10.1037/a0031976

Fogaça, J. L., Quartiroli, A., & Wagstaff, C. R. D. (2024). Professional development of sport psychology practitioners: From systematic review to a model of development. *Psychology of Sport & Exercise*, *70*, 102550. https://doi.org/10.1016/j.psychsport.2023.102550

Fogaça, J. L., Zizzi, S. J., & Andersen, M. B. (2018). Walking multiple paths of supervision in American sport psychology: A qualitative tale of novice supervisees' development. *The Sport Psychologist, 32*(2), 156–165. https://doi.org/10.1123/tsp.2017-0048

Fox, B., Moffett, G. E., Kinnison, C., Brooks, G., & Case, L. E. (2019). Physical activity levels of children with Down syndrome. *Paediatric Physical Therapy*, *31*(1), 33–41 https://doi.org/10.1097/PEP.0000000000000556

García-Álvarez, D., & Faubel, R. (2020). Strategies and measurement tools in physical activity promotion interventions in the university setting: A systematic review. *International Journal of Environmental Research and Public Health*, *17*(18), 6526. https://doi.org/10.3390/ijerph17186526

Ginis, K. A. M., van der Ploeg, H. P., Foster, C., Lai, B., McBride, C. B., Ng, K., Pratt, M. P., Shiraziour, C. H., Smith, B. H., Vásquez, P. M., & Heath, G. W. (2021). Participation of people living with disabilities in physical activity: A global perspective. *The Lancet*, *398*(10298), 443–455. https://doi.org/10.1016/S0140-6736(21)01164-8

Greiwe, J., & Nyenhuis, S. M. (2020). Wearable technology and how this can be implemented into clinical practice. *Current Allergy and Asthma Reports*, *20*, 1–10. https://doi.org/10.1007/s11882-020-00927-3

Grus, C. L., Shen-Miller, D., Lease, S. H., Jacobs, S. C., Bodner, K. E., Van Sickle, K. S., Veilleux, J., & Kaslow, N. J. (2018). Professionalism: A competency cluster whose time has come. *Ethics& Behavior*, *28*(6), 450–464. https://doi.org/10.1080/10508422.2017.1419133Ha

Guthold, R., Stevens, G. A., Riley, L. M., & Bull, F. C. (2020). Global trends in insufficient physical activity among adolescents: A pooled analysis of 298 population-based surveys with 1· 6 million participants. *The Lancet Child & Adolescent Health*, *4*(1), 23–35. https://doi.org/10.1016/S2352-4642(19)30323-2

Hagger, M. S., Cameron, L. D., Hamilton, K., Hankonen, N., & Lintunen, T. (Eds.). (2020). *The handbook of behavior change*. Cambridge University Press. https://doi.org/10.1017/9781108677318

Hendrix, J. A., Amon, A., Abbeduto, L., Agiovlasitis, S., Alsaied, T., Anderson, H. A., Bain, L., Baumer, N., Bhattacharyya, A., Dusan, B., Botterton, K. N., Capone, G., Chandan, P., Chase, I., Chicoine, B., Cieuta-Walti, C., DeRuisseau, L. R. Durand, S., Esbensen, A., & Yi, J. S. (2020). Opportunities, barriers, and recommendations in Down syndrome research. *Translational Science of Rare Diseases*, 5(3–4), 99–129. https://doi.org/10.3233/TRD-200090

Herrmann, S. D., Willis, E. A., Ainsworth, B. E., Barreira, T. V., Hastert, M., Kracht, C. L., Schuna Jr, J. M., Cai, Z., Quan, M., Tudor-Locke, C., Whitt-Glover, M. C., & Jacobs Jr, D. R. (2024). 2024 Adult compendium of physical activities: A third update of the energy costs of human activities. *Journal of Sport and Health Science*, *3*(1), 6–12. https://doi.org/10.1016/j.jshs.2023.10.010

Hutchesson, H., Dollman, J., Baker, A., & Kernot, J. (2021). Barriers and enablers to implementing mental well-being programs through Australian rural football clubs—A qualitative descriptive study. *Health Promotion Journal of Australia*, *32*(2), 326–334. https://doi.org/10.1002/hpja.358

Hutchison, A. J., & Johnston, L. H. (2013). Exploring the potential of case formulation within exercise psychology. *Journal of Clinical Sport Psychology*, *7*(1), 60–76. https://doi.org/10.1123/jcsp.7.1.60

Hutter, R. I. V., van der Zande, J. J., Rosier, N., & Wylleman, P. (2018). Education and training in the field of applied sport psychology in Europe. *International Journal of Sport and Exercise Psychology*, *16*(2), 133–149. https://doi.org/10.1080/1612197X.2016.1162189

Johnson, S., Van Hoye, A., Donaldson, A., Lemonnier, F., Rostan, F., & Vuillemin, A. (2020). Building health-promoting sports clubs: A participative concept mapping approach. *Public Health*, *188*, 8–17. https://doi.org/10.1016/j.puhe.2020.08.029

Jooste, J., Kruger, A., Steyn, B. J. M., & Edwards, D. J. (2016). Essential competencies in contemporary applied sport psychology: Comparative perspectives from South Africa and the United Kingdom psychology. *African Journal for Physical Activity and Health Sciences, 22*(1-1), 1–32.

Kelly, R. K., & Snow, S. (2019). The importance of corporate wellness programs for psychological health and productivity in the workplace. In Ronald J. Burke, & Astrid M. Richardsen (Eds.), *Creating psychologically healthy workplaces* (pp. 411–430). Edward Elgar Publishing.

Knowles, Z., Goss, H., Shearer, C., & Turner, F. (2023). 'It isn't all child's play' Working with children and young people. In A. Borrie, C. Chandler, A. Hooton, A. Miles, & P. Watson (Eds.), *The applied sport and exercise practitioner* (pp. 176–186). Routledge.

Kornspan, A. S., & Quartiroli, A. (2019). A brief global history of sport psychology. In M. H. Anshel, T. A. Petrie, & J. A. Steinfeldt (Eds.), *APA handbook of sport and exercise psychology: Sport psychology* (pp. 3–16). American Psychological Association. https://doi.org/10.1037/0000123-001

McEwan, H. E., & Tod, D. (2015). Learning experiences contributing to service-delivery competence in applied psychologists: Lessons for sport psychologists. *Journal of Applied Sport Psychology, 27*(1), 79–93. https://doi.org/10.1080/10413200.2014.952460

Meredith, S. J., Wagstaff, C. R. D., & Dicks, M. (2019). Getting to the heart of the matter: An ethnography of emotions and emotion regulation in cardiac rehabilitation, *Qualitative Research in Sport, Exercise and Health, 11*(3), 364–381, https://doi.org/10.1080/2159676X.2018.1548373

Motomura, M., Koohsari, M. J., Lin, C. Y., Ishii, K., Shibata, A., Nakaya, T., Kaczynski, A. T., Veitch, J., & Oka, K. (2022). Associations of public open space attributes with active and sedentary behaviors in dense urban areas: A systematic review of observational studies. *Health & Place, 75*, 102816. https://doi.org/10.1016/j.healthplace.2022.102816

Neimeyer, G. J., Taylor, J. M., & Rozensky, R. H. (2012). The diminishing durability of knowledge in professional psychology: A Delphi Poll of specialties and proficiencies. *Professional Psychology: Research and Practice, 43*, 364–371. https://dx. doi.org/10.1037/a0028698

Nieuwenhuijsen, M. J. (2020). Urban and transport planning pathways to carbon neutral, liveable and healthy cities; A review of the current evidence. *Environment International, 140*, 105661. https://doi.org/10.1016/j.envint.2020.105661

Norton, L. W. (2020). The business of consulting psychology: Lessons from the field. *Consulting Psychology Journal: Practice and Research, 72*(1), 68–76. https://doi.org/10.1037/cpb0000159

Ntoumanis, N., Ng, J. Y. Y., Prestwich, A., Quested, E., Hancox, J. E., Thøgersen-Ntoumani, C., Deci, E. L., Ryan, R. M., Lonsdale, C., & Williams, G. C. (2021). A meta-analysis of self-determination theory-informed intervention studies in the health domain: Effects on motivation, health behavior, physical, and psychological health. *Health Psychology Review, 15*(2), 214–244. https://doi.org/10.1080/17437199.2020.1718529

O'Neill, S., & Kremer, J. (2017). Physical activity and self-concept: A humanistic intervention. In S. Cotterill, N. Weston, & G. Brelin (Eds.), *Sport and exercise psychology practitioner case studies* (pp. 334–353). John Wiley & Sons.

Oldridge-Turner, K., Kokkorou, M., Sing, F., Klepp, K. I., Rutter, H., Helleve, A., Sinclair, B., Meincke, L., Mitrou, G., Wiseman, M., & Allen, K. (2022). Promoting physical activity policy: The development of the MOVING framework. *Journal of Physical Activity and Health, 19*(4), 292–315. https://doi.org/10.1123/jpah.2021-0732

Pao, P. S. (2023). Social stigma centred around menstruation: A reflective review. *Frontier Anthropology, 11*, 51–58. https://doi.org/01.2023-14175947

Parker, P. C., Perry, R. P., Coffee, P., Chipperfield, J. G., Hamm, J. M., Daniels, L. M., & Dryden, R. P. (2021). The impact of student-athlete social identity on psychosocial adjustment during a challenging educational transition. *Psychology of Sport and Exercise*, *56*, 101979. https://doi.org/10.1016/j.psychsport.2021.101979

Pham, T., Green, R., Neaves, S., Hynan, L. S., Bell, K. R., Juengst, S. B., Zhang, R., Driver, S., & Ding, K. (2023). Physical activity and perceived barriers in individuals with moderate-to-severe traumatic brain injury. *PM&R*, *15*(6), 705–714 https://doi.org/10.1002/pmrj.12854

Pickett, A. C., & Cunningham, G. B. (2017). Physical activity for every body: A model for managing weight stigma and creating body-inclusive spaces. *Quest*, *69*(1), 19–36. https://doi.org/10.1080/00336297.2016.1145129

Poczwardowski, A., Andersen, M. B., Van Raalte, J. L., Harwood, C., Si, G., Tshube, T., & Noce, F. (2023). ISSP position stand: Competent supervision in sport psychology. *International Journal of Sport and Exercise Psychology, 21*(6), 931–950. https://doi.org/10.1080/1612197X.2023.2229342

Poczwardowski, A., Sherman, C. P., & Ravizza, K. (2004). Professional philosophy in the sport psychology service provision: Building on theory and practice. *The Sport Psychologist, 18,* 445–463. https://doi.org/10.1123/tsp.18.4.445

Portenga, S. T., Aoyagi, M. W., & Cohen, A. (2017). Helping to build a profession: A working definition of sport and performance psychology. *Journal of Sport Psychology in Action, 8,* 47–59. https://doi.org.1080/21520704.2016.1227413

Price, D., Wagstaff, C. R. D., & Thelwell, R. C. (2022). Opportunities and considerations of new media and technology in sport psychology service delivery*, Journal of Sport Psychology in Action, 13*(1), 4–15. https://doi.org/10.1080/21520704.2020.1846648

Prochaska, J. O., & DiClemente, C. C. (1982). Transtheoretical therapy: Toward a more integrative model of change. *Psychotherapy: Theory, Research & Practice*, *19*(3), 276–288. https://doi.org/10.1037/h0088437

Proper, K. I., & van Oostrom, S. H. (2019). The effectiveness of workplace health promotion interventions on physical and mental health outcomes – A systematic review of reviews. *Scandinavian Journal of Work, Environment & Health, 45*(6)*,* 546–559. https://doi.org/10.5271/sjweh.3833

Quartiroli, A., Etzel, E. F., Knight, S. M., & Zakrajsek, R. A. (2019). Self-care as key to others' care: The perspectives of globally situated experienced senior-level sport psychology practitioners. *Journal of Applied Sport Psychology, 31*(2), 147–167. https://doi.org/10.1080/10413200.2018.1460420

Quartiroli, A., Fogaça, J. L., & Wagstaff, C. R. D. (2023). Professional training and development: The bedrock of ethical, competent, and sustainable sport psychology. *Journal of Applied Sport Psychology, 35*(3), *349–371.* https://doi.org/10.1080/10413200.2022.2043485

Quartiroli, A., Harris, B. S., Brückner, S., Chow, G. M., Connole, I. J., Cropley, B., Fogaça, J., Gonzalez, S. P., Guicciardi, M., Hau, A., Kao, S., Kavanagh, E. J., Keegan, R. J., Li, H. Y., Martin, G., Moyle, G. M., Noce, F., Peterson, K., Roy, J., … Zito, M. (2021). The International Society of Sport Psychology Registry (ISSP-R) ethical code for sport psychology practice. *International Journal of Sport and Exercise Psychology, 19*(6), 907–928. https://doi.org/10.1080/1612197X.2020.1789317

Quartiroli, A., Hunter, H., & Martin, D. R. (2022). Practising What We Preach: Self-Care as an Avenue for Effective Practice. In V. Shanmuganathan-Felton & S. Smith (Eds.), *Developing a sport psychology consultancy practice* (pp. 160–175). Routledge.

Quartiroli, A., Knight, S. M., Etzel, E. F., & Zakrajsek, R. A. (2019). Fostering and sustaining sport psychology professional quality of life: The perspectives of senior-level, experienced sport psychology practitioners. *The Sport Psychologist, 33*, 148–158. https://doi.org/10.1123/tsp.2017-0140

Quartiroli, A., Schinke, R. J., Griffin, C., Vosloo, J., & Fisher, L. A., (2023). Cultural competence in a multinational group of sport psychology professionals. *Journal of Applied Sport Psychology, 35*(6), 919–940. https://doi.org/10.1080/10413200.2022.2140224

Quartiroli, A., Vosloo, J., Fisher, L., & Schinke, R. (2020). Culturally competent sport psychology: A survey of sport psychology professionals' perception of cultural competence. *The Sport Psychologist, 34*(3), 242–253. https://doi.org/10.1123/tsp.2019-0075

Quartiroli, A., Vosloo, J., Schinke, R. J., Anderson, S. N., Fisher, L. A., & Giffin, C. E. (2021). Sport psychology professionals' perceptions of the roadblocks to cultural sport psychology. *Sport, Exercise, and Performance Psychology, 10*(2), 240–256. https://doi.org/10.1037/spy0000256

Quartiroli, A., Wagstaff, C. R., Herms, M., & Kemmel, C. (2021). The future of continuing education and lifelong learning in sport psychology professionals: A Delphi study. *Professional Psychology: Research and Practice*, *52*(2), 173–185. https://dx. doi.org/10.1037/pro0000362

Quartiroli, A., Wagstaff, C. R., Hunter, H., & Martin, D. R. (2022). The identity of the sport psychology profession: A multinational perspective. *Psychology of Sport and Exercise*, *60*, 102140. https://doi.org/10.1016/j.psychsport.2022.102140

Quartiroli, A., Wagstaff, C. R., & Thelwell, R. (2022). The what and the how of self-care for sport psychology practitioners: A delphi study. *Journal of Applied Sport Psychology, 34*(6), 1352–1371. https://doi.org/10.1080/10413200.2021.1964107

Razon, S., & Sachs, M. (2017). *Applied exercise psychology.* Taylor & Francis.

Riseth, L., Nilsen, T. I. L., Mittet, Ø., Steinsbekk, A. (2021). The effect of initial support on fitness center use in new fitness center members, A randomised controlled trial. *Preventive Medicine Reports 24,* 101605. https://doi.org/10.1016/j.pmedr.2021.101605

Roberts, C., Faull, A. L., & Tod, D. (2016). Blurred lines: Performance enhancement, common mental disorders and referral in the U.K. Athletic population. *Frontiers in Psychology*, 7, 1067. https://doi.org/10.3389/fpsyg.2016.01067

Rodolfa, E., Bent, R., Eisman, E., Nelson, P., Rehm, L., & Ritchie, P. (2005). A cube model for competency development: Implications for psychology educators and regulators. *Professional Psychology: Research and Practice*, *36*(4), 347–354. https://doi.org/10.1037/0735-7028.36.4.347

Rodolfa, E., Greenberg, S., Hunsley, J., Smith-Zoeller, M., Cox, D., Sammons, M., Caro., C., & Spivak, H. (2013). A competency model for the practice of psychology. *Training and Education in Professional Psychology*, *7*(2), 71–83. https://doi.org/10.1037/a0032415

Russell, S. (2019). *The bowel cancer recovery toolkit*. Hammersmith Health Books.

Ryba, T. V., Schinke, R. J., Quartiroli, A., Wong, R., & Gill, D. L. (2024). ISSP position stand on cultural praxis in sport psychology: Reaffirming our commitments to the ethics of difference, cultural inclusion, and social justice, *International Journal of Sport and Exercise Psychology*, *22*(3), 533–552. https://doi.org/10.1080/1612197X.2024.2310988

Saglam, H. Y., & Orsal, O. (2020). Effect of exercise on premenstrual symptoms: A systematic review. *Complementary Therapies in Medicine*, *48*, 102272. https://doi.org/10.1016/j.ctim.2019.102272

Sallis, J. F., Floyd, M. F., Rodríguez, D. A., & Saelens, B. E. (2012). Role of built environments in physical activity, obesity, and cardiovascular disease. *Circulation*, *125*(5), 729–737. https://doi.org/*10.1161/CIRCULATIONAHA.110.969022*

Schinke, R. J., Si, G., Zhang, L., Elbe, A. M., Watson, J., Harwood, C., & Terry, P. C. (2018). Joint position stand of the ISSP, FEPSAC, ASPASP, and AASP on professional accreditation. *Psychology of Sport and Exercise*, *38*, 107–115. https://doi.org/10.1016/j.psychsport.2018.06.005

Schinke, R., Wylleman, P., Henriksen, K., Si, G., Wagstaff, C. R., Zhang, L., Tshepang, T., Noce, F., & Li, Y. (2023). International Society of Sport Psychology position stand: Scientist practitioners. *International Journal of Sport and Exercise Psychology*, *22*(1), 1–23. https://doi.org/10.1080/1612197X.2023.2174681

Schneider, C. M., Dennehy, C. A., Carter, S. D. (2003). *Exercise and cancer recovery.* Human Kinetics Publishers Inc.

Seal, E., Nicholson, M., McNeil, N., Stukas, A., O'Halloran, P., & Randle, E. (2022). Fear of judgement and women's physical (in) activity experiences. *International Review for the Sociology of Sport*, *57*(3), 381–400. https://doi.org/10.1177/10126902211016631

Shah, E. J., de Cruz, N., & Keegan, R. (2023). International routes to sport and exercise psychology. In V. Shanmuganathan-Felton and S. Smith (Eds.), *Developing a sport psychology consultancy practice: A toolkit for students and trainees* (pp. 54–69). Routledge. https://doi.org/10.4324/9781003196280-5

Shannon, V. R., & Zizzi, S. J. (2017). Professional and ethical issues in applied exercise psychology. In S. Razon & M. Sachs (Eds.), *Applied exercise psychology* (pp. 445–452). Routledge.

Sly, D., Mellalieu, S. D., & Wagstaff, C. R. (2020). "It's psychology Jim, but not as we know it!": The changing face of applied sport psychology. *Sport, Exercise, and Performance Psychology*, *9*(1), 87–101. https://doi.org/10.1037/spy0000163

Sparkes, A. C., & Smith, B. (2014). *Qualitative research methods in sport, exercise and health.* Routledge.

Stout, N. L., Santa Mina, D., Lyons, K. D., Robb, K., & Silver, J. K. (2021). A systematic review of rehabilitation and exercise recommendations in oncology guidelines. *CA: A Cancer Journal for Clinicians*, *71*(2), 149–175. https://doi.org/10.3322/caac.21639

Sue, S., Zane, N., Nagayama Hall, G. C., & Berger, L. K. (2009). The case for cultural competency in psychotherapeutic interventions. *Annual Review of Psychology, 60*(1), 525–548. https://doi.org/10.1146/annurev.psych.60.110707.163651

Swedlund, C. (2023). Embedding exercise psychology into fitness. In E. Prior and T. Holder (Eds.), *Navigating applied sport and exercise psychology: Reflections and insights from emerging practitioners* (pp. 170–180). Routledge.

Swift, S., Green, M., Hillage, J., & Nafilyan, V. (2016). Impact of the cycle to work scheme. *Institute for Employment Studies*. https://socialvalueuk.org/wp-content/uploads/2016/09/impact-of-cycling-to-work-scheme.pdf

Takemura, N., Ho, M.-H., Cheung, D. S. T., & Lin, C.-C. (2023). Effectiveness of motivational strategies on physical activity behavior and associated outcomes in patients with cancer: A systematic review and meta-analysis. *Worldviews on Evidence-Based Nursing*, *21*(3), 253–262. https://doi.org/10.1111/wvn.12691

Tam, G., & Yeung, M. P. S. (2018). A systematic review of the long-term effectiveness of work-based lifestyle interventions to tackle overweight and obesity. *Preventive Medicine*, *107*, 54–60. https://doi.org/10.1016/j.ypmed.2017.11.011

Teixeira, D. S., Ekkekakis, P., Andrade, A. J., Bastos, V., & Palmeira, A. L. (2023). Exploring the impact of individualized pleasure-oriented exercise sessions in a health club setting: Protocol for a randomized controlled trial. *Psychology of Sport & Exercise*, *67*, 102424. https://doi.org/10.1016/j.psychsport.2023.102424

Teixeira, D. S., Rodrigues, F., Cid, L., & Monteiro, D. (2022). Enjoyment as a predictor of exercise habit, intention to continue exercising, and exercise frequency: The intensity traits discrepancy moderation role. *Frontiers in Psychology, 13.* https://doi.org/10.3389/fpsyg.2022.780059

Thedinga, H. K., Zehl, R., & Thiel, A. (2021). Weight stigma experiences and self-exclusion from sport and exercise settings among people with obesity. *BMC Public Health*, *21*, 1–18. https://doi.org/10.1186/s12889-021-10565-7

Tod, D., McEwan, M. B., & Andersen, M. P. (2021 [1951]). When to refer athletes to other helping professionals. In J. M. Williams & V. Krane (Eds.), *Applied sport psychology* (pp. 433–450). McGraw Hill.

Toomey, E., Hardeman, W., Hankonen, N., Byrne, M., McSharry, J., Matvienko-Sikar, K., & Lorencatto, F. (2020). Focusing on fidelity: Narrative review and recommendations for improving intervention fidelity within trials of health behaviour change interventions. *Health Psychology and Behavioral Medicine, 8*(1), 132–151. https://doi.org/10.1080/21642850.2020.1738935

Van Hoye, A., Johnson, S., Geidne, S., Donaldson, A., Rostan, F., Lemonnier, F., & Vuillemin, A. (2021). The health promoting sports club model: An intervention planning framework. *Health Promotion International*, *36*(3), 811–823. https://doi.org/10.1093/heapro/daaa093

Wade, M., Mann, S., Copeland, R. J., & Steele, J. (2020). Effect of exercise referral schemes upon health and well-being: Initial observational insights using individual patient data meta-analysis from the National Referral Database. *Journal of Epidemiology and Community Health*, *74*(1), 32–41. https://dx. doi.org/10.1136/jech-2019–212674

Wagstaff, C. R. D., & Quartiroli, A. (2020). Psychology and psychologists in search of an identity: What and who are we, and why does it matter? *Journal of Sport Psychology in Action, 11*(4), 254–265. https://doi.org10.1080/21520704.2020.1833124

Watson, P. M. (2023). What it means to be an applied exercise psychologist: Reflections from 2003 to 2023. *Case Studies in Sport and Exercise Psychology*, *7*(1), 122–134. https://doi.org/10.1123/cssep.2023-0038

Wiradendi Wolor, C., Kurnianti, D., Zahra, S. F., & Martono, S. (2020). The importance of work-life balance on employee performance millennial generation in Indonesia. *Journal of Critical Reviews*, *7*(9), 1103–1108. https://dx. doi.org/10.31838/jcr.07.09.203

Yi, S., Lee, Y. W., Connerton, T., & Park, C. Y. (2021). Should I stay or should I go? Visit frequency as fitness centre retention strategy. *Managing Sport and Leisure*, *26*(4), 268–286. https://doi.org/10.1080/23750472.2020.1763829

Zizzi, S., & Fogaça, J. L. (2018). *Supervision in Exercise Settings*. Oxford Research Encyclopedia of Psychology. Retrieved 8 Oct. 2025, from https://oxfordre.com/psychology/view/10.1093/acrefore/9780190236557.001.0001/acrefore-9780190236557-e-323

INDEX

Note: **Bold** page numbers refer to tables and *italic* page numbers refer to figures.